Contributions to Economics

More information about this series at http://www.springer.com/series/1262

Hasan Dincer • Ümit Hacioglu • Serhat Yüksel
Editors

Global Approaches in Financial Economics, Banking, and Finance

 Springer

Editors
Hasan Dincer
Istanbul Medipol University
Istanbul, Turkey

Ümit Hacioglu
Istanbul Medipol University
Istanbul, Turkey

Serhat Yüksel
Istanbul Medipol University
Istanbul, Turkey

ISSN 1431-1933   ISSN 2197-7178 (electronic)
Contributions to Economics
ISBN 978-3-319-78493-9   ISBN 978-3-319-78494-6   (eBook)
https://doi.org/10.1007/978-3-319-78494-6

Library of Congress Control Number: 2018944625

Printed on acid-free paper

This Springer imprint is published by the registered company Springer International Publishing AG part of Springer Nature.
The registered company address is: Gewerbestrasse 11, 6330 Cham, Switzerland

Contents

Part I
Financial Economics and Growth Dynamics

Chapter 1
Regional or Local Damage? Contagion Effects of Greek Debt Crisis Revisited

Melik Kamışlı, Serap Kamışlı, and Fatih Temizel

Abstract The term contagion has become one of the central topics in the financial literature after devastating effects of Asian Crisis. In general terms, contagion is the increase in the relationships between the markets after a shock that occur in a country or in a group of countries. The consecutive crises that the world is facing in recent years caused an increase in the number of studies that try to find the answer if the crises change the volatility spillovers between the countries and cause contagion effects or not. When the contagion is considered as the initiation of volatility spillover from the financial markets of crisis-originating country to the financial markets of other countries, capital markets of emerging markets are expected to become very fragile due to the foreign capital flows. For this reason, the effects of crises are felt more profoundly in these markets, and these markets are exposed to contagion effects more than developed countries. The determination of contagion effects is crucial especially for international investors that aim to decrease portfolio risk by international diversification. Also it will provide valuable information to policy makers that can be used in decision processes. There are various econometric methodologies that detect the contagion effects and one of them is frequency domain causality approach. In this context, in the study, contagion effects of Greek debt crisis on 34 European stock markets are analyzed by traditional and frequency domain causality approach. According to the results, there are contagion effects from Greek stock market to Czech Republic, Spain, Estonia, Hungary, Ireland, Iceland, Lithuania, Luxembourg, and Portugal stock markets.

M. Kamışlı (✉) · S. Kamışlı
Department of Banking and Finance, School of Applied Sciences, Bilecik Seyh Edebali University, Bilecik, Turkey
e-mail: melik.kamisli@bilecik.edu.tr; serap.kamisli@bilecik.edu.tr

F. Temizel
Faculty of Economics and Administrative Sciences, Anadolu University, Eskişehir, Turkey
e-mail: ftemizel@anadolu.edu.tr

© Springer International Publishing AG, part of Springer Nature 2018
H. Dincer et al. (eds.), *Global Approaches in Financial Economics, Banking, and Finance*, Contributions to Economics, https://doi.org/10.1007/978-3-319-78494-6_1

Introduction

Portfolio management decisions of the investors are affected from too many factors, notably the relationships between the financial markets. One of these factors is the financial crises. Because, on the one hand, crises cause deteriorations in economic and financial variables, on the other hand, they affect the other markets through the contagion channels. This situation and the recent crises cause increase in the number of the studies which investigate that if the crises cause contagion effect or not, and the relationships between the markets are analyzed on the basis of the crises. But, despite the increase in the number of studies on contagion effects, there is no consensus on the theoretical or empirical definition of the contagion. Yet, determination and measurement of the contagion is quite important for both academic researches and for policy makers (Gómez-Puig and Rivero 2014).

The term contagion is a relatively new term for the financial literature. This term was not used in financial world until 1990s and emerged after devastating effects of 1997 Asian Crisis. After this crisis, the financial researches generally analyzed the effects of crisis on the emerging markets. Especially, capital markets of emerging countries are fragile in both downtrends and uptrends (Tiryaki and Ekinci 2015). For this reason, the effects of crises on these countries are greater, and contagion effects are seen much in these countries. But, 2008 Global Crises showed that contagion is not a phenomenon that affects only the emerging countries; this is an event that may affect whole of the financial system through different channels (Kolb 2011).

In general terms, contagion is an event which occurred in one country, and has a rapid effect on many countries. Forbes and Rigobon (2002) defines the contagion as the increase in the relationships between the markets after a shock that occurred in one of the markets, while Masson (1999) defines the contagion as the beginning of the crisis in one country, that cannot be explained by macroeconomic factors, because of the crisis that occurred in another country. With reference to the definitions, it can be said that contagion causes change in the market sensitivity, and after the crisis the new information in the market is interpreted differently than it was in the past. Definitions also indicate that if the markets display high degree of co-movements in stable times and after a shock the interrelation is still high, then this is not a contagion (Gómez-Puig and Rivero 2014). On the other hand, if the effects are gradual, this is referred to as a spillover (Kolb 2011).

According to Naoui et al. (2010), significant increase in the possibility of crisis in one country increases because of the crisis that occurred in another country. To another definition, contagion is significant increases in the relationships, which are measured by the co-movements of the asset prices and financial flows, after a shock compared to stable periods (Dornbusch et al. 2000). Contagion can be described on the basis of market volatility too. In terms of volatility, contagion can be defined as the beginning of volatility spillover from the crisis country to the other.

In the light of this explanation, to qualify the increases in the relationships as contagion, the following features should be determined (Claeys and Vasicek 2014):

- Great and significant changes in the relationships.
- Sudden changes in the relationships.
- To be unable to explain the changes by macro-economical connections.

In recent years, there occurred unforeseen crises in too many countries in different regions of the world. Especially, the crisis that started in America in 2008 affected almost all the regions of the world. While the effects of this crisis are not understood properly, The Greek debt crisis started in Euro area.

The Greek economy is a relatively small economy in Euro area with its GDP which is less than 3% of total Eurozone GDP (Bhanot et al. 2012). But the crisis that occurred in this country in November 2009 has affected almost all countries in the region. These effects have been caused by financial transactions besides trade relations. Especially due to the financial liberalization, the relationships between the financial markets have increased and the markets have become interconnected. Therefore, especially stock markets in the Eurozone have been affected more from the Greek debt crisis. Three potential transition channels for the crises may be identified. Firstly, investors make analogies between the crisis country and the countries that they invest in, and this situation affects their investment decisions. Secondly, in crisis periods increasing volatility affects the attitudes of the investors towards risk and risk aversion increases. Investors prefer to invest in safety areas (Vayanos 2004). Thirdly, losses that occurred due to the crises may cause decreases in funding sources of the institutions in the other countries.

Arghyrou and Tsoukalas (2011) explained the development of the crisis in five stages ranging from 2007 USA Sub-Prime Crisis to announcements of the new Greek government. The first stage begins with the increases in Greek CDS spreads due to the Sub-Prime Crisis, the second stage includes the effects of the peak of Global Crisis, and the third stage covers the period in which recovery packages were started to be applied between April and August 2009. The fourth stage of the crisis includes three important events: snap election; the new government's announcements about the previous government; and in mid-November 2009, submission of the proposed public budget of Greece to the European Commission. The third event was also stated as the beginning of the final stage.

In the light of these explanations, the purpose of this research is to investigate the contagion effects of 2009 Greek debt crisis and to present valuable information to the investors that they can use in their risk management and portfolio allocation decisions.

Literature Review

There are too many studies in the literature that analyze the contagion effects of crises. Mink and Haan (2013) analyzed the contagion effects of Greek debt crisis on the basis of banking sector, while Samitas and Tsakalos (2013) investigated the contagion effect on stock markets. Similarly, Mollah et al. (2016) determined the contagion effects of Global Financial and European debt crisis on stock markets. In the studies of Dungey and Gajurel (2014) and Luchtenberg and Vu (2015), the contagion effects of 2008 global crisis on stock markets were researched. But the contagion phenomenon is not the event that only affects the stock markets; there may be contagion effects in other markets too. So, Missio and Watzka (2011) analyzed the contagion for government bond yields after the European debt crisis. Dua and Tuteja (2016) studied on the contagion effects of Global Financial and European debt crisis on currencies.

The contagion effects of the crises can be determined by many econometric methodologies, and there are too many studies in the literature that use traditional approaches in the analyses. But in recent years, the new methods, which allows the researcher to analyze the time-varying structure and frequency dimensions of the causality dynamics, have been developed. Bodart and Candelon (2009), Ciner (2011a, b, c), Mermod and Dudzeviciute (2011), Aslanoğlu and Deniz (2012), Bozoklu and Yılancı (2013), Joseph et al. (2014), and Tiwari (2014) used frequency domain causality test in their study to investigate the relationships between the markets.

Bodart and Candelon (2009) examined the contagion effects of Latin America and Asian Crises and found that crisis showed regional contagion. Ciner (2011b) found that there are spillovers between currency futures in crisis periods. Mermod and Dudzeviciute (2011), Aslanoğlu and Deniz (2012), Bozoklu and Yılancı (2013), and Tiwari (2014) used frequency domain causality approach to analyze the relationships between macroeconomic variables. Similarly, Ciner (2011a) investigated the relationships between commodity prices and inflation by using frequency domain causality test. In his another study, Ciner (2011c) examined the relationships between currencies and interest rates with the same methodology. Joseph et al. (2014) determined the relationships between spot and future market by applying frequency domain causality test.

But there are limited studies in the literature that analyze the contagion effects of 2009 Greek debt crisis. In this context, it is thought to contribute to the literature with this method and large dataset.

Data and Methodology

The purpose of this research is to analyze the contagion effects of Greek debt crisis on frequency dimension differently from the traditional approaches. In this context, the main hypothesis of the research can be expressed as follows:

H_0 Greek debt crisis does not show contagion effect on the basis of stock returns.

H_1 Greek debt crisis shows contagion effect on the basis of stock returns.

In the research, both the traditional and the frequency-based causality tests are used to determine the contagion effects. Traditional causality tests produce one test statistic for the relationship between the variables. But to accept that the relationships do not change over the time is not realistic without discriminating the short, mid, and long-run. In this context, the frequency-based causality approach refuses the fundamental assumption of traditional causality test that "one test summarizes the relationship which is valid for all frequencies between the variables" by producing more than one test statistic for different frequencies. Therefore, frequency-based causality approach gives the opportunity of investigating the causality dynamics in different frequencies instead of depending on one test statistic as it is in traditional analyses (Ciner, 2011b). This situation was firstly stated in the studies of Geweke (1982) and Hosoya (1991). Later Breitung and Candelon (2006) developed the frequency domain causality based on these studies.

Breitung and Candelon analysis depends on the studies of Geweke (1982) and Hosoya (1991) which consider finite (p) order VAR model that has two dimensional vectors Y_t and X_t.

The causality criteria that is proposed by Geweke (1982) is as follows:

$$M_{X \to Y}(\omega) = \log \left[1 + \frac{\|\psi_{12}(e^{-i\omega})\|^2}{\|\psi_{11}(e^{-i\omega})\|^2} \right] \qquad (1.1)$$

If $\left| \psi_{12}(e^{-i\omega}) \right| = 0$, There is no Granger causality from X_t to Y_t at frequency ω.

$$(1.2)$$

In testing hypothesis, that is "X_t is not cause of Y_t at frequency ω," the null hypothesis is as follows:

$$M_{X \to Y}(\omega) = 0 \qquad (1.3)$$

Breitung and Candelon (2006) developed the following linear restrictions to test the hypothesis above

$$\sum_{k=1}^{p} \theta_{12,k} \cos (k\omega) = 0 \qquad (1.4)$$

$$\sum_{k=1}^{p} \theta_{12,k} \sin (k\omega) = 0 \qquad (1.5)$$

Based on the linear restrictions, the null hypothesis "$M_{X \to Y}(\omega) = 0$" is expressed as follows:

$$H_0 = R(\omega)\beta \qquad (1.6)$$

Here, β is the vector of Y_t coefficients and

$$R(\omega) = \begin{bmatrix} \cos(\omega) & \cos(2\omega)\ldots & \cos(p\omega) \\ \sin(\omega) & \sin(2\omega)\ldots & \sin(p\omega) \end{bmatrix} \tag{1.7}$$

Therefore, the null hypothesis that there is no Granger causality at frequency ω can be tested by using F test for the linear restrictions. F test distributes approximately as $F(2, T - 2p)$ for $\omega \in (0, \pi)$. Here, 2 states the restriction number, T is the number of observations, and p is the lag length of VAR model.

In the research stock returns calculated based on the weekly price data of Austria (AUT); Belgium (BEL); Bosnia-Herzegovina (BIH); Bulgaria (BGR); Croatia (HRV); Cyprus (CYP); Czech Republic (CZE); Denmark (DNK); Estonia (EST); Finland (FIN); France (FRA); Germany (DEU); Greece (GRC); Hungary (HUN); Iceland (ISL); Ireland (IRL); Italy (ITA); Latvia (LVA); Lithuania (LTU); Luxembourg (LUX); Macedonia (MKD); Malta (MLT); the Netherlands (NLD); Norway (NOR); Poland (POL); Portugal (PRT); Romania (ROU); Serbia (SRB); Slovakia (SVK); Slovenia (SVN); Spain (ESP); Sweden (SWE); Switzerland (CHE); Turkey (TUR); and United Kingdom (GBR) stock markets. Returns are calculated as follows:

$$R_t = ln\left(\frac{F_t}{F_{t-1}}\right) \tag{1.8}$$

F_t refers to closing price at t^{th} week.

The data set is limited between 09/16/2008–7/25/2015 and divided into two periods. The first period starts with the collapse of Lehman Brothers that is accepted as the beginning of the Global Crisis (15/09/2008) and finishes at 11/03/2009. The second period starts with the statement of financial falsification by the new government that came to power in Greece, that is accepted as the beginning of the Greek debt crisis (11/04/2009), and finishes on 7/25/2015. Therefore, 358 weekly stock market return data belongs to aforementioned countries are used in the analyses. The data was gathered from Thomson Reuters Datastream.

To investigate the contagion effect, first standard VAR-Granger causality test is applied. The test results show that there is no causality in the first period, but there is causality in the second period indicating that there is contagion effect from Greek stock market to stock markets of selected countries. After applying VAR-Granger causality test, the contagion effect is tested by frequency causality test based on the study of Bodart and Candelon (2009). Depending on this study, the existence of contagion is proved by the existence of high frequency relationship ($w > 2.00$) in the postcrisis period while there is no low frequency relationship ($w < 0.05$) in the precrisis period.

In light of this information, the steps of the research are as follows:

- Determination of descriptive statistics of Euro area stock markets' return and analysis of the stationarity of the series.
- Calculation of the unconditional correlations between Greek stock market and stock markets of European countries.

- Investigation of contagion effect of 2009 Greek debt crisis to European stock markets by VAR-Granger causality test.
- Determination of contagion effect of 2009 Greek debt crisis to European stock markets by frequency domain causality test.

Empirical Results

The determination of the contagion effect is very important for risk management and portfolio allocation decisions. But besides the determination of the contagion effects, descriptive statistics of the series presents valuable information for the investors. The descriptive statistics must be analyzed also for checking that if the prior conditions of the further analyses are satisfied or not. Therefore, the descriptive statistics of the European stock markets' returns are given in Table 1.1 before investigating the contagion effects.

When Table 1.1 is investigated, it is seen that most of European stock markets have negative average returns between 2008 global crisis and 2009 Greek debt crisis. The stock markets that have lowest average returns are Iceland, Bulgaria, Serbia, Latvia, and Croatia stock markets, respectively. In this period, Turkey, Sweden, and Bosnia-Herzegovina stock markets have positive average returns. On the other hand, in the mentioned period, stock markets of Cyprus and Serbia have the highest standard deviations. Stock market returns of developed countries such as Switzerland, United Kingdom, France, and Sweden have lower risk relative to stock market returns of other countries. All of the countries except Slovakia, Denmark, Malta, and Bosnia-Herzegovina have negative skewness values, and kurtosis values of all of the stock markets are higher than three. This situation indicates that almost all of the stock markets in Euro area move away normal distribution due to the shocks which occurred depending on the 2008 global crisis.

In order to check the prior condition of VAR-Granger causality and frequency domain causality test, the stationarity of the stock returns is tested by augmented Dickey–Fuller (ADF) (1981) and Phillips–Perron (PP) (1988) unit root tests, and the results are presented together with the descriptive statistics in Table 1.1. Both ADF and PP tests show that none of the series has unit root; in other words all of the stock markets in Euro Area are stationary in the first period.

It is seen from Table 1.2 that there are important changes in average returns of European stock markets in the second period. The stock markets that have negative average returns are Cyprus, Greece, Bosnia-Herzegovina, Portugal, Macedonia, Slovenia, Czech Republic, Croatia, Spain, Serbia, and Italy, respectively. All of the European stock markets except these countries have positive average returns. On the other hand, the stock markets that have the highest standard deviations are Cyprus, Greece, Italy, Spain, and Portugal stock markets. But differently from the first period, returns of the stock markets of developed countries such as Germany, France, Finland, and Norway have high risk too in the second period. Also, all of the stock markets have high skewness values except Bulgaria, Cyprus, Macedonia,

Table 1.1 Descriptive statistics of 1st period

	Mean	Median	Std. Dev.	Skewness	Kurtosis	Jarque-Bera	ADF	PP
AUT	−0.0043	0.012	0.060	−0.979	3.960	11.89*	−6.59*	−6.60*
BEL	−0.0039	0.003	0.043	−1.020	4.310	14.69*	−4.99*	−4.86*
BGR	−0.0131	−0.002	0.064	−1.011	4.975	19.97*	−5.10*	−5.21*
BIH	0.0015	−0.002	0.085	3.281	20.453	869.2*	−7.06*	−7.09*
CHE	−0.0020	0.003	0.032	−1.155	5.302	26.59*	−6.94*	−6.94*
CYP	−0.0058	0.002	0.074	−0.411	3.289	1.90	−5.04*	−5.04*
CZE	−0.0023	0.003	0.055	−0.735	4.121	8.55*	−5.99*	−5.99*
DEU	−0.0020	0.002	0.043	−0.716	3.627	6.11**	−6.00*	−5.87*
DNK	−0.0028	0.004	0.068	0.651	6.720	38.84*	−9.37*	−9.47*
ESP	0.0005	0.007	0.038	−0.894	3.570	8.81*	−6.36*	−6.36*
EST	−0.0044	−0.005	0.048	−0.208	3.691	1.63	−5.08*	−5.18*
FIN	−0.0039	0.004	0.041	−0.636	3.070	4.06	−6.07*	−6.03*
FRA	−0.0024	0.007	0.038	−0.892	3.831	9.68*	−6.10*	−5.99*
GBR	−0.0007	0.002	0.035	−0.814	4.193	10.19*	−6.02*	−5.91*
GRC	−0.0028	0.005	0.051	−0.910	3.786	9.82*	−5.47*	−5.50*
HRV	−0.0077	−0.009	0.055	−0.484	3.484	2.93	−5.33*	−5.42*
HUN	0.0005	0.004	0.059	−0.934	4.464	14.07*	−6.14*	−6.11*
IRL	−0.0066	0.007	0.055	−0.927	4.146	11.88*	−6.09*	−6.06*
ISL	−0.0333	−0.004	0.154	−5.849	39.637	697.7*	−3.28**	−7.24*
ITA	−0.0036	0.006	0.047	−0.695	3.065	4.84*	−5.76*	−5.78*
LTU	−0.0068	−0.001	0.057	−0.051	5.469	15.27*	−4.77*	−4.93*
LUX	−0.0055	0.003	0.049	−1.051	4.736	18.57*	−5.63*	−5.62*
LVA	−0.0083	0.002	0.046	−0.661	3.193	4.46	−5.60*	−5.60*
MKD	−0.0062	−0.010	0.058	−0.397	3.710	2.83	−4.98*	−5.02*
MLT	−0.0033	−0.004	0.022	0.741	3.737	6.84**	−5.68*	−5.71*
NLD	−0.0041	0.003	0.044	−0.814	3.510	7.27**	−5.52*	−5.47*
NOR	−0.0006	0.008	0.054	−0.913	4.015	10.92*	−6.42*	−6.42*
POL	−0.0013	0.001	0.049	−0.650	3.316	4.47	−6.32*	−6.29*
PRT	0.0003	0.005	0.035	−1.439	7.107	62.88*	−7.15*	−7.18*
ROU	−0.0022	0.008	0.060	−0.971	4.308	13.71*	−6.19*	−6.34*
SBR	−0.0089	−0.002	0.073	−0.583	4.124	6.55**	−5.93*	−6.05*
SVK	−0.0068	−0.006	0.030	0.529	5.623	20.00*	−5.90*	−5.90*
SVN	−0.0064	0.000	0.040	−1.349	5.660	35.88*	−7.01*	−7.09*
SWE	0.0019	0.007	0.040	−0.724	4.297	9.45*	−6.65*	−6.58*
TUR	0.0040	0.011	0.052	−0.744	3.390	5.91***	−6.51*	−6.54*

*,**,*** indicates significance levels for 1%, 5% and 10% respectively

Croatia, Estonia, Bosnia-Herzegovina, and Latvia. Kurtosis values of all of the stock markets are higher than three in the second period. High skewness values and the kurtosis values which are higher than three show that series are far away normal distribution in the second period too, but this time due to the shocks that occurred depending on the 2009 Greek debt crisis. ADF and PP unit root tests show that stock markets in Euro Area are stationary in the second period too.

Table 1.2 Descriptive statistics of 2nd period

	Mean	Median	Std. Dev.	Skewness	Kurtosis	Jarque-Bera	ADF	PP
AUT	0.0006	0.002	0.024	−0.535	4.871	78.01*	−17.10*	−17.10*
BEL	0.0012	0.002	0.019	−0.519	4.666	64.68*	−18.67*	−18.63*
BGR	0.0012	0.001	0.017	−0.061	4.158	22.75*	−14.09*	−14.60*
BIH	−0.0018	−0.003	0.013	1.169	8.230	551.1*	−14.22*	−14.01*
CHE	0.0009	0.002	0.017	−0.988	6.378	257.2*	−15.23*	−16.88*
CYP	−0.0091	−0.006	0.054	0.077	6.588	216.6*	−16.21*	−16.09*
CZE	−0.0003	0.001	0.019	−0.834	5.818	180.1*	−16.00*	−15.70*
DEU	0.0020	0.003	0.022	−0.573	5.420	120.3*	−17.24*	−17.25*
DNK	0.0027	0.005	0.020	−0.639	4.830	83.68*	−16.87*	−16.83*
ESP	−0.0002	0.000	0.026	−0.074	3.345	2.37	−17.20*	−17.10*
EST	0.0027	0.002	0.018	1.127	10.159	945.9*	−13.68*	−13.43*
FIN	0.0011	0.003	0.022	−0.636	6.018	180.1*	−18.27*	−18.28*
FRA	0.0008	0.002	0.022	−0.327	4.631	51.87*	−17.89*	−17.81*
GBR	0.0009	0.001	0.017	−0.379	4.762	61.78*	−17.53*	−17.55*
GRC	−0.0029	−0.001	0.041	−0.202	3.694	10.84*	−17.04*	−17.11*
HRV	−0.0003	−0.001	0.014	0.477	8.495	522.3*	−13.47*	−13.72*
HUN	0.0014	0.002	0.022	−0.318	4.654	52.73*	−16.35*	−16.35*
IRL	0.0020	0.004	0.020	−0.663	5.149	107.1*	−17.79*	−17.74*
ISL	0.0026	0.002	0.014	−0.196	3.839	14.42*	−16.38*	−16.51*
ITA	−0.0001	0.001	0.027	−0.295	3.799	16.56*	−16.87*	−16.86*
LTU	0.0020	0.001	0.015	−0.315	12.691	1583.6*	−15.07*	−15.00*
LUX	0.0007	0.001	0.020	−0.247	4.924	66.25*	−16.62*	−16.59*
LVA	0.0030	0.002	0.018	1.448	11.402	1326.3*	−13.77*	−13.59*
MKD	−0.0008	−0.001	0.017	0.100	6.194	172.01*	−14.90*	−15.11*
MLT	0.0009	0.001	0.011	−0.111	7.562	350.4*	−15.19*	−15.31*
NLD	0.0013	0.003	0.020	−0.412	4.710	60.57*	−17.55*	−17.41*
NOR	0.0019	0.004	0.021	−0.723	5.869	173.3*	−18.02*	−17.94*
POL	0.0001	0.001	0.020	−0.457	4.267	40.95*	−16.83*	−16.78*
PRT	−0.0012	−0.001	0.025	−0.323	3.910	20.90*	−16.88*	−16.79*
ROU	0.0015	0.003	0.020	−0.555	6.887	274.32*	−15.40*	−15.40*
SBR	−0.0002	0.001	0.019	−0.188	5.935	147.02*	−13.75*	−13.87*
SVK	0.0004	0.002	0.017	−1.342	10.056	957.4*	−18.81*	−18.81*
SVN	−0.0006	0.000	0.017	−0.156	4.617	45.52*	−15.59*	−15.59*
SWE	0.0013	0.003	0.019	−0.522	5.833	153.1*	−18.63*	−18.61*
TUR	0.0020	0.004	0.027	−0.618	4.144	47.67*	−16.68*	−16.70*

* indicates significance levels for 1%

To decrease portfolio risk and benefit from diversification, it is needed that there is negative or low correlation between the financial assets. For this reason, in the next step unconditional correlations between the returns of Greek and European stock markets are calculated and given in Table 1.3.

The unconditional correlations given in Table 1.3 show the direction and magnitude of the relationships between the returns of Greek and European stock markets

Table 1.3 Unconditional correlations between Greek stock market returns and stock market returns of European countries for the 1st and 2nd period

	1. Period	2. Period		1. Period	2. Period
AUT–GRC	0.530	0.668	ISL–GRC	0.183	0.308
BEL–GRC	0.509	0.640	ITA–GRC	0.591	0.663
BGR–GRC	0.202	0.314	LTU–GRC	0.201	0.347
BIH–GRC	0.005	0.254	LUX–GRC	0.444	0.586
CHE–GRC	0.409	0.562	LVA–GRC	0.140	0.188
CYP–GRC	0.479	0.647	MKD–GRC	0.099	0.341
CZE–GRC	0.487	0.592	MLT–GRC	−0.125	0.184
DEU–GRC	0.463	0.628	NLD–GRC	0.461	0.647
DNK–GRC	0.397	0.435	NOR–GRC	0.408	0.601
ESP–GRC	0.578	0.581	POL–GRC	0.431	0.530
EST–GRC	0.216	0.392	PRT–GRC	0.587	0.621
FIN–GRC	0.446	0.615	ROU–GRC	0.304	0.512
FRA–GRC	0.511	0.619	SBR–GRC	0.199	0.397
GBR–GRC	0.436	0.588	SVK–GRC	0.053	0.071
HVR–GRC	0.240	0.419	SVN–GRC	0.185	0.431
HUN–GRC	0.335	0.546	SWE–GRC	0.428	0.521
IRL–GRC	0.460	0.558	TUR–GRC	0.305	0.501

by periods. As it is seen from the table that there is negative correlation only between Greek and Malta stock market returns in the first period. Also, there are low correlations between Greek and Bulgaria, Bosnia-Herzegovina, Estonia, Croatia, Iceland, Lithuania, Latvia, Macedonia, Serbia, Slovakia, and Slovenia stock market returns. But results indicate that the correlations between the returns of Greek stock market and stock market of European countries increased after the Greek debt crisis. There is no negative correlation between Greek and European stock markets in the second period. On the other hand, there are low correlations between Greek and Bosnia-Herzegovina, Latvia, Malta, and Slovakia stock market returns. According to the unconditional correlation results, investors who invest in Greek stock market can diversfy their portfolios by investing in Bosnia-Herzegovina, Latvia, Malta, and Slovakia stock markets. However, it is not realistic to assume that the relations between stock markets are stable within the specified period. The contagion effect of regional and global crises may affect the relationships between the markets in different periods. Therefore, in the next step of the research contagion effect of Greek debt crisis from Greek stock market to European stock markets are first investigated with VAR-Granger causality test, and results are presented in Table 1.4.

The results of VAR-Granger causality test indicate causality between Greek and Austria, Bulgaria, Germany, Estonia, Finland, Croatia, Ireland, Iceland, Lithuania, Macedonia, Romania Slovakia, and Slovenia stock markets for the period between 2008 global crisis and 2009 Greek debt crisis. There is no causality between Greek and rest of the other European stock markets for the same period. But after the Greek debt crisis, causality between Greek and Denmark, Iceland, Luxembourg, Portugal,

Table 1.4 VAR-Granger causality test results

	1. Period	2. Period		1. Period	2. Period
GRC ≠> AUT	Yes	No	GRC ≠> ISL	Yes	Yes
GRC ≠> BEL	No	No	GRC ≠> ITA	No	No
GRC ≠> BGR	Yes	No	GRC ≠> LTU	Yes	No
GRC ≠> BIH	No	No	GRC ≠> LUX	No	**Yes**
GRC ≠> CHE	No	No	GRC ≠> LVA	No	No
GRC ≠> CYP	No	No	GRC ≠> MKD	Yes	No
GRC ≠> CZE	No	No	GRC ≠> MLT	No	No
GRC ≠> DEU	Yes	No	GRC ≠> NLD	No	No
GRC ≠> DNK	No	**Yes**	GRC ≠> NOR	No	No
GRC ≠> ESP	No	No	GRC ≠> POL	No	No
GRC ≠> EST	Yes	No	GRC ≠> PRT	No	**Yes**
GRC ≠> FIN	Yes	No	GRC ≠> ROU	Yes	Yes
GRC ≠> FRA	No	No	GRC ≠> SBR	No	No
GRC ≠> GBR	No	No	GRC ≠> SVK	Yes	No
GRC ≠> HVR	Yes	No	GRC ≠> SVN	Yes	Yes
GRC ≠> HUN	No	No	GRC ≠> SWE	No	No
GRC ≠> IRL	Yes	No	GRC ≠> TUR	No	No

Optimal VAR lag length is selected based on AIC information criteria and diagnostic tests
Bold "yes" indicates contagion effect from Greek stock market to related stock market

Romania, and Slovenia stock markets there can be seen. In determining the contagion effect with VAR-Granger causality test, the existence of contagion is accepted if there is causality in postcrisis period while there is no causality before the crisis period. Therefore, according to VAR-Granger causality test results, the Greek debt crisis shows contagion effect to Denmark, Luxembourg, and Portugal stock markets.

According to Forbes and Rigobon (2002), contagion is significant increases in the relationships between the markets after a shock that occurred in one of the markets. If the markets display high degree of co-movements in stable times and after a shock the interrelation is still high, then this is not a contagion (Gómez-Puig and Rivero 2014). For this reason, the contagion effect can be determined healthier if the causality relations between the markets are analyzed for precrisis and postcrisis periods considering the frequency dimensions. But VAR-Granger causality test method produces one test statistic to test the causality relationships for the determined periods. In this context, in the next step of the research to investigate the contagion effect of Greek debt crisis, the causality between Greek stock market and stock market of European countries are investigated by frequency domain causality test for the first and second period. The graphics of frequency domain causality test results are given in Appendix, and summarized version of the results is shown in Table 1.5.

Analyses show that there are causality relationships between Greek stock market return and return of many of the European stock markets in short, mid, and long run

Table 1.5 Evidence of contagion

	1. Period			2. Period			Contagion
	Low Freq.	Mid Freq.	High Freq.	Low Freq.	Mid Freq.	High Freq.	
GRC ≠> AUT	–	✓	✓	✓	✓	–	–
GRC ≠> BEL	–	–	✓	–	–	–	–
GRC ≠> BGR	✓	✓	✓	✓	✓	✓	–
GRC ≠> BIH	✓	–	–	–	–	–	–
GRC ≠> CHE	–	–	–	–	–	–	–
GRC ≠> CYP	–	–	–	✓	✓	✓	✓
GRC ≠> CZE	–	✓	✓	✓	✓	–	–
GRC ≠> DEU	–	✓	–	–	✓	✓	–
GRC ≠> DNK	✓	–	–	✓	✓	✓	✓
GRC ≠> ESP	–	✓	✓	–	✓	✓	✓
GRC ≠> EST	–	✓	✓	–	✓	–	–
GRC ≠> FIN	–	✓	✓	–	–	–	–
GRC ≠> FRA	–	✓	–	–	–	–	–
GRC ≠> GBR	–	✓	–	–	–	–	–
GRC ≠> HRV	✓	–	✓	✓	✓	✓	✓
GRC ≠> HUN	–	–	✓	✓	✓	✓	✓
GRC ≠> IRL	–	–	–	✓	✓	✓	✓
GRC ≠> ISL	–	✓	✓	✓	–	–	–
GRC ≠> ITA	–	–	✓	–	–	✓	–
GRC ≠> LTU	–	✓	–	✓	✓	✓	✓
GRC ≠> LUX	–	–	✓	✓	–	–	✓
GRC ≠> LVA	–	–	✓	–	–	✓	–
GRC ≠> MKD	✓	–	✓	–	–	✓	–
GRC ≠> MLT	✓	–	✓	–	–	✓	–
GRC ≠> NLD	–	–	–	–	–	–	–

GRC ≠> NOR	↘	—	—	↘	↘	↘	—
GRC ≠> POL	—	—	—	—	—	—	—
GRC ≠> PRT	—	↘	↘	↘	↘	↘	↘
GRC ≠> ROU	—	↘	↘	↘	—	↘	—
GRC ≠> SRB	↘	—	↘	↘	↘	—	—
GRC ≠> SVK	↘	↘	—	—	↘	↘	—
GRC ≠> SVN	↘	↘	↘	↘	—	↘	—
GRC ≠> SWE	—	—	—	—	—	—	—
GRC ≠> TUR	—	↘	↘	—	↘	—	—

for the period between 2008 global crisis and 2009 Greek debt crisis. But there is no causality between Greek stock market and Switzerland, Cyprus, Czech Republic, Spain, France, Hungary, Ireland, Italy, Luxembourg, Netherlands, Poland, and Sweden stock markets in this period. On the other hand, on the basis of mid and high frequencies, it is determined that return of Greek stock market is the cause of Austria stock market return for the frequency between 0.96–3.14; Germany stock market return for the frequency between 1.22–2.39; Estonia stock market return for the frequencies between 0.82–1.51 and 2.17–3.14; Finland stock market return for the frequency between 1.63–2.31; United Kingdom stock market return for the frequency between 1.29–2.06; Lithuania stock market return for the frequencies between 1.30–1.77 and 2.53–3.14; Portugal stock market return for the frequencies between 1.67–1.79 and 1.96–2.54; and Romania stock market return for the frequency between 1.12–1.68 and 2.41–3.14. On the basis of high frequency, return of Greek stock market is the cause of Belgium, Iceland, and Latvia stock market returns for the frequencies between 3.04–3.14, 2.61–2.82, and 2.38–2.64, respectively. Turkey is the sole country that has causality only in the mid run with Greek stock market with the frequency between 1.50 and 1.62.

In the first period that begins with the 2008 global crisis, it is determined that return of Greek stock market is the cause of Bulgaria stock market return for the frequency between 0.01–1.36; Bosnia-Herzegovina stock market return for the frequency between 0.01–0.60; Denmark stock market return for the frequency between 0.01–0.44; Croatia stock market return for the frequency between 0.01–0.56; Macedonia stock market return for the frequency between 0.01–0.60; Malta stock market return for the frequency between 0.01–0.61; Norway stock market return for the frequency between 0.01–0.36; Serbia stock market return for the frequency between 0.01–0.50; Slovakia stock market return for the frequency between 0.01–1.25; and Slovenia stock market return for the frequency between 0.01–0.34 on the basis of low frequency (in the long run). In other words, the causality from Greek stock market return to Bulgaria, Bosnia-Herzegovina, Denmark, Croatia, Macedonia, Malta, Norway, Serbia, Slovakia, and Slovenia stock market returns start at 5th, 10th, 14th, 11th, 10th, 10th, 17th, 13th, 5th, and 18th week, respectively. According to the results of the first period, there are causality relationships between Greek stock market return and stock market return of Bulgaria, Bosnia-Herzegovina, Denmark, Croatia, Macedonia, Malta, Norway, Serbia, Slovakia, and Slovenia. To qualify the causality from Greece as contagion, there should not be causality in the low frequency in precrisis period. Therefore, these countries are excluded from the scope of contagion investigation.

It is seen that important changes occurred in the relationships between Greek stock market and stock markets of European countries on high, mid, and low frequency dimensions after the 2009 Greek debt crisis. There is no causality between Greek stock market return and stock market returns of Belgium, Bosnia-Herzegovina, Switzerland, Finland, France, United Kingdom, Croatia, Italy, Latvia, Netherlands, Poland, and Sweden in the second period. On the basis of low frequency, there is only causality between Greek stock market return and stock market return of Cyprus for the frequency between 0.17–0.30. On the basis of mid frequency, there is only causality between Greek stock market and stock market return of Germany for the frequency between 1.19–1.25. On the basis of high frequency, Greek stock market return is the cause of Hungary stock market return for the frequency between 2.34–3.14; Lithuania stock market return for the frequency between 2.90–3.14; Macedonia stock market return for the frequency between 2.15–2.48; Malta stock market return for the frequency between 2.43–2.78; and Slovakia stock market return for the frequency between 2.07–2.21 and 2.53–2.62.

On the basis of low and mid frequencies, Greek stock market return is the cause of Austria stock market return for the frequency between 0.01–1.29; Romania stock market return for the frequency between 0.01–1.63; and Turkey stock market return for the frequency between 0.01–1.52. There are causality relationships between Greek stock market return and stock market returns of Denmark and Slovenia for the frequencies 0.54–0.59, 2.40–2.56, 2.65–2.75 and 0.17–0.24, 0.50–0.64, 2.55–2.66, respectively, on the basis of low and high frequencies. On the basis of mid and high frequencies, Greek stock market return is the cause of Spain stock market return for the frequencies between 1.21–1.42, 1.76–1.92, 2.83–2.96 and Estonia stock market return for the frequencies between 1.59–1.74, 2.28–2.73.

In the research, the evidence of causality relationships between Greek stock market return and stock market returns of some of the European countries is found after the 2009 Greek debt crisis for low, mid, and high frequencies. The return of Greek stock market is the cause of Bulgaria stock market return for the frequencies between 0.01–0.12, 0.51–0.53, 1.65–1.74, 2.39–2.45; Czech Republic stock market return for the frequencies between 0.53–0.59, 1.90–2.04, 2.64–2.74; Ireland stock market return for the frequencies between 0.50–0.53, 1.22–1.23, 1.58–1.75, 3.07–3.14; Luxembourg stock market return for the frequencies between 0.56–0.62, 1.59–1.99, 2.58–3.14; Norway stock market return for the frequencies between 0.64–0.82, 1.22–1.38, 2.97–3.14; Portugal stock market return for the frequencies between 0.43–0.59, 1.17–1.40, 2.78–2.95; and Serbia stock market return for the frequencies between 0.11–0.13, 1.03–1.16, 1.71–2.15. Also there is causality between Greek stock market return and Iceland stock market return for all frequencies.

According to empirical results and the contagion theory, there are contagion effects from Greece stock market to stock market of Czech Republic, Spain, Estonia, Hungary, Ireland, Iceland, Lithuania, Luxembourg, and Portugal after the 2009 Greek debt crisis. On the other hand, there are relationships between Greek stock market and stock market of Austria, Bulgaria, Germany, Denmark, Macedonia, Malta, Norway, Romania, Serbia, Slovakia, Slovenia, and Turkey in both precrisis and postcrisis periods that cannot be considered as contagion. Results also show that there is no causality relationship between Greece stock market and stock market of Switzerland, France, Italy, Poland, Netherlands, and Sweden in both precrisis and postcrisis periods. So, investors who invest in Greek stock market can diversify their portfolios by investing in these markets, and vice versa. Another important finding of the research is that the causality between Greek stock market and stock market of Belgium, Bosnia-Herzegovina, Finland, United Kingdom, Croatia, and Latvia has disappeared after the 2009 Greek debt crisis.

Conclusion

The purpose of this research is to investigate the contagion effects of 2009 Greek debt crisis and to present valuable information to the investors that they can use in their risk management and portfolio allocation decisions. In line with this purpose, the causality relations between Greek stock market and stock markets of 34 European countries are analyzed with both traditional and newly developed approaches for the precrisis and postcrisis periods. The analyses that are made with traditional approach show that there is contagion effect of the Greek debt crisis only to Denmark, Luxembourg, and Portugal stock markets.

After the traditional approach, the relationships between Greek stock market and stock markets of 34 European countries are investigated on frequency dimension based on the current contagion literature. Findings of the frequency-based approach prove that there are contagion effects from Greek stock market to stock markets of Czech Republic, Spain, Estonia, Hungary, Ireland, Iceland, Lithuania, Luxembourg, and Portugal after the 2009 Greek debt crisis. This situation shows that Czech Republic, Estonia, Hungary, Lithuania, and Luxembourg stock markets are affected from the crisis besides Spain, Ireland, Iceland, and Portugal that are frequently criticized countries in the European Debt Crisis period.

It is determined by the research that the relationships between Greek stock market and stock markets of Belgium, Bosnia-Herzegovina, Finland, United Kingdom, Croatia, and Latvia are disappeared in the debt crisis period while there are relationships for different frequencies in the precrisis period. Results also indicate that investors can diversify their portfolios by investing in Switzerland, France, Italy, Poland, the Netherlands, and Sweden stock markets when they invest in Greek stock market, and vice versa.

Appendix: Graphics of Frequency Domain Causality Test Results

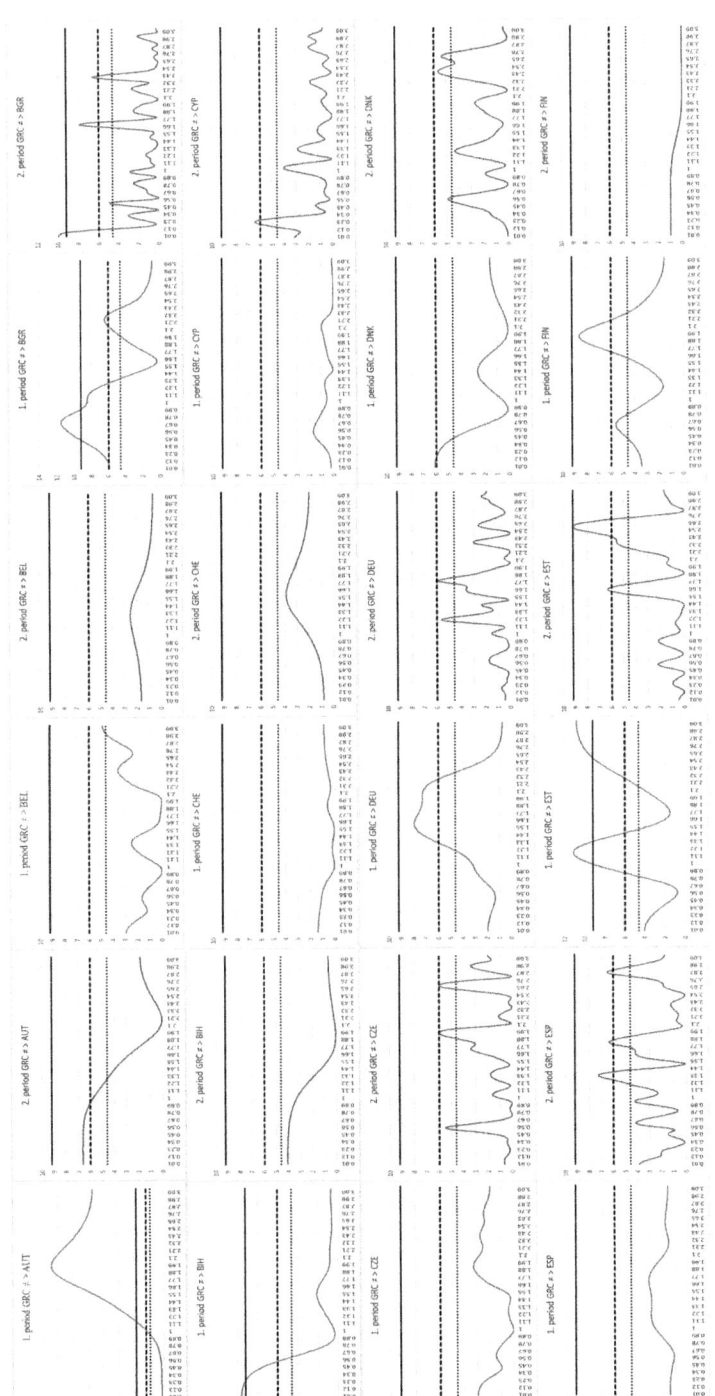

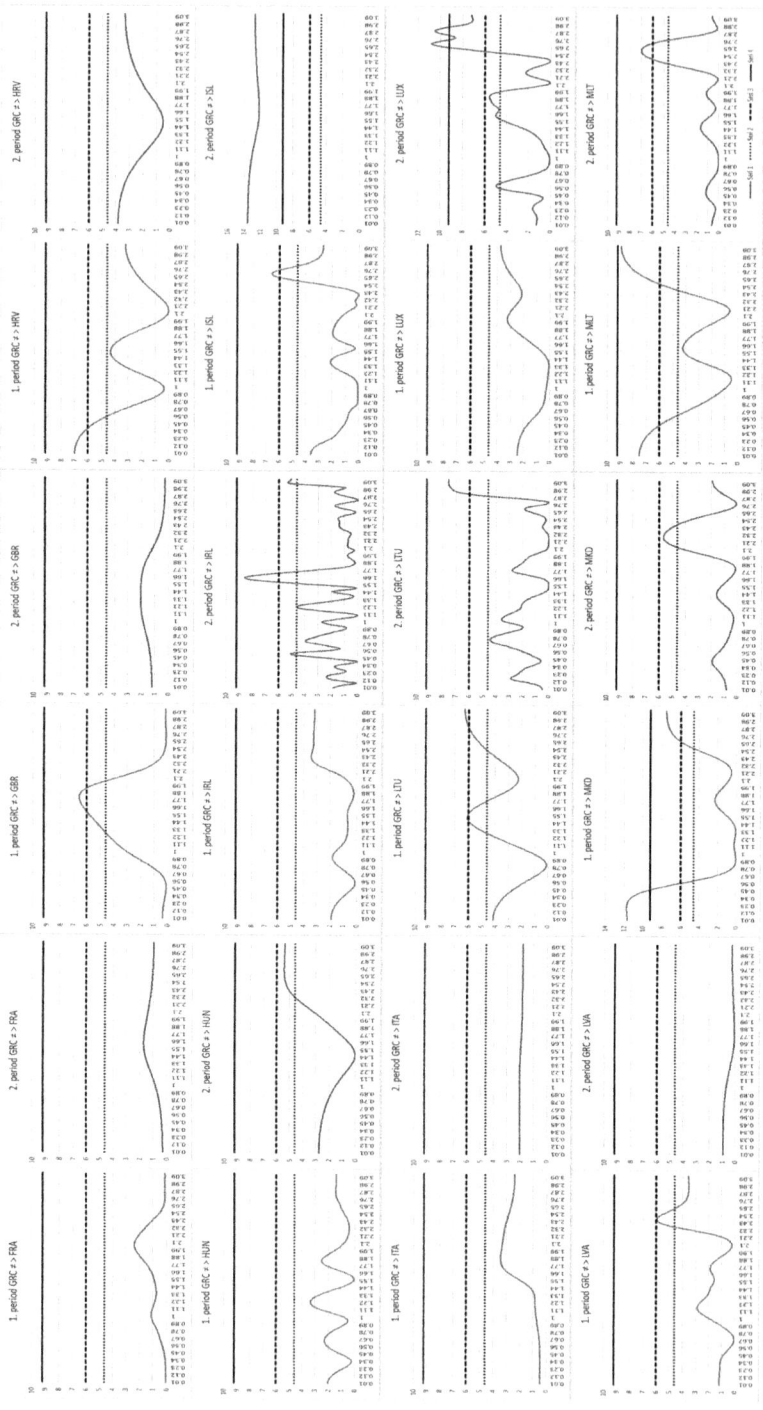

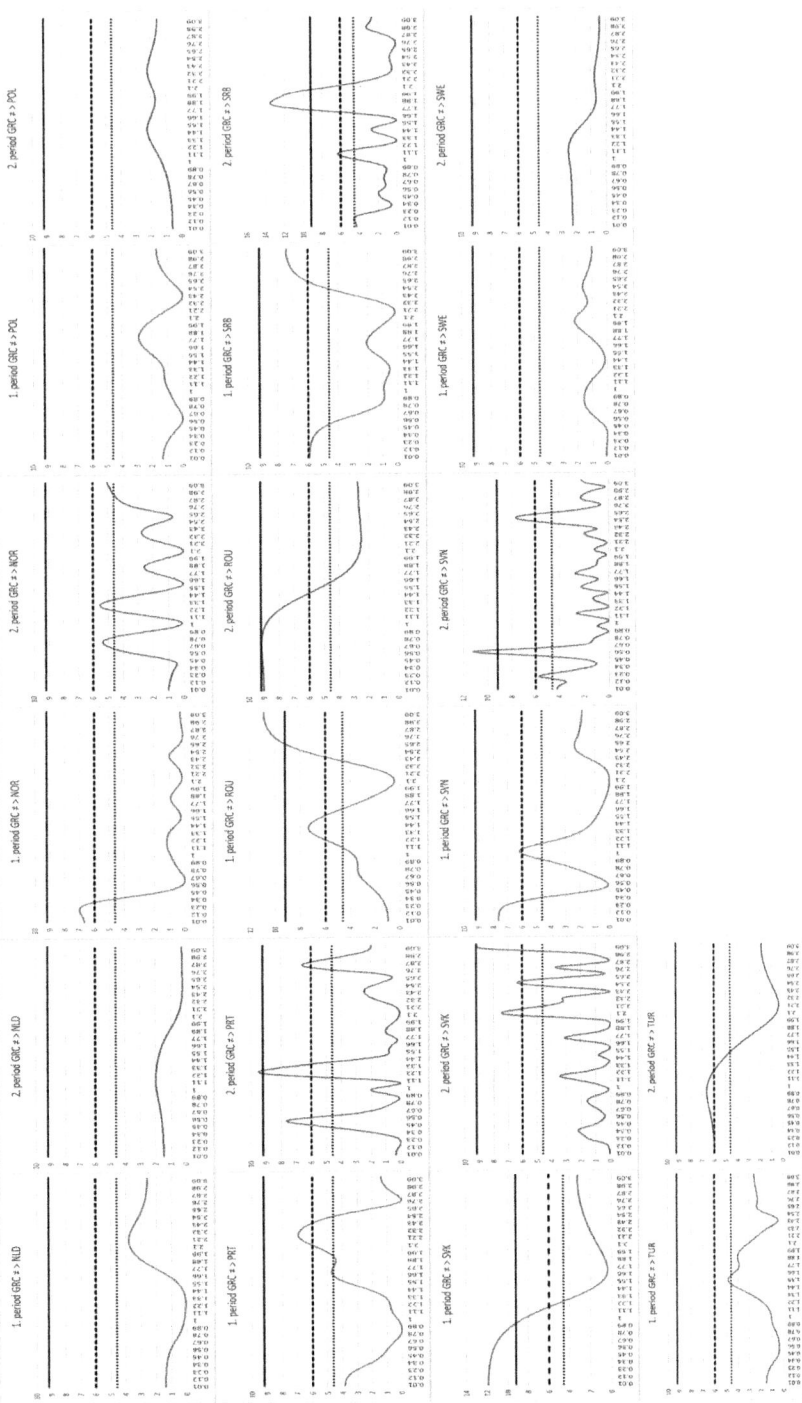

References

Arghyrou, M. G., & Tsoukalas, J. D. (2011). The greek debt crisis: Likely causes, mechanics and outcomes. *The World Economy, 34*(2), 173–191. https://doi.org/10.1111/j.1467-9701.2011. 01328.x.

Aslanoğlu, E., & Deniz, P. (2012). How does stability in financial openness affect growth? *Topics in Middle Eastern and African Economies, 14*, 164–189. http://ecommons.luc.edu/cgi/ viewcontent.cgi?article=1156&context=meea.

Bhanot, K., Burns, N., Hunter, D. & Williams, M. (2012). *Was there contagion in Eurozone sovereign bond markets during the Greek debt crisis?*, The University of Texas at San Antonio, College of Business Working Paper Series, No:# 006FIN-73-2012. http://business.utsa.edu/ wps/fin/0006FIN-073-2012.pdf

Bodart, V., & Candelon, B. (2009). Evidence of interdependence and contagion using a frequency domain framework. *Emerging Markets Review, 10*(2), 140–150. https://doi.org/10.1016/j. ememar.2008.11.003.

Bozoklu, S., & Yılancı, V. (2013). Energy consumption and economic growth for selected OECD countries: Further evidence from the Granger causality test in the frequency domain. *Energy Policy, 63*, 877–881. https://doi.org/10.1016/j.enpol.2013.09.037.

Breitung, J., & Candelon, B. (2006). Testing for short and long-run causality: A frequency-domain approach. *Journal of Econometrics, 132*(2), 363–378. https://doi.org/10.1016/j.jeconom.2005. 02.004.

Ciner, Ç. (2011a). Commodity prices and inflation: Testing in the frequency domain. *Research in International Business and Finance, 25*(3), 229–237. https://doi.org/10.1016/j.ribaf.2011.02. 001.

Ciner, Ç. (2011b). Information transmission across currency futures markets: Evidence from frequency domain tests. *International Review of Financial Analysis, 20*(3), 134–139. https:// doi.org/10.1016/j.irfa.2011.02.010.

Ciner, Ç. (2011c). Eurocurrency interest rate linkages: A frequency domain analysis. *International Review of Economics and Finance, 20*(4), 498–505. https://doi.org/10.1016/j.iref.2010.09.006.

Claeys, P., & Vasicek, B. (2014). Measuring bilateral spillover and testing contagion on sovereign bond markets in Europe. *Journal of Banking and Finance, 46*, 151–165. https://doi.org/10. 1016/j.jbankfin.2014.05.011.

Dickey, D. A., & Fuller, W. A. (1981). Likelihood ratio statistics for autoregressive time series with a unit root. *Econometrica, 49*(4), 1057–1072. https://doi.org/10.2307/1912517.

Dornbusch, R., Park, Y. C., & Claessens, S. (2000). Contagion: Understanding how it spreads. *The World Bank Research Observer, 15*(2), 177–197. https://doi.org/10.1093/wbro/15.2.177.

Dua, P., & Tuteja, D. (2016). Financial crises and dynamic linkages across international stock and currency markets. *Economic Modelling, 59*, 249–261. https://doi.org/10.1016/j.econmod.2016. 07.013.

Dungey, M., & Gajurel, D. (2014). Equity market contagion during the global financial crisis: Evidence from the world's eight largest economies. *Economic Systems, 38*(2), 161–177. https:// doi.org/10.1016/j.ecosys.2013.10.003.

Forbes, K. J., & Rigobon, R. (2002). No contagion, only interdependence: Measuring stock market comovements. *The Journal of Finance, 57*(5), 2223–2261. https://doi.org/10.1111/0022-1082. 00494.

Geweke, J. (1982). Measurement of linear dependence and feedback between multiple time series. *Journal of the American Statistical Association, 77*, 304–324. https://doi.org/10.1080/ 01621459.1982.10477803.

Gómez-Puig, M., & Rivero, S. S. (2014). Causality and contagion in EMU sovereign debt markets. *International Review of Economics and Finance, 33*, 12–27. https://doi.org/10.1016/j.iref.2014. 03.003.

Hosoya, Y. (1991). The decomposition and measurement of the interdependence between second-order stationary processes. *Probability Theory and Related Fields, 88*(4), 429–444. https://doi.org/10.1007/BF01192551.

Joseph, A., Sisodia, G., & Tiwari, A. K. (2014). A frequency domain causality investigation between futures and spot prices of Indian commodity markets. *Economic Modelling, 40*, 250–258. https://doi.org/10.1016/j.econmod.2014.04.019.

Kolb, R. W. (2011). What is financial contagion? In R. W. Kolb (Ed.), *Financial contagion* (pp. 3–10). Hoboken: Wiley. https://doi.org/10.1002/9781118267646.

Luchtenberg, K. F., & Vu, Q. V. (2015). The 2008 financial crisis: Stock market contagion and its determinants. *Research in International Business and Finance, 33*, 178–203. https://doi.org/10.1016/j.ribaf.2014.09.007.

Masson, P. (1999). Contagion: Macroeconomic models with multiple equilibria. *Journal of International Money and Finance, 18*(4), 587–602. https://doi.org/10.1016/S0261-5606(99)00016-9.

Mermod, A. S., & Dudzeviciute, G. (2011). Frequency domain analysis of consumer confidence, industrial production and retail sales for selected European countries. *Journal of Business Economics and Management, 12*(4), 589–602. https://doi.org/10.3846/16111699.2011.599406.

Mink, M., & Haan, J. (2013). Contagion during the Greek sovereign debt crisis. *Journal of International Money and Finance, 34*, 102–113. https://doi.org/10.1016/j.jimonfin.2012.11.006.

Missio, S., & Watzka, S. (2011). *Financial contagion and the European debt crisis*, CESIFO Working Paper No. 3554. http://www.cesifo-group.de/DocDL/cesifo1_wp3554.pdf

Mollah, S., Quoreshi, A. M. M. S., & Zafirov, G. (2016). Equity market contagion during global financial and Eurozonecrises: Evidence from a dynamic correlation analysis. *Journal of International Financial Markets, Institutions and Money, 41*, 151–167. https://doi.org/10.1016/j.intfin.2015.12.010.

Naoui, K., Khemiri, S., & Liouane, N. (2010). Crises and financial contagion: The subprime crisis. *Journal of Business Studies Quarterly, 2*(1), 15–28.

Phillips, P. C. B., & Perron, P. (1988). Testing for a unit root in time series regression. *Biometrika, 75*(2), 335–346. https://doi.org/10.2307/2336182.

Samitas, A., & Tsakalos, I. (2013). How can a small country affect the European economy? The Greek contagion phenomenon. *Journal of International Financial Markets, Institutions and Money, 25*, 18–32. https://doi.org/10.1016/j.intfin.2013.01.005.

Tiryaki, H. N., & Ekinci, A. (2015). Financial contagion in global crises and its effect on Turkish economy. *Sakarya İktisat Dergisi, 4*(1), 1–30. http://www.sdu.dergipark.gov.tr/download/article-file/319613.

Tiwari, A. K. (2014). The frequency domain causality analysis between energy consumption and income in the United States. *Economia Aplicada, 18*(1), 51–67. https://doi.org/10.1590/1413-8050/ea307.

Vayanos, D. (2004). *Flight to quality, flight to liquidity, and the pricing of risk*. NBER Working Paper Series, No: 10327. http://www.nber.org/papers/w10327

Chapter 2
A Hardheaded Look: How Did India Feel the Tremors of Recent Financial Crises?

Sovik Mukherjee and Asim K. Karmakar

Abstract The last half century has witnessed an unprecedented number of financial crises and episodes of great price and output volatility. Given the economic, financial, and trade inter-linkages of the global economy, both the US Subprime crisis and the 2010 Eurozone crisis spilled over into the emerging and developing economies and India was no exception. In this background, this chapter starts off with a whirlwind rundown of the existing literature, giving emphasis to the different generations of financial crisis models and shows how these have characterized the crises across the globe. Theoretically, the contribution of this chapter lies in proposing a macroeconomic model based on the Keynesian line of argument to explore the episodes of crises and the response of macro-variables in such a setup. This is in turn followed by the construction of a crisis index (*CI*), at monthly frequency which functions as the binary response variable in a probit model in conglomeration with some other macroeconomic variables which have played a role during the periods of crisis. Formulating the probit model empirically brings out the magnitude to which each macroeconomic variable have contributed to the probability of a crisis happening. The novelty of this chapter lies in the theoretical and the empirical portrayal of the crisis periods in conjunction with bringing out the most significant policy variables responsible in this regard.

Introduction

The flow of foreign capital gradually increased for the emerging economies since 1990s. The main reason behind these economies becoming a hub of global capital lies in the fact that these EDEs are integrated with the global financial markets. This fairy tale also has a darker side when bigger capital inflows consequently result in larger current account deficits when there is an appreciation in the exchange rate. In

S. Mukherjee (✉)
Department of Commerce (Evening), Shri Shikshayatan College, Kolkata, West Bengal, India

A. K. Karmakar
Jadavpur University, Kolkata, West Bengal, India

© Springer International Publishing AG, part of Springer Nature 2018
H. Dincer et al. (eds.), *Global Approaches in Financial Economics, Banking, and Finance*, Contributions to Economics, https://doi.org/10.1007/978-3-319-78494-6_2

this context of volatility of global markets, the probability that a country will get affected from the contagion rises. In the Indian circumstance, sticking to the premise of successive crisis waves being dissimilar, the effect of the contagion, in case of both the crises considered, has little in common to what had happened in the past. Moving away from the third-generation crisis models, the crises that this chapter talks about are a result of exogenous macroeconomic shocks generating either from the domestic environment or from outside. From the authors' perspective, the background story of the two crises considered is widely different but the "external shocks" are something communal between them. It should be clarified that this chapter attempts to answer the research question that how the external shocks, as discussed in this chapter, can destabilize an otherwise stable economy.

The year 2008 turned out to be an *annus horribilis* for the global economy. It was followed by skyrocketing oil and food prices and the contagion soon spread to Asia. Once the avalanche started, the soundness of the decoupling theory became questionable. The reason for the failure of the decoupling theory was the trade and the financial linkages that Asian economies had with the developed world. With the onset of the 2008 crisis, import demand in the USA, UK, and other advanced economies plummeted; abrupt falls in exports and industrial production were recorded in Asia (Athukorala and Kohpaiboon 2009). The decoupling hypothesis became a flawed theory for most of the EMEs but China, India, and Indonesia were the only exceptions where the GDP growth did not become negative and could stand resiliently in the face of global crisis though the growth rates had started to slow down (Das 2010). Going down memory lane, the phase between 2003 and 2007 marked India's unparalleled rise in the growth rate coupled with an outpour of foreign investments. Then out of the blue, India was seen fighting out the 2008 US subprime mortgage market crisis. The inter-connectedness among the macroeconomic channels added fuel to the fire. During 2008–2009, there was a slide in the growth rate but the economy quickly recovered in 2009–2010. But in 2011–2012, the situation was different and in addition to the global recession two major modifications (shocks emanating from within the domestic economy) were introduced in the Union Budget, viz., RBI's restrictions on FPI and FII and also the General Anti-Avoidance Rule (GAAR) declared in the Union Budget in February 2012 wreaked havoc. The Eurozone crisis did not affect India to a great extent and it quickly recovered, but the shocks as mentioned above proved to be drastic for India. The exchange rate increased unswervingly till August'12 and then was subject to constant minor fluctuations; the inflation rate boomed up and growth rate tumbled (RBI 2013).

The present chapter contextualizes this issue by developing a theoretical macroeconomic model in section "A Macro-theoretic Model" which essentially portrays the consequential impacts of the two major financial crises on India since 2008. In section "The Empirical Analysis", the spotlight is on the empirical modeling of the crises. In particular, the probit model has been designed to mark off the noteworthy factors liable for the occurrence of these crises. This chapter concludes by highlighting future research possibilities in this regard.

Review of Select Literature

The analysis of first-generation models initiated with the works of Kouri (1976) and Krugman (1979) which explain financial crisis as an outcome arising out of an irregularity linking the pegged exchange rate regime with the monetary and fiscal techniques the government pursues; i.e., in that fixed exchange rate regime, the target of the monetary experts was to predetermine a strategy in line with government's deficit on the budget front. According to Krugman (1979), imbalances in the levels of fiscal deficit lead to a deficit on the external sector, but to keep the exchange rate fixed there is a persistent collapse in the quantity of foreign exchange (FOREX) reserves. A fall in FOREX reserves below a minimum level finally culminates into a currency crisis. However, Krugman's highly simplified macro-model with an incomplete modeling of the balance of payments side is not realistic. In a more realistic setup, considering an open economy financial market, Flood and Garber (1984), Connolly and Taylor (1984), Sachs (1987), and Helpman et al. (1988) have all contributed to extending Krugman (1979).

The second-generation models, contrary to the first-generation ones, model the minimization of an explicit objective function [specifically, a quadratic loss function which is a function of how much the output deviates from its natural rate and inflation; for details refer to Barro and Gordon (1983)] to decide as to when the central bank should abandon the fixed exchange rate regime. There may not be a unique equilibrium coupled with the presence of multiple equilibria is what this model champions. The crisis that took place in 1992–1993 in the European exchange rate structure is an example of this multiple equilibrium approach (Karmakar 2014). To explain this multiple equilibrium case, consider two speculators. It is known to one that the selling of holdings by the other speculator will lead to a depreciation of the domestic currency and consequently the worth of his holdings reduce. Neither wants to be stubborn when the other considers selling. Therefore, a form of prisoner's dilemma situation prevails when both of them have to sell even though everyone may be worse off after the devaluation. A priori, can one comment on the conditions as to when a country happens to be susceptible to a speculative attack? A sufficiently low level of FOREX reserves makes it known to each speculator that selling their domestic currency will deplete the foreign reserves that the central bank has at its disposal, and devaluation becomes inevitable. But if the fundamentals are strong, i.e., if the level of reserves with the central bank is adequately high so that both speculators know that even if they sell their domestic currency, devaluation is not imminent and there is no reason to launch a speculative assault. This is one possibility. But the intermediate range throws up an interesting case. If the horribility of the situation is not too severe, the country lies in the "zone of vulnerability." In such a case, then both outcomes are equally probable, i.e., either launch a speculative attack or do not. This was the case with Sweden and UK. The willingness shown to raise the interest rates by both the countries in 1992 as a measure of defense for the krona and the pound failed to create an impression among the speculators and persistent speculative attacks continued against such currencies (Frankel and Wei 2005). Given the construction of the second-generation crisis model, there can be a unique equilibrium when a policy change is consistent with what the speculators expect [see Obstfeld (1996)].

Going by the third-generation models, interpretation of crises is a problem of moral hazard. In the light of this argument, "crony capitalism" suddenly became popular and placed emphasis on how the financial structure in the developing economies was distorted. In technical terms, this means the financial sector crisis arising out of government guaranteeing poorly regulated banks and corporate debtors. In the background of the formation of domestic asset price bubbles is the misconception people have of financial intermediaries doing well when they invest. In reality, it's not and hence the explosion leading to these financial intermediaries becoming insolvent, and as prices collapse, severe capital flight occurs. An example of such a situation is the East Asian crisis of 1997–1998. All of a sudden Asian countries did not develop structural flaws for the first time in 1997. Then the question of why the crisis suddenly cropped up was doing the rounds. The arrival of the attack again is the brainchild of the speculators who calculate it. They have a fear in their mind that if they wait for long, sufficient foreign exchange reserves will not be left to cash in. The key difference between the first-generation and the third-generation crisis models that the literature has pointed out lies in the timing of the attack. In the first-generation models, FOREX reserves steadily fall off over time and the attack happens when reserves sink in below a critical level. But in the later case, the steady rise in the level of liabilities over time, artificially encouraged by a situation of moral hazard, determines the time of attack. Now, big businessmen and banks borrow from abroad to finance risky projects on the belief that if things go wrong then government will come to their rescue even when the government declares well in advance of the usual disclaimer (Frankel and Wei 2005). There is as such no critical level but when speculators form a belief that if they hang on for longer, their money would get stuck up and the chances of recovery falls. Thus, speculative attack routinely happens and the central bank is forced to do away with that exchange rate. The four generations of crisis models have been summarized in Table 2.1.

Modifying a third-generation crisis model by bringing in asset prices to act in the lead role and constructing a general crisis model and not a currency crisis one per se gave birth to the class of fourth-generation crisis models (Krugman 2001). Extending the argument in line with Krugman (2001), the work by Breuer (2004) identifies ethnic/religious tension, politics, law and order, trust, sociocultural customs, property-related rights, and nature of governance, be it control over the financial sector or the external sector as significant determinants of financial crisis (Tularam and Subramanian 2013). Both the crises that this chapter talks about, viz., the US Subprime crisis and the Eurozone crisis are in essence third-generation models, but based on the analytical procedure followed one can think of them as fourth-generation models. Also, statistical analysis on fourth-generation models include Kaminsky and Reinhart (1999, 2000) and Liu and Lindholm (2006) developing composite pressure indices based on the behavior of some macroeconomic

Table 2.1 Summarizing the four generations of crisis models

Generational models	Leading economists	Main variables
First:	Salant, Henderson, Kouri, Krugman	• The ratio of fiscal deficit to GDP • The money balance in real terms M_1 • Government consumption/GDP ratio • Growth of credit availability • M_2 growth • Capital and current account balance • Evolution process of real effective exchange rate
Second:	Ecichengreen, Rose, Obstfeld, Jeane, Wyplosz, Masson	• Exports • Imports • Real effective exchange rate • Terms of trade • Production levels • Real interest rates.
Third:	Krugman, Mckinnon, Corsetti, Pesenti, Roubini, Bhattacharya, Claessens, Ghosh, Hernandez, Alba	• Ratio of domestic credit to GDP • Ratio of M_2 to international reserves • Money multiplier in terms of M_2 • Stock prices • Bank deposits
Fourth:	Krugman	• Asset prices • Ethnic and religious tension • Policies of the government • Law and order • Sociocultural customs • Property-related rights

Source: Compiled by the authors from Tularam and Subramanian (2013)

variables like exchange rate, current account balances, FOREX reserves, etc. at the time of crisis. Moving on to the Greek financial crisis in 2015 (which did not have much of an effect on India), it has opened up a new avenue of research where the concept of "Optimum Currency Areas (OCA)" of Mundell (1961) has taken center stage. OCA theory maintains that you cannot have a common currency for a group of very dissimilar economies. Until and unless there is a strong similarity between the participating economies or at least some strong convergence process—a common currency could end up in a disaster. This is exactly what happened with Greece in 2015–2016 (Karmakar and Mukherjee 2017).

With reference to the other three-generational models, fourth-generational crisis models are still under development and relatively less work has been carried out. In an endeavor to contribute to the existing studies on fourth-generation models, the authors try to introduce a theoretical and empirical synthesis of how the above-mentioned crises had an impact on India.

A Macro-theoretic Model

India's golden period which started from 2003 to 2004 witnessed an unparalleled rise in the growth rate coupled with an environment of stable and favorable balance of payments (BOP) situation followed by a highly uncertain phase of global recession and unfavorable balance of payments situation. The theoretical model developed is based on the standard Keynesian notion of open economy modeling with imperfect capital mobility as the nucleus. To model India's case, certain modifications have been made and those will be accordingly clarified as and when required. The period being examined is a short-run context so GDP is assumed to be demand determined. Also, to model the price level and the inflation rate determination thereof, the supply side has been incorporated. The model basically is a three sector model comprising of the real market, financial sector and the external sector. Now, the authors move on to the construction of the model.

To start off with, firstly, the authors will introduce two analytical simplifications consistent with the Indian scenario. Following the work of Lahiri et al. (2015), the rate of interest has become a policy variable and is regulated by the RBI using Liquidity Adjustment Facility (LAF) and Open Market Operations. Thus, it is fixed up at a particular level. Also, imported intermediate inputs, say, for example, petroleum and petroleum products, fertilizers, electronic apparatus, etc. are very much essential for production along with indirect taxes, denoted as $\bar{t}$, constituting an important source of tax revenue. As firms take short-term loans to finance their purchases of factor services and intermediate inputs, $\bar{r}$ has become a determinant of the marginal cost of production. Thus,

$$r = \bar{r} \text{ and } P = P(e, \bar{t}, \bar{r}) \tag{2.1}$$

Modeling the goods market: $Y = C\big[(1-t)(1-\bar{t})Y\big]$
$$+ I(\bar{r}, D, eP^*) + G + NX(Y, Y^*, eP^*, P)$$

$$\text{or } Y = E(Y, Y^*, P^*, e, \bar{r}, D, G, t, \bar{t}) \tag{2.2}$$

In Eq. (2.2), $Y \equiv$ NDP at factor cost as per national income terminology, C is consumption which is a function of disposable income, $I \equiv$ investment, $r \equiv$ interest rate, $D \equiv$ Central bank's credit to the commercial banks, and $t \equiv$ direct tax rate. Investment is a function of rate of interest the exchange rate while $P^* \equiv$ foreign price in foreign currency, $e \equiv$ nominal exchange rate, $P \equiv$ domestic price level, $NX \equiv$ net exports, and $Y^* \equiv$ GDP of whole of the other countries of the world except the domestic economy. Given the small country assumption holds, P^* and Y^* are assumed to be given. To deliberate more about the assumption of interest rates being fixed at a specific level and how money market reacts to this is something worth exploring. Consider a stylized balance sheet of a Central Bank, say RBI for instance in Table 2.2,

Table 2.2 A Central bank's stylized Balance Sheet

Liabilities	Assets
Domestic currency in circulation (H)	Foreign Exchange Reserve (F)
Reserves of commercial banks (R)	Credit extended to domestic agents including commercial banks (D)

From the balance sheet identity $H + R = D + F$. (Note that here F is given in terms of domestic currency, i.e., at the exchange rates at which foreign currencies were procured by the central bank.) Using this, the money market equilibrium condition turns out to be

$$\frac{H}{P} + \frac{R}{P} = \frac{D}{P} + \frac{F}{P} = L(\bar{r}, Y). \tag{2.3}$$

That there is no interference on the part of the central bank epitomizes a flexible exchange rate regime. Hence, the foreign exchange reserve of the central bank, F, may be considered as fixed. Given the CRR, SLR and REPO rates are regulated by the central bank exogenously; the amount of reserves becomes exogenous in such a context. Also, it has been assumed that domestic agents hold a negligible part of their total financial wealth in the form of foreign assets (Lahiri et al. 2015). In Eq. (2.3), there are three endogenous variables—Y, D, and P. Corresponding to any given Y, one can solve for the value of D that satisfies it, given P and the exogenous policy variables. Take any (Y, D) that satisfies Eq. (2.3). Let us denote it by (Y_0, D_0) and one can write

$$\frac{D_0}{P} + \frac{F}{P} = L(\bar{r}, Y_0). \tag{2.4}$$

Now, suppose Y increases *ceteris paribus* from Y_0 by a given amount dY. Then, demand for real balance goes up by $L_y(\bar{r}, Y_0)dY$ creating an excess demand for real balance of the same amount. This encourages domestic agents to sell off, both domestic and foreign bonds to increase their holding of real balance bringing about an excess supply in the domestic bond market. The excess supply of domestic bonds puts downward pressure on the domestic interest rate. Since the central bank wants to keep r at $\bar{r}$, it has to buy up the domestic bonds offered for sale with the domestic currency. The central bank's intention of purchasing bonds from domestic agents through open market operations imply an increase in D, and, therefore, that increases $(H + R)$ by the value of purchase. Thus, as long as there is excess demand for real balance, the excess supply of domestic bonds will persist and the supply of real balance will increase through the increase in D.

Fittingly, $\frac{H+R}{P}$ and $\frac{D}{P}$ will increase by $L_y(\bar{r}, Y_0)dY$. This is how central bank keeps r at $\bar{r}$.

Moving on to the characterization of the BOP equilibrium, it follows from Eqs. (2.2) and (2.3) that if the goods market and money market are in equilibrium, the external sector or BOP is also in equilibrium. This can be proved by using the Walra Law which states that if all markets except one are in equilibrium, then that particular market has to be in equilibrium. Formally, it is stated as "the values of excess demand (or, excess market supplies) must sum to zero" (Lange 1942). That is,

$$\sum_{j=1}^{m} p_j(D_j - S_j) = 0 \qquad (2.5)$$

The literature on financial crises so far has talked stuff which does not model the Indian context per se. This model includes both Y and Y^* in the net capital inflow function. Including Y^* is in line with the impact of capital inflow from the rest of the world. Therefore,

$$K = K(\bar{r} - r^*, \theta, \varphi, Y, Y^*, e).$$

where $(\bar{r} - r^*)$ represents the interest rate differential and r^* represent the foreign interest rate, which is given to the domestic economy. θ in the model means the belief that foreign investors have about investment in India, completely an exogenous factor; may be political in nature. Also tax rates applicable are an important determinant. The parameter φ captures the legal restrictions on both FDI and FPI. There are legal caps imposed by GoI and the RBI on certain sectors like multi-brand retail. Following the argument in Eq. (2.5), BOP equilibrium is given as

$$K = K(\bar{r} - r^*, \theta, \varphi, t, \bar{t}\, Y, Y^*, e) + NX(Y, Y^*, P^*, P, e) = 0$$
$$\Rightarrow B(\bar{r} - r^*, \theta, \varphi, t, \bar{t}\, Y, Y^*, e, P^*) = 0 \qquad (2.6)$$

In this framework, there are four unknown variables and four equations. So the model is solvable. In addition to that, among the four variables, if one solves for e, P can be solved directly given the value of indirect tax rate. Therefore, the model actually reduces to three variables. It needs to be noted that this model is a kind of a short period model highlighting short-run situations, say, over a year, quarter, or a month, etc. and as a result, one cannot use it for long-run predictions. The diagrammatic setup of the determination of equilibrium process follows in Fig. 2.1.

Given the specifications of the model, it contains four key equations, (2.1), (2.2), (2.3), and (2.6), and has four endogenous variables D, Y, e, and P. Equation (2.2) gives the value of Y that keeps the goods market in equilibrium, when e and D are at such a value that it is not only the money market but also the FOREX market which is in equilibrium. Diagrammatically deriving Eq. (2.2) (left side panel), where the EE schedule provides the value of aggregate planned demand for goods and services, given by the right-hand side of (2.2). The equilibrium Y corresponds to the point of intersection of the AD schedule and the 45° line. Figure 2.1 illustrates that $(NX + K)$ schedule gives the values of $(NX + K)$ corresponding to different values of e, for

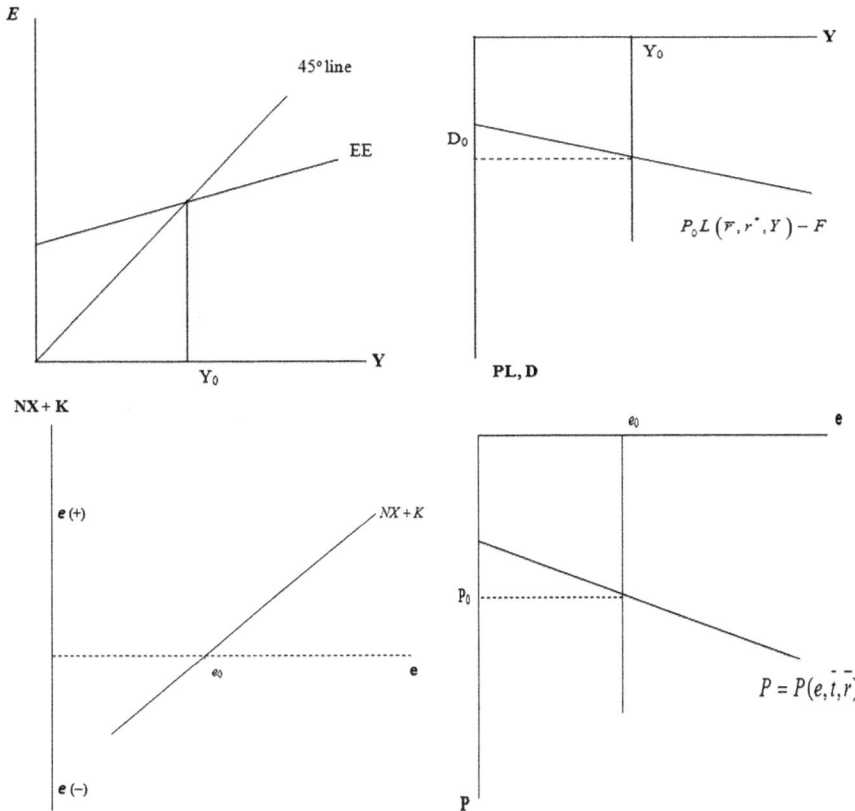

Fig. 2.1 Diagrammatic representation of the equilibrium

given values of Y, P, and the other control variables. Since, following an increase in e, net export has been assumed to rise (thus satisfying the "Bickerdike–Robinson–Metzler"[1] condition) leading to the $(NX + K)$ schedule being positively sloped signifying both negative and positive BOP situations. The equilibrium e is labeled e_0 in Fig. 2.1. From (2.1), given everything else, it solves for P corresponding to the value of all the policy and exogenous variables. The P function in (2.1) is an increasing function of its parameters and has been accordingly labeled. The sequence actually gets portrayed in Fig. 2.1. Hence, substituting the equilibrium value of e, as given by Eq. (2.6), in Eq. (2.1), one can derive the equilibrium value of P in terms of Y and other policy and exogenous variables. Again, substitute these equilibrium values of e and P in Eqs. (2.2) and (2.3) to simultaneously solve for the equilibrium values of D and Y. The solution system becomes:

---

[1]The condition that depreciation will improve the position of trade balance of a country is known as the Bickerdike–Robinson–Metzler condition or, in particular, the Marshall–Lerner condition (for details see Rose and Yellen 1989).

$$Y = f\left(Y^*, P^*, \bar{r}, r^*, G, t, \bar{t}, \varphi, \theta\right) \tag{2.7}$$
$$D = f\left(Y^*, P^*, \bar{r}, r^*, G, t, \bar{t}, \varphi, \theta\right). \tag{2.8}$$
$$e = f\left(Y^*, P^*, \bar{r}, r^*, G, t, \bar{t}, \varphi, \theta\right) \tag{2.9}$$
$$P = f\left(Y^*, P^*, \bar{r}, r^*, G, t, \bar{t}, \varphi, \theta\right) \tag{2.10}$$

The purpose of the model is to explain growth and inflation of an open (small) economy in the short run but the process in which equilibrium values are determined takes up a secondary role here. The authors will start off with situations to show that how changes in different exogenous parameters have landed India into trouble during the last 10 years. These comparative static results explain the different crises that Indian economy has encountered since 2008.

In the recent literature (like Lahiri et al. 2015) on the employment of macroeconomic modeling to explain financial crisis, the incorporation of the money market in the equilibrium process has been ignored through the assumption of the rate of interest being fixed at a certain level. But to maintain this assumption, as already explained, the money market is very much functional and should be analyzed in conjunction with the BOP situation and the goods market. In this chapter, the storyline remains the same but the methodological setup has been revamped.

Proposition 1 (a) *A decrease in θ will tend to lower Y, raise e and hence inflation.*
(b) *But a decrease in Y* will tend to lower Y unambiguously while e fluctuates on account of short-run adjustments.* □

To sum up the consequential aftermath of the subprime crisis, insights on three most important macroeconomic indicators, specifically, growth, exchange rate, and inflation, will be decisive. The crisis was mostly on account of flawed monetary policy taken up by the Federal Reserve which simply did not have anything to do with India. Thus, it is the prerogative of this model to explain how an exogenous impact led to the contagion. The period before the financial crisis saw the GDP growth expanding at 9% with the deficit on the current account placed at 1.3% of the GDP. The inflation rate, being 4.7%, was also under control with a strong foreign capital inflow. In due course, the effect of the contagion became prominent with the insolvency of Lehman Brothers' in mid of September in 2008. The consequential impacts started with the FII outflows from the equity markets leading to a credit crunch and creating a contemporaneous pressure in the foreign exchange market across the globe; India was no exception.

In this period of financial turmoil, the rupee depreciated sharply from Rs. 48 per US$ to Rs. 49 per US$ and by November, 2008 was standing at Rs. 50 per US$ (circled part in Fig. 2.2). It is also clear from Fig. 2.2 that the exchange rate follows a rising trend. The deceleration in growth happened and it stood at 6.7% registering a massive drop of 2.1% from the previous 5-year period average growth of 8.8% (Dullien et al. 2010). In the second week of June 2008, food price inflation was soaring high on account of a significant ramble in global food and fuel prices. Figure 2.3 reflects percentage changes that took place in the CPI inflation rate during that period along with the percentage change in real GDP as compared to the past

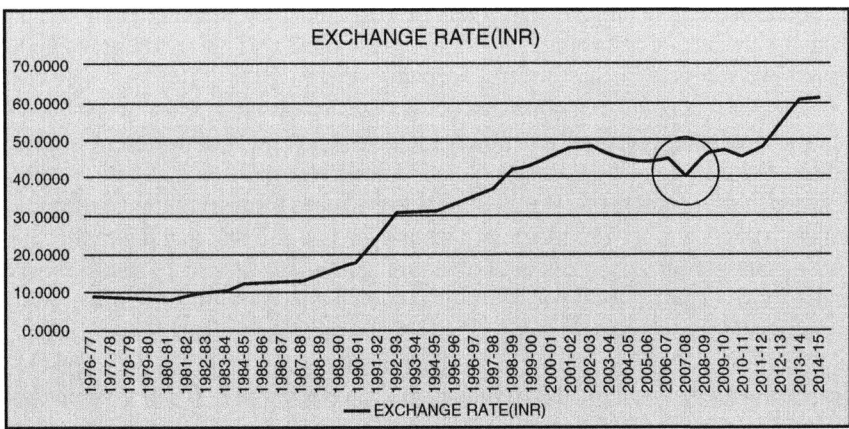

Fig. 2.2 NEER (Rupee vis-à-vis US$) movements between 1976 and 2015. Source: Compiled from various RBI bulletins

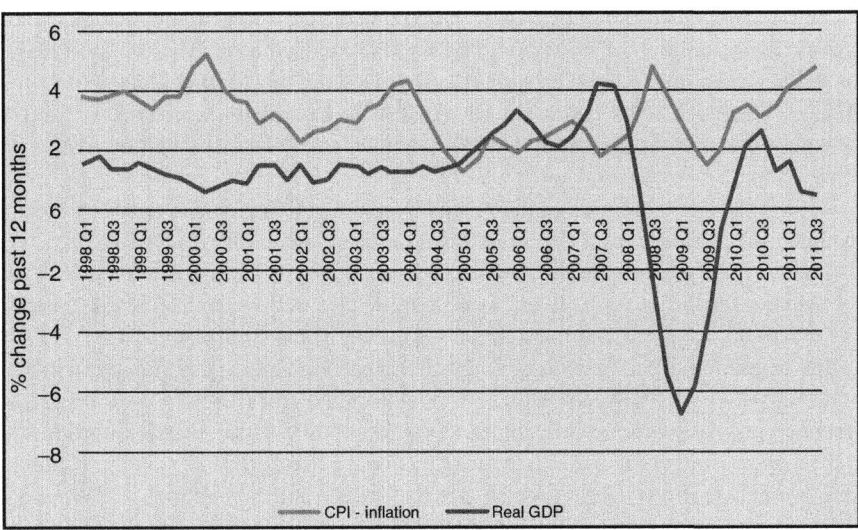

Fig. 2.3 Growth-inflation movements (percentage changes). Source: Compiled from various RBI bulletins (For the mathematical derivation of proposition 1, refer to Appendix A.1 and A.2)

12 months. For the first time in India's economic history, inflation crossed the double digit mark reaching 11% in spite of RBI's continued monetary tightening operations. The decline in exports coupled with capital outflows and the intensification in the dollar value against key currencies was the cause of the unrelenting downward pressure on the rupee.

Things slowly started changing. The results of the general elections created a sense of political stability, and propped up by market sentiments, the persistent depreciation of the rupee staged a fantastic turnaround. The rupee which depreciated sharply from 39.99 to 50.95 between March, 2008 and 2009, stabilized to 45.14 per US dollar by the end of March, 2010. Moving on to the next part of the story, India entered into recession again since the second quarter of 2011–2012.

The Indian economy's performance in this period was epitomized by slowdown in growth and high-pitched inflation with expanding fiscal and current account deficits. Weakening of both domestic and external demand coupled with a global recession in the rest of the world added fuel to the fire. The onset of global recession through a decline in Y^* brings about a decline in Y, a rise in e and hence a rise in inflation rates. Intuitively, it can be argued that a fall in the value of Y^* brings about a decline in net exports, leading to a rise in e through the rightward shift of the ($NK + K$) curve in Fig. 2.1 (external sector equilibrium in quadrant 3). This leads to a rise in the degree of inflation through an increase in the value of P. These results are consistent with the theoretical predictions given in Appendix B.1. The repercussion effect led to a fall in the growth rate; it stood at 6.5% in 2011–2012 as compared to 8.4% in the previous year. In this process of adjustment, as the level of GDP started to come down it kind of corrected the BOP deficit as the nominal effective exchange rate from Rs. 52.6769 in December 2011 fell to Rs. 49.1671 in February 2012 (RBI 2012a, b). Only this piece of evidence on account of very short-run fluctuations goes against the assumption of satisfying the "Bickerdike–Robinson–Metzler" condition for India. But in other cases, as supported by the data, the "Bickerdike–Robinson–Metzler" condition holds good. The fluctuations in e on the back of a fall in the Y^* have been captured in Appendix A.2 *[The mathematical derivation of the results in proposition 2 are given in Appendix B.1]*.

Recession in the euro area accompanied by an uncertain global economic climate damaged the prospects of a rise in external demand. According to RBI (2012a, b), "Domestic policy uncertainties, governance, and corruption issues amidst lack of political consensus on reforms led to a sharp deterioration in investment climate." The recession deepened and marked the beginning of the Eurozone crisis.

The beginning of the volatile period was marked with an almost 17% jump in the value of the rupee between August and December, 2011. The Eurozone crisis deepened and lack of plausible solutions on top of two major changes introduced in the Union Budget, viz., RBI's restrictions on FPI and FII and also the General Anti-Avoidance Rule (GAAR) declared in the Union Budget in February 2012 along with the retrospective modification of the income tax laws relating to the indirect transfer of Indian assets. These ripples gave a massive blow to the foreign investment inflows as credit rating agencies (such Fitch, S&P, etc.) downgraded India (Fitch Ratings 2011). In Fig. 2.4, the downward trend in FDI inflows can be attributed to these reasons. The situation since 2011–2012 has seen a fall in the growth rate plus a steep rise in the inflation rate following an escalation in the exchange rate which has been shown in this model through a rise in φ.

Proposition 2 *An increase in φ will lower Y and raise e.* □

There was an adverse impact on the foreign investors' confidence as a result of the downgrading of India's sovereign ratings by credit rating agencies in April, 2012 and then again in June, 2012. Correspondingly, there took place a substantial decline

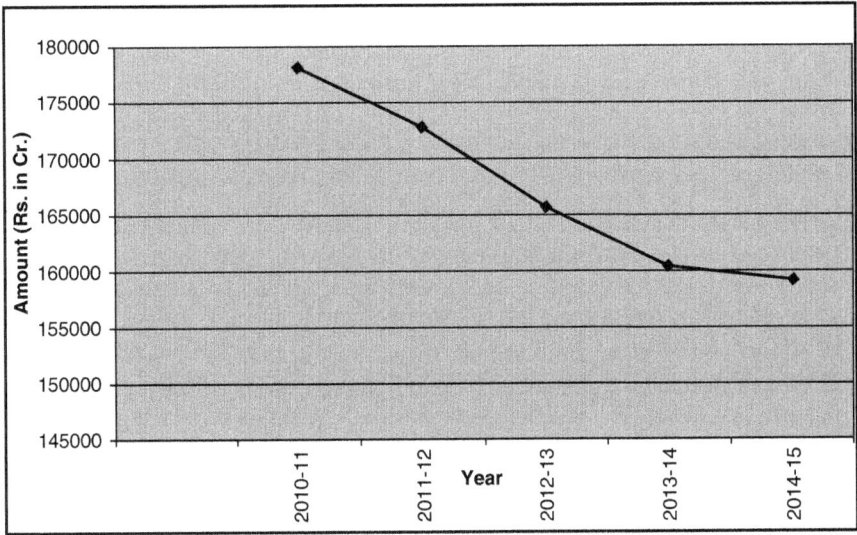

Fig. 2.4 FDI Inflows in India from 2010–2011 to 2014–2015 (Focus period 2012–2013). Source: Compiled from Handbook of Statistics on the Indian Economy, RBI (2012a, b, 2013, 2014, 2015)

in the inflow of the net foreign direct investments (refer to Fig. 2.4). The predictions of this model are reminiscent of the fact that growth rate declined in tandem with skyrocketing exchange rates. This unsettled the government at the center and a currency crisis became inevitable. But, India could avoid such a crisis. A fusillade of measures was adopted to reinstate the confidence of the foreign investors. The first step was the change of guard at the finance ministry thereby postponing the implementation of GAAR and the retrospective amendment of income tax laws. In addition to this, FDI norms were relaxed in the retail and insurance sectors along with an increase in FII limits in the corporate and government debt markets (RBI 2013). The reversal of the foreign capital inflows put the economy in good shape but unfavorable effects stemming from an increase in the indirect tax rates badly affected growth (refer to Appendix C.1). Summing up, macroeconomic well-being of India continued to worsen, notwithstanding the reversal in the net foreign capital inflows.

The Empirical Analysis

Methodology

This chapter has characterized "transmission" as a situation when financial and/or macroeconomic variables of two or more countries face a considerable increase in the correlation (can be positive or negative) on account of an external shock (Edwards and Susmel 1999). The effects of two major crises that India has faced during the period of study are the 2008 US Subprime Mortgage market crisis and the Eurozone debt crisis in 2011 coupled with the global recession. Starting off with monthly and quarterly data (2008–2013) compiled from the RBI Handbook of Statistics database on Indian economy (https://rbi.org.in), database of World Bank (data.worldbank.org), www.indiastat.com, and www.indexmundi.com, the empirical model has been developed. The methodology has been discussed below.

1. At the outset, the chapter builds up a crisis index (CI), at monthly frequency as percentage change in NEER devaluation (relative to the last month) + percentage loss in foreign exchange reserves (relative to the last month) + percentage of GDP lost (relative to the last month) + GDP growth during the month. The index developed is a convex combination of the indices used by Frankel and Rose (1996), Eichengreen and Rose (1995), and Frankel and Wei (2005).
2. A particular month, m in the Indian context will be called a "month of crisis" if

$$CI(m) \geq 20\%$$
$$CI(m) - CI(m - 1) \geq 5\%$$

3. It should be noted that data points for GDP growth in every month were not accessible for 2010 and 2013, so the data had to be interpolated accordingly by using Newton's Forward and Backward Interpolation method.[2]
4. This model will make use of two dummy variables. The first one will tackle the intra-crisis cases and the second one will be related to inter-crisis cases. A variable $ECRI(m) = 1$ if it is a crisis month and 0 otherwise. The other dummy variable, Y_t, will take value 1, when the data pertains to 2008 US financial crisis, i.e., data till March 2010 will come under the period under consideration for the 2008 US crisis and the rest will make way for the Eurozone debt crisis.
5. A response variable, Y, is binary, that is it can have only two probable outcomes which will be denoted as 1 or 0 otherwise. There exists a vector of regressors X, which can possibly influence the outcome variable Y. Specifically, the model takes the form:

$$\Pr(ECRI = 1/X) = \Phi(X^T \beta) + \varepsilon$$

---

[2]Newton's forward and backward interpolation formula is used to interpolate the missing values and they look like,

- *Newton's forward interpolation formula*:
  $$U_{a+rh} = U_a + r_{C_1} \Delta U_a + r_{C_2} \Delta^2 U_a + \ldots r_{C_n} \Delta^n U_a; \quad r = \frac{x - x_0}{h}$$
  where, h is the difference between two consecutive step values and x_0 is the initial value.
- *Newton's backward interpolation formula*:
  $$U_{n+vh} = U_n + v\Delta U_{n-1} + \frac{v(v+1)}{1 \times 2} \Delta^2 U_{n-2} + \ldots \frac{v(v+1)\ldots(v+n-1)}{1 \times 2 \times \ldots \times n} \Delta^n U_a; \quad v = \frac{x - x_n}{h}$$
  where, h is the difference between consecutive step two values and x_n is the terminal value.

Table 2.3 LM test for normality test result

Observations	Chi-square	P value	Normality result
72	0.07	0.97	Yes

Source: Calculations done by the author in STATA 12

where ε assumes a standard normal distribution, Φ is the cumulative distribution function, and X is the vector of regressors, and it consists of:

(a) Trade openness, measured by the Trade Orientation Ratio, *TOR* as

$$TOR = \frac{Exports + Imports}{GDP}$$

(b) External debt to GDP ratio, *ED*
(c) FDI + equity inflows (percentage of GDP), *FDI*
(d) Rate of inflation with one period lag, i_{-1}, to tackle the multicollinearity issue
(e) Budget deficit as a share of GDP, *BD*
(f) The time dummy, Y_t

6. Before estimation of the model, the first robustness check is the validity of the "normality assumption." At this point, Amadou (2010) test of normality of residuals in a probit model has been conducted. That the population is normally distributed forms the null hypothesis and if the *p*-value is less than the preferred level, then the rejection of the null hypothesis is confirmed and there is evidence that the data points being tested are from a non-normal population. One more methodological issue that needs to be addressed before beginning. When variables are drawn from a list of potential candidates that figure prominently in this regard, many of them are undoubtedly endogenous. So, the technique used is Heckit corrections (Nicoletti and Peracchi 2001) for multivariate probit to control for endogeneity. Following Maddala (1986), this method says that including the correlations between the endogenous regressors and the error term should be included as additional variables in the model. This is how we have actually controlled for the endogeneity problem in our model.

7. *skprobit* is the function in STATA statistical software that carries out a Lagrange Multiplier Test to check out the normality positions of the residuals of a Probit model. The results reported in Table 2.3 indicate that residuals are indeed normal as the presupposition of normality gets accepted under the null hypothesis.

8. In trying to estimate this model, the second robustness verification is checking out whether the model suffers from multicollinearity or not. Imprecisely, *TOR* may be correlated with *FDI* but that does not hamper the results. The result of the multicollinearity check is given in Table 2.4. The VIF value defined by

$$VIF = \frac{1}{1 - R^2}.$$

The rule of thumb is that VIFs over and above the value of 10 demand further investigation, but in this model the value is well within the stipulated bounds and as a result it does not suffer from multicollinearity. Perhaps one cannot rule out a certain

Table 2.4 VIF results

Variable	VIF
TOR	2.73
ED	1.61
FDI	4.58
i_{-1}	3.04
BD	2.97
Y_t	0.56
Mean VIF	2.58

Source: Calculations done by the author in STATA 12

degree of correlation amongst the focus variables. The estimation results of the probit model follow.

Results and Discussions Thereof

Before moving on to the estimation results, an assumption based on which this empirical model has been executed states that an imminent threat of a crisis cannot bring in additional financing from across the globe, and funds for recovery comes only when the crisis has set in. Hence, it is considered to be an unobserved factor which has not been modeled.

The authors will begin with the interpretation of the pseudo R squared reported in the model. STATA actually reports the one proposed by McFadden. It is defined as

$$R^2 = 1 - \frac{\ln L(M_{\text{full}})}{\ln L(M_{\text{intercept}})}$$

When likelihood value of "only intercept" model is low, then log of the likelihood is definitely of a higher magnitude as compared to the log of a "full blown" model. In that case, the ratio of log likelihoods becomes small indicative of the fact that the full model is a better fit than the "only intercept" model considered. Consequently, the pseudo R squared value will be very high (Veall and Zimmermann 1992). Interpretation of the coefficients in case of probit regressions needs to be done very cautiously. When the coefficient for any forecaster variable turns out to be positive, it implies that a unit rise in the value of that variable actually leads to an increase in the value of the expected probability. Correspondingly, for a negative coefficient, the connotation is precisely the opposite. Furthermore, given the values of other predictor variables, this unit increase in the value of a particular predictor powers the probability value depending on the starting value from which it is changing. For instance, a change from 1 to 2 may not be the same as the change from 3 to 4 even if the extent of change is same.

As predicted by the model, TOR, FDI, I, and BD (BD only in the later case) have had very strong influences in powering a crisis. A positive coefficient for TOR implies that more open is the economy, the higher will be the likelihood of encountering a situation of crisis. Analogous is the effect of inflation in the Indian context. Next comes budget deficit. During 2008, budget deficits did not have a significant influence but in the budget for the financial year 2012–2013, reduction in cooking gas subsidy, a hike in the excise and service tax rates by 2%, rise in the freight fares, etc. have all contributed to a fall in the budget deficit (GoI 2012, RBI 2013). This brought the growth rate down, fuelled up the inflation and year-on-year exchange rate fluctuation continued (refer to Appendix C.1). The sign of the *FDI* coefficient means that less FDI means greater is the chance of a crisis happening. When the global recession was in full force and FDI outflows had become a common phenomenon, growth rates slumped, inflation knew no bounds in addition to the depreciation of the rupee, and India was on the verge of a crisis in later part of 2012. As already mentioned in section "A Macro-theoretic Model", two "sudden domestic shocks," viz., the "General Anti-Avoidance Rule (GAAR)" and "amendment to the income tax law retrospectively" were tabled in February'12 which worsened the scenario. Eventually, these measures had to be rolled back which cemented the way for rise in FDI inflows. But since this model is not concerned about the recovery phase, the issues pertaining to how things came back on track have not been dealt with. Last but not the least, comes the issue of external debt.

But the question is external debt has not turned out to be significant in this context. Why?

In a bulletin by the Department of Economic Affairs, Ministry of Finance, GoI (2010) testifies the fact that,

> Though India's external debt has increased in absolute terms during 2009–2010, key debt sustainability indicators suggest that India's external debt remains at a comfortable level. This was made possible because of the external debt management policy of the Government of India, which focuses on monitoring long and short-term debt, raising sovereign loans on concessional terms with longer maturities, regulating external commercial borrowings (ECB) through end-use and all-in-cost restrictions, and rationalizing interest rates on Non-Resident Indian deposits.

Subsequently, moving to the global recession phase, the position of external debts in powering a crisis still remained insignificant. In this background, as stated by the then Finance Minister, GoI, Mr. P. Chidambaram,

> A cross country comparison also shows that India continues to be among the less vulnerable countries with its external debt indicators comparing well with the other indebted countries, particularly in respect of the share of concessional credit in total debt, debt-to-GNI and debt-service ratios, and the share of short-term in total external debt. (GoI 2012).

In spite of the widening current account deficits, rupee depreciation, and a hostile global economic situation, the volume of external debt in India has stayed well inside governable limits (GoI 2016). This actually sums up why external debts have become insignificant in this analysis. Consequently, one can calculate the expected probability of the crisis occurring during the above-mentioned time periods by using these coefficients (insignificant regressors have been omitted), i.e.,

Case 1: $\Phi([0.003 \times TOR] + [-0.008 \times FDI] + [0.001 \times i])$

Case 2: $\Phi([0.006 \times TOR] + [-0.011 \times FDI] + [0.003 \times i] + [-0.477 \times BD])$

On the basis of the results given in Table 2.5, TOR epitomizes the "transmission channel" and is a "likely" contributor to the two major financial crises that India has experienced in the recent past. While the FDI channel validates the theoretical

Table 2.5 Summary of the Probit Regression Results

Variables	2008 to March, 2010	April, 2010 onwards	Contributor to crisis
TOR	0.003 (0.00)	0.006 (0.00)	Likely
ED	−0.131 (0.17)	−0.261 (0.19)	Not likely
FDI	−0.008 (0.003)	−0.011 (0.005)	Likely
i_{-1}	0.001 (0.00)	0.003 (0.00)	Likely
BD	0.001 (0.19)	−0.477 (0.00)	Likely
Pseudo R^2 : 0.56			

Source: Calculations done by the author in STATA 12

arguments proposed in section "A Macro-theoretic Model", the theoretical as well as empirical models are based on the dissection of the crisis period and has nothing to do with the recovery phase or the policies that eventually bailed out India. The main objective is to show how economic theory can explain such events along with an econometric justification.

Conclusion

Summing up the results briefly, all the regressors considered are "likely" contributors of a crisis except *ED*. It is worth mentioning that for countries like India, the probability of encountering a debt crisis reduces as it does not have unsustainable levels of debt at the outset. *FDI* variable is negatively related to the probability of a crisis that is justified on the ground that fall in the level of FDI inflows actually culminates into a kind of financial crisis while the others are positively related to the probability of a crisis happening (refer to section "A Macro-theoretic Model" for theoretical foundations). This analysis even supports Frankel and Wei's (2005) observation that more is the openness of an economy, the lesser is the chance of the economy being stable given that the coefficient of *TOR* is positive. Also, fall in budget deficit kind of motivates a crisis to occur as per the results.

This narrative sets out for the policy makers the tribulations from which one can draw lessons for future reference. The notion of developing such a model was not to emphasize on what caused the crisis or how the crisis spread but to specifically highlight how India was affected. This kind of sets the tone for bringing in panel data analysis across the countries in times of crisis where the crisis index can be calculated by making use of Principal Component Analysis (PCA). This would be indeed worth exploring. In addition to this, the theoretical model has tried to put its best foot forward in explaining the situation during the crisis periods, but to avoid unnecessary complications in the process of framing the model, very short-term fluctuations (say, daily basis) have been ignored. Moreover, this chapter does not make an attempt to predict when and where crises will next appear; instead it reminds us not to trust our hunches and be ready to solve the puzzles of crisis as and when they crop up. The application of such theoretical and econometric tools will be certainly constructive for the researchers working with macroeconomic modeling of crises of other countries round the globe.

Keywords and Definitions

US Subprime Crisis In simple language, the mortgage meltdown in point of fact started with the bursting of the US housing bubble which began in 2001 and reached its peak in 2005 and eventually culminated into a crisis in the autumn of 2008. Following the Federal Reserve's low interest rates, credit availability was made easy and most of the borrowers got credits without correctly examining their ability to pay. A sense of optimism about housing values led to a boom in the housing market and new houses started coming up. But, with supply more than demand, housing prices fell unexpectedly and borrowers who were planning to resale their houses at a higher price and settle the mortgage started defaulting. Global investors having mortgage-backed securities (including many of the banks) started incurring losses and eventually by the 4th quarter of 2008, the subprime mortgage market crisis had struck USA with repercussion effects being felt across the world.

Eurozone Crisis The European debt crisis (often also referred to as the Eurozone crisis or the European sovereign debt crisis) is a multiyear phenomenon that started in the Eurozone since the end of 2009 and continued till the end of 2016. Quite a few Eurozone member countries like Greece, Portugal, Ireland, Spain, and Cyprus were unable to assist over-indebted banks under their national control without the help from third party financial institutions like other Eurozone countries, the European Central Bank (ECB), or the International Monetary Fund (IMF). The aftermath of the crisis had adverse impacts with towering unemployment rates in Greece and Spain reaching around 27% coupled with economic growth plummeting. Also, one of the political fallouts was a change of authority in 10 out of the 19 Eurozone countries, including Greece, Ireland, France, Italy, Portugal, Spain, Slovenia, Slovakia, Belgium, and the Netherlands, as well as outside of the Eurozone, in the UK.

Macroeconomic Modeling A macroeconomic model is an analytical design to illustrate the operations of the different sectors of an economy and how such operations tend to influence the overall macroeconomic situation. This chapter makes use of a standard Keynesian open economy model with imperfect capital mobility at its core to understand how the behavior of certain macro-variables like growth, exchange rate movements, inflation, etc. affects the economy.

Probit Model In econometrics, a probit model represents a type of a regression model where the dependent variable is an ordinal or binary response variable, i.e., it can take only two values, for example, say, a crisis period or a noncrisis period. The objective is to classify observations into two specific categories and thereby assess the predicted probabilities of the occurrence of a particular situation. A response variable, Y, is a binary variable, i.e., it can have only two probable outcomes which will be denoted as 1 or 0 otherwise. There exist a vector of regressors X, which are assumed to influence the outcome Y. Specifically, the model is of the form:

$$\Pr(Y = 1/X) = \Phi(X^T \beta)$$

Trade Orientation Ratio Trade orientation ratio, TOR, is a measure of the extent of the trade openness of a country. It is defined as

$$TOR = \frac{Exports + Imports}{GDP}$$

Budget Deficit The term budget deficit represents a situation when the federal government's expenditure goes beyond its revenue. A budget deficit is a pointer of the financial health of an economy. There are three types of budget deficit:

1. Revenue deficit = Total revenue expenditure − Total revenue receipts.
2. Fiscal deficit = Total expenditure − Total receipts excluding borrowings.
3. Primary deficit = Fiscal deficit − Interest payments.

External Debt External debt (or foreign debt) can be termed as the total value of debt a country owes to foreign creditors, accompanied by internal debt owed to domestic lenders. The debt may include money owed to private commercial banks, central banks of other nations, governments of other nations, or the international financial institutions such as International Monetary Fund (IMF), World Bank, Asian Development Bank (ADB), etc.

Appendix A.1

The standard adjustment mechanisms are applicable and by using Taylor's rule, Eqs. (2.2) and (2.6) have been linearized around the equilibrium values.

The Impact of a Fall in θ

Differentiating Eqs. (2.2), (2.3), and (2.6) with respect to θ and keeping other exogenous variables constant, given the adjustment conditions, the result is

$$E_Y \frac{\partial Y}{\partial \theta} + E_e \frac{\partial e}{\partial \theta} = 0. \tag{2.11}$$

$$PL_Y \frac{\partial Y}{\partial \theta} = \frac{\partial D}{\partial \theta} \tag{2.12}$$

$$-B_Y \frac{\partial Y}{\partial \theta} - B_e \frac{\partial e}{\partial \theta} - B_\theta = 0 \tag{2.13}$$

Writing in matrix notation,

$$\begin{pmatrix} E_Y & E_e & 0 \\ PL_Y & 0 & -1 \\ -B_Y & -B_e & 0 \end{pmatrix} \begin{pmatrix} \dfrac{\partial Y}{\partial \theta} \\ \dfrac{\partial e}{\partial \theta} \\ \dfrac{\partial D}{\partial \theta} \end{pmatrix} = \begin{pmatrix} 0 \\ 0 \\ B_\theta \end{pmatrix} \tag{2.14}$$

Using Cramer's rule, the values of $\dfrac{\partial Y}{\partial \theta}$ and $\dfrac{\partial e}{\partial \theta}$ are

$$\frac{\partial Y}{\partial \theta} = \frac{\begin{vmatrix} 0 & E_e & 0 \\ 0 & 0 & -1 \\ B_\theta & -B_e & 0 \end{vmatrix}}{\begin{vmatrix} E_Y & E_e & 0 \\ PL_Y & 0 & -1 \\ -B_Y & -B_e & 0 \end{vmatrix}} = \frac{-B_\theta E^\theta e}{-E_Y B_e + E_e B_Y} > 0$$

$$\frac{\partial e}{\partial \theta} = \frac{\begin{vmatrix} E_Y & 0 & 0 \\ PL_Y & 0 & -1 \\ -B_Y & B_\theta & 0 \end{vmatrix}}{\begin{vmatrix} E_Y & E_e & 0 \\ PL_Y & 0 & -1 \\ -B_Y & -B_e & 0 \end{vmatrix}} = \frac{E_Y B_\theta}{-E_Y B_e + E_e B_Y} < 0$$

Since the objective is to look at the partials of Y and e with respect to θ, the authors have not calculated the value of the partial of D with respect to θ. Coming to the sign of the partials, if the perceptions of the foreigners improve regarding investment in India, capital inflows will come into the economy and the balance of payments position would improve so $B_\theta > 0$. An increase in income, i.e., a rise in Y will induce imports to rise so the balance of payments position deteriorates $\Rightarrow B_Y < 0$. PL_Y is the monetary value of the change in money demand as income changes, which is positive given the specifications of the money demand function. Moving onto the sign of E_e, there is a doubt regarding the sign. To explain this, the authors have made an assumption that investment in India is more sensitive to exchange rate as compared to income based on Lahiri et al. (2015). An increase in the value of e raises prices of foreign goods in terms of the domestic currency. Since production and investment in India are heavily import dependent, an increase in e value not only leads to a depression of investor sentiments but also due to very high import intensities, imports fall and as a result NX improves. This kind of also justifies why $B_e > 0$. But what about E_e? As argued by Lahiri et al. (2015), the negative impact on investor sentiments outweighs the positive effect of improvement in NX and thus $E_e < 0$. Coming on to the sign of E_Y, where E_Y is the expenditure propensity. As Y rises, imports will rise along with a rise in C. So, on the one hand, there is a positive effect (C rises) and on the other there is a negative effect of a rise in imports. Here, also, it has been assumed that net effect of a rise in imports dominate the rise in C, given India's heavy dependence on imports. So, the value of $E_Y < 0$. Consequently, the results follow. As the exchange rate depreciates, inflation will rise given the specifications of the model and the stability condition:

$$\begin{vmatrix} E_Y & E_e & 0 \\ PL_Y & 0 & -1 \\ -B_Y & -B_e & 0 \end{vmatrix} > 0$$

An increase in the value of $Y*$ has a positive effect both on the balance of payments positions as well as the expenditure function through an improvement in the value of net exports. One more result needs to be highlighted for use in Appendix A.2. Given the construction and specifications in Eqs. (2.2) and (2.6),

$$\frac{E_Y}{E_{Y*}} < \frac{B_Y}{B_{Y*}} \quad \text{or} \quad \frac{E_Y}{E_{Y*}} > \frac{B_Y}{B_{Y*}}.$$

The magnitude of these ratios will be crucial in determining whether exchange rate rises or falls. So, the fluctuations in Fig. 2.2 during 2011–2012 and 2012–2013 clearly got reflected.

Appendix A.2

The Impact of a Fall in Y*

Differentiating Eqs. (2.2), (2.3), and (2.6) with respect to $Y*$ and keeping other exogenous variables constant, and then similarly using Cramer's rule, the result is

$$E_Y \frac{\partial Y}{\partial Y*} + E_e \frac{\partial e}{\partial Y*} + E_{Y*} = 0. \tag{2.15}$$

$$PL_Y \frac{\partial Y}{\partial Y*} = \frac{\partial D}{\partial Y*}. \tag{2.16}$$

$$-B_Y \frac{\partial Y}{\partial Y*} - B_e \frac{\partial e}{\partial Y*} - B_{Y*} = 0. \tag{2.17}$$

Writing in matrix notation,

$$
\begin{pmatrix}
E_Y & E_e & 0 \\
PL_Y & 0 & -1 \\
-B_Y & -B_e & 0
\end{pmatrix}
\begin{pmatrix}
\dfrac{\partial Y}{\partial Y^*} \\
\dfrac{\partial e}{\partial Y^*} \\
\dfrac{\partial Y^*}{\partial D} \\
\partial Y^*
\end{pmatrix}
=
\begin{pmatrix}
-E_{Y*} \\
0 \\
B_{Y*}
\end{pmatrix}
\tag{2.18}
$$

Using Cramer's rule, the values of $\frac{\partial Y}{\partial Y^*}$ and $\frac{\partial e}{\partial Y^*}$ can be derived as

$$
\frac{\partial Y}{\partial Y^*} =
\frac{
\begin{vmatrix}
-E_{Y*} & E_e & 0 \\
0 & 0 & -1 \\
B_{Y*} & -B_e & 0
\end{vmatrix}
}{
\begin{vmatrix}
E_Y & E_e & 0 \\
PL_Y & 0 & -1 \\
-B_Y & -B_e & 0
\end{vmatrix}
}
= \frac{E_{Y*}B_e - B_{Y*}E_e}{-E_Y B_e + E_e B_Y} > 0
$$

$$
\frac{\partial e}{\partial Y^*} =
\frac{
\begin{vmatrix}
E_Y & -E_{Y*} & 0 \\
PL_Y & 0 & -1 \\
-B_Y & B_{Y*} & 0
\end{vmatrix}
}{
\begin{vmatrix}
E_Y & E_e & 0 \\
PL_Y & 0 & -1 \\
-B_Y & -B_e & 0
\end{vmatrix}
}
= \frac{E_{Y*}B_y - B_{Y*}E_y}{-E_y B_e + E_e B_Y}
$$

Given the intuitive arguments mentioned earlier, the results are hence proved.

Appendix B.1

The Impact of a Rise in φ

Following the same line of attack and carrying out the differentiation with respect to φ, the result in the matrix form comes out to be

$$
\begin{pmatrix}
E_Y & E_e & 0 \\
PL_Y & 0 & -1 \\
-B_Y & -B_e & 0
\end{pmatrix}
\begin{pmatrix}
\dfrac{\partial Y}{\partial \varphi} \\
\dfrac{\partial e}{\partial \varphi} \\
\dfrac{\partial Y^*}{\partial D} \\
\partial \varphi
\end{pmatrix}
=
\begin{pmatrix}
0 \\
0 \\
B_\varphi
\end{pmatrix}
\tag{2.19}
$$

Using Cramer's rule, the values of $\dfrac{\partial Y}{\partial \varphi}$ and $\dfrac{\partial e}{\partial \varphi}$ are

$$\frac{\partial Y}{\partial \varphi} = \frac{\begin{vmatrix} 0 & E_e & 0 \\ 0 & 0 & -1 \\ B_\varphi & -B_e & 0 \end{vmatrix}}{\begin{vmatrix} E_Y & E_e & 0 \\ PL_Y & 0 & -1 \\ -B_Y & -B_e & 0 \end{vmatrix}} = \frac{B_\varphi E_e}{-E_Y B_e + E_e B_Y} < 0$$

$$\frac{\partial e}{\partial \varphi} = \frac{\begin{vmatrix} E_Y & 0 & 0 \\ PL_Y & 0 & -1 \\ -B_Y & B_\varphi & 0 \end{vmatrix}}{\begin{vmatrix} E_Y & E_e & 0 \\ PL_Y & 0 & -1 \\ -B_Y & -B_e & 0 \end{vmatrix}} = \frac{E_Y B_\varphi}{-E_Y B_e + E_e B_Y} > 0$$

It should be noted that the sign of B_φ is negative. The more the government places restrictions on FDI and FPI, the lesser will be the capital inflow. There are sectoral ceilings or caps on FDI, and this cap varies across sectors. For details, one can go through RBI (2013). The caps are on the amount of Foreign Institutional Investment (FIIs) in any Indian company. In addition to this, the "General Anti Avoidance Rule (GAAR)" and the "retrospective amendment to the income tax law" kind of hampered the prospects, so growth rate deteriorated further.

Appendix C.1

The Impact of a Rise in $\bar{t}$

Following the same line of attack and carrying out the differentiation with respect to $\bar{t}$, the result in the matrix form comes out to be

$$\begin{pmatrix} E_Y & E_e & 0 \\ PL_Y & 0 & -1 \\ -B_Y & -B_e & 0 \end{pmatrix} \begin{pmatrix} \dfrac{\partial Y}{\partial \bar{t}} \\ \dfrac{\partial e}{\partial \bar{t}} \\ \dfrac{\partial D}{\partial \bar{t}} \end{pmatrix} = \begin{pmatrix} -E_{\bar{t}} \\ 0 \\ B_{\bar{t}} \end{pmatrix} \qquad (2.20)$$

Using Cramer's rule, $\dfrac{\partial Y}{\partial \bar{t}}$ and $\dfrac{\partial e}{\partial \bar{t}}$ turns out to be

$$\frac{\partial Y}{\partial \bar{t}} = \frac{\begin{vmatrix} -E_{\bar{t}} & E_e & 0 \\ 0 & 0 & -1 \\ B_{\bar{t}} & -B_e & 0 \end{vmatrix}}{\begin{vmatrix} E_Y & E_e & 0 \\ PL_Y & 0 & -1 \\ -B_Y & -B_e & 0 \end{vmatrix}} = \frac{E_{\bar{t}}B_e - B_{\bar{t}}E_e}{-E_YB_e + E_eB_Y} < 0$$

$$\frac{\partial e}{\partial \bar{t}} = \frac{\begin{vmatrix} E_Y & -E_{\bar{t}} & 0 \\ PL_Y & 0 & -1 \\ -B_Y & B_{\bar{t}} & 0 \end{vmatrix}}{\begin{vmatrix} E_Y & E_e & 0 \\ PL_Y & 0 & -1 \\ -B_Y & -B_e & 0 \end{vmatrix}} = \frac{E_YB_{\bar{t}} - B_YE_{\bar{t}}}{-E_YB_e + E_eB_Y}$$

Rise in the indirect tax rates restrains production a bit, so the sign of $E_{\bar{t}} < 0$.

The signs of the other partials have already been explained in Appendix A.1. Hence, the results follow.

The sign of $\frac{\partial e}{\partial \bar{t}}$ is ambiguous depending on the strength of the horizontal shifts, i.e., $\frac{E_Y}{E_{\bar{t}}}$ and $\frac{B_Y}{B_{\bar{t}}}$ in Eqs. (2.2) and (2.6) as a result of a unit increase in $\bar{t}$. So this actually explains the fluctuations that took place at that point of time.

References

Amadou, D. I. (2010). SKPROBIT: Stata module to perform Lagrange Multiplier Test for Normality for Probit model. *Statistical Software Components*.

Athukorala, P. C., & Kohpaiboon, A. (2009). *East Asian exports in the global economic crisis: The decoupling fallacy and post-crisis policy challenges*. The Australian National University, Arndt-Corden Department of Economics.

Barro, R. J., & Gordon, D. B. (1983). Rules, discretion and reputation in a model of monetary policy. *Journal of Monetary Economics, 12*(1), 101–121.

Breuer, J. B. (2004). An exegesis on currency and banking crises. *Journal of Economic Surveys, 18* (3), 293–320.

Connolly, M. B., & Taylor, D. (1984). The exact timing of the collapse of an exchange rate regime and its impact on the relative price of traded goods. *Journal of Money, Credit and Banking, 16* (2), 194–207.

Das, D. (2010). *Financial globalization: Growth, integration, innovation and crisis*. Springer.

Dullien, S., Kotte, D. J., Márquez, A., & Priewe, J. (2010). *The financial and economic crisis of 2008-2009 and developing countries*. UNCTAD, United Nations.

Edwards, S., & Susmel, R. (1999). *Contagion and volatility in the 1990s* (No. 153). Universidad del CEMA.

Eichengreen, R., & Rose, A. (1995). Wyplosz 1995. *Speculative attacks on pegged exchange rates: An empirical exploration with special reference to the European monetary system*. Federal Reserve Bank of San Francisco.

F&P (FitchRatings). (2011). *Press note (May 24)*, New Delhi/Singapore. Accessed at https://www.fitchratings.com/site/pr/712961

Flood, R. P., & Garber, P. M. (1984). Collapsing exchange-rate regimes: Some linear examples. *Journal of International Economics, 17*(1–2), 1–13.

Frankel, J. A., & Rose, A. K. (1996). Currency crashes in emerging markets: An empirical treatment. *Journal of International Economics, 41*(3), 351–366.

Frankel, J., & Wei, S. (2005). Managing macroeconomic crises: Policy lessons. In J. Aizenman & B. Pinto (Eds.), *Managing economic volatility and crises* (pp. 315–405). Cambridge: Cambridge University Press.

GoI (Government of India). (2010). *India's external debt: A status report 2009-10*. Press Information Bureau, Ministry of Finance, Government of India, India.

GoI (Government of India). (2012). *India's external debt: A status report 2011-12*. Press Information Bureau, Ministry of Finance, Government of India, India.

GoI (Government of India). (2016). *India's external debt: A status report 2015-16*. Press Information Bureau, Ministry of Finance, Government of India, India.

Helpman, E., Razin, A., & Sadka, E. (Eds.). (1988). *Economic effects of the government budget*. Cambridge, MA: MIT Press.

http://data.worldbank.org/

http://www.indexmundi.com/

http://www.indiastat.com/default.aspx

Kaminsky, G. L., & Reinhart, C. M. (1999). The twin crises: The causes of banking and balance-of-payments problems. *American Economic Review, 89*, 473–500.

Kaminsky, G. L., & Reinhart, C. M. (2000). On crises, contagion, and confusion. *Journal of International Economics, 51*(1), 145–168.

Karmakar, A. K. (2014). Contagious financial crises in the recent past and their implications for India. In *Analytical issues in trade, development and finance* (pp. 499–533). Springer India.

Karmakar, A. K., & Mukherjee, S. (2017). Mortgaging the future? Contagious financial crises in the recent past and their implications for BRICS economies. In *Global financial crisis and its ramifications on capital markets* (pp. 175–190). Springer International Publishing.

Kouri, P. J. (1976). The exchange rate and the balance of payments in the short run and in the long run: A monetary approach. *The Scandinavian Journal of Economics, 78*, 280–304.

Krugman, P. (1979). A model of balance-of-payments crises. *Journal of Money, Credit and Banking, 11*(3), 311–325.

Krugman, P. (2001, March). Crises: The next generation. In *Razin conference*, Tel Aviv University (pp. 25–26).

Lahiri, H., Ghosh, A., & Ghosh, C. (2015). India's recent macroeconomic performance and foreign capital inflows. *Contemporary Issues and Ideas in Social Sciences, 7*, 1–53.

Lange, O. (1942). Say's law: A restatement and criticism. In Lange, O., F. McIntyre, T.O. Matema (Eds) Studies in mathematical economics and econometrics (pp. 49–68). Chicago, IL: University of Chicago Press.

Liu, S., & Lindholm, C. K. (2006). Assessing early warning signals of currency crises: A fuzzy clustering approach. *Intelligent Systems in Accounting, Finance and Management, 14*(4), 179–202.

Maddala, G. S. (1986). Disequilibrium, self-selection, and switching models. *Handbook of Econometrics, 3*, 1633–1688.

Mundell, R. A. (1961). A theory of optimum currency areas. *The American Economic Review, 51*(4), 657–665.

Nicoletti, C., & Peracchi, F. (2001, July). *Two-step estimation of binary response models with sample selection*. In first British Household Panel Survey research conference held in Colchester.

Obstfeld, M. (1996). Models of currency crises with self-fulfilling features. *European Economic Review, 40*(3), 1037–1047.

RBI (Reserve Bank of India). (2012a). *Handbook of statistics on the Indian economy*. RBI database.

RBI (Reserve Bank of India). (2012b). *The economy: Review and prospects*. The annual report on the working of the Reserve Bank of India (pp. 16–74).

RBI (Reserve Bank of India). (2013). *Handbook of statistics on the Indian economy*. RBI database.
RBI (Reserve Bank of India). (2014). *Handbook of statistics on the Indian economy*. RBI Database.
RBI (Reserve Bank of India). (2015). *Handbook of statistics on the Indian economy*. RBI database.
Rose, A. K., & Yellen, J. L. (1989). Is there a J-curve? *Journal of Monetary Economics, 24*(1), 53–68.
Sachs, J. D. (1987). The Bolivian hyperinflation and stabilization. *American Economic Review, 77*(2), 279–283.
Tularam, G. A., & Subramanian, B. (2013). Modeling of financial crises: A critical analysis of models leading to the global financial crisis. *Global Journal of Business Research, 7*(3), 101–124.
Veall, M. R., & Zimmermann, K. F. (1992). Pseudo-R 2's in the ordinal probit model. *Journal of Mathematical Sociology, 16*(4), 333–342.

Chapter 3
The Extreme Value Forecasting in Dynamics Situations for Reducing of Economic Crisis: Cases from Thailand, Malaysia, and Singapore

Chukiat Chaiboonsri and Satawat Wannapan

Abstract This chapter was successfully proposed to clarify the complicated issue which is the dynamic prediction in the extreme events in economic cycles and computationally estimated its impacts on economic systems in ASEAN-3 countries such as Thailand, Malaysia, and Singapore by employing econometric tools, including the Markov-Switching Bayesian Vector Autoregressive model (MSBVAR), Bayesian Non-Stationary Extreme Value Analysis (NEVA), and Bayesian Dynamic Stochastic General Equilibrium approach (BDSGE). Technically, the yearly time-series variables such as Thailand's gross domestic products, Malaysia's gross domestic products, and Singapore's gross domestic products were observed during 1961–2016. Empirically, the results showed the economic trends in the countries containing fluctuated movements relied on the real business cycle concept (RBC model). Additionally, these trends had unusual points called "extreme events" which should be mentioned as an economic alarming signal. Furthermore, the speedy economic adjustments estimated by BDSGE indicated that the extreme fluctuated rates of GDP in ASEAN-3 countries can be the harmful factor to face capital bubble crises, chronic unemployment, and even overpricing indexes. Accordingly, practical policies and private collaboration regarding economic alarming announcements in advance should be intensively considered.

Introduction

In the history of world financial catastrophes, the Great Depression of the 1930s was critically the worst recession period for the world's economic system. Its negative impacts lasted 5 years, overhauling the world's purchasing power, increasing unemployment rates, and terminating financial markets. This critical time was caused by uncontrollable, worldwide economic expansion in 1920. After that, the Asian Financial Crisis, called the bubble burst, was a similar financial emergent case during

C. Chaiboonsri (✉) · S. Wannapan
Faculty of Economics, Chiang Mai University, Chiang Mai, Thailand

© Springer International Publishing AG, part of Springer Nature 2018
H. Dincer et al. (eds.), *Global Approaches in Financial Economics, Banking, and Finance*, Contributions to Economics, https://doi.org/10.1007/978-3-319-78494-6_3

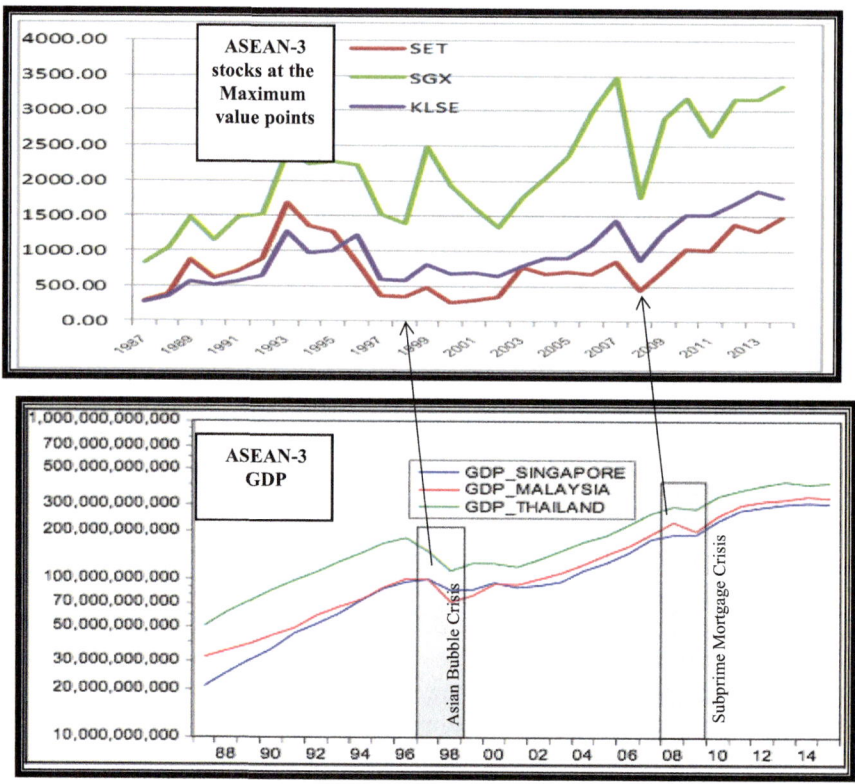

Fig. 3.1 The presentation of ASEAN-3 economic expansions and economic crises [modified from Chaiboonsri et al. (2016)]

1997. This crisis brought an enormous amount of financial companies in Asia to collapse, especially banking systems in Southeast Asian countries. As shown in Fig. 3.1, the blue box displays the perilous signal in ASEAN countries (Thailand, Singapore, and Malaysia) before 1997s bubble crisis surfaced. Afterward, the second Global Financial Crisis occurred which stated that the "Subprime Mortgage Crisis" critically affected the purchase of properties around the world in 2008. Its harmful signals dramatically decreased the world's security of debts as well as economic expansion rates in USA and Europe. This debt crisis also negatively impacted Thailand's exports (Chaiboonsri 2015). In other words, this insecure sign is shown in the red box of Fig. 3.1. The uncontrollable property debt expansion in the USA between 2002 and 2007 caused the 2008 subprime crisis and the economic recession in ASEAN countries. Considering recent economic expansion trends, Thailand's gross domestic product increased from 262,942.65 million US$ to 404,823.95 million US$ between 2007 and 2014 (Bank of Thailand 2016). Similarly, the ASEAN Economic Community's economic augmentation continuously grew during the same period, which was a 94.14% increment from 1,325,823 million US$ to 2,574,000 million US$ (Association of Southeast Asian Nation 2016). Asia's economic trend also grew between 2007 and 2014, which was an approximate 65.16%

increase from 26,442,979 million US$ to 43,674,155 million US$ (Asian Development Bank 2016). Likewise, the world economy experienced a 35.51% enlargement from 57,532,027.10 million US$ to 77,960,606.59 million US$. As we look at the rising movement of economic trends, it is reasonable to state that the alarming economic signal should be systematically considered.

Currently, business cycle computing and the procedures of economic beliefs in the field are the major facts that authorities are curious to diurnally realize. Considerably, the problematic issues of implying the restrictions of acceptance upon "economic liberalizing tendency" are being discussed in the new era of economic research (Chaiboonsri et al. 2016). This leads the authors to enthusiastically adapt the statistical forecasting models that can explain extreme situations in economic movements and precisely alarm critical points in time. The multiplicative predictions in extreme models for alarming economic crisis are employed to statistically investigate the extraordinary points in macroeconomic indicators of Thailand and ASEAN economies. Furthermore, the empirical results in this research are going to be clarified by using the Dynamic Stochastic General Equilibrium model (DSGE) based on Bayesian inference procedures to econometrically study the movements of institutionally economic scenarios when macroeconomic factors are dynamically fluctuated. This process will present many useful points onward from the economic cycle in Thailand as well as ASEAN's economy for reducing economic crises in the upcoming future.

Relate to Literature Review

To explore negative outcomes and policy responses regarding global economic crises is confirmed by international scholars. However, the lack of sensible alarming signals is still the obstruction to broadly influence authorities and investors for being aware of upcoming economic crises. To forecast historical data for alarming economic crisis requires business cycle theory and empirical researches regarding financial crises, fiscal policies, and monetary policies. Duca (2007) examined a casual inspection of stock market prices and GDP in developed market economies. The study called "The Relationship Between the Stock Market and the Economy: Experience From International Financial Markets" summarized that an effective and efficient regulatory framework can prevent the occurrence of runaway prices in domestic stock markets. Sánchez (2011) studied the financial crisis called "Bubbles and Recurrent Crises," which surfaced in 2007. This study named "Financial Crises: Prevention, Correction, and Monetary Policy" stated that monetary policies are ill-suited for directly abating bubbles, and it is better to use regulatory and supervisory implements to target the source of problems.

Econometrically, the global financial crises have also been highlighted by many economists. For instance, Zare et al. (2013) explored the asymmetric effects of monetary policy on real output in Bull and Bear phases of stock markets in five ASEAN economies (Malaysia, Singapore, Indonesia, the Philippines, and Thailand) by using the pooled mean group technique (PMG). The research result stated that interest rates are the major factor in ASEAN-5 countries, and this implied a suitable monetary policy indicator must be utilized. Boudebbous (2015) studied the differences between boom-bust cycles of economic activities and of the stock market for six developed countries during the period from February 1990 to May 2013 by applying an autoregressive Markov regime-switching model. The results concluded that the transfer of shocks from the stock market to the real economy is significant, and that the interdependent relationship between these two entities is considerable. Chaiboonsri et al. (2016) studied the multiplex of forecasting in ASEAN extreme stock data (SGX, KLSE, and SET) during the period of 1987 to 2015 by using Generalized Pareto distribution (GPD) and Bayesian theorem. The result of the empirical research stated that the Bayesian approach was implemented to estimate the Generalized Pareto Distributions (GPD) as the predictive value of the minimum index points. This allowed the authors to conclude that regulators must concentrate on changes in investing behaviors or returns when attempting stabilization policy in general to stimulate the economy after current easing policies.

In order to computationally conduct a precise signal for alarming economic crises, the authors necessitate the statistical inference which can avoid unreasonable assumptions and efficiently enable collected data to inform its real stories. Bayesian statistics is chosen. Interestingly, this subjective inference mentioned in this chapter has been recently being recognized by many researchers in the econometric field since few decades. For example, Geweke (1989, 1998), Bauwens et al. (2000), Spirtes (2005), Koop et al. (2008), Geweke and Amisano (2014), and Kline and Tamer (2016). Hence, this inference would be applied in every step of estimations.

The first section of the research is to employ Bayesian inference for investigating economic cycling trends. The authors combine Bayesian statistics with the Markov-Switching Vector Autoregressive model, and it is defined as the MSBVAR model. Following several academic researches such as Mallick and Sousa (2009), Brandt et al. (2011), Moreira et al. (2013), and Adenomon et al. (2015), this approach is, therefore, applied to better understand the movements of economic trends in ASEAN-3 countries.

According to the second section which is to computationally explore unusual events in ASEAN's macroeconomic indicators, the researchers then apply the statistical method called Non-Stationary Extreme Value Analysis (NEVA) to investigate a rare critical point in economic growth trends. Historically, the NEVA approach has being specifically employed in meteorology. For example, Hundecha et al. (2008), Collier (2010), Cheng et al. (2014), and Hounkpe et al. (2015). Interestingly, the authors originally adapt this extreme-value analysis to econometrically indicate the extreme point, which is used to set the economic alarming signal.

Considering a dynamic econometric model for forecasting economic crises, the researchers employ Bayesian inference in the Dynamic Stochastic General Equilibrium model (DSGE), which is combined with the Markov Chain Monte Carlo (MCMC) simulation and Metropolis–Hasting (MHs) algorithm, to express the sensibly predictive trends that can be the parallel supporter for setting the alarming indicator. The BDSGE model is interested by many researchers in many academic fields, for instance, Adolfson et al. (2007), Fernández-Villaverde (2010), and Kliem and Uhlig (2013). However, it is no evidence that the BDSGE model has been usually used to deeply clarify predictively systematic trends in economics.

From previous literature, it is reasonable to conclude that studies on the alarming macroeconomic indicators of ASEAN countries should not be ignored. Bayesian statistics, extreme value computing, and dynamically predictive models are very essential. As a result, to start with, econometric models and simulation methods for policy recommendations in this chapter to alarm the potential occurrence of economic crises in the upcoming future should be implemented.

Objective of the Chapter

Econometrically, the main object of this paper is to computationally examine the multi-modeling on the predictively extreme value that can identify the level of crisis before potential occurrences based on macroeconomic indicators of ASEAN-3 countries as well as the forecasting using BDSGE model to investigate the dynamics situations of households and firms behaviors in Thai economy, Malaysia economy and Singapore economy (ASEAN-3 countries) respectively.

The Conceptual Framework and Methodologies

To describe the objectives more obviously, Fig. 3.2 represents business cycle and the predictive points for alarming the potential occurrence of economic crises. Point A is the maximum forecasting point in the extreme situation of economic expansible

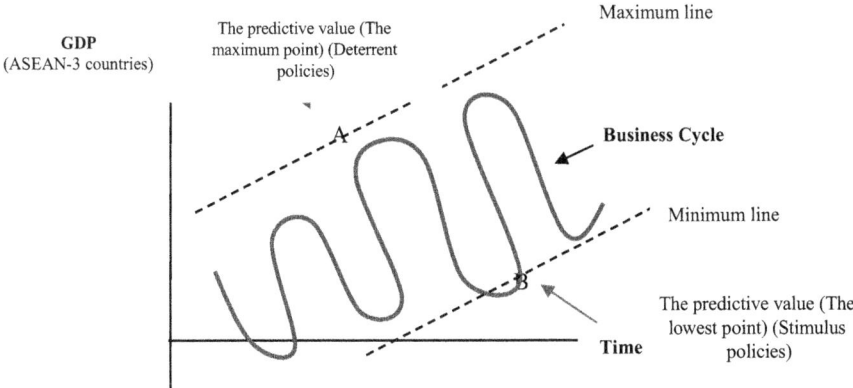

Fig. 3.2 The presentation of business cycle and the predictive point for alarming the potential occurrence in extreme cases

periods. This can provide the level of dangerous signals for launching deterrent policies. Point B is the lowest predictive spot in the extreme cases of economic recession periods. It can provide the level of risky signals for launching stimulus policies. From Chart 3.1, it describes the process of methodologies to estimate and predict the economic cycling parameters. The first method is the regime-switching approach based on Real Business Cycle theory (RBC) which is called Markov-Switching Bayesian Vector Autoregressive (MSBVAR). The second process is extreme value estimating based on Bayesian inference, which is defined as Nonstationary Extreme Value Analysis (NEVA). Lastly, the highlighted section for setting economic alarming signal is the Bayesian Dynamic Stochastic General Equilibrium model (BDSGE).

The Theory of Real Business Cycles

Theoretically explaining about economic fluctuations, the real business cycle theory (RBC), which provides a successful description of recessions and booms, makes the notable contribution of showing that fluctuations in economic activities are consonant with competitive general equilibrium environments in which all agents are rational maximizers (Stadler 1994). In both classical and Keynesian perspectives, many sorts of disturbances can in principle generate fluctuations in real business cycle models. For instance, governments' expenditures, taxations, and even the relative price of oil (Mankiw 1989). Moreover, short-run dynamic relationships between money measures, inflation, and output reflect both the way in which private agents respond to economic disturbances and the way in which the monetary policy authority responds to those same disturbances. For this reason, cross-countries monetary activities are being more important for policy implementations in the recent moment (Walsh 2010).

Bayes Inference for Econometrics

Fundamentally, we obtained the posterior density based on the Bayes' theorem $\pi(\theta|D)$ which stands for a probability distribution of parameters θ. This can be expressed as

$$\pi(\theta|D) \alpha L(D|\theta)\pi(\theta). \tag{3.1}$$

The details in Eq. (3.1) are the prior density for θ. Because the functional form of $\pi(\theta)$ was not known and assumed to be constant. This can be explained in Eq. (3.1) (Takaishi 2010):

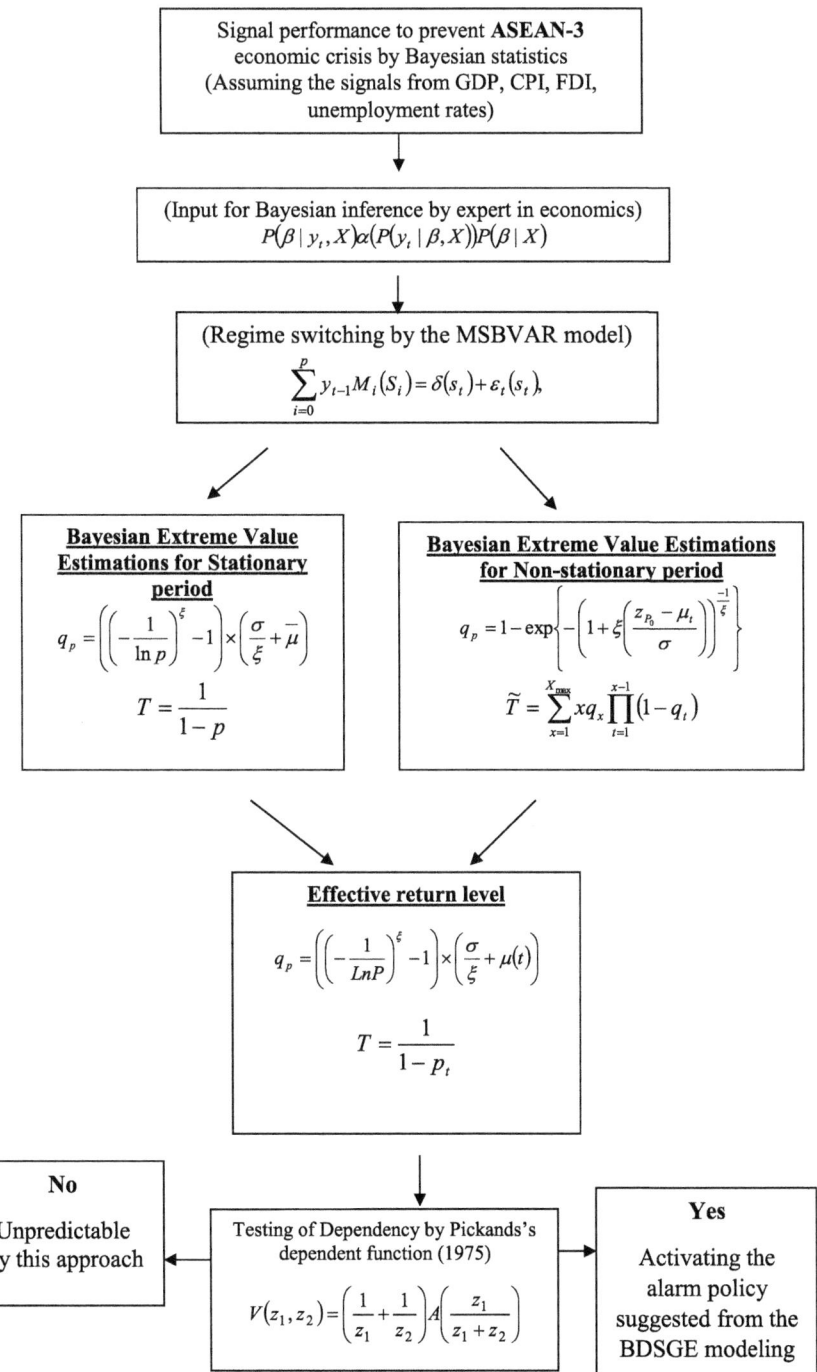

Chart 3.1 The methodology applied to reduce ASEAN-3 economic risks

$$\{\theta\} = \frac{1}{Z} \int \theta \pi(\theta|D) d\theta, \tag{3.2}$$

and

$$Z = \int \pi(\theta|D) d\theta. \tag{3.3}$$

From Eqs. (3.2) and (3.3), the estimated posterior density $\{\theta\}$ cannot be analytically performed. Bayesian modeling requires a joint distribution, which is conveniently factored into a prior distribution for the parameters, and the complete-data likelihood function is written in Eq. (3.4):

$$L(D|\theta) = \prod_{i=1}^{n} \frac{1}{\sqrt{2\pi\sigma_t^2}} \exp\left(-\frac{D_t^2}{2\sigma_t^2}\right), \tag{3.4}$$

where D refers to the time-series data of n observations, $D = (d_1, d_2, \ldots, d_n)$ and θ stands for the estimated parameters. Considering Eq. (3.4), the parameters in the log-likelihood function can be maximized as expressed in Eq. (3.5):

$$LnL(D|\theta) = -\frac{1}{2} \sum_{i}^{n} \ln\left(2\pi\sigma_t^2\right) - \sum_{i}^{n} \frac{D_t^2}{2\sigma_t^2}. \tag{3.5}$$

Markov-Switching Bayesian Vector Autoregressive (MSBVAR)

Based on the journal paper of Hamilton (1989) who introduced a Markov-switching autoregressive model to study on the quarterly data of US GNP, the Markov-switching version of Bayesian vector autoregressive model is conducted and mentioned for breaking down normality assumptions in time-series forecasting. The structural equation of Markov-switching Bayesian VAR (MS-BVAR) is given by

$$\sum_{i=0}^{p} y_{t-1} M_i(S_i) = \delta(s_t) + \varepsilon_t(s_t), \quad t = 1, 2, \ldots, T. \tag{3.6}$$

Considering details in Eq. (3.6), $S_t = j$ is a h-dimensional vector state of the switching process and j is the term of integer labels for the state, with a $h \times h$ Markov transition matrix. The matrix is given by the probability of transitioning from the state S_{t-1} to S_t, which can be mathematically defined as $Pr(S_t = k|S_{t-1} = j)$. For setting the prior in the MSBVAR model, the parameters M_i and δ are determined by sensible beliefs, the random walk prior in the Sims and Zha model (Sims and Zha 1998). Thus, the predictions from a Markov-switching VAR model like Eq. (3.7) are the weighted combination of the forecasts for each state or phase.

The Forecasting in Extreme Value of Non-stationary and Stationary

Fundamentally, studying on the class of issues where the behavior of the distributions, which are over (below) a high (small) threshold, is characterized as extreme events. A random quantity with distribution function $F(X)$ underneath certain conditions shown by Pickands (1975), $F(x|u) = P(X \leq u + x | X > u)$, can be estimated by a Generalized Pareto distribution (GPD). This can be expressed as

$$G(x|\xi, \sigma, u) = \begin{cases} 1 - \left(1 + \frac{\xi(x-u)}{\sigma}\right)^{-1/\xi}, & if \quad \xi \neq 0 \\ 1 - \exp\left\{-\frac{(x-u)}{\sigma}\right\}, & if \quad \xi = 1 \end{cases}, \qquad (3.7)$$

where $\sigma > 0$ and ξ are the scale and shape parameter. The data deliberately display heavy tail behavior when $\xi > 0$. To conduct the threshold coming from a GPD introduced in Eq. (3.7), the authors assume the proposed model that contains observations under the threshold, u, which are generated from a certain distribution with parameters, η. The model is, therefore, defined as $H(.|\eta)$. Consequently, the distribution function F of any observation X can be enumerated as

$$F(x|\eta, \xi, \sigma, u) = \begin{cases} H(x||\eta), & if \ x < u \\ H(u|\eta) + (1 - H(u|\eta))G(x|\xi, \sigma, u), & if \ x \geq u. \end{cases} \qquad (3.8)$$

For an Eq. (3.8) which is a sample size n, $x = (x_1, \ldots, x_n)$ from F, parameter vectors $\theta = (\eta, \sigma, \xi, u)$, $A = (i : x_i) < u$, and $B = (i : x_i)$ with the likelihood function are defined as

$$L(\theta; x) = \prod_A h(x|\eta) \prod_B (1 - H(u|\eta)) \left[\frac{1}{\sigma}\left(1 + \frac{\xi(x_i - u)}{\sigma}\right)\right]_+^{-(1+\xi)/\xi}, \qquad (3.9)$$

$$\xi \neq 0, \text{ and } L(\theta; x) = \prod_A h(x|\eta) \prod_B (1 - H(u|\eta)) \left\{\left(\frac{1}{\sigma}\exp\frac{[(x_i - u)]}{\sigma}\right)\right\}, \quad \text{for } \xi = 0.$$

The threshold, u, detailed in Eq. (3.8) is the point where the density has a discontinuity, which depends on the larger or smaller jumped density. In each case, the choice of observations will be considered as exceedances that can be more obvious or less evident. The smaller jumped density is more difficult to estimate the threshold. Thus, strong discontinuities, or large jumps, indicate separation of the data such that it is expected the parameter estimation would be easier (Behrens et al. 2004).

To extend the concept of GPD estimating, Cheng et al. (2014) introduced Non-stationary Extreme Value Analysis (NEVA) for forecasting extreme value based on Bayesian statistics. This new technique is conducted to examine both the nonstationary time series and stationary time series, especially in the extreme cases of financial critical periods. In this research, the non-stationary extreme value analysis offers a usual measure for linking the predictive value of macroeconomic indicators. The model of the predictive value of Thailand's macroeconomic indicators was described in Eq. (3.10):

$$P(y|\beta, X) = \prod_{t=1}^{N_t} (P(y_t|\beta, X(t))) = \prod_{t=1}^{N_t} (P(y_t|\mu(t), \sigma, \xi)) \qquad (3.10)$$

$P(y|\beta, \chi)$ = the estimation of parameter in GPD under non-stationary based calculated on Bayes theorem
$\mu(t)$ = the location parameter depends on time
σ = the scale parameter
ξ = the shape parameter
X = the time-series data (historical data)
y = the predictive value (the highest and lowest value of macroeconomic indicators)
$X(t)$ = the time-series data both stationary and nonstationary data (historical data)
y_t = predictive value both stationary and nonstationary data (the highest and lowest value of macroeconomic indicators)

To connect the impact of extreme value in ASEAN-3 countries, Pickands' dependence function (Pickands 1975) was employed and defined as follows:

$$V(z_1, z_2) = \left(\frac{1}{z_1} + \frac{1}{z_2}\right) A\left(\frac{z_1}{z_1 + z_2}\right), \qquad (3.11)$$

which satisfied max(t, $1 - t$) $\leq A(t)$ for t belongs to [0, 1] and $A(t) = 1$ for independent data. The dependent function is convex and it can be written as

$$A(t) = 1 - t + 2 \int_0^t Q([0, w])dw, \quad 0 \leq t \leq 1. \qquad (3.12)$$

This formula enabled one to compute Q from A, since

$$Q([0, w]) = \begin{cases} 1 + A'(w) & 0 \leq w < 1 \\ 2 & w = 1 \end{cases}, \qquad (3.13)$$

where A' is the right-hand derivative of A.

The Bayesian Dynamic Stochastic General Equilibrium Model (BDSGE)

For this study, the BDSGE model was relied on a standard real business cycle (RBC modeling) adapted from Collard and Juillard (2001) and Griffoli (2013). Basically, the economy consists of an infinitely living representative agent who values consumption C_t and labor service h_t, and this can be described as the utility function:

$$U_t \sum_{\tau=t}^{\infty} \beta^{\tau-1} \left[\log(c_t) - \theta \frac{h_t^1 + \phi}{} \right], \tag{3.14}$$

where the discount factor is defined as $0 < \beta < 1$, the disutility of tourism labors is $\theta > 0$, and the elasticity of labor supplies is defined as $\phi > 0$. For activating policies, a social planner optimizes this utility function subjected to the resource constraint, which is explained in Eq. (3.15).

$$c_i + i_t = y_t, \tag{3.15}$$

where i_t is investment and y_t output. Consumers are owners of the firms. In a real economy, the output can be consumed and partly invested in the form of physical capital. Thus, the law of motions of capital is defined as

$$k_{t+1} = \exp(b_t)i_t + (1 - \delta)k_t, \tag{3.16}$$

where b_t is a shock affecting incorporated technological progress. Physical depreciation δ is expressed as $0 < \delta < 1$. Also, a standard constant return to scale is assumed to produce output. The form of the production function is given by

$$y_t = \exp(a_t)k_t^\alpha h_t^{1-\alpha}, \tag{3.17}$$

where α is the capital elasticity in the production function, with $0 < \alpha < 1$, and a_t stands for a stochastic shock (or Solow residual). For describing a shock structure, shocks are allowed to display persistence across time and correlation in the recent period. This can be shown in Eq. (3.12).

$$\begin{Bmatrix} a_t \\ b_t \end{Bmatrix} = \begin{Bmatrix} \rho & \tau \\ \tau & \rho \end{Bmatrix} \begin{Bmatrix} a_{t-1} \\ b_{t-1} \end{Bmatrix} + \begin{Bmatrix} \varepsilon_t \\ \mu_t \end{Bmatrix}, \tag{3.18}$$

where $|\rho + \tau| < 1$ and $|\rho + \tau| < 1$ to confirm stationarity. We define ρ is the coefficient of persistence and τ is the coefficient of cross-persistence, and we assume $E_t(\varepsilon_t) = 0$ and $E_t(\mu_t) = 0$ to be the contemporaneous variance–covariance matrix of the innovations ε_t and μ_t, which is described by

$$\begin{bmatrix} \sigma_\varepsilon^2 & \psi \sigma_\varepsilon \sigma_\mu \\ \psi \sigma_\varepsilon \sigma_\mu & \sigma_\mu^2 \end{bmatrix}, \tag{3.19}$$

where the variance–covariance correlation $\mathrm{corr}(\varepsilon_t \mu_t) = 0$ and the variance–covariance correlation $\mathrm{corr}(\mu_t \mu_t) = 0$ for all $t \neq s$.

Technically, the econometric estimation of the BDSGE model is proposed to employ two computational approaches, including the Markov Chain Monte Carlo simulation (MCMC) and Metropolis–Hastings (MH) algorithm. The model and its details are given by

$$P_{MH}(\theta_{i-1}, \theta) == \min\left[1, \frac{P(\theta_i)}{P((\theta_{\theta-1}))}\right], \quad (3.20)$$

where θ_i is the candidate with a probability of $P_{MH}(\theta_{i-1}, \theta)$. When θ_i is refused, we retain θ_{i-1}. After that, the MH procedure will be a loop back to generate a new value θ_i from a certain proposal density $g(\theta_i|\theta_{i-1})$ again. Finally, when the proposal density is not related to the previous value which is $g(\theta_i|\theta_{i-1}) = g(\theta_i)$, we obtain

$$P_{MH}(\theta_{i-1}, \theta_i) = \min\left[1, \frac{P(\theta_i)}{P(\theta_{i-1})} \frac{g(\theta_{i-1})}{g(\theta_i)}\right]. \quad (3.21)$$

From Eq. (3.18), there is a symmetric proposal density $g(\theta_i|\theta_{i-1}) = g(\theta_i|\theta_{i-1})$. This indicates that the Metropolis algorithm is reduced and the Metropolis accepted probability is expressed by

$$P_{MH}(\theta_{i-1}, \theta_i) = \min\left[1, \frac{P(\theta_i)}{P(\theta_{i-1})}\right]. \quad (3.22)$$

For setting sensibly calibrated parameters in the Bayesian way, we conducted priors such as α, ρ, τ, β, δ, ψ, θ, ε and μ to be the initial values for estimating simulated posteriors. The details were represented in Table 3.1.

The Empirical Results of Research

Descriptive Information

Basically, the economic growth trends of ASEAN-3 countries such as Thailand, Malaysia, and Singapore were displayed in Fig. 3.3. It is obvious that the trends were fluctuated during 1961 to 2016. Interestingly, unusual economic movements were observed in at least four sections. The first case is a dramatic jump of growth rates in 1973, which is referred to as "Oil Crisis." This extreme event accompanied a result of many factors culminating in a hugely economic storm, for example, world crop failures, surging in world food prices, the extraordinary increases in oil prices, and the sharp deceleration of productivity (Burns 1979).

Speaking to other three unusual cases in economic growth trends, the economic crises during 1985 to 2009 were defined as depression collapse. Firstly, the drawn-out process of financial deregulation in Sweden and Finland during 1985 to 1990. Its negative impacts called "financial liberalization and overheating" widely caused short-term debt crisis to world economy (Jonung et al. 2008). Secondly, the Asian financial crisis in 1997 originally occurred in Thailand financial systems that enormously built up a high level of debt related to reserves. Since weakness in banking systems and lack of alarming announcements, the country could not tolerate a vast amount of outflow capital and this collapse widely caused a great economic depression to other Asian countries (Berg 1999). Lastly, the bursting of the housing bubble

Table 3.1 Calibrated parameters for prior distributions

Country	Parameters	Description	Initial value (Normal case)	Initial value (Boom)	Initial value (Recess)
Thailand	y	Economic growth rate[a]	0.024	0.150	−0.230
	c	Share of domestic goods in consumption[b]	0.075	0.469	−0.469
	h	Labor supply[b]	0.640	2.900	0.080
	k	Share of capital in production function[a]	1.200	7.500	1.200
	α	The capital elasticity in the production function[a]	0.180	0.306	0.180
	ρ	Persistence of shocks[c]	0.950	0.833	0.120
	τ	Cross-persistence of shocks[c]	0.025	0.156	0.680
	β	Discount factor[a]	0.993	0.993	0.993
	δ	Physical depreciation[b]	0.025	0.025	0.025
	ψ	The labor supply elasticity[b]	1.050	1.200	0.099
	θ	The disutility of labor[a]	1	1	1
	ε	The variance of persistence shocks[c]	0	0	0
	μ	The variance of cross-persistence shocks[c]	0	0	0
Malaysia	y	Economic growth rate[d]	0.065	0.245	−0.15
	c	Share of domestic goods in consumption[d]	0.422	1.662	−1.662
	h	Labor supply[d]	0.990	1.200	0.900
	k	Share of capital in production function[d]	3.000	8.000	0.800
	α	The capital elasticity in the production function[d]	0.350	0.490	0.220
	ρ	Persistence of shocks[d]	0.885	0.500	0.045
	τ	Cross-persistence of shocks[d]	0.012	0.500	0.850
	β	Discount factor[d]	0.985	0.985	0.985
	δ	Physical depreciation[d]	0.025	0.025	0.025
	ψ	The labor supply elasticity[d]	0.720	2.735	0.010
	θ	The disutility of labor[e]	1	1	1
	ε	The variance of persistence shocks[c]	0	0	0
	μ	The variance of cross-persistence shocks[c]	0	0	0

(continued)

Table 3.1 (continued)

Country	Parameters	Description	Initial value (Normal case)	Initial value (Boom)	Initial value (Recess)
Singapore	y	Economic growth rate[e]	0.040	0.300	−0.350
	c	Share of domestic goods in consumption[e]	0.600	5.550	−0.070
	h	Labor supply[e]	−0.100	0.650	0.040
	k	Share of capital in production function[e]	2.500	7.000	1
	α	The capital elasticity in the production function[e]	0.300	0.300	0.300
	ρ	Persistence of shocks[e]	0.800	0.400	0.010
	τ	Cross-persistence of shocks[e]	0.100	0.500	0.800
	β	Discount factor[e]	0.980	0.980	0.980
	δ	Physical depreciation[f]	0.020	0.020	0.020
	ψ	The labor supply elasticity[f]	0.500	1.000	0.040
	θ	The disutility of labor[c]	1	1	1
	ε	The variance of persistence shocks[c]	0	0	0
	μ	The variance of cross-persistence shocks[c]	0	0	0

Source: Author's computed
[a]Tanboon (2008)
[b]Alp and Elekdag (2012)
[c]Griffoli (2013)
[d]Shaari (2008)
[e]Chow-Tan et al. (2014)
[f]Chow and McNelis (2010)

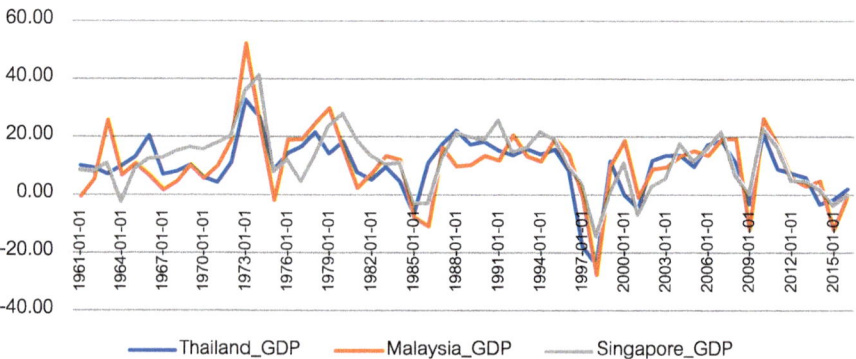

Fig. 3.3 Presenting descriptive economic trends of ASEAN-3

in the USA during 2008 had quickly caused long shadow on the economic fortunes to many countries. This crisis called "Great Recession" surprised many policymakers, multilateral agencies, academics, and investors (Verdick and Islam 2010).

Accordingly, as the review of descriptive facts, crises and their outcomes damaged world economic systems inevitably, alarming signals are more and more crucial. Additionally, this can be confirmed that the trends contained economic cycles.

Estimated Durations of Regimes by the MSBVAR Model

As economic cycles in ASEAN-3 countries were found and demographically explained as descriptive information, the process of regime switching by the MSBVAR model was employed to clarify the type of economic situations. Considering Table 3.2, economic trends of ASEAN-3 countries were classified as booming and recessing states. In Thailand, there were 24 time periods for economic expansions. On the other hand, there were 31 time periods contained in the economic depressions. In the case of Malaysia, the empirical estimation showed that there were 36 time periods for economic booming cycles. Conversely, the downtrends of Malaysian economy were found and there were 19 time periods during 1961 to 2016. Lastly, in the case of Singapore economy, 24 time periods of economic expansions and 31 time periods of economic depressions were observed during 55 years, respectively. In conclusion, the results estimated by the MSBVAR model can emphasize that the real business cycles obviously occurred in ASEAN-3 countries' economic systems.

The Results of Nonstationary Bayesian Extreme Value Analysis

The Nonstationary Extreme Value analysis (NEVA) employed in this study confirmedly provided the unusual points of economic trends in ASEAN-3 countries, which were complied with the real business cycle theory and economic cycling results estimated by the MSBVAR model. The NEVA approach is the essential component

Table 3.2 Presentation switching numbers of time periods in economic cycles

	Booming cycles (yearly time periods)	Recessing cycles (yearly time periods)
Gross domestic products of Thailand	24	31
Gross domestic products of Malaysia	36	19
Gross domestic products of Singapore	24	31

Source: From computing by R software [Package called MSBVAR adapted from Brandt (2009)]

Table 3.3 Presentation of the extreme values in booming and recessing cycles estimated by the NEVA approach

	Booming cycles (Peak value)	Recessing cycles (Downsizing value)
Thailand GDP (%)	15.00	−23.00
Malaysia GDP (%)	24.05	−15.00
Singapore GDP (%)	30.00	−35.00

Source: Author's computed

which is used to set an upper bound (the highest critical event in economic trends) and lower bound (the lowest critical point). The empirical findings shown in Table 3.3 indicated that Thailand's GDP contains 15% of economic expansion rates to be the critical upper bound. On the other hand, the extremely critical value for recessing periods is −23%. The details were graphically showed in Figs. 3.5 and 3.6 in Appendix. Considering the case of Malaysia, the highest critical point for booming periods is 24.05%. Conversely, the extreme signal of economic depressions is −15%. This information was presented in Fig. 3.7 and Fig. 3.8 in Appendix. Speaking to extreme situations in Singapore economy, the results displayed in Figs. 3.9 and 3.10 implied that 30% of economic growth was set to be the critical upper bound for booming period. Reversely, −35% of growth rates was calibrated to be the critical point for recessing cases. Moreover, the estimated results of Pickands' dependence distribution were graphically displayed in Fig. 3.4. The details indicate that strongly extreme dependences were found in three bivariate extreme distributions (similar to V shape). As a result, this ensured that the economic shocks from each country in ASEAN-3 have extremely impacted to others' economic systems.

The Results of Bayesian Dynamic Stochastic General Equilibrium Estimating

Based on three cases such as normally economic movements, booming situations, and recessions, the results of BDSGE testing were represented in Table 3.4. For

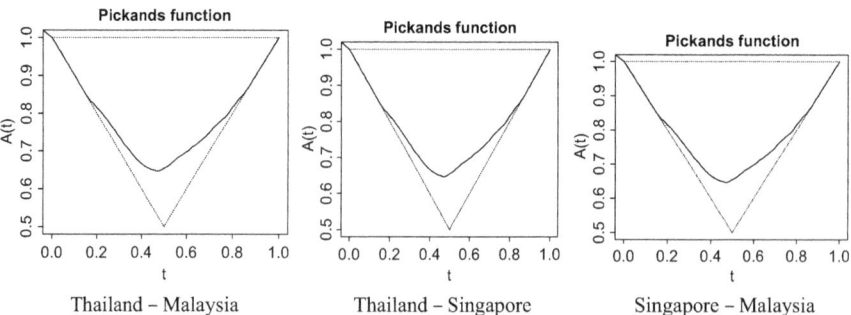

Fig. 3.4 Pickands' extreme dependent distributions in ASEAN-3 countries

Table 3.4 Estimated parameters of prior and posterior distributions by the BDSGE model

Country	Symbol	Type	Normal cases		Booming periods		Recessing periods	
			Prior mean	Posterior mean	Prior mean	Posterior mean	Prior mean	Posterior mean
Thailand	α	Beta	0.200	0.307	0.400	0.367	0.400	0.294
	β	Beta	0.990	0.990	0.990	0.990	0.990	0.990
	δ	Beta	0.030	0.024	0.030	0.026	0.030	0.029
	ψ	Gamma	1.100	1.017	2.000	2.057	2.000	1.356
	ρ	Beta	0.950	0.951	0.950	0.962	0.950	0.701
	θ	Gamma	3.000	2.972	3.000	2.772	3.000	2.952
	τ	Beta	0.006	0.005	0.030	0.029	0.030	0.029
	ε	Inverse Gamma	0.010	0.001	0.010	0.010	0.010	0.024
Initial value of the log posterior			782.7042		1516.1867		−755.9166	
Log data density			1440.5219		1498.9930		983.4505	
Malaysia	α	Beta	0.400	0.421	0.400	0.492	0.400	0.263
	β	Beta	0.990	0.990	0.990	0.990	0.990	0.990
	δ	Beta	0.030	0.027	0.030	0.028	0.030	0.025
	ψ	Gamma	1.100	0.957	3.000	3.151	3.000	2.863
	ρ	Beta	0.950	0.902	0.950	0.972	0.950	0.931
	θ	Gamma	3.000	3.159	3.000	3.144	3.000	3.177
	τ	Beta	0.020	0.019	0.020	0.022	0.020	0.016
	ε	Inverse Gamma	0.010	0.010	0.010	0.011	0.010	0.029
Initial value of the log posterior			1422.4958		816.5289		−1005.7267	
Log data density			1415.1198		1479.5770		978.2583	

(continued)

Table 3.4 (continued)

Country	Symbol	Type	Normal cases		Booming periods		Recessing periods	
			Prior mean	Posterior mean	Prior mean	Posterior mean	Prior mean	Posterior mean
Singapore	α	Beta	0.400	0.368	0.400	0.390	0.400	0.366
	β	Beta	0.990	0.990	0.990	0.990	0.990	0.990
	δ	Beta	0.030	0.027	0.030	0.030	0.030	0.032
	ψ	Gamma	1.100	1.070	1.100	0.903	1.100	1.001
	ρ	Beta	0.950	0.902	0.950	0.867	0.950	0.701
	θ	Gamma	3.000	3.060	3.000	3.175	3.000	2.829
	τ	Beta	0.020	0.020	0.020	0.021	0.020	0.028
	ε	Inverse Gamma	0.010	0.011	0.010	0.011	0.010	0.021
Initial value of the log posterior			1317.7148		1356.6974		66.5367	
Log data density			1355.3893		1377.2524		1028.2971	

Source: Author's computed

explaining the prior distributions, the remaining eight parameters were in line with the literature review. Fundamentally, the selection of the distributions were as follows: the beta distribution was employed to clarify parameters bounded between zero and unity, and the gamma distribution was used to describe parameters assumed to be positive values. Technically, in the section of posterior estimations, the results were relied on a total of 500 simulated observations obtained through the Metropolis–Hastings sampling algorithm. Consequently, the comparison between prior and posterior means for three situational types was displayed in Table 3.4. Moreover, in appendix, the figures representing the comparison between prior and posterior distributions for Thailand's RBC modeling were illustrated in Fig. 3.11. For Malaysian's economy, details were displayed in Fig. 3.12. For Singapore's economic system, all of prior and posterior distributions were shown in Fig. 3.13.

Considering speedy adjustments of economy theoretically based on the RBC model, in the case of Thailand, details predicted in the next 30 years were graphically shown in Figs. 3.14 and 3.15 (Appendix). At the extreme event in which economic growth raised more than 15%, the predictive adjustment indicated that Thailand economy (y), capital growth (k), and even consumption (c) would not be closed to the equilibrium and trend to be bubble burst. Especially, the indicators of consumptions and capital accumulations in extremely economic expansions are anxious. The impulse responses showed that over quantities of these two factors would be blown up in 5 years approximately. Furthermore, the danger signal was labor supply which has continuously fallen into the minus area. This implied that the extreme economic growth would cause the problem of unemployment. In the case of recessions, -23% decreasing in economic growth would cause Thailand's economic system, capital growth, consumption, and labor services (h) to decline earlier than the normal case. In other words, the index of economic growth (y) would be approximately dropped in 10 years. Capital growth (k) would be continuously falling during the next 10 years. Moreover, the labor supply would be completely shut during the upcoming 5 years. As a result, these signals are the alarming ring for recovering economy.

Speaking to Malaysian's economy, the empirical findings were graphically displayed in Figs. 3.16 and 3.17 in Appendix; a 25.4% increment in economic growth hugely caused negative impacts to economic systems. The results showed the bubble burst signal in economy would be occurring in 5 years and this would redundantly grow in consumptions (c) and capital growth (k). In particular, the impulse response line of economic growth (y) obviously displayed that the booming crises would be immediately occurring in less than 2 years if extreme rates of economic expansions are uncontrollable. On the other hand, the effects from recessing periods are worse. A -15% in economic growth negatively affected labor supply (h), which would relate to chronic unemployment crisis during approximate 10 years. The capital growth would also continuously decline between 10 and 20 years. At last, the Malaysian economy would be dying in the next 15 years.

According to Singapore's economy, the results were presented in Figs. 3.18 and 3.19 in Appendix. In booming situations, a 30% increase in economic growth can be a harmful signal for labor forces (h), which would fall to minus area in the next 10 years and it implied to the problem of chronic unemployment, even though this hugely economic expansion has driven capital growth (k) and consumptions (c).

Furthermore, the extremely expansion rate negatively impacts on the economic trend. If the uncontrollable rising growth often happens, this would cause an unrelenting decline of Singapore's economy for 15 years at least. Conversely, the case of recessions is more anxious. The -32% declining rate in economic growth would cause unemployment (labor supply (h)) to occur earlier in the upcoming 5 years. Additionally, the economic system (y) would be a fluctuated declining trend in upcoming 10 years as well as capital growth (k) would be continuously decreasing in the next 10 years.

Accordingly, the estimated impulse lines of speedy adjustments when extreme economic shocks have existed strongly confirmed that the economic systems in ASEAN-3 countries would face economic crises such as chronic unemployment, great recession in consumptions, and even economic bubble bursts from overheat investments. Thus, the computational findings of this paper are intensively emphasizing that sensibly economic alarming signals should be provided beforehand and the center of special economic crises research should be practically activated.

Conclusion and Policy Suggestions

The complicated issues which is the dynamic stochastic prediction of the extreme events in economic cycles and its possible impacts on economic systems in ASEAN-3 countries such as Thailand, Malaysia, and Singapore is successfully clarified in this paper. The yearly time-series variables such as Thailand GDP, Malaysia GDP, and Singapore GDP were collected during 1961 to 2016. This paper was aimed to statistically employ "Bayesian Inference" to econometrically investigate empirical results of the economic cycling adjustments in extreme events. In the regime-switching approach (MSBVAR), the results were relied on the Business Cycle theory (RBC model), and they showed the economic regimes were divided into two states, including booming periods and recessions. This strongly confirmed that these three countries' economic trends cannot be estimated by linear-parametric testing. In the subsequent process, this section is one of important components for setting up the economic alarming signal to investigate. The NEVA approach provided the unusual points of economic trends and this can be called "Extreme Point." Obviously, the extreme economic events in ASEAN-3 countries have negatively affected each other. Thus, these empirical findings can be efficiently used to announce the critical upper bound and the harmful lower bound for economic trends.

Another highlighted issue of this chapter is the BDSGE analysis. This powerful econometric tool combined with the simulation method (Markov Chain Monte Carlo: MCMC) and Metropolis–Hastings (MH) algorithm can be employed to computationally estimate the predictive economic adjustments for setting the precise alarm signal in time. Empirically, the most critical points when economic shocks have threatened are the section of labors and domestic consumptions. Accordingly, the policies to maintain the stability in labor supplies and consumer price indexes are extremely crucial. In the issue regarding capital growth and economic expansions, the results indicated that the extreme rates of GDP in ASEAN-3 countries, especially a huge increasing rate, would be the negative cause of bubble crises in capital accumulations and economic growth to occur earlier. Consequently, to stimulate economic systems for measuring the high rate of growth cannot be the best solution anymore. Moreover, an alarming signal and precisely predictive trend to dynamically take care economic movements are essential and need to be intensively emphasized as a practical policy.

Keywords Definitions

Real Business Cycle Real business cycle theory (RBC theory) is a class of macroeconomics models and theories, which regards to the periodic up and down movements in the economy, which are measured by fluctuations in real GDP and other macroeconomic factors. There are sequential phases of the business cycle that demonstrate rapid growth (defined as expansions or booms) followed by periods of stagnation or decline (known as recessions or declines).

Bayesian Statistics Bayesian statistics is a mathematical procedure that applies probabilities to statistical problems. It provides people the tools to update their beliefs in the evidence of new data. In the Bayesian paradigm, degrees of belief in states of nature are specified. These are non-negative, and the total belief in all states of nature is fixed to be one. Bayesian statistical inferences start with existing "prior" beliefs, and update these using data to give "posterior" beliefs, which may be used as the basis for inferential decisions.

Markov Chain Monte Carlo Simulation (MCMC) The MCMC technique is the method for sampling from probability distributions using Markov chains. This method is used in data modeling, especially for Bayesian inference and numerical integration.

Metropolis–Hastings (MH) Algorithm The MH algorithm is a Markov chain Monte Carlo (MCMC) method for obtaining a sequence of random samples from a probability distribution, which direct sampling is often difficult. The key idea is to construct a Markov Chain that converges to the given distribution as its stationary distribution. After that, drawing samples from a Markov Chain's stationary distribution can be approximated by simulating the Markov Chain.

Markov Process A Markov process is either discrete state space or discrete index set (often representing time). The defining property of the Markov process is commonly called the Markov property; it was first stated by A.A. Markov.

Extreme Event An extreme event analysis is relied on the extreme value theory or extreme value analysis (EVA), which is a branch of statistics dealing with the extreme deviations from the median of probability distributions. The EVT provides a solid probabilistic foundation for studying the distribution of extreme events in many academic fields such as hydrology, climate sciences, even finance and insurance etc.

Non-stationary Data Non-stationary data are unpredictable and cannot be modeled or forecasted. The results obtained by using non-stationary time series may be spurious in that they may indicate a relationship between two variables where one does not exist. The non-stationary process contains a variable variance and a mean that do not closely remain, or return to a long-run mean over time.

Dynamic Stochastic General Equilibrium (DSGE) Dynamic stochastic general equilibrium modeling is a branch of applied general equilibrium theory that influences in contemporary macroeconomics. Technically, the DSGE methodology is proposed to explain aggregate economic phenomena, including economic growth, business cycles, and the effects of monetary and fiscal policies.

Speedy Economic Adjustment Economic adjustments usually involve a combination of free market policies such as privatization, fiscal austerity, free trade and deregulation. In recent moment, the adjustments have been also defined to structurally relate to 'poverty reduction'.

Appendix

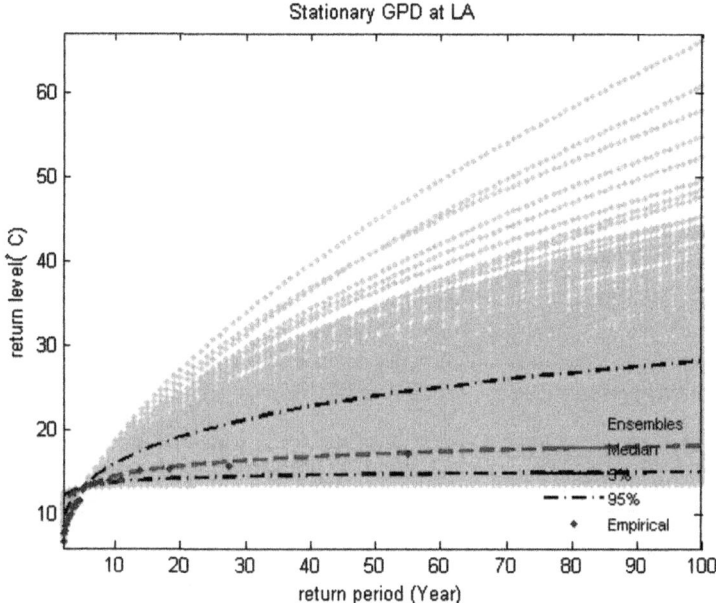

Fig. 3.5 Presentation extreme information for booming cycles in Thailand

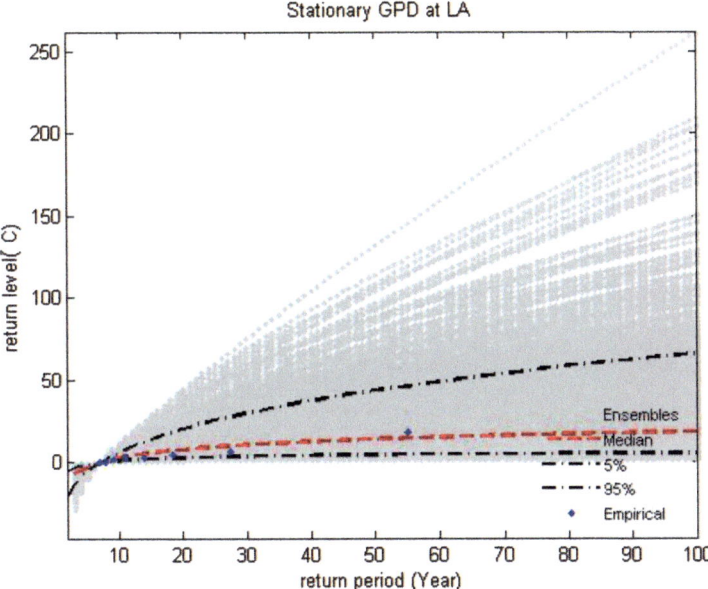

Fig. 3.6 Presentation extreme information for recessing cycles in Thailand

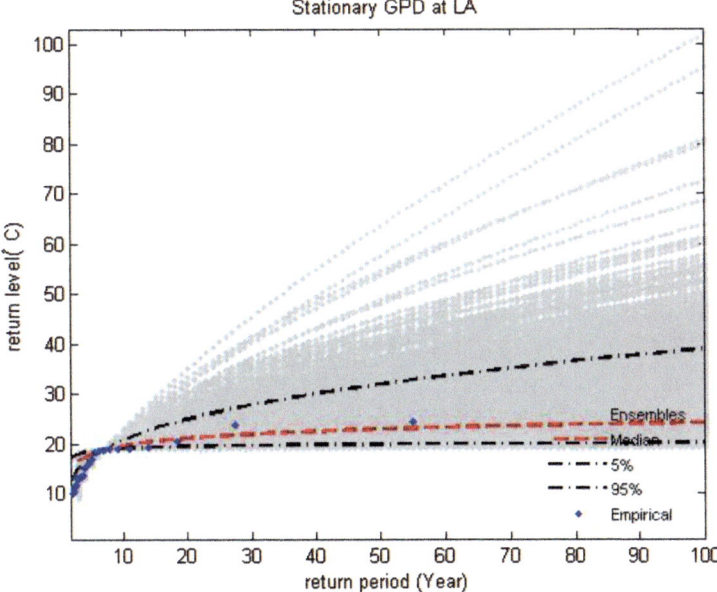

Fig. 3.7 Presentation extreme information for booming cycles in Malaysia

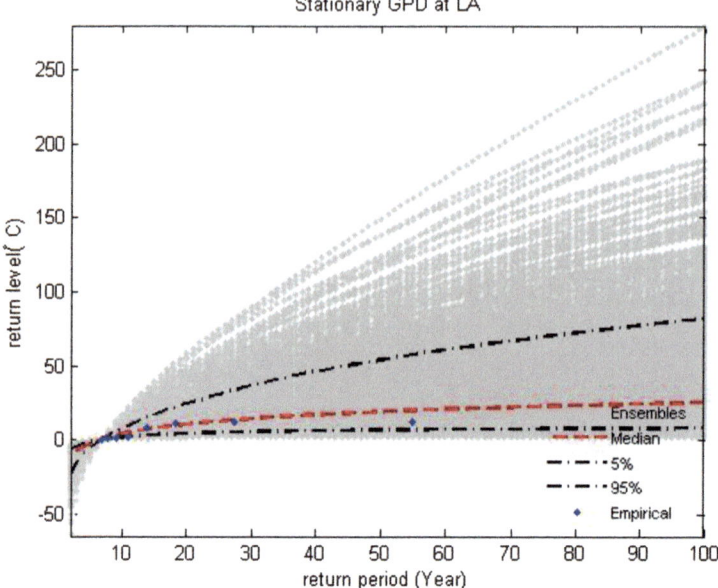

Fig. 3.8 Presentation extreme information for downsizing cycles in Malaysia

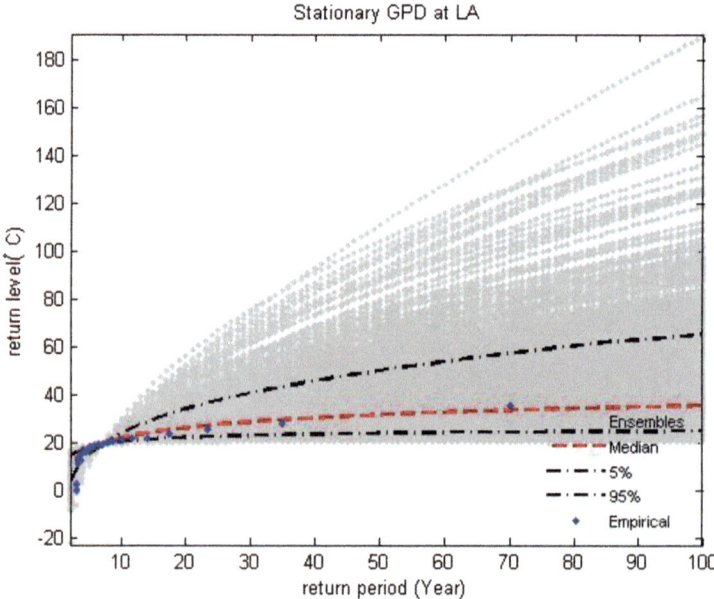

Fig. 3.9 Presentation extreme information for booming cycles in Singapore

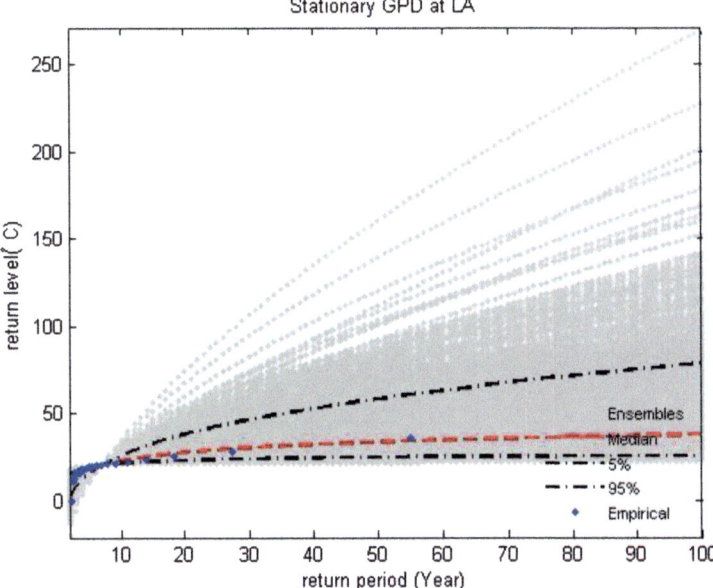

Fig. 3.10 Presentation extreme information for recessing cycles in Singapore

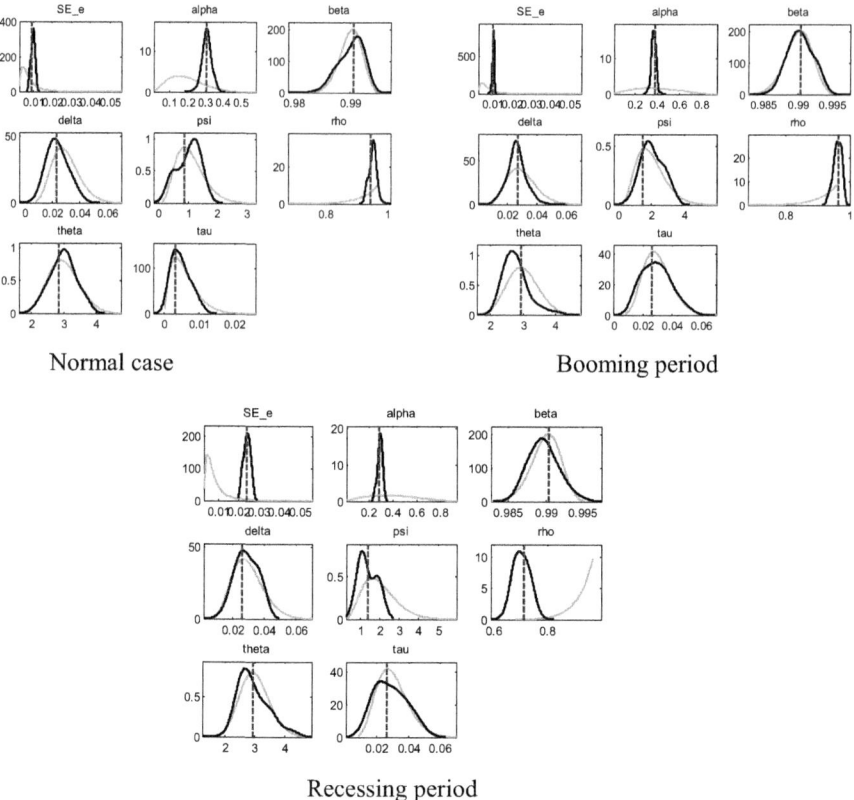

Normal case   Booming period

Recessing period

Fig. 3.11 Prior and posterior distributions of Thailand by BDSGE modeling

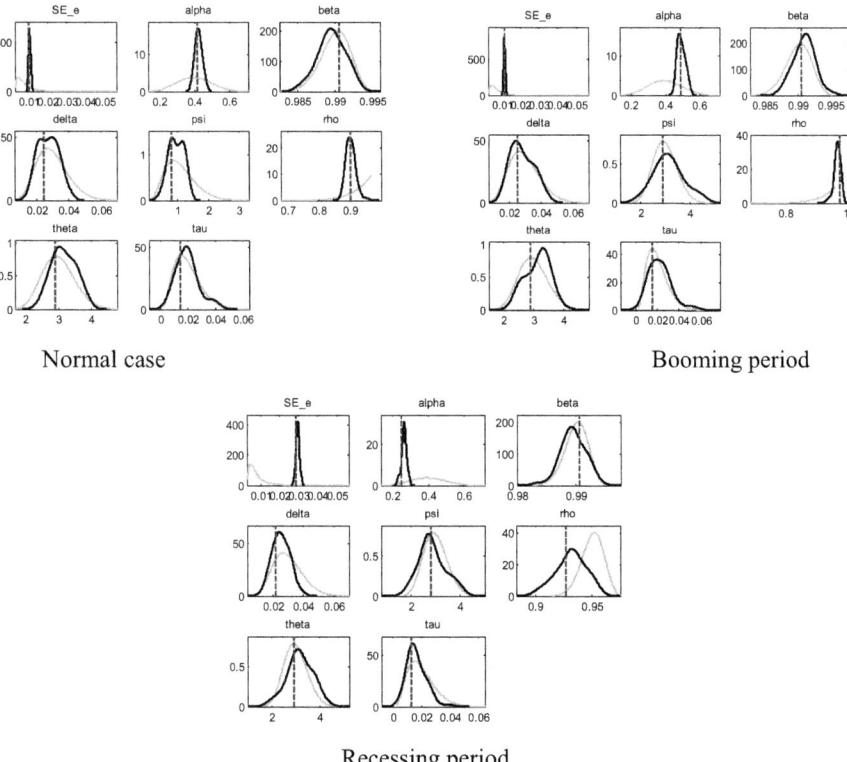

Fig. 3.12 Prior and posterior distributions of Malaysia by BDSGE modeling

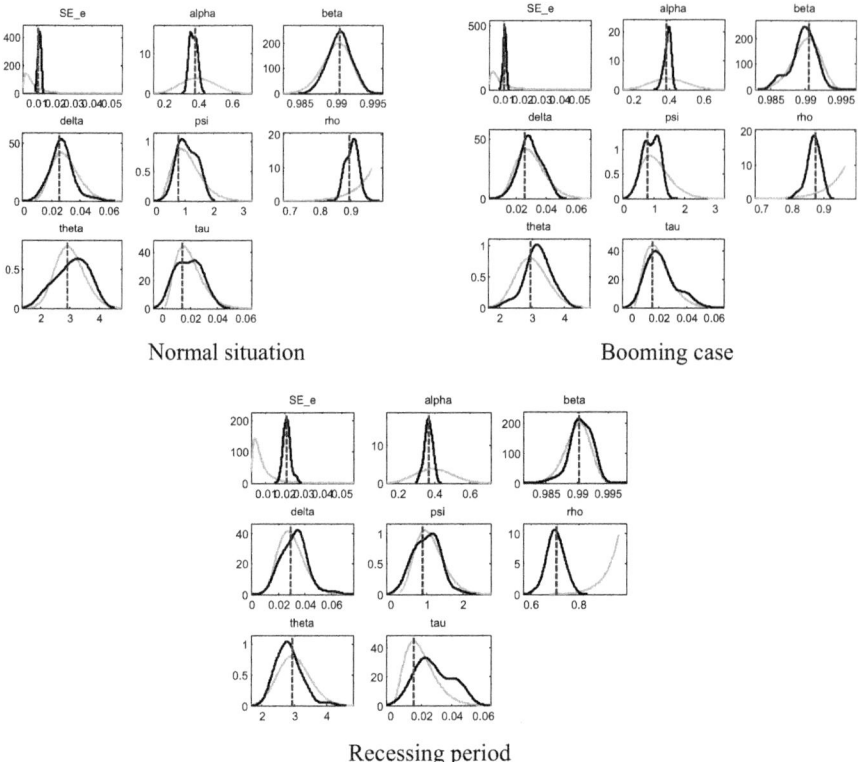

Fig. 3.13 Prior and posterior distributions in economic booming cases of Singapore

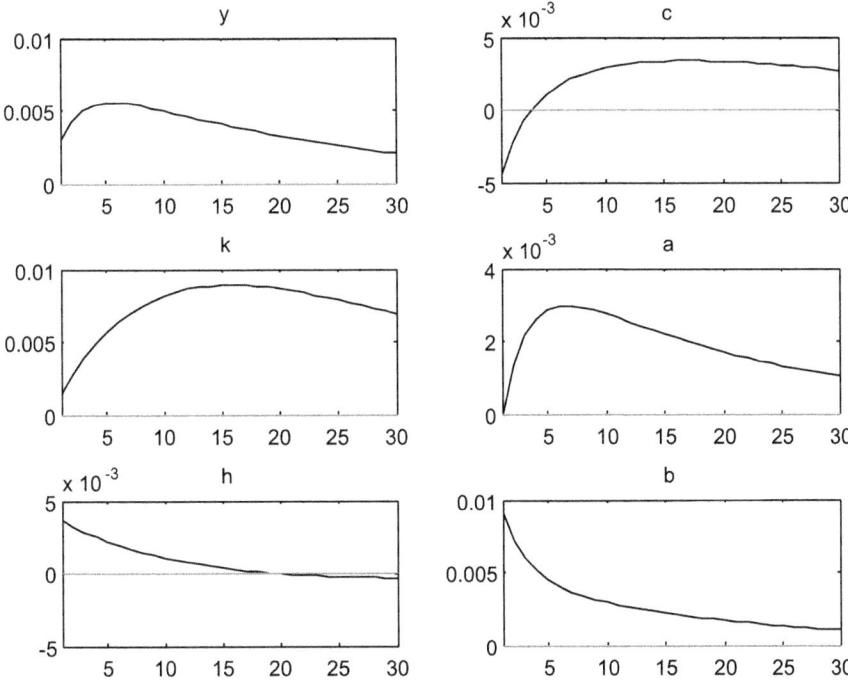

Fig. 3.14 Speedy adjustments of structurally economic variables in normal situations of Thailand

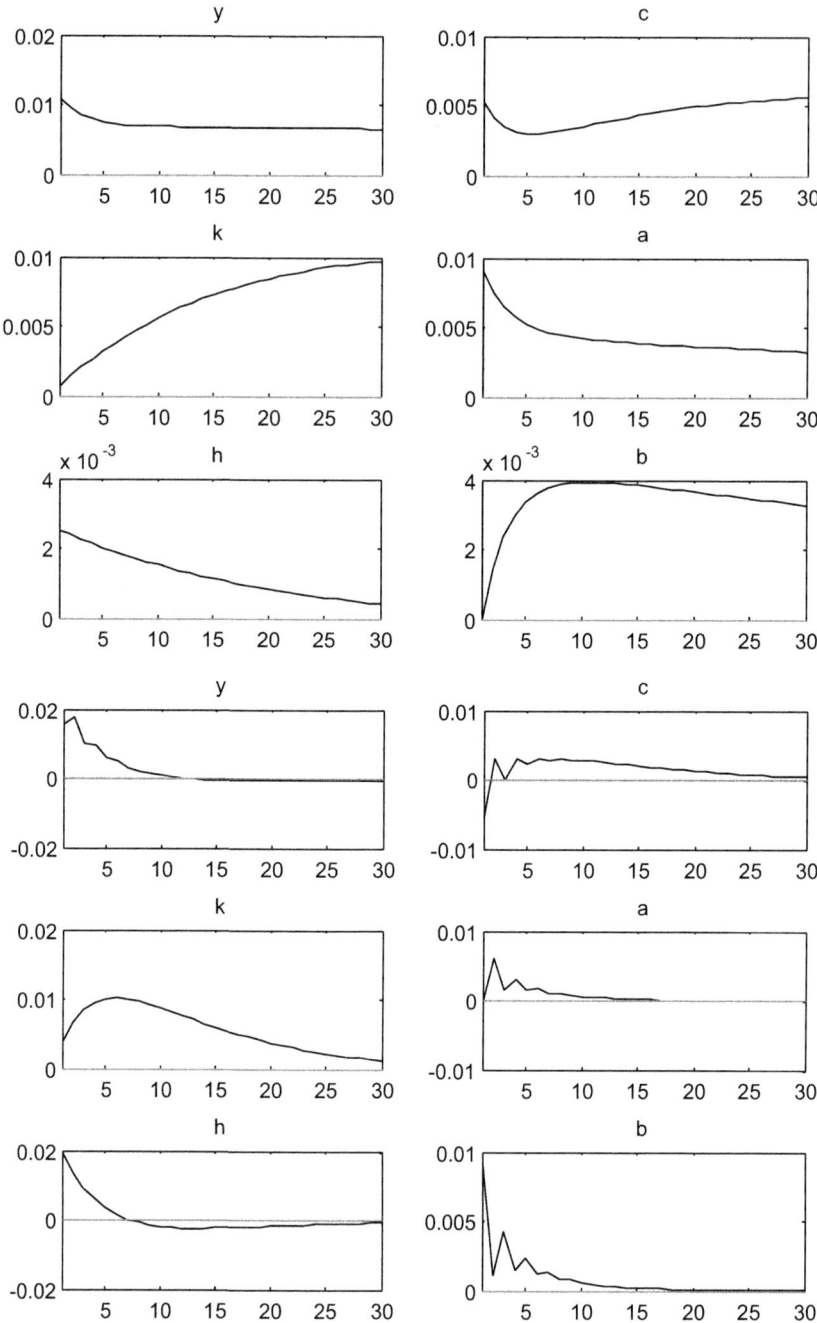

Fig. 3.15 Speedy adjustments of structurally economic variables in boom and recess periods of Thailand

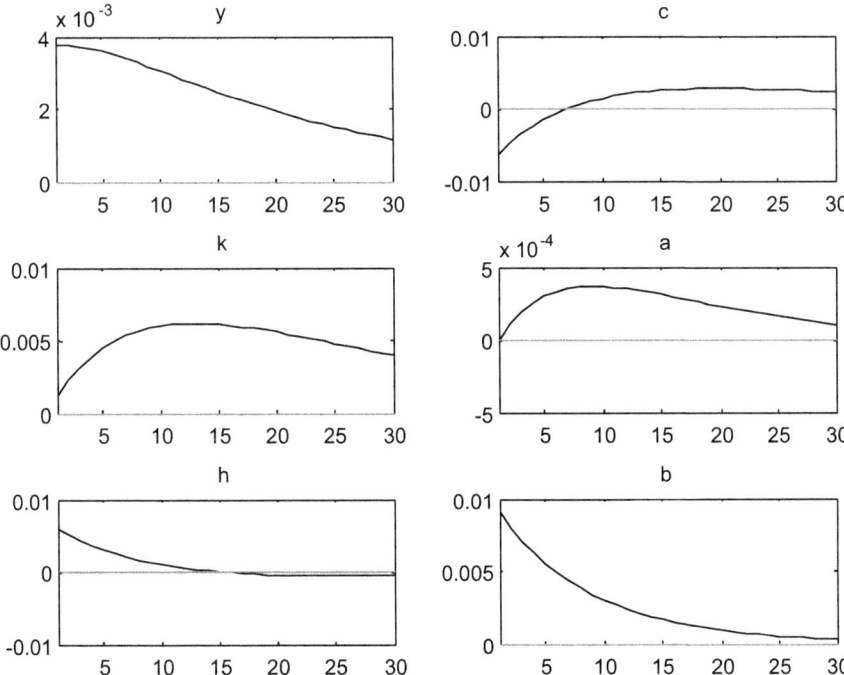

Fig. 3.16 Speedy adjustments of structurally economic variables in normal situations of Malaysia

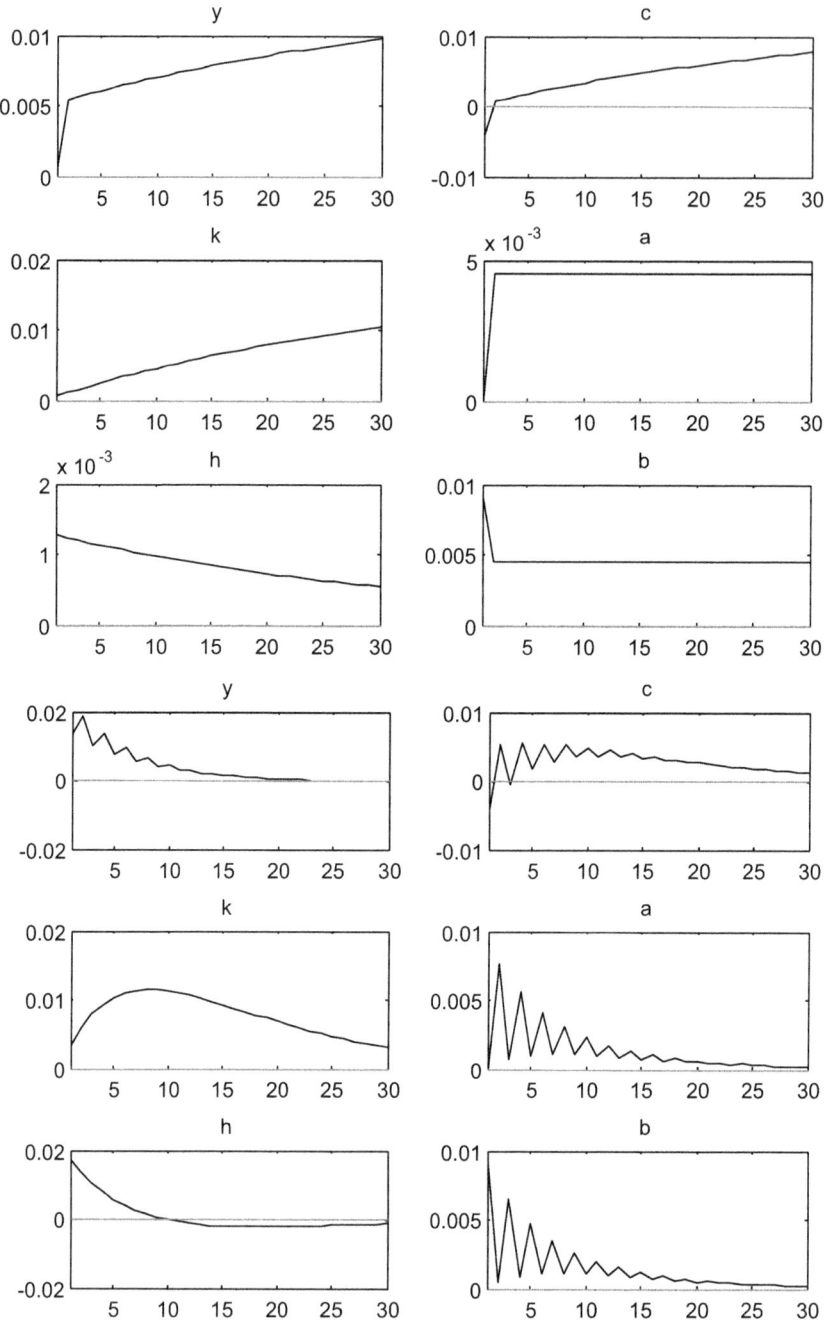

Fig. 3.17 Speedy adjustments of structurally economic variables in boom and recess periods of Malaysia

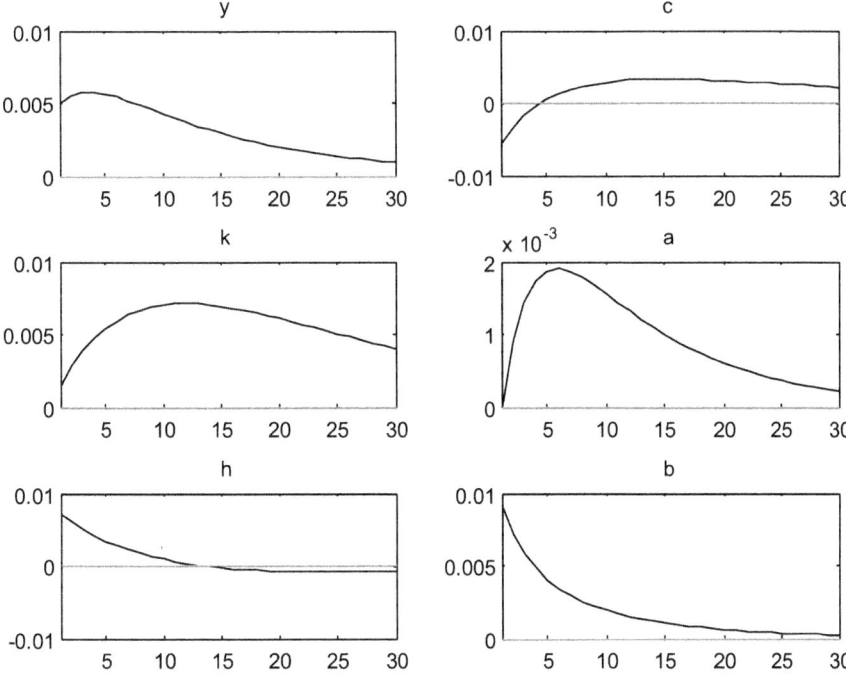

Fig. 3.18 Speedy adjustments of structurally economic variables in normal situations of Singapore

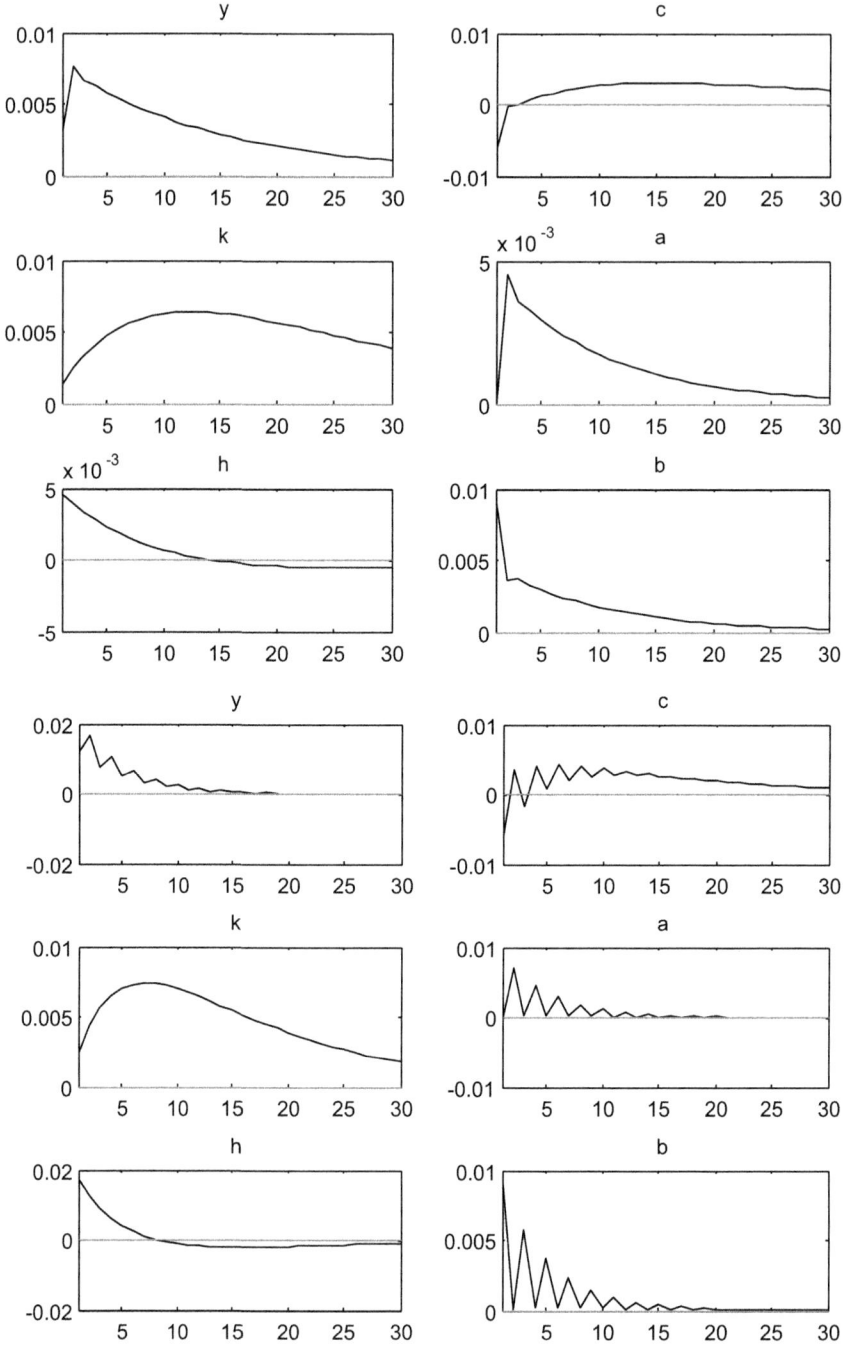

Fig. 3.19 Speedy adjustments of structurally economic variables in boom and recess periods of Singapore

References

Adenomon, M. O., Michael, V. A., & Evans, O. P. (2015). Short term forecasting performance of classical VAR and Sims-Zha Bayesian VAR models for time series with collinear variables and correlated error terms. *Open Journal of Statistic, 5*, 742–753.

Adolfson, M., Laseén, S., Lindé, J., & Villani, M. (2007). Bayesian estimation of an open economy DSGE model with incomplete pass-through. *Journal of International Economics, 72*(2), 481–511.

Alp, H., & Elekdag, S. (2012). *Shock therapy! What role for Thai monetary policy?*. IMF Working Paper 12/269. Asia and Pacific Department, International Monetary Fund.

Asian Development Bank. (2016). *Key indicators for Asia and the Pacific 2015*. Available at http://www.adb.org/sites/default/files/publication/175162/ki2015-rt-economy-output.pdf

Association of Southeast Asian Nation. (2016). *Asean statistical yearbook 2014*. Available at http://www.asean.org/wp-content/uploads/images/2015/July/ASEAN-Yearbook/July%202015%20-%20ASEAN%20Statistical%20Yearbook%202014.pdf

Bank of Thailand. (2016). *Thailand's macro economic indicators 1*. Available at http://www2.bot.or.th/statistics/ReportPage.aspx?reportID=409&language=eng

Bauwens, L., Lubrano, M., & Richard, J. F. (2000). *Bayesian inference in dynamic econometric models* (1st ed.). Oxford: Oxford Scholarship Press.

Behrens, C. N., Lopes, H. F., & Gamerman, D. (2004). Bayesian analysis of extreme events with threshold estimation. *Statistical Modelling, 4*, 227–244.

Berg, A. (1999). *The Asia crisis: Causes, policy responses, and outcomes*. IMF Working Paper No. 138. Asia and Pacific Department, International Monetary Fund.

Boudebbous, T. (2015). Stock market bear regime and recession: Are they synchronized? *International Journal of Economics and Finance, 7*(2), 261–272.

Brandt, P. T. (2009). *Empirical, regime-specific models of international, inter-group conflict, and politics*. Paper presented at the annual meeting of the Midwest Political Science Association 67th Annual National Conference. The Palmer House Hilton, Chicago, IL (Online). November 29, 2014, from http://citation.allacademic.com/meta/p360983_index.html

Brandt, P. T., Freeman, J. R., & Schrodt, P. A. (2011). Real time, time series forecasting of inter- and intra-state political conflict. *Conflict Management and Peace Science, 28*(1), 41–64.

Burns, A. F. (1979). *The anguish of central banking offsite link*. The 1979 Per Jacobsson Lecture, Belgrade, Yugoslavia, September 30, 1979.

Chaiboonsri, C. (2015). *Business cycle theory* (1st edn). Faculty of Economics, Chiang Mai University. isbn:978-616-382-383-0.

Chaiboonsri, C., Chaitip, P., & Chokethaworn, K. (2016). *The multiplex of forecasting in extreme data: Evidences from ASEAN stock exchanges*. Presented at the SIBR 2016 Conference on Interdisciplinary Business and Economics Research, 2nd–3rd June 2016, Bangkok.

Cheng, L., AghaKouchak, A., Gilleland, E., & Katz, R. (2014). Non-stationary extreme value analysisin a changing climate. *Climatic Change, 127*(2), 353–369. https://doi.org/10.1007/s10584-014-1254-5.

Chow, H. K., & McNelis, P. D. (2010). *Need Singapore fear floating? A DSGE-VAR approach*. Working Paper No. 29. Research Collection School of Economics. Available at http://ink.library.smu.edu.sg/soe_research/1250

Chow-Tan, H. K., Lim, G. C., & McNelis, P. D. (2014). Monetary regime choice in Singapore: Would a Taylor rule outperform exchange-rate management? *Journal of Asian Economics, 30*, 63–81.

Collard, F., & Juillard, M. (2001). Accuracy of stochastic perturbation methods: The case of asset pricing models. *Journal of Economic Dynamics and Control, 25*(6–7), 979–999.

Collier, A. J. 2010. *Extreme value analysis of non-stationary processes – A study of extreme rainfall under changing climate*. Doctor of Philosophy, School of Civil Engineering and Geosciences, University of Newcastle.

Duca, G. (2007). The relationship between the stock market and the economy: Experience from international financial markets. *Bank of Valleta Review, 36*, 1–12.

Fernández-Villaverde, J. (2010). The econometrics of DSGE models. *SERIEs, 1*, 3–49. https://doi.org/10.1007/s13209-009-0014-7.

Geweke, J. (1989). Bayesian inference in econometric models using Monte Carlo integration. *Econometrica, 57*(6), 1317–1339.

Geweke, J. 1998. *Using simulation methods for Bayesian econometric models: Inference, development, and communication*. Research Department Staff Report 249, Federal Reserve Bank of Minneapolis.

Geweke, J., & Amisano, G. (2014). Analysis of variance for Bayesian inference. *Econometric Reviews, 33*, 270–288.

Griffoli, T. M. (2013). *An introduction to the solution and estimation of DSGE models*. Boston, MA: The Free Software Foundation.

Hamilton, J. (1989). A new approach to the economic analysis of nonstationary time series and business cycle. *Econometrica, 57*(2), 357–384.

Hounkpe, J., Diekkrüger, B., Badou, D. F., & Afouda, A. A. (2015). Non-stationary flood frequency analysis in the Ouémé River Basin, Benin Republic. *Hydrology, 2*, 210–229.

Hundecha, Y., St-Hilaire, A., Ouarda, T. B. M. J., & El Adlouni, S. (2008). A nonstationary extreme value analysis for the assessment of changes in extreme annual wind speed over the Gulf of St. Lawrence, Canada. *Journal of Applied Meteorology and Climatatology, 47*, 2745–2757.

Jonung, L., Kiander, J., & Vartia, P. (2008). *The great financial crisis in Finland and Sweden: The dynamics of boom, bust and recovery, 1985–2000*. Economic Papers 350. Directorate-General for Economic and Financial Affairs, European Commission.

Kliem, M., & Uhlig, H. (2013). *Bayesian estimation of a DSGE model with asset prices*. Working Paper No. 37. Deutsche Bundesbank, Frankfurt, Germany.

Kline, B., & Tamer, E. (2016). Bayesian inference in a class of partially identified models. *Quantitative Economics, 7*, 329–366.

Koop, G., Leon-Gonzalez, R., & Strachan, R. (2008). Bayesian inference in a cointegrating panel data model. In S. Chib, W. Griffiths, G. Koop, & D. Terrell (Eds.), *Bayesian econometrics (Advances in econometrics)* (Vol. 23, pp. 433–469). Bingley: Emerald Group.

Mallick, S., & Sousa, R. M. (2009) *Monetary policy and economic activity in the BRICS*. Working Paper No. 27. NIPE, The Portuguese Foundation Science and Technology.

Mankiw, N. G. (1989). Real business cycles: A new Keynesian perspective. *Journal of Economic Perspectives, 3*(3), 79–90.

Moreira, R. R., Chaiboonsri, C., & Chaitip, P. (2013). Relationships between effective and expected interest rates as a transmission mechanism for monetary policy: Evidence on the Brazilian economy using MS-models and a Bayesian VAR. *Procedia Economics and Finance, 5*, 562–570.

Pickands, J. (1975). Statistical inference using extreme order statistics. *Annals of Statistics, 3*, 110–131.

Sánchez, M. (2011). Financial crises: Prevention, correction, and monetary policy. *Cato Journal, 31*(3), 521–534.

Shaari, M. H. (2008). *Analyzing bank Negara Malaysia's behavior in formulation monetary policy: An empirical approach*. A thesis for the degree of Doctor of Philosophy. College of Business and Economics. The Australian National University.

Sims, C. A., & Zha, T. A. (1998). Bayesian methods for dynamic multivariate models. *International Economic Review, 39*(4), 949–968.

Spirtes, P. (2005). Graphical models, causal inference, and econometric models. *Journal of Economic Methodology, 12*(1), 1–33.

Stadler, G. W. (1994). Real business cycles. *Journal of Economics Literature, 32*, 1750–1783.

Takaishi, T. (2010). Bayesian inference with an adaptive proposal density for GARCH models. *Journal of Physics: Conference Series, 221*.

Tanboon, S. (2008). *The bank of Thailand structural model for policy analysis.* Discussion Paper. Bank of Thailand.

Verdick, S., & Islam, I. (2010). *The great recession of 2008–2009: Causes, consequences and policy responses.* Discussion Paper No. 4934. The Institute for the Study of Labor, Bonn, Germany.

Walsh, C. E. (2010). *Monetary theory and policy* (3rd ed.). Cambridge, MA: The MIT Press.

Zare, R., Azali, M., Habibullah, M. S., & Azman-Saini, W. N. W. (2013). Monetary policy effectiveness and stock market cycles in ASEAN-5. *PROSIDING PERKEM VIII*, 1, pp. 480–492.

Chapter 4
External Borrowing Issue in Ottoman Empire (1854–1876 Term)

Kenan Demir

Abstract By the beginning of the Nineteenth century, foreign borrowing was put on the agenda since it was understood that fiscal structure of the state could not be sustained by internal dynamics; yet, foreign borrowing did not materialize in that period. The state, which could not afford increasing war expenditures during Crimean war in 1853, borrowed from abroad for the first time in 1854. After this initial borrowing from England and France, foreign borrowing was started to be seen as a state policy by the state, who signed several debt treaties in succession. The newspapers that started to emerge in the Ottoman state in that period penned articles regarding borrowing policy of the state. In these newspapers, there were no direct criticisms regarding borrowing per se, rather the state was criticized mainly on the grounds that it borrowed money when it was in trouble, not to make investments. This study explains foreign borrowings made by the Ottoman State from 1854 and analyzes the views of the intellectuals of the period regarding them.

Introduction

From the ending of the eighteenth century, big issues have started to appear and frequent fiscal deficits have started to emerge in Ottoman treasury. In this term, the long wars with Russia brought extra costs to government. Besides, after 1750s, many industrial production facilities started to close down one by one because of the problems in the Ottoman economy. The increase of cheap foreign products in Ottoman market due to deepening trade relations with West expedited the close-downs in those years. This caused a significant loss of income for the government. Decreasing of income as a result of both costs of the war and the regression in the industry accelerated the aggravation of Ottoman economy.

In an attempt to save its economy, Ottoman Empire put internal borrowing policy into effect in 1774, but it did not work. Due to the inability to enhance the sources of

K. Demir
İstanbul Medipol University, İstanbul, Turkey
e-mail: kdemir@medipol.edu.tr

© Springer International Publishing AG, part of Springer Nature 2018   91
H. Dincer et al. (eds.), *Global Approaches in Financial Economics, Banking, and Finance*, Contributions to Economics, https://doi.org/10.1007/978-3-319-78494-6_4

income and the inefficacy of internal borrowing, the thought of external borrowing was first formed in 1784. Yet the government did not make any attempt in this regard. In the era of Selim III, even though the thought to borrow from Europe emerged, this idea has been abandoned because there was no example bygone. Although, there were attempts to borrow in the period of Mahmud II, there was no result. Bureaucrats of Tanzimat Reform Era also attempted to borrow from Western countries. The Crimean War in 1854 further increased the costs to economy and as a result, Ottoman Empire has made the first foreign borrowing.

After the first borrowing, Ottoman Empire chose borrowing policy in every economical crisis and borrowed from European countries. From the first borrowing year 1854 to 1876 moratorium when the state declared bankrupt, 15 debt agreements had been signed. In this study, the financial problems that pushed Ottoman Empire into debt are addressed, and the chronology of borrowings is given with an explanation of their conditions. In the following sections, debts' effects on the economy are explained and later on, views and criticisms of Ottoman scholars of the period which they had written in newspapers are expressed.

Financial State and Policies of Ottoman Empire

Eighteenth century was the period when Ottoman economy started to centralize; in other words, it was a time new institutions were being established in order to estimate income and expenses beforehand and to balance them. In this era, while the influence of domestic forces was growing, the salary system was becoming widespread on centralized bureaucracy. All of the measures taken amplified the financial bureaucracy and augmented the workload. The state which could not break through in agriculture and industry during eighteenth century was trying to save the day with financial measures and prosecutions (Ortaylı 2000: 131). As from 1774, Ottoman statesmen started the stock shares method which is sort of an internal borrowing as it was understood that the present incomes were unable to cover the expenses (Cezar 1986: 79). The stock shares method was the selling of cash incomes—under the name of "*muaccele*"—separated into sagittal slices which belonged to some of the tax secretaries known as "*mukataa*" to private individuals in return for ready cash (Genç 1995: 376). During the Abdul Hamid I period when the financial problems intensified, it was understood that incomes provided by confiscation, internal borrowing, and donation (iane) were not enough to free from difficulties. In 1788, thought of borrowing from Dutch, Spanish, or French merchants was formed. However, after the meetings with the ambassador of the Netherlands yielded no results, the traditional financial method took place and the carat of coin lowered again (Berkes 2003: 102).

Ottoman financial system entered a brand new era with the new regulations in the period of Selim III (Cezar 1985: 929). With reforms, new taxes, new register systems, and new bureaucracy were born. Financial means were slogged to the full extent with the creation of new taxes and raises on taxes like poll tax (jizya) in this period. Need for a big reform was being openly perceived (Ortaylı 2000: 131). In Mahmut II period, radical reformation attempts were undertaken in financial institutions. In 1837, The Ministry of Finance was found (Suvla 1999: 268). In order to cover the expenses of the new army which was found in 1827 after the disjoint of guild of janissaries, timar fields were transferred to central treasury; thus income of central treasury increased (Cezar 1985: 930). During the periods of Selim III and Mahmud II, the goals to form a treasury that is able to pay its debts and create a steady currency could not be reached. In the first years of nineteenth century, top brass has continued to devalue the currency in order to provide balanced budget. Under the reign of Mahmut II, Ottoman currency system was changed 35 times in gold and 37 times in silver (Lewis 2004: 110–111). With the adulteration made in this period, content of silver coin was reduced to 85% (Pamuk 2004: 1082). After 1844, adulteration system has come to an end (Şahin 2001–2002: 59). The reason behind the adulteration in Ottoman Empire was that in the face of a market in crisis, the state was bringing side income by printing money. In Ottoman, adulteration can be referred not only as devaluation but also as the state's additional coin to cover budget deficits (Pamuk 2005: 115).

Along with the Tanzimat Reform Era, Ottomans produced a banknote called "kaime" with intent to cover the expenses of Ottoman treasury (Toprak 1985: 761). Even though it was announced that the banknotes were current money, they were payments of interest. At first, in 1840, 160 million kuruş (coin) worth "*kaime*" was released to the market (Kıray 2008: 26). Because of disorganized and perpetual striking and widely expulsion of imitations into the market, there was a fall at an unprecedented pace in "*kaime*'s" value. The state began to experience problems paying "*kaime*" interests (Dumont 2007: 84). With monetized "kaimes" till 1860, there were 12.5 million banknotes circulating (10 million lira banknotes and 2.5 million lira interest); thus, the economy was in a dire situation. In order to get off the hook, bureaucrats borrowed from England and pulled all banknotes from the market (Eren 1999: 247). In this period, the irregularity in fiscal policy was being observed at every level of hierarchy. The expenditure and collection of government revenues was not subject to any specific control. It was hard to get information about the true quality of government's revenues and expenses on accounts (Engelhardt 1999: 277). In Tanzimat Reform Era, financial management of Ottoman was reorganized, and Ministry of Finance was turned into an institution carrying on all the financial affairs of the state (Güran 1998: 79–80). After announcement of the Rescript of Gülhane, in order to restore the financial status of the state, Ottoman bureaucrats sent a decree to provinces and wanted these measures to be taken: removal of civil taxes, determination of taxes according to everyone's income, removal of tax farming from tithe, levying the cattle tax once and for all, improvement of tribute and poll tax, and removal of tax in kind and the taxes received from public as compensation for the salaries and expenses of civil servants (Çakır 2001: 23).

In the first years of Tanzimat Era, financial policies were performed with regard to fiscal policies as it was before. In the limitation of state's duties and expenditures, designation of taxes mostly according to utility theory, considering the relationship between the increase in state revenue and the increase in production as positive, and adoption of the consumer state comprehension state's financial interests were taken into account in every step (Şener 2000: 275). After the declaration of Tanzimat, a schedule for a budget balance was established by calculating the revenues and expenses of the previous year for the first time at the end of 1844 (Karal 1983: 207). There were no budget deficits in first schedules; however, as the expenses increased, large increases in the amount of budget deficits have occurred (Güran 2003: 10). After 1848, Ottoman economy faced crises in tandem. Revenues were not enough to bear the expenses and they were unable to find new sources of income. Statesmen were convinced that it was a time for external borrowing (Karal 1983: 208). According to Engelhardt, one of the witnesses of the period, these crises originated from three reasons: floating banknotes without any assurance by the state, lack of a safe and certain budget of the state, and lack of an administrative order to control the expenses and revenues of the state (Engelhardt 1999: 101–102). Their additional burdens to the state's budget wars and domestic riots were one of the most important reasons for the treasure to fall into financial distress. The Crimean War of the time was one of the most financially influential events for the state. For the first time, treasury of the state borrowed from foreign countries after the Crimean War (Şener 2000: 278).

External Borrowings of Ottoman Empire (1854–1876)

In order to close the budget deficit and supply the financial need, Ottoman Empire traditionally adopted adulteration, borrowing from Galata bankers and exchangers, and exportation of banknotes methods (Anbar 2009: 29). Because these methods were not able to provide a permanent solution, Ottoman Empire continuously dealt with financial difficulties (Sayar 2006: 180–181). In 1783, due to the war that started with the Russian occupation of Crimea, military expenses of the state increased (Akar and Al 2003: 3). Thus, the idea of borrowing was first observed in Ottoman statesmen in 1784, yet the idea was not passed on (Çakır 2001: 65). When Selim III inherited to the throne, treasury was in a really bad state. On top of that, the state was at war. To get rid of this, the idea of borrowing from European states occurred again. However, it was a terrible thought to be in debt to European states and there was no example in the past; so the idea was dropped (Karal 1983: 209). Thereupon, the mayors of Algeria and Tunisia were consulted for financial support but they were also in a bad economic situation. Later on, Ottoman Empire consulted to Morocco since it was an Islamic state, but this attempt also did not materialize (Koraltürk 1995: 54). In the period of Mahmut II, there was an attempt to borrow from England. Even though there were negotiations about borrowing one million pounds from England for supply of timber and wheat to the British fleet in the Mediterranean, there was no result due to the absence of strong warrants for British (Aysal 2013: 5). At first, reformers kept away from the idea of borrowing; due to that they would reorganize the finance. Yet later, they adopted the idea because of increasing irregularities in finance (Karal 1983: 209). Despite the loan taken in 1840 from

Bank of Dersaadet founded by Galata bankers Alleon and Baltaci is introduced as first external borrowing by some sources, this borrowing had the characteristics of domestic borrowing since the capital of this bank was not from foreign capital markets (Yılmaz 2002: 195). The external borrowing became a current issue again in 1850 when Britain's Istanbul Ambassador Canning wrote a memorandum to Sultan Abdulaziz noting that external borrowing was obligatory for Ottoman Empire. However, despite the Mustafa Reşit Paşa's positive approach, the borrowing didn't take place because the Sultan was ill-disposed to do so (Akar and Al 2003: 3).

Europeans suggested borrowing under favorable conditions to state authorities. Not convinced, Ottoman authorities were going to be convinced after Crimean War in 1854 and carry out the first external borrowing (Buluş and Mercan 2002: 251). In 1854, the modern war expenses and the opportunities offered by war allies directed Ottoman government to borrow from Paris and London's money market (Al 2007: 44). Taking the previous negativities from the borrowing attempts into account, Babıali (Ottoman government) employed two foreign traders named Black and Durand in the matter of keeping the negotiations (Akar and Al 2003: 7). On August 4th, 1854, the Sultan enacted authorizing three million pound borrowing. Interest of this debt agreement was 6%, amortization was 1%, and export price was 80 pound (Lewis 2004: 446). In return for the loan, Ottoman government guaranteed 30 million piastre of Egypt's treasury revenues (Karal 1983: 210). Warranted percentage of the tax was going to be split up evenly by "*Bank of England*" and "*Bank of France*" (Akar and Al 2003: 8). Not long after the first debt, on 27 June 1855, Babıali borrowed five million English pounds from Londoner Rothschilds in order to cover the expenses of the war. Under the guarantee of British and French governments, this debt had 4% interest and 102% export price. In exchange for the loan, rest of Egypt's treasury and some parts of Syrian and Izmir customs were given (Tekin 2000: 253). The guarantee of British and French on debts ensured better conditions. However, offences against the Ottoman's financial freedom were seen for the first time with these agreements. Guarantor countries obtained the right to assign officials to determine the use of debts for wars, to monitor the use of funds, and to examine treasury accounts. Even though these officials' jobs were being deactivated by Ottoman officials, there was a supervision task of foreigners for the first time (Lewis 2004: 446). The interests of Babıali's debt agreements were much more than other countries' debt interests (Tekin 2000: 252). The revenues obtained from the debts were spent for the capital and interest payments arising from the loan and current expenditure, especially for military and municipal institutions for the bureaucracy's salaries (Kazgan 1975–1976: 70). On the Crimean War, in order to prevent the strengthening of Russia, British and French governments were encouraging European fundholders to give credits to Ottoman with regard to international policies due to the fact that the Ottoman state lacks sufficient resources to continue the war (Akar and Al 2003: 9).

Even after the Crimean War, Ottoman treasury's distress was increasing. Treasury's need for money went up. In 1858, another debt agreement was signed to remove the banknotes of which value had fallen sharply (Lewis 2004: 446–447). 5.5 million gold Ottoman liras (five million British pounds) were borrowed externally with the debt agreement signed with the British institutions "Dent, Palmer and Partners." The government pledges İstanbul customs revenue and head taxes on security as debt allowance. The borrowed 3 million 784 thousand golden liras were all spent for the withdrawal of Ottoman banknotes "kaime" of which market values had fallen to 30%. The borrowed money was insufficient to withdraw the Ottoman paper money entirely from the market (Özdemir 2010: 51). In 1860, Babıali made a bid for borrowing as to pay internal and external debts. Banker M. Mires and Ottoman state signed a debt contract of 16 million pound over 53.75% export price. In addition to the commission of 1.50% on the principal at the borrowing contract, Mires was going to receive 273,000 franc in the year over the entire payment period. Borrowing price was going to be paid to Ottoman government in equal installments of 18 months; however, Ottoman state had to pay interest payments immediately. Ottoman state collateralized custom, salt, and fish taxes, and Plovdiv attar of roses tax, Edirne silk tax, Midilli and İzmit olive tithe, Samsun and neighbor tobacco and customs taxes (Sağlam 2013: 13–14). The state went worse financially for reasons like inability to obtain the benefits of 1860 Mires borrowing, to restrain incidents in Syria and to spread to other provinces, and the appraisal of Galata bankers' capitals in European markets. As a result, the government attempted to borrow again in order to withdraw banknotes which had become gangrenous in the economy from the market. The state signed a debt contract of 200 million frank with an export price of 68%, an interest rate of 6%, a redemption rate of 2% with European fundholders providing that 40% of the banknotes (kaime) was going to pay with money, and 60% was going to pay with "esham-ı cedide" (stock shares). Tobacco, salt, stamp tax incomes, and dividend tax incomes were pledged as collateral for this loan (Sayar 1977: 211).

The borrowing resorted to cover the expenses and the banknotes withdrawn from the market were now being used as an important financial method to cover the fiscal deficits (Blaisdell 1979: 38). In 1863, Ottoman state was preparing for its first budget in Western sense. The department of finance was made the center in charge of state's financial affairs; revenues and expenses of the state were kept in budget procedures. The statesmen' search for a balanced budget could not be materialized despite their efforts to diversify the taxes and increase the revenue items as the expantion of the tax base considering the foreign cost specialists' reports. Thus, in 1863, financial bureaucrats made 6,248,000 liras borrowing debt provision of 8,800,000 liras (200,000,000 French franc) together with the partnership of newly established "Ottoman Bank" and "Credit Mobilier." With this loan, an important part of state's expense, some part of internal debts, and Galata bankers' debt payable were paid (Özdemir 2010: 57). Bursa and Edirne's silk tithe; İzmir, Balıkesir, and Midilli's olive tithe; some city's tobacco and salt tithe; and customs tithe were collateralized in return for 200 million franc debt (Çakır 2001: 68). In 1865, Ottoman Empire made two external borrowings. The first one was called as "cattle tax borrowing" referring to the collateralization of cattle taxes and the second one was called as "Public Shares Borrowing (Esham-ı Umumiye)" which was a general debt agreement (Açba 1995a: 63). Participating "Ottoman Bank," "Credit Mobilier," and "Societe Generale," the first was 150 million francs worth debt agreement which had 6% of interest, 2.44% of amortization, and 66% of export price. The government collateralized Anatolian cattle taxes and Ergani copper mines in return for the loan. (Teper 2008: 60). The government had to make another debt agreement in 1865. The borrowing made in 1863 had helped to pay internal borrowings which were due, but there were still stock shares banknotes in the market. Ottoman Empire was wishing to draw foreign capital into the country by transforming the bond papers in the market into long-term foreign debt. In this regard, bureaucrats made several attempts to borrow from European countries. After a couple of attempts banker M. Metron's borrowing project was approved and a debt contract was signed with *"General Credit and Finance Corporation"* in London. What was collateralized in return to the loan was all the incomes of the state. 40 million Ottoman golds (about 900 million francs) were taken as a debt which had 5% of interest, 1% of amortization, and 50% of export price (Açba 1995a: 64–65).

In 1869, another external borrowing agreement was made with France in order to pay the short-term debts and resolve the budget deficit. 300 million francs debt was taken with an agreement signed with *"Comptoir d'Escompte Bank"* from Paris. Export price of the each 500 francs stocks was 270 francs. The amount of this loan in Ottoman golds was 24,444,442 liras. However, what was gained with this agreement was 13,200,000 liras. Interest price of the debt was 6% and amortization was 1%. The state collateralized some percentages of Adana, Syria, Yanya, Trabzon, Bursa, Bosnia, Aydın, Menteşe, Konya, and Baghdat tithes and cattle taxes (Yılmaz 2011: 49–50). In 1870, Ottoman government made Rumelian railroads borrowing, the most important deal in terms of usage but the worst borrowing deal financially. Ottoman Empire gave privileges of the 2000 km of two railroads linking the Empire and Europe to Baron Hirsch, a banker from Brussels. Starting from Istanbul, one of the railroads was reaching to Bosnia and Sava rivers, and the other one to Edirne, Plovdiv, İnos, Burgaz, and Salonica with its branch offices. In 1870, Hirsch established Rumeli railway operating company. Baron Hirsch signed a borrowing contract for a portion of the capital required for construction (Sağlam 2013: 21–22). Having 11,193,177 liras clear revenue, 34,848,000 liras worth (792 million French franc) lottery debt had an interest of 3%, amortization of 1%, and export price of 32,125%. It had the least export price (Özdemir 2010: 60). The government committed to issue debt shares for the construction of railways. Accordingly, the government issued 1,980,000 copies of stock certificates each par value of 400 francs. A variety of bonuses were given every 2 months to the number of hits that were taken. The government was to pay 2,936,398 francs with gathered bonuses (Teper 2008: 60). The state pledged Egypt's tax as collateral in return for this agreement (Yılmaz 2011: 50).

In order to close the budget deficit and pay the interests of external debts, in 1871, Ottoman Empire attempted to borrow from Europe again. With Ottoman bureaucrats' initiatives, having an interest of 6%, 5,700,000 pounds worth debt agreement was signed through the agency of *"Credit Cohen Sons"* and *"Dent Palmer and Company"* banks. What was provided as collateral was the left of Egypt's taxes. According to agreement, Ottoman earned 4,577,100 liras out of 6,270,000 liras debt (Çakır 2001: 69). In 1872, Ottoman made another debt agreement with *"Ottoman*

Table 4.1 External debts of ottoman empire according to Parvus Efendi

Loan	Amount of the loan	Price of issue	Buyers' value according to export price
1854	75,000,000 francs	80%	60,000,000 francs
1855	125,000,000 francs	100%	125,000,000 francs
1858	125,000,000 francs	76%	95,000,000 francs
1860	50,930,500 francs	62.5%	31,831,562 francs
1862	200,000,000 francs	68%	136,000,000 francs
1863	200,000,000 francs	68% and 72%	136,000,000 francs
1865	150,000,000 francs	66%	99,000,000 francs
1865	909,091,000 francs	50%	454,545,500 francs
1869	555,555,500 francs	61%	388,885,500 francs
1870–1872	792,000,000 francs	125% and 32%	254,430,000 francs
1871	142,500,000 francs	73%	104,025,000 francs
1872	278,155,000 francs	98.5%	273,972,675 francs
1873	694,444,500 francs	59.5%	413,194,477 francs
1874	1,000,000,000 francs	43.5%	435,000,000 francs
Total	5,297,676,500 francs		3,012,884,714 francs

Source: Parvus Efendi, Türkiye'nin Can Damarı Devlet-i Osmaniye'nin Borçları ve Islahı, Prepared by: Filiz Dığıroğlu, İstanbul, Taş Mektep Yayınları, 2014, p. 24

Bank," "*Banque Austro- Ottomane*," and "*Credit General Ottoman*" with a high interest of 9%. In accordance with the contract, 10,403,004 Ottoman liras of 12,238,820 liras debt were paid to Ottoman government. Salonica, Edirne, and Tuna's incomes and Anatolia's cattle taxes were collateralized (Yılmaz 2011: 52). At the end of 1872, Ottoman stock market was seen to be refreshing due to Ottoman bank and other banks taking care of treasury's needs, the state lionizing stock shares and bonds, while tramway, tunnel corporations, and financial establishments were lionizing stock certificates. In 1873, desiring to take advantage of the situation, statesmen made an application for changing the borrowings by introducing a new law. 22,252,400 liras national debt was recorded to the national debt agreement made in 1865. It was decided to be replaced with medium-term stock shares which were due to be paid in 1876, 1877, and 1878. The export price of the agreement was 98.5% and the interest rate was 9% (Sayar 1977: 218–219). The last debt agreement of the Ottoman Empire before its bankruptcy was signed with Ottoman Bank in 1874. 40 million pound worth agreement had an interest of 5%, an amortization of 1%, and an export price of 43.5%. Because of the lower export price, Ottoman government became indebted with 44 million liras in exchange for 19,140,000 liras debt (Teper 2008: 62) (Table 4.1).

Results of External Borrowings and Their Affects to Economy

Babıali had continued borrowing attempts until on October 6th 1875, with the decision of the moratorium, Mahmud Nedim Paşa government announced that the government was able to pay only half of borrowings and interests reaching 14 millions per annum and was going to give 5 year bonds which had an interest of 5% for the other half (Timur 2005: 58). As of 1865, Ottoman Empire had difficulties to pay back the debts. Both advances taken from Ottoman Bank and new subprime borrowings retarded the process (Yılmaz 2011: 60). Soon afterwards the announcement of moratorium, interior, and exterior reactions increased. Due to moratorium, a lot of internal bankers suffered, as for European debtees tried to domineer the Ottoman government by making propaganda against it in European media. Demonstrations held in several European capitals against Ottoman (Açba 1995b: 137). After the moratorium, the term between 1875 and 1881 was called "*time between two decrees.*" On the first date, the payments were reduced by half. On the second date, postponed with "*Muharrem Kararnamesi (Muharram Decree)*" borrowing policy was cured for certain with the establishment of "*Duyun-ı Umumiy İdaresi (Ottoman Public Debt Administration)*" (Sağlam 2013: 42).

Until 1875, Ottoman Empire had only revenue of 3 billion francs although it borrowed 5.3 billion francs. For 20 years period, Ottoman Empire paid 2 billion francs to both intermediary firms and bondholders (Sağlam 2013: 34). Debt burden of the state increased a bit more each year. Till early 1860s, external borrowing payments had formed 10% of state spendings; this rate reached 33% at the end of 1860s and 57% in 1874 (Kıray 2008: 11–12). Even though the interests of external borrowings seemed low (around 5–6%), interests rose to 12% veraciously due to low export prices of stocks (Yılmaz 2011: 58). Babıali's wrong policies and palace and state officials' extravagancies were the reasons behind first borrowings. Only one in eight percent of revenues provided from external debts was spent on investments. 25 million liras were spent on railway construction, 1 million liras on İstanbul Port, and 1 million liras on Konya province irrigation operations (Tezel 2002: 85). Ottoman's external borrowing is categorized as "*borrowing for consumption model*" because it was spent mostly on current expenditure (Kazgan 1975–1976: 69–82). As the debts increased, the domestic spendings also increased. Ottoman Empire preferred external borrowing over trying to increase the control over tithe and to make this taxing more beneficial for the state because it was easier. Ottoman government's choice was beneficial for European bankers and Western states; accordingly they were promoting the external borrowing policy of the Ottoman (Teper 2008: 64).

In 1874, revenues of Ottoman Empire had increased; however, the amount of external debts had grown further. 55% of the treasury revenues were being given to foreigners as a repayment of the debts. State spendings were increasing and the government was looking for money lenders to cover the expenses. Borrowing by collateralizing the tithes of following years was easier than cutting current expenditure. The state was making internal borrowings into external borrowings continuously (Blaisdell 1979: 40). Important factors affecting the low credibility of Ottoman Empire on borrowing were that there were no reports about Ottoman finance enough to give information to foreign shareholders and the malfunctions in administrative structure. Having insufficient information, shareholders were not insistent on credits to give Ottoman Empire, and this caused an increasing on borrowing costs (Akar and Al 2003: 4).

During the 22 years after the first external borrowing in order to cover the military expenses of 1854 Crimean War, Ottoman Empire had to borrow large amounts of money from London, Paris, Vienna, and other European markets on increasingly worse conditions (Pamuk 2008: 145). The first term of borrowing 1854–1876 borrowing account ended with a heavy fall after a short term. This process which culminated in the establishment of "*Duyun-u Umumiye İdaresi*" in order to give debt owned by the creditors as a result of 22 years of borrowing policy brought higher costs to the treasury than the internal financing methods applied before 1854 (Pamuk 2008: 145). First term of external debts of Ottoman Empire played the role of an intermediary of transferring wealth resources of the country to foreign countries. Instead of output growth, the funds obtained from borrowings were used for the state's current expenditures mostly and thus the state's debt amount increased. The increase in debts has led to a large part of the government's public revenues being taken over by foreigners (Kepenek 2009: 11). European fund holders who traded with Ottoman Empire have supported to grant loans to the Empire. The fundholders were gaining profits from the debts borrowed by Ottoman Empire because those debts were primarily used for the repayment of old debts and for the guarantees of foreign capital investors (Keyder 1993: 59). External borrowings accelerated Ottoman state's integration with European economy. With the debts borrowed, importation of consumer goods increased more than importation of capital goods. With this increase in imports, rival companies that meet domestic consumption collapse rapidly. A specialization was actualized in the exported goods with the expectation of an increase in exports in order to repay debts. Besides, with the funds obtained through this borrowing policy, a progress was also made towards the realization of westernization reforms (Kıray 2008: 15).

The View, Criticism, and Solution Offers of Ottoman Intellectuals to State's Borrowing Policy

In the newspapers of the period, the borrowing policy of the state was consumingly criticized. Borrowing issue appeared vastly in newspaper columns. In evaluations, it was constantly and repeatedly emphasized that the bureaucrats were going to push the state into a debt spiral in 10–15 years. The most important points criticized in those articles were the use of borrowing as a policy and statesmen' inability to turn the debts into an investment. In the media of the period, the first article about borrowing was titled "*İstikrazlar Hakkında.*" In this article, the borrowing policy of the state was not criticized directly; however, its damages were referred implicitly. Stating a country that had gained safety among other countries would face borrowing as long as there would be a financial difficulty; Namık Kemal specified that the borrowings would only gain temporary favor. He told that in the past the states had used to confiscate the wealth of their own people on the basis of confiscation, afterwards instead of confiscation borrowing applied as a precaution. Stating that even though only a few statesmen made the borrowings, the whole nation was affected; Kemal said that most of the borrowings were spent on unnecessary expenses and the state's revenues were in the hook by paying these (Kemal 1866: 1). According to Namık Kemal, due to the increase in the variety of debt securities and the high prices, the demands of wealth owners had increased. This situation caused a decrease in transactions and also reduced the endeavor to work due to high earnings on debt security (Kemal 1866: 1). Namık Kemal stated that Ottoman stock shares were more useful than external borrowings (Kemal 1866: 1). He said that stock shares were not have much to pay so it would not affect the trade, and they did not depend on European procedures so their damage would be less. According to Namık Kemal, as a result of internal borrowings neither big capitals would be prevented from trading nor big bankrupts would be experienced. After specifying the benefits of stock shares, Namık Kemal also stated that thanks to stock shares a security was provided for those who were not able for arts and commercials since there was no such thing as safety funds in the country (Kemal 1866: 1–2).

Published in Hürriyet Daily News, "*Sekizinci Numaradaki Maliye Bendine Zeyl*" titled article also criticized the state's borrowing policy. Noting that Babıali had been against Egypt's borrowing from Europe because it was harmful for the country's benefits, Kemal stated that in Abdulaziz period, required precautions for financial reforms were collected under two titles. One of them was increasing the revenues, and the other one was borrowing. Namık Kemal told that if the state's revenues would have been increased with right precautions, the state's wealth would be folded 8–10 times in 10–15 years. According to Kemal, this was not able to materialize because of the increase in tax rates. Kemal reflected borrowing should not be applied in cases such as rescuing homeland from major disasters. Namık Kemal criticized Babıali for resorting to borrowing method every time when in trouble (Kemal 1868: 1). Kemal also criticized the government's acceptance of borrowing as an income instead there were other methods like increasing the state's wealth by making the people work in agriculture, industrial, and trade sectors. Criticizing the example of the European states resorting to borrowing while the state was attempting to borrow, Namık Kemal set France as an example. Kemal told that France had been borrowing for hundred years; however, its 80 million pouch debt was not more than five times their revenues. While starting to borrowing in 1854, Ottoman Empire's debt had reached 20 million pouch and it was seven times Empire's revenues. Namık Kemal stated that the state's internal and external debts corresponded to one-third of the revenues (Kemal 1868: 1). Later, Kemal informed about Ottoman's debts based on German newspaper (Kemal 1868: 2).

On the article published in Hürriyet's 62nd issue, providing convenience on budget's borrowing issue was mentioned. According to Namık Kemal, the debt agreements were signed at high prices by issuing double deed and due to treasury was not capable of repaying the debt that was paid with another debt. And this caused a budget deficit every year increasingly. As long as there were ways for new borrowings with the encouragement of the foreign countries, the state would not be freed from borrowing funds. If the state wanted to borrow by courtesy of the treasury, the budget balance were in a very bad situation to allow that. Namık Kemal criticized that the only precaution for increasing the reputation of the budget was shown as a new debt agreement (Kemal 1869c: 2). On the 47th issue of Hürriyet, telling that if this borrowing would continue, soon they would not be able to find a coin even with an interest of 50%. Kemal said, "We are unable to describe how the treasury's going to end at this rate. It should be well thought that it is not 'The state can not live unsteady'; it is 'The state can not live only with borrowing'" and criticized the borrowing policy of the state (Kemal 1869b: 2).

On the 22nd issue of Hürriyet, the state's borrowing policy was reviewed through historical process on an article titled "*İstikraz-ı Cedid Üzerine Yeni Osmanlılar Cemiyetinin Mütalaatı.*" According to Ziya Paşa, from its foundation till 1854, Ottoman Empire had cared to stand on its own feet despite domestic and external incidents, wars, and distresses and had not borrowed even a coin. In 1854, with the beginning of copying Europe trend, the expenses of the palace and ministries increased extremely and because the state was unable to pay this surplus, banknotes were launched to the market. Supposing a worthless piece of paper as an endless fund, waste and splurged increased. When the time of payment of the banknotes has come, Ottoman state wanted to pay again with printing new banknotes; however, Europeans collected the debts in cash. Instead of trimming the sails, decreasing wastage, and increasing incomes, the officials increased the taxes to get out of this debt (Ziya Paşa 1868: 1–2). Later, Ziya Paşa wrote about the first borrowings of the state. Borrowing precaution was thought as an alternative during Russian War, for both to cover the cost of war and to remove various documents from the market. Bureaucrats leaned towards the debt agreements to promote relations with Europe against Russian threat. First, five million pounds worth debt agreement was signed. The money gained from the agreement returned to Europe because of big wastages and arms payments. Getting the idea that they found a treasure as they did while printing the banknotes, bureaucrats acted the same way and the wastes accelerated still more. Next year, three million pounds debt agreement was signed. Instead of investment and repayment of the aids taken from the public, these debts were spent on bureaucrats' wastages and construction of buildings like Çırağan Palace. In 1858, in order to pay the interests of the debts, an agreement worth of five million pounds was also signed. Some of the money was used to pay old debts' interests and a part of debts to Galata moneylenders. What was left was wasted on prodigality. Two years later, after a loss of two million francs worth agreement, European states said that it was wrong and after that they would lend in order to invest. Later, Babıali borrowed under cover of investment. And these loans were wasted on inutile expenses. As the time of debt payments came, treasury started to print banknotes. When everything went worse, in 1862, the deedless banknotes were removed from the market by borrowing 8 million pounds. In 1863, 6 million worth; in 1864, 2 million worth; in 1865, 6 million worth debt agreements were signed (Ziya Paşa 1868: 2–3). According to Ziya Paşa, 14 years before, Ottoman Empire did not have any external debt even a coin. but got into 750,000 pouch coins external debt thanks to the current administration. Ziya Paşa noted that the treasury was obliged to pay 974,640 pouches interest every year. Paşa indicated that the amount of debt was seven fold of state's revenues; however, the interests it was paying were equivalent to half of state's incomes (Ziya Paşa 1868: 4). He said that when the finance was in this dire situation, Babıali attempted to borrow five million and it was rumored that a portion of the incomes would be collateralized and an interest of 10% and an interest of 3% as a commission would be paid. Gainsayer to this agreement, Ziya Paşa expressed that even though the borrowing would work for Babıali, the public was totally against it (Ziya Paşa 1868: 5).

Reintegration of the state into borrowing attempts from European in 1868 was met with a strong reaction in the press. Harsh articles and deeds of protest were seen in newspapers in succession. Repeated several times the first deed of protest was declared in Muhbir Newspaper by Ali Suavi. On behalf of ummah, Suavi declared that the borrowings of Babıali was unacceptable (Le Mukhbir 1868b, c, d, e: 4, 1, 1, 1). Another deed of protest seen at the press was "*Babıali'nin Akdedeceği İstikrazı Ümmet-i Osmaniye'nin Kabul Etmeyeceğini Havi İstanbul'dan Yüz İki İmza ile Aldığımız Protestonamedir*" published in Hürriyet's 21st issue. Kanizade Rıfat indicated a rumor that Babıali was about to get under 125 million francs debt promising that it would not make a debt deal anymore in return. Kanızade was against this policy under five articles: (1) Earlier, 40 million liras debt agreement had been made promising there would be no more debts; however, they made another exorbitant sum borrowing agreements. (2) Even though it had been announced that the borrowings would be spent on civil and financial measures like roads to be built, education would be advanced, and old debts would be closed, none of these was done. Instead, the money was spent on building mansions, pavilions, and palaces for administrators. (3) The community was not aware of the borrowings and did not express an opinion about it. In accordance with the decisions of only some of the bureaucrats like Grand vizier and foreign service officers, these agreements were signed. (4) The interests of the debts were paid by part of state revenues. (5) - European bankers continued to give loan even though they knew poorly about the state's condition, because they were getting high interest and commission (Kanızade Rıfat Bey 1868: 1). In his article, after ranking these five objects, Kanizade wanted the debt agreement to be protested because it would help neither to Ottoman State nor its people (Kanızade Rıfat Bey 1868: 1–2).

The borrowing made by the state in 1868 was criticized in an article of Hürriyet's 38th issue titled "*Yeni İstikraz.*" Namık Kemal indicated that wandering Europe in order to sign a debt agreement for conceivable railway between İstanbul and Belgrade, bureaucrats finally made a 150 million liras worth borrowing. Kemal emphasized the objections of the agreement under five articles: (1) The money gained from the agreement was 1,759,277 liras per year both capital and the interest;

however, the four-part income shown as a provision was worth around 2,680,000 liras. (2) To be given the revenue to the company at the time of the delivery, Ottoman state was not entrusted and the management of the incomes was given to company. (3) 1–2% commission was given in such instabilities; however, in this borrowing 4% commission was given. (4) State's income was going to be in foreigners' hand for 5 years. (5) 12.5% of interest was paid in this agreement although a debt settlement giving more than 5% was not found in Europe (Kemal 1869a: 1–2). According to Kemal, Babıali has made a living with borrowing a principle for 15 years. Disrepute of the state increased with debt agreements and this paved the way for even giving an administration of state incomes to foreigners. In 1869, with a debt agreement Ottoman lost Danube, Edirne, and Salonica's tithes and Anatolian cattle taxes and duties. The state would lose different incomes for the next years in need of new debt agreements (Kemal 1869a: 2).

Published on İbret, in an article titled "*İstikraz,*" those reviews were made. According to Reşad Bey, a state should be in a difficult situation while borrowing. If an order in finance has been broken, state should make reforms and the expenses should be decreased. Ignoring this fact, if the state resorts to external borrowing, the rescue of the state would be eddying (Reşad Bey 1872: 1). Reşad stated that as the taxes would increase with borrowing, social problems would arise. He was against a passed down debt. He said that this debt did not have a place in Qur'an and it was an arbitrary debt (Reşad Bey 1872: 1). He criticized Fuat Paşa's saying; "This state can not live without borrowing." He criticized the bureaucrats thereby asking if the state had been living with borrowing since its foundation. He said that the state had become needy after being governed safe and sound for five to six centuries and it was not suitable for political ethics that turning a debtless state into an indebted state and then saying the state could not live without borrowing. He explained that financial indicator of the time showed that the state could not live without borrowing, yet the bureaucrats were the reason (Reşad Bey 1872: 1). According to Reşad, the state had a large source of wealth. The state and the public should have worked to evaluate these worthy of treasure sources in order to pay the state's debts. So, the state would live without borrowing and would reach to a point to give loans to other countries (Reşad Bey 1872: 1).

On Muhbir's several issues, news and criticisms towards state's borrowing policy were published. Published on the 11th issue of Muhbir, on the first news, Ali Suavi criticized the debt taken in order to remove the banknotes and the transformation of the interest-free debts into interest-bearing debts (Le Mukhbir 1867: 3). On the news published on Muhbir's 25th issue, the debt agreement between bureaucrats and England and an objection against this agreement were stated (Le Mukhbir 1868a: 3). In an article titled "*İstikraz*" published on 14th issue, it was stated that the government should have given importance to equalizing the expenses and revenues. Suavi indicated that the state should not have borrowed except for war and invest-ment expenses, and the necessity of paying attention to the agreements' borrowing's conditions that it should not have a high interest rate. Suavi said that the borrowings increased with the encouragement of European governments and the treasury went down into a situation that it became even unable to pay 1.5 million pouchs interest it should pay each year (Ali Suavi 1867: 1–2).

However in articles published in Terakki Newspaper, the state's policy was not criticized as sharply as the other articles mentioned above. In fact, the benefits of the debts were mentioned and how the debts saved the economy of the state was explained. Firstly, on Terakki's 228th issue, in an article titled "*Devletlerin Borçları*," it was mentioned that the debt agreements between states gained mutual advantages. Later, it was told that the states should make internal borrowings more than external borrowings. According to Hayrettin Bey, the borrowings between states benefited the states. While the debtor was out of a tight corner thanks to the debt, the lender exploited from return of the debt due to the interest of the debt (Hayrettin Bey 1869: 1). Hayrettin notes that the reason how a state that had a debt burden could find a debt easier than a state with a less debt was that the safety shown in debt payment was taken into account. The borrowed country was saved from a difficult situation that it had fallen due to the debt it received. Besides, it would raise the wealth and prosperity of the country by running the money it received (Hayrettin Bey 1869: 1–2). Hayrettin Bey drew attention to importance of a state's internally borrowing rather than externally. He told how England fixed the economy by borrowing internally after years of borrowing from France. The purpose of this example was to show that people pay attention to the fact that the benefits to the Ottoman state should not be left in the hands of the foreigners by taking the example of the Europeans (Hayrettin Bey 1869: 2). He indicated that the people should have worked ardently in order to save the treasury from falling into need for foreign capital and to overcome this problem. He said that in case treasury would need a loan, people should have to fight with each other for loaning to state without the need from foreign capitals (Hayrettin Bey 1869: 2).

In an untitled article published on Terakki's 317th issue, it was stated that the Ottoman Empire had increased its share of the borrowing monies, and the debt treaties were mentioned one by one. The writer noted that in the early days, Ottoman stock shares were approached with suspicion by European states because of the war news and Empire's bad economic situation and later on, with the increasing of state's revenues through reforms the demand to Ottoman stock shares increased affirmatively. According to the writer, in the wake of construction of roads in the country, establishment of major railways, and financial reforms, the confidence of the Ottoman state in the financial succession consolidated compared to 3–4 years before. As a result, demand on Ottoman stock shares increased (Terakki 1870: 2). The writer expressed that it was clear that the roads and railways to be built with loans would benefit substantially the treasury (Terakki 1870: 2).

According to an article titled "*Umur-ı Maliye*" published in Terakki's 113th issue, the state had almost 2 billion francs debt and 875 million of it was external borrowings. There were two ways in order to both close the fiscal deficit and pay the debts. One of them was borrowing and the other one was taxes. Borrowing would provide temporary relief to the state. In general, applied by the states due to a very dire situation, this method should not have been preferred because paying the debts back with an interest would bring more burden to the public (Terakki 1869a: 2).

According to the writer, since the amount of interest to be paid after the debts were collected from the public, the benefit from borrowing would usually be resulted in negativity. When borrowing was done, most of the debts were in the hands of the Europeans, so the beneficiaries were not the Ottoman people but the foreigners. If borrowing was made for investment, benefits would be observed in the long run (Terakki 1869a: 2).

Published on Terakki, "*Gayet Mühim Bir Madde*" addressed to negativities of borrowing. According to the writer, Ottoman Empire had a deficit of a couple millions coins in exchanges with Europe every year. If it would have continued that way, there would not be left any coin in treasury. When the debt agreements are examined, it is observed that due to high interests paid to debts every year, the capital flows to foreign countries. Even though the state gained 15–20 million liras of capital from the borrowings, it paid back four or five times more. In short, the borrowings did great harm to the state (Terakki 1869b: 3).

Published in Terakki's 181th issue, an article expressed that the place the foreign capitalist came the least was Ottoman Empire even though the state's incomes were increasing (Terakki 1869e: 2). According to the author, while Empire had been taking debts with a high interest in the past, during those days it could borrow as much as it desired with relatively low interests. There were hesitations on London and Paris's stock markets for exportation of stock shares at the beginning; later on, trend toward Ottoman stock shares increased due to the goodwill Ottomans showed in the contracts and the safety shown in the exchanges (Terakki 1869e: 2). The author indicated that the borrowings contributed to reformation of the economy; yet, the loans should be used where needed. He also recommended the repayments of the installments and interests should be made in time (Terakki 1869e: 2–3).

The last article about the borrowing policy on Terakki was "*Bütçe Risalesi.*" The writer indicated that the bureaucrats decided to remove banknotes as precaution because they thought that a budget balance would be impossible with banknotes on the market. The writer expressed that 5 million liras borrowed in 1858 to remove banknotes and almost 1 millions of 1,200,000 pouch money was removed. Later on, the treasury needed to mint banknotes again in order to cover the debts and expenses of Montenegro riot (Terakki 1869c: 2–3). The writer said that the treasury had 2 million pouchs banknotes debt and 3.5 million pouchs other debts because the state had not increased the revenues and decreased the expenses (Terakki 1869c: 3). In the next issue, the writer indicated that the bureaucrats who observed the predicament of the treasury was convinced that gaining its reputation back was not possible for the treasury as long as the banknotes would stay in the market. Because the state did not have enough capital, bureaucrats attempted to remove the banknotes from market for second time through borrowing. According to the writer, in 1862, Ottoman Empire borrowed 8 million liras from London and minted 2 million new stock shares (esham-ı cedide). Even though some of the debt of the state was paid with it, the state needed to borrow again and a year later it borrowed 8 millions from Paris. And in following years, the state also made another borrowing worth 6 millions (Terakki 1869d: 1–2).

Conclusion

During the rising time, Ottoman Empire did not have any troubles because the revenues were much more than the expenses. This era was called "the golden times" in terms of finance. Major problems began to appear in the state finances due to decrease in the expenses and the increase of current expenditures since the end of sixteenth century and the rise of domestic disturbance and wars. Ottoman state adopted methods like adulteration, confiscation, internal borrowing, and contribution in order to overcome economical problems in seventeenth and eighteenth centuries. Along with the nineteenth century, Ottoman state's external borrowing attempts were experienced with the decrease of the state's revenues due to further expansion of the foreign trade deficit with European states. Because an external borrowing had not been observed in 500 years of state tradition, the current state acted timidly. At first the Sultan and an important part of the bureaucrats objected to borrow from foreign countries. However, in 1853, Ottoman Empire had to take the first step for borrowing, which was being recommended for half a century, due to the treasury was not strong enough to cover the expenses of Crimean War fought with Russia and the encouragement of two allied countries England and France on borrowing.

From the first borrowing in 1854 till the declaration of bankruptcy in 1876 Moratorium, Ottoman Empire signed 15 debt agreements with European governments and bankers. Ottoman was obliged to make first borrowing to cover the expenses of Crimean War. However, latter agreements were signed because borrowing was seemed to be the financial solution to fiscal deficits. Bureaucrats resorted to borrowing method in every economical crisis. As a consequence, external debts became an important income source for the state. The state did not benefit from the agreements because they were spent for current expenditures mostly. Only a little part of the borrowings was spent for investment expenditures and this worsened the state of treasury.

In 1873, state's economical status got heavier due to problems finding hot money in Europe because of world economical crisis and large droughts experienced in the Empire. The Grand Vizier of the period Mahmud Nedim Paşa notified that the state would not be able to repay the debts. European bankers reacted to this decision and Ottoman borrowing's first era came to an end. After long negotiations between the Empire and debtors, in 1881 Public Debt Administration (*Duyun-ı Umumiye İdaresi*) was found with Muharrem Decree. It was agreed that this Administration would collect the large part of incomes in remuneration for European bankers' loans. Ottoman Empire's borrowing policy between 1854 and 1876 failed. The state could not adequately benefit from the borrowings and the borrowings resulted the government to lose its right to manage major revenue sources.

In Ottoman Empire, a public opinion free from government has been formed along with the development of press from the second half of the nineteenth century. On media organs of the period, the state's economical and political issues appeared in detail and the policies of the state were evaluated and criticized extensively.

Scholars of the period evaluated the economic and financial issues of the state and brought various proposals to the state on these issues. The borrowing policy was mentioned infinitely in the newspapers and exposed to harsh criticisms. The intellectual of the era frequently wrote upon harms brought by the debt agreements signed by bureaucrats to the state, in their columns. However, in some of the newspapers, there was no direct criticism to borrowing policy. Rather, it was mentioned that borrowings benefited the state. Intellectuals criticized that the state made borrowing in every time when in trouble and did not turn the loans into investments. In this period, it was said openly that the state's source of wealth was wasted with borrowings. Being taken mortgage about the half of state's incomes due to borrowings was criticized consumingly.

Bibliography

Açba, S. (1995a). *Osmanlı Devletinin Dış Borçlanması (1854-1914)*. Afyon: Afyon Kocatepe Üniversitesi Yayınları.
Açba, S. (1995b). *Devlet Borçlanması*. Afyon: Afyon Kocatepe Üniversitesi Yayınları.
Akar, Ş. K., & Al, H. (2003). *Osmanlı Dış Borçları ve Gözetim Komisyonları 1854-1856*. İstanbul: Osmanlı Bankası Arşiv ve Araştırma Merkezi, Kasım.
Al, H. (2007). *Uluslararası Sermaye ve Osmanlı Maliyesi*. Osmanlı Bankası Arşiv ve Araştırma Merkezi, Aralık: İstanbul.
Anbar, A. (2009). *Osmanlı İmparatorluğunun Avrupa'yla Finansal Entegrasyonu: 1800-1914*. Maliye Finans Yazıları Dergisi, Yıl:23, Sayı:84, Temmuz.
Aysal, N. (2013). *Kırım Savaşından Lozan Barış Antlaşmasına Osmanlı Dış Borçlarının Tarihsel Gelişim Süreci (1854-1923)*. Ankara Üniversitesi Türk İnkılap Tarihi Enstitüsü Atatürk Yolu Dergisi, Sayı:53, Lozan Anlaşması Özel Sayısı.
Berkes, N. (2003) Türkiye'de Çağdaşlaşma, İstanbul, Yapı Kredi Yayınları, 5.Baskı, Ekim.
Bey, K. R. (1868). *Babıâli'nin Akdedeceği İstikrazı Ümmet-i Osmaniye'nin Kabul Etmeyeceğini Havi İstanbul'dan Yüz İki İmza ile Aldığımız Protestonamedir*. Hürriyet, Sayı:21, s.1–2, 6 Şaban 1285/22 Kasım.
Bey, H. (1869). *Devletlerin Borçları*. Terakki, Sayı:228, s.1–2, 14 Cemaziyelahir 1286/8 Eylül.
Bey, R. (1872). *İstikraz*. İbret, Sayı:19, s.1, 27 Haziran 1288/9 Temmuz.
Blaisdell, D. C. (1979). *Osmanlı İmparatorluğunda Avrupa Mali Denetimi Duyunuumumiye*. İstanbul: Doğu-Batı Yayınları.
Buluş, A-M., Mercan, B. (2002). *Son Dönem Osmanlı İktisat Politikaları*. Liberal Düşünce, Y:7, S:28, Güz.
Çakır, C. (2001). *Tanzimat Dönemi Osmanlı Maliyesi*. İstanbul: Küre Yayınları, Ekim.
Cezar, Y. (1985). *Tanzimat'a Doğru Osmanlı Maliyesi*. Tanzimat'tan Cumhuriyet'e Türkiye Ansiklopedisi, C:4. İstanbul: İletişim Yayınları.
Cezar, Y. (1986). *Osmanlı Maliyesinde Bunalım ve Değişim Dönemi*. Mayıs: Alan Yayıncılık.
Dumont, P. (2007) *Tanzimat Dönemi, 1839*. Der:Robert Mantran, Osmanlı İmparatorluğu Tarihi, C:2 Duraklamadan Yıkılışa, İstanbul, Alkım Yayınları, 8.Basım.
Engelhardt, E. P. (1999). *Tanzimat ve Türkiye*. İstanbul: Kaknüs Yayınları.
Eren, A. (1999). *Osmanlı Ekonomisinde Kurumsal Gelişmeler*. Ankara: Osmanlı Ansiklopedisi, İktisat, Yeni Türkiye Yayınları.
Genç, M. (1995). *Esham*. İslam Ansiklopedisi, C:11. İstanbul: Türk Diyanet Vakfı.
Güran, T. (1998). *Tanzimat Dönemi Osmanlı Maliyesi*. İstanbul: İstanbul Üniversitesi İktisat Fakültesi Mecmuası, C:49, 60.Yıl Özel Sayısı.

Güran, T. (2003). *Osmanlı Mali İstatistikleri Bütçeler 1842–1918.* Ankara: Başbakanlık Devlet İstatistik Enstitüsü Yayınları, Eylül.

Karal, E. Z. (1983). *Osmanlı Tarihi,* C:6, Ankara, Türk Tarih Kurumu Basımevi, 3.Baskı.

Kazgan, H. (1976). *Osmanlı Modeli Tüketim İçin Borçlanma.* İstanbul Üniversitesi İktisat Fakültesi Mecmuası, C:35, Sayı:1–4, Ekim 1975-Eylül.

Kemal, N. (1866). *İstikrazlar Hakkında.* Tasvir-i Efkâr, Sayı:445, s.1–3, 13 Şaban 1283/21 Aralık.

Kemal, N. (1868). *Sekizinci Numaradaki Maliye Bendine Zeyl.* Hürriyet, Sayı:10, s.1–2, 13 Cemaziyelevvel 1285/31 Ağustos.

Kemal, N. (1869a). *Yeni İstikraz.* Hürriyet, Sayı:38, s.1–2, 1 Zilhicce 1285/15 Mart.

Kemal, N. (1869b) *Esham-ı Umumiye Üzerine.* Hürriyet, Sayı:47, s.2, 5 Safer 1286/17 Mayıs.

Kemal, N. (1869c). *Muvazene-i Maliye 1 Hizmet.* Hürriyet, Sayı:62, s.2, 22 Cemaziyelevvel 1286/30 Ağustos.

Kepenek, Y-Y. (2009) *Nurhan, Türkiye Ekonomisi.* İstanbul, Remzi Kitabevi, 22. Basım, Eylül.

Keyder, Ç. (1993). *Türkiye'de Devlet ve Sınıflar.* İstanbul, İletişim Yayınları, 3. Baskı, Mayıs.

Kıray, E. (2008). *Osmanlı'da Ekonomik Yapı ve Dış Borçlar.* İstanbul, İletişim Yayınları, 3.Baskı.

Koraltürk, M. (1995). *Osmanlı Dış Borçları ve 1875 Moratoryumu.* Tarih ve Toplum, C:24, Sayı:142, Ekim.

Le Mukhbir. (1867). Sayı:11, s. 3, 7 Novembre (Kasım).

Le Mukhbir. (1868a). Sayı:25, s. 3, 29 Fevrier (Şubat).

Le Mukhbir. (1868b). Sayı:34, s. 4, 13 Mai (Mayıs).

Le Mukhbir. (1868c) Sayı:36, s. 1, 27 Mai (Mayıs).

Le Mukhbir. (1868d). Sayı:37, s. 1, 3 Juin (Haziran).

Le Mukhbir. (1868e). Sayı:38, s. 1, 12 Juin (Haziran).

Lewis, B. (2004). *Modern Türkiye'nin Doğuşu.* Ankara, Türk Tarih Kurumu Basımevi, 9.Baskı.

Ortaylı, İ. (2000), *İmparatorluğun En Uzun Yüzyılı.* İstanbul, İletişim Yayınları, 6.Baskı.

Özdemir, B. (2010). *Osmanlı Devleti Dış Borçları.* Ankara, Maliye Bakanlığı Strateji Geliştirme Başkanlığı Yayınları, 2. Baskı, Şubat.

Pamuk, Ş. (2004). *Osmanlı İmparatorluğu'nda Para 1326–1914.* Der. Halil İnalcık-Donald Quataert, Osmanlı İmparatorluğu'nun Ekonomik ve Sosyal Tarihi 1600–1914, C:2. İstanbul: Eren Yayıncılık.

Pamuk, Ş. (2005). *Osmanlı-Türk İktisadi Tarihi 1500–1914.* İstanbul: İletişim Yayınları, 2.Baskı.

Pamuk, Ş. (2008). *Seçme Eserleri 1 Osmanlı Ekonomisi ve Kurumları.* İstanbul: Türkiye İş Bankası Kültür Yayınları, 11. Baskı, Eylül.

Parvus, E. (2014). *Türkiye'nin Can Damarı Devlet-i Osmaniye'nin Borçları ve Islahı,* Haz.: Filiz Dığıroğlu. İstanbul: Taş Mektep Yayınları.

Paşa, Z. (1868). *İstikraz-ı Cedid Üzerine Yeni Osmanlılar Cemiyetinin Mütalaatı.* Hürriyet, Sayı:22, s.1–6, 13 Şaban 1285/29 Kasım.

Sağlam, M. H. (2013). *Osmanlı Devletinde Moratoryum 1875-1881, Rüsum-ı Sitteden Duyun-ı Umumiyye'ye.* İstanbul: Tarih Vakfı Yurt Yayınları, 2. Basım, Kasım.

Şahin, C. (2001–2002). *Yeni Bir Çalışma Işığında Osmanlı'da Dış Borçlanma ve Mali İflas Üzerine.* Doğu-Batı, Yıl:4, Sayı:17, Kasım-Aralık-Ocak.

Sayar, N. S. (1977). *Türkiye İmparatorluk Dönemi Mali Olayları.* İstanbul: Meter Matbaası.

Sayar, A. G. (2006). *Osmanlı İktisat Düşüncesinin Çağdaşlaşması.* İstanbul: Ötüken Yayınevi, 3. Baskı.

Şener, A. (2000). *Tanzimat ve Meşruiyet'te İktisadi ve Mali Politikalar.* Yeni Türkiye, Osmanlı Özel Sayısı 2, Ekonomi ve Toplum, Y:6, S:32, Mart-Nisan.

Suavi, A. (1867). *İstikraz.* Le Mukhbir, Sayı:14, s. 1–2 28 Novembre (Kasım).

Suvla, R. Ş. (1999). *Tanzimat Devrinde İstikrazlar.* Tanzimat C:1, Komisyon. İstanbul: Milli Eğitim Bakanlığı Yayınları.

Tekin, A. (2000). *Osmanlı Devleti Dış Borçlanması (1854–1874).* Yeni Türkiye, Osmanlı Özel Sayısı 2, Ekonomi ve Toplum, Mart, Y:6, S:32, Nisan.

Teper, N. (2008). *Bizde (Osmanlı Devletinde) İlk Devlet Borçları Duyun-ı Umumiye.* İstanbul: Yeni Asya Matbaası.

Terakki. (1869a). *Umur-ı Maliye*. Terakki, Sayı:113, s.2–3, 27 Zilhicce 1285/29 Mart.

Terakki. (1869b). Gayet Mühim Bir Madde. Terakki, Sayı:114, s.3, 29 Zilhicce 1285/31 Mart.

Terakki. (1869c). *Bütçe Risalesi 2*. Terakki, Sayı:199, s.2, 2 Cemaziyelevvel 1286/29 Temmuz.

Terakki. (1869d). *Bütçe Risalesi 3*. Terakki, Sayı:200, s.1–2, 3 Cemaziyelevvel 1286/30 Temmuz.

Terakki. (1869e) Sayı:181, s.2–3, 5 Rebiülahir 1286/3 Temmuz.

Terakki. (1870). Sayı:317, s.2, 26 Zilhicce 1286/16 Mart.

Tezel, Y. S. (2002). *Cumhuriyet Dönemi İktisadi Tarihi*. İstanbul: Tarih Vakfı Yurt Yayınları, 5. Baskı, Ekim.

Timur, T. (2005). *1875 Osmanlı Mali Krizi*. Toplumsal Tarih, Sayı:134, Şubat.

Toprak, Z. (1985). *Osmanlı Devleti'nde Para ve Bankacılık*. Tanzimat'tan Cumhuriyet'e Türkiye Ansiklopedisi, C:3. İstanbul: İletişim Yayınları.

Yılmaz, B. E. (2002). *Osmanlı İmparatorluğunu Dış Borçlanmaya İten Nedenler ve İlk Dış Borç*. Akdeniz Üniversitesi İktisadi İdari Bilimler Fakültesi Dergisi, Sayı:4.

Yılmaz, F. (2011). *Osmanlı'nın Borç Batağı Duyun-ı Umumiye*. İstanbul: İz Yayıncılık.

Chapter 5
Rethinking the Schumpeterian Revolution: The Linkage Between Financial Development, Technology, and Economic Growth

Gönül Yüce Akıncı

Abstract Since the pioneering work done by Schumpeter, the linkage between finance, technology, and growth has been widely examined. Schumpeter claims that developed financial markets accelerate technologic progress and hence the level of economic growth increases because of the rising potential of technology. This idea is now understood that the development of financial markets is vital for both technological progress and economic growth. Therefore, this chapter aims to determine the linkages between finance, technology, and economic growth using unbalanced panel simultaneous equation system in the EU-member countries in the period from 1995 to 2013. The general results of the simultaneous equation system point out that growth and finance are in congruity indirectly, suggesting that economic growth process improves financial development level. Besides, the results reveal that in the first stage the financial development process of accelerating the technology level measured as R&D expenditures as a percent of gross domestic product and in the second stage a rise in technology level improve the economic growth. In general, it is said that the Schumpeterian hypothesis claiming the positive effect of finance on technology and positive effect of technology on growth is valid.

Introduction

One of the most debated topics in the economics is the cause of growth differences among countries, regions, and even provinces. The main element of the sustainable economic development and growth is thought to be the elimination of these differences and, therefore, the convergence hypothesis formed by neoclassical and the endogenous growth theories introduced in the economic literature. Although the neoclassical theory asserts that the poor countries grow much faster than rich countries, the experiences of the real world have shown that the relationship has become reversed: Poor countries have become poorer, while rich ones have become richer. From this aspect, the equal distribution of income shares taken by countries

G. Y. Akıncı (✉)
Ordu University, Ordu, Turkey

© Springer International Publishing AG, part of Springer Nature 2018   111
H. Dincer et al. (eds.), *Global Approaches in Financial Economics, Banking, and Finance*, Contributions to Economics, https://doi.org/10.1007/978-3-319-78494-6_5

from economic growth and development is a subject that is widely investigated in many countries. Because many countries attempt to establish more equally income distribution and balanced economic growth and development process, implementing more comprehensive public policies and legal regulations as well as free market conditions gain importance among countries. However increasing commercial, industrial, financial, and technological competitions among countries create more complicated economic relations and policy applications to reach the sustainable and balanced economic growth and development process. Therefore, the growth and development theories arising from the studies aiming to find a solution for this problem concentrate on both of the causes of regional and interregional imbalances and the solution suggestions for these imbalances.

Introduced by the neoclassical theory and then had found a significant place in the growth theories, the assumption that the poor countries would grow faster than the rich ones has been named "convergence analysis." But, on the other hand, the endogenous growth theories emphasized the dominance of divergence dynamics. From this aspect, it is the situation, in which the convergence process becomes reversed and the difference between the poor countries or provinces and relatively richer ones was named "divergence." For this reason, the narrowing of gap during the development process on behalf of the poor country has been named convergence, whereas the enlargement on behalf of the richer country has been named divergence. The convergence analyses leaped forward significantly and were studied in various growth theories and model, and the spillover effects of growth were comprehensively examined for decades (Gerni et al. 2015: 315).

Schumpeter (1911), who correlated the financial sector to the literature of economics, examined spillover effects of financial markets and technological innovations, and stated that the real sector can develop together with the financial markets reaching at their optimum functional level, is one of the thinkers leading the analysis of economic system from a wide perspective. Schumpeter argued that the capitalist economic system has a static structure but the capitalist economic system has a structure renewing itself automatically with new products and manufacturing methods using the existing resources, and that the entire actual system is in a constant change having the same meaning with economic development (Erdoğan and Canbay 2016: 33).

As emphasized by Schumpeter (1911), the financial markets completely fulfilling their functions provide the entrepreneurs with the best options for the execution of new product and production methods by giving them the resources and funds they need (Yüce et al. 2013: 112; Yüce Akıncı et al. 2014a: 57, 2014b: 34). Thus, it can be said that finance stimulates growth process by providing the required capital and increasing the efficiency of capital and investment. Following the leading study of Schumpeter (1911), many authors examined the linkage between financial development and economic growth, and the character of this relationship and the causation were firstly systematized in the first study carried out by Patrick (1966). Patrick (1966) stated that the finance–growth relationships might manifest themselves around two axes. *Demand following*, the first one of them, was grounded on the idea that the financial sector would develop in parallel with the acceleration of economic growth process. Within this context, it can be stated that, when the real market develops, the request for miscellaneous financial services would become effective and this request would be satisfied by the financial side of the economy. *Supply leading*, the second axis, was suggested by Diamond and Verrecchia (1982) and Jensen and Murphy (1990) as the hypothesis that finance encourage long-term growth process, accelerates the acquisition and sharing of knowledge by stimulating the specialization level, and contributes to the increase of investment volume by reducing the costs. Moreover, a developed financial system reducing the basic administrative problems directs the attention of administrators and capitalists to the maximization of firm value and thus is capable of increasing the level of corporate control.

When considered from the aspect of finance–growth relationship, the importance of total factor efficiency is based on understanding the dynamism created by the financial development on the efficiency process. The first of mechanisms leading this dynamism is that the conformity to the newly developed technologies requires a significant amount of stock-in-trade that can be easily mobilized within the developed financial system. The second one is that the advanced capital markets and corporations ensure and encourage the access to long-term production technologies by reducing the liquidity risks investors. The third and last one is that the financial markets and corporations play an accelerating role for the technical development process due to the function of procurement of hedge and other risk distribution means. In this parallel, the countries having an advanced banking system and capital market can achieve high level of technical advancement speed, efficiency benefits, and economic growth dynamism (Tadesse 2005: 1–2).

The technological development is the most vital determinant playing a role in accelerating the growth process by ensuring the structural adjustment in industry, because the technology is directly or indirectly effective on the demand and trade volume and the labor and capital efficiencies, and has positive effect on the industrial performance. From a general perspective, the innovations in production process and the innovative products increase the productivity and, thus, lead to the growth by increasing demand (Karluk 2007: 63; Akıncı and Sevinç 2013: 7–8). In the theories that have been developed, it has been argued that the technological developments and consequently the R&D investments play effective role in succession the process of growth. The classical growth models suggested that the economic growth depends on the factors such as capital stock, labor force, and natural resources. The economic effects stimulated by the technological developments were firstly statistically analyzed by Schumpeter (1911), and it was reported that the R&D activities having an important role in accelerating the technical innovations accelerate the economic growth process by increasing the amount of product per labor force.

Besides the theory introduced by Schumpeter, it has been frequently stated in various growth theories that the technological developments and thus the R&D investments have an important part in achieving the growth. Since 1980s, the liberalization of capital movements forced the countries to find and develop new production methods for sustaining their economic growths. From this aspect, the development level of countries was believed to be directly proportional to their capacity of developing and using the existing technology (Akıncı and Sevinç 2013: 7–8). The classical growth models emphasized that the economic growth is based on the factors such as capital stock, labor force, and natural resources. Even though it is emphasized in classical theory that the capital is subjected to diminishing returns, Solow (1956, 1970) suggested that the production process including the technological development has increasing revenues according to the scale and thus the marginal efficiency of capital increases and this level is maintained. Corroborating the idea of Solow, Jones (1998) also stated that the externalities and spillover effects arising from the R&D investments of companies remove the conditions of decreasing income and cause the increasing revenues, and that this process increases the economic growth rate.

In literature, the studies generally examine the relationships between finance and growth, and technological developments playing a significant role in potential welfare and efficiency increases that might be achieved in long term are generally ignored. To close the gap in literature, the present study aims to investigate the linkage between finance, growth, and technology for EU-member countries from 1995 to 2013 by using panel system two-stage least squares (2SLS) analysis method. In this context, this chapter consists of five sections. In the next section, the related literature is presented. In third stage titled "Dataset, Model, and Methodology", the methods, data set, and model regarding the econometric practice part of the study are exhibited. In fourth section, the study findings are discussed. This study ends with a conclusion for discussing from a general perspective.

Review of Related Literature

In the light of the convergence and divergence analysis introduced by neoclassical and endogenous growth theories, one of the most important questions of why some countries are wealthier and others are not and what mechanisms give rise to wealth and poverty has been emerged in the economic literature. To reply to the question, the determinants of the process of economic growth are classified into two categories: *proximate determinants of growth* and *deep determinants of growth*. Proximate determinants of growth assert that the conglomeration of human and physical capital, labor, and technology, in other words increasing productivity, are the main factors which drive economic growth. As Bloch and Tang (2004) noted, we learn little from the neoclassical model about what drives the growth of total factor productivity and how to improve it. Besides, it is impossible for us to know why and how technology arises, and, therefore, total factor productivity is regarded as *manna from heaven*. Moreover, the same problems emerge when the accumulation of human capital has been taken into consideration. Since we accept technological progress as manna from heaven, we cannot measure total factor productivity and it just remains as a *measurement of our ignorance* as Solow (1956) noted. In order to get through the problems of how total factor productivity is measured and what factors drive productivity growth, the endogenous growth theories have emerged.

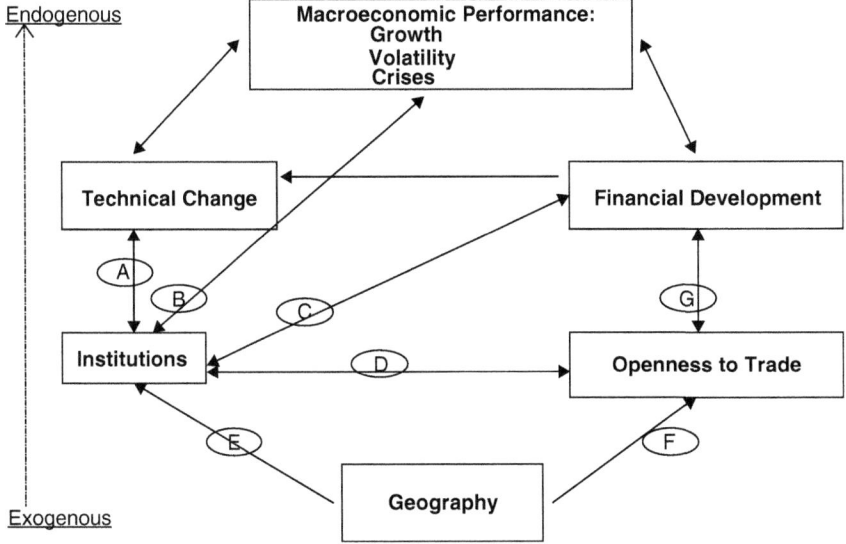

Fig. 5.1 Deep determinants of growth. Source: Bloch and Tang (2004: 252)

With the help of multiple variables as part of endogenous growth theories, the importance of institutions, openness of trade, geographical factors, culture, process of economic integration, diseases, rule of law, economic freedom, life expectancy, financial sector development, spatial spillovers, and schooling rates come in sight as deep determinants of growth. Therefore, Fig. 5.1 summarizes the deep determinants of growth, economic volatility, and crisis.

As it is seen in Fig. 5.1, it is possible to observe a two-way linkage between technical change and growth and between finance and growth. Accordingly, it is possible to say that growth process and financial development are the mutually reinforcing factors, which have to be commonly taken into consideration for sustainable economic progress. Besides, there is a unidirectional linkage from the process of financial development to total factor productivity. With the help of developed financial markets, capital funds can be transferred from financial institutions to innovators who create and improve technology, and the real sector markets working with rising technology accelerate the process of economic growth. In other words, a well-designed financial market accelerates the technical development processes, decreases the potential financial problems of entrepreneurs, ensures the effective distribution of capital, and stimulates the growth dynamics for the whole economy. Moreover, financial deepening provide the real sector with high level of capital supply and, depending on the capital accumulation, the advanced technologies lead to low marginal costs and such a process both strengthens the comparative advantages and improves the dynamism of economic growth. Furthermore, it can be argued that there are close nexus between financial markets development and technology. Financial markets easing potential economic risks allow investors to create new technologies. Therefore, it is possible to say that the adoption of improved technologies requires developed financial systems through capital transfer mechanism. With the help of decreasing investors' liquidity risk, long-run investment projects can be applied. In the light of this mechanism, development process of financial markets warrants firms to reduce cost of transferring capital which makes the production process more profitable and enhances economic growth. As noted by Tadesse (2005), by providing investors to reduce risk through the process of portfolio diversification, developed financial systems allow more division of labor, raise capital/labor ratio, and give rise to higher productivity. Furthermore, owing to the fact that the process of financial development supports innovations via making financial funds cheaper and available, firms depending on external finance methods for new technologies can benefit more from financial markets and increase their profits for future investment project. These processes that enhance the marginal efficiency of capital allow economy to remain sustainable growth path.

On the other hand, some empirical evidences argue that geography affects the process of economic growth through institutional quality and openness to external trade mechanism. Figure 5.1 shows that there are unidirectional linkages from geography to institution and to openness to trade. In the next step, the dynamism of economic growth is affected by technical change, financial development process, and foreign trade, mutually. Since financial markets and institutions have reciprocal linkages with economic growth, technical progress is said to boost the economic growth process, also. In this sense, it is highly possible to say the validity of interrelated linkages between growth, finance, and technology.

Through various transmission mechanisms, as noted above, the effectively functioning advanced capital markets might lead to acceleration of technological developments and increase in efficiency level. The adaptability to the technological developments and ensuring the technical advancement require more effective move of capital within an advanced financial market. Even though the effect of financial markets on the technique improvement has been systematically analyzed by Schumpeter (1911), the linkage between finance and technological preferences has been firstly emphasized by Hicks (1969) while explaining the rise of industrial revolution. Arguing that the industrial development can be achieved by adopting the investment-based technologies, Hicks (1969) noted that the process of industrial revolution was not effective in developing new technologies, but all the innovations have been made before the industrial revolution. Hicks (1969), who drew attention to the role of financial systems that ensure liquidity to investors in achieving the needed labor- or capital-intense technologies, emphasized that there are direct relationships between the technological development of the countries and the development of their financial systems (Tadesse 2005: 8). Even though the subjects of financial development, economic growth, and technological development drew the attention of leading economics since early twentieth century, it is a fact that there is limited number of empirical studies discussing all the parameters in finance and economics literature.

As emphasized by Rajan and Zingales (1998) and Guiso et al. (2004), a well-designed financial structuring accelerates the technical development processes, decreases the potential financial problems of entrepreneurs, ensures the effective distribution of capital, and stimulates the growth dynamics for the whole economy. Emphasizing that the risk level will be reduced through such a diversification of financial system, Saint-Paul (1992) asserted that the division of labor, high efficiency, and comparative advantages would be achieved. Moreover, he also stated that a financial system that has the sufficient depth would provide the real sector with high level of capital supply and, depending on the capital accumulation, the advanced technologies offering low marginal costs and consequently the comparative advantages. Furthermore, in his multiple balance analyses, Saint-Paul (1992) stressed that there are close relationships between financial progress and technology. The author reported that, in case of an underdeveloped financial market, the technologies offering low level of efficiency but higher elasticity would be preferred. He also asserted that, based on the underdeveloped financial structuring, the advanced but risky technical processes would be chosen.

Levine and Zervos (1998), who used the panel data analysis method for investigating the linkage between the stock markets and banks constituting the financial system and the process growth and productivity for the period between 1976 and 1993 using the data of 47 countries, reported that the financial development process would increase the productivity depending on the economic growth, capital accumulation, and technical development speed.

Beck et al. (2000), who used panel data analysis for analyzing the relationship between growth and technology level for the period of 1960–1995 in 77 countries, determined that the wide financial markets positively influence the total factor productivity and accelerate the growth.

Alfaro et al. (2004) used the panel data analysis for examining the relationships between direct foreign investments, economic growth, financial development, and technical spillover processes among 20 OECD-member countries and 51 - non-member countries from 1975 to 1995. The findings showed that the direct foreign investment is one of the most vital determinants contributing to the growth of the overall economy. Besides that, the authors also stated that the main factor playing role in achieved result is the development process observed in financial markets. Thus, in order for the direct foreign investments to be effective on economic growth, a strong financial structuring is required. Moreover, it was specified that various spillover effect including the technology and originating from the presence of insufficient financial market would not be seen.

Investigating the linkage between finance and growth at various stages of development levels by applying generalized method of moments (GMM) in 74 countries, Rioja and Valev (2004) reported that the depth observed in financial markets of developed countries increases the technical development and thus the total factor productivity, and that the impacts of finance on output are seen through the capital accumulation in underdeveloped countries.

Levine (2005), who used Generalized Method of Moments (GMM) for 77 country groups to analyze the linkage between financial progress, growth, and productivity increase considered as technology for the period of 1960–1995, determined that the financial development process is the main factor accelerating the technological progress and the process of growth.

Using the system equations of panel GMM, Zagorchev et al. (2011) analyzed the impacts of finance and technological development process on the process of growth as well as the impacts of financial markets on the telecommunication technologies in 8 EU-member Middle and Eastern European countries for the period of 1997–2004. The results showed that the financial markets and the investments in telecommunication technologies affect the process of economic growth positively. Moreover, the authors also stated that the financial development process positively influences the telecommunication technologies and, in parallel with the advancements in telecommunication technologies, financial development level slightly but positively in response to this.

Ilyina and Samaniego (2011), who used panel data analyses for examining the nexus between technology and financial market progress in 28 industrial sectors in 41 countries for the period of 1970–1999, determined that the industrial branches having the potential of rapid growth in financially developed countries would achieve gradually increasing rates of R&D intensity. Thus, the authors emphasized that the financial markets, which fulfill their functions completely, stimulate the growth dynamics depending on the R&D activities, and that it acts as a direct resource in this system. Similar findings were reported by Deng and Su (2012).

Applying panel vector autoregressive (VAR) model, Pradhan et al. (2016) examined the linkage between finance, growth, and innovations in 18 Euro-zone-member countries from 1961 to 2013 and asserted that the financial sector development and increase in innovative capacity positively affected the economic growth dynamism.

Data, Model, and Methodology

In this study, the panel system Two-Stage Least Squares (2SLS), one of the simultaneous equation systems, is applied to investigate the nexus between growth, finance, and technology. To estimate the linkages among the variables mentioned above in the EU-member countries, the time span from 1995 to 2013 is taken into consideration. For this purpose, in order to determine the level of financial sector progress, the domestic credits to private sector by banks as a percentage of gross domestic product are used. Though there are some other variables to measure the development of financial market progress such as the ratio of M2 money supply to gross domestic product, the ratio of total bank deposits to gross domestic product, and the ratio of financial system deposits to gross domestic product, the papers investigating the nexus between finance and growth generally take into account the domestic credits by banks as a proxy of finance. Following the studies done by Clarke et al. (2006), Beck et al. (2007), Ang (2010), Yüce Akıncı et al. (2014b), and Park and Shin (2015), the domestic credits provided by banks as a percentage of gross domestic product is taken into account for the proxy of finance. The annual percentage change of per-capita gross domestic product in constant prices (*Growth*) is also considered as a proxy for the process of growth. In order to measure technology level (*Technology*), R&D expenditures as a percent of gross domestic product is taken into consideration. Besides, following Beckfield (2006), the impacts of the economic integration (*Integration*) process of the European Union-member countries into world economy on finance–growth–technology nexus are examined. A country's export level which goes to the world economy as a percentage is used a proxy for the economic integration variable. With the help of this measure, it can be said that the process of economic integration rises if trade level of the member countries within the world economy raise and vice versa. In addition, following Afonso et al. (2010), the study analyzes the impact of economic/financial-market crisis (*Crisis*) on the nexus of finance–economic growth–technology using a dummy variable which indicates the situation of the economy, "crisis" or "normal." For this purpose, *Crisis* is used as a dummy taking the value of "1" if a financial/economic crisis exists in the starting and the following year of the crisis, and *Crisis* takes the value of "0" in other situation. The data are taken from the web pages of the World Bank-World Development Indicators and Eurostat.

Firstly, the chapter tries to determine the linkages between growth and finance in the light of demand following and supply leading. Secondly, this study analyzes whether economic growth or financial development affects technology level. Therefore, our analysis of demand following or supply leading can be investigated by two different kinds of regression equations. If demand following phenomenon is true ($\beta_1 > 0$), it will be assumed that financial development process will have an effect on technology, and rising technology level enhances the process of economic growth. Therefore, the equation systems can be described as follows:

$$
\begin{aligned}
Finance_{it} &= \beta_0 + \beta_1 Growth_{it} + e_{1it} \\
Technology_{it} &= \alpha_0 + \alpha_1 Finance_{it} + e_{2it} \\
Growth_{it} &= \gamma_0 + \gamma_1 Technology_{it} + e_{3it}
\end{aligned}
\tag{5.1}
$$

On the other hand, if supply leading phenomenon is true ($\psi_1 > 0$), it will be supposed that economic growth process will have an effect on technology and rising technology level improves the development process of financial services. Therefore, the equation systems can be introduced as follows:

$$
\begin{aligned}
Growth_{it} &= \psi_0 + \psi_1 Finance_{it} + e_{1it} \\
Technology_{it} &= \xi_0 + \xi_1 Growth_{it} + e_{2it} \\
Finance_{it} &= \varphi_0 + \varphi_1 Technology_{it} + e_{3it}
\end{aligned}
\tag{5.2}
$$

In order to examine the impacts of the enlargement progression of the EU-member countries into world economy and financial/economic crises on the linkage between finance, growth, and technology, the equations numbered (5.1) and (5.2) can be rewritten as follows:

$$
\begin{aligned}
Finance_{it} &= \beta_0 + \beta_1 Growth_{it} + e_{1it} \\
Technology_{it} &= \alpha_0 + \alpha_1 Finance_{it} + e_{2it} \\
Growth_{it} &= \gamma_0 + \gamma_1 Technology_{it} + \gamma_2 Integration_{it} + \gamma_3 Crisis_{it} + e_{3it}
\end{aligned}
\tag{5.3}
$$

$$Growth_{it} = \psi_0 + \psi_1 Finance_{it} + e_{1it}$$
$$Technology_{it} = \xi_0 + \xi_1 Growth_{it} + e_{2it} \qquad (5.4)$$
$$Finance_{it} = \varphi_0 + \varphi_1 Technology_{it} + \varphi_2 Integration_{it} + \varphi_3 Crisis_{it} + e_{3it}$$

When demand following phenomenon is emerged ($\beta_1 > 0$), it will be assumed that financial development process will have an effect on technology and rising technology level enhances the growth process of overall economy. Additionally, the effects of the integration process and financial/economic crises on growth and finance are observed in the light of the sign of the coefficient of γ_2, γ_3, φ_2 and φ_3. Similar statements can be made in the case of the validity of supply leading phenomenon ($\psi_1 > 0$).

A simultaneous system model is a series of regressions including uncharted parameters. Systems are predicted taking into account a few multivariable analyses that consider the interdependencies among the regression equations which are included in the system. The form of a panel system can be summarized as

$$f(y_{it}, x_{it}, \beta) = \varepsilon_{it} \qquad (5.5)$$

where y_{it} is a vector of intrinsic variables, x_{it} is a vector of external variables, and ε_{it} is a white-noise error term. The aim of the estimation process is to predict the parameters of β.

2SLS, extension of the standard OLS analysis, is a single regression equation estimation procedure that is suitable when some of the variables used in the model are intrinsic. Besides, 2SLS method is an econometric mechanism which is applied in the case of structural regression equations. It is more suitable to apply 2SLS method when the error terms of the dependent variable are interrelated with the independent variables. In addition, if there are feedback cycles in the model, it is appropriate to use 2SLS analysis technique. Furthermore, it does not require any distributional assumptions and isolates specification errors. Also, this method provides interaction effects between multiple regression equations. As Bollen (1996) noted, 2SLS method may ensure more robust estimation results in small samples than any other econometric techniques. Additionally, with the help of instrumental variables, more robust results can be obtained. In the context of the advantages of 2SLS method, it should be more appropriate to apply this technique to solve the equations numbered from (1) to (4). Re-writing the j-th regression equation of the system as follows:

$$Y\Gamma_{ij} + XB_{ij} + \varepsilon_{ij} = 0 \qquad (5.6)$$

or, alternatively:

$$y_{ij} = Y_{ij}\gamma_{ij} + X_{ij}\beta_{ij} + \varepsilon_{ij} = Z_{ij}\delta_{ij} + \varepsilon_{ij} \qquad (5.7)$$

where $\Gamma'_{ij} = \left(-1, \gamma'_{ij}, 0\right), B'_{ij} = \left(\beta'_{ij}, 0\right), Z'_{ij} = \left(Y'_{ij}, X'_{ij}\right)$, and $\delta'_{ij} = \left(\gamma'_{ij}, \beta'_{ij}\right)$. Y is the matrix of intrinsic variables and X is the matrix of external variables; Y_{ij} is the matrix of intrinsic variables not including y_{ij}. Firstly, the regression process begins with the estimation of the right-hand side intrinsic variables of y_{ij} on all external variables X and get the fitted values:

$$\widehat{Y}_{ij} = X(X'X)^{-1}X'Y_{ij} \tag{5.8}$$

Secondly, the regression process continues with the estimation of y_{ij} on $\widehat{Y}_{ij}$ and X_{ij} to obtain

$$\widehat{\delta}_{2SLS} = \left(\widehat{Z}'_{ij}\widehat{Z}_{ij}\right)^{-1}\widehat{Z}'_{ij}y \tag{5.9}$$

where $\widehat{Z}_{ij} = \left(\widehat{Y}_{ij}, X_{ij}\right)$. The residuals obtained from the equation taking into account these coefficients can be considered for weights.

Empirical Findings

Table 5.1 introduces descriptive stats and correlation coefficients for the period 1995–2013. Consistent with previous studies, growth is correlated with finance positively and significantly, and vice versa. Besides, both growth and finance are correlated with technology level positively and significantly. Additionally, the process of economic integration is correlated with the process of growth and financial market improvement positively and significantly, also. Therefore, it is highly possible to observe a positive effect of integration on economic growth process and finance in the estimation results. In addition, it can be observed that crisis hinders both the process of growth and finance.

Table 5.2 reports the estimations for equations numbered (1) and (2). In the first stage, the aim is to determine the linkages between growth and finance in the light of demand following and supply leading. In the second stage, the effects of growth and finance on technology are estimated. Lastly, in the third stage, the impacts of technology on growth of real side of economy and financial market improvement are predicted. The findings of the simultaneous equation systems are pointed out in Table 5.2.

The results shown in Table 5.2 assert that the link between growth and finance is in congruity that is compatible with most of the recent empirical work in this area, suggesting that economic growth improves financial markets and vice versa. That's why, the results of the panel system 2SLS analysis point out the presence of both demand following and supply leading phenomenon, because of positive and statistically significant coefficients of *Growth* (3.783) and *Finance* (2.213), respectively. Nonetheless, it can be said that demand following hypothesis is more superior to supply leading hypothesis, since the significance level of the coefficient of *Growth* (1%) is higher than that of *Finance* (5%). In addition, our analysis goes further by attempting to investigate the possible linkage between growth, finance, and

Table 5.1 Descriptive statistics and correlation coefficients

Panel A: Descriptive statistics

Variable	Obs	Mean	Std. dev	Min	Max
Growth	532	2.388	1.745	−16.589	13.267
Finance	532	88.294	54.453	7.115	304.951
Technology	532	1.515	0.956	0.228	3.725
Integration	532	62.115	29.880	38.217	83.421

Panel B: Correlation coefficients

		Growth	Finance	Technology	Integration	Crisis
Growth	Correlation	1.000				
	t-stat	–				
	Probability	–				
Finance	Correlation	0.783***	1.000			
	t-stat	5.088	–			
	Probability	0.000	–			
Technology	Correlation	0.441***	0.512***	1.000		
	t-stat	2.881	3.012	–		
	Probability	0.003	0.001	–		
Integration	Correlation	0.691***	0.115*	0.113**	1.000	
	t-stat	3.550	1.961	2.331	–	
	Probability	0.000	0.080	0.027	–	
Crisis	Correlation	−0.204***	−0.076*	0.118	0.315	1.000
	t-stat	2.776	1.993	1.123	1.035	–
	Probability	0.008	0.072	0.421	0.463	–

Note: ***, **, and * indicate significance at 1%, 5%, and 10%, respectively

technology level. The findings show that financial sector progress increases technology level and the process of economic growth raises technology, also. Besides, that the impact of finance on technology (0.633) is higher than that of growth (0.522) supports the Schumpeterian theory which asserts that developed financial sector improves the level of technology. Besides, it can obviously be observed from Table 5.2 that the level of technology boosts the process of economic growth (0.722) more than financial development (0.118).

Additionally, our analysis goes further by attempting to investigate the possible effects of economic integration and crises as well as economic growth and finance on technology and vice versa. Table 5.3 which point out the consistent results with the Table 5.2 shows the similar findings. In other words, the validity of both demand following and supply leading hypothesis, because of positive and statistically significant coefficients of *Growth* (3.358) and domestic credits (1.312), respectively, can be clearly shown. Besides, it is possible to state the dominance of demand following phenomenon than supply leading because the significance level of the coefficient of *Growth* (1%) is higher than that of *Finance* (10%). Besides, alongside the level of financial sector progress and the growth process of overall economy enhanced by technology, finance stimulates technology (0.542) more than growth

Table 5.2 The results of the panel system two-stage least squares

Panel A: The results of simultaneous equation system				Main equations			
Variable	**Coefficient**	***t*-stat**	**Probability**	$Finance_{it} = \beta_0 + \beta_1 Growth_{it} + e_{1it}$			
β_0(constant)	2.995***	3.862	0.003	**Statistics of the model**			
β_1(growth)	3.783***	4.116	0.000				
α_0(constant)	1.158	1.338	0.244	**R^2:**	**F:**	**Prob(F):**	**DW:**
				0.538	3.428***	0.005	1.947
α_1(finance)	0.633***	3.412	0.007	$Technology_{it} = \alpha_0 + \alpha_1 Finance_{it} + e_{2it}$			
γ_0(constant)	0.359	1.548	0.213	**Statistics of the model**			
γ_1(technology)	0.722***	3.641	0.005				
Instrumental variable							
Constant (C)	Growth (−1)	Finance (−1)	Technology (−1)	**R^2:**	**F:**	**Prob(F):**	**DW:**
				0.679	3.776***	0.003	2.012
Statistics of the general model				$Growth_{it} = \gamma_0 + \gamma_1 Technology_{it} + e_{3it}$			
R^2: 0.648	**F:** 3.773***	**Prob(F):** 0.004	**DW:** 2.011	**Statistics of the model**			
				R^2:	**F:**	**Prob(F):**	**DW:**
				0.616	3.616***	0.009	1.912
Panel B: The results of simultaneous equation system				**Main equations**			
Variable	**Coefficient**	***t*-stat**	**Probability**	$Growth_{it} = \psi_0 + \psi_1 Finance_{it} + e_{1it}$			
ψ_0(constant)	1.884*	1.953	0.083	**Statistics of the model**			
ψ_1(finance)	2.213**	2.716	0.044				
ξ_0(constant)	1.047	1.227	0.356	**R^2:**	**F:**	**Prob(F):**	**DW:**
				0.501	2.991***	0.003	1.887
ξ_1(growth)	0.522**	2.696	0.048	$Technology_{it} = \xi_0 + \xi_1 Growth_{it} + e_{2it}$			
φ_0(constant)	0.110	1.437	0.347	**Statistics of the model**			
φ_1(technology)	0.118*	1.945	0.087				
Instrumental variable							
Constant (C)	Growth (−1)	Finance (−1)	Technology (−1)	**R^2:**	**F:**	**Prob(F):**	**DW:**
				0.536	2.665**	0.015	2.034
Statistics of the general model				$Finance_{it} = \varphi_0 + \varphi_1 Technology_{it} + e_{3it}$			
R^2: 0.526	**F:** 2.889***	**Prob(F):** 0.006	**DW:** 1.873	**Statistics of the model**			
				R^2:	**F:**	**Prob(F):**	**DW:**
				0.528	2.778***	0.008	1.937

Note: ***, **, and * indicate significance at 1%, 5%, and 10%, respectively. Values in parenthesis show the optimum lag lengths determined by taking AIC and SIC into consideration

(0.351). With the help of rising technology, the level of growth and finance accelerates, but the impact of technology on growth is more dominant compared to finance (the statistically significant coefficients of technology on growth and finance are 0.761 and 0.101, respectively). Furthermore, the linkages between growth, finance, and technology are strengthened by adding two control variables into the

Table 5.3 The results of the panel system two-stage least squares

Panel A: The results of simultaneous equation system

Variable	Coefficient	t-stat	Probability	Main equations
				$Finance_{it} = \beta_0 + \beta_1 Growth_{it} + e_{1it}$
β_0(constant)	1.114	1.356	0.445	**Statistics of the model**
β_1(growth)	3.358***	3.774	0.005	**R²:** 0.555 **F:** 3.539*** **Prob(F):** 0.004 **DW:** 1.977
α_0(constant)	1.094	1.227	0.530	$Technology_{it} = \alpha_0 + \alpha_1 Finance_{it} + e_{2it}$
α_1(finance)	0.542***	3.502	0.008	**Statistics of the model**
γ_0(constant)	−0.048	−1.176	0.647	**R²:** 0.658 **F:** 3.660*** **Prob(F):** 0.000 **DW:** 2.098
γ_1(technology)	0.761***	3.824	0.001	$Growth_{it} = \gamma_0 + \gamma_1 Technology_{it} + \gamma_2 Integration_{it} + \gamma_3 Crisis_{it} + e_{3it}$
γ_2(integration)	0.144**	2.858	0.035	**Statistics of the model**
γ_3(crisis)	−0.153*	−2.330	0.057	**R²:** 0.608 **F:** 2.445** **Prob(F):** 0.028 **DW:** 1.818

Instrumental variable

Constant (C)	Growth(−1)	Finance(−1)	Technology(−1)	

Statistics of the general model

R²: 0.616	**F:** 3.294***	**Prob(F):** 0.007	**DW:** 1.898	

Panel B: The results of simultaneous equation system

Variable	Coefficient	t-stat	Probability	Main equations
ψ_0(constant)	0.762	0.922	0.629	$Growth_{it} = \psi_0 + \psi_1 Finance_{it} + e_{1it}$
ψ_1(finance)	1.312*	2.210	0.059	**Statistics of the model**
ξ_0(constant)	0.816	1.113	0.605	**R²:** 0.516 **F:** 3.045*** **Prob(F):** 0.000 **DW:** 2.110
ξ_1(growth)	0.351**	2.457	0.047	$Technology_{it} = \xi_0 + \xi_1 Growth_{it} + e_{2it}$
φ_0(constant)	0.056	0.886	0.959	**Statistics of the model**
φ_1(technology)	0.101*	1.911	0.091	
φ_2(integration)	0.152**	2.776	0.043	
φ_3(crisis)	−0.226*	−2.647	0.052	

Instrumental variable

Constant (C)	Growth(−1)	Finance(−1)	Technology(−1)	R²: 0.496	F: 2.554**	Prob(F): 0.031	DW: 1.888
Statistics of the general model				$Finance_{it} = \varphi_0 + \varphi_1 Technology_{it} + \varphi_2 Integration_{it} + \varphi_3 Crisis_{it} + e_{3it}$			
R²: 0.440	F: 2.748**	Prob(F): 0.047	DW: 1.926	**Statistics of the model**			
				R²: 0.356	F: 2.224*	Prob(F): 0.067	DW: 1.794

Note: ***, **, and * indicate significance at 1%, 5%, and 10%, respectively. Values in parenthesis show the optimum lag lengths determined by taking AIC and SIC into consideration models: economic integration and economic/financial crisis. It is clearly observed that the process of economic integration among the EU-member countries raises economic growth and financial development almost equally (because of positive and statistically significant coefficient of economic integration, 0.144 and 0.152). Lastly, in times of the economic/financial crisis, the process of economic growth and financial development becomes narrow, because of negative and significant coefficient of *Crisis*, −0.153 and − 0.226.

Conclusion Remarks and Policy Suggestions

In this chapter, the relationships between financial market improvement, economic growth, and technological development were examined using panel system two-stage least squares method for EU-member countries for the period of 1995–2013. For this purpose, the relationships between finance and growth within the scope of demand following and supply leading processes were examined firstly, and then the effects of finance and growth on the technological progress were analyzed. On the other hand, it was tried to estimate the impacts of a rise in technology level on the finance and economic growth.

The findings on the link between growth and finance show that growth and finance are in congruity, suggesting that growth improves finance and vice versa. Hence, it can be said the existence of both demand following and supply leading phenomenon. Nonetheless, it can be said that the validity of the hypothesis of demand following is stronger than supply leading with the help of regression results. In addition, our analysis goes further by investigating the possible linkage between economic growth, finance, and total factor productivity, in other words technology level. The findings show that financial development increases technology level and the process of economic growth raises technology, also. Besides, the findings of the analysis support the Schumpeterian theory because the effect of financial development on technology is higher than that of growth. Besides, it is observed that the level of technology boosts the process of economic growth more than financial development. Additionally, our analysis goes further by attempting to investigate the possible effects of economic integration and crises as well as economic growth and finance on total factor productivity and vice versa. Alongside the level of financial market progress and the process of growth enhanced by technology, finance stimulates technology more than growth. With the help of rising technology, the level of growth and finance accelerates, but the impact of technology on growth is more dominant compared to finance. Furthermore, the linkages between growth, finance, and technology are strengthened by adding two control variables into the models: economic integration and economic/financial crisis. It is clearly observed that the process of economic integration among the EU-member countries raises growth and finance equally. Lastly, in times of the economic/financial crisis, the process of growth and financial market improvement deteriorate.

In general, the results of the analysis indicating that finance and growth processes have effects on each other suggest that, for the analyzed period, *demand following* hypothesis was valid for the EU-member countries. As emphasized by Schumpeter, the financial development process generally affected positively from the economic growth dynamism was observed to stimulate the technological development. Moreover, it was also observed that the development of technology contributes to the growth of real sector. It was reported that the economic integration of EU-member countries accelerated the economic growth, and that the economic/financial crises reversed this process. When the obtained results are considered as a whole, it can be seen that the economic growth can be used as a policy tool for accelerating the financial development process, and that the effectively functioning financial sector stimulates the technological advancements by ensuring the optimal distribution of resources. Based on the Schumpeterian hypothesis that can be seen as the guiding light of Neoclassical model and Endogenous Growth Theories, it can be asserted that the accelerating technical innovations might provide the economy with an additional dynamism. In order for aforementioned process to be sustainable, it is necessary to achieve the growth rates that are capable of supporting the financial development. It can also be asserted that the funds to be allocated by financial sector to market actors leading the technological innovations might lead to vertical integration of inventions, trigger the innovations through the creative destruction mechanism, increase the profit opportunities by achieving the monopolist position in global markets, and thus accelerate the growth process. This cycle providing the system with sustainability might pave the way for the organization of a self-feeding market and also enable the effective operation of real and financial markets. The fact that the driving force of the system is the savings and capital accumulation directed from real sector to finance sector and then to the efficient entrepreneurs indicates that the main focus of economy policies should be the economic measures aiming to increase the volume of savings. In addition to increasing the savings, it can also be recommended to support these policy measures with the capital flows to be directed to EU-member countries. Moreover, it can also be stated that it is important to prepare various stimulus packages in order to allocate the capital stock to be achieved via the aforementioned economic policies to the technology-intense leading sectors.

Although a comprehensive literature claims that growth accelerates finance, it does not mean that the process of financial development improves technological progress or total factor productivity. In many countries, especially in rich countries, in the first stage, economic growth has been accompanied by rising financial sector progress and technology and in the second stage growth improves in the light of spillover effects. In order to trigger the growth process and development, the growth itself may be important, but the quality of growth is the undoubted way to make this process sustainable. In the process of redistribution with growth policies, employment of unskilled labor can be encouraged, the assets of the poor can be directed to the productive investment, the development of financial markets can be achieved, and total factor productivity can be fastened with the help of developed financial markets to boost economic growth process. The way in which these factors could be combined into an effective growth policy package can improve the income growth, and the cooperation of real and financial markets can create high technology level which gives rise to process of sustainable growth. Besides, the central implication of the study is that the process of economic integration is a significant part for increasing growth process. Since it is trying to create homogeneous economic and financial markets in the context of common competition policy in the EU, it can be argued that the higher is the homogeneity bias, the higher is the enlargement process of the economic integration and therefore total factor productivity which is supported by financial markets. With the help of optimum economic and financial policies, the destructive effects of economic crises on the growth process may be alleviated. In the context, the EU-member countries should make provision for rising finance-intensive growth which culminates in more influential fund allocation and in higher technology.

References

Afonso, A., Grüner, H. P., & Kolerus, C. (2010). *Fiscal policy and growth: Do financial crises make a difference?* (European Central Bank Working Paper Series No. 1217).

Akıncı, M., & Sevinç, H. (2013). AR&GE harcamaları ile ekonomik büyüme arasındaki ilişki: 1990-2011 Türkiye örneği. *Uluslararası Sosyal Araştırmalar Dergisi, 6*(27), 7–17.

Alfaro, L., Charanda, A., Kalemli-Özcan, Ş., & Sayek, S. (2004). FDI and economic growth: The role of local financial markets. *Journal of International Economics, 64*(1), 89–112.

Ang, J. B. (2010). Finance and inequality: The case of India. *Southern Economic Journal, 76,* 738–761.

Beck, T., Demirgüç-Kunt, A., & Levine, R. (2007). Finance, inequality and the poor. *Journal of Economic Growth, 12,* 27–49.

Beck, T., Levine, R., & Loayza, N. (2000). Finance and the sources of growth. *Journal of Financial Economics, 58*(1–2), 261–300.

Beckfield, J. (2006). European integration and income inequality. *American Sociological Review, 71,* 964–985.

Bloch, H., & Tang, S. H. K. (2004). Deep determinants of economic growth: Institutions, geography and openness to trade. *Progress in Development Studies, 4*(3), 245–255.

Bollen, K. A. (1996). An alternative two stage least squares (2sls) estimator for latent variable equations. *Psychometrika, 61,* 109–121.

Clarke, G. R. G., Xu, L. C., & Zou, H. (2006). Finance and income inequality: What do the data tell us? *Southern Economic Journal, 72,* 578–596.

Deng, H., & Su, J. (2012). The research on the mechanism of financial development promote technical progress. *Future Communication, Computing, Control and Management, 142,* 113–123.

Diamond, D. W., & Verrecchia, R. E. (1982). Optimal managerial contracts and equilibrium security prices. *Journal of Finance, 37*(2), 275–287.

Erdoğan, S., & Canbay, Ş. (2016). İktisadi büyüme ve araştırma & geliştirme (ar-ge) harcamaları ilişkisi üzerine teorik bir inceleme. *Muş Alparslan Üniversitesi Sosyal Bilimler Dergisi, 4*(2), 29–44.

Gerni, C., Sarı, S., Sevinç, H., & Emsen, Ö. S. (2015). Bölgesel dengesizliklerin giderilmesinde yatırım teşviklerinin rolü ve başarı kriteri olarak yakınsama analizleri: Türkiye örneği. In: *International conference on eurasian economies,* pp. 311–320.

Guiso, L., Sapienza, P., & Zingales, L. (2004). Does local financial development matter? *The Quarterly Journal of Economics, 119*(3), 929–969.

Hicks, R. (1969). *A theory of economic history*. Oxford: Clarendon Press.

Ilyina, A., & Samaniego, R. (2011). Technology and financial development. *Journal of Money, Credit and Banking, 43*(5), 899–921.

Jensen, M. C., & Murphy, K. J. (1990). Performance pay and top management incentives. *Journal of Political Economy, 98*(2), 225–264.

Jones, C. (1998). *Introduction to economic growth*. New York: W.W. Norton & Company.

Karluk, R. (2007). *Uluslararası Kuruluşlar (Küreselleşen Dünyada)*. Ankara: Beta Basım.

Levine, R. (2005). Finance and growth: Theory and evidence. In P. Aghion & N. S. Durlauf (Eds.), *Handbook of economic growth* (Vol. I, pp. 866–923). Amsterdam: North Holland Publishing.

Levine, R., & Zervos, S. (1998). Stock markets, banks and economic growth. *The American Economic Review, 88*(3), 537–558.

Patrick, H. T. (1966). Financial development and economic growth in underdeveloped countries. *Economic Development and Cultural Change, 14*(2), 174–189.

Pradhan, R. P., Arvin, M. B., & Nair, M. (2016). Innovation, financial development and economic development in eurozone countries. *Applied Economics Letters, 23*(16), 1141–1144.

Park, D., & Shin, K. (2015). *Economic growth, financial development and income inequality* (ADB Economics Working Paper Series No. 441).

Rajan, R. G., & Zingales, L. (1998). Financial dependence and growth. *The American Economic Review, 88*(3), 559–586.

Rioja, F., & Valev, N. (2004). Finance and the sources of growth at the various stages of economic development. *Economic Inquiry, 42*(1), 127–140.

Saint-Paul, G. (1992). Technological choice, financial markets and economic development. *European Economic Review, 36*(4), 763–781.

Schumpeter, J. A. (1911). *The theory of economic development*. Cambridge: Harvard University Press.

Solow, R. M. (1956). A contribution to the theory of economic growth. *Quarterly Journal of Economics, 70*(1), 65–94.

Solow, R. M. (1970). *Growth theory: An exposition*. New York: Oxford University Press.

Tadesse, S. (2005). *Financial development and technology* (William Davidson Institute Working Paper No. 749).

Yüce, G., Akıncı, M., & Yılmaz, Ö. (2013). Finansal kalkınma ile iktisadi büyüme arasındaki nedensellik ilişkisi: çok ülkeli bir zaman serisi analizi. *Finansal Araştırmalar ve Çalışmalar Dergisi, 4*(8), 111–144.

Yüce Akıncı, G., Akıncı, M., & Yılmaz, Ö. (2014a). Finansal kalkınma sürecinin ar-ge harcamaları üzerindeki etkisi: Schumpeter haklı mıydı? *Maliye Dergisi, 166*, 56–74.

Yüce Akıncı, G., Akıncı, M., & Yılmaz, Ö. (2014b). Financial development-economic growth nexus: A panel data analysis upon OECD countries. *Hitotsubashi Journal of Economics, 55*(1), 33–50.

Zagorchev, A., Vasconcellas, G., & Bae, Y. (2011). Financial development, technology, growth and performance: Evidence from the accession to the EU. *Journal of International Financial Markets, Institutions & Money, 21*(5), 743–759.

Chapter 6
Defense Expenditures and Economic Growth Relationship: A Panel Data Approach for NATO

Güldenur Çetin, Hasan Hüseyin Yıldırım, Ayben Koy, and Cihat Köksal

Abstract One of the rules of being successful in the international competition is having technology-intensive manufacturing areas. The investments made in the defense industry, and the recognition of the products that are being produced in this area as *technology-intensive* products, are increasing the importance of the defense expenditures and the economic growth relationship. Increases in defense spending cause greater investments in industrial sectors. Secondly, economic growth affects the competitiveness of the countries prominently. Thirdly, public expenditures can lead to an increase in investments and growth. This study brings to light the relationship between military expenditures and economic growth for NATO member countries. In the period from 2000 to 2015 for 27 NATO member countries, the two-way direction of the relationship is found by using panel data techniques.

Introduction

Today, the level of international competitiveness is based on the technology-intensive manufacturing. Especially, the investments made in the defense industry, and the recognition of the products that are being produced in this area as *technology-intensive* products, are increasing the importance of the defense expenditures (DE) and economic growth (EG) relationship. This relationship is among the mostly studied and econometrically analyzed topics in the economy literature.

Manufacturing of defense industry goods not only allows the country to gain higher monetary benefits but also allows the countries to dominate the structure of the defense industry goods importing countries which dependent on the exporting ones. Exportation of the technology-intensive products has a considerable

G. Çetin · A. Koy (✉) · C. Köksal
İstanbul Ticaret University, İstanbul, Turkey
e-mail: gadiguzel@ticaret.edu.tr; akoy@ticaret.edu.tr; ckoksal@ticaret.edu.tr

H. H. Yıldırım
Balıkesir University, Balıkesir, Turkey
e-mail: hhyildirim@balikesir.edu.tr

© Springer International Publishing AG, part of Springer Nature 2018   131
H. Dincer et al. (eds.), *Global Approaches in Financial Economics, Banking, and Finance*, Contributions to Economics, https://doi.org/10.1007/978-3-319-78494-6_6

Fig. 6.1 Total number of armed conflicts and the regional distribution 2006–2015. Source: SIPRI Yearbook (2016)

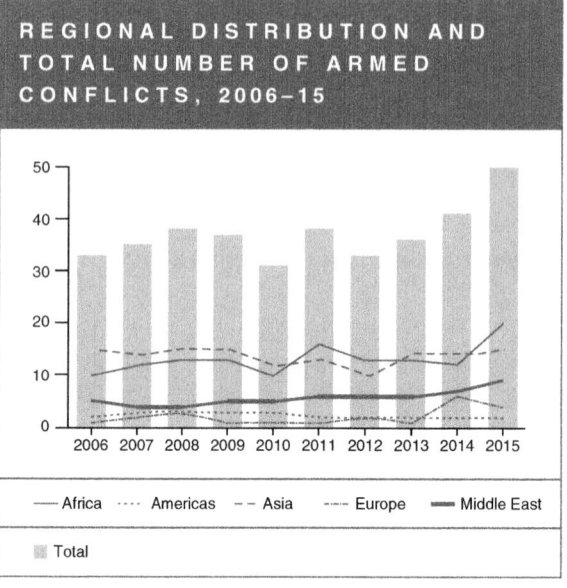

impact on the balance of payments of the countries and plays an important role for their EG. Export productivity of the defense industry is not enough to consider. Relationships with other countries, effects on the other country's approaches, and totality of the country are some other factors that cannot be ignored. Moreover, EG affects the competitiveness of the countries prominently (Hämäläinen 2003; Porter et al. 2001). However, there is not a compromise on the effects of DE on economy.

How important is the DEs in the twenty-first century? It can clearly be seen in Fig. 6.1, 2016 as a dark year. There were many terrorist attacks in Middle East and Europe. By the increasing number of armed conflicts, many people left their home country. As a result of the wars in Iraq and Syria, 4 million Iraqi and 12 million Syrian refugees are mostly hosted by Jordan, Lebanon, and Turkey. In addition, active armed conflicts increased to 50 in 2015, substantially related with enlargement activities of the Islamic State (IS) into new territories in 12 countries. One of the conflicts occurred between India and Pakistan; however, the rest of the conflicts were between the states and concerned government, territory, or both of them. Eventually, peace is not rising in the twenty-first century. On the contrary, armed conflicts and total DEs have got a widespread outlook (Figs. 6.1 and 6.2).

In this study, from the above-mentioned viewpoints, relationship between the DEs and the EG of the North Atlantic Treaty Organization (NATO) member countries has been analyzed. NATO has the power to guarantee the freedom and security of the member countries. This is enabled via their military and diplomatic acts. NATO also has the ability to take over crisis-management operations if diplomatic efforts fail. From The Washington Treaty (North Atlantic Treaty) 1949, which forms the basis of NATO, it commits members to protect each other.

27 NATO member countries and 432 annually observations are used in the study. The analyzing period is beginning from 2000 to 2015. When the top ten countries,

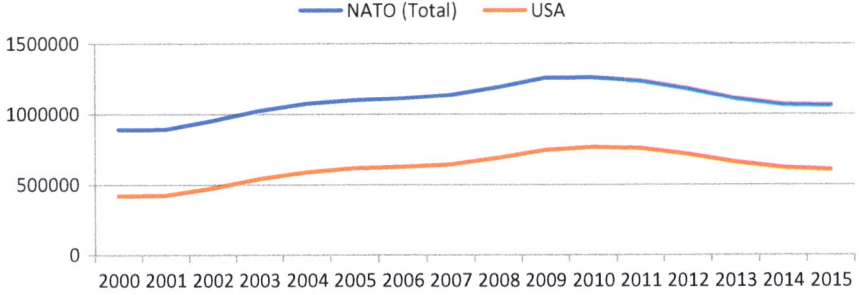

Fig. 6.2   Military expenditures of NATO and USA (2001–2015). Source: SIPRI

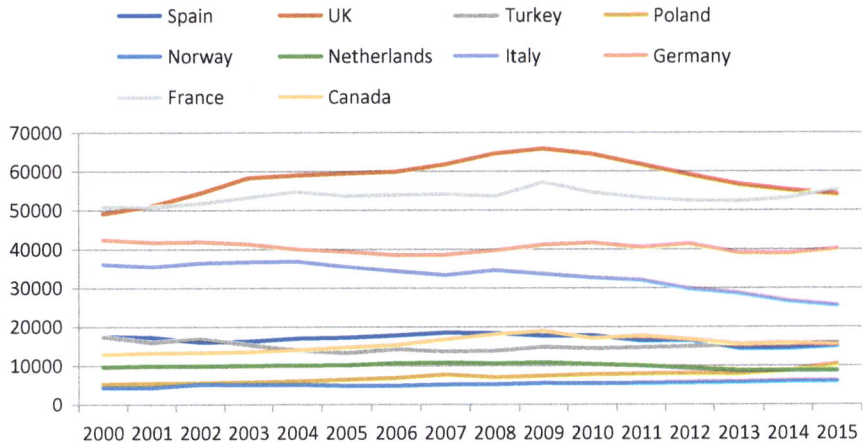

Fig. 6.3   Military expenditures of top ten countries except USA (2001–2015). Source: SIPRI

which have the largest military expenditures (MEs), are analyzed, it is seen that the rising outlook is related with the expenditures of USA (Figs. 6.2 and 6.3). The highest MEs are shown in 2009. In the top ten countries with highest ME, variables that belong to USA, UK, France, and Canada are highest in 2009 too.

Regarding the effects of DEs on the EG, there are different approaches. These are Keynesian approach, neo-classical approach, Marxist approach, and institutionalist approach.

Keynesian approach considers DEs as a part of public expenditure, and DEs can lead to an increase in investments and growth (Kaya 2013). This is the case when the total demand is insufficient and the state using DEs as a reflection of public spending to increase total production (Duyar and Koçolu 2014). According to Keynesian approach, one unit increase in the public expenditure enhances the national income more than one unit. This effect of public expenditures on the national income is explained via multiplier mechanism (Bekmez and Destek 2015). Keynesian models involving explicit production functions have been criticized by many researchers for not taking into consideration the problems of supply side issues (Dunne 1996). There is another point in Keynesian approach that under the excess production capacity assumption, if the demand from any side in economy increases, it has got a positive impact on total production (Faini et al. 1984).

Neo-Classicalists suggest that defense spending negatively affects EG approach. They also reveal that defense spending also creates a crowding out effect on other investments, such as other public expenditures. When the output and income levels will begin to increase primarily with the increase in DEs which is in public expenditure and growing income will increase the demand for money. By the rising of demand for money, interest rates and the cost of borrowing will increase too. As a result of this relationship, the investments will decrease (Taş et al. 2013). According to the neo-classical approach, DEs reduce investments for education, health, investment, and exports (Tuncay 2017).

Militarism and military spending are handled on a social and sociopolitical aspect from Marxist approach. They defend that DEs prevent crises and implement an informal industrial policy. According to the Marxist approach, the economic aspects are not the main focused details of MEs (Dunne and Nikolaidou 2012).

The institutionalist approach unites the Keynesian approach with a different focus which shows that the high DEs that can lead to industrial inefficiencies. According to this approach, strong stakeholder groups consisting of the households, companies, and organizations which utilize from high DEs are named as military industrial complex (MIC). The MIC tries to increase ME by doing some pressure to the state even when there is not any need to do such spending (Dunne and Uye 2014).

Literature Review

There are many studies about DEs and EG relationship. In the literature section of the study, explanations are given related with the research variables, such as DEs and EG, and some of studies in the literature related with the variables are included. Some of them have evidence on one-way causality from DEs to EG (Benoit 1973; Alptekin and Levine 2012) while some of them are vice versa (Kollias et al. 2004; Dritsakis 2004; Gokmenoglu et al. 2015). Also there are studies which say there is evidence on nonexistence or bidirectional relationship (Dakurah et al. 2001; Chang et al. 2001) too. Some of the similar studies in the literature are emphasized in Table 6.1.

In an early study, Benoit (1973) supports the Keynesian approach for some developing countries with the evidence that MEs have got positive impact on the EG. One of the next study of Benoit (1978) reviews other analysis on defense and growth and gives indicators of defense and development for sample countries. Following Benoit (1973, 1978), the popularity and importance of studies on DE has gained significantly. Additionally, the studies related with the sectors and EG put the researches in a new way. Feder (1983) interested with the efficiency of export-productivity of the sectors and found these sectors as GDP growth drivers. Bringing a new approach to literature, Ram (1986) and Biswas, Ram (1986) analyzes as

Table 6.1 Literature review

Author(s)	Methodology	Conclusion
Benoit (1978)	Multiple regression	Heavy defense burden is related with the most rapid rate of growth
Deger and Smith (1983)	Cross-sectional analysis	MEs have negative effect on EG
Macnair et al. (1995)	The model of Feder and ram on three sector analysis	Comparing the impacts of nondefense and defense spending, an increase in nondefense public expenditure is found having higher impact on growth
Kollias (1997)	Granger causality analysis	There isn't any evidence found on the relationship between DE and EG
Sezgin (2000)	Granger causality analysis	Direction of causality is found from DE to EG
Dakurah et al. (2001)	Granger causality analysis	One-way directional causality is found in 23 countries out of 62 developing countries
Dunne et al. (2001)	Granger causality analysis	Direction of causality is found from ME to EG. The sign of effect is negative
Abu-Bader and Abu-Qarn (2003)	Multivariable co-integration and variance decomposition	Direction of causality is found from ME to EG. The sign of effect is negative in Egypt, Israel, and Syria
Yıldırım and Sezgin (2003)	ARDL bound testing	ME negatively affects employment in Turkey
Dritsakis (2004)	Granger causality analysis	Causality direction is found from EG to ME for Turkey and Greece
Kollias et al. (2004)	Co-integration analysis and causality tests	Direction of causality is found from EG to ME
Giray (2004)	Statistical comparison analysis	5% of GNP has been spent for defense and national security in Turkey, whereas in most of the other NATO member countries, the ratio is smaller
Halicioğlu (2004)	Multivariate co-integration analysis	The long-run relationship is found positive and strong between DE and GDP in Turkey
Yıldırım et al. (2005)	Cross-section and dynamic panel estimation techniques	ME increases GDP in the middle eastern countries
Cuaresma and Reitschuler (2004)	ARIMA model analysis	In USA, a level-dependent effect of ME on EG is found
Pieroni (2009)	Cross-section estimations	ME and EG are in a negative relationship in the countries having above average military costs
Chang et al. (2001)	Co-integration test and VAR analysis	Two-sided relationship of granger causality between DEs and EG for Taiwan
Yılancı and Özcan (2010)	Gregory–Hansen co-integration analysis and Toda Yamamato analysis	Direction of causality is found from EG to ME

(continued)

Table 6.1 (continued)

Author(s)	Methodology	Conclusion
Ozun and Erbaykal (2011)	Granger causality analysis is applied to Toda–Yamamoto analysis	One-way directional causality exists for the seven NATO member countries. The direction of causality varies from one country to another one. For five countries, no causal relationship is found
Alptekin and Levine (2012)	Meta-regression analysis	ME affects EG in developed countries
Shahbaz et al. (2013)	The autoregressive distribution delay boundary test approach for co-integration	Co-integration relationship is found between DEs and EG for Pakistan
Altay et al. (2013)	Panel data analysis	Negative impacts of terror on all of the economic variables have been found
İpek (2014)	ARDL bound testing	One-way directional causality from DE to inflation rate is found for Turkey. Negative relationship between DE and EG is found for Israel
Korkmaz (2015)	Panel data analysis	ME effects EG negatively and it increases unemployment
Yang et al. (2015)	Johansen co-integration analysis and granger causality analysis	One-way directional relationship from EG to ME is found
Gokmenoglu et al. (2015)	Johansen co-integration analysis and granger causality analysis.	ME and EG are co-integrated. One-way directional relationship from EG to ME is found
Fatah and Salihoglu (2016)	Time series methods	Correlation between DEs and GDP growth varies with country

defense and nondefense sectors and their effect on EG from 1951 to 1988. Similarly, Macnair et al. (1995) used a three-sector Feder–Ram model including a sample of ten aliens of NATO. In the study that the sector differences impact on EG is analyzed, there is evidence that a decrease in defense spending has got a lower impact contrary to the increase in nondefense public spending.

In the widening literature, there is not a consensus if the high defense spending is the result of high growth rates or vice versa. Kollias et al. (2004) study the relationship between ME and EG for 15 European Union members beginning from the year 1961 to 2000. It has been found that there is a causality relationship from EG to MEs. It can be concluded that the EU countries decide their MEs based on their EG rate. In another research, similar findings were reached by Cuaresma and Reitschuler (2004) for USA. They found a level-dependent impact of ME on GDP growth. In a number of 90 countries' sample, Pieroni (2009) shows evidence that the relationship between ME and EG might have some nonlinearity. Another finding is that in the countries with high military power, relationship of the ME and growth is found negative.

In Dakurah et al. (2001), one-way directional causality is found in 23 countries out of 62 developing countries; however, the causality direction varies from one country to another. In seven countries, the evidence indicated that the causality between ME and EG is two sided. In the study, Greece and Turkey have been analyzed in Dritsakis (2004); the one-way directional causality from EG to ME is found for both countries. It is a good example that Ozun and Erbaykal (2011) analyzed selected 13 countries of NATO in a period from 1949 to 2006. By using Granger causality and Toda–Yamomato approach, the evidence showed that the direction of relationship varies on countries. In developed countries such as France, United Kingdom, and Norway, a unilateral relationship from ME to EG is found. The unilateral relationship from EG to MEs are also appeared for Portugal and the Netherlands. Besides no relationship is found for five countries in the results, the bilateral causal relationship is also seen for Turkey.

Some selected macroeconomic variables like GDP growth rate, current account balance, inflation rate, and DE are analyzed in İpek (2014). Including the period from 1980 to 2012, one-way directional causality from DE to inflation rate is found for Turkey, and relationship between DE and EG is found negative for Israel.

There are a number of researches carried out regarding the countries outside of NATO members. Different results have been obtained; however, most of them also show the strong relationship between DEs and EG (Khiui and Mahmood 1997; Stroup and Heckelman 2001; Abu-Bader and Abu-Qarn 2003; Korkmaz 2015).

Khiui and Mahmood (1997) bring to light the impact of DEs on Pakistan's EG and other economic variables between the years 1972 and 1995. Bidirectional relationship between the DE and GDP growth is found in the study. In another study, the influence of DE and military labor use on EG is investigated. Stroup and Heckelman (2001) used panel data approach for 44 countries in Africa and Latin America for the period beginning from 1975 to 1989. A nonlinear relationship is found between DE and EG that low levels of MEs increase EG while increasing levels of MEs decrease growth. In a following study (Abu-Bader and Abu-Qarn 2003), government expenditures and EG for Egypt, Israel, and Syria by multivariate co-integration and variance decomposition techniques for the past three decades are investigated. The evidence is found that ME affects EG negatively for all of the countries named in the analysis.

Chang et al. (2001) studied the sample Taiwan and China beginning from 1952 to 1995. The study showed evidence on the bidirectional causality for Taiwan and one-directional causality from EG to DEs for China. Pakistan is studied by Shahbaz et al. (2013). Results of the autoregressive distribution delay boundary test approach for co-integration show that there is a stable co-integration relationship between DEs and EG. Middle Eastern countries and Turkey are analyzed in Yıldırım et al. (2005). By using cross-section and dynamic panel estimation techniques for time period between 1989 and 1999, increasing effect of ME on EG is found.

Coping with terrorism is an important reason for countries to increase their DEs. Altay et al. (2013), in which panel data analysis method is used, the observation period is from 1996 to 2010. The study negatively influences terror on all of the economic variables particularly including tourism that were subject to analysis and can evidently be seen in the analysis. The authors have evidence that the countries which are prone to terrorism increase their DEs; however, the EG rate which is dependent on economic activities might be negatively influenced as the spending won't be enough to be able to increase the EG itself alone.

The disarray in the Arab regions after the Arab regions and the Mediterranean region have strategic priorities, 10 countries have been selected in the Mediterranean region and the panel data analysis has been carried out for the years from 2005 to 2012 in the study of Korkmaz (2015). The effect of ME of these countries on EG and unemployment is studied. The results of the analysis show that, while military expenditure affects EG of countries negatively, the unemployment increases.

The examination of the effect of ME on EG is the main aim of Alptekin and Levine (2012) using Meta Regression Analysis. They have evidence that ME has positive effect on EG in some of the developed countries. However the relationship between these variables is neither valid nor significant in general.

Methodology

Data Set

This study includes 27 NATO Member Countries with 432 annual observations. Data from 2000 to 2015 for DE are obtained from Stockholm International Peace Research Institute (SIPRI) and data for GDP (per capita) are obtained from United Nations Conference on Trade and Development (UNCTAD) for the same period. Excel 2010 and Stata 13 package programs have been used to implement data processing and econometric analyses.

Methods

In the panel analyses, the data are ready to use for both time series and cross section in the same analysis. The panel data have space as well as time dimensions. Nowadays, there are increasing economic researches on using panel data models. Cross-sectional data of units such as individuals, households, companies, and countries can be combined for a certain period by the panel data method (Tatoğlu 2012).

Economic and financial data often contain unit roots and nonstationary. When unit root data is used, spurious regressions may occur. In the equations with spurious regressions, the R^2 value is high even if the variables may totally be unrelated. In other words, when nonstationary data are applied by the standard regression techniques, the results might be seen significant and look "good" in standard measures (significant coefficient estimates and high R^2), but in reality the results might be valueless to consider as evidence.

Literature has shown that panel-based unit root tests are more powerful than unit root tests based on individual time series in examining stationarity.[1] In this study, the most popular tests of stationarity (or non-stationarity) over the past years are used. These are Augmented Dickey Fuller (ADF); Philips Perron (PP); and Levin, Lin, and Chu unit root tests.

$$\Delta Y_t = \delta Y_{t-1} + u_t \tag{6.1}$$
$$\Delta Y_t = \beta_1 + \delta Y_{t-1} + u_t \tag{6.2}$$
$$\Delta Y_t = \beta_1 + \beta_2 t + \delta Y_{t-1} + u_t \tag{6.3}$$

The Fisher ADF test uses the classical ADF test for time series and the Fisher PP test uses classical PP test for each series separately for each time series. ADF test is conducted by "augmenting" [Eqs. (6.1)–(6.3)] when the lagged values of ΔY_t are added. The ADF test consists of estimating the following regression:

$$\Delta Y_t = \beta_1 + \beta_2 t + \delta Y_{t-1} + \sum_{i=1}^{m} \alpha_i \Delta Y_{t-i} + u_t \tag{6.4}$$

$$u_t = \text{white noise error term}$$
$$\Delta Y_{t-1} = (Y_{t-1} - Y_{t-2}), \Delta Y_{t-2} = (Y_{t-2} - Y_{t-3}) \text{ etc.}$$

The number of lagged difference terms in formula is often determined empirically.

By using nonparametric statistical methods in the PP test, the aim is to remove the serial correlation in the error terms except from including lagged difference terms (Gujarati 2004).

$$\Delta Y_{it} = \rho Y_{it-1} + u_{it} \tag{6.5}$$
$$\Delta Y_{it} = \alpha_{0i} + \rho Y_{it-1} + u_{it} \tag{6.6}$$
$$\Delta Y_{it} = \alpha_{0i} + \alpha_{0i} t + \rho Y_{it-1} + u_{it} \tag{6.7}$$

Levin, Lin, and Chu (LLC) (Levin et al. 2002) developed the panel unit root test Levin and Lin (1992, 1993), and in 2002 it was finalized. LLC panel unit root test, first panel unit root test, was developed to analyze the effect of agglomeration and deterministic trend. The LLC (2002) test is described in three different ways as in Eqs. (6.1)–(6.3). The test is based on the hypothesis that there is a unit root for the alternative hypothesis, which states that the same autoregressive parameter does not have a unit root in all units.

It can be decided whether there is a long-term or short-term relationship between the variables, after the decision that variables don't have any unit roots. Besides, the co-integration relationship in a panel setting has already been focused in literature, for example, by Pedroni (1999), Pedroni 2004, Kao (1999) and Maddala and Wu (1999).

---

[1]Levin et al. (2002), Breitung (2000) and Im et al. (2003), Fisher-type tests using ADF and PP tests (Maddala and Wu 1999; Choi 2001; Hadri 2000).

Table 6.2 The unit root test results, $I(0)$

Unit root test type	Variables		
	Include in test equation	Military expenditure (USD million[a])	GDP per capita (USD million[b])
Levin, Lin, and Chu	Individual intercept	−0.21948 (0.4131)	−5.43921 (0.001)
	Individual intercept and trend	0.54921 (0.7086)	3.56698 (0.9998)
ADF–Fisher chi-square	Individual intercept	52.1679 (0.5454)	55.7498 (0.4088)
	Individual intercept and trend	36.8743 (0.9639)	5.67195 (1.000)
PP–Fisher chi-square	Individual intercept	42.8775 (0.8619)	67.9263 (0.0964)
	Individual intercept and trend	31.1069 (0.9947)	2.53562 (1.000)

[a]US Dollars at current prices in millions. Constant 2015 prices
[b]US Dollars at current prices in millions. Constant 2005 prices

Pedroni (1999) panel co-integration test suggests tests based on the null hypothesis that there is no co-integration between panel data series. For this purpose, seven test statistics were developed to examine the long-term relationship between the series. Four tests of these are called within-groups and the other three tests are called between-group test statistic. The difference between these two groups occurs in the ρ_i autoregressive coefficient. The model to be examined for the Pedroni (1999) test is regulated according to whether it has trend and mean or not. The co-integration which is trend and average is shown in Eq. (6.8).

$$Y_{it} = \alpha_i + \delta_i t + \beta_{1i} X_{1it} + \ldots + \beta_{ki} X_{ki,t} + \varepsilon_{it} \tag{6.8}$$

Panel causality tests are examined according to panel co-integration results. In the structure of causality tests, Vector Error Correction Model and VAR model can be used.

Empirical Results

In this analysis, DE and GDP (per capita) data have been used for 27 NATO member countries (Albania, Belgium, Bulgaria, Canada, Croatia, Czech Republic, Denmark, Estonia, France, Germany, Greece, Hungary, Italy, Luxembourg, Lithuania, Latvia, Netherlands, Norway, Portugal, Poland, Romania, Spain, Slovenia, Slovakia, Turkey, United Kingdom, and United States). The relationship between ME and GDP (per capita) of the sample is investigated by Panel data analysis. The stationary of the variables is tested by Levin, Lin, and Chu, ADF, PP panel unit root tests. The results are demonstrated in Table 6.2.

Table 6.3 Results of unit root test, $I(1)$

Unit root test type	Variables Include in test equation	DE	GDP per capita
Levin, Lin, and Chu	Individual intercept	−9.95010 (0.0001)	−4.67605 (0.0001)
	Individual intercept and trend	−9.34068 (0.0001)	−13.1452 (0.0001)
ADF-Fisher chi-square	Individual intercept	176.845 (0.0001)	89.7327 (0.0016)
	Individual intercept and trend	136.942 (0.0001)	168.176 (0.0001)
PP-Fisher chi-square	Individual intercept	179.262 (0.0001)	107.762 (0.0001)
	Individual intercept and trend	158.764 (0.0001)	208.463 (0.0001)

The stationarity level for the series of two variables is shown in Table 6.3 under these hypotheses:

H0: There is a unit root. Variable is nonstationary.
H1: There is no unit root. Variable is stationary.

The null hypothesis cannot be accepted at 5% significance level for both variables. Because the variables are not stationary at individual constant, and individual constant and trend. Stationary processes must be applied to the variables.

When there is first difference for the both variables, they become stationary at 5% significance level which is shown in Table 6.3. In the following stage, a co-integration test has been applied to realize the relationship between DE and EG. Table 6.4 shows the results as follows:

The null and alternative hypotheses are as follows:

H0: There is no co-integration
H1: There is co-integration

Pedroni test statistics confirms with majority (*) that the co-integration relationship exists. The results have evidence that the difference of ME and GDP per capita for 27 NATO member countries are co-integrated in the long run, and they move together. Following co-integration test, the results of the causality test are shown in Table 6.5.

From the results examined, it can be concluded that there is a two-way relation between the first degree difference of ME and the first degree differences of GDP per capita. In other words, GDP per capita causes ME and also ME causes GDP per capita. It can be said with the given results that MEs have causality relationship in the direction of GDP per capita and GDP per capita have causality relationship in the direction of MEs. These variables can affect each other and can be influenced by each other.

Table 6.4 Pedroni (Engle-Granger based) panel co-integration test results

Deterministic trend specification type	Test statistics	Military expenditure dependent variable		GDP per capita dependent variable	
		Statistic	Prob.	Statistic	Prob.
Individual intercept	Panel v-statistic	−1.329766	0.9082	1.14394	0.1263
	Panel rho-statistic	1.456398	0.9274	−4.3405	0.0001*
	Panel PP-statistic	1.167114	0.8784	−4.9707	0.0001*
	Panel ADF-statistic	−2.933836	0.0017*	−5.3494	0.0001*
	Grup rho-statistic	−3.092296	0.0010*	−2.5216	0.0058*
	Grup PP-statistic	−10.04881	0.0001*	−5.1003	0.0001*
	Grup ADF-statistic	−8.053512	0.0001*	−4.1712	0.0001*
Individual intercept and individual trend	Panel v-statistic	−1.792400	0.9635	−3.4290	0.9997
	Panel rho-statistic	−1.071978	0.1419	0.0628	0.5251
	Panel PP-statistic	−6.956254	0.0001*	−8.6156	0.0001*
	Panel ADF-statistic	−8.762238	0.0001*	−10.033	0.0001*
	Grup rho-statistic	−0.187824	0.4255	2.0011	0.9773
	Grup PP-statistic	−12.83343	0.0001*	−12.418	0.0001*
	Grup ADF-statistic	−9.126376	0.0001*	−11.352	0.0001*
No intercept or trend	Panel v-statistic	1.176199	0.1198	0.4455	0.3279
	Panel rho-statistic	−0.422900	0.3362	−2.4890	0.0064*
	Panel PP-statistic	−1.076554	0.1408	−2.8056	0.0025*
	Panel ADF-statistic	−10.50981	0.0001*	−2.5986	0.0047*
	Grup rho-statistic	−5.257030	0.0001*	−3.2654	0.0005*
	Grup PP-statistic	−11.06025	0.0001*	−6.1284	0.0001*
	Grup ADF-statistic	−9.666907	0.0001*	−4.1808	0.0001*

Table 6.5 Granger causality–block exogeneity Wald test results

	Dependent	Independent	Chi-square	Df	Prob.	Direction
Models	Military expenditure, $I(1)$	GDP per capita, $I(1)$	56.00219	3	0.0001	Unidirection
	GDP per capita, $I(1)$	Military expenditure, $I(1)$	82.17343	3	0.0001	Unidirection

Table 6.6 The correlation results of variables for $I(0)$ and $I(1)$

	$I(0)$		$I(1)$	
	Defense expenditure	GDP per capita	Defense expenditure	GDP per capita
Military expenditure	1.000	0.970	1.000	0.064
GDP per capita	0.970	1.000	0.064	1.000

In the preliminary expectation of economic model to be established, there is a relation from MEs to GDP growth and a relation from GDP growth to ME with respect to the causality results. The power of the relationship between two variables is shown as correlation results in the following table.

The results in Table 6.6 show that, while the correlation is 0.970 in raw data, it declines to 0.064 by doing the same analysis with the first differences. These findings indicate that the variables have got a long run relation.

Two models are formed according to the preliminary expectations:

$$\textbf{Model 1: } \text{Military Expenditure}_{it} = \beta_0 + \beta_1 \text{GDP}_{it} + u_{it} \qquad (6.9)$$
$$\textbf{Model 2: } \text{GDP}_{it} = \beta_0 + \beta_1 \text{Military Expenditure}_{it} + u_{it} \qquad (6.10)$$

Process sequence with three steps is followed for Models 1 and 2:

In the first step, Lagrange Multiplier test (LM) of Breusch and Pagan (1980) is used to test cross-sectional dependence. Breusch–Pagan LM test is used to take the average of the squared pair-wise correlation coefficients of the residuals and testing the null hypothesis specified by $\left(H_0 : \sigma_\mu^2 = 0 \right)$ (Pesaran et al. 2008; Tatoğlu 2012: 173). Breusch–Pagan LM test statistic's formula is given as follows:

$$LM = \frac{NT}{2(T-1)} \left[\frac{\sum\limits_{i=1}^{n} \left(\sum\limits_{t=1}^{T} u_{it} \right)^2}{\sum\limits_{i=1}^{n} \sum\limits_{t=1}^{T} u_{it}^2} - 1 \right]^2 \qquad (6.11)$$

u_{it}'s in the formula are residuals that are obtained from the estimation of the pooled least square model. This test statistic fits to the freedom chi-squared distribution's first degree. Result of the LM test statistic is compared with the chi-squared table: If the H_0 hypothesis is not rejected, unit effects are not accepted and the classical model is appropriate. In the opposite case, with the rejection of H_0 hypothesis, it is concluded that the classical model is not suitable. The model's assumptions will be tested after it is decided whether the data is a pooled or panel.

The tests of the assumptions which the models should provide are given in the second step. The results in the first step point out the classical model in the first step. The heteroskedasticity and autocorrelation test should be applied in accordance with the classical model (Tatoğlu 2012). In the classical model, the presence of heteroskedasticity is investigated by Breusch–Pagan/Cook–Weiesberg's Test and White Test, and the presence of autocorrelation is searched out by Durbin–Watson's Test, Breusch–Godfrey's Test, and Wooldridge's Test.

Consistent estimators are used in the third step in accordance with the results in the second step. In other words, consistent estimators and their methods are used whether the characteristics of panel data have got the assumptions of heteroskedasticity and autocorrelation or not.

Many methods of consistent estimators as Huber–Eicker–White's, Arellano Froot–Rogers', Wooldridge's, Newey–West's, Anselin's maximum likelihood, Parks–kmenta's, Beck–kactz', and Driscoll and Kraay's may be used. By the assumption results of two models, it is found appropriate to use Arellano–Froot–Rogers' in the study.

The three steps' results of two models are given in Table 6.6. Breusch–Pagan is used to understand if the data is panel or classical (pooled panel model) in the first step. Applying the classical model is decided according to the probability which is bigger than 0.05 in both of the two models. The heteroskedasticity and autocorrelation, which are two assumptions both models would provide, are tested in the second step. By Breusch–Pagan/Cook–Weiesberg's Test and White Test, heteroskedasticity is found in the models. Furthermore, autocorrelation is found in both of the models by Wooldridge's test. Finally, carrying the characteristics of heteroskedasticity and autocorrelation, classical model is found appropriate for Model 1 and Model 2.

While the assumptions of heteroskedasticity and autocorrelation are not provided in the classical model, Arellano–Froot–Rogers estimator is used to identify the regression results for Model 1 and Model 2.

The results owned to the third step are given in Table 6.8. After analyzing the assumptions of the classical model, the following Arellano–Froot–Rogers Test's results give the explanatory power and significance of the independent variables on the dependent variable.

The power and significance of the effect of the independent variable GDP growth on MEs are shown in Table 6.7. $P > [t] = 0.073$ means that the explanation of independent variable GDP growth on dependent variable MEs is significant. One unit change of independent variable GDP causes 0.003298's unit change in dependent variable MEs in the same direction. The explanatory power and significance of the independent variable MEs on the dependent variable GDP growth are shown in Model 2. $P > [t] = 0.000$ means that the explanation of independent variable MEs on dependent variable GDP growth is significant. Additionally, one unit change of independent variable MEs causes 1.245166's unit change in dependent variable GDP growth in the same direction.

Table 6.7 Assumptions' results for Models 1 and 2

First Step : Breusch-Pagan Test Results	
Model 1: $Military\ Expenditure_{it} = \beta_0 + \beta_1 GDP_{it} + u_{it}$	Model 2: $GDP_{it} = \beta_0 + \beta_1 Military\ Expenditure_{it} + u_{it}$
Breusch and Pagan Lagrangian multiplier test for random effects Military Expenditure[crossid,t] = Xb + u[crossid] + e[crossid,t] Estimated results: 　　　　　　　　　　　　Var　　sd = sqrt(Var) Military Expenditure　5.68e+07　7536.85 　　　　e　5.34e+07　7306.134 　　　　u　　0　　0 Test: Var(u) = 0 　　　　chibar2(01) =　0.00 　　　Prob > chibar2 =　1.0000	Breusch and Pagan Lagrangian multiplier test for random effects gdp[crossid,t] = Xb + u[crossid] + e[crossid,t] Estimated results: 　　　　　　Var　　sd = sqrt(Var) gdp　2.14e+10　146439.2 　e　1.23e+10　110916.6 　u　　0　　0 Test: Var(u) = 0 　　　chibar2(01) =　0.00 　　Prob > chibar2 =　1.0000
Applying the classical model is decided according to the probability which is bigger than 0.05.	Applying the classical model is decided according to the probability which is bigger than 0.05.
Second Step: Assumptions' Tests on The Classical Model	
Model 1: $Military\ Expenditure_{it} = \beta_0 + \beta_1 GDP_{it} + u_{it}$	Model 2: $GDP_{it} = \beta_0 + \beta_1 Military\ Expenditure_{it} + u_{it}$
Heteroskedasticity (Breush-Pagan / Cook-Weisberg Tests' Results)	
Breusch-Pagan / Cook-Weisberg test for heteroskedasticity Ho: Constant variance Variables: fitted values of dexpend chi2(1)　=　1402.74 Prob > chi2　=　0.0000	Breusch-Pagan / Cook-Weisberg test for heteroskedasticity Ho: Constant variance Variables: fitted values of gdp chi2(1)　=　4.75 Prob > chi2　=　0.0293
The probability is smaller than 0.05 . The H_0 hypothesis off constant variance is rejected. There is enough evidence of heteroskedasticity.	The probability is smaller than 0.05 . The H_0 hypothesis off constant variance is rejected. There is enough evidence of heteroskedasticity.
Otocorrelation (WooldridgeTest Results)	
Wooldridge test for autocorrelation in panel data H0: no first-order autocorrelation 　F(1,　26) =　494.285 　　　Prob > F =　0.0000	Wooldridge test for autocorrelation in panel data H0: no first-order autocorrelation 　F(1,　26) =　80.486 　　　Prob > F =　0.0000
Probability is smaller than 0.05. The H_0 hypothesis off no autocorrelation is rejected.	Probability is smaller than 0.05. The H_0 hypothesis off no autocorrelation is rejected.

Conclusion

Having technology-intensive manufacturing areas is one of the rules of being successful in the international competition. The investments made in the military industry, and the recognition of the products that are being produced in this area as *technology-intensive* products, are increasing the importance of the MEs and EG relationship. Especially, exportation of the technology-intensive products has a considerable impact on the balance of payments of the countries and plays an important role for their EG. Secondly, EG affects the competitiveness of the countries prominently.

In the world of the twenty-first century, where peace does not rise, moreover armed conflicts and total DEs have got a widespread outlook, studies on subjects related with military and defense still concern many. By using ME and GDP per capita data set between the years of 2000–2015, the relationship between the variables in 27 NATO member countries has been analyzed.

This study brings to light the relationship between ME and EG for NATO member countries. Applying Granger co-integration to the series which became stable, short and long-term causality relationships have been detected. The evidence

Table 6.8 Regression results in step 3

Arellano-Froot-Rogers Test's Results						
Model 1: $Military\ Expenditure_{it} = \beta_0 + \beta_1 GDP_{it} + u_{it}$						

Linear regression

```
Number of obs  =     405
F( 1,    26)   =    3.50
Prob > F       =  0.0726
R-squared      =  0.0041
Root MSE       =  7530.7
```

(Std. Err. adjusted for 27 clusters in crossid)

Military Expenditure	Coef.	Robust Std. Err.	t	P>|t|	[95% Conf. Interval]	
gdp	.0032983	.0017625	1.87	0.073	-.0003245	.0069211
_cons	307.829	329.6996	0.93	0.359	-369.8782	985.5361

Model 2: $GDP_{it} = \beta_0 + \beta_1 Military\ Expenditure_{it} + u_{it}$

Linear regression

```
Number of obs  =     405
F( 1,    26)   =   59.22
Prob > F       =  0.0000
R-squared      =  0.0041
Root MSE       =  1.5e+05
```

(Std. Err. adjusted for 27 clusters in crossid)

dgdp	Coef.	Robust Std. Err.	t	P>|t|	[95% Conf. Interval]	
Military Expenditure	1.245166	.1618074	7.70	0.000	.9125661	1.577766
_cons	38905.78	18662.58	2.08	0.047	544.2905	77267.27

of the two-way direction indicates that ME and GDP per capita variables can affect each other and can be influenced by each other. The relation from GDP growth to ME and the relation from ME to GDP growth are supported with the correlation results too. Finally, carrying the characteristics of heteroskedasticiy and autocorrelation, classical model is found appropriate for the two models explaining GDP growth and ME relationship. By the Arellano–Froot–Rogers Test's results, it is found that two of the variables have significance explanatory power on each other. In literature, there is not a consensus if the high defense spending is the result of high growth rates, one of these variables is cause of the others, or vice visa for both hypothesis.

There is a widening literature and difference evidences on the relationship between DE and EG. Where some studies have evidence on one-way directional relationship from DE to EG (Benoit 1973; Alptekin and Levine 2012) or conversely one-way directional relationship from EG to DE (Kollias et al. 2004; Dritsakis 2004; Gokmenoglu et al. 2015), there is evidence on nonexistence or bidirectional relationship too (Dakurah et al. 2001; Chang et al. 2001). However, when the varying evidence for NATO member countries are considered in the literature, findings of the study support Dakurah et al. (2001), and Ozun and Erbaykal (2011).

In theoritical view, our findings support the Keynesian approach and institutional approach. Keynesian approach considers DEs as a part of public expenditure, and

DEs can lead to an increase in investments and growth. With a complementary role, the institutionalist approach emphasizes that there are strong interest groups consisting of individuals, companies, and organizations which utilize from high defense spending named as MIC.

References

Abu-Bader, S., & Abu-Qarn, A. S. (2003). Government expenditures, military spending and economic growth: Causality evidence from Egypt, Israel, and Syria. *Journal of Policy Modeling, 25*(6), 567–583.

Alptekin, A., & Levine, P. (2012). Military expenditure and economic growth: A meta-analysis. *European Journal of Political Economy, 28*(4), 636–650.

Altay, H., Ekinci, A., & Peçe, M. A. (2013). Ortadoğu'da Terörün Ekonomik Etkileri: Türkiye, Mısır Ve Suudi Arabistan Üzerine Bir İnceleme. *Dumlupinar University Journal of Social Science/Dumlupinar Üniversitesi Soysyal Bilimler Dergisi, 37*, 267–288.

Bekmez, S., & Destek, M. A. (2015). Savunma Harcamalarında Dışlama Etkisinin İncelenmesi: Panel Veri Analizi, *Siyaset. Ekonomi ve Yönetim Araştırmaları Dergisi, 3*(2), 91–110.

Benoit, E. (1973). *Defence and economic growth in developing countries*. Boston, MA: Lexington Books.

Benoit, E. (1978). Growth and defense in developing countries. *Economic Development and Cultural Change, 26*(2), 271–280.

Breitung, J. (2000). The local power of some unit root tests for panel data. In B. Baltagi (Ed.), *Nonstationary panels, panel cointegration, and dynamic panels. Advances in econometrics* (Vol. 15, pp. 161–178). Amsterdam: JAI.

Breusch, T. S., & Pagan, A. R. (1980). The Lagrange multiplier test and its applications to model specification in econometrics. *The Review of Economic Studies, 47*(1), 239–253.

Chang, T., Fang, W., Wen, L. F., & Liu, C. (2001). Defence spending, economic growth and temporal causality: Evidence from Taiwan and mainland China, 1952-1995. *Applied Economics, 33*(10), 1289–1299.

Choi, I. (2001). Unit root tests for panel data. *Journal of International Money and Finance, 20*(2), 249–272.

Cuaresma, J. C., & Reitschuler, G. (2004). A non-linear defence-growth nexus? Evidence from the US economy. *Defence and Peace Economics, 15*(1), 71–82.

Dakurah, A. H., Davies, S. P., & Sampath, R. K. (2001). Defense spending and economic growth in developing countries: A causality analysis. *Journal of Policy Modeling, 23*(6), 651–658.

Deger, S., & Smith, R. (1983). Military expenditure and growth in less developed countries. *Journal of Conflict Resolution, 27*, 335–353.

Dritsakis, N. (2004). Defense spending and economic growth: An empirical investigation for Greece and Turkey. *Journal of Policy Modeling, 26*(2), 249–264.

Dunne, J. P. (1996). Chapter 13: Economic effects of military expenditure in developing countries: A survey. In N. P. Gleditsch, A. Cappelen, O. Bjerkholt, R. Smith, & P. Dunne (Eds.), *The peace dividend* (pp. 439–464). North-Holland: Amsterdam. Contributions to Economic Analysis, Emerald. Published online: 8 Mar 2015.

Dunne, P., & Nikolaidou, E. (2012). Defence spending and economic growth in the Eu15. *Defence and Peace Economics, 23*(6).

Dunne, P., Nikolaidou, E., & Vougas, D. (2001). Defence spending and economic growth: A causal analysis for Greece and Turkey. *Defence and Peace Economics, 12*(1), 5–26.

Dunne, J. P., & Uye, M. (2014). Defence spending and development. In A. Tan (Ed.), *The global arms trade: A handbook* (p. 293). London: Europa.

Duyar, M., & Koçolu, M. (2014). Askeri Harcamalarin Ekonomik Büyüme Üzerine Etkisi Sahra Alti Afrika Örneği. *Uluslararası Sosyal Araştırmalar Dergisi, 7*(33).

Faini, R., Annez, P., & Taylor, L. (1984). Defense spending, economic structure, and growth: Evidence among countries and over time. *Economic Development and Cultural Change, 32*(3), 487–498.

Fatah, A. A., & Salihoglu, S. A. (2016). Comparative study of the impact of defense expenditures on economic growth in Indonesia and Turkey. *The Journal of Defense Sciences, 15*(1), 55–77.

Feder, G. Ö. (1983). On exports and economic growth. *Journal of Development Economics, 12*(1–2), 59–73.

Giray, F. (2004). Savunma Harcamalari ve Ekonomik Büyüme. *Cumhuriyet Üniversitesi İktisadi ve İdari Bilimler Dergisi, 5*(1), 181–199.

Gokmenoglu, K. K., Taspinar, N., & Sadeghieh, M. (2015). Military expenditure and economic growth: The case of Turkey. *Procedia Economics and Finance, 25*, 455–462.

Gujarati, D. (2004). *Basic econometrics*. West Point, NY: United States Military Academy.

Hadri, K. (2000). Testing for stationarity in heterogeneous panel data. *The Econometrics Journal, 3*(2), 148–161.

Halicioğlu, F. (2004). Defense spending and economic growth in Turkey: An empirical application of new macroeconomic theory. *Review of Middle East Economics and Finance, 2*(3), 193–201.

Hämäläinen, T. J. (2003). *National competitiveness and economic growth. New horizons in institutional and evolutionary performance in the world economics series*. Cheltenham: Edward Elgar Publishing.

Im, K. S., Pesaran, M. H., & Shin, Y. (2003). Testing for unit roots in heterogeneous panels. *Journal of Econometrics, 115*(1), 53–74.

İpek, E. (2014). Savunma Harcamalarının Seçilmiş Makroekonomik Değişkenler Üzerine Etkisi: ARDL Sınır Testi Yaklaşımı. *Anadolu Üniversitesi Sosyal Bilimler Dergisi, 37*, 113–125.

Kao, C. (1999). Spurious regression and residual-based tests for cointegration in panel data. *Journal of Econometrics, 90*(1), 1–44.

Kaya, S. S. (2013, December). Türkiye'de Savunma Harcamalarinin İktisadi Etkileri Üzerine Nedensellik Analizi (1970-2010). *Trakya University Journal of Social Science, 15*(2).

Khiui, N. M., & Mahmood, A. (1997). Military expenditures and economic. *Pakistan Development Review, 36*(4 Part II), 791–808.

Kollias, C. (1997). Defence spending and growth in Turkey 1954–1993: A causal analysis. *Defence and Peace Economics, 8*(2), 189–204.

Kollias, C., Manolas, G., & Paleologou, S. M. (2004). Defence expenditure and economic growth in the European Union: A causality analysis. *Journal of Policy Modeling, 26*(5), 553–569.

Korkmaz, S. (2015). The effect of military spending on economic growth and unemployment in Mediterranean countries. *International Journal of Economics and Financial Issues, 5*(1), 273.

Levin, A., & Lin, C. F. (1992). *Unit root tests in panel data: Asymptotic and finite sample properties* (Discussion paper 92–23). University of California, Department of Economics.

Levin, A., & Lin, C. F. (1993). *Unir root tests in panel data: New results* (Discussion paper 93–56). University of California, Department of Economics.

Levin, A., Lin, C. F., & Chu, C. S. J. (2002). Unit root tests in panel data: Asymptotic and finite-sample properties. *Journal of Econometrics, 108*(1), 1–24.

Macnair, E. S., Murdoch, J. C., Pi, C. R., & Sandler, T. (1995). Growth and defense: Pooled estimates for the NATO alliance, 1951-1988. *Southern Economic Journal*, 846–860.

Maddala, G. S., & Wu, S. (1999). A comparative study of unit root tests with panel data and a new simple test. *Oxford Bulletin of Economics and Statistics, 61*(S1), 631–652.

North Atlantic Treaty Organization. www.nato.int.

Ozun, A., & Erbaykal, E. (2011). *Further evidence on defence spending and economic growth in NATO countries* (Koç University-TÜSİAD Economic Research Forum Working Paper Series).

Pedroni, P. (1999). Critical values for cointegration tests in heterogeneous panels with multiple regressors. *Oxford Bulletin of Economics and Statistics, 61*(S1), 653–670.

Pedroni, P. (2004). Panel cointegration: Asymptotic and finite sample properties of pooled time series tests with an application to the PPP hypothesis. *Econometric Theory, 20*(3).

Pesaran, M. H., Ullah, A., & Yamagata, T. (2008). A bias-adjusted LM test of error cross section independence. *The Econometrics Journal, 11*(1), 105–127.

Pieroni, L. (2009). Military expenditure and economic growth. *Defence and Peace Economics, 20*(4), 327–339.

Porter, M., Sachs, J., & McArthur, J. (2001). Executive summary: Competitiveness and stages of economic development. *The Global Competitiveness Report, 2002,* 16–25.

Ram, R. (1986). Government size and economic growth: A new framework and some evidence from cross-section and time series data. *American Economic Review, 76,* 191–203.

Sezgin, S. (2000). A casual analysis of Turkish defence-growth relationships. *Ankara Üniversitesi SBF Dergisi, 55*(2).

Shahbaz, M., Afza, T., & Shabbir, M. S. (2013). Does defence spending impede economic growth? Cointegration and causality analysis for Pakistan. *Defence and Peace Economics, 24*(2), 105–120.

SIPRI Yearbook. (2016). https://www.sipri.org/yearbook/2016

Stockholm International Peace Research Institute. https://www.sipri.org/.

Stroup, M. D., & Heckelman, J. C. (2001). Size of the military sector and economic growth: A panel data analysis of Africa and Latin America. *Journal of Applied Economics, 4*(2).

Taş, S., Örnek, İ., & Aksoğan, G. (2013). Türkiye'de Savunma Harcamaları, Büyüme ve Gelir Eşitsizliği, 1970-2008: Ekonometrik Bir İnceleme. *Gaziantep University Journal of Social Sciences, 12*(3).

Tatoğlu, F.Y. (2012). Panel veri ekonometrisi: stata uygulamalı. *Beta Basım Yayın.*

Tuncay, Ö. (2017). Finansal Serbestleşme Sonrası Dönem Savunma Harcamalarının Ekonomik Analizi. *Uluslararası Ekonomik Araştırmalar Dergisi, 3*(1).

United Nations Conference on Trade and Development. unctad.org.

Yang, H., Hong, C., Jung, S., & Lee, J. D. (2015). Arms or butter: The economic effect of an increase in military expenditure. *Journal of Policy Modeling, 37*(4), 596–615.

Yılancı, V., & Özcan, B. (2010). Yapısal kırılmalar altında Türkiye için savunma harcamaları ile GSMH arasındaki ilişkinin analizi. *CÜ İktisadi ve İdari Bilimler Dergisi, 11*(1), 21–33.

Yıldırım, J., & Sezgin, S. (2003). Military expenditure and employment in Turkey. *Defence and Peace Economics, 14*(2), 129–139.

Yıldırım, J., Sezgin, S., & Öcal, N. (2005). Military expenditure and economic growth in middle eastern countries: A dynamic panel data analysis. *Defence and Peace Economics, 16*(4), 283–295.

Chapter 7
Grouping OECD Countries Based on Energy-Related Variables Using *k*-Means and Fuzzy Clustering

Abdulkadir Hiziroglu, Ayhan Kapusuzoglu, and Erhan Cankal

Abstract The main purpose of this study is to examine the relationships between energy consumption, CO_2 emission and economic growth for 28 OECD countries and to form clusters based on the findings. The study is carried out under the 1990–2010 period, considering the annual data, the average annual values for each country are calculated and the countries are grouped by taking into account the main energy variables. This study examined OECD countries into three groups to form more specific clustering, rendering to test the hypotheses in current empirical studies, and examining the relationships of the interacted variables for within and inter-cluster countries.

Introduction

The relationship between energy consumption and economic growth has been one of the primary discussion topics in the last decade due to rising overall demand of economic agents on energy sources and its effect on decisions for expenditures by economic units such as households, firms and countries (Lin and Wesseh 2014).

Energy consumption can affect economies via various channels. Countries need energy sources for maintaining their production activities as well as transportation of raw materials and products. As a result, energy proves to be one of the main significant factors in contributing to economic development of the countries (Nasreen and Anwar 2014).

High prices of energy sources that arise from 1970s energy crisis led to protectionist energy policies for the countries to follow. In this context, when it is assumed that the energy consumption is the cause of the economic growth, a reduction in energy consumption will lead to a decline in output and a rise in unemployment level. However, in a case where economic growth is a causation of energy

A. Hiziroglu
Izmir Bakircay University, Izmir, Turkey

A. Kapusuzoglu (✉) · E. Cankal
Ankara Yildirim Beyazit University, Ankara, Turkey

© Springer International Publishing AG, part of Springer Nature 2018 151
H. Dincer et al. (eds.), *Global Approaches in Financial Economics, Banking, and Finance*, Contributions to Economics, https://doi.org/10.1007/978-3-319-78494-6_7

consumption, a protective energy policy in force may not lead to negative effects or minimal negative effects on the economy (Bozoklu and Yilanci 2013). According to Stern (2000), since energy is a primary factor in production process, the likelihood of a reduction in economic activities and an increase in unemployment is caused by a decline in energy consumption.

There are four different views as to the causation between energy consumption and economic growth (Salahuddin and Gow 2014; Omri and Kahouli 2014; Narayan and Smyth 2007; Odhiambo 2009). First is the growth hypothesis, which suggests that the energy consumption causes economic growth. In other words, economic growth is dependent on energy consumption. This approach argues that a decline in energy consumption will likely affect the economic growth downward. The second view is the conservation hypothesis that emphasises the importance of real sector activities. An expansion in real sector activities has the potential to demand more energy. The third view is the feedback hypothesis. This approach argues that the two-way causation exists between energy consumption and economic growth. A protectionist energy policy will lead the economic growth to shrink, and a slow economic growth further slowdowns the energy consumption. Finally, the fourth view, the neutrality hypothesis, rejects the causality between energy consumption and economic growth. According to Dagher and Yacobian (2012), national energy and environmental policies should be designed carefully in evaluating the relationship between energy and GDP based on the first approach.

In the literature of energy economies, the relationship between economic growth and CO_2 emission has a remarkable place as well and is demonstrated by environmental Kuznet Curve. This U-shaped relationship involves linear and nonlinear variations in GDP (per capita). At the first stages of economic growth, emission level increases, and at the following phases, it reaches a threshold level and then starts declining.

Energy sources are important components of economic growth. Especially, the fossil fuels are the most common type of energy sources and can be placed on the top of the list. However, the energy consumption in both developed and developing countries has caused a rapid global increase in emission levels, which further inevitably requires the use of renewable energy sources.

The reason that CO_2 is included within the context of this research is because of its importance in discussions on sustainable growth and protectionist environmental policies. The indicators for economic growth are closely related to energy consumption. The efficient and high-level energy consumption potentially leads to high economic growth rate. In the relevant literature, there is no consensus. As such, the relationship needs some further investigations.

The aim of this study is to decompose the OECD countries for the 1990–2010 period into similar subgroups in terms of their energy consumptions, CO_2 emission levels, and economic growth and to evaluate the emerging country groups resulting from the decomposition. In the relevant literature, the countries on the basis of energy-related variables can be classified according to their growth levels and development parameters, as well as according to whether they are in a position that export energy sources. Therefore, the main contribution of this research to the literature in this framework is to divide the OECD countries into similar subgroups and reach more specific findings and catch the opportunity to make more accurate inferences in the light of these findings.

The subsequent sections of the study are organised as follows: the literature on energy-related variables will be examined in the second part and the methodological framework will be presented in the third section. The empirical findings will be provided in the subsequent part and the evaluation and inferences of the findings will take place in the final section.

Literature Review

There are a number of empirical research studies that examine the relationships between energy consumption (EC), economic growth (EG) and CO_2 emission (CE) and reveal different findings.

In this study, firstly, the empirical studies examine the relationships between energy consumption and economic growth. In this context, the various types of relationships between variables are pointed out as mentioned before.

As the earlier studies are examined, a unidirectional causality (growth hypothesis) from energy consumption to economic growth (Kraft and Kraft 1978; Akarca and Long 1980; Yu and Choi 1985; Lin and Wesseh 2014; Saidi and Hammami 2015; Yang and Zhao 2014; Omri 2013; Bozoklu and Yilanci 2013; Dergiades et al. 2013; Wandji 2013; Pirlogea and Cicea 2012; Yildirim et al. 2012; Wolde-Rufael 2009), unidirectional causality (conservation hypothesis) from economic growth to energy consumption (Shahbaz et al. 2017; Omri and Kahouli 2014; Salahuddin and Gow 2014; Bozoklu and Yilanci 2013; Herrerias et al. 2013; Saboori and Sulaiman 2013; Akinlo 2008), two-way causal relationship (feedback hypothesis) between energy consumption and economic growth (Santos Gaspar et al. 2017; Nasreen and Anwar 2014; Omri and Kahouli 2014; Sebri and Ben-Salha 2014; Dagher and Yacobian 2012; Eggoh et al. 2011; Erdal et al. 2008; Saidi et al. 2017) and the absence of any causal relationship (neutrality hypothesis) between energy consumption and economic growth (Rahman and Mamun 2016; Wandji 2013; Pirlogea and Cicea 2012; Jafari et al. 2012; Akinlo 2008) are revealed. As it can be seen, there is no consensus regarding the presence and direction of the relationship between energy consumption and economic growth in the literature (Table 7.1).

It is possible to come across the studies that reveal that energy consumption and economic growth are unidirectional causality on CO_2 emission (Begum et al. 2015; Kivyiro and Arminen 2014; Omri 2013; Hamit-Haggar 2012) as well as the studies that argue that CO_2 emission is a unidirectional causality on energy consumption and economic growth (Sebri and Ben-Salha 2014; Saidi and Hammami 2015). In addition, there are some studies that detect two-way causal relationship between the variables (Salahuddin and Gow 2014; Yang and Zhao 2014; Omri 2013; Saboori and Sulaiman 2013; Hamit-Haggar 2012), while one can also see the studies that

Table 7.1 Energy consumption/economic growth

Author	Period	Methodology	Countries	Causal relation
Lin and Wesseh (2014)	1971–2010	Granger causality	South Africa	EC → EG
Nasreen and Anwar (2014)	1980–2011	Granger causality	Asian countries	EC ↔ EG
Omri and Kahouli (2014)	1990–2011	Granger causality	High income	EC ↔ EG
			Middle income	EC ↔ EG
			Low income	EG → EC
Salahuddin and Gow (2014)	1980–2012	Granger causality	Gulf Cooperation Council countries	EG → EC
Saidi and Hammami (2015)	1990–2012	Simultaneous-equations models	58 countries	EC → EG
Sebri and Ben-Salha (2014)	1971–2010	ARDL bounds tests VECM	BRICS countries	EC ↔ EG
Yang and Zhao (2014)	1970–2008	Granger causality	India	EC → EG
Omri (2013)	1990–2011	Granger causality	14 MENA countries	EC ↔ EG
Bozoklu and Yilanci (2013)	1970–2011	Granger causality	20 OECD countries	EC → EG EG → EC
Dergiades et al. (2013)	1960–2008	Granger causality VEC	Greece	EC → EG
Wandji (2013)	1971–2009	Granger causality	Cameroon	EC → EG
				No causal relation
Herrerias et al. (2013)	1995–2009	Panel co-integration	China	EG → EC
	1999–2009	VAR		
Saboori and Sulaiman (2013)	1980–2009	ARDL bounds tests co-integration	Malaysia	No causal relation
				EG → EC
Pirlogea and Cicea (2012)	1990–2010	Granger causality	Spain	EC → EG
			Romania	EC → EG
			EU	No causal relation
Dagher and Yacobian (2012)	1980–2009	Toda–Yamamato VEC	Lebanon	EC ↔ EG
Yildirim et al. (2012)	1949–2010	Granger causality	USA	EC → EG
	1960–2010			
	1970–2010			No causal relation

(continued)

Table 7.1 (continued)

Author	Period	Methodology	Countries	Causal relation
Jafari et al. (2012)	1971–2007	Toda–Yamamato	Indonesia	No causal relation
Eggoh et al. (2011)	1970–2006	Panel co-integration	African countries	EC ↔ EG
		Panel causality		
Wolde-Rufael (2009)	1971–2004	Granger causality	African countries	EC → EG
Akinlo (2008)	1980–2003	ARDL bounds tests	11 sub-Sahara African countries	EC ↔ EG
		VECM		EG → EC
				No causal relation
Erdal et al. (2008)	1970–2006	Granger causality	Turkey	EC ↔ EG

EC Energy consumption, *EG* Economic growth

detect no causality (Ozturk and Acaravcı 2010). These relationships are demonstrated in Table 7.2.

Methodology

Data Set

As mentioned in the previous section, the connections between economic growth (GDP will be taken into account as an indicator), energy consumption and carbon dioxide (CO_2) emissions for the considered 28 OECD countries [*(Australia—(C1), Austria—(C2), Belgium—(C3), Canada—(C4), Chile—(C5), China—(C6), Denmark—(C7), Finland—(C8), France—(C9), Germany—(C10), Greece—(C11), Ireland—(C12), Israel—(C13), Italy—(C14), Japan—(C15), Korea—(C16), Luxembourg—(C17), Mexico—(C18), Netherlands—(C19), New Zealand—(C20), Norway—(C21), Portugal—(C22), Spain—(C23), Sweden—(C24), Switzerland—(C25), Turkey—(C26), United Kingdom—(C27), United States—(C28)*] are examined, and relationship-based clustering is formed for 1990–2010 period accordingly. The energy consumption (kg of oil equivalent per capita) and CO_2 emission (metric tons per capita) data obtained from the World Bank Data Center (www.data.worldbank.org). In an effort to use the obtained data efficiently for the analyses, they are converted to specific average values for each country and variable for the examined period.

Table 7.2 Energy consumption/economic growth/CO_2 emissions

Author	Period	Methodology	Countries	Causal relation
Begum et al. (2015)	1970–1980	ARDL bounds tests	Malaysia	EC → CE
	1980–2009			EG → CE
Salahuddin and Gow (2014)	1980–2012	Granger causality	Gulf Cooperation Council countries	EC ↔ CE
Sebri and Ben-Salha (2014)	1971–2010	ARDL bounds tests	BRICS countries	CE → EG
		VECM		CE → EC
Yang and Zhao (2014)	1970–2008	Granger causality	India	EC → CE
				EG ↔ CE
Saidi and Hammami (2015)	1990–2012	Simultaneous-equations models	58 countries	CE → EG
Kivyiro and Arminen (2014)	1971–2009	ARDL bounds tests	Sub-Saharan Africa	EC → CE
		Granger causality		EG → CE
Omri (2013)	1990–2011	Granger causality	14 MENA countries	EC → CE
				EG ↔ CE
Saboori and Sulaiman (2013)	1971–2009	ARDL bounds tests	ASEAN countries	EC ↔ CE
		VECM		
Hamit-Haggar (2012)	1990–2007	Granger causality	Canada	EC ↔ CE
				EG → CE
Ozturk and Acaravcı (2010)	1968–2005	ARDL bounds tests	Turkey	No causal relation
		Granger causality		

EC Energy consumption, *EG* Economic growth, CE CO_2 emissions

Research Methodology

The methodological foundation of this study stems from clustering theory. Clustering is the method of classifying certain number of items into groups. However, the number of groups is unknown to the person who performs clustering. In other terms, it can be defined as unsupervised classification or categorisation of data (Changchien and Lu 2001). It is related to many disciplines including statistics, machine learning and pattern recognition and has been applied to many areas of business, management and finance. The main target of clustering is to ensure that items or objects within a group are similar while objects in different groups possess dissimilar attributes or behaviours (Tan et al. 2006). Suppose that a data matrix is comprised of n rows (observations) and p columns (variables), the clustering objective function will differentiate object in a way that objects within the same group are homogenous and objects in different groups are heterogeneous one from the other (Giudici 2003). The relationship between the objects is represented via a proximity matrix (for example, Euclidean distance), which is the unique input to be able to perform a clustering algorithm (Jain and Dubes 1948).

There are different taxonomies available for clustering in the related literature; however, the two most common ones are the following: exclusive versus non-exclusive and hierarchical versus non-hierarchical or partitional. Regarding the first classification, exclusive assignment of objects considers only a unique belongingness. Each observation is exactly assigned to only one cluster whereas non-exclusive considers the situations in which a point can be placed in more than one cluster. The term "non-exclusive" is also called overlapping which means that there are overlaps or intersections among clusters. Fuzzy clustering (FC) is a type of non-exclusive clustering. Detailed information regarding overlapping clustering are obtainable in the related literature (Arabie et al. 1981; Jain and Dubes 1948). The second categorisation is based on the fact that whether clusters are nested or un-nested, aka. Hierarchical or partitional (Jain and Dubes 1948; Tan et al. 2006). Hierarchical clustering obtains sub-clusters each associated with subsequent level of clustering. Partitioning data in hierarchical clustering is represented via dendogram (similar to tree structure). Every node (cluster) associated with sub-clusters (members) and the root of the tree comprises of all the items in the tree structures. Partitional (non-hierarchical) clustering divides the data into specific number of separate sets by complying the condition of homogeneity (Giudici 2003; Han and Kamber 2001; Hand et al. 2001). In order to perform a partition-based clustering, let us say to form k clusters, one would need to find a search space of possible assignments of k points. The aim here is to find a solution that minimises or maximises the score functions of the algorithms (Hand et al. 2001). Although there have been many methods for performing a partitional clustering, the algorithms based on iterative improvement process, particularly k-means, seems to be the most popular and the most common in the related literature (Giudici 2003). According to the background information provided above, representative of two clustering approaches, namely fuzzy clustering and k-means, will be utilised in order to carry out the analyses. Following subsections provide some details on the clustering techniques utilised.

Fuzzy Clustering

Fuzzy clustering (FC) is a method that is extensively used in order to obtain fuzzy models. It can be considered as an unsupervised technique both for data compression and data categorisation (Hu and Sheu 2003). Fuzzy clustering method divides data into overlapping groups according to a similarity or distance measurement (Setnes 2000).

Compared to the hard (crisp) clustering, the FC has some differences (Sato-Ilic and Jain 2006). In the crisp methods, one can discriminate whether a data or item belongs to a group (cluster) or not; a data point either only belongs to a cluster and its membership is represented by "1" or it does not belong to a cluster and its membership is represented by "0". But, this partition may be insufficient to model the real situations. Thus, a data points' membership in a cluster is expressed between 0 and 1, with a different membership value. In other words, a data point can be a member of more than one cluster at the same time with varying membership degrees. Also, knowledge of the degree to which objects belong to the formed clusters becomes available, and the sum of the total membership values of the objects to a certain cluster is equal to 1 (Sato-Ilic and Jain 2006). This situation is described usually as an objective function by maximising the total membership values of data in the same cluster and the distance between the cluster centres of each cluster (Dimitriadou et al. 2002; Torkul et al. 2006).

Fuzzy-clustering-based algorithms can be divided into three categories in terms of their algorithmic running methodology. The first methodology is based on a fuzzy relation concept to carry out the clustering, the second group utilises an objective function in order to obtain fuzzy cluster while the third one makes use of the nearest neighbour rule (Hsu et al. 2000; Yang 1993). In this chapter, the second type of fuzzy clustering methodology was applied. Within this scope of the study, one of the most common techniques of fuzzy clustering algorithms (fuzzy c-means) was utilised. Fuzzy c-means algorithm was developed from the well-known partitional clustering algorithm (k-means); however, it incorporates a parameter that is known as fuzzifier constant or fuzzification coefficient (notated as m) that defines the degree of fuzziness. The fuzzy c-means algorithm recognises the data objects in a p-dimensional space, and each cluster is represented by its centre (Höppner et al. 1999).

k-Means

The algorithmic procedure of k-means technique will be described based on some references (Balakrishnan et al. 1996; Giudici 2003; Han and Kamber 2001; Hand et al. 2001; Shin and Sohn 2004; Tan et al. 2006). The algorithm has three steps, namely, initialisation, transfer evaluation and repetition. At the initialisation step, the algorithm starts by randomly choosing k initial centroid or centre points among n objects, where k is a user-defined parameter and represents the number of clusters. Each element of k represents a cluster mean or centre. At the transfer evaluation step, each remaining object or data points ($n–k$ items) are assigned to its nearest cluster based on similarity or distance between the object and the cluster centres. The distance between the objects and the centres of the clusters is calculated by Euclidean distance. Finally, the cluster centres are updated based on the assignment of the new objects. Updating process continues until the cluster centres remain the same or the difference is very small compared to the previous clustering structure.

Empirical Findings

Descriptive Results

Descriptive statistics were presented as shown in Table 7.3 in order to have a better understanding of the data. The results showed that average CO_2, GDP and EC values were found to be approximately 9.26, 26640.66 and 4042.48, respectively. Regarding the distribution of the clustering variables, it could be said that the distribution of CO_2 variable was not normal while the distributions of GDP and EC variables were found to be normal. This could be observed through looking at the skewness and kurtosis values of the corresponding variables as well as the histograms of the variables as shown in Fig. 7.1.

Also, another way to check non-normality is to look at some test statistics regarding normality status including Shapiro–Wilk, Anderson–Darling, Martinez–Iglewicz and Kolmogorov–Smirnov tests, which were presented in Table 7.4. According to the test statistics, the normality status of the variables was found to be the same as it was mentioned in the results section of the kurtosis and skewness tests.

In fact, the above results could also be observed through the histograms of the variables as they were shown in the followings figures.

Clustering Results

To be able to provide a performance measurement for different clustering structures (different number of clusters), some clustering validity tests were carried out. The

Table 7.3 Descriptive statistics for the clustering variables

Clustering variables	Min	Max	Mean	Skewness	Kurtosis
CO_2	3.3	22.37	9.26	1.17	4.09
GDP	1407.37	62088.78	26640.66	0.25	3.24
EC	1096.52	8408.72	4042.48	0.57	2.77

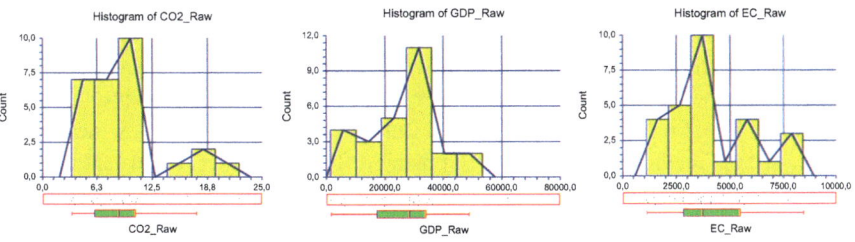

Fig. 7.1 Histogram representation of the variables

Table 7.4 Test statistics for normality

Clustering variables	Normality test	Test value	Prob./CV (5%)	Decision (5%)
CO_2	Shapiro–Wilk W	0.88	0.003	Reject
	Anderson–darling	1.17	0.004	Reject
	Martinez–Iglewicz	1.43	1.24	Reject
	Kolmogorov–Smirnov	0.20	0.16	Reject
GDP	Shapiro–Wilk W	0.96	0.43	Cannot reject
	Anderson–darling	0.44	0.29	Cannot reject
	Martinez–Iglewicz	1.04	1.24	Cannot reject
	Kolmogorov–Smirnov	0.10	0.16	Cannot reject
EC	Shapiro–Wilk W	0.95	0.17	Cannot reject
	Anderson–darling	0.48	0.23	Cannot reject
	Martinez–Iglewicz	1.04	1.24	Cannot reject
	Kolmogorov–Smirnov	0.16	0.16	Cannot reject

Table 7.5 Percent of variations for k-means clustering results

Number of clusters (c)	PV
2	53.45
3	27.21
4	19.82
5	14.06
6	10.26
7	7.86
8	6.95

first clustering validity test is based on a goodness-of-fit criterion (Jain and Dubes 1948). That criterion includes the value of within-cluster sum of squares, and the percent variation of this measurement, PV, is used as the cluster validity index. One should observe a spot where this percentage fails to decrease dramatically in order to find optimum number of clusters. Second cluster validity test was conducted for fuzzy clustering which observes the changes in two different validity indices. The first index is Dunn's (1974) partition coefficient which measures the "fuzziness" in a solution. In other words, it measures how close the fuzzy clustering solution compared to crisp clustering result. A normalised version of this partition, represented as $Fc(U)$, takes values between 0 (fuzzy cluster) and 1 (hard cluster). Another partition coefficient mentioned by Kaufman and Rousseeuw (2005) and the normalised version of this coefficient notated as $Dc(U)$ takes value from 0 (hard cluster) to $1-1/c$ (fuzzy cluster). These two coefficients provide an indication for optimum number of fuzzy clusters. In order to spot the optimum number of clusters, one should look for large $Fc(U)$ and small $Dc(U)$ values. In this study, k-means and fuzzy c-means methods were carried out using different number of clusters ranging from 2 to 8. Optimum number of clusters for each method were determined using the above-mentioned validity measurements. The results can be found in Tables 7.5 and 7.6, respectively.

Table 7.6 $Fc(U)$ and $Dc(U)$ values for fuzzy clustering results

Number of clusters (c)	Fuzzification coefficient ($m = 1.5$)		Fuzzification coefficient ($m = 1.75$)		Fuzzification coefficient ($m = 2$)	
	$Fc(U)$	$Dc(U)$	$Fc(U)$	$Dc(U)$	$Fc(U)$	$Dc(U)$
2	0.50	0.15	0.27	0.30	0.13	0.46
3	0.63	0.14	0.40	0.25	0.21	0.44
4	0.59	0.14	0.37	0.30	0.22	0.52
5	0.60	0.14	0.34	0.35	0.19	0.61
6	0.60	0.13	0.32	0.41	0.18	0.60
7	0.55	0.19	0.28	0.48	0.17	0.61
8	0.64	0.13	0.31	0.48	0.22	0.57

Table 7.7 Cluster means for k-means ($c = 3$)

Variables/clusters	Cluster 1	Cluster 2	Cluster 3
CO_2	0.18	0.87	0.71
GDP	0.39	0.84	0.48
EC	0.14	0.85	0.56
Number of countries	4	9	15
Group status	L, L, L	H, H, H	H, L, L

Table 7.8 Cluster means for fuzzy clustering ($c = 3$ and $m = 1.5$)

Variables/clusters	Cluster 1	Cluster 2	Cluster 3
CO_2	0.38	0.93	0.73
GDP	0.40	0.89	0.55
EC	0.23	0.93	0.63
Number of countries (crisp assignment)	7	6	15
Group status	L, L, L	H, H, H	H, L, H

According to the results, the optimum number of clusters for k-means occurred at cluster number 3 where the PV value has a substantial change. As far as the results for fuzzy clustering are concerned, for each fuzzification coefficient the optimum number of cluster can be found to be three too. After determining the optimum number of clusters for k-means and fuzzy c-means methods, the clustering results for both approaches were obtained via using the three variables (CO_2, GDP and EC values) as clustering inputs. The cluster means of each cluster and the pertaining number of objects (countries) assigned to those clusters were shown in Tables 7.7, 7.8 and 7.9. According to Table 7.7, more than 60% of the countries were assigned to cluster 3. In fact, the same conclusion can be drawn for fuzzy clustering results. Also, Table 7.7 indicates that fuzzy clustering results yielded the same clustering structure for fuzzification coefficients 1.75 and 2.

However, one should notice that the number of countries assigned to each group are the crisp assignments of fuzzy clustering results. The assignments were carried out according to the highest belongingness of the corresponding clusters. The following tables also include information that show the group status of a cluster.

Table 7.9 Cluster means for fuzzy clustering ($c = 3$ and $m = 1.75$ and 2)

Variables/clusters	Cluster 1	Cluster 2	Cluster 3
CO_2	0.26	0.93	0.73
GDP	0.42	0.89	0.53
EC	0.17	0.93	0.60
Number of countries (crisp assignment)	5	6	17
Group status	L, L, L	H, H, H	H, L, H

Fig. 7.2 3D representation of k-means clustering results ($c = 3$)

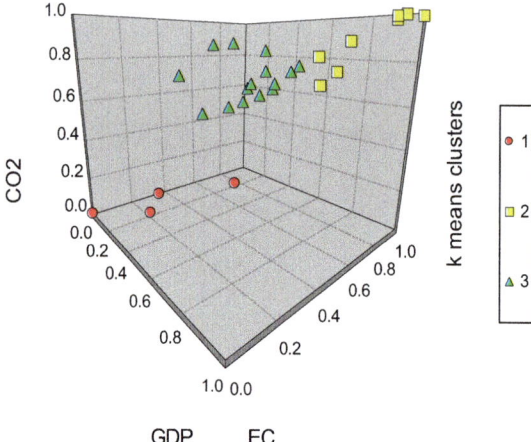

The group status information were obtained via comparing the average values of the variables for each cluster with the overall average values of the corresponding variables. In order to acquire the group status information, the following rule was applied for each variable. If the average value of a variable for a cluster exceeds the overall corresponding average value, then that variable is labelled high or low depending on the comparison. The group status information in these tables help in identifying if the clusters that are obtained are distinctive or differentiable. In this respect, k-means results can be considered different than the fuzzy clustering results.

For simplification purpose, from now on fuzzy clustering results with fuzzification coefficient equals to 1.75 will be taken into consideration for future analyses. In order to visualise the results of the two comparative approaches, three-dimensional representations were presented in Figs. 7.2 and 7.3, respectively.

Comparison of the Clustering Methods

The comparison of the clustering was performed based on three types of analyses. The first analysis helps us to understand how identifiable the clusters are in terms of the variables used. One-way variance analysis (ANOVA) was utilised in order to answer that question. It should be noted that the fuzzy results with crisp assignments

Fig. 7.3 3D representation of fuzzy clustering results ($c = 3$ and $m = 1.75$)

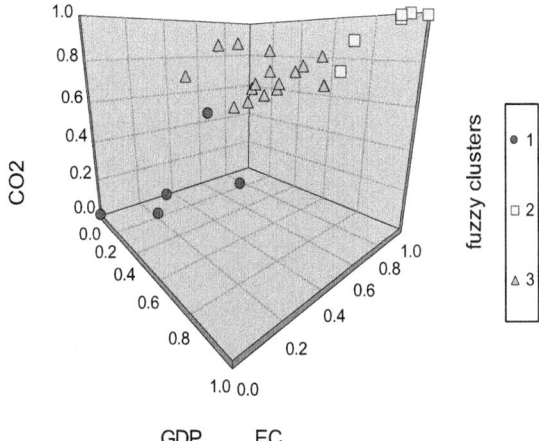

Table 7.10 ANOVA results for k-means and fuzzy clustering

Variables	k-means clustering ($c = 3$)		Fuzzy clustering ($c = 3$ and $m = 1.75$)	
	F-values	Sig.	F-values	Sig.
CO_2	52.51	0.00	45.02	0.00
GDP	20.86	0.00	14.51	0.00
EC	37.63	0.00	50.31	0.00

Table 7.11 Comparison of fuzzy clustering and k-means results ($c = 3$ and $m = 1.75$)

Test	Value	df	Asymp. sig. (2-sided)
Pearson chi-square	36.61	4	0.00
Kappa index	0.75	N/A	0.00

were taken into account to conduct the analysis. At each variable level, the differences in clusters were analysed. The results of the analyses were given (Table 7.10). Based on the test results, it was proved that there were significant differences between the clusters according to the variables used for the comparative approaches.

The second analysis was carried out to observe the similarity or difference between the chosen methods (see Table 7.11). For this purpose, a statistical measurement of agreement was used, aka. Kappa index. The results of the similarity test show that there is a good agreement between the results of the comparative clustering methods at a percentage level of 75%. However, the remaining 25% of indifference must be explained. In order to accomplish that Pearson Chi-Square analysis was performed. The results indicated that k-means and fuzzy methods have different clustering results which mean that there is significant difference between the clustering structures that cannot be explained by chance.

The third analysis is based on a subjective evaluation that provides information regarding the potential managerial implications of the results produced by the comparative approaches. Since fuzzy clustering produces an overlapping clustering structure, it is also feasible to extract information regarding the degree of

Table 7.12 Membership values for fuzzy clustering and their corresponding crisp assignments versus cluster assignments of k-means results ($c = 3$ and $m = 1.75$)

Fuzzy cluster ID	MD in $C1$	MD in $C2$	MD in $C3$	k-means cluster ID
1	0.70	0.09	0.21	1
3	0.06	0.06	0.88	3
3	0.41	0.10	0.50	3
1	0.82	0.06	0.12	1
2	0.02	0.95	0.03	2
2	0.04	0.89	0.07	2
3	0.15	0.09	0.76	3
1	0.60	0.09	0.31	3
3	0.11	0.13	0.76	3
3	0.10	0.06	0.84	3
2	0.11	0.51	0.39	2
3	0.09	0.08	0.83	3
3	0.12	0.32	0.56	2
3	0.09	0.22	0.69	3
3	0.09	0.06	0.85	3
3	0.16	0.31	0.52	2
1	0.65	0.13	0.22	1
2	0.02	0.95	0.03	2
3	0.22	0.08	0.70	3
3	0.13	0.19	0.67	3
3	0.43	0.13	0.44	3
2	0.06	0.76	0.18	2
3	0.10	0.42	0.48	2
3	0.28	0.15	0.57	3
3	0.21	0.19	0.60	3
2	0.02	0.93	0.05	2
3	0.06	0.06	0.88	3
1	0.83	0.06	0.12	1

belongingness of each country to different clusters. In addition, the crisp assignment of the countries to the clusters could also be obtained. The degree of belongingness of each cluster is represented by membership degrees (MD) or values and it can be utilised for managerial purpose. The membership degrees of the countries, respectively, ($C1$, $C2$,..., $C28$) with the corresponding fuzzy and crisp assignments were presented in Table 7.12.

According to the results provided in Table 7.12, k-means method assigned each country to only one cluster as it can be observed in the last column of the table. Similarly, the fuzzy approach produced a crisp cluster result and assigned each country to a specific cluster where the highest membership value occurs or a country belongs to a cluster the most (see the second column). However, fuzzy approach also gave information on belongingness of each country (membership degree values) to the available clusters. This belongingness shows the extent to which countries share the same features of a given cluster. The values marked bold indicate the highest belongingness of the countries, and there are various types of memberships in terms of degree of belongingness in the table. Firstly, some countries e.g., Austria, Chile and Ireland, are clearly closer to a single cluster than they are to any other cluster. Secondly, some countries share the characteristics or attributes of two clusters at almost the same degree or level (e.g., Norway and Spain). For a country to be considered, a member of more than one cluster surely depends on an alpha-cut (threshold) value. The determination of alpha-cut value is subjective on one hand. However, on the other hand, a certain rule can be developed. Fuzzy clustering literature assumes that a measure of $1/c$ can be taken into consideration as a threshold value for an object (country) to belong to a certain cluster. Alternatively, this alpha-cut value could be determined by taking into account the smallest value of the average membership of each cluster. The first alternative was taken into consideration in this study and the value of that measurement is set to 0.33. Therefore, if a cluster has a degree of membership for a specific object (country) more than 66% where three clusters exist, then it could be assumed that there is a crisp assignment to the corresponding cluster at a strong level.

Conclusion and Discussions

The main purpose of this study is to examine the relationships between energy consumption, CO_2 emission and economic growth for 28 OECD countries and to form clusters. It is carried out under the 1990–2010 period, considering the annual data, the average annual values for each country are calculated and the countries are grouped by taking into account the basic energy variables. The literature is rich; however, there is no clear consensus as to the existence of the relationship and its direction (positive or negative).

The scope of this chapter aims to reflect ecological approach via emphasising the fact that energy is one of the most needed factors of production that have great impact on production and investment. The CO_2 emission that is included in this relationship chain is also seen as the reflection of energy consumption and is also thought that depending on the rise in the emission, energy consumption increases and this process is interactive with economic growth. However, the quality of energy sources consumed by countries may affect the amount of emission. In other words, poor quality energy sources lead to high amount of emission. Therefore, a high emission amount may not always be an indication of a high-energy consumption in that country. That is why the grouping of countries based on their energy-related parameters or potential to export energy sources is insufficient in order to provide accurate macroevaluations, and a different opinion is needed. In this respect, as a result of the analyses, three different groups were formed based on the considered variables for the corresponding countries. While each group contains similar countries, some countries such as Norway and Spain are found to reflect multiple group characteristics. The countries that are located in the first group are Australia, Canada, Finland, Luxembourg, and the USA The second group countries are comprised of Chile, China, Greece, Mexico, Norway, Portugal, and Turkey. The third group countries are Austria, Belgium, Denmark, France, Germany, Ireland, Israel, New Zealand, Norway, Spain, Sweden, Switzerland, and the UK.

When countries are evaluated within their formed groups, none of the groups seem to form an accurate group based on geographical and regional structure. However, when it is considered that economic growth can be related to geographical proximity of the countries, the countries that are in close proximity can be placed into the same groups depending on the relevant variable. For instance, it is seen that Portugal and Turkey that are located in the second group are similar while the third group countries are the European countries that are relatively alike in terms of economic achievement. In addition, the vast majority of the grouped countries do not have underground energy sources, but their economic growth levels may show similarity depending on their economic development since they have the opportunity to establish robust and sustainable energy supply. The formation of the groups carried out by the analyses seem to be constructed realistically in terms of the corresponding energy supply potentials. It should be emphasised that especially fuzzy clustering-based groupings is in good accordance with real life and enables flexibility in forming groups. As stated earlier, a clear consensus as to the presence of relationship between energy consumption and CO_2 emission resulted from energy consumption, and economic growth does not exist. The findings of this study support this lack of consensus.

This study makes a major contribution to the relevant literature by splitting up the examined OECD countries into three groups to form more specific clustering, rendering to test the hypotheses in current empirical studies, and examining the short- and long-term relationships of the interacted variables for within and inter-cluster countries.

Keywords Definitions

Energy consumption: Energy consumption is the total energy consumed by end users.

CO_2 emission: It means the release of the gases into the atmosphere over a specified area and period of time.

Economic growth: Economic growth is an increase in the output level by a country over a certain period of time.

Fuzzy clustering: Fuzzy clustering is a method that divides data into overlapping groups according to a similarity or distance measurement.

References

Akarca, A. T., & Long, T. V. (1980). On the relationship between energy and GNP: A re-examination. *Journal of Energy Development, 5*, 326–331.

Akinlo, A. E. (2008). Energy consumption and economic growth: Evidence from 11 sub-Sahara African countries. *Energy Economics, 30*, 2391–2400.

Arabie, P., Carroll, J. D., DeSarbo, W., & Wind, J. (1981). Overlapping clustering: A new method for product positioning. *Journal of Marketing Research, 18*(3), 310–317.

Balakrishnan, P. V. S., Cooper, M. C., Jacob, V. S., & Lewis, P. A. (1996). Comparative performance of the FSCL neural net and k-means algorithm for market segmentation. *European Journal of Operational Research, 93*(2), 346–357.

Begum, R. A., Sohag, K., Abdullah, S. M. S., & Jaafar, M. (2015). CO_2 emissions, energy consumption, economic and population growth in Malaysia. *Renewable and Sustainable Energy Reviews, 41*, 594–601.

Bozoklu, S., & Yilanci, V. (2013). Energy consumption and economic growth for selected OECD countries: Further evidence from the Granger causality test in the frequency domain. *Energy Policy, 63*, 877–881.

Changchien, S. W., & Lu, T. Z. (2001). Mining association rules procedure to support on-line recommendation by customers and products fragmentation. *Expert Systems with Applications, 20*(4), 325–335.

Dagher, L., & Yacobian, T. (2012). The causal relationship between energy consumption and economic growth in Lebanon. *Energy Policy, 50*, 795–801.

Dergiades, T., Martinopoulos, G., & Tsoulfidis, L. (2013). Energy consumption and economic growth: Parametric and non-parametric causality testing for the case of Greece. *Energy Economics, 36*, 686–697.

Dimitriadou, E., Dolnicar, S., & Weingessel, A. (2002). An examination of indexes for determining the number of clusters in binary data sets. *Psychometrika, 67*(3), 137–160.

Dunn, J. C. (1974). Well-separated clusters and the optimal fuzzy partitions. *Journal of Cybernetics, 4*(1), 95–104.

Eggoh, J. C., Bangake, C., & Rault, C. (2011). Energy consumption and economic growth revisited in African countries. *Energy Policy, 39*, 7408–7421.

Erdal, G., Erdal, H., & Esengun, K. (2008). The causality between energy consumption and economic growth in Turkey. *Energy Policy, 36*, 3838–3842.

Gaspar, J. S., Marques, A. C., & Fuinhas, J. A. (2017). The traditional energy-growth nexus: A comparison between sustainable development and economic growth approaches. *Ecological Indicators, 75*, 286–296.

Giudici, P. (2003). *Applied data mining: Statistical methods for business and industry*. West Sussex: Wiley.

Hamit-Haggar, M. (2012). Greenhouse gas emissions, energy consumption and economic growth: A panel cointegration analysis from Canadian industrial sector perspective. *Energy Economics, 34*, 358–364.

Han, J., & Kamber, M. (2001). *Data mining: Concepts and techniques*. London: Academic.

Hand, D., Mannila, H., & Smyth, P. (2001). *Principles of data mining*. MIT Press: London.

Herrerias, M. J., Joyeux, R., & Girardin, E. (2013). Short- and long-run causality between energy consumption and economic growth: Evidence across regions in China. *Applied Energy, 112*, 1483–1492.

Höppner, F., Klawonn, F., Kruse, R., & Runkler, T. (1999). *Fuzzy cluster analysis: Methods for classification, data analysis and image recognition*. Chichester: Wiley.

Hsu, T., Chu, K., & Chan, H. (2000). *The fuzzy clustering on market segment*. Paper presented at the the 9th IEEE international conference on fuzzy systems and published at fuzzy systems, 2000 (pp. 621–626).

Hu, T., & Sheu, J. (2003). A fuzzy-based customer classification method for demand-responsive logistical distribution operations. *Fuzzy Sets and Systems, 139*(2), 431–459.

Jafari, Y., Othman, J., & Nor, A. H. S. M. (2012). Energy consumption, economic growth and environmental pollutants in Indonesia. *Journal of Policy Modeling, 34*, 879–889.

Jain, A. K., & Dubes, R. C. (1948). *Algorithms for clustering data*. Prentice Hall: New Jersey.

Kaufman, L., & Rousseeuw, P. J. (2005). *Finding groups in data: An introduction to cluster analysis*. New York: Wiley.

Kivyiro, P., & Arminen, H. (2014). Carbon dioxide emissions, energy consumption, economic growth, and foreign direct investment: Causality analysis for sub-Saharan Africa. *Energy, 74*, 595–606.

Kraft, J., & Kraft, A. (1978). On the relationship between energy and GNP. *Journal of Energy Development, 3*, 401–403.

Lin, B., & Wesseh, P. K. (2014). Energy consumption and economic growth in South Africa reexamined: A nonparametric testing approach. *Renewable and Sustainable Energy Reviews, 40*, 840–850.

Narayan, P. K., & Smyth, R. (2007). Energy consumption and real GDP in G7 countries: New evidence from panel cointegration with structural breaks. *Energy Economics, 30*, 2331–2341.

Nasreen, S., & Anwar, S. (2014). Causal relationship between trade openness, economic growth and energy consumption: A panel data analysis of Asian countries. *Energy Policy, 69*, 82–91.

Odhiambo, N. M. (2009). Energy consumption and economic growth nexus in Tanzania: An ARDL bounds testing approach. *Energy Policy, 37*(2), 617–622.

Omri, A. (2013). CO_2 emissions, energy consumption and economic growth nexus in MENA countries: Evidence from simultaneous equations models. *Energy Economics, 40*, 657–664.

Omri, A., & Kahouli, B. (2014). Causal relationships between energy consumption, foreign direct investment and economic growth: Fresh evidence from dynamic simultaneous-equations models. *Energy Policy, 67*, 913–922.

Ozturk, I., & Acaravcı, A. (2010). CO_2 emissions, energy consumption and economic growth in Turkey. *Renewable and Sustainable Energy Reviews, 14*, 3220–3225.

Pirlogea, C., & Cicea, C. (2012). Econometric perspective of the energy consumption and economic growth relation in European Union. *Renewable and Sustainable Energy Reviews, 16*, 5718–5726.

Rahman, M. M., & Mamun, S. A. K. (2016). Energy use, international trade and economic growth nexus in Australia: New evidence from an extended growth model. *Renewable and Sustainable Energy Reviews, 64*, 806–816.

Saboori, B., & Sulaiman, J. (2013). CO_2 emissions, energy consumption and economic growth in Association of Southeast Asian Nations (ASEAN) countries: A cointegration approach. *Energy, 55*, 813–822.

Saidi, K., & Hammami, S. (2015). The impact of energy consumption and CO_2 emissions on economic growth: Fresh evidence from dynamic simultaneous-equations models. *Sustainable Cities and Society, 14*, 178–186.

Saidi, K., Rahman, M. M., & Amamri, M. (2017). The causal nexus between economic growth and energy consumption: New evidence from global panel of 53 countries. *Sustainable Cities and Society, 33*, 45–56.

Salahuddin, M., & Gow, J. (2014). Economic growth, energy consumption and CO_2 emissions in Gulf Cooperation Council countries. *Energy, 73*, 44–58.

Sato-Ilic, M., & Jain, L. C. (2006). *Innovations in fuzzy clustering: Theory and applications*. Springer: Berlin.

Sebri, M., & Ben-Salha, O. (2014). On the causal dynamics between economic growth renewable energy consumption,CO_2 emissions and trade openness: Fresh evidence from BRICS countries. *Renewable and Sustainable Energy Reviews, 39*, 14–23.

Setnes, M. (2000). Supervised fuzzy clustering for rule extraction. *IEEE Transactions on Fuzzy Systems, 8*(4), 416–424.

Shahbaz, M., Van Hoang, T. H., Mahalik, M. K., & Roubaud, D. (2017). Energy consumption: Financial development and economic growth in India: New evidence from a nonlinear and asymmetric analysis. *Energy Economics, 63*, 199–212.

Shin, H. W., & Sohn, S. Y. (2004). Segmentation of stock trading customers according to potential value. *Expert Systems with Applications, 27*(1), 27–33.

Stern, P. C. (2000). Toward a coherent theory of environmentally significant behavior. *Journal of Social Issues, 56*(3), 407–424.

Tan, P., Steinbach, M., & Kumar, V. (2006). *Introduction to data mining*. Pearson Education: Boston.

Torkul, O., Cedimoglu, I. H., & Geyik, A. (2006). An application of fuzzy clustering to manufacturing cell design. *Journal of Intelligent and Fuzzy Systems, 17*(2), 173–181.

Wandji, Y. D. F. (2013). Energy consumption and economic growth: Evidence from Cameroon. *Energy Policy, 61*, 1295–1304.

Wolde-Rufael, Y. (2009). Energy consumption and economic growth: The experience of African countries revisited. *Energy Economics, 31*, 217–224.

Yang, M. (1993). A survey of fuzzy clustering. *Mathematical Computer Modelling, 18*(11), 1–16.

Yang, Z., & Zhao, Y. (2014). Energy consumption, carbon emissions, and economic growth in India: Evidence from directed acyclic graphs. *Economic Modelling, 38*, 533–540.

Yildirim, E., Sarac, S., & Aslan, A. (2012). Energy consumption and economic growth in the USA: Evidence from renewable energy. *Renewable and Sustainable Energy Reviews., 16*, 6770–6774.

Yu, S. H., & Choi, J. Y. (1985). The causal relationship between energy and GNP: An international comparison. *Journal of Energy Development, 10*, 249–272.

Chapter 8
The Determinants of Total Factor Productivity in European Union

Murat Akkaya and Deniz Güvercin

Abstract The aim of this study is to investigate the effect of construction sector on Total Factor Productivity (TFP) in European Union economy by using panel data analysis and analyzing cross-sectional data of 24 European Union countries for the period 2003–2014. To this end, building permits, house prices, and construction index are used to examine the effect of housing sector dynamics and construction sector productivity on the total factor productivity in the general economy. The aim of study is to explain variation in the TFP across countries by the intensity of construction sector activities. It is observed that the coefficients of changes in nominal house prices and building permits are positive, and they have significant relationship with TFP as the coefficient of construction index is negative. Positive coefficients of changes in nominal house prices and building permits support our model. Construction index that measures that how costly the construction activity is also expected to have negative parameters that imply that as construction activity becomes more costly the contribution to TFP growth becomes less. That is, house construction and permits and house demand have positive effects on total factor productivity.

Introduction

This study investigates whether activity level in the construction sector leads to TFP growth in the European Union economy. The primary concern isn't TFP in a construction sector. To this extent, it searches empirically the link between the size of construction industry and overall TFP growth.

Construction industry has specific role in initial phases of economic development. Almost all countries begin developing their economies by investing in construction industry particularly in infrastructure. Dynamics in the construction sector contributes to the general economic performance through house consumption, construction, and

M. Akkaya (✉) · D. Güvercin
Faculty of Economics and Administrative Sciences, T.C. İstanbul Arel Üniversitesi, Istanbul, Turkey
e-mail: muratakkaya@arel.edu.tr

© Springer International Publishing AG, part of Springer Nature 2018   171
H. Dincer et al. (eds.), *Global Approaches in Financial Economics, Banking, and Finance*, Contributions to Economics, https://doi.org/10.1007/978-3-319-78494-6_8

linkages with interconnected sectors. It contributes to the growth of interconnected sectors through forward and backward linkages and has significant contribution on employment, particularly creates job opportunities for unskilled and semi-skilled workers, and economic growth. From this particular view, if the price elasticity of house supply is high, then the increasing construction activity might lead to immigration, solve local unemployment problems, and generate more balanced economic development as well. If the construction activity in metropolitan cities is high, and there is sufficient housing supply as well as infrastructure, urbanization and structural economic transformation would boost. Therefore, construction activity containing house supply and infrastructure if sufficiently satisfy the demand for house and infrastructure, local labor would move from unproductive activities to productive, industrial activities and increase the competition in metropolitan local markets which prompt for skill accumulation that would prompt the economic transformation and TFP growth.

Furthermore, construction activity is characterized by labor market that is flexible. Because of the flexible labor market, firing and employing workers is easy which would prompt labor-saving technologies, reduce the shirking behavior, and brings new fresh workers more easily to the production line.

However, it is argued that (Yiu et al. 2004) the initial role of the construction boom in economic development diminishes in advanced stages because it is relatively inefficient in productivity improvement and capital accumulation. Additionally, Tse and Ganesan (1997) argue the contracting effects of the growing construction activities on the general economy: raising interest rates through putting pressures on credit demand, which crowds out more productive investment opportunities and reduce TFP level, additionally put pressure on general price level and raise inflation expectations. They also mention about the multiplier effect of the construction activity and high capacity of increasing GDP which would lead higher demand for construction activity that would increase the long-run stock of capital.

It is expected that because construction sector is the locomotive sector, it affects demand intensity in all inter-connected sectors and therefore TFP in the general economy. Infrastructural investment in development phase and in preceding stages of development increases overall efficiency so that TFP grows in general economy. Infrastructure is public good such as highways that decreases transportation cost so that competition between firms increases and the relevant blocks are eliminated on entrance to the markets; hence, infrastructure boom leads to TFP growth.

However, the overinvestment in construction sector might lead to misallocation of resources across sectors that might halt the economic growth and TFP growth. Borensztein and Lee (2002) reports that there are positive associations between economic growth and house price depreciations because of improvement in capital allocation efficiency. Benjamin and Meza (2009) reports that a reallocation of resources towards low productivity sectors following the 1997 Korean Crisis resulted in a fall in TFP. Therefore, they argue that as the economic activity in the construction sector decreases it would imply higher TFP growth. This chapter investigates whether intensity in construction industry implies TFP growth or not.

The main findings in the literature on the TFP argue that technological intensity in production-labor saving technology, the speed of change in technological dimension of capital goods which is regarded as technological progress, the intensity of ICT and human capital prompt TFP growth in general economy, and sectoral TFPs with different degrees. Ruddock (2006) reports that in the USA and the UK, the ICT investment level is lower in construction sector than industry which they argue is due to "under financed" firms. Human capital usage level in the construction industry relatively, and particularly its absorption capacity of female human capital, is very limited. Human capital is stock of knowledge of labor force which can be increased through training and education that can keep up with technological advancements in the world. In construction sector, the education opportunities and R&D possibilities and knowledge externalities are lower than services and industry or energy sectors which restrict the human capital stock in the general economy. Therefore, the level of labor-saving technological advancement so that TFP growth would be limited.

Slowing down or boosting up of sectoral innovation such as advancement in building techniques or sticking with old fashioned building practices would affect TFP growth in construction sector. Furthermore, secular decline in labor skills, education and qualifications would diminish the TFP growth in construction sector, thus, TFP in general economy. Thus, if increase in the size of the construction industry implies that the size of the less efficient and productive sectors diminishes where the technological advancement is slower and qualification and skill acquisition of labor is lower, the TFP growth in general economy would get higher. In other words, if the increase in the size of construction sector drives structural transformation where the less efficient sectors drain, then construction industry leads high TFP growth in the general economy.

Additionally, an increase in TFP growth might get housing prices up which would increase investment level in construction industry which would then result in more TFP growth. In this circular relation, TFP growth affects construction sector beforehand. However, particularly before crisis, before the burst of housing bubbles, the misallocation of resources might block TFP growth in general economy that cuts the circular relation.

Literature

There are researches in the literature focusing on the calculation of TFP growth in construction industry. Zhi et al. (2003) used Jorgensen's method to calculate TFP growth rates in Singapore construction sector. Choy et al. (2015) calculated TFP growth in construction sector of Malaysia, and they figured out that more advanced building practices in the construction sector lead to TFP growth in the period of 1998–2012. Navaratna and Jayawardane (2007) uses Tornqvist method to calculate TFP growth in Sri Lanka's construction sector. Fan and Yu (2016) measure the TFP of Chinese construction sector and estimate the TFP index and its decomposition (technical efficiency, scale effects, allocative efficiency) by Stochastic Frontier

Analysis. Abdel-Wahab and Vogl (2011) compared productivity growth in construction sector of Europe, the USA, and Japan and report that labor productivity in construction is lower than industry sector in Europe, the USA, and Japan which they claim that is the result of poor TFP growth in construction sector compared to industry. Chau (2009) investigated sources of TFP growth in Hong Kong building industry that they argue are technology transfer and real interest changes. Koike and Wada (2013) calculated TFP for Japanese construction sector and other sectors and report that construction sector's TFP declines for the period examined. They also compare firms operating in Japanese construction sector in terms of TFPs and report that high level TFP firms experience rise whereas low level firms experience fall in TFPs. Goodrum and Haas (2004) examines 200 construction activities in the USA from 1976 to 1998 and report that activities experiencing significant changes in equipment technology have greater long-term improvements in labor productivity. Wang et al. (2013) measured Chinese construction sector's TFP through DEA-Malmquist index and investigated spatial differences in the construction industry TFP through spatial clustering analyses. Allen (1985) argues that productivity decline in the US from 1968 to 1978 by 8.8% results from a shift in the mix of output from large scale commercial, industrial, and institutional projects to single family houses.

There are very few studies focusing on the construction sector's impact on productivity in general economy. Moro and Nuño (2011) investigated the role of differences in TFP growth in construction sector and the general economy. To this end, they employed growth accounting methods by which they reveal the effect of TFP growth differential between construction and general economy on construction prices. They show that TFP growth differential between construction sector and general economy explains the boom in construction prices for the USA and Germany. García-Santana et al. (2016) have comparative study on sectors' effect on TFP level in Spain argue that misallocation of resources particularly towards construction sector reduces potential TFP which is more than misallocation in other sectors. Valence (2011) emphasizes the vivid role of construction sector in creating knowledge externalities and negligible potential of laying ground for technological advancement in general economy so that low potential of generating significant TFP growth in general economy. The literature is biased against the calculation of TFP in construction sector; this study is the first attempt to empirically evaluate the effect of construction sector on the TFP in general economy.

Data and Methodology

Variables

Before giving theoretic details about calculation of TFP, it is discussed that why TFP growth is the focus in this study other than some other productivity measure. Productivity can be measured simply by taking ratio of output to single inputs. To illustrate, labor productivity is a ratio of output to labor used. This measurement of productivity does not take an account of composition of inputs and effect of change in quality and quantity of inputs together. For example, increasing the number of machines in the production process would increase labor productivity which is not captured by Single Productivity measurement. For example, Single Productivity measurement does not give details about the underlying causes of labor productivity differences in two production processes even if they have same production technology. One producer may face with lower capital prices which renders its production more capital intensive resulting in higher labor productivity. However, TFP, which is also called as multifactor productivity, measurement does not depend on intensity of observable factors. Under TFP measurement, relative price change does not induce production increase and thus isoquant shift, but it induces movement along isoquant.

Productivity growth may occur with changes in allocative efficiency and technical efficiency. Allocative efficiency refers to the input combination giving minimum cost. The maximum amount of output by input combination means technical efficiency. In order to measure productivity growth, scholars used different estimation methods such as Stochastic Frontier Analysis, Productivity Index, and Data Envelopment Analysis (Carson and Abbott 2012). Further theoretical information regarding theory of production indexes can be found in Caves et al. (1982).

Rather than partial productivity measures referred in the beginning, TFP takes the substitutability of inputs into account. TFP, namely, measures technological advancement that is regarded as an improvement in the efficiency in usage of all inputs. TFP indexes, Tornqvist Index is accepted by majority of scholars, are based on the calculation of a ratio (total aggregate output quantity index/a total aggregate input quantity index). TFP growth implies the movement of production possibility frontier further without any increase in the amount of inputs. TFP growth is driven by finding new advanced techniques and regulations of production and institutions that enhance efficiency of inputs. As it is explained below it is residual which is unexplained part of economic growth after taking into account of growth in inputs. Economic growth, therefore, can be sustained without having input growth by TFP growth which is driven by innovation and invention, know-how, efficient management methods, and advancement in Information Technologies.

Dependent variable is TFP growth whereas the independent variables are construction index, changes nominal housing prices, building permits along with control variables. Construction index reflects the input price level in construction sector.

Total Factor Productivity

Robert Solow (1956) is first in literature to discuss total factor productivity (TFP). He defines TFP as follows (Adak 2009):

$$Y = A(t) * F * [K(t), \ L(t)] \qquad (8.1)$$

Y: Aggregate production,
A: the factor neutral shifter (TFP in this framework),
K: Physical capital,
L: Labor force.

Technological progress influences the whole production function as shown in Eq. (8.1). Function can be shown in terms of growth rates by taking differences of Eq. (8.1):

$$\frac{\dot{Y}_t}{Y} = \frac{\dot{A}_t}{A} + \frac{F_K}{F[K(t), L(t)]} \dot{K}_t + \frac{F_L}{F[K(t), L(t)]} \dot{L}_t \qquad (8.2)$$

where F_K and F_L are the marginal products of capital and labor, respectively. Using (8.1) in Eq. (8.2) gives us the following:

$$\frac{\dot{Y}_t}{Y} = \frac{\dot{A}_t}{A} + \frac{A_t F_K K_t}{Y_t} \frac{\dot{K}_t}{K} + \frac{A_t F_L L_t}{Y_t} \frac{\dot{L}_t}{L} \qquad (8.3)$$

In a competitive market, the factors are paid according to their marginal product. Return to capital is (r-interest rate)

$$\frac{dY}{dK} = A\frac{dF}{dK} = AF_K = r \qquad (8.4)$$

Return to labor (w-wage)

$$\frac{dY}{dL} = A\frac{dF}{dL} = AF_L = w \qquad (8.5)$$

Using (8.4) and (8.5) in (8.3) gives the following:

$$\frac{\dot{Y}_t}{Y} = \frac{\dot{A}_t}{A} + r\frac{K_t}{Y_t} \frac{\dot{K}_t}{K} + w\frac{L_t}{Y_t} \frac{\dot{L}_t}{L} \qquad (8.6)$$

$s_k = r\frac{K_t}{Y_t}$ is the share of physical capital income in total income.
$s_l = w\frac{L_t}{Y_t}$ is a part of labor income in total income.

The sum of s_k and s_l equals to 1 in constant return to scale production.

$$\frac{\dot{Y}_t}{Y} = \frac{\dot{A}_t}{A} + s_k\frac{\dot{K}_t}{K} + s_l\frac{\dot{L}_t}{L} \qquad (8.7)$$

A is TFP. TFP is part of output not explained by observed inputs.

There are two methods of estimation for TFP. First method is regressing the output to factors of production and residual (TFP term with constant coefficient) can be used to gauge TFP (due to constant is common for all units). Another approach that can be taken is estimating the input elasticities by making constant returns to scale and perfect competition assumptions. Under these assumptions, first-order conditions link the factor shares to input elasticities which can be calculated from real data, and TFP can be calculated by using found input elasticities in production function.

In Firm level, one of the determinants of the TFP growth is the managerial practice; manager combines the inputs and coordinates the production process; therefore, the managerial expertise in maintaining optimal production results in sustaining TFP growth. Bushnell and Wolfram (2009) find that performance of the managers in power plant firms affects performance of the power plant firm. Human capital factor is also effective in determining the size of TFP. Ilmakunnas and others (2004) use Finnish worker-plant data to show that productivity is increasing in workers' education and age. Capital can be in intangible form such as know-how, reputation, loyal customer base which would affect the efficiency and TFP (Syverson 2011). ICT usage as explained before is one of the significant source of the TFP growth that Bloom and others (2012) emphasized that human capital interacts with the ICT that affect TFP growth.

Dacy (1965) made the first contribution of explaining the sources of labor productivity in the construction sector: increase in capital per worker, shifts in the construction production mix, shifts in the geographical distribution of construction, increase in the corporate shares in the contract construction, and the declining average age of construction workers. Stokes (1981) and Allen (1985) examined the causes of productivity decline in the USA between 1968–1978 by focusing on economies of scale, labor quality, capital–labor ratio, and the percentage of unionized workers. However, significant amount of productivity growth is not accounted by these factors that they argue that can be attributable to the factors such as R&D expenditure and technological progress. R&D expenditure moves the technology absorption capacity and frontier forward which eases the adoption of technology originated outside. Kendrick (1981) argues that three factors affect technology progress:

- Domestic R&D outlays.
- Changes in average age of fixed capital goods.
- Rate of international technology transfer.

Construction technology is related to construction methods, work task particularly: materials, equipment technology, techniques, and information systems. These methods are used in constructing, designing, planning, and maintaining buildings and infrastructure (Ofori 1994). The TFP level in the construction sector is also related with whether new construction is more weighed than maintenance and repair construction since the latter generally has relatively low productivity.

Additionally, the construction sector is very deeply connected with other sectors through input linkages; hence, technological progress particularly equipment and information technology developed in the construction industry would affect other industries and be affected from them. Bernard and others (2010) argue that more variation and type of products produced by firm, the more TFP can be generated. Because construction sector has significant backward linkages, variation in materials, and equipment and products in these input providing sectors would increase the product variation in the construction sector and increase TFP growth.

Construction technology can spill over other sectors through subcontracting, licensing, training, trade, joint venture, international technology transfer, and replacement of capital goods (Kendrick 1981). Furthermore, if the constructions are replaced rapidly, more advanced technology intensive constructions would be built which would affect technology progress in general and affect positively TFP growth. Additionally, energy prices and inflation rate affect the technological investment, capital formation and TFP growth rate in the construction sector and in an economy.

Other factors affecting TFP can be the institutional structure and dynamics which affect the cost and profit levels. Therefore, efficiency through cost minimization, incentive structure that economic actors find that investing in technology is profitable, can be sustained through well-established institution structures. Legal structure and property rights define particular characteristics of the institutional structure that affect the physical and human capital investment level, level of competition among economic players that affect efficiency level.

Construction Index (CI)

There is strong link between TFP in construction sector and construction prices. Moro and Nuño (2011) argue that surge in construction prices with sluggish growth in TFP in construction sector relative to TFP growth in general economy is an empirically supported fact. However, this study focuses on the role of construction cost on the TFP. With regard to principle of duality in production theory; the cost function determines the transformation of inputs into outputs so that technological capacity. Construction input prices index is used as a proxy for the cost function (translog cost function can be used to estimate TFP).

By construction price indices, one can follow changes in the prices of both inputs or outputs of construction activity. But, price indices terminology for construction activity differs between countries.[1]

Changes in Nominal House Prices (HP)

House price appreciations might lead to overinvestment in housing construction which would decrease the available funds left to be used in other industries. House price bubble thus creates imperfect resource allocation where the marginal revenues

---

[1]https://stats.oecd.org/glossary/detail.asp?ID=5851

can be increased after reallocating resources from housing construction to services or industry which would increase TFP growth. Therefore, house price needs to be considered to explain variation in TFP growth.

It is a percentage change and computed annually by using house price indices. Nominal house prices indices also show changes in house prices for a given period. Nominal house prices indices consist of data of a number of countries collected by Eurostat (EMF HYPOSTAT 2015).

House price indices measure inflation in the property market of a country. It reflects price changes of all new and existing residential property bought by households including flats, detached houses and terraced houses, etc. HPI includes only market prices. Therefore, self-build dwellings are out of consideration. Also, land component of the residential property is added. House price indices are sum of results obtained from National Statistical Institutes. NSIs conduct these works by the framework of the owner-occupied housing pilot project under Eurostat coordination.

Building Permits (BP)

"A building permit is an authorization to start work on a building project. As such, a permit is the final stage of planning and building authorizations from public authorities, prior to the start of work. In Hypostat, the building permit concerns only dwellings."[2] By building permits, cities, town, and municipalities enforce their building codes to satisfy the minimum safety. The standards are updated every few years as new building equipment, materials, and techniques are introduced.

The content of the building codes is highly related to construction supply. If the building permits involve high land and building methods restrictions, then it would discourage investors and cut off number of construction projects which would increase house prices and reduce the speed of adjustment of the construction sector against demand and cost shocks. As argued above, such an effect would reduce the variety of products the sector produced and reduce TFP in general economy.

Economic Freedom Index (EFI)

Economic freedom explains the protection of private property rights and the freedom of voluntary transactions (Gwartney et al. 1996). James Gwartney defines Economic Freedom as: "Individuals have economic freedom when property they acquire without the use of force, fraud, or theft is protected from physical invasions by others and they are free to use, exchange, or give their property as long as their actions do not violate the identical rights of others. An index of economic freedom should measure the extent to which rightly acquired property is protected and individuals are engaged in voluntary transactions."

---

[2]EMF HYPOSTAT (2015), **a.g.e.**

The goal of economic freedom is not simply an absence of government coercion or constraint. It is also the creation and maintenance of a mutual sense of liberty for all. The index of economic freedom takes a comprehensive view of economic freedom.[3]

The index of economic freedom is constructed through analysis of 10 specific components of economic freedom, which are grouped for ease of reference into four key categories or pillars.

• Rule of law (property rights, freedom from corruption).
• Limited government (fiscal freedom, government spending).
• Regulatory efficiency (business freedom, labor freedom, monetary freedom).
• Open markets (trade freedom, investment freedom, financial freedom).

Some of the 10 components are themselves composites of additional quantifiable measures. Each of the 10 economic freedoms is graded on a scale from 0 to 100. The 10 component scores are equally weighted and averaged to get an overall economic freedom score for each economy."

Foreign Direct Investment (FDI)

FDI is change in ownership of a company in another country by purchasing an asset or a significant amount of stock. By foreign direct investment, firms acquire continuing interest in and virtual control over another firm in a country. Foreign direct investment has an important role in modern economy. It is obvious that foreign direct investment has significant relation with factor productivity and income growth for host countries. Particularly, technological gap between domestic firms and multinational corporations get reduced by FDI which increases productivity in the host country.

Control Variables

Gross Domestic Products (GDP) To control the level of GDP across countries which affect certain development indicators such as the level of infrastructure, life expectancy, and child mortality, the level of quality of education in the economy is included.

Trade Openness The trade-to-GDP ratio is an indicator of the relative importance of international trade in the economy of a country. It is used as a measure of the economic openness of a country. Trade is one of the mechanisms that can close technological gap between countries. Additionally, competition between domestic and foreign firms on global markets pushes the domestic firms to apply cost efficient production techniques which involve costly installments.

Polity2 "The polity2 coding rules for the creation of what seems to be a measure of the level of democracy and produce democracy scores for some affected country years that lack face validity." (Plümper and Neumayer 2010). Current level of technology

---

[3]http://www.heritage.org/index/pdf/2016/book/index_2016.pdf, pp. 21–24.

and technological progress is endogenous to institutional factors. Rodrik (2000) argues that economic institutions are endogenous to the deeper political parameters such as whether the society is governed by dictatorship or democracy. It is obvious that in dictatorships to satisfy the sustainment of power, the dictator would keep the power groups in check so that economic power and technological capacities would be under check by the dictator. In democracy where the separation of powers are enforced by law, the capacity of installing technological facilities, equipment, and applying cutting-edge production methods is not restricted and feasible. Additionally, citizens that are not under any political powers' pressure would give feedbacks and more insightful information regarding institutional quality, technological capacity of the economic organizations which is almost completely free of political biasedness, and fear from political regime. Therefore, TFP levels would differ across countries that have different political regimes and the quality of democracy.

Population Boserup (1981) and Simon (2014) claim that productivity resulting from innovation, invention, creating economies of scale, and specialization stems from population growth. Even though greater population growth means less capital per worker, the greater the pool of information about technological methods of production, the greater the variety of communication channels which would increase population growth would result in rapid circulation of technique knowledge, increase in stock of knowledge that would give high TFP growth.

Internet Usage Jorgenson et al. (2006) argues that increase in TFP speeding up in USA is dominated by industries using information technology creatively and inno-vatively. Internet usage does not just accelarate the dissemination of technical knowledge but also increase the exposure to market competition through advertise-ments which would give more efficient and continuously updated production methods, equipment technology, and so higher total factor productivity.

Data

Total factor productivity (TFP),[4] construction index (CI), changes in nominal house prices (HP),[5] building permits (BP) (Gwartney et al. 1996), economic freedom index (EFI),[6] foreign direct investment (FDI),[7] gross domestic products (GDP) (Plümper and Neumayer 2010), trade openness (TO) (Plümper and Neumayer 2010), polity2,[8] population (Plümper and Neumayer 2010), loans to GDP (Gwartney et al. 1996), and

---

[4]Total Factor Productivity (TFP) data has been gathered from TED Economy Database via The conference Board.

[5]Changes in nominal house prices (HP), building permits (BP), and loans to GDP data from EMF HYPOSTAT (2015).

[6]Economic Freedom Index data from CESifo Group Munich's official site.

[7]Foreign direct investment, gross domestic products, trade openness, population, and internet user data from The World Bank DataBank.

[8]Polity2 data from http://www.systemicpeace.org/polity/polity4.htm.

internet user (Plümper and Neumayer 2010) have been included in analysis in the study.

This study investigates relationship between TFP growth and construction in a sample of 24 countries[9] in European Union over the period 2003–2014. Countries with poor data collection are excluded.

Annual changes in data covering 2003–2014 period which includes 3.456 observations, considering data limitations is used.

Methodology

This study uses balanced panel regression model shown below in examining determinants of TFP:

$$\text{TFP}_{it} = \alpha_0 + \beta_1 \text{CI}_{it} + \beta_2 \text{HP}_{it} + \beta_3 \text{BP}_{it} + \sum_{m=1}^{M} \gamma_m X_{mit} + \mu_i + \lambda_t + \varepsilon_t$$

In the model,

i = country index,
t = time index,
TFP = total factor productivity of capital and labor,
CI = construction index,
HP = changes in nominal house prices.
BP = building permits.
X = usual vector of control variables.

In the robustness checks, the baseline model is extended to include control for gross domestic products (GDP), trade openness (TRADE), polity2, population, and internet user (Internet).

Model includes country fixed effects μ_i to find omitted factors stemming from country's specific situation that are relatively stable over time. Model also uses time dummies, λ_t, to consider individual and time effects over all countries in a given period. M indicates the number of control variables used in the model.

Endogeneity

An endogeneity problem takes place when an explanatory variable is correlated with the error term. Endogeneity can occur as a result of measurement error, autoregression with autocorrelated errors, simultaneous causality (Instrumental variable), and omitted variables. There are two common causes: an uncontrolled confounder causing both independent and

---

[9]EU contries: Austria, Belgium, Czech Republic, Denmark, Estonia, Finland, France, Germany, Greece, Hungary, Ireland, Italy, Latvia, Lithuania, Luxembourg, the Netherlands, Poland, Portugal, Slovak Republic, Slovenia, Spain, Sweden, Turkey, and the UK.

dependent variables of a model and a loop of causality between the independent and dependent variables of a model. (Wooldridge 2013)

There are two solutions offered in the literature to the endogeneity problem: structural specification and instrumental variables. In structural specification: additional equations are specified that can explain the correlation between independent variables and error term. Second approach is instrumental variables approach that involves adding dependent variables correlated with original dependent variables but not error term into the model. Using instrumental variables enable estimation of model through ordinary least square methods, because estimated parameters become consistent. (Greene 2012).

Sargan Test and Davidson–Mac Kinnon Test can be used to test the endogeneity and the exogeneity of regressors. Sargan test determines overall quality of adjustment and of instruments's relevance.

Davidson and MacKinnon (1993) test for the presence of endogeneity is used. Davidson and MacKinnon form an augmented regression test including residuals of each endogenous right-hand side variable in a regression of the original model as a function of all exogenous variables (Davidson and MacKinnon 1993).

There is endogeneity problem in construction index variable on estimated model. The endogeneity of the CI variables creates an econometric issue. CI variables are treated as endogenous using first degree lagged values instead of contemporaneous values to control for this endogeneity problem.

Cross-Sectional Dependence

Particularly following financial integration of countries, countries experience economic common shocks and countries spatially close; group of countries affected by the same unobservable common factors also perform the same particular pattern which results in cross-sectional dependence. It is first necessary to determine whether cross-sectional dependency exists.

Cross-sectional dependence in the error term of the estimated model leads inconsistent coefficient estimates if independent variables are correlated with the unspecified common variables or shocks. (Pesaran 2007).

Breusch and Pagan (1980) test is used for testing cross-sectional dependence when time dimension (T) is larger than cross-section dimension (N). However, when time dimension is lower than cross-section dimension $T < N$, then Breusch and Pagan (1980) test does not have desirable statistical properties. Friedman and Pesaran's CD test is used for this purpose to test the presence of cross-sectional dependence. Cross-sectional dependence is not observed on our estimated model. So one of the first generation unit root tests can be applicable.

Peseran's CD test can be followed along the following lines:

Standard panel data model follows as

$$y_{it} = \alpha_i + \beta' x_{it} + u_{it}, \quad i = 1, \ldots, N \text{ and } T = 1, \ldots, N$$

Null hypothesis is.

1. u_{it} is assumed to be independent and identically distributed (i.i.d.) over time periods.
2. across cross-sectional units.

Alternative hypothesis emphasizes that u_{it} may be correlated across cross-sections. However no serial-correlation assumption remains.

$$H_0 = \rho_{ij} = \rho_{ji} = \text{cor}(u_{it}, u_{jt}) = 0 \text{ for } i \neq j$$

vs.

$$H_1 = \rho_{ij} = \rho_{ji} = \text{cor}(u_{it}, u_{jt}) \neq 0 \text{ for some } i \neq j$$

where ρ_{ij} is correlation coefficient of the disturbances

$$\rho_{ij} = \rho_{ji} = \frac{\sum_{t=1}^{T} u_{it}.u_{jt}}{\left(\sum_{t=1}^{T} u^2_{it}\right)^{1/2} \left(\sum_{t=1}^{T} u^2_{jt}\right)^{1/2}}$$

$$CD = \sqrt{\frac{2}{N(N-1)}} \left(\sum_{i=1}^{N-1} \sum_{j=i+1}^{N} \sqrt{T_{ij}}\widehat{\rho}_{ij}\right)$$

where T_{ij} is the number of common time series observations between units i and j.

Null hypothesis suggests no cross-sectional dependence. That is, $CD \xrightarrow{d} N(0,1)$ for $N \to \infty$ where T is sufficiently large.

Unit Root Test

Cross-sectional dependence can lead to serious problems testing the null hypothesis that all variables are non-stationary. Since cross-sectional dependence is not observed in estimated model, Levin–Lin–Chu unit root test as the first generation test is applied.

Xtunitroot command of Stata in panel datasets is used to testing unit roots or stationarity. Harris–Tzavalis (1999), Breitung (2000; Breitung and Das 2005), Fisher-type (Choi 2001), Levin–Lin–Chu (2002), and Im–Pesaran–Shin (2003) tests examine the existence of stationary in panel data analysis. These tests have null hypothesis, that is, variables contain a unit root.

Unit root test, Levin–Lin–Chu, shows that time series data of all variables are stationary at 1% significancy level. Levin–Lin–Chu test works well and has significant power if time dimension is between 5 and 250 and cross-section dimension is between 10 and 250, and it relies critically on the absence of cross-sectional dependence (Baltagi 2013).

Empirical Analysis

This study examines the effects of construction index (CI), changes in nominal house prices (HP), and building permits (BP) on total factor productivity using panel techniques. Also, it examines the effects of economic freedom index (EFI), foreign direct investment (FDI), gross domestic products (GDP), trade openness (TO), polity2, population, loans to GDP, and internet ser1 data as control variables on TFP.

Results

The model involves two econometric problems. The first one comes from correlation between the error term and plus the variables resulting from the dynamic nature of the data. Furthermore, test statistic indicates the presence of auto correlation. The second issue results from heteroskedasticity of the explanatory variables. Generalized method of moments (GMM) which is introduced by Hansen (1982) implements orthogonality conditions to allow for efficient estimation in which heteroscedasticity exists. Under the heteroskedasticity, GMM estimator is more efficient. Additionally, in previous stages, it is determined that the construction index is endogenous regressor. To deal with endogeneity, lagged values of Construction Index is included into the model which is estimated by Arellano–Bond GMM difference estimator. Additionally, there are unobservable country time invariant fixed effects that may be correlated with regressors. Arellano and Bond (1991) developed two-step system generalized method of moments (GMM) that takes into account these problems in this study.

The model results are presented in Table 8.1.

The coefficients of the GMM show that there is significant relation in annual changes between construction index (CI), changes in nominal house prices (HP), building permits (BP) and total factor productivity. The coefficient of construction Index (CI) is negative. In the model, positive relation is expected. But negative relation is observed. This negative coefficient may occur due to taking first difference of construction index (CI) to get rid of endogeneity. Because of the coefficients of changes in nominal house prices (HP), building permits (BP) are positive and they have significant relationship with TFP.

Table 8.1 GMM two-step results

GMM two step		
	Wald chi	3234.88
	Prob > Chi^2	0.0000
	Statistics	**P-value**
CI L1	−8.5716	0.0000
HP	0.1437	0.0000
BP	2.1187	0.0000

Table 8.2 GMM two-step results with control variables

GMM two step			
	Wald chi		1603
	Prob > Chi^2		0.0000
	Statistics		**P-value**
CI L1	−8.4465		0.0200
FDI L1	−0.1742		0.0450
Internet L1	8.2064		0.0200

Table 8.3 Arellano–Bond test results

Order	z	Prob > z
Arellano-bond test		
1	−3.1360	0.0170
2	−1.7871	0.0739

Table 8.2 presents our model results with control variables.

The coefficients of the GMM with control variables show that there is significant relation only between total factor productivity and construction index (CI), foreign direct investment (FDI), and internet users. The coefficient of construction index (CI) is again negative. In the model, any significant relationship with other instrumental variables is observed. The robustness of TFP results with instrumental variables is examined and there is observable relationship.

Robustness

The robustness of TFP results using Arellano–Bond test and Sargan test is shown in Table 8.3.

Sargan test.

Ho: Overidentifiying restrictions.

$$Chi^2(19) = 20.5903$$
$$Prob > Chi^2 = 0.3599$$

Conclusion

TFP literature that examines the construction activity is not very exhausting all the relations involved. Particularly, scholars search for techniques of calculating TFP and using techniques referred in the literature to calculate TFP levels in construction activity. There are very few studies relating TFP growth in general economy and the indicators of the construction activity. This study is the first attempt of evaluating

TFP growth in general economy in terms of influence of construction activity. It includes set of indicators that measure the construction activity at different dimensions. Cross-sectional data for a panel of 24 European Union countries for the period 2003–2014 is analyzed in order to observe the relationship between Construction Index, Changes in Nominal House Prices, and Building Permits on total factor productivity.

Two-step GMM system approach is applied to deal with heteroscedasticity and endogeneity across regressors and error term problems. It is observed that the coefficients of changes in nominal house prices and building permits are positive, and they have significant relationship with TFP as the coefficient of construction index is negative. Positive coefficients of changes in nominal house prices and building permits supports in model. In the model, positive relation is expected. But negative relation is observed. This negative coefficient may occur due to taking first difference of construction index (CI) to get rid of endogeneity. Because the coefficients of changes in nominal house prices (HP) and building permits (BP) are positive and they have significant relationship with TFP. That is, house construction and permits and house demand has positive effects on total factor productivity. Construction index that measures that how costly the construction activity is also expected to have negative parameters that imply that as construction activity becomes more costly, the contribution to TFP growth becomes less.

References

Abdel-Wahab, M., & Vogl, B. (2011). Trends of productivity growth in the construction industry across Europe, US and Japan. *Construction Management and Economics, 29*(6), 635–644.

Adak, M. (2009). Total factor productivity and economic growth. *İstanbul Ticaret Üniversitesi Sosyal Bilimler Dergisi, 8*(15), 49–56.

Allen, S. (1985). *Why construction industry productivity is declining* (NBER Working Paper No. 1555).

Arellano, M., & Bond, S. (1991). Some tests of specification for panel data: Monte Carlo evidence and an application to employment equations. *The Review of Economic Studies, 58*, 277–297.

Baltagi, B. H. (2013). *Econometric analysis of panel data* (5th ed.). West Sussex: Wiley.

Benjamin, D., & Meza, F. (2009). Total factor productivity and labor reallocation: The case of the Korean 1997 crisis. *The BE Journal of Macroeconomics, 9*(1), 1–41.

Bernard, A. B., Redding, S. J., & Schott, P. K. (2010). Multiple-product firms and product switching. *American Economic Review, 100*(1), 70–97.

Bloom, N., Floetotto, M., Jaimovich, N., Saporta-Eksten, I., & Terry, S. J. (2012). *Really uncertain business cycles* (No. w18245). National Bureau of Economic Research.

Borensztein, E., & Lee, J.-W. (2002). Financial crisis and credit crunch in Korea: Evidence from firmlevel data. *Journal of Monetary Economics, 49*, 853–875.

Boserup, E. (1981). *Population and technological change: A study of lone-term trends*. Chicago: University of Chicago Press.

Breitung, J. (2000). The local power of some unit root tests for panel data. In B. H. Baltagi (Ed.), *Nonstationary panels, panel cointegration and dynamic panels* (pp. 161–177). Amsterdam: Elsevier.

Breitung, J., & Das, S. (2005). Panel unit root tests under cross-sectional dependence. *Statistica Neerlandica, 59*(4), 414–433.

Breusch, T. S., & Pagan, A. R. (1980). The Lagrange multiplier test and its applications to model specification in econometrics. *The Review of Economic Studies, 47*(1), 239–253.

Bushnell, J. B., & Wolfram, C. (2009). The guy at the controls: Labor quality and power plant efficiency. In *International differences in the business practices and productivity of firms.* Chicago: University of Chicago Press.

Carson, C., & Abbott, M. (2012). A review of productivity analysis of the New Zealand construction industry. *Construction Economics and Building, 12*(3), 1–15.

Caves, D. W., Laurits, R. C., & Diewert, W. E. (1982). The economic theory of index numbers and the measurement of input, output, and productivity. *Econometrica, 50*(6), 1393–1414.

Chau, K. W. (2009). Explaining total factor productivity trend in building construction: Empirical evidence from Hong Kong. *International Journal of Construction Management, 9*(2), 45–54.

Choi, I. (2001). Unit root tests for panel data. *Journal of International Money and Finance, 20*(2), 249–272.

Choy, C. F., Skitmore, M., & Yan Yan, F. Y. (2015). *Total factor productivity in the Malaysian construction sector.* In 21st Annual Pacific-Rim Real Estate Society Conference, Malaysia.

Dacy, D. C. (1965). Productivity and price trends in construction since 1947. *The Review of Economics and Statistics, 47*, 406–411.

Davidson, R., & MacKinnon, J. G. (1993). *Estimation and inference in econometrics.* Canada: Oxford University Press.

EMF HYPOSTAT. (2015). *A review of Europe's mortgage and housing markets.* European Mortgage Federation.

Fan, J., & Yu, X. (2016). *Total factor productivity growth of China's construction industry: A stochastic frontier approach.* In International Conference on Construction and Real Estate Management.

García-Santana, M., Moral-Benito, E., Pijoan-Mas, J., & Ramos, R. (2016). *Growing like Spain: 1995-2007* (Banco De Espana Documentos de Trabajo No. 1609).

Goodrum, P. M., & Haas, C. T. (2004). Long-term impact of equipment technology on labor productivity in the US construction industry at the activity level. *Journal of Construction Engineering and Management, 130*(1), 124–133.

Greene, W. H. (2012). *Econometric analysis* (7th ed.). London: Pearson Education.

Gwartney, J. D., Lawson, R., & Block, W. (1996). *Economic freedom of the world, 1975–1995.* Vancouver: The Fraser Institute.

Hansen, L. P. (1982). Large sample properties of generalized method of moments estimators. *Econometrica: Journal of the Econometric Society, 50*, 1029–1054.

Harris, R. D., & Tzavalis, E. (1999). Inference for unit roots in dynamic panels where the time dimension is fixed. *Journal of Econometrics, 91*(2), 201–226.

Ilmakunnas, P., Maliranta, M., & Vainiomäki, J. (2004). The roles of employer and employee characteristics for plant productivity. *Journal of Productivity Analysis, 21*(3), 249–276.

Im, K. S., Pesaran, M. H., & Shin, Y. (2003). Testing for unit roots in heterogeneous panels. *Journal of Econometrics, 115*(1), 53–74.

Jorgenson, D. W., Ho, M., & Stiroh, K. (2006). *The sources of the second surge of U.S. productivity and implications for the future* (Working Paper).

Kendrick, J. W. (1981). International comparisons of recent productivity trends. In W. Fellner (Ed.), *Essays in contemporary economic problems: demand, productivity, and population.* Washington: American Enterprise Institute.

Koike, A., & Wada, S. (2013). Productivity growth of the construction industry in Japan, using by Total factor productivity. *Journal of Japan Society and Civil Engineers, 69*(4), 265–272.

Levin, A., Lin, C. F., & Chu, C. S. J. (2002). Unit root tests in panel data: Asymptotic and finite-sample properties. *Journal of Econometrics, 108*(1), 1–24.

Moro, A., & Nuño, G. (2011). *Does TFP drive housing prices? A growth accounting exercise for four countries.* Madrid: Banco de España.

Navaratna, D., & Jayawardane, A. K. W. (2007). Total factor productivity in the building construction industry in Sri Lanka. *Engineer: Journal of the Institution of Engineers, Sri Lanka, 40*(1), 63–70.

Ofori, G. (1994). Construction industry development: Role of technology transfer. *Construction Management and Economics, 12*, 379–392.

Pesaran, M. H. (2007). A simple panel unit root test in the presence of cross-section dependence. *Journal of Applied Econometrics, 22*(2), 265–312.

Plümper, T., & Neumayer, E. (2010). The level of democracy during interregnum periods: Recoding the polity2 score. *Political Analysis, 18*(2), 206–226.

Rodrik, D. (2000). Institutions for high-quality growth: What they are and how to acquire them. *Studies in Comparative International Development, 35*(3), 3–31.

Ruddock, L. (2006). ICT in the construction sector: Computing the economic benefits. *International Journal of Strategic Property Management, 10*(1), 39–50.

Simon, J. L. (2014). *Population and development in poor countries: Selected essays.* Princeton: Princeton University Press.

Solow, R. M. (1956). A contribution to the theory of economic growth. *The Quarterly Journal of Economics, 70*(1), 65–94.

Stokes, K. (1981). An examination of the productivity decline in the construction industry. *Review of Economics and. Statistics, 63*, 495–502.

Syverson, C. (2011). What determines productivity? *Journal of Economic Literature, 49*(2), 326–365.

Tse, R. Y., & Ganesan, S., IV. (1997). Causal relationship between construction flows and GDP: Evidence from Hong Kong. *Construction Management and Economics, 15*(4), 371–376.

Valence, G. (2011). Defining an industry: What is the size and scope of the Australian building and construction industry. *Construction Economics and. Building, 1*(1), 53–65.

Wang, X., Chen, Y., Liu, B., Shen, Y., & Sun, H. (2013). A total factor productivity measure for the construction industry and analysis of its spatial difference: A case study in China. *Construction Management and Economics, 31*(10), 1059–1071.

Wooldridge, Jeffrey M. (2013). Introductory Econometrics: A Modern Approach (Fifth international ed.). Australia: South-Western. pp. 82–83. ISBN 978-1-111-53439-4.

Yiu, C. Y., Lu, X. H., Leung, M. Y., & Jin, W. X. (2004). A longitudinal analysis on the relationship between construction output and GDP in Hong Kong. *Construction Management and Economics, 22*(4), 339–345.

Zhi, M., Hua, G. B., Wang, S. Q., & Ofori, G. (2003). Total factor productivity growth accounting in the construction industry of Singapore. *Construction Management and Economics, 21*(7), 707–718.

Chapter 9
The Role of Religion on Tax Revenue: A *Global Religious Perspective*

Gökhan Dökmen

Abstract The obligation of the government to provide public services raises the need for tax revenues. As the production factors increase mobility due to globalization, tax revenues have become even more critical. In this process, there has been an increase in the studies that analyze economic and behavioral factors that have an influence on tax revenue performance. In this study, the relationship between religion and tax revenues has been examined by panel data method using dummy variables for world religions. In countries with the highest Christian Protestant population have been found that their tax revenues are increasing. However, in countries where the population is predominantly Orthodox and Muslim, the tax revenues are decreasing due to various reasons.

Introduction

Today, public expenditure is rapidly increasing in many developed and developing countries. This case brings up the discussions on the financing of public expenditures. For this reason, the funding public expenditure by raising taxes is of great importance regarding policymakers. Indeed, in the current literature on the public financial system, there are many studies on the impact of various economic, social, and psychological factors on tax revenue. It is also seen that fundamental studies have been made especially for the effect of religion on tax compliance behaviors in the recent period. The primary purpose of the study is to try to establish religion-tax revenue relationship by looking at the religious intensity of the population in the countries. Christianity, Islam, Hinduism, and Buddhism, which are the most important religions globally, will be examined to analyze the relationship between religion and taxation using a panel data approach. The article aims to contribute to the tax literature by showing how religions of the world affect the level of tax revenues.

G. Dökmen
Bülent Ecevit University, Zonguldak, Turkey
e-mail: gokhan.dokmen@beun.edu.tr

© Springer International Publishing AG, part of Springer Nature 2018 191
H. Dincer et al. (eds.), *Global Approaches in Financial Economics, Banking, and Finance*, Contributions to Economics, https://doi.org/10.1007/978-3-319-78494-6_9

The organization of the study is as follows. In section "Determinants of the Tax Revenue: Theoretical Considerations", I briefly review the determinants of the tax revenue. Section "Literature on the Relationship Between Taxation and Religion" summarizes the literature on the relationship between taxation and religion. Section "Empirical Analysis" consists of the data and variables, empirical methodology, and results of the model. Section "Conclusion and Policy Suggestions" presents the findings and evaluations.

Determinants of the Tax Revenue: Theoretical Considerations

The relationship between taxation and the determinants of tax revenue collection is one of the most important economic issues to be discussed in the recent period. This relationship is especially evident in developing countries due to poor financial performance. This issue is also crucial in developed countries in terms of ensuring financial sustainability (Aloo 2012).

Tax revenues collected in one country are affected by three components. The first of these components is the *tax base*, which is defined as the sum of the taxable assets, income, and property. Extension of the tax base is significant regarding increasing tax incomes. If the tax base in a country is too narrow, the collected taxes are insufficient. However, if the tax base is broad, it increases the number of taxpayers and the reported income levels. The second is the *tax rate*, which is expressed as a percentage of taxable income or by the tax base. If the tax rates are determined at a very high level, the expected revenue cannot be achieved. For this reason, the tax rate should not be exceeded at the optimal level. Tax revenue ultimately depends on the principles and performance of the *tax administration* (Karran 1985: 366–367). The primary task of the tax administration should be to increase tax *productivity* by applying tax laws. In this context, the performance of tax administrations is determined according to three basic criteria as efficiency, productivity, and equality.

These three factors affecting tax revenue performance are changing with the effect of different areas. Taxation is among the subjects of academics in law, politics, administration, history, psychology, and sociology, especially economics. There are five different approaches to taxation. Since the state receives taxes on income, expenditure, and wealth, taxation tends to depend on economic relations such as production and consumption. In this context, the relationship between economic structure and taxation is in the first place in economists' work. In addition to economic structure, tax behavior also depends on factors such as ethics, culture, and beliefs. This perspective, which is addressed in the context of the second approach, is influential on the voluntary tax compliance. The third approach examines the role of various external factors, such as war and natural disaster, on the efficiency of revenue administration. Another approach is to explain the differences between the functions of the government and the tax system. According to the last approach, which is called the fiscal contract model by Bräutigam (2008), taxpayers want to minimize the taxes they pay, while the revenue administration wants to maximize the taxes it collects (Bräutigam 2008: 4–5).

Although there are many different approaches to explain tax behavior, especially economic and behavioral factors are at the point of influencing the compliance behavior of taxpayers (Devos 2014). Taxation has direct or indirect effects in virtually every area of production and distribution in modern economies. There is a positive relationship between economic development and tax revenue. Developments in the economic structure are expected to lead to some changes in the tax system such as tax rate and capital structure, tax legislation, and the tax resources. At this point, it is particularly important that the economic growth causes an increase in tax revenues (Gupta 2007: 4; Morrissey et al. 2016).

Another important economic factor that determines tax revenues is the level of trade openness that emerges with globalization. Globalization is a process characterized by an increasing degree of trade openness and more integration. Along with globalization, the importance of the understanding of the nation-state has decreased, and an integrated world concept has emerged. Following the exposure of many countries to globalization, a significant strand of literature has started to focus on whether openness may affect the national tax policies. In the light of these discussions, two fundamental changes are expected in the literature of taxation. Firstly with globalization, countries have become more dependent on changes in tax policy in other countries. If one country reduces tax rates to attract foreign capital, it negatively affects the tax base of other countries. This effect of globalization is explained by the concept of *fiscal externalities*. Secondly, increasing globalization limits the power of national policies in the field of taxation. In other words, countries have reduced their independence in determining tax policies. The decline in the importance of national policies in the global economy has brought about the concept of tax competition. In the context of globalization, three hypotheses have been proposed theoretically concerning tax competition. Firstly, as the integration of a country into capital markets increases, it is expected to decrease at the level of capital taxes. Secondly, if the integration into the capital market increases, the taxes paid on labor will be so high compared to capital taxes. Finally, if the integration is above a certain threshold level, large countries will have the chance to implement higher rates in capital taxes compared to small countries (Giray 2005: 102, 203).

Fluctuations in tax revenues are also affected by inflation. In the case of high inflation, government tax revenues are eroded by the rise of the informal sector and the underground economy. As a result of which, the real value of tax revenues diminishes (Rodrik 1998). The literature also points to the erosion of the real value of taxation depending on tax collection lags. The decrease in tax revenues based on inflation is called Olivera-Tanzi effect. If tax collection delays are too long, the loss of real tax revenue might be sizeable. However, in most modern economies, the size of the Olivera-Tanzi effect has been reduced because tax collection lags have decreased due to developments in information and communication technology and the existence of tax prepayments in the tax system (Prammer and Reiss 2015: 28).

The tax revenues collected by the state depend on the willingness of individuals to pay as well as economic factors. The willingness of taxpayers to obey tax laws is called tax compliance (Andreoni et al. 1998). Whether people are willing or unwilling to pay tax, which is an essential indicator of tax compliance, is determined by social factors. The first studies on tax compliance have examined the issue of risk-taking behavior and the deterrence of punishment. According to Allingham and Sandmo (1972: 324), the tax declaration decision is an uncertainty decision. Because when taxpayers do not declare their full income to tax authorities, they do not automatically receive a penalty. At this point, the taxpayer will either declare his actual income or declare less than his real income. Which strategy the taxpayer chooses will depend on his motivation for risk-taking and the effectiveness of the tax audit system. If the audit system is working efficiently, the revenues will be closer to declaring real income. However, under any circumstance, the taxpayer can take less risk and declare less income.

There is increasing evidence that the probability of detection and the penalty structure is not sufficient to explain the compliance behavior of taxpayers (and attitudes to taxation). Frey and Feld (2002) stated that the factors affecting tax revenue are mainly handled in the literature by taxpayer's attitudes and behaviors. He stressed that factors such as the structure and functioning of tax administrations are not examined adequately. However, the attitudes and behaviors of tax administrations directly affect taxpayer behavior in response to taxation. Taxpayers observe the policies of tax administration and shape their behavior according to this policy. If tax officials are honest, fair, transparent, and uncorrupted, the level of voluntary compliance and the desire to pay taxes are positively affected. In contrast, if tax administration sees the taxpayers as liable to pay taxes under all circumstances, in such a case, the taxpayers will tend to have a tax evasion in return (Frey and Feld 2002).

Recent studies are related to taxpayers' views on state and tax administration. These studies suggest a new model by synthesizing different research paradigms on tax behavior. The model, called slippery slope framework by Kirchler et al. (2008), is based on the idea that the tax climate in society will be shaped by the interaction between the taxpayer and the state. This tax climate is called a synergistic climate if the taxpayer is working together with the tax administration. If the taxpayer and the administration conflict, it is called the antagonistic climate. According to slippery slope framework, tax compliance can be influenced through the power of state's authorities and trust in government. While increasing the power of the tax authorities rises the enforced compliance, growing confidence in state institutions encourages voluntary compliance (Kaplanoglou and Rapanos 2015: 21). It is called voluntary compliance that taxpayers meet their obligations without any external force. There are four components required for voluntary fulfillment of tax liability: (1) the taxable income must be fully declared, (2) accurate indication of deductions in income tax declaration, (3) filling in the tax return on time, and (4) correct calculation of declared tax. Enforced tax compliance means that fulfilling tax liabilities is achieved with force by the tax administration (Roth and Scholz 1989; Randlane 2016).

Tax compliance is also related to the government performance in terms of providing public goods and services. Pommerehne and Frey (1992: 9–10) stated that tax compliance behavior is affected not only the amount of public expenditure but also expenditure by individuals' preferences. If taxpayers are satisfied with public goods and services, they tend to pay the tax on time and comply with the tax laws. Moreover if government performance is weak because of corruption, heavy-duty bureaucracy and government failure to provide public services, complexity of the tax system, high compliance costs, lack of integrity of tax officials due to inadequate salary structures, and insufficient law enforcement, taxpayers may refuse to pay taxes (Mangoting and Sukoharsono 2015). In addition to the reduced government performance, taxpayers' perception toward fairness is also affecting tax compliance. Richardson (2008) stated that if taxpayer tends to perceive tax systems as being unfair, they either incline tax evasion or tax avoidance.

In the broad field of tax compliance literature, historically, many of the researchers have analyzed economic factors affecting tax revenue. However, this trend has been criticized in some studies that examine the effects of noneconomic factors on taxpayer behavior. Recent studies have emphasized the internal values of taxpayers such as value, norm, and morality. However, even in these studies, the phenomenon of religion, which can be considered within the scope of internal values, has not been examined sufficiently. Religiosity has been excluded from the tax literature by many scholars and has not been considered as a variable that influences taxpayer psychology. This deficiency was eliminated by scholars like Torgler (2003), Stack and Kposowa (2006), and Anderson (1988), and it emphasized the significance of religiosity in tax compliance.

Religious values are expected to prevent the negative behavior of the individual. Therefore, it is hoped that religiosity will encourage voluntary compliance. In other words, there is a belief that taxpayers with high religious tendencies will fulfill their tax liabilities promptly and will have a more positive attitude about tax management (Eiya et al. 2016). Furthermore religious sensitivities will contribute to social peace, and taxpayers will be more fair and honest in economic relations. Based on this acceptance, religious rules will prevent negative behaviors such as tax evasion and fraud and will protect the economic values to be used in the financing of public services (Stack and Kposowa 2006).

From a theoretical perspective, there are three main possibilities regarding the role of religiosity on tax revenue. The first is that religion does not have a determinable or measurable effect. The second is that religion has discernable or measurable gradual (or linear) effect on tax compliance. The last is that religion has a discernable or measurable effect once a certain level of a threshold is reached, i.e., the level of tax compliance is higher once a certain level of religiosity is reached (Pope and Mohdali 2010).

Religion rules can withstand a divine order as Abrahamic religions, or it can stem from own dynamics of the social structure. In this respect, religious orders differ from country to country. This differentiation changes taxpayers' voluntary compliance according to religious sensitivities. In other words, religions are different, especially about beliefs and practices. It is stated that the holy book of the Christians,

Bible, deals with the relationship between the state and the individual and includes various tax regulations. When Jesus is asked whether citizens should pay taxes to Caesar or not, Jesus replied that *So give back to Caesar what is Caesar's, and to God what is God's* (Matthew 22: 17, 21). According to McGee (2012a: 5), this issue has not been elaborated by Jesus. So there are lots of discussion on the particular nature of the sin in the Christian literature. While some Christians think that tax evasion is unethical all the time, others think that it is not unethical at least sometimes (McGee 2012b: 209).

The religion of Islam has explicit provisions on many issues. However, on some topics, especially taxation, there are no explicit texts because current taxes did not exist at the time of the Prophet Muhammad (peace and blessings be upon him). Therefore, Muslim scholars struggle to provide Islamic provisions for tax behavior. Some scholars are opposed to taxation, and others believe in government's right to force taxes on its citizens (Al-Ttaffi and Abdul-Jabbar 2015).

In the literature much has not been written about the taxation from the Jewish religion. According to Cohn (1998), the following characteristics of Jewish religion affect the taxation:

1. A Jewish citizen must obey and follow the rules of his own country. This obligation requires compliance with tax laws.
2. Jewish laws are strongly opposed to lying. This rule requires tax liabilities to be declared correctly.
3. A Jewish citizen is prohibited from doing anything contrary to the rules of religion. This prohibition covers all kinds of crimes against the state.
4. A Jewish citizen should be integrated into every aspect of society. This integration also includes the area of taxation.

Cohn (1998) stated, based on these four factors, why a Jewish person should not be a tax evader according to Jewish law.

Literature on the Relationship Between Taxation and Religion

There is an extensive and comprehensive literature on the difference in tax revenues across countries. Researchers have included several factors such as economic development, which is usually represented by the gross domestic product per capita (Tanzi 1992; Gupta 2007; Bahl 2004; Bird et al. 2006), the structure of the economy that can be studied through the sectoral composition of the GDP (Bird et al. 2006; Baunsgaard and Keen 2010; Moore 2013), the economic stability that is measured by consumer price index (Bayoumi and Gagnon 1996), and the structure of the tax system (Kirchler et al. 2008) and external factors such as the level of foreign direct investment (Bond and Samuelson 1986; Gropp and Kostial 2000) and trade (Mahdavi 2008; Gupta 2007). Demographic factors like taxpayers' age

(Dubin and Wilde 1988; Clotfelter 1983; Kirchler 1999; Fjeldstad and Semboja 2001), gender (Spicer and Hero 1985; Friedland et al. 1978), and education (Richardson 2006) also affect taxpayer behavior.

More recent studies have been based on social and psychological factors affecting tax revenue. Social and psychological factors like probability of detection, fairness, perceived role of government, moral beliefs and attitudes, and trust in the government are also considered determinants of tax revenue (Snavely 1990; Torgler and Schneider 2007; Torgler 2005; Raskolnikov 2009; Pope and Mohdali 2010; Verboon and Van Dijke 2011; Pommerehne et al. 1994; Alm et al. 1992).

There has been much work in the literature regarding the factors affecting tax revenues, but no consensus has been reached about what are the factors affecting the behavior of taxpayers (Devos 2014: 13). Because, in tax literature, many issues affecting tax compliance behaviors such as religion have not yet been studied intensively.

Studies on the influence of religious belief on the taxpayers' behavior are two different formats. The first one concentrated on the evidence of a link between religion and tax, and the second one examined the religious types' impact on tax revenues. Torgler (2003: 546–557) stated that tax evasion tendencies are low in people with religious sensitivities. In other words, religion can be considered as a decision-making variable that affects tax evasion. It has been found that religiosity in the light of the data obtained from the World Values Survey is a value that raises tax ethics. Empirical analyzed by Grasmick et al. (1991a) indicated that religious precision and church attendance reduced the inclination to tax evasion. In a study by Feld and Torgler (2007), the tax moral variable obtained by World Values Survey is explained by a vector of various variables including religion and regional dummy variables (East or West Germany). It is indicated in the study that religious sensitivities change taxpayer behavior positively for East and West German society. Grasmick et al. (1991b) stated that a person would be more inclined to tax evasion if he did not have a religious affiliation. Similarly, the findings of Stack and Kposowa (2006) showed that the tax fraud trends are higher for people who do not have religious beliefs.

Benk et al. (2016) presented statistical evidence that religiosity in Turkey affects tax compliance. According to the analysis results, intrapersonal religiosity only increases voluntary compliance. When it comes to intrapersonal religiosity, any statistical evidence that affected voluntary and compulsory compliance could not be reached. In a study by Agbetunde et al. (2015), it is showed that religion has a more significant impact than culture to decrease tax evasion. In other words, this situation showed that taxpayers are found to be more influenced by their religion than culture in relation to tax evasion. Moreover, it is concluded that religion is a very significant factor to consider by authorities when targeting significant reduction in tax evasion especially in developing countries like Nigeria. By examining Christian adherence in the United States, according to Boone et al. (2013), states with more religiosity tend to have less tax evasion behavior.

Palil et al. (2013) investigated the effect of religiosity in the relationship between tax consciousness and tax education. The results of the study show that religious values play a very crucial role for tax compliance. Welch et al. (1991) stated that tax evasion is related to an individual's religiosity. Similar results have been found including Christianity (Torgler and Murphy 2004; Lago-Peñas and Lago-Peñas 2010; Strielkowski and Čábelková 2015), Islam (Murtuza and Ghazanfar 1998; Demir 2008; Mohdali and Pope 2012, 2014; Mohd Ali 2013; Benk et al. 2016; McGee et al. 2012), and Judaism (McGee and Cohn 2006).

The second direction of research concentrates on religious types' effect on collected tax revenues. Guiso et al. (2003) distinguished religious denominations to identify the relationship between the intensity of religious beliefs and economic attitudes like taxation. It is found that taxpayers who believe in Jewish religion are more resistant to paying taxes compared to other religions such as Protestant, Catholic, Hindu, and Muslim. In the study by Torgler (2004), tax morale is analyzed in several Asian countries for the period 1995–1997. He reached the result that the taxpayers who believe in Christian religion did not fulfill their tax obligations under certain conditions compared to other religious groups. Also, it has been observed that Muslims and people without any religious view had higher tax ethics than Hindus. Two years later, Torgler (2006) indicated a strong correlation between religious beliefs and tax morality, and religious beliefs were found to be a significant factor in increasing tax morality. Torgler (2006) analyzed seven different religious beliefs, Catholic, Protestant, Orthodox, Judaism, Islam, Hindu, and Buddhist, and found a statistically significant relationship between tax morality and some religious beliefs. It has observed the tendency that Catholics, Hindus, and Buddhists behave more sensitively in fulfilling tax obligations when compared to Protestants and Orthodox.

A study by involving 149 graduate students from the business department showed that Christians were more sensitive to tax evasion than were Hindus (McGee and George 2008). In a study with 315 business, philosophy, and seminar students, it has been found that Muslims are less opposition to tax evasion than Catholics (McGee and Bose 2007). McGee and Goldman (2012) stated that Catholics and other Christian sects had the same negative attitudes toward tax evasion. In a study by Gupta and McGee (2010), it was found that Buddhists were more inclined to tax evasion when compared to Catholics. Ross and McGee (2011) conclude that Protestants are the most religious structures against tax evasion when compared to Roman Catholics, Muslims, Hindus, and Buddhists.

Empirical Analysis

The research design used in the literature on determinants of tax revenues may change from research to research. Econometric modeling has been used in this study.

Data and Variables

The determinations of tax revenue were carried out by panel data analysis. The dataset consists of a panel observation of 79 countries[1] over the years 1990–2013.[2] The following variables are used in the study: tax revenue as a percent of GDP (TAX), per capita growth (annual %) (GDP), private capital stock (percentage change from the same month of the previous year) (CAPITAL), general government final consumption expenditure as a percent of GDP (GOV), foreign direct investment, net inflows as a percent of GDP (FDI), current account balance as a percent of GDP (CURRENT), and inflation (GDP deflator, annual %) (INF). The data are obtained from World Bank databank and IMF *Government Finance Statistics*. Religion dummy variables were created using the methodology of The Global Religious Landscape report.

Empirical Methodology

To estimate the determinants of tax revenues in the study, the following form is used:

$$TAX_{it} = \beta_1 TAX_{i,t-1} + \beta_2 X_{it} + \beta_3 R_{it} + u_{it} \qquad (9.1)$$

where i and t stand for countries and periods, respectively, β_j are the estimated parameters, and TAX *stands for* tax revenue as a percentage of GDP. $TAX_{i,\,t-1}$ in the model indicates the dynamic nature of tax revenue. X_{it} stands for a matrix of the control variables, namely, GDP, CAPITAL, GOV, FDI, CURRENT, and INF. Variable R_{it} includes our variables of religion dummy: Protestant, Catholic, Orthodox, Muslim, Hindu, Buddhist, and *Unaffiliated*. u is the error term; $u_{it} = \mu_i + \varepsilon_{it}$, μ_i being the unobservable individual specific effects and ε_{it} the remaining disturbance.

In this study, system GMM is used to estimate a tax revenue determination as in Eq. (9.1). System GMM, developed by Arellano and Bover (1995) and Blundell and Bond (1998), is considered more outstanding than difference GMM. For dynamic panel data models, Bond et al. (2001) asserted that this method has significant

---

[1]The country sample includes Argentina, Australia, Bahrain, Belize, Benin, Brazil, Bulgaria, Burundi, Cameroon, Canada, Chile, China, Colombia, Costa Rica, Denmark, Dominica, Dominican Republic, Ecuador, Egypt Arab Republic, El Salvador, Finland, France, Germany, Ghana, Greece, Grenada, Guatemala, Iceland, India, Indonesia, Italy, Jordan, Kenya, Korea Republic, Malaysia, Mauritius, Mexico, Morocco, the Netherlands, Norway, Pakistan, Panama, Paraguay, Peru, the Philippines, Poland, Portugal, Romania, Saudi Arabia, Senegal, Sierra Leone, Singapore, South Africa, Spain, Sri Lanka, St. Kitts and Nevis, St. Lucia, Sweden, Switzerland, Tanzania, Thailand, Togo, Trinidad and Tobago, Tunisia, Turkey, the United Kingdom, the United States, Uruguay, Austria, New Zealand, Ireland, Iran Islamic Republic, Yemen Republic, Oman, Central African Republic, Guinea, Guinea-Bissau, Nepal, and Burkina Faso.

[2]Israel was removed from the sample because it was a data problem. For this reason, Jewish religious dummy variable was not formed.

advantages over simple cross-sectional regressions and other estimation methods. Initially, estimates will no longer be biased by any omitted variables that are constant over time. Secondly, the use of instrumental variables allows parameters to be estimated consistently in endogenous right-hand side variables including models. Thirdly, the use of instruments potentially allows consistent estimation even in the presence of measurement error (Nayan et al. 2013).

Empirical Results

In this study, dynamic panel data analysis is estimated by the generalized method of moments (GMM). It is applied to determine the elements affecting tax revenue. Before using *the system GMM analysis*, the panel unit root test must be used first to identify the stationary properties of the variables. In this study, we choose three panel unit root tests, Levin et al. (2002); Im et al. (2003); and Maddala and Wu (1999). Test results are shown in Table 9.1.

The panel test results indicate that TAX, GDP, GOV, FDI, CURRENT, and INF are stationary at a level according to Levin, Lin, and Chu, Fisher ADF, and Fisher PP. CAPITAL variables are nonstationary in their individual intercept form in Levin, Lin, and Chu test. However, in their individual intercept and trend form, this variable is stationary.

Table 9.1 Results of panel unit root tests

Variables	Levin, Lin, and Chu		Im, Pesaran, and Shin		ADF-Fisher	
	Individual intercept	Individual intercept and trend	Individual intercept	Individual intercept and trend	Individual intercept	Individual intercept and trend
TAX	-3.193 $(0.000)^*$	-2.179 $(0.014)^{**}$	-3.430 $(0.000)^*$	-6.273 $(0.000)^*$	251.230 $(0.000)^*$	297.481 $(0.000)^*$
GDP	-17.969 $(0.000)^*$	-16.203 $(0.000)^*$	-18.506 $(0.000)^*$	-15.734 $(0.000)^*$	653.139 $(0.000)^*$	529.319 $(0.000)^*$
CAPITAL	-0.763 (0.222)	-2.037 $(0.020)^{**}$	-1.272 $(0.101)^{***}$	-3.981 $(0.000)^*$	201.696 $(0.010)^{**}$	261.790 $(0.000)^*$
GOV	-5.271 $(0.000)^*$	-4.337 $(0.000)^*$	-5.104 $(0.000)^*$	-4.887 $(0.000)^*$	253.867 $(0.000)^*$	248.627 $(0.000)^*$
FDI	-10.186 $(0.000)^*$	-7.312 $(0.000)^*$	-11.944 $(0.000)^*$	-10.130 $(0.000)^*$	439.749 $(0.000)^*$	382.781 $(0.000)^*$
CURRENT	-34.006 $(0.000)^*$	-21.812 $(0.000)^*$	-30.538 $(0.000)^*$	-24.174 $(0.000)^*$	1083.45 $(0.000)^*$	792.576 $(0.000)^*$
INF	-395.451 $(0.000)^*$	-570.474 $(0.000)^*$	-74.987 $(0.000)^*$	-117.344 $(0.000)^*$	993.167 $(0.000)^*$	1073.55 $(0.000)^*$

Note: Automatic lag length selection (Akaike Info Criterion) is used. *Display significance at the 1% level, **display significance at the 5% level, ***display significance at the 10% level

Table 9.2 Results of the estimation by system GMM, 1990–2013

Independent variables	
TAX (−1)	0.9678 (0.000)*
GDP	0.1225 (0.007)*
CAPITAL	−12.6663 (0.000)*
GOV	−0.0827 (0.049)**
FDI	0.0267 (0.356)
CURRENT	−0.0068 (0.642)
INF	−0.0018 (0.360)
Religious dummy	
Protestant	2.8565 (0.031)**
Orthodox	−9.0523 (0.087)***
Muslim	−4.9339 (0.067)***
Hindu	47.0658 (0.112)
Buddhist	−5.6900 (0.615)
Unaffiliated	−20.5667 (0.215)
Number of groups	79
Number of obs.	1817
Wald chi2 (prob)	(0.000)
Sargan Chi2	23.85 (0.470)
A–B test for AR(1)	−6.12 (0.000)
A–B test for AR(2)	−0.30 (0.765)

Notes: (1) *Display significance at the 1%, **display significance at the 5%, and ***display significance at the 10%; AB stands for Arellano-Bond. (2) Stata dropped Catholic religion dummy variable due to collinearity. (3) Israel was removed from the sample because it was a data problem. For this reason, Jewish religious dummy variable was not formed

These results support the assumption that the variables in the system GMM approach are stationary. For this reason, the system GMM approach has been estimated in the following stages. The results are shown in Table 9.2.

Before interpreting the panel regression results in Table 9.2, the consistency of the system GMM predictors was tested. At this point, Wald test, Sargan test, and Arellano-Bond (AB) test were applied. The Wald test shows whether the variables used in the model are significant as a whole. The Sargan test is performed to check whether the *instrumental* variables used in the model are valid. AB test shows whether there is an autocorrelation problem in the model. Wald chi2 test results show that the model is significant as a whole. The validity of the instrumental variables was tested with the null hypothesis indicating the relationship between the instrumental variables and the error terms, and the result is that the instrumental variables are valid. The AB test is the autocorrelation problem in AR (1), but in AR (2) it does not have autocorrelation.

When the panel regression results are analyzed, the results are partially suited to expectations. If there is no instability in the conjuncture, there may not be extreme differences between the periods in the tax revenues depending on the continuity of the production process. In other words, the tax revenues will show a trend depending on the previous period level. The regression results show that tax revenues are positively and statistically significant about the previous year's value. There is also a positive relationship between tax revenues and per capita growth in line with expectations. This result indicates that tax revenues are in line with economic fluctuations; in other words, tax flexibility is high. The relationship between fixed capital investments and tax revenues has also been examined in this study. As a result of the realization of fixed capital investments in the private sector, it is thought that these investments will increase the national income and lead to the development of the country with the assumption that the production of goods and services will increase in the economy. For this reason, a positive relationship is expected between the fixed capital investments and the taxation in the long run. According to panel test results, there was a negative relationship between tax revenues and private sector fixed capital investments. This result can be explained by the fact that the fixed capital investments caused the financing needs and accordingly the private sector had difficulties in paying taxes. Another variable discussed in the analysis is public expenditure. There is no consensus in the literature about the direction of the causality relationship between taxation and public expenditure. Some studies show that direction of causality has been gone from the public expenditure to taxation; others stated that the causal relationship flows from taxation to expenditures. This study expects that an increase in public expenditures has a positive impact on tax revenue. However, the results indicate that there is a negative relationship between tax revenue and public expenditures. This result can be explained by the fact that public expenditures are crowding out private sector investments. The negative impact of public spending on private sector investments, called the crowding out hypothesis in the literature, can cause a reduction in revenue by affecting tax capacity.

Concepts such as tax ethics and tax compliance are areas affected by taxpayer religious beliefs. For this reason, the basis of the study was dealt with to cover various world religions. According to the results of the study, dummy variables related to Protestant, Orthodox, and Muslim religions are statistically significant. Dummy variables related to Hindu, Buddhist, and *Unaffiliated* are not statistically significant. The dummy variable for Protestant religion received a positive value. This result shows that tax revenues are increasing in countries where Protestant religion is dominant. Protestant business ethics has always been associated with capitalism. Max Weber claims that this tendency derives from the capitalist spirit in the presence of the Protestant denomination. Due to this relationship between Protestantism and capitalism, it is expected that the capital accumulation and the tax base will be high in countries where the Protestant population is concentrated.

When the countries with the highest percentage of Orthodox Christians population are analyzed, Orthodox religion dummy variable is a negative sign. These countries are predominantly the former eastern bloc countries. It can be expected that the tax base will be low in these countries where the capital accumulation process has not yet been fully developed. Similarly, the dummy variable in the countries with the highest Muslim population is negative and statistically significant.

Because some of the Muslim countries are predominantly rich in natural resources, especially oil and natural gas, their requirements for tax revenues may not be very high. On the other hand, some Muslim countries economically insufficiently developed, so tax resources are insufficient. This structure in Muslim countries can be considered as an element that weakens tax compliance and tax ethics.

Conclusion and Policy Suggestions

Tax revenues follow a fluctuating trend in today's developed and developing countries. Many economic and noneconomic factors have a direct and indirect influence on tax revenue performance. An essential component of economic factors is per capita income. Per capita income as a proxy for the development of economic structure is expected to be positively correlated with tax revenue. The sectoral structure of the economy is considered as one of the economic factors affecting tax revenues. Some sectors, such as agriculture, are taxed at a different level than other sectors. The level of openness of the economy and inflation also affects the tax revenue performance. If the openness of the economy is taken as a sign of the globalization process, it may be expected that there will be some changes in the tax bases of countries due to tax competition. Inflation can reduce public revenues by affecting the real values of tax revenues.

In addition to the macro variables mentioned, the policies of the tax administration also affect tax compliance behavior and therefore tax revenue. If the tax office sees taxpayers as persons with only specific duties and focuses on an audit-oriented management system, taxpayers may tend to tax evasion. For this reason, the tax administration should take into account the taxpayers' psychology. Another variable that taxpayers take into account in the taxation process is public service perceptions. If the taxpayers feel that the taxes they pay are reflected in the form of public goods and services, they will fulfill their tax obligations voluntarily and without any compulsion. The attitudes and behaviors of taxpayers are based not only on external factors but also on sociological and psychological factors such as norms, beliefs, and religion. However, these factors especially religion have not been studied much in the tax literature. Religious affiliations shape the taxpayer's behavior. More religious people can be expected to have higher tax morals. However, this does not mean that atheists' tax morals are low. It is meant that individuals with high religious sensitivities may be more sensitive to compliance with tax laws.

This study was done to analyze the relationship between religion and tax revenues. Religious dummy variables were formed by classifying the countries according to the religious structure of the population, and the relationship between tax revenues and religion was examined econometrically by panel data analysis. In this study involving 79 countries, the Protestant religion dummy variable was positive and statistically significant. This conclusion shows that tax revenue has increased to the countries with the highest percentage of Protestant population. Protestant countries, where capital accumulation is intense, have a high tax base.

For this reason, it is expected that tax revenues will have a high performance. However, this does not apply to Orthodox countries where capital accumulation is low because of the low level of income. Orthodox religion dummy variable is negative and statistically significant. Looking at Orthodox countries, it is seen that they are less developed and problematic countries. These countries do not base their capital accumulation process on a historical background. These countries are mostly former eastern bloc countries, and the tax base is not very developed. A similar tendency applies within Muslim countries. Muslim religion dummy variable is also negative and statistically significant. The tax revenues of Muslim countries some of which are rich in natural resources and others are developing and underdeveloped are much lower than those of developed countries. Given the economic conditions of Muslim and Orthodox countries, it is not surprising that tax revenue performance is low.

As a conclusion, the level of economic development and capital accumulation is affecting the tax revenue performance. Also, tax revenue performances differ among countries with different religious beliefs. The most fundamental limitation of this study is that it cannot examine religious sensitivities on an individual basis. In the study, countries were classified according to their religious affiliation, and tax revenue performance was examined. For this reason, it is not possible to make an assessment that any religious order will cause more or less tax revenue.

Keywords Definitions

Government: Government means that a group of people that govern a community. It administers public policy and levy tax for public expenditure.

Tax revenue: Tax revenue is defined as the revenues collected from taxes on income and profits, taxes levied on goods and services, payroll taxes, and taxes on the ownership and transfer of property. Taxation is the main source of income for a state.

Religion: Religion is the set of beliefs, feelings, and practices that define the relations between human being and sacred.

Panel data analysis: Panel data analysis is a statistical method, widely used in social science.

References

Agbetunde, L. A., Adedokun, L. B., & Fadipe, A. O. (2015). A cross-cultural survey of ethical reasons for tax evasion among Nigerian taxpayers. *Research Journal of Finance and Accounting, 6*(23), 9–15.

Allingham, M. G., & Sandmo, A. (1972). Income tax evasion: A theoretical analysis. *Journal of Public Economics, 1*(3–4), 323–338.

Alm, J., McClelland, G. H., & Schulze, W. D. (1992). Why do people pay taxes? *Journal of Public Economics, 48*(1), 21–38.

Aloo, O. E. (2012). *The determinants of tax revenue in Kenya*. Unprinted dissertation, University of Nairobi, Kenya.

Al-Ttaffi, L. H. A., & Abdul-Jabbar, H. (2015). A conceptual framework for tax non-compliance studies in a Muslim country: A proposed framework for the case of Yemen. *International Postgraduate Business Journal, 7*(2), 1–16.

Anderson, G. M. (1988). Mr. Smith and the preachers: The economics of religion in the wealth of nations. *Journal of Political Economy, 96*(5), 1066–1088.

Andreoni, J., Erard, B., & Feinstein, J. (1998). Tax compliance. *Journal of Economic Literature, 36* (2), 818–860.

Arellano, M., & Bover, O. (1995). Another look at the instrumental variable estimation of error-components models. *Journal of Econometrics, 68*, 29–51.

Bahl, R. (2004). Reaching the hardest to tax: Consequences and possibilities. *Contributions to Economic Analysis, 268*, 337–354.

Baunsgaard, T., & Keen, M. (2010). Tax revenue and (or?) trade liberalization. *Journal of Public Economics, 94*(9–10), 563–577.

Bayoumi, T., & Gagnon, J. (1996). Taxation and inflation: A new explanation for capital flows. *Journal of Monetary Economics, 38*(2), 303–330.

Benk, S., Budak, T., Yüzbaşı, B., & Mohdali, R. (2016). The impact of religiosity on tax compliance among Turkish self-employed taxpayers. *Religions, 7*(4), 37.

Bird, R. M., Martinez-Vazquez, J., & Torgler, B. (2006). Societal institutions and tax effort in developing countries. *The Challenges of Tax Reform in a Global Economy, 283*.

Blundell, R., & Bond, S. (1998). Initial conditions and moment restrictions in dynamic panel data models. *Journal of Econometrics, 87*, 115–143.

Bond, E. W., & Samuelson, L. (1986). Tax holidays as signals. *The American Economic Review, 76* (4), 820–826.

Bond, S., Hoeffler, A., & Temple, J. (2001). *GMM estimation of empirical growth models*. CEPR Discussion Paper, 3048. Retrieved from https://ssrn.com/abstract=290522

Boone, J. P., Khurana, I. K., & Raman, K. K. (2013). Religiosity and tax avoidance. *The Journal of the American Taxation Association, 35*(1), 53–84.

Bräutigam, D. (2008). Introduction: Taxation and state-building in developing countries. In B. Deborah et al. (Eds.), *Taxation and state-building in developing countries*. New York: Cambridge University Press.

Clotfelter, C. T. (1983). Tax evasion and tax rates: An analysis of individual returns. *The Review of Economics and Statistics, 65*(3), 363–373.

Cohn, G. (1998). The Jewish view on paying taxes. *Journal of Accounting, Ethics & Public Policy, 1*(2), 109–120.

Demir, İ. C. (2008). *Vergi ahlakı ve belirleyenleri: Ege Bölgesi örneği*. Unprinted dissertation, University of Dokuz Eylül, Turkey.

Devos, K. (2014). *Factors influencing individual taxpayer compliance behaviour*. Netherlands: Springer.

Dubin, J. A., & Wilde, L. L. (1988). An empirical analysis of federal income tax auditing and compliance. *National Tax Journal, 41*, 61–74.

Eiya, O., Ilaboya, O., & Okoye, A. (2016). Religiosity and tax compliance: Empirical evidence from Nigeria. *Igbinedion University Journal of Accounting, 1*, 27–41.

Feld, L. P., & Torgler, B. (2007). *Tax morale after the reunification of Germany: Results from a quasi-natural experiment*. CESifo Working Paper, No. 1921. Retrieved from https://ssrn.com/abstract=965414

Fjeldstad, O. H., & Semboja, J. (2001). Why people pay taxes: The case of the development levy in Tanzania. *World Development, 29*(12), 2059–2074.

Frey, B. S., & Feld, L. P. (2002). *Deterrence and morale in taxation: An empirical analysis*. CESifo Working Paper Series, 760. Retrieved from https://ssrn.com/abstract=341380

Friedland, N., Maital, S., & Rutenberg, A. (1978). A simulation study of income tax evasion. *Journal of Public Economics, 10*(1), 107–116.

Giray, F. (2005). Küreselleşme sürecinde vergi rekabeti ve boyutlar. *Akdeniz İİBF Dergisi, 9*, 93–122.

Grasmick, H. G., Bursik, R. J., & Cochran, J. K. (1991a). Render unto Caesar what is Caesar's. *The Sociological Quarterly, 32*(2), 251–266.

Grasmick, H. G., Kinsey, K., & Cochran, J. K. (1991b). Denomination, religiosity and compliance with the law: A study of adults. *Journal for the Scientific Study of Religion, 30*(1), 99–107.

Gropp, R., & Kostial, K. (2000). *The disappearing tax base: Is foreign direct investment eroding corporate income taxes?*. IMF Working Papers, WP/00/173.

Guiso, L., Sapienza, P., & Zingales, L. (2003). People's opium? Religion and economic attitudes. *Journal of Monetary Economics, 50*(1), 225–282.

Gupta, A. (2007). *Determinants of revenue efforts in developing countries*. IMF Working Papers, WP/07/184, 1–39.

Gupta, R., & McGee, R. (2010). Study on tax evasion perceptions in Australasia. *Australian Tax Forum, 25*, 507–534.

Im, K. S., Pesaran, M. H., & Shin, Y. (2003). Testing for unit roots in heterogeneous panels. *Journal of Econometrics, 115*(1), 53–74.

Kaplanoglou, G., & Rapanos, V. T. (2015). Why do people evade taxes? New experimental evidence from Greece. *Journal of Behavioral and Experimental Economics, 56*, 21–32.

Karran, T. (1985). The determinants of taxation in Britain: An empirical test. *Journal of Public Policy, 5*(3), 365–386.

Kirchler, E. (1999). Reactance to taxation: Employers' attitudes towards taxes. *Journal of Socio-Economics, 28*(2), 131–138.

Kirchler, E., Hoelzl, E., & Wahl, I. (2008). Enforced versus voluntary tax compliance: The "slippery slope" framework. *Journal of Economic Psychology, 29*(2), 210–225.

Lago-Peñas, I., & Lago-Peñas, S. (2010). The determinants of tax morale in comparative perspective: Evidence from European countries. *European Journal of Political Economy, 26*(4), 441–453.

Levin, A., Lin, C. F., & Chu, C. S. J. (2002). Unit root tests in panel data: Asymptotic and finite-sample properties. *Journal of Econometrics, 108*(1), 1–24.

Maddala, G. S., & Wu, S. (1999). A comparative study of unit root tests with panel data and a new simple test. *Oxford Bulletin of Economics and Statistics, 61*(S1), 631–652.

Mahdavi, S. (2008). The level and composition of tax revenue in developing countries: Evidence from unbalanced panel data. *International Review of Economics & Finance, 17*(4), 607–617.

Mangoting, Y., & Sukoharsono, E. G. (2015). Developing a model of tax compliance from social contract perspective: Mitigating the tax evasion. *Procedia – Social and Behavioral Sciences, 211*, 966–971.

McGee, R. W. (2012a). Four views on the ethics of tax evasion. In R. W. McGee (Ed.), *The ethics of tax evasion* (pp. 3–33). New York: Springer.

McGee, R. W. (2012b). Christian views on the ethics of tax evasion. In R. W. McGee (Ed.), *The ethics of tax evasion* (pp. 201–210). New York: Springer.

McGee, R. W., & Cohn, G. (2006). *Jewish perspectives on the ethics of tax evasion*. Andreas School of Business Working Paper Series. Retrieved from http://ssrn.com/abstract=929027

McGee, R. W., & Bose, S. (2007). *The ethics of tax evasion: A survey of Australian opinion*. Retrieved from https://ssrn.com/abstract=979410

McGee, R. W., & George, B. (2008). Tax evasion and ethics: A survey of Indian opinion. *Journal of Accounting, Ethics & Public Policy, 9*(3), 301–332.

McGee, R. W., & Goldman, G. A. (2012). Ethics and tax evasion: A survey of South African opinion. In R. W. McGee (Ed.), *The ethics of tax evasion* (pp. 337–356). New York: Springer.

McGee, R. W., Benk, S., Ross, A. M., & Kılıçaslan, H. (2012). Cheating on taxes if you have a chance: A comparative study of tax evasion opinion in Turkey and Germany. In R. W. McGee (Ed.), *The ethics of tax evasion* (pp. 357–369). New York: Springer.

Mohd Ali, N. R. (2013). *The influence of religiosity on tax compliance in Malaysia.* Ph.D. thesis, Curtin University, Curtin Business School, School of Economics and Finance.

Mohdali, R., & Pope, J. (2012). The effects of religiosity and external environment on voluntary tax compliance. *New Zealand Journal of Taxation Law and Policy, 18*, 119–139.

Mohdali, R., & Pope, J. (2014). The influence of religiosity on taxpayers' compliance attitudes: Empirical evidence from a mixed-methods study in Malaysia. *Accounting Research Journal, 27* (1), 71–91.

Moore, M. (2013). *Obstacles to increasing tax revenues in low income countries.* International Centre for Tax and Development Working Paper, 15.

Morrissey, O., Von Haldenwang, C., Von Schiller, A., Ivanyna, M., & Bordon, I. (2016). Tax revenue performance and vulnerability in developing countries. *The Journal of Development Studies, 52*(12), 1689–1703.

Murtuza, A., & Ghazanfar, S. M. (1998). Taxation as a form of worship: Exploring the nature of zakat. *Journal of Accounting, Ethics & Public Policy, 1*(2), 134–161.

Nayan, S., Kadir, N., Ahmad, M., & Abdullah, M. S. (2013). Revisiting energy consumption and GDP: Evidence from dynamic panel data analysis. *Procedia Economics and Finance, 7*, 42–47.

Palil, M. R., Akir, M. R., & Ahmad, W. F. (2013). The perception of tax payers on tax knowledge and tax education with level of tax compliance: A study the influences of religiosity. *ASEAN Journal of Economics, Management and Accounting, 1*(1), 118–129.

Pommerehne, W. W., & Frey, B. S. (1992). *The effects of tax administration on tax morale.* Diskussionsbeiträge: Serie II, Sonderforschungsbereich 178 "Internationalisierung der Wirtschaft", Universität Konstanz, No. 191. Retrieved from http://hdl.handle.net/10419/101488

Pommerehne, W. W., Hart, A., & Frey, B. S. (1994). Tax morale, tax evasion and the choice of policy instruments in different political systems. *Public Finance, 49*, 52–69.

Pope, J., & Mohdali, R. (2010). The role of religiosity in tax morale and tax compliance. *Australian Tax Forum, 25*, 565–596.

Prammer, D., & Reiss, L. (2015). Impact of inflation on fiscal aggregates in Austria. *Monetary Policy & The Economy, Q1*(15), 27–41.

Randlane, K. (2016). Tax compliance as a system: Mapping the field. *International Journal of Public Administration, 39*(7), 515–525.

Raskolnikov, A. (2009). Revealing choices: Using taxpayer choice to target tax enforcement. *Columbia Law Review, 109*(4), 689–754.

Richardson, G. (2006). Determinants of tax evasion: A cross-country investigation. *Journal of International Accounting, Auditing and Taxation, 15*(2), 150–169.

Richardson, G. (2008). The relationship between culture and tax evasion across countries: Additional evidence and extensions. *Journal of International Accounting, Auditing and Taxation, 17* (2), 67–78.

Rodrik, D. (1998). Why do more open economies have bigger governments? *Journal of Political Economy, 106*(5), 997–1032.

Ross, A. M., & McGee, R. W. (2011). A demographic study of Malaysian views on the ethics of tax evasion. In *Allied academies international conference. Academy of legal, ethical and regulatory issues. Proceedings 15*(1). Jordan Whitney Enterprises.

Roth, J. A., & Scholz, J. T. (1989). *Taxpayer compliance, Volume 1: An agenda for research* (Vol. 1). Philadelphia: University of Pennsylvania Press.

Snavely, K. (1990). Governmental policies to reduce tax evasion: Coerced behavior versus service and values development. *Policy Science, 23*(1), 57–72.

Spicer, M. W., & Hero, R. E. (1985). Tax evasion and heuristics: A research note. *Journal of Public Economics, 26*(2), 263–267.

Stack, S., & Kposowa, A. (2006). The effect of religiosity on tax fraud acceptability: A cross-national analysis. *Journal for the Scientific Study of Religion, 45*(3), 325–351.

Strielkowski, W., & Čábelková, I. (2015). Religion, culture, and tax evasion: Evidence from the Czech Republic. *Religions, 6*(2), 657–669.

Tanzi, V. (1992). Structural factors and tax revenue in developing countries: A development economies: Structural adjustment and agriculture. In I. Goldin & L. A. Winters (Eds.), *Open economies: Structural adjustment and agriculture* (pp. 267–281). New Delhi: Cambridge University Press.

Torgler, B. (2003). *Tax morale: Theory and empirical analysis of tax compliance*. Doctoral dissertation, University of Basel.

Torgler, B. (2004). Tax morale in Asian countries. *Journal of Asian Economics, 15*(2), 237–266.

Torgler, B. (2005). Tax morale and direct democracy. *European Journal of Political Economy, 21* (2), 525–531.

Torgler, B. (2006). The importance of faith: Tax morale and religiosity. *Journal of Economic Behavior & Organization, 61*(1), 81–109.

Torgler, B., & Murphy, K. (2004). Tax morale in Australia: What shapes it and has it changed over time. *Journal of Australian Taxation, 7*(2), 298–335.

Torgler, B., & Schneider, F. (2007). What shapes attitudes toward paying taxes? Evidence from multicultural European countries. *Social Science Quarterly, 88*(2), 443–470.

Verboon, P., & van Dijke, M. (2011). When do severe sanctions enhance compliance? The role of procedural fairness. *Journal of Economic Psychology, 32*(1), 120–130.

Welch, M. R., Tittle, C. R., & Petee, T. (1991). Religion and deviance among adult Catholics: A test of the "moral communities" hypothesis. *Journal for the Scientific Study of Religion, 30*(2), 159–172.

Chapter 10
Assessing the Twin and Triple Deficit Hypotheses in Developing Economies: A Panel Causality Analysis

Arzu Tay Bayramoğlu and Zafer Öztürk

Abstract Twin deficit hypothesis, regarding Keynesian and Ricardian perspective, introducing of the linkage between budget deficit and current account deficit is broadly investigated. The literature on triple deficits which advance twin deficit hypothesis by associating savings and fixed investments is limited. The aim of this chapter is to explore whether the twin and triple deficit hypotheses are valid in developing economies. To this end, the twin and triple deficit hypotheses are examined by testing Dumitrescu and Hurlin (Economic Modelling 29(4): 1450–1460, 2012) panel causality approach for 15 developing country economies. The Czech Republic, Hungary, Estonia, Lithuania, Latvia, Ukraine, Brazil, India, Malaysia, Slovak Republic, Romania, Poland, Russian Federation, South Africa, and Turkey were analyzed, and the period is between 2000 and 2015 in the study. According to the panel causality results, there is a unidirectional causality from budget deficit to current account deficit. It is concluded that hypothesis of twin deficits is valid for the country group analyzed. In the field of the triple deficit hypothesis, a strong interrelationship between domestic savings and the current account is reached, while a causal relationship between fixed capital investments and the current account balance cannot be determined. In this context, when considering domestic savings as the decisive variable in the saving-investment gap, it is concluded that the theory of triple deficit is partially valid for the group of developing countries.

Introduction

The most important criteria for ensuring macroeconomic equilibrium in the economy are the budget balance and the current account balance. The budget deficit and current account deficit and the long duration of these deficits cause many permanent and significant problems in economies. A large-scale budget deficit raises interest

A. T. Bayramoğlu (✉) · Z. Öztürk
Bulent Ecevit University, Zonguldak, Turkey
e-mail: arzutb@beun.edu.tr; zaferozturk@beun.edu.tr

© Springer International Publishing AG, part of Springer Nature 2018
H. Dincer et al. (eds.), *Global Approaches in Financial Economics, Banking, and Finance*, Contributions to Economics, https://doi.org/10.1007/978-3-319-78494-6_10

rates and therefore leads the crowding out of private investments. Similarly, a current account deficit causes some problems such as a decrease in competitive power, the depletion of foreign exchange reserves, and the transfer of wealth to foreign countries (Ahmad et al. 2015: 80). The monetary and fiscal policies to be followed to cover the deficits affect other macroeconomic variables and make the problems more complicated.

One of the main issues to economic growth in developing countries is the low investment rates. The reason for the inadequacy of investments is the low saving rate and the insufficient capital that is caused by this. When the domestic resources required for financing growth and development are not sufficient, foreign resources are used. Foreign savings are obtained from abroad with a certain cost according to the risk premium of the country. Financing of investments with external savings increases vulnerability by leading to the outward-oriented growth and influenced by the fluctuations of the international economy. After the 1980s, liberalization of goods, services, and financial markets has facilitated the outsourcing of countries to obtain foreign resources. In this process, the developing economies with low savings rates and high consumption rates have a problem that is current account deficit. Meanwhile, the public budget deficit has arisen in the development process, in developing countries, where all three balances as public, current account, and saving-investment have a deficit.

Budget deficits and current account deficits are serious problems for all countries, whether they are developed or developing countries. In the literature, the existence of these two types of deficits in an economy and is related to each other is called twin deficits. The problems of the budget deficit and the current account deficit, which have mostly risen in many economies from the 1980s until today, have been discussed and investigated in the literature.

Considering recent developments in world economies, however, it can be observed that there is a growing current account deficit problem, while positive developments in important macroeconomic indicators such as the budget deficit, inflation, and interest rates are experienced. This situation led to the questioning of the hypothesis of the twin deficit, and it turned out that current account deficits affect not only budget deficits but also a saving-investment gap. In this context, in the literature, the deficit in the current account balance, composing external balance, the saving-investment gap, and the budget deficit together, is called "triple deficit." In other words, the twin deficit hypothesis is expanded and is saving gap added to the budget and the current account deficit to create a triple deficit hypothesis.

Although there are lots of studies, examining the hypothesis of the twin deficit in the literature, there are no much studies testing the triple deficit hypothesis. The motivation of this chapter is to explore whether the triple deficit hypothesis is valid in developing economies. Following the introduction part, the second part provides the theoretical framework in terms of different approaches. In the third part of the chapter, the relevant literature is given in a wide range. Data set, econometric model and methodology, and model outputs are stated in the fourth section. In the last part, the concluding remark is given.

Theoretical Framework

In the literature, the relationship between the budget deficit and the current account deficit is explained in different ways. The most common approaches to explain this relationship are "traditional Keynesian approach" and "Ricardian equivalence hypothesis" (Berke et al. 2015: 68). The Keynesian perspective argues that there is a positive correlation between the current account deficit and the budget deficit. According to this approach, budget deficits as a result of the expanding fiscal policies applied in an economy create an increase in consumption expenditures and national income. Increased national income leads to a rise in imports, and therefore current account deficits grow. Also, increasing of budget deficits causes to rise of domestic interest rates. A rise in interest rates also increases capital inflows to the country and leads to the evaluation of national currency. This process results in a deficit of the current account. This approach following an indirect route, in which budget deficits causes to increase current account deficits by raising interest rates, is called the Feldstein chain approach in the literature (Feldstein 1986: 2). According to the Feldstein chain approach, the interrelation between current account deficit and budget deficit depends on the free movement of capital. A rise in interest rates accelerates capital inflows to the country. While capital mobility is high, short-term capital inflows increase, and demand for national money also increases at the same rate. In other words, in this hypothesis, where there is high capital mobility, savings and investments are not related, and in such a case, the budget deficit and the current account deficit act together (Marinheiro 2008: 1042).

Undoubtedly, an important factor that determines the effect of the budget deficit on the current account deficit is how the funding is financed. The intensive use of domestic borrowing in the financing of budget deficits leads to a rise in interest rates in emerging economies where the savings level is inadequate and alternative sources of funding for public deficits and economic growth are extremely limited. Increase in interest rates also leads to a deterioration of the public budget, crowding out, and a negative impact on investment-saving balance.

In addition to the theoretical approaches that budget deficits directly or indirectly affect current account deficits, current account deficits also consider budget deficits unilaterally. From this perspective, the current account deficit decreases the growth rates, which causes budget deficits. It is argued that this is especially true in developing open economies (Baharumshah et al. 2006: 335) in that they do not have enough domestic savings to realize economic development, and they need intensive foreign capital inflows.

The Ricardian equivalence hypothesis, on the other hand, asserts that there is no connection between current account deficit and budget deficit. The hypothesis says, if a budget deficit arising in an economy is financed by borrowing, then this does not affect consumption, savings, investment, and current account in that economy. When public debts increase, taxes which will arise in the future to finance these debts are perceived by the private sector in the current period. Despite the decrease in taxes in the current period, households will not increase their consumption because they know that the tax will increase in the future. For this reason, the savings increase, while taxes decrease. The decrease in public savings, as a result of the budget deficit, will be neutralized by the rise in private savings, so the interest rates, investments, and the current account balance will not be affected since total savings do not change (Barro 1989; Yıldırım et al. 2016: 449).

The validity of this hypothesis depends on that intergenerational transfers exist or that the lifespan is infinite under the assumption of full employment. However, many studies have shown that tax reductions in the current period increased consumption. It is revealed that the Ricardian equivalence hypothesis does not work because of factors such as the different time dimension of the government and households, uncertainty, liquidity limitations, the presence of households in each generation without children, or households not paying attention to the welfare of their children (Yıldırım et al. 2016: 450).

In an economy, the existence of a current account deficit is due to the saving gaps as the result of imbalances between investments and savings that are the source of growth and the budget deficits as the result of public revenue-expenditure imbalances. For this reason, budget balance and saving-investment balance are some of the main factors for macroeconomic stability in economies. These economic indicators and the current account deficit caused by them are among the variables that policymakers closely follow and value for the permanent stability and economic growth. Recently, in the developing economies, these indicators do not establish equilibrium, and deficits have been observed (Özdemir et al. 2014).

In recent years, triple deficit hypothesis is another issue discussed in the literature, depending on the hypothesis of twin deficits. In an economy, if a budget deficit, saving-investment gap, and foreign trade deficit arise in the same period, it is called a triple deficit. In the case of triple deficits, simultaneous deficits of the public sector revenue-expenditure balance and the private sector saving-investment balance, which constitute the domestic economic balance, cause a deficit in the external balance (Szakolczai 2006).

In order to express the concept of triple deficits as an equation, first of all, it is necessary to explain how macroeconomic equilibrium occurs. The concept of deficit means that there is no equilibrium in three important macroeconomic variables. From this point, the theoretical bases of the triple deficit hypothesis can be explained by Keynesian national income identity (İpek and Ayvaz Kızılgöl 2016; Yıldırım et al. 2016: 102):

$$Y = C + I + G + (X - M) \tag{10.1}$$

In Eq. (10.1), (C) denotes expenditures of consumption, (I) is represented expenditures of investment, (G) presents expenditures of public, (X) represents exports of goods and services, (M) denotes imports of goods and services, and accordingly $(X–M)$ refers to net exports. All of the consumption, investment, and public expenditures in an economy imply aggregate expenditures (AE) as seen in Eq. (10.2). When the left side of Eq. (10.2) is written in the first equation, Eq. (10.3) is obtained. When this last equation is rearranged, Eq. (10.4) is obtained. In

Eq. (10.4), the left side of the equation indicates the internal balance, and the right side shows the external balance.

$$AE = C + I + G \qquad (10.2)$$
$$Y = AE + (X - M) \qquad (10.3)$$
$$Y - AE = (X - M) \qquad (10.4)$$

If the expenditures are more than the production in an open economy, the left-hand side of Eq. (10.4) takes a negative value, and the internal deficit occurs in that economy. In such a case, the right-hand side of the equation will also have a negative value to provide equilibrium, which means that external deficit also occurs.

The sources of external deficits that arise in an economy can be the private sector and the public sector. This can be explained by the leaks and injections in an open economy. Investments (I), government expenditures (G), and exports (X), which cause an increase in demand for domestic goods, constitute injections in an economy. On the contrary, savings (S), taxes (T), and imports (M) reduce demand for domestic goods, leading to leaks in that economy (Yıldırım et al. 2016: 175). The total expenditure for goods supplied in an economy is given in Eq. (10.5), and the use of revenue obtained from this supply is shown in Eq. (10.6).

$$AE = C + I + G + X \qquad (10.5)$$
$$Y = C + S + T + M \qquad (10.6)$$

Equations (10.5) and (10.6) are equated to each other since the expenditure must be made as much as the good produced to ensure equilibrium in the economy, and Eq. (10.7) is obtained.

$$C + S + T + M = C + I + G + X \qquad (10.7)$$

Equation (10.8) obtained by rearranging Eq. (10.7) shows that the injections in the economy are equal to the leaks.

$$S + T + M = I + G + X \qquad (10.8)$$

Equation (10.9), indicating the sources of external deficits in the economy, is obtained when the necessary arrangements are made in Eq. (10.8).

$$(S - I) + (T - G) = (X - M) \qquad (10.9)$$

In Eq. (10.9), the internal and external balance of an economy is expressed. On the left side, $(S–I)$ is the balance of private sector saving-investment; $(T–G)$ indicates the balance of public sector budget. The expression $(X–M)$ on the right side shows the external equilibrium. This equation shows that if the economy has an external deficit, it can be due to private sector saving-investment gap and/or the budget deficit. If the external balance is accompanied by a budget deficit, the economy has twin deficits. The saving gap that arises due to the inefficiency of domestic savings in meeting domestic investments is accompanied by the twin deficit problem and creates triple deficits (Szakolczai 2006). Eğilmez (2012) defines triple deficits as the "balance of imbalance." According to Eğilmez, the triple deficit is expressed as a situation where the two equilibria that constitute the domestic economic equilibrium have deficits and as a situation where this deficit is balanced by the external deficit.

Literature Review

In the literature, there are many studies test the hypothesis of twin deficits. While some of these studies have reached conclusions that support the traditional Keynesian approach, others have come to the conclusion that they support the Ricardian equivalence hypothesis. Dibooglu (1997), Akbostancı and Tunç (2002), Piersanti (2000), Acaravci and Ozturk (2008), Kalou and Paleologou (2012), Perera and Liyanage (2012), Saeed and Khan (2012), and Ahmad et al. (2015) have obtained results that support the traditional Keynesian approach in their work for the United States, for Turkey, for the OECD countries, for Greece, for Sri Lanka, for Pakistan, and for African countries, respectively. On the other hand, Feldstein (1992), Daly and Siddiki (2009), Aksu and Başar (2009), Afonso and Rault (2009), and Bolat et al. (2011) have reached results that support the Ricardian equivalence hypothesis in their studies for the United States, for 23 OECD countries, for Turkey, for OECD and EU countries, and for Turkey, respectively.

In addition to researchers that test the twin deficit hypothesis, there are some studies on triple deficits that include savings and investment variables in the analysis and use different empirical methods. Some of these studies analyze the relationship of variables with each other or with other variables, while some of them investigate the triple deficit hypothesis directly. The results obtained from studies that test the triple deficit hypothesis vary. While some studies have concluded that confirm the hypothesis, others do not seem to confirm the hypothesis.

Zaidi's (1985) study on developing countries' foreign debt by using time series analysis indicates that there is pressure on savings because of the increase in investment expenditures and the rise in budget deficits leads to negative impacts on external deficits. Hence, it is stated that the hypothesis of triple deficits is acceptable in the countries mentioned in the analysis. This work is also one of the first studies on triple deficits.

Roubini's (1988) research includes 18 member states of the OECD. As a result of the different regressions, using data over the 1960–1985 period, he concludes that saving gap leads to increase in the budget deficits and budget deficits also increase external deficits, based on the triple deficit context.

Doménech et al. (2000) conducted VAR analysis for 18 OECD countries in their study. The result of the analysis is that permanent savings shocks have a temporary impact on the balance of the budget. Contrary to the traditional view, it is stated that the Ricardian equivalence hypothesis is acceptable, and in this context, it is stated that the hypothesis of triple deficits is not acceptable in the mentioned countries.

Chowdhury and Saleh (2007) have investigated the interrelationship among the budget deficit, saving-investment gap, current account deficit, and trade openness for the short and long term in Sri Lanka. They have used ARDL method and a data set covering over the 1970–2005 period. According to empirical results, Keynesian perspective, which argues there is a meaningful linkage among the budget deficit, saving-investment gap, and current account deficit, is supported. In addition to this, the coefficient of the trade openness variable is statistically insignificant and positive in the model, in which the current account deficit is the dependent variable.

Karaçor et al. (2012) examined the triple deficit hypothesis by using VAR analysis and Granger causality test for the Turkish economy with the data over the period 1980–2010. According to the results of the VAR analysis, there is bilateral causality between current account deficit and public deficit, which means current account deficit leads to rising in public deficit and public deficit also increases current account deficit. In addition to this, there is no short-term causality relationship between the mentioned variables.

Akıncı and Yılmaz (2012) analyzed the existence of the hypothesis of triple deficits in Turkey by the ARDL boundary test approach for the period 1975–2010. According to the results of the analysis, the savings gap and budget deficits influence on the current account deficit positively in short and long term and the hypothesis of triple deficits exist in the Turkish economy in the mentioned period.

Yaraşır Tülümce (2013) explored the hypothesis of triple deficits in the Turkish economy using the VAR model for the period 1984–2010. In view of the analysis, the hypothesis of triple deficits was not confirmed for Turkey. However, a relation between current account deficit and savings gap is determined, and hence the reason of current account deficits is found as the savings gap.

Türkay (2013) investigated the interrelationship among the current deficit, the budget deficit, and the investment-saving gap in Turkey in the study. In the analysis part of the research, using data from 1980 to 2012, the relation between the variables has been investigated by the Engle-Granger two-stage method and the dynamic ordinary least square approach. In view of the analysis, the validity of a long-term linkage between the budget deficit, the current account deficit, and the investment-saving gap has been determined.

Tang (2014) analyzed the hypothesis of triple deficits in the United States during the period from 1960 (Q1) to 2013 (Q1). ARDL and Toda-Yamamoto causality methods are used in the study. As a result of the analysis, budget deficits, trade deficits, and financial account deficits have a correlation in the long term. For the American economy, the triple deficit hypothesis is valid.

Şen et al. (2014) analyzed the hypothesis of triple deficits in the Turkish economy with the data set covering 1980–2010 periods by the VAR and Dolado-Lütkepohl causality test. The analysis outcomes imply that the hypothesis of triple deficits is existed in the Turkish economy.

In the study of Akbas and Lebe (2016), bootstrap panel cointegration method has been used to examine the triple deficit hypothesis in G7 countries for the time period from 1994 to 2011. They have determined that there are two bilateral causality relationships between the savings gap and current account deficit and between the budget deficit and the savings gap. Also, according to the analysis, triple deficit hypothesis is valid for G7 countries.

Akbaş et al. (2014) have investigated the existence of the hypothesis of triple deficits during the time period from 1960 to 2012 in Turkey. Confirming to Toda-Yamamoto causality test results, there are two bilateral causalities between the budget deficit and current account deficit and between the savings gap and current account deficit. Thus, they have confirmed the triple deficit hypothesis in Turkey.

İpek and Ayvaz Kızılgöl (2016) investigated the existence of a triple deficit hypothesis for the Turkish economy. ARDL boundary test and Toda-Yamamoto causality methods are performed using the data over the period 2004:1–2014:3. Findings from empirical analyses indicate that the hypothesis of triple deficits is existed in the mentioned period in the Turkish economy.

Karanfil and Kılıç (2015), in their study, analyze triple deficit hypothesis in the Turkish economy with the data set covering 1980–2013 period by Granger causality and cointegration analysis. The results of the analysis indicate that there are one-way causality relationships from the current deficit to saving gap and to the budget deficit in the Turkish economy, and a bilateral relationship among savings gap and budget deficit, and hence the hypothesis of triple deficits is valid.

Shastri et al. (2017) have analyzed the validity of triple deficit hypothesis in five South Asian countries for the years from 1985 to 2015. According to the results obtained from panel cointegration tests, a long-term interrelationship exists among the variables budget balance, current account balance, and savings gap. The study reveals that triple deficit hypothesis is valid in the mentioned countries since the long run coefficients of budget balance and savings gap are positive.

Şen and Kaya (2016) have employed the Granger causality method to examine the hypothesis of twin and triple deficits in their study. The year-end data set covers the time period 1994–2012. Also the analysis includes six postcommunist countries. The results of the study indicate that there is not any causality between the budget deficits and trade deficits or savings gap or current account deficits. Çoban and Balıkçıoğlu (2016) used a dynamic panel data method in the study of the presence of the hypothesis of triple deficit in 24 transition countries. As a result of the study covering the years of 2002–2013, no relation between current deficit and savings gap was found.

Objective of the Chapter

The purpose of the present chapter is to explore the linkage between budget deficit/surplus, domestic saving, fixed investments, and current account deficit by panel causality technique to test the twin and triple deficit hypotheses for developing economies, the Czech Republic, Hungary, Estonia, Lithuania, Latvia, Ukraine, Brazil, India, Malaysia, Slovak Republic, Romania, Poland, Russian Federation, South Africa, and Turkey in the period between 2000 and 2015.

Data Set, Econometric Method, and Empirical Results

As the hypothesis of twin deficit, public balance affects the balance of the current account. Triple deficit hypothesis says that the public budget balance and private sector investment-saving balance have an influence on the current account deficit. The model is examined in Eq. (10.10):

$$\text{CA}_{it} = \alpha_0 + \alpha_1 \sum_{i=1}^{n} S_{it} + \alpha_2 \sum_{i=1}^{n} I_{it} + \alpha_3 \sum_{i=1}^{n} \text{DS}_{it} + \mu_{it} \qquad (10.10)$$

In Eq. (10.10), CA represents current account, S gross domestic savings, I the gross fixed capital investments, and DS budget deficit/surplus, and μ_{it} denotes the error term, (t) is the model's time dimension, and (i) is the model's cross dimension.

Data Set

In this model, panel data analysis covers selected 15 developing country economies, the Czech Republic, Hungary, Estonia, Lithuania, Latvia, Ukraine, Brazil, India, Malaysia, Slovak Republic, Romania, Poland, Russian Federation, South Africa, and Turkey, and the period is between 2000 and 2015. The data (CA, S, I, DS), in current US dollars, are in proportion to GDP. They are obtained from the World Bank database.

Panel Data

Panel data analysis method which has significant advantages compared to other techniques was chosen in the chapter. The most important feature of this analysis is that it allows building a data set with both time and cross-section dimensions, by compounding cross-section and time series. Panel data analysis seems to have various advantages when examined in contrast with cross-section and time series analysis. At first, by compounding cross section with time series observations means that large observation provides a high degree of freedom and reduces the likelihood of high linear correlation between explanatory variables. Then, panel data can better observe and determine impacts, easily cannot be detected in a cross-section or a time series data.

Another benefit of panel data analysis is that it provides the establishment and examining of more complex behavioral models than cross-section or time series. This advantage does not cause any significant problem in the panel data analysis of excluded variables leading to significant deviations in estimation results in studies using time series or cross-section data (Baltagi 2008: 295).

Cross-section Dependence

Regarding econometrics, cross-section independence refers that there is no connection between individuals forming the panels and error terms in the model; see in Eq. (10.11). According to the economics perspective, it could be inferred that in a situation in which the panel units are forming, the panel is not influenced by a shock; the other panel units will be influenced too (Akbaş et al. 2013).

$$y_{it} = \alpha_i + \beta_i x_{it} + \varepsilon_{it}$$
$$\mathrm{Cov}(\varepsilon_{it}, \varepsilon_{ij}) \neq 0 \tag{10.11}$$

Then, traditional ordinary least square (OLS)-based estimations are inefficient, biased, and inconsistent in case of cross-section dependence. Hence, the existence of cross-section dependence in the panel should be tested before proceeding to the panel analyses (Pesaran 2004; Breusch and Pagan 1980). Pesaran et al. (2008) added the mean and the variance to the test statistics to the adjusted Breusch and Pagan (1980) Lagrange multiplier test and cross dependence test advanced by Pesaran (2004). Then, this test known as the LM test adjusted according to the bias method ($\mathrm{LM}_{\mathrm{adj}}$) is in below:

$$\mathrm{CD} = \sqrt{\frac{2T}{N(N-1)}} \left[\sum_{i=1}^{N-1} \sum_{j=i+1}^{N} \widehat{\rho}_{ij} \right] \quad N(0,1) \tag{10.12}$$

In Eq. (10.12), $\widehat{\rho}_{ij}$ represents the correlation coefficient between the residuals acquired from each regression by using ordinary least square (OLS). Test hypotheses are:

H_0: no cross-section dependence
H_1: cross-section dependence

From the test results, if the H_0 is not rejected, the analysis is needed to be continued with the first generation of panel unit root tests. However, if the H_0 is rejected and there is a cross-section dependence among panel units, then the analysis should be continued with second generation of panel unit root tests (Baltagi 2008: 284).

The cross-section dependency in the series was checked by Pesaran (2004) CDLM test, and the outcome is shown in Table 10.1. As seen in Table 10.1, the null hypothesis is rejected strongly because the probability value of statistic CDLM is smaller than 0.05. From here it is concluded that the shocks of the variables in one of the country also affect other countries.

Table 10.1 Cross-sectional dependency

CD test	Stat.	Prob.
Pesaran CD	3.862	0.0001

According to the CD test results obtained in Table 10.1, there is a significant relationship among the individuals of the panel. Hence, it is rejected the null hypothesis (H_0) says that the series are not dependent on each other, and it is revealed that a cross-sectional dependence exists in the panel data model.

Panel Unit Root

Panel-based unit root tests, which are called first-generation tests, are devised under the hypothesis that the panel individuals are independent of each other, while panel-based unit root tests called second-generation tests are built on the assumption that the individuals are not independent of each other.

Cross-section dependence influences the test structures used in statistical analysis. It needs to apply to second-generation panel unit root test because of the existence of cross-sectional dependence in the model. Therefore, it was used as one of the second-generation unit root tests by Pesaran (2007) CADF (cross-sectionally augmented Dickey-Fuller) test for the analysis of stationary. Second-generation tests are applied as CADF, and CIPS (cross section Im, Pesaran, and Shin) unit root test process can be considered as follows:

$$\Delta y_{it} = \alpha_i + b_i y_{i,t-1} + c_i \bar{y}_{t-1} + d_i \Delta \bar{y}_t + u_{it} \tag{10.13}$$

In Eq. (10.13), α_i is constant, $\Delta \bar{Y}_{t-1}$ is the differences' a lag, and $\bar{Y}_{t-1}$ is the one lag of $\bar{Y}_t$. The hypotheses of null and alternative for CADF testing are in below:

$H_0 = \beta 1 = \beta 2 =..... \beta n = 0$ (series contains a unit root)
$H_A = \beta 1 \neq \beta 2 \neq..... \beta n \neq 0$ (series are stationary)

The CADF test cannot analyze the stationarity of all panels; thus, the CIPS test developed by Pesaran (2007) fills a gap of the CADF test. This test can analyze for all panels which series is stationary under the null hypothesis and use the Pesaran critical value. Equation (10.13) stability analysis is tested in CADF by comparing the statistical values of the t values for the b_i coefficients with of the Pesaran (2007) table critical values obtained from the Monte Carlo simulations. Unit root test outcomes are shown in Table 10.2.

Table 10.2 Panel unit root results (CADF)

	CADF (constant)		CIPS statistics (constant)	
	Level	I(1)		
Variable	Z[t-bar] prob.	Z[t-bar] prob.	Level	I(1)
CA	2.886 (0.998)	−2.735 (0.003)[*]	−1.426	−3.348[*]
S	3.198 (0.999)	−2.801 (0.003)[*]	−1.546	−3.548[*]
I	2.991 (0.999)	−1.554 (0.060)[***]	−1.282	−3.255[*]
DS	3.019 (0.999)	−3.638 (0.000)[*]	−1.928	−4.293[*]

Note: "*," "**," and "***" are implied that provided stationary in 1%, 5%, and 10% according to the Pesaran (2007: 274, 281) critical values of constant and trend models

According to the unit root results obtained from the CADF and CIPS statistics in Table 10.2, CA, S, I, and DS are not stationary; they have a unit root at the level. As in Table 10.2, $D(I)$, $S(I)$, and $DS(I)$ are stationary at 1% level, and the I variable is stationary at 10% level. In this case, it needs to get the variables' first differences for the panel causality analysis.

Panel Causality

The causality analysis developed by Granger (1969) estimates whether other variables provide useful information when estimating the future value of a variable. After Holtz-Eakin et al. (1988) have begun to examine the panel data causality framework, new techniques have been introduced to the literature for the causality relationship. The main reason for the Granger causality test for panel data framework is the desire to benefit from the advantages of the structure of the panel data models. Panel data permits more flexible modeling of unit behavior than traditional time series analysis and at the same time has more observations than the singular time series, resulting in more effective results than the Granger tests in a traditional context, especially in short-time periods. As indicated by Dumitrescu and Hurlin (2012), there is a high likelihood that a causality relationship applicable to a country in terms of an economic fact is valid for other countries. For this reason, the causality relationship can be tested more effectively with more observations in the panel data framework (Bozoklu and Yılancı 2013: 174).

The cross-section dependency affects the selection of the panel causality technique. All of the panel causality tests estimate under the hypothesis of no cross-section dependence. Only the Dumitrescu and Hurlin (2012) methodology can be applied to approximate both cross-section independence and cross-section dependence and achieve effective results (Dumitrescu and Hurlin 2012: 1).

The main benefit of the Dumitrescu and Hurlin's (2012) method over the other tests is that the absence of a homogeneous Granger causality relation under the basic hypothesis is tested against the alternative hypothesis at least one cross section has this relationship. That is, the test considers the cross-section dependency among the panel countries. Apart from that, the other superior aspect of the test is that it is insensitive to the size difference between time dimension and cross-section size. That is, the test can produce effective results in all cases (Bozoklu and Yılancı 2013: 175).

The test of the Dumitrescu and Hurlin (2012) is similar to the Granger causality test for heterogeneous panel units. This test expresses the individual Wald tests' average calculated for cross-sectional units under the Granger causality test, notices both heterogeneity and cross-section dependence. In the panel Granger causality methodology advanced by Dumitrescu and Hurlin (2012), the following linear heterogeneous model is considered for each unit (i) at time t, when X and Y denote the two stationary processes obtained for T units for N units:

$$y_{i,t} = \alpha_i + \sum_{k=1}^{K} \gamma_i^{(k)} y_{i,t-k} + \sum_{k=1}^{K} \beta_i^{(k)} x_{i,t-k} + \varepsilon_{i,t} \tag{10.14}$$

where K is the same lag of the cross sections and $\beta_i = (\beta^{(1)}, \ldots .\beta^{(k)})$. In the panel Granger causality test of Dumitrescu–Hurlin, the absence of a homogeneous Granger causality relation under the null hypothesis is examined against the alternative hypothesis that at least one cross section has this relation. The null and alternative hypotheses established for the above equation are as follows (Dumitrescu and Hurlin 2012: 4):

$$
\begin{aligned}
H_0 &= \beta_i = 0 \quad \forall_i = 1, \ldots, N \\
H_1 &= \beta_i = 0 \quad \forall_i = 1, \ldots, N_1 \qquad 0 \le N_1/N \prec 1 \\
\beta_i &\ne 0 \qquad\quad \forall_i = N_1 + 1, \ldots N
\end{aligned}
$$

It is calculated the Wald statistics $W_{i,T}$ for cross-sectional units to examine the null and alternative hypotheses and obtained the panel's Wald statistic $W_{N,T}^{HNC}$ by getting the average of these statistics. $W_{i,T}$ represents the Wald test statistic used to test Granger causality for the country of i in Eq. (15):

$$W_{N,T}^{HNC} = 1/N. \sum_{i=1}^{N} W_{i,T} \tag{15}$$

Dumitrescu and Hurlin (2012) suggest using the $Z_{N,T}^{HNC}$ statistic with asymptotic distribution in case of the cross-sectional dimension is smaller than the time dimension but recommends using the Z_N^{HNC} statistic in case of the cross-sectional dimension is larger than the time dimension. $Z_{N,T}^{HNC}$ moreover, Z_N^{HNC} test statistics are calculated as follows (Dumitrescu and Hurlin 2012: 4–5):

$$Z_{N,T}^{HNC} = \sqrt{\frac{N}{2K}}\left(W_{N,T}^{HNC} - K\right) \xrightarrow[N\to\infty]{d} N(0,1) \tag{16}$$

and

$$Z_N^{HNC} = \frac{N^{-1/2}.\left[W_{N,T}^{HNC} - N^{-1}.\sum_{i=1}^{N} E(W_{i,T})\right]}{\sqrt{N^{-1}.\sum_{i=1}^{N} \mathrm{Var}(W_{i,T})}} \xrightarrow[N\to\infty]{d} N(0,1) \tag{17}$$

The results of the $Z_{N,T}^{HNC}$ test statistic were used to specify the directions of causality interrelations of the series in the model. According to Table 10.3, the outcomes of the causality analysis are as follows: there is (1) a two-way causality between current account and savings, (2) a one-way causal relation from the budget balance to the current account balance, (3) no causality between fixed investments and current account balance, (4) a two-way causality between savings and fixed

Table 10.3 Dumitrescu and Hurlin (2012) panel causality test results

Null hypotheses			$W_{N,T}^{HNC}$	$Z_{N,T}^{HNC}$	Z_N^{HNC}
CA	Does not Granger cause	S	3.1936	6.2043 (0.0000)*	3.8169 (0.0001)*
S	Does not Granger cause	CA	1.8465	2.3942 (0.0167)*	1.2087 (0.2268)
I	Does not Granger cause	CA	1.3900	1.1030 (0.2700)	0.3248 (0.7453)
CA	Does not Granger cause	I	1.4633	1.3103 (0.1901)	0.4667 (0.6407)
DS	Does not Granger cause	CA	2.0203	2.8859 (0.0039)**	1.5453 (0.1223)
CA	Does not Granger cause	DS	0.7286	0.7678 (0.4426)	-0.9558 (0.3392)
S	Does not Granger cause	I	1.7445	2.1058 (0.0352)**	1.0112 (0.3119)
I	Does not Granger cause	S	2.5009	4.2452 (0.0000)*	2.4758 (0.0133)**
DS	Does not Granger cause	S	1.9357	2.6466 (0.0081)*	1.3814 (0.1671)
S	Does not Granger cause	DS	1.9012	2.5490 (0.0108)**	1.3146 (0.1886)
DS	Does not Granger cause	I	1.4433	1.2540 (0.2099)	0.4281 (0.6686)
I	Does not Granger cause	DS	1.6769	1.9145 (0.0556)***	0.8803 (0.3787)

Note: Values in parentheses indicate p-probability values; *, **, and *** indicate significance at 1%, 5%, and 10%, respectively

investments, (5) a bi-directional causality budget deficits and savings, and (6) a one-way causal relation from fixed capital investments to budget balance.

Concluding Remarks

The hypothesis of twin deficit explains the linkage between public budget deficit and current account deficit in the economy. According to the hypothesis of triple deficits, private sector saving-investment deficit affects the current account deficit with the public budget deficit. This effect is significant in developing economies where savings rates are lower than developed economies. Hence, the domestic saving-investment gap is compensated by foreign savings, which leads to the current account deficit.

In this chapter, the linkage between domestic savings, fixed capital investments, public budget balance, and current account deficits in developing economies was analyzed by the panel causality method based on the twin and the triple deficit hypotheses. Dumitrescu and Hurlin (2012) panel causality test results show that there is a one-way causality relationship from the public budget balance to the current account balance. In this framework, the hypothesis of twin deficits is valid for the country group analyzed. Within the scope of the hypothesis of the triple deficits, bi-directional causality between domestic savings and the current account is reached, while a causal relationship between fixed capital investments and the current account balance cannot be determined. In this context, when considering domestic savings as the decisive variable in the saving-investment gap, it is concluded that the triple deficit theory is partially valid for the group of developing countries. Additionally, when the causality relation between the other variables apart from the current account deficit is examined, it is concluded that there is a mutual relationship between savings and investments and the budget balance and the savings in accordance with the macroeconomic theory. Also, the findings imply that savings, which have the causality relation with all variables, are very important macroeconomic variable for the economies.

Keywords Definitions

Twin deficit hypothesis: The hypothesis that explains budget deficit has influence on current account deficit.

Triple deficit hypothesis: It refers to the situation in the economy, the public budget deficit, the saving-investment deficit, and the current account deficit occurring at the same time.

Budget deficit: It means that government revenue is smaller than the government expense.

Current account: It is defined as the sum of net exports of goods and services, net primary income, and net current transfers.

Saving gap: Private sector savings minus fixed capital investments.

Panel data analysis: It is a type of analysis where cross-sectional observations of units such as individuals, countries, companies, and households are assembled at a certain time period.

References

Acaravci, A., & Ozturk, I. (2008). Twin deficits phenomenon: Empirical evidence from the ARDL bound test approach for Turkey. *Bulletin of Statistics & Economics, 2*(A08), 57–64.

Afonso, A., & Rault, C. (2009). *Budgetary and external imbalances relationship: A panel data diagnostic.* Cesifo Working Paper No. 2559, 1–38.

Ahmad, A. H., Aworinde, O. B., & Martin, C. (2015). Threshold cointegration and the short-run dynamics of twin deficit hypothesis in African countries. *The Journal of Economic Asymmetries, 12*(2), 80–91.

Akbas, Y. E., & Lebe, F. (2016). Current account deficit, budget deficit and saving gap: Is the twin or triplet deficit hypothesis valid in G7 countries? *Prague Economic Papers, 25*(3), 271–286.

Akbas, Y. E., Senturk, M., & Sancar, C. (2013). Testing for causality between the foreign direct investment, current account deficit, GDP and total credit: Evidence from G7. *Panoeconomicus, 60*(6), 791–812.

Akbaş, Y. E., Lebe, F., & Zeren, F. (2014). Testing the validity of the triplet deficit hypothesis for Turkey: Asymmetric causality analysis. *Journal of Business and Economics, 7*(14), 137–154.

Akbostancı, E., & Tunç, G. İ. (2002). *Turkish twin effects: An error correction model of trade balance*. Economic Research Center Working Paper in Economics, No. 01/06. Middle East Technical University.

Akıncı, M., & Yılmaz, Ö. (2012). Validity of the triple deficit hypothesis in Turkey: Bounds test approach. *Istanbul Stock Exchange Review, 13*(50), 1–28.

Aksu, H., & Başar, S. (2009). Türkiye için ikiz açıklar hipotezi'nin tahmini: Bir sınır testi yaklaşımı. *Ankara Üniversitesi SBF Dergisi, 64*(04), 001–014.

Baharumshah, A. Z., Lau, E., & Khalid, A. M. (2006). Testing twin deficits hypothesis using VARs and variance decomposition. *Journal of the Asia Pacific Economy, 11*(3), 331–354.

Baltagi, B. (2008). *Econometrica* (4th ed.). Berlin, Heidelberg: Springer.

Barro, R. J. (1989). The Ricardian approach to budget deficits. *The Journal of Economic Perspectives, 3*(2), 37–54.

Berke, B., Temiz, D., & Karakurt, E. (2015). Üçüz açık ve büyüme ilişkisi: Türkiye örneği. *Eskişehir Osmangazi Üniversitesi İİBF Dergisi, 10*(2), 67–89.

Bolat, S., Belke, M., & Aras, O. (2011). Türkiye'de ikiz açık hipotezinin geçerliliği: Sınır testi yaklaşımı. *Maliye Dergisi, 161*, 347–364.

Bozoklu, Ş., & Yılancı, V. (2013). Finansal gelişme ve iktisadi büyüme arasındaki nedensellik ilişkisi: Gelişmekte olan ekonomiler için analiz. *Dokuz Eylül Üniversitesi İktisadi ve İdari Bilimler Fakültesi Dergisi, 28*(2), 161–187.

Breusch, T. S., & Pagan, A. R. (1980). The Lagrange multiplier test and its applications to model specification in econometrics. *The Review of Economic Studies, 47*(1), 239–253.

Chowdhury, K., & Saleh, A. S. (2007). *Testing the Keynesian proposition of twin deficits in the presence of trade liberalisation: Evidence from Sri Lanka*. Faculty of Business Economics Working Papers, University of Wollongong, No: 07-09, 2–35.

Çoban, H., & Balıkçıoğlu, E. (2016). Triple deficit or twin divergence: A dynamic panel analysis. *The International Journal of Economic and Social Research, 12*(1), 271–280.

Daly, V., & Siddiki, J. U. (2009). The twin deficits in OECD countries: Cointegration analysis with regime shifts. *Applied Economics Letters, 16*(11), 1155–1164.

Dibooglu, S. (1997). Accounting for US current account deficits: An empirical investigation. *Applied Economics, 29*(6), 787–793.

Doménech, R., Taguas, D., & Varela, J. (2000). The effects of budget deficit on national saving in the OECD. *Economics Letters, 69*(3), 377–383.

Dumitrescu, E. I., & Hurlin, C. (2012). Testing for Granger non-causality in heterogeneous panels. *Economic Modelling, 29*(4), 1450–1460.

Eğilmez, M. (2012). *İkiz açık, üçüz açık.* 15.09.2017. http://www.mahfiegilmez.com/2012/10/ikiz-ack-ucuz-ack.html

Feldstein, M. (1986). *The budget deficit and the dollar*. NBER Working Paper, No. 1898, 1–62.

Feldstein, M. (1992). *The budget and trade deficits aren't really twins*. NBER Working Paper, No. 3966, 1–11.

Granger, C. W. (1969). Investigating causal relations by econometric models and cross-spectral methods. *Econometrica: Journal of the Econometric Society, 37*(3), 424–438.

Holtz-Eakin, D., Newey, W., & Rosen, H. S. (1988). Estimating vector autoregressions with panel data. *Econometrica: Journal of the Econometric Society, 56*(6), 1371–1395.

İpek, E., & Ayvaz Kızılgöl, Ö. (2016). Türkiye ekonomisinde üçüz açık. *Ege Akademik Bakış, 16* (3), 425–442.

Kalou, S., & Paleologou, S. M. (2012). The twin deficits hypothesis: Revisiting an EMU country. *Journal of Policy Modeling, 34*(2), 230–241.

Karaçor, Z., Alptekin, V., Akar, T., & Akar, G. (2012). İstikrar mı, istikrarsızlık mı? Türkiye'de üçüz açık analizi. *Türkiye Ekonomi Kurumu 3. Uluslararası Ekonomi Konferansı*, 1–3 Kasım.

Karanfil, M., & Kılıç, C. (2015). Türkiye ekonomisinde üçüz açık hipotezinin geçerliliği: Zaman serisi analizi. *Uluslararası Yönetim İktisat ve İşletme Dergisi, 11*(24), 1–20.

Marinheiro, C. F. (2008). Ricardian equivalence, twin deficits, and the Feldstein–Horioka puzzle in Egypt. *Journal of Policy Modeling, 30*(6), 1041–1056.

Özdemir, D., Buzdağlı, Ö., Emsen, Ö. S., & Çelik, A. A. (2014). Geçiş ekonomilerinde üçüz açık hipotezinin geçerliliği. *International Conference on Eurasian Economies*. Accessed September 26, 2017, from http://avekon.org/papers/991.pdf

Perera, A., & Liyanage, E. (2012). An empirical investigation of the twin deficit hypothesis: Evidence from Sri Lanka. *Staff Studies, 41*(1&2), 41–87.

Pesaran, M. H. (2004). *General diagnostic tests for cross section dependence in panels*. University of Cambridge Working Papers in Economics, No. 0435.

Pesaran, M. H. (2007). A simple panel unit root test in the presence of cross-section dependence. *Journal of Applied Econometrics, 22*(2), 265–312.

Pesaran, M. H., Ullah, A., & Yamagata, T. (2008). A bias-adjusted LM test of error cross-section independence. *The Econometrics Journal, 11*(1), 105–127.

Piersanti, G. (2000). Current account dynamics and expected future budget deficits: Some international evidence. *Journal of International Money and Finance, 19*(2), 255–271.

Roubini, N. (1988). *Current account and budget deficits in an intertemporal model of consumption and taxation smoothing. A solution to the "Feldstein-Horioka Puzzle"?*. NBER Working Paper Series, No. 2773.

Saeed, S., & Khan, M. A. (2012). Twin deficits hypothesis: The case of Pakistan 1972–2008. *Academic Research International, 3*(2), 155–162.

Şen, H., & Kaya, A. (2016). *Are the twin or triple deficits hypotheses applicable to post-communist countries?*. BOFIT Discussion Papers, Bank of Finland, 3.

Şen, A., Şentürk, M., Sancar, C., & Akbaş, Y. E. (2014). Empirical findings on triplet deficits hypothesis: The case of Turkey. *Journal of Economic Cooperation and Development, 35*(1), 81–102.

Shastri, S., Giri, A. K., & Mohapatra, G. (2017). Assessing the triple deficit hypothesis for major South Asian countries: A panel data analysis. *International Journal of Economics and Financial Issues, 7*(4), 292–299.

Szakolczai, G. (2006). The triple deficit of Hungary. *Hungarian Statistical Review, 84*(10), 40–62.

Tang, T. C. (2014). *Fiscal deficit, trade deficit, and financial account deficit: Triple deficits hypothesis with the US experience*. Monash University Department of Economics Discussion Paper, No. 06/14, 1–13.

Türkay, H. (2013). Türkiye'de cari açık, bütçe açığı ve yatırım-tasarruf açığı ilişkisi. *Cumhuriyet Üniversitesi İktisadi ve İdari Bilimler Dergisi, 14*(2), 253–269.

Yaraşır Tülümce, S. (2013). Türkiye'de üçüz açığın ampirik analizi (1984–2010). *Maliye Dergisi, 165*, 97–114.

Yıldırım, K., Karaman, D., & Taşdemir, M. (2016). *Makroekonomi*. Seçkin Yayıncılık.

Zaidi, I. M. (1985). Saving, investment, fiscal deficits, and the external indebtedness of developing countries. *World Development, 13*(5), 573–588.

Chapter 11
Stability Analysis of Some Dynamic Economic Systems Modeled by State-Dependent Delay Differential Equations

Sertaç Erman

Abstract The research subject of many studies is the asymptotical behavior of dynamic systems with both continuous and discrete time scales for economical approaches. The qualitative theory of differential or difference equations is the main basis of these studies. When modeling using ordinary differential equations, the delays in the system are always ignored. However, even a small amount of delay in the system can cause significant changes in the system. For this reason, it is more realistic to use delayed differential equations while modeling the majority of the problems encountered. Moreover, some research showed us that some delays in the systems vary with respect to the internal effects of the system. In this case, using of state-dependent delay differential equations is much more suitable.

In this paper, Kaldorian macro dynamic model with Kaleckian investment delay and models of goods market with supply delay are investigated. First, the classical models are introduced, and then the effects of the delays in the system are discussed. Finally, general systems of state-dependent delay differential equations covering these models are analyzed.

Introduction

Mathematical models are often used to investigate systemic structures on various disciplines such as physics, biology, or social science. One reason for this is that mathematical models reveal some equations relating to the variables and the parameters in the system. These equations enable you to have indicators allowing to predict about behavior of the system in different circumstances. It is obvious that the mathematical models describe the actual process approximately. There is a certain margin of error depending on mathematical model between predictions and actual values of the system. The margin of error can be reduced by using more realistic

S. Erman
İstanbul Medipol University, Istanbul, Turkey
e-mail: serman@medipol.edu.tr

© Springer International Publishing AG, part of Springer Nature 2018   227
H. Dincer et al. (eds.), *Global Approaches in Financial Economics, Banking, and Finance*, Contributions to Economics, https://doi.org/10.1007/978-3-319-78494-6_11

mathematical model. The more realistic model means more parameter, more variable, and more relations. In this case, since the mathematical model becomes more complex form, the analysis of the model is more challenging and may even be impossible with known methods. There is almost always a trade-off between efficiency and simplicity. Both are desirable, but a gain in one usually includes a loss in the other.

It is supposed that t is independent real variable and $y(t)$ is another real variable which is depended on t. Let us use $\Delta t = t_1 - t_0$ to denote change of t from t_0 to t_1. Also let us use $\Delta y(t) = y(t_1) - y(t_0)$ to denote change of y when t changes from t_0 to t_1. Average rate of change of y with respect to t is described as follows:

$$\frac{\Delta y(t)}{\Delta t} = \frac{y(t_0 + \Delta t) - y(t_0)}{\Delta t}.$$

Limit of average rate of change of y as Δt tends to 0 give us instantaneous rate of change of y with respect to t as follows:

$$\frac{dy(t)}{dt} = \lim_{\Delta t \to 0} \frac{\Delta y(t)}{\Delta t} = \lim_{\Delta t \to 0} \frac{y(t_0 + \Delta t) - y(t_0)}{\Delta t}$$

that is definition of differentiation of y with respect to t. It is also shown as $\dot{y}(t)$.

If the change in the variable of the considered system effects to system's dynamics continuously, equations including differentiation of variable are used when the system is being modeled. These equations are called differential equations.

This paper is primarily concerned with two different dynamic economic systems modeled by ordinary differential equations with delay term. The variable t represents time and $y(t)$ represents some quantities in economical systems that vary continuously with time.

Let us consider the mathematical model of the gross domestic product (GDP) over time. In Zhang (2005a), this model is explained as follows:

"If y is considered state of the GDP of the economy, the rate of the change of the GDP is proportional to the current GDP.

$$\dot{y}(t) = gy(t)$$

where $\dot{y}(t)$ is the differentiation of the function y with respect to t." The instantaneous change of growth rate of the GDP is $\dfrac{\dot{y}(t)}{y(t)}$. Thus, the GDP at t is given by solving the differential equation if the growth rate g is given any time t. When g is a constant, the above differential function can be solved explicitly.

According to Zhang (2005a), "it is reasonable to assume that the growth rate is affected by many factors, such as international environment, accumulated knowledge of the economy, the current state of the economic system, and many other conditions. This means that the growth rate may take on a complicated form $g(y,t)$." Hence the growth rate of the GDP is described by

$$\frac{\dot{y}(t)}{y(t)} = g(t, y(t)) \tag{11.1}$$

Moreover, it can be assumed that the growth rate is not only affected by the instantaneous state of the factors but also by some earlier state of the factors. In this case, the model becomes

$$\frac{\dot{y}(t)}{y(t)} = g(t, y(t), y(t - \tau)) \tag{11.2}$$

where $\tau > 0$ is delay or time lag. Differential Eq. (11.2) is called delay differential equation.

In Eq. (11.2), delay term τ is considered as a constant, but more realistically, the delay in the system depends on state of the system. Hence, the model is expressed as

$$\frac{\dot{y}(t)}{y(t)} = g(t, y(t), y(t - \tau(y(t)))) \tag{11.3}$$

where $\tau(y(t)) > 0$ is called state-dependent delay function and Eq. (11.3) is called state-dependent delay differential equation.

The mathematical theory and methods for solving linear differential equations are highly developed. In contrast, for nonlinear differential equations, the theory is more complicated, and methods of solution are less satisfactory. General analytic solution of a nonlinear differential equation may not be obtained as well. On the other hand, most of the mathematical models lead to nonlinear differential equations. Thus, obtaining a linear differential equation approximating a nonlinear differential equation is an extremely important process. This process of approximating a nonlinear differential equation by a linear one is called linearization. Linearization ordinarily is applied at a point and works at near of the point efficiently. The near of this point can be expressed as an interval. That is, the analysis of the linear equation obtained by linearization at point t_0 approximates the nonlinear differential equation in interval $(t_0 - r, t_0 + r)$ where r is small enough real number.

For instance, Eq. (11.1) is a nonlinear differential equation. It is rewritten as

$$\dot{y}(t) = G(t, y) \tag{11.4}$$

where $G(t, y) = g(t, y)y$. Let $G_t(t, y) = \frac{\partial G(t, y)}{\partial t}$ and $G_y(t, y) = \frac{\partial G(t, y)}{\partial y}$, then linearization of Eq. (11.4) at (t_0, y_0) is

$$\dot{y}(t) = G_0 + G_1 t + G_2 y(t)$$

where $G_1 = G_t(t_0, y_0)$, $G_2 = G_y(t_0, y_0)$ and $G_0 = G(t_0, y_0) - G_1 t_0 - G_2 y_0$.

Even though linearization generally transforms nonlinear linear equations to tractable form, convergence of approximation or length of interval of approximation may not be convincing. Additionally, in Driver (1977), it is mentioned that applying above linearization to delay terms may change behavior of the solution of the delay differential equation. Thus, if the equation

$$\dot{y}(t) = G(t, y(t - \tau(y)))$$ (11.5)

is considered in order to reach linearized form, the argument $y(t - \tau(y))$ should be regarded as completely different argument. However, the approximated equation obtained by this procedure is still nonlinear because the equation includes $y(t - \tau(y))$ term. Linearization of state-dependent delay differential equation is done heuristically by freezing the value of the state-dependent delay at its equilibrium value. Justification of this approach is shown in Hartung et al. (2006). On the other hand, in Erman and Demir (2016), range of the solution of this type equation is determined by the means of coefficients and stability of the solution is investigated.

Nonlinear mathematical models are used widely to consider dynamics of economy. The range of the applications includes many topics, such as trade cycles, economic development, economic growth, economic chaos, sexual division of labor, etc. For some application of nonlinear theory to economics, see Rosser (1991), Zhang (1991, 2005b), Puu (2000), Shone (2002), Lorenz (1993).

In this paper, dynamics of commodity price fluctuations based on Walrasian theory and business cycle based on Kaldorian macro dynamic model are considered with supply delay and Kaleckian investment delay, respectively.

Dynamics of Commodity Price Fluctuations

The dependence of production, consumption, and price of a commodity is investigated by dynamic formalization of relationship between market price, demand, and supply as follows:

$$\frac{dP}{dt} = (D(P) - S(P_s))P$$ (11.6)

where $S(P)$ and $D(P)$ are supply and demand functions, respectively, and $P(t)$ is market price in time t in Mackey (1987).

The differential Eq. (11.6) is based on Walrasian theory. It is assumed that a simple balance between supply and demand governs relative variations in market price $P(t)$ with respect to the theory.

It is acceptable to assume that all buying decisions are formed on the current market price. Thus, demand is taken as a function whose argument is P.

Nonetheless, the argument of the supply, P_S, should be approached more sophisticated because of relation with supply price and current market price. In Mackey (1987), the following two factors incorporated in this model are considered: "First, before a decision to adjust production is translated into an actual difference in supply, most commodities need to elapse a finite minimum time $t_{min} \geq 0$. Second, certain commodities, once produced, may be stocked for a variable period of time (denoted by ∇) until the producer deems the market price advantageous for selling. Generally, it would be expected that the maximum storage period ∇_{max} occurs when the market price is about the production price, and as market prices increase, the storage period seems to fall. Thus, the total production delay τ may be either a humped or a monotone decreasing function of current market price:

$$\tau(P) = \tau_{min} + \nabla(P), \tag{11.7}$$

where $\tau_{min} \leq \tau(P) \leq \tau_{min} + \nabla_{max}$."

As a result, due to above two factors in the model, current supply price $P_S(t)$ is affected from only the market price at a time $t - \tau(P)$. Hence, the argument of the supply function is described by previous market price from the current market price:

$$P_s(t) = P(t - \tau(P)).$$

Therefore, the model equation is

$$\dot{P}(t) = P(t)\left[D(P(t)) - S\left(t - \tau(P(t))\right)\right] \tag{11.8}$$

where the delay function is defined by expression (11.7). In Mackey (1987), the linearized stability of an equilibrium solution P^* is studied using freezing the value of the state-dependent delay at its equilibrium value.

A related problem is studied in Bobalova and Novotna (2015) where demand and supply function are assumed as follows:

$$\tilde{D}(P(t)) = P(t)D(P(t)) = d_1 + d_2P(t), \quad d_2 < 0$$
$$\tilde{S}(P(t)) = P(t)S(P(t - \tau)) = s_1 + s_2P\left(t - \tilde{\tau}\right), \quad s_2 > 0$$

where $\tilde{\tau}$ is positive constant delay and stands for the time required to produce a difference in the supply. Thus, the model can be rewritten as follows:

$$\dot{P}(t) = k_1\left(d_1 - s_1 + d_2P(t) - s_2P\left(t - \tilde{\tau}\right)\right) \tag{11.9}$$

where $k_1, s_1, s_2 > 0$, d_1, and $d_2 < 0$ are real parameters.

However, for more realistic modeling, the delay term should be taken as depending on current market price. In this case, the system again can be described by Eqs. (11.8) and (11.9) as follows:

$$\dot{P}(t) = -A_1P(t) - A_2P(t - \tilde{\tau}(P)) + A_3 \tag{11.10}$$

where $A_1 = -k_1d_2$, $A_2 = k_1s_2$, and $A_3 = k_1d_1 - k_1s_1$. In the sequel, applying transformation $P(t) = x(t) + \frac{A_3}{A_1+A_2}$ to Eq. (11.10), the following equation is obtained:

$$\dot{x}(t) = -A_1 x(t) - A_2 x(t - \tau(x(t))) \tag{11.11}$$

where $\tau(x(t)) = \widetilde{\tau}\left(x + \dfrac{A_3}{A_1 + A_2}\right)$.

The range of the solution of the Eq. (11.11) is determined for delay function τ $(x(t)) = \frac{a+bx(t)}{c+dx(t)}$ in Erman and Demir (2016). This type of delay function can be considered as [1/1] Pàde approximation of any continuous function. Moreover, in Erman and Demir (2016), some criteria of asymptotic stability are given in the terms of upper bound of the delay function and coefficient of the equation.

Application of the Model (11.11)

Bobalova and Novotna summarized the evolution of the meat market in the Czech Republic from 1960 to 2014 in Bobalova and Novotna (2015) as follows:

"For the past several decades, in particular from the 1960s, meat consumption in the Czech Republic has been increasing. The reason for this increase is that in the past, production of agricultural commodities and products was subsidized by the state. Meat consumption in the Czech Republic reached its peak in 1989 and 1990— 97.4 and 96.5 kg per person and year, respectively. Afterward there was a decline in meat sales which was due to an increase in prices and price liberalization. A new increase in the consumption of this meat was caused by favorable price relations in comparison with other kinds of meat, the spread of higher finalization products on the domestic market, easy and fast kitchen preparation, and in the 1990s also findings on dietological properties of different kinds of meat. In the last few years, poultry meat has been the cheapest meat on the domestic market in comparison with other kinds of meat.

A significant change in the poultry meat consumption occurred in 2003, when this meat experienced a moderate decline. The next year, however, the consumption increased again to 25.3 kg per person and year. A record increase in poultry meat consumption occurred in 2005—26.1 kg per person. For a comparison, consumption in EU countries is around 23 kg. In 2007, there was a decline in poultry meat consumption, which was most probably caused by consumers having concerns about bird flu. At the moment, poultry meat consumption in the Czech Republic ranges between 24 and 25 kg per person and year."

Data from outlook and situation reports of the Ministry of Health of the Czech Republic was used in order to compile their model. By utilizing annual data for the years 2002–2014 with regression analysis, the corresponding coefficients were obtained. It was assumed that the length of the delay corresponds to ability of adaptation of the poultry meat producers to new market conditions and it is a constant. Thus, Bobalova and Novotna have established the following model:

$$\dot{P}(t) = k_1(209.2 - 0.78P(t) - 1.78P(t - 0.5))$$

with history function $P_0(t) = 0.181t^2 + 3.4t + 67$ for $t \in [-0.5, 0]$. The coefficient k_1, which represents sensitivity of the market to changing conditions, was used as parameter to identify behavior of the solution. It was illustrated that the solution oscillates at the moment when the parameter k_1 is bigger than the value 1.0779. The solution is not asymptotically stable if parameter k_1 is bigger than the value 3.402.

The above equation was investigated with constant delay 0.5. However, it is more realistic that the ability of the adaptation to new market conditions varies with respect to current market price. Hence, we assume that range of the delay of the system is in interval [0, 0.7]. The model with state-dependent delay term is recompiled as follows:

$$\dot{P}(t) = k_1(209.2 - 0.78P(t) - 1.78P(t - \widetilde{\tau}(P(t))))$$
$$\widetilde{\tau}(P(t)) > 0, \forall t \in IR^+$$

Since the delay term is a function of solution of the equation, identifying of delay term is important. To ensure positivity of delay term while taking the value in the desired range, we use the following theorem which is given in Erman and Demir (2016):

Theorem 1: Let $A_0, A_1 \in IR^+$, $\tau(u(t)) = \frac{a+bu(t)}{c+du(t)}$, $\mu = -\frac{c}{d}$, and $\sigma = -\frac{a}{b}$. The delay differential equation

$$u'(t) = -A_0 u(t) - A_1 u(t - \widetilde{\tau}(u(t)))$$

$$\widetilde{\tau}(u(t)) = \max\{0, \tau(u(t))\} \geq 0, \qquad \forall t \in IR^+$$

has a unique solution $u(t) \in C^1([0, \infty), (L_0, M_0))$ if Lipschitz history function $u_0(t) : [-\tau, 0] \to (L_0, M_0)$ exists such that

$$(L_0, M_0) = \begin{cases} \left(\sigma, -\dfrac{\sigma A_1}{A_0}\right); & \mu < \sigma < 0 \\[2mm] \left(-\dfrac{\sigma A_1}{A_0}, \sigma\right); & 0 < \sigma < \mu \\[2mm] (\sigma, \mu); & \sigma < 0 < \mu, \quad -\dfrac{\sigma A_1}{A_0} < \mu \\[2mm] (\mu, \sigma); & \mu < 0 < \sigma, \quad \mu < -\dfrac{\sigma A_1}{A_0} \end{cases}$$

and $\tau = \max\limits_{u(t) \in (L_0, M_0)} \{\widetilde{\tau}(u(t))\} > 0$.

When transformation $P(t) = x(t) + \frac{209.2}{2.56}$ applies to the equation, the following equation is obtained:

$$\dot{x}(t) = -k_1 0.78x(t) - k_1 1.78x(t - \tau(x(t)))$$
$$\tau(x(t)) = 0.2133 + 0.0125x(t)$$

where $\tau(x(t)) = \widetilde{\tau}\left(x(t) + \dfrac{209.2}{2.56}\right)$. By applying the same transformation, history function $x_0(t) = 0.181t^2 + 3.4t - 14.71875$ is obtained. Moreover, the above state-dependent delay differential equation satisfies conditions of Theorem 1. Thus, the range of the solution of the equation can be determined as $(L_0 = -17.064, M_0 = 38.9416)$. In this model, delay of the system varies from 0 to 0.7 with respect to current value market price.

In Erman and Demir (2016), the following theorems are written in order to investigate of stability by using upper bound of state-dependent delay term. First, we introduce these theorems and then apply them to our system to get a criterion for stability.

Theorem 2: The solution of the Eq. (11.11) with delay term which satisfies $0 < \tau(x(t)) < M_1$ for all $t \in IR^+$ is asymptotically stable if and only if the following conditions are satisfied:

($\tilde{a}$) $-\frac{1}{M_1} < A_1$

($\tilde{b}$) $-A_1 < A_2 < \frac{\omega}{\sin(\omega M_1)}$, where ω is root of $A_1 = \frac{-\omega \cos(\omega M_1)}{\sin(\omega M_1)}$ such that $\omega M_1 \in (0, \pi)$.

From Theorem 2, the equation is asymptotically stable if $k_1 1.78 < \frac{\omega}{\sin(0.7\omega)}$ where ω is root of $0.78 = \frac{-\omega \cos(0.7\omega)}{\sin(0.7\omega)}$ such that $0.7\omega \in (0, \pi)$. These equations are solved by fsolve command on Maple, and it is obtained that the system is asymptotically stable if $k_1 < 1.553293617$.

Theorem 3: Let $\tau_p = \frac{2}{\sqrt{A_2^2 - A_1^2}} \left(\arctan \left(\frac{\sqrt{A_2^2 - A_1^2}}{A_2 - A_1} + p\pi \right) \right)$, $p \in Z$ and τ_n denote least τ_p value which is greater than 0. The solution of the Eq. (11.11) with delay term $x(t)$ which satisfies $0 < \tau(x(t)) < M_1$ for all $t \in IR^+$ is asymptotically stable under the condition $0 < A_1 + A_2$ and $M_1 < \tau_n$.

Because of Theorem 3, the system is asymptotically stable if $k_1 < 1.807494663$.

Kaldor-Kalecki Model

One of the most readable theories of business cycle was investigated by Nicolas Kaldor (1940). Kaldor introduced nonlinear relations with variable. Specifically, he simulated that investment and saving function will nonlinearly depend on capital stock and output level. The Kaldor model can be expressed as follows:

$$\dot{Y}(t) = \alpha[I(Y(t), K(t)) - S(Y(t))]$$
$$\dot{K}(t) = I(Y(t), K(t)) - \delta K(t)$$

where variable and parameters are defined as:

Y and K output level and capital stock, respectively
$I(Y,K)$ investment function $\left(\frac{dI}{dY} > 0, \quad \frac{dI}{dK} < 0 \right)$
$S(Y)$ saving function $\left(0 < \frac{dS}{dY} < 1 \right)$
α a positive adjustment parameter
δ a positive capital depreciation rate

Investment varies directly proportional to income as well as indirectly proportional to capital, so $\frac{dI}{dY} = I_Y > 0$ and $\frac{dI}{dK} = I_K < 0$. Saving depends on income in the usual way, i.e., $0 < \frac{dS}{dY} = S_Y < 1$.

Moreover, Kalecki added a delay between the installation of investment goods and the investment decision.

In paper (Matsumoto and Szidarovszky 2010), The Kaldor-Kalecki model is described as follows:

"The Kaldor-Kalecki model is a combination of nonlinear investment and a time lag in the capital accumulation. Then the Kaldor-Kalecki model can be written as

$$\dot{Y}(t) = \alpha[I(Y(t), K(t)) - S(Y(t))]$$
$$\dot{K}(t) = I(Y(t - \tau), K(t)) - \delta K(t) \tag{11.12}$$

where τ is positive constant delay."

Since the system (11.12) is investigated by linearization with respect to τ around $\tau = 0$ in paper (Matsumoto and Szidarovszky 2010), the analysis is convenient for small enough delay.

Let us investigate the Kaldor-Kalecki model using the following linear approximation at an equilibrium point (Y^*, K^*). Thus, the system (11.12) can be rewritten as

$$\dot{Y}(t) = \alpha[(I_2 - S_2)Y(t) - I_3 K(t) - (I_1 - S_1)]$$
$$\dot{K}(t) = I_2 Y(t - \tau) - (I_3 + \delta)K(t) + I_1 \tag{11.13}$$

where $I_2 = I_Y(Y^*, K^*) > 0, I_3 = -I_K(Y^*, K^*) > 0, I_1 = I(Y^*, K^*) - I_2 Y^* - I_3 K^*$, $S_2 = S_Y(Y^*)$, and $S_1 = S(Y^*) - S_2 Y^*$.

We assume that $I(0, 0) = 0$ and $S(0) = 0$. In the sequel, the equilibrium point is obtained as $(0, 0)$, and the system (11.13) is transformed to the following system:

$$\dot{Y}(t) = \alpha[(I_2 - S_2)Y(t) - I_3 K(t)]$$
$$\dot{K}(t) = I_2 Y(t - \tau) - (I_3 + \delta)K(t) \tag{11.14}$$

Stability Analysis of Kaldor-Kalecki Model

Let $Z(t) = [Y(t), K(t)]$ be solution vector of the system (11.14). The solution vector can be written as form $Z(t) = \left[\sum_j a_j e^{\lambda_j t}, \sum_j b_j e^{\lambda_j t} \right]$ where λ_j are solutions of the characteristic equation.

When determining to asymptotic behavior of the system by using characteristic equation, the following statements are investigated.

"If the characteristic roots have negative real parts, i.e., $\text{Re}(\lambda_j) < 0$ for all $j = 1$, $2, \cdots$ then the solution of (11.14) is asymptotically stable and if at least one of the characteristic roots have positive real parts, i.e., $\mathrm{Re}(\lambda_j) > 0$ for some $j = 1, 2, \cdots$ then the solution of (11.14) is unstable." Therefore, pure imaginary roots, $\lambda = i\omega$, changing stability behavior of the system are critical roots.

The stability and instability of the system in the terms of parameters (I_2, S_2) are determined by using the following characteristic equation:

$$g(\lambda) = \lambda^2 + (I_3 + \delta - \alpha(I_2 - S_2))\lambda - \alpha(I_2 - S_2)(I_3 + \delta) + \alpha I_2 I_3 e^{-\lambda\tau} = 0. \quad (11.15)$$

For $\lambda = 0$, it is obtained from Eq. (11.15) as follows:

$$C_* : I_2\delta - S_2(I_3 + \delta) = 0$$

which forms a line in parameter space (I_2, S_2). Substituting $\lambda = i\omega$ and equating to zero the real and imaginary parts in characteristic Eq. (11.15), we find the following equations:

$$\mathrm{Re}(g(i\omega)) = -\omega^2 - \alpha(I_2 - S_2)(I_3 + \delta) + \alpha I_2 I_3 \cos(\omega\tau) = 0$$
$$\mathrm{Im}(g(i\omega)) = (I_3 + \delta - \alpha(I_2 - S_2))\omega - \alpha I_2 I_3 \sin(\omega\tau) = 0$$

The curve equation determining border of the changing points of the stability in parameter space (I_2, S_2) is obtained by solving the above equations for I_2 and S_2 as follows:

$$I_2 = \frac{\omega^3 + \omega(I_3 + \delta)^2}{\alpha I_3((I_3 + \delta)\sin(\omega\tau) + \omega\cos(\omega\tau))} \quad (11.16)$$

$$S_2 = \frac{\omega^3 + I_3 \sin(\omega\tau)\omega^2 + \omega(I_3 + \delta)(I_3 + \delta - \cos(\omega\tau)I_3)}{\alpha I_3((I_3 + \delta)\sin(\omega\tau) + \omega\cos(\omega\tau))} \quad (11.17)$$

where ω is a real parameter. Equations (11.16) and (11.17) have singularity for ω such that

$$\tan(\omega\tau) = -\frac{\omega}{\delta + I_3}. \quad (11.18)$$

Since period of $\tan(\omega\tau)$ is $\frac{\pi}{\tau}$, there is a root, ω_k, of Eq. (11.18) in interval $\left(\frac{k\pi}{\tau}, \frac{(k+1)\pi}{\tau}\right)$. The intervals $J_k = (\omega_k, \omega_{k+1})$ are introduced and the curve is denoted by C_k for $\omega \in J_k$.

These results are illustrated for various values of parameters. The curves C_k and the straight line C_* are shown in Fig. 11.1 for $I_3 = 0.25$, $\alpha = 4$, $\delta = 1.75$, and $\tau = 1$. Additionally, evaluation of the curves is illustrated for $\tau = 1, 2$, and 3 in Fig. 11.2.

It is possible to assign a number h which is the number of roots with positive real parts of the characteristic equation in the different regions bordered by the curves. Among the regions of this decomposition can be also found regions in which $h = 0$. These regions are regions of asymptotic stability of solutions.

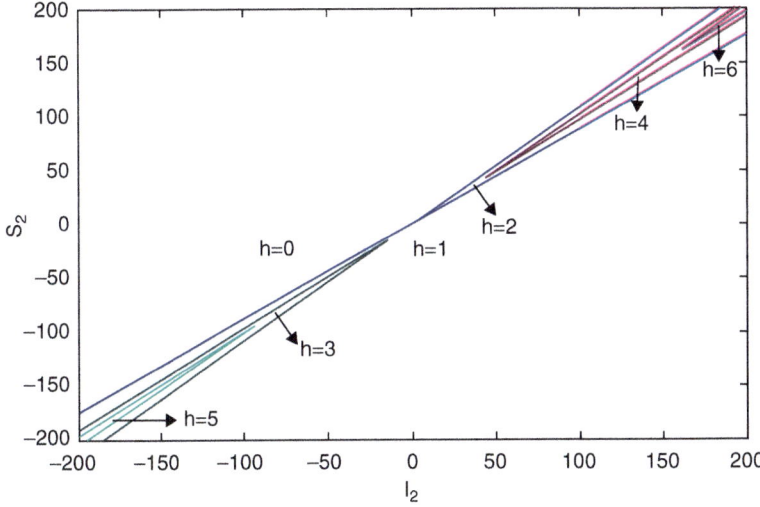

Fig. 11.1 Number of the roots with positive real parts of the characteristic equation for $I_3 = 0.25$, $\alpha = 4$, $\delta = 1.75$, and $\tau = 1$

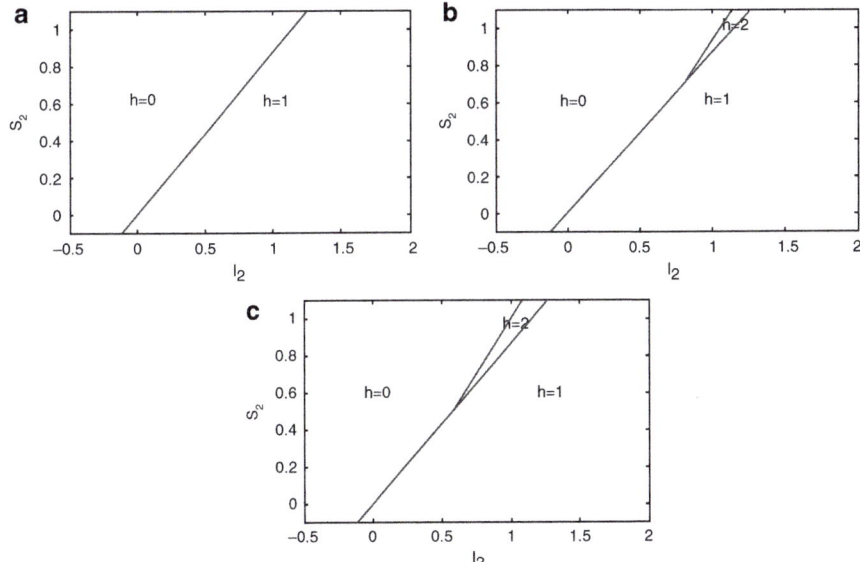

Fig. 11.2 Evaluation of the curves is illustrated for (**a**) $\tau = 1$, (**b**) $\tau = 2$, and (**c**) $\tau = 3$

Kaldor-Kalecki Model with State-Dependent Delay

In the system (11.14) delay is considered as constant. However, more realistically, delay between the installation of investment goods and the investment decision depends on state of output level in the model. Thus, the following model is considered:

$$\dot{Y}(t) = \alpha[(I_2 - S_2)Y(t) - I_3 K(t)]$$
$$\dot{K}(t) = I_2 Y(t - \tau(Y(t))) - (I_3 + \delta)K(t) \tag{11.19}$$

where $\tau(Y(t)) > 0$ is a state-dependent delay function.

If function $\tau(Y(t))$ takes negative values, then predicted delay in the system is not properly modeled. To guarantee that solutions to Eq. (11.19) do not terminate because delay function takes negative value, the range of the parameter values must be restricted under consideration.

Theorem 1: Let $A_1 \in IR^-$, A_2, B_1, $B_2 \in IR^+$, and $\tau(Y(t))$ be a continuous function. The delay differential equation system

$$\dot{Y}(t) = A_1 Y(t) - A_2 K(t)$$
$$\dot{K}(t) = B_1 Y(t - \tilde{\tau}(Y(t))) - B_2 K(t) \quad ; \quad \tilde{\tau}(Y(t)) = \max\{0, \tau(Y(t))\} \tag{11.20}$$

has a unique solution $[Y(t), K(t)] \in (L, M) \times (P, R)$ for all $t \in IR^+$ if Lipschitz history function $Y_0(t) : [-\tau, 0] \rightarrow (L, M)$ and $K(0) = k \in (P, R)$ exist such that $B_2 P \le B_1 L \le B_1 M \le B_2 R, A_1 M \le A_2 P \le A_2 R \le A_1 L$, and $\tau = \max\limits_{Y(t) \in (L,M)} \{\tilde{\tau}(Y(t))\}$.

Proof Suppose not, then there exists $t_0 > 0$ such that $[Y(t), K(t)] \in (L, M) \times (P, R)$ for all $t < t_0$, but $K(t_0) = P$ or R when $Y(t_0) \in (L, M)$ or $Y(t_0) = L$ or M when $K(t_0) \in (P, R)$

In the sequel, the following two cases are considered.

Case 1: If $K(t_0) = P$ when $Y(t_0) \in (L, M)$, then it implies that $\dot{K}(t_0) \le 0$. Furthermore

$$\dot{K}(t_0) = B_1 Y(t_0 - \tilde{\tau}(Y(t_0))) - B_2 K(t_0) > B_1 L - B_2 P > 0$$

which contradicts the assumption. In a similar way, if $K(t_0) = R$ when $Y(t_0) \in (L, M)$, then it implies that $\dot{K}(t_0) \ge 0$. Furthermore

$$\dot{K}(t_0) = B_1 Y(t_0 - \tilde{\tau}(Y(t_0))) - B_2 K(t_0) < B_1 M - B_2 R < 0$$

which contradicts the assumption.

Case 2: If $Y(t_0) = L$ when $K(t_0) \in (P, R)$, then it implies that $\dot{L}(t_0) \le 0$. Furthermore

$$\dot{Y}(t_0) = A_1 Y(t_0) - A_2 K(t_0) > A_1 L - A_2 R > 0$$

which contradicts the assumption. In a similar way, if $Y(t_0) = M$ when $K(t_0) \in (P, R)$, then it implies that $\dot{L}(t_0) \ge 0$. Furthermore

$$\dot{Y}(t_0) = A_1 Y(t_0) - A_2 K(t_0) < A_1 M - A_2 P < 0$$

which contradicts the assumption.

As a result, there is no such $t_0 \in IR^+$ and $[Y(t), K(t)] \in (L, M) \times (P, R)$ for all $t \in IR^+$.

Since the right side of the equation in (11.20) is Lipschitz with respect to each their argument, local existence and uniqueness of the solution follow from Driver (1977).

Let us assume that $I_2 - S_2 < 0$ and $\tau(Y(t)) = a + bY(t)$ where $a \neq 0$ is any real number and b is positive real number in the system (11.19). It is clear that $\tau(Y(t)) > 0$ for $Y(t) \in \left(L = -\frac{a}{b}, M\right)$. Thus, $\widetilde{\tau}(Y(t))$ and $\tau(Y(t))$ are equal and Theorem 1 also holds for the system (11.19).

Conclusion

Two specific dynamic models in economy are considered by using state-dependent delay differential equations.

First, Walras model of market price, demand, and supply is modeled by delay term depending on state of current market price. When the model is investigated, Eq. (11.11) is obtained. In Erman and Demir (2016), the range of the solution of the Eq. (11.11) and its stability depending on this range were studied.

Second, Kaldorian macro dynamic model with Kaleckian investment delay is determined by two-dimensional delay differential equation. In this study, the model is presented by delay term as a function of current output level of the system. For the positivity of delay term, the some restrictions on the range of parameters are assigned by Theorem 1. Moreover, Theorem 1 can be used to determine to the interval in which the delay term has a value. Having such an interval is very important in the analysis of the stability. The stability regions are investigated for any values of parameters and illustrated their evolution with time delay in Figs. 11.1 and 11.2 for some specific values of parameters.

References

Bobalova, M., & Novotna, V. (2015). The use of functional differential equations in the model of the meat market with supply delay. In *Procedia – Social and Behavioral Sciences* (Vol. 213, pp. 74–79). Kaunas: Elsevier.

Driver, R. D. (1977). *Ordinary and delay differential equations*. New York: Springer.

Erman, S., & Demir, A. (2016). An analysis on the stability of a state dependent delay differential equation. *Open Mathematics, 14*(1), 425–435.

Hartung, F., Krisztin, T., Walther, H. O., & Wu, J. (2006). Functional differential equations with state-dependent delays: theory and applications. In A. Canada, P. Drabek, & A. Fonda (Eds.), *Handbook of differential equations: Ordinary differential equations* (Vol. III, pp. 435–545). Amsterdam: Elsevier/North-Holland.

Kaldor, N. (1940). A model of the trade cycle. *The Economic Journal, 50*(197), 78–92.

Lorenz, H. W. (1993). *Nonlinear dynamic economics and chaotic motion*. Berlin: Springer.

Mackey, M. C. (1987). Commodity price fluctuations: Price dependent delays and nonlinearities as explanatory factors. *Journal of Economic Theory, 48*(2), 497–509.

Matsumoto, A., & Szidarovszky, F. (2010). Delay differential nonlinear economic models. In G. Bischi, C. Chiarella, & L. Gardini (Eds.), *Nonlinear dynamics in economics, finance and social sciences*. Berlin, Heidelberg: Springer.

Puu, T. (2000). *Attractors, bifurcations, and chaos: Nonlinear phenomena in economics*. Berlin: Springer-Verlag Telos.

Rosser, J. B., Jr. (1991). *From catastrophe to chaos: A general theory of economic discontinuities*. Boston: Kluwer Academic.

Shone, R. (2002). *Economic dynamics-phase diagrams and their economic application*. Cambridge: Cambridge University Press.

Zhang, W. B. (1991). *Synergetic economics*. Berlin: Springer.

Zhang, W. B. (2005a). *Differential equation, bifurcations and chaos in economics*. Singapore: World Scientific.

Zhang, W. B. (2005b). *Economic growth theory*. London: Ashgate.

Part II
Finance and Banking

Chapter 12
Troubled Credits Selling of State Banks to Asset Management Companies in Turkey

Mustafa Tevfik Kartal

Abstract Turkish Banking Sector has grown substantially in recent years. Turkish Banking Sector's total asset size of sector has reached TL 2972 billion, and total credit size has reached TL 1919 billion as of 2017 June. On the other hand, an increment is being seen in the troubled credits with credit growth. Total troubled asset size has reached TL 61 billion as of 2017 June.

Banks try to dispose troubled credits in their balance sheet. In this context, one of the options that banks carry out is to sell of troubled credits to asset management companies. When examining practices in Turkey, it can be seen that private banks have been using this option. However, state banks cannot be able to use the option because of regulation absence. Banking Regulation and Supervision Agency issued a charter to make up the deficiency about state banks' troubled credit selling to asset management companies on 08.11.2017. Hence, state banks can transfer and benefit from troubled credit selling to asset management companies.

This paper was prepared to make an evaluation about the charter and its probable effects. As a result of study, it was determined that state banks need to be able to sell credit to asset management companies because their rivals who are private banks have such an opportunity. So, in order to be able to compete with private banks, the regulation is really a need for state banks. Also, state banks' various indicators which are asset quality, profitability, growth, and industry share would be improved by means of the regulation. On the other hand, troubled credits selling of state banks to asset management companies in Turkey may cause reputation risk for state banks because of collection processes and practices of asset management companies.

In general, it can be said that new regulation proposed by Banking Regulation and Supervision Agency would be beneficial to state banks. Taken into consideration that troubled asset size in state banks has reached TL 17 billion as of 2017 March, importance and benefits of new regulation can be understood very well. However, it would be the best that effects of new regulation should be followed up strictly by

M. T. Kartal (✉)
Borsa İstanbul, Istanbul, Turkey

© Springer International Publishing AG, part of Springer Nature 2018   243
H. Dincer et al. (eds.), *Global Approaches in Financial Economics, Banking, and Finance*, Contributions to Economics, https://doi.org/10.1007/978-3-319-78494-6_12

regulatory authorities specifically Banking and Regulation Supervision Agency. Necessary amendments should be made if negative effects were seen.

This paper is the first academic study handling the subject which is about Banking Regulation and Supervision Agency's charter for state banks' troubled credit selling to asset management companies.

Introduction

The main role of banks is to provide financing to individuals and corporations who need funds. Banks do this duty by giving and collecting credits. Hence banks aim at making profit. For this reason, credits are the most important asset item in banks' balance sheets. Credits are also important due to fact that they reflect asset quality.

Banks provide a substantial amount of credits. However, collecting credits back on time is unlikely possible in practice. Borrowers sometimes have in trouble to repay their credits on time. Specifically repayment difficulties are seen widely in economic dislocation times. Not to be repaid credits by borrowers is a big problem for banks, and they can be named as troubled credits. Troubled credits are defined as credits which are not repaid on time and have probability of never repaid (Aktaş 2000). Taking into consideration that banks can give credits by collecting deposits, management of troubled credits are also important for asset-liability balance.

Banks try to find solution/way to get rid of troubled credits. Banks have two options to do this. One is applying legal follow-up, and second is selling troubled credits to asset management companies (AMC). Banks deploy follow-up because it is a legal obligation issue. However, legal follow-up requires long and detailed procedures, and its result is not foreseen. Also legal follow-up processes cause credits' return after for a long time against planned time. For this reason, banks occasionally prefer to sell troubled credits to AMC. Hence, banks can have opportunity to get rid of troubled credits' disadvantages which are to decrease banks' profits and liquidity. Banks can also prevent deterioration in asset quality.

Banks sell troubled credits and collect cash in return. Private banks have been selling their troubled credits to AMC in Turkey practice. 23 different banks have sold troubled credits 186 times from 2008 to today. In these transactions, banks have sold troubled credits to AMCs at amount of total TL 25.5 billion and collected TL 3.1 billion cash in return. Hence, private banks have disposed of troubled credits and generated income.

Although private banks can benefit from selling troubled credits to AMC, state banks cannot benefit from this opportunity. Taken into consideration that total TL 17 billion troubled credits exist in state banks' assets as of 2017 March, disadvantages of state banks against their rivals can be understood better. In order to enhance state banks condition, Banking Regulation and Supervision Agency (BRSA) issued a charter about troubled credit selling of state banks to AMC on 08.11.2017. After this time, state banks can sell their troubled credits to AMC and benefit from troubled credit selling.

This paper was prepared to make an evaluation about BRSA's regulation which is named as *Troubled Credits Selling of State Banks to Asset Management Companies* (shortly BRSA Charter). With this study, it is aimed at to determine advantages and disadvantages of the new regulation and practice. This paper is the first academic study handling the subject which is about Banking Regulation and Supervision Agency's charter for state banks' troubled credit selling to AMC. This study will contribute to by bringing in the subject to literature.

This study consists of six parts. After the introduction part, information about Turkish Banking Sector, state banks, credits, and troubled credits are shared in part II. Within the context of literature review, studies about troubled credits and troubled credit selling to AMCs are examined because of the fact that there is no study about BRSA's charter for state banks' troubled credit selling to AMC in part III. Troubled credits, their cost, advantages, and disadvantages of credit selling are handled in part IV. BRSA's regulation and its probable effects with regard to state banks, TBS, and Turkish economy are examined in part V. Finally an evaluation is made in part VI.

Turkish Banking Sector, State Banks and Credits

After banking crises in 2001 and 2002 in Turkey, restructuring of work was started in order to make economy stronger. In this context, new Banking Law became effective in 2005, and BRSA is authorized to make secondary regulations related with Banking Law (Banking Law 2005). BRSA has made so many secondary regulation related with Banking Law from that time to today. In this process, Turkish Banking Sector (TBS) began to grow. TBS has reached TL 2972 billion total asset size and TL 1919 billion total credit size as of 2017 June. In addition to this, there has been operating by 51 banks, 11,705 branches and 210,369 personnel in TBS as 2017 June (BDDK 2017a, b).

As it was stated above, total credit size has reached TL 1919 billion as of 2017 June. While total credit size has been growing, troubled credit size also grows. Total troubled asset size has reached TL 61 billion as of 2017 June. Because of increasing size, troubled credits are one of the most important issues and problems for banks in Turkey. So, banks try to dispose troubled credits. In this context, banks could sometimes choose to sell troubled credits to asset management companies.

In Turkey practices, banks can sell troubled credits to asset management companies if they want to sell and complete necessary steps. This option has been deployed fully by private banks. However, state banks cannot be able to use this option because of the fact that there is no regulation for which enables state banks to use this option. In order to fill gap, Banking Regulation and Supervision Agency issued a charter about state banks' troubled credit selling to asset management companies on 08.11.2017, and state banks can no longer transfer and benefit from troubled credit selling to asset management companies.

According to bank type, there are 51 banks operating actively. 33 of them are deposit banks, 5 of them participation banks, and 13 of them development and

Table 12.1 State banks in Turkey

Bank name	Bank type	Scale
T.C. Ziraat Bankası A.Ş.	Deposit	Big
Türkiye Halk Bankası A.Ş.	Deposit	Big
Türkiye Vakıflar Bankası T.A.O.	Deposit	Big
Türkiye İhracat Kredi Bankası A.Ş.	Development and investment	Medium
İller Bankası A.Ş.	Development and investment	Small
İstanbul Takas ve Saklama Bankası A.Ş.	Development and investment	Small
Türkiye Kalkınma Bankası A.Ş.	Development and investment	Small
Ziraat Katılım Bankası A.Ş.	Participation	Micro
Vakıf Katılım Bankası A.Ş.	Participation	Micro

Source: BDDK 2017b

Table 12.2 Total credit size of state banks in Turkey—summary (TL 1000)

Year/ period	Deposit banks	Development and investment banks	Participation banks	Grand total
2010/12	146,001,008	11,998,519	–	157,999,527
2011/12	184,323,316	17,742,814	–	202,066,130
2012/12	204,048,769	24,615,506	–	228,664,275
2013/12	281,163,099	37,354,513	–	318,517,612
2014/12	345,954,639	46,620,587	–	392,575,226
2015/12	434,716,461	60,064,927	1,690,106	496,471,494
2016/12	536,189,374	83,197,146	8,504,389	627,890,909
2017/3	571,972,307	83,688,180	10,227,398	665,887,885

Source: Derived from Appendix 1

investment banks in Turkey (BDDK 2017b). According to another classification, there are two banks in Saving Deposit Insurance Fund, 24 foreign banks, 16 private banks, and 9 state banks. State banks in Turkey are included in Table 12.1.

As it can be seen from Table 12.1, there are nine state banks in Turkey. State banks consist of two participation banks, three deposit banks, and four development and investment banks (BDDK 2017b). Also state banks can be categorized according to scale. There are three big scale banks, one medium scale bank, three small scale bank, and two microscale banks.

State banks provide substantial credits to borrowers and national economy. Total credit size provided by state banks has reached TL 665 billion as of 2017 March. Details of credits provided by state banks are included in Appendix 1, and its summary is included in Table 12.2.

Deposit banking has the highest share in state banks. Deposit banking's share is calculated as 85.90%. Participation banking and development and investment banking share in state banks is relatively low in comparison with deposit banking. As it can be seen from Table 12.2, total credit size of state banks has reached TL 665,887,885,000 as of 2017 March.

Table 12.3 Total troubled credit size of state banks in Turkey—summary (TL 1000)

Year/ period	Deposit banks	Development and investment banks	Participation banks	Grand total
2010/12	4,878,539	201,201	–	5,079,740
2011/12	4,688,615	211,620	–	4,900,235
2012/12	6,742,162	211,803	–	6,953,965
2013/12	8,194,044	244,585	–	8,438,629
2014/12	10,390,953	238,710	–	10,629,663
2015/12	11,964,475	241,289	2	12,205,766
2016/12	15,770,682	360,995	14,130	16,145,807
2017/3	16,631,168	392,546	29,248	17,052,962

Source: Derived from Appendix 2

Table 12.4 Total troubled credits/total credits ratios of state banks in Turkey—summary

Year/ period	Deposit banks	Development and investment banks	Participation banks	Grand total
2010/12	3.34%	1.68%	–	3.22%
2011/12	2.54%	1.19%	–	2.43%
2012/12	**3.30%**	0.86%	–	**3.04%**
2013/12	2.91%	0.65%	–	2.65%
2014/12	**3.00%**	0.51%	–	**2.71%**
2015/12	2.75%	0.40%	0.00%	2.46%
2016/12	**2.94%**	**0.43%**	**0.17%**	**2.57%**
2017/3	2.91%	**0.47%**	**0.29%**	2.56%

Source: Derived from Appendix 3

While credit size has been growing, unfortunately troubled credits size also grows. Total troubled credit size provided by state banks has reached TL 17 billion as of 2017 March. Details of troubled credits provided by state banks are included in Appendix 2, and its summary is included in Table 12.3.

Deposit banking has the highest share in state banks. Deposit banking's share is calculated as 97.53%. Participation banking and development and investment banking share in state banks is relatively low in comparison with deposit banking. As it can be seen from Table 12.3, total troubled credit size of state banks has reached TL 17,052,962,000 as of 2017 March. When evaluating total credit size and total troubled credit size together, it can be understood that state deposit banks have higher share in troubled credit size (97.53%) in comparison with total credits (85.90%).

Although states banks' troubled credits have been growing, it is essential to make a thorough evaluation that total troubled credits/total credits ratios be analyzed. Details of total troubled credits/total credits ratio of state banks are included in Appendix 3, and its summary is included in Table 12.4.

Because of the fact that deposit banking has the highest credit share in state banks, deposit banking's total troubled credits/total credits ratio is higher than participation banks and development and investment banks. In addition to this, as it can be seen from Table 12.4, total troubled credits/total credits ratios changed negatively in some periods. For example, the ratio has increased against prior period in 2012/12, 2014/12, and 2016/12 for deposit banks and overall state banks. Total troubled credits/total credits ratio is 2.56% as of 2017 March.

When total troubled credits/total credits ratios are analyzed at bank and year bases, total troubled credits/total credits ratio has increased against prior period for Ziraat Bank, Halk Bank, and Vakıflar Bank in 2012/12; Vakıflar Bank and Kalkınma Bank in 2013/12; Halk Bank and Takas ve Saklama Bank in 2014/12; Vakıflar Bank in 2015/12; eight state banks' ratios except for İller Bank increased in 2016/12; Halk Bank, Vakıflar Bank, İhracat Kredi Bank, Ziraat Katılım Bank, and Vakıf Katılım Bank in 2017/3. Bank and year bases details can be viewed in Appendix 3.

Literature Review

There is no study about state banks' troubled credit selling to asset management companies in Turkey in the context of BRSA Charter. However, there are various studies related with troubled credits and troubled credit selling to AMCs. Within the context of literature review, some of selected studies are included in Table 12.5.

Troubled Credits and Credit Selling

Troubled credits are defined as credits which are not repaid on time and have probability of never repaid (Aktaş 2000). Troubled credits can also be named as nonperforming loan (NPL). NPL are credits of whom borrowers do not fulfill their obligations to banks on time (Mesutoğlu 2001; Ağaoğlu 2011). In some definition, delaying minimum of 90 days is a requirement to describe credits as troubled credits (Yüksel 2016).

Banks expect that credits which were given to borrowers will be repaid on time. Repayment on time is very important for banks because of the fact that repaid credits are used to provide new credits to borrowers and they are also used to pay deposit withdrawal to depositors. For these reason, troubled credits cause some inconveniences and costs.

Banks try to dispose of disadvantages of troubled credits either by collecting with using follow-up processes or using credit selling method. Taken into consideration that follow-up processes takes a longer time, troubled credit selling method is an important option for banks. But, troubled credit selling has also some advantages and disadvantages. On the other hand, management of troubled credits is also important for asset-liability balance.

Table 12.5 Some selected studies in Turkey

Author	Year	Results
Aydoğan	1990	He stated that there is a negative relationship between provisions and nonperforming loan which shows asset quality
Barr et al.	1994	They concluded that banks which have high troubled credits go bankrupt
Berger and DeYoung	1997	They determined that there is negative relationship between troubled credits and banks' capital ratio
Kaya	2002	It was stated that troubled credits is one of the determinants of profitability
Güngör	2007	It was stated that micro and macro factors which affects troubled credits have important effects on banks' profitability
Espinoza and Prasad	2010	They stated that there is negative relationship between troubled credits and growth rate
Şahbaz	2010	She reached a conclusion that there is positive relationship between credit increase and troubled credits
Yücememiş and Sözer	2010	They determined that total troubled credits/total credits ratio has increased relatively low in 2008 global crisis against 2001 banking crisis in Turkey and the ratio is very low against numerous European Union countries
Ağaoğlu	2011	It was concluded that an AMC should be established with Saving Deposit Insurance Fund's participation as 20% shareholder after 2001 crisis in Turkey for solution of troubled assets
Gülhan and Uzunlar	2011	They stated that troubled credits have a meaningful effect on return on assets
Koyuncu and Saka	2011	They concluded that credits which have been provided to private sector are affected by troubled credits negatively
Castro	2013	He stated that there is relation between troubled credits and credit growth rate
Ćurak et al.	2013	She stated that there is relation between troubled credits and banks' profitability
Makri et al.	2014	They concluded that troubled credits are affected from unemployment rate, growth rate, and banks' capital sum
Şahbaz and İnkaya	2014	It was determined that troubled credits are related with economic variables in the long run
Chaibi and Fititi	2015	They concluded that troubled credits are affected from growth rate, interest rate, unemployment rate and foreign currency exchange rates.
Selimler	2015	He stated that troubled credits affect banks' capital adequacy and asset quality and liquidate ratio negatively
Kaya et al.	2016	They stated that total troubled credits/total credits ratio affects total credits/total assets negatively
Yüksel	2016	He determined that increase in foreign currency exchange rates causes increase in troubled credits, while increase in growth rate and banks' interest incomes causes decrease in troubled credits
Kartal and Demir	2017a	It was determined that credits growth rate in participation banking should be increased in order to reach 15% industry share target

(continued)

Table 12.5 (continued)

Author	Year	Results
Kartal and Demir	2017b	They stated that participation banks could use the option of selling troubled credits to AMCs by selling credit receivables either in return for a commodity or in return for a benefit
Yüksel	2017	He concluded that decrease in industry production index is the most important determinant of the increase in nonperforming credits

Source: Authors

Troubled Credits' Costs to Banks

As it was mentioned above, troubled credits cause some inconveniences and costs. These can be summarized as follows (Suadiye 2006; Yücememiş and Sözer 2010; Yuca 2012; Alhassan et al. 2013; Kaya et al. 2016):

- Troubled credits cause losses. Because of losses, banks' profitability and capital sum and capital adequacy ratio would decrease. Hence, troubled credits affect banks' performance negatively.
- Troubled credits cause decrease in banks' risk appetite. Banks do not take new risk along with decreasing risk appetite. Hence, credit volume to be provided to borrowers and markets would be decreased/minimized.
- Increase in troubled credits and provisions impairs banks' asset quality.
- Troubled credits prevent banks' personnel from productive works because of the fact that troubled credits require much more attention and follow-up and they cause increase in follow-up and law expenses.
- High amount of troubled credits prevent banks' growth and jeopardize image of banks. They also slow banks' growth and affect negatively and decrease banks' competitive power.
- Motivation and performance of banks' personnel could be negatively affected because of the fact that there is a tight growth.
- Banks would be suffered from income losses because of the fact that some funds are devoted to substitute for troubled credits.
- Banks would recall some credits due to fact that banks have high amount of troubled credits. This could result in increase in interest rates, grege in credit conditions, and restrict in credit limits.
- High amount of troubled credits makes banks vulnerable to external shocks about recession, inflation, budget deficit, foreign currency exchange rate, interest rate, current deficit, and capital inflow and outflow.

Troubled credits show repayment capacity of debt of household and real sector. Therefore, troubled credits are a pioneer indicator in the view of real economy. In recession periods, it is seen to increase in troubled credits due to fact that households are faced with unemployment and welfare loss and real sector are faced with income loss.

Important Points that Banks Should Take into Consideration About Troubled Credits

As mentioned in the subunit above, troubled credits cause different type of costs to banks. So, banks should follow up troubled credits carefully in order to prevent deterioration in asset quality and increment in troubled asset volume. In this context, banks should take into consideration some points as follows (Kartal and Demir 2017b):

- Banks should establish follow-up systems for continuous follow-up of troubled credits in order to make follow-up activities efficiently.
- Follow-up systems should be for all customers in different strategic business units of banks and they should use banks' all data and intelligence sources.
- Follow-up systems should follow up specifically credits which are in branch authority.
- Follow-up systems should produce early warning signals and make some actions automatic which are determined previously if necessary.
- Customers, who have troubled credits, should be provided by the change by banks to restructure their credits before customers' financial positions get worse if there were not a legislation limitation.
- Banks' collaterals should be increased and preserved throughout credit debt maturity if customers' debts were restructured.
- An internal process in order to dispose of troubled credits should be prepared and approved by board of directors of bank. The process should be compliant with regulations, and troubled credits selling should be evaluated according to this process.

Selling troubled credits to AMCs should also be evaluated as an option in managing troubled credits. Banks should manage selling process living up to fairness, transparency, and accountability principles if they decided to sell their troubled credits. Banks should also provide competition environment, select the best time to obtain the best bidding, invite AMCs who has BRSA license to auction, and make nondisclosure agreements with AMCs who will take role in selling auction. In addition to these, banks' law, allocation, risk management, internal control, internal audit, and other related departments should work together in order to prevent probable problems in troubled credit selling process.

Advantages and Disadvantages of Selling of Troubled Credits to Banks

Credit selling to AMCs is an important option for banks to dispose of troubled credits. Credit selling to AMCs contains some advantages. These can be summarized as follows (Çan 2014):

- Troubled credits amount will be decreased in total assets after selling to AMCs. Hence, banks' troubled credits/total credits ratio will decrease at a considerable amount depending on how large-scale troubled credits are sold to AMCs.
- Banks' legal capital requirement will decrease, and hence banks' capital adequacy ratios will increase.
- Banks could gain liquid fund depending on how large-scale troubled credits are sold to AMCs.
- Banks' profits will be increased due to fact that banks made provisions for troubled credits already.
- Banks' return on assets will be affected positively by selling troubled credits to AMC.

Although credit selling to AMCs has advantages for banks, unfortunately it has some disadvantages too. These advantages can be summarized as follows (Mesutoğlu 2001):

- Credit selling to AMCs will decrease capacity of banks' in usage corporate information about borrower and debt.
- Credit selling to AMCs could make banks laxer in credit allocating and follow-up.
- Some AMCs which are established or managed by public could work without making good pricing and hence could work inefficiently.

When banks sell troubled credits to AMCs, disconnection would occur between borrower, debt, and bank. Hence, borrowers, who previously did not repay their credits, could reach to obtain credit again, so some borrowers can think that there will be nothing if they do not repay their credits. This will be a bad physiological environment for banks to operate in.

Disposal Methods of Troubled Credits in Selected Countries

The methods that are used to dispose of troubled credits can be changed from country to country. Some countries choose to deploy a central institution, while some countries prefer to use other methods. Countries' choices change according to countries' own conditions. Some countries' choices are included in Table 12.6.

As it can be seen from Table 12.6, countries can select different methods. Central/national asset management institution, asset management institution based on each bank, collector bank, asset management to be applied with rehabilitation and liquidation are methods that can be deployed by banks. For example, FDIC and RTC are responsible from troubled assets in the USA, while FOBAPROA deals with banks' troubled credits and tries to liquid them in Mexico. Both of them deploy asset management to be applied with rehabilitation and liquidation as method. Similarly, BAD bank is responsible from troubled assets in Albania, while investment and

Table 12.6 Disposal methods of troubled credits in selected countries

Institution type	Country samples
Central or national asset management institution	Czech Republic: Konsolidation Bank France: Consortium de Realisation Indonesia: Indonesian Restructuring Agency South Korea: Korea Asset Management Company (KAMCO) Mongolia: Mongolian Asset Realization Malesia: Pengurusan Danaharta Nasional Berhad
Asset management institution based on each bank	Finland: Two agencies Mexica: Loan restructuring programs Sweden: Securum
Collector bank	Albania: BAD bank Hungary: Investment and development bank
Asset management to be applied with rehabilitation and liquidation	USA: Federal Deposit Insurance Corporation (FDIC), Resolution Trust Corporation (RTC) Mexico: FOBAPROA (El Fondo Bancario de Protección al Ahorro), Deposit Protection Agency, Asset and Valuation and Sale Agency (VVA), Coordinating Unit for Corporate Loans (UCABE) Japan: Deposit Insurance Company, Resolution and Collection Bank, Housing Loan Administration Corporation Spain: Deposit Guarantee Fund Slovenia: Bank Rehabilitation Agency

Source: Dziobek (1998), Duvan (2001), Selimler (2006), Acar (2013)

development bank deals with banks' troubled credits in Hungary. Both of them deploy collector bank method.

In Turkey practices, banks try to dispose troubled credits firstly by follow-up processes. If troubled credits cannot be collected in follow-up processes, then bank could prefer to use credit selling option to AMCs.

When analyzing troubled credit selling practices in Turkey, it can be seen that 23 different private banks including deposit and participation banks have sold troubled credits 186 times from 2008 to today. In these sales, average sale price/portfolio volume became 12.16%.

Complete list takes place in Appendix 4. In these practices, banks have sold troubled credits to AMCs at amount of total TL 25.5 billion. In this volume, deposit banks have sold at amount of total TL 24.1 billion, and participation banks have sold at amount of TL 1.4 billion troubled credits to AMCs. As a result of credit sales, 23 banks have collected TL 3.1 billion cash in return. Hence, private banks have disposed of troubled credits, enhanced asset quality, generated income, and increased their profits.

An Evaluation upon Banking Regulation and Supervision Authority's Regulation About Credit Selling of State Banks to Asset Management Companies (BRSA Charter) in Turkey

Selling of Troubled Credits in the View of Regulations in Turkey

State banks and their activities are subject to Banking Law in terms of legislation (Banking Law 2005). Besides this, state banks are subject to Public Law due to fact that they are state banks. Banks' selling troubled credits are regulated by Banking Law, Public Law, and BRSA's regulations in Turkey. So, credit selling of state banks should be handled in terms of legislation made related with Banking Law and Public Law.

There is no restriction in Banking Law to sell state banks' troubled assets. When BRSA Charter about establishment and activities of asset management companies is reviewed, it is also concluded that there is no restriction about the subject. According to this charter, AMCs could purchase all banks' receivables including state banks' troubled credits (BDDK 2006).

When the subject is handled in terms of Public Law, however, there is no absolute regulation that enables state banks to sell their troubled credits to AMCs. There was a loophole in the law. State banks have not sold their troubled credits to AMCs because of the fact that there is no special regulation for state banks. So, making a new regulation was a must. For this reason, BRSA issued new charter about troubled credit selling of state banks to AMC on 08.11.2017 named as *Troubled Credits Selling of State Banks to Asset Management Companies*. After on 08.11.2017, state banks, which have not benefitted previously from credit selling, can sell their troubled credits to AMC and benefit from troubled credit selling.

BRSA Charter of Troubled Credits Selling of State Banks to Asset Management Companies

In Turkey practices, banks can sell troubled credits to asset management companies if they want to sell and complete necessary steps. Troubled credit selling to AMCs option has been deployed fully by private banks by now. In order to make state banks enable to use the option, BRSA issued a draft charter about state banks' troubled credit selling to asset management companies on 04.24.2017. The draft charter became effective on 08.11.2017.

BRSA Charter has total of six articles. These are as follows (BDDK 2017c):

- Article 1: Objective and scope
- Article 2: Base
- Article 3: Descriptions and abbreviations
- Article 4: Determination and closure of receivables to be sold

- Article 5: Enforcement
- Article 6: Execution

According to Article 1, state banks can sell troubled credits to AMCs. According to Article 2, BRSA Charters is issued based on Article 93 and 143 of Banking Law no. 5411. Descriptions and abbreviations take place in Article 3. According to Article 4, the board of directors of banks must determine necessary conditions about credit selling to AMCs taking into consideration productivity principles, market conditions, payment potentials, collateral conditions, wealth of borrowers, and potential results that can be reached at the end of legal proceedings. Also banks' internal processes should be compliant with Banking Law and BRSA's regulations. In these processes, minimum requirements, sales method, tender period, and tender process must take place. In addition, necessary disclosures should be published to public about being sold troubled credits. Enforcement and execution also take place in Article 5 and 6. According to them, the charter becomes effective on 08.11.2017 and is executed by BRSA Chairman (BDDK 2017c).

BRSA Charter's Effects to State Banks

The first, and the most important, effect of BRSA Charter is that state banks can sell their troubled assets to AMCs with becoming BRSA Charter effective. Using troubled credit selling option, state banks could receive benefits as follows:

- Troubled credits in balance sheets would be reduced.
- Troubled credits/total credits ratio would be decreased.
- Legal capital requirement would decrease.
- Asset quality would be improved.
- There would be improvement in some financial indicators:

  - Provisions would be decreased.
  - Profits would be increased.
  - Return on assets would be affected increased.
  - Liquidity would be increased.
  - Capital adequacy ratio would be increased.
  - Growth rate would be accelerated and industry share would be increased in time.

Degree of effects could change depending on how a large-scale troubled credits are sold to AMCs by state banks. Taken into consideration that state banks have TL 665,887,885,000 credit volumes and TL 17,052,962,000 troubled credit volume as of 2017 March and average sale price/portfolio volume is at 12.16% in practice, state banks could have cash inflow at amount of TL 2,073,640,000 if they sell all troubled credits at average sale price/portfolio volume. This is a substantial amount and as mentioned above, it could result in so many positive effects on state banks' financial indicators.

Although credit selling to AMCs has state banks many advantages, unfortunately it has some disadvantages too. The first, and the most important, disadvantages of state banks' credit selling option is reputation risk. AMCs deploy different collection processes and practices. Some of them are to scare borrowers, to call borrowers' relatives, etc. These methods are looked askance at borrowers and society. So, when state banks sell their troubled assets to AMCs and AMCs deploy these unpreferable methods, society and potential borrowers do not take kindly state banks' credit selling decision to AMCs.

BRSA Charter's Effects to Turkish Banking Sector and Turkey Economy

Along with starting state banks' troubled credit selling, there would be not only improvement state banks' financial indicators but also Turkish Banking Sector and hence Turkey economy's some indicators.

In view of Turkish Banking Sector, state banks' troubled credit selling would make similar effects with state banks on TBS. Depending on state banks' practices and credit selling volume, TBS's troubled credits/total credits ratio and provisions would be decreased; capital adequacy ratio, liquidity, profits, and return on asset would be increased. Also TBS's asset quality is affected from troubled credit selling of state banks positively. In addition to these, improvements in mentioned financial indicators would support TBS' growth in time. Hence, TMS's total volume would be much bigger than ever before.

In the view of Turkish economy, state banks' troubled credit selling to AMCs could also make effects. Due to improvements in financial indicators, state banks and TBS could provide much more credits to economy, businesses, and individuals. Hence, macro economy is supported by banking sector. So, this shows that Turkey economy would be supported by credit channel and economic growth would be accelerated.

When effects of BRSA Charters on Turkish Banking Sector and Turkey economy are evaluated, it can be said that new practice, which is selling troubled credits of state banks to AMC, would be beneficial for all stakeholders including state banks, TBS, and Turkey economy. However, it should not be forgotten that possible negative effects of new practice be followed up by regulatory authorities specially by BRSA and be taken necessary measures if negative effects were seen on state banks, TBS, and Turkey economy.

Conclusion

Banks' main function is to provide finance. In this context, banks provide credits to who needs funds. In this process, troubled credits are one of the most important problems for banks while operating. Troubled credit selling is one option for banks to dispose of troubled credits. Troubled credit selling is preferred and supported by both banks' management and regulatory authorities due to fact that it provides cash in return for worthless credits, it enhances some financial ratios, it cleans balance sheets in the view of bank management, it cleans and enhances balance sheets, and it gives possibility to analyze balance sheets of Turkish Banking Sector much more correctly in the view of regulatory authorities.

When Turkey practices examined, it can be seen that state banks cannot benefit from troubled credit selling option although private banks have used the option 186 times from 2008 to today. Hence, private banks have sold TL 25.5 billion troubled credits and have collected TL 3.1 billion in return. However, state banks have not been able to use troubled credit selling option until 08.11.2017. BRSA issued a charter named as *Troubled Credits Selling of State Banks to Asset Management Companies* to enable state banks to sell troubled credits to AMCs. This shows that the need for troubled credit selling of state banks is responded by regulatory authorities. After on 08.11.2017, state banks can sell troubled credits to AMCs and benefit from this option. Hence, state banks can compete with private banks under more equal conditions.

State bank would benefit reducing troubled credits in balance sheet, decreasing troubled credits/total credits ratio, decreasing legal capital requirement, enhancing asset quality, and also improving some financial ratios such as provision, profits, return on asset, liquidity, and capital adequacy from troubled credit selling to AMCs. Troubled credit selling of state banks will provide not only benefits to state banks, but it also affect Turkish Banking Sector and Turkish economy. It is expected that Turkish Banking Sector and Turkish economy will be affected positively in some areas such as growth in credits and growth in gross national product in general by state banks' troubled credit selling.

When it is taken into consideration that state banks have TL 17,052,962,000 troubled credits as of 2017 March, state banks could have cash inflow at amount of TL 2,073,640,000 if they sell all troubled credits at average sale price/portfolio volume which is 12.16%. This is a substantial amount for state banks, and this could result in so many positive effects on state banks' financial indicators as mentioned above.

Although troubled credit selling of state banks is evaluated as positive in general, unfortunately it has some disadvantage too. The method could result in reputation risk for state banks because of the fact that AMCs' collection processes and practices have some negative insight in the view of public. So, when AMCs deploy unpreferable methods, credit selling of state banks is not taken kindly by society and potential borrowers.

As a general evaluation, it can be said that the regulation is really a need for state banks. So, BRSA's regulation is evaluated as a positive improvement. It is thought that the regulation will be beneficial to related parties such as state banks, Turkish Banking Sector, and Turkish economy. However, the regulation's probable positive and negative effects should be followed up by regulatory authorities specifically by BRSA and should be taken necessary measures if negative effects were seen.

Appendices

Appendix 1 Credit volume of state banks in Turkey (TL 1000)

Bank name	2010/12	2011/12	2012/12	2013/12	2014/12	2015/12	2016/12	2017/3
T.C. Ziraat Bankası A.Ş.	57,161,350	71,173,260	70,630,294	110,253,435	141,129,911	185,942,859	232,392,086	251,674,445
Türkiye Halk Bankası A.Ş.	44,003,264	55,949,446	65,550,830	84,413,441	100,481,286	125,799,124	157,178,296	167,130,112
Türkiye Vakıflar Bankası T.A.O.	44,836,394	57,200,610	67,867,645	86,496,223	104,343,442	122,974,478	146,618,992	153,167,750
Türkiye İhracat Kredi Bankası A.Ş.	4,159,138	8,065,619	13,352,060	23,035,036	31,889,864	43,156,126	61,520,461	60,676,959
İller Bankası A.Ş.	6,669,608	7,784,913	8,949,749	11,358,967	11,477,528	12,884,980	16,227,751	16,982,158
İstanbul Takas ve Saklama Bankası A.Ş.	19,054	81,405	107,306	282,291	169,177	172,112	98,945	106,776
Türkiye Kalkınma Bankası A.Ş.	1,150,719	1,810,877	2,206,391	2,678,219	3,084,018	3,851,709	5,349,989	5,922,287
Ziraat Katılım Bankası A.Ş.	–	–	–	–	–	1,690,106	5,557,942	6,504,876
Vakıf Katılım Bankası A.Ş.	–	–	–	–	–	–	2,946,447	3,722,522
Total (Deposit)	146,001,008	184,323,316	204,048,769	281,163,099	345,954,639	434,716,461	536,189,374	571,972,307
Total (development and investment)	11,998,519	17,742,814	24,615,506	37,354,513	46,620,587	60,064,927	83,197,146	83,688,180
Total (participation)	–	–	–	–	–	1,690,106	8,504,389	10,227,398
Grand total	157,999527	202,066130	228,664275	318,517612	392,575226	496,471494	627,890909	665,887885

Source: Deposit and development and investment banks' data were obtained from Turkish Banking Association. Participation banks' data were obtained from banks' own web sites

Appendix 2 Troubled credits of state banks in Turkey (TL 1000)

Bank name	2010/12	2011/12	2012/12	2013/12	2014/12	2015/12	2016/12	2017/3
T.C. Ziraat Bankası A.Ş.	855,070	863,041	2,057,553	2,417,441	2,716,920	3,140,524	4,217,097	4,331,998
Türkiye Halk Bankası A.Ş.	1,757,753	1,668,695	1,959,646	2,245,176	3,699,661	3,973,738	5,140,082	5,570,837
Türkiye Vakıflar Bankası T.A.O.	2,265,716	2,156,879	2,724,963	3,531,427	3,974,372	4,850,213	6,413,503	6,728,333
Türkiye İhracat Kredi Bankası A.Ş.	120,766	114,853	112,383	117,478	127,478	131,688	233,087	266,012
İller Bankası A.Ş.	461	466	563	563	562	556	555	555
İstanbul Takas ve Saklama Bankası A.Ş.	1637	1637	1637	1637	1637	1574	1574	1574
Türkiye Kalkınma Bankası A.Ş.	78,337	94,664	97,220	124,907	109,033	107,471	125,779	124,405
Ziraat Katılım Bankası A.Ş.	–	–	–	–	–	2	10,483	19,602
Vakıf Katılım Bankası A.Ş.	–	–	–	–	–	–	3647	9646
Total (deposit)	**4,878,539**	**4,688,615**	**6,742,162**	**8,194,044**	**10,390,953**	**11,964,475**	**15,770,682**	**16,631,168**
Total (development and investment)	**201,201**	**211,620**	**211,803**	**244,585**	**238,710**	**241,289**	**360,995**	**392,546**
Total (participation)	–	–	–	–	–	**2**	**14,130**	**29,248**
Grand total	**5,079,740**	**4,900,235**	**6,953,965**	**8,438,629**	**10,629,663**	**12,205,766**	**16,145,807**	**17,052,962**

Source: Deposit and development and investment banks' data were obtained from Turkish Banking Association. Participation banks' data were obtained from banks' own web sites.

Appendix 3 Troubled credit/total credit ratios of state banks

Bank name	2010/12	2011/12	2012/12	2013/12	2014/12	2015/12	2016/12	2017/3
T.C. Ziraat Bankası A.Ş.	1.50%	1.21%	**2.91%**	2.19%	1.93%	1.69%	**1.81%**	1.72%
Türkiye Halk Bankası A.Ş.	3.99%	2.98%	**2.99%**	2.66%	**3.68%**	3.16%	3.27%	**3.33%**
Türkiye Vakıflar Bankası T.A.O.	5.05%	3.77%	**4.02%**	**4.08%**	3.81%	**3.94%**	4.37%	**4.39%**
Türkiye İhracat Kredi Bankası A.Ş.	2.90%	1.42%	0.84%	0.51%	0.40%	0.31%	**0.38%**	**0.44%**
İller Bankası A.Ş.	0.01%	0.01%	0.01%	0.00%	0.00%	0.00%	0.00%	0.00%
İstanbul Takas ve Saklama Bankası A.Ş.	8.59%	2.01%	1.53%	0.58%	**0.97%**	0.91%	**1.59%**	1.47%
Türkiye Kalkınma Bankası A.Ş.	6.81%	5.23%	4.41%	**4.66%**	3.54%	2.79%	2.35%	2.10%
Ziraat Katılım Bankası A.Ş.	–	–	–	–	–	0.00%	**0.19%**	**0.30%**
Vakıf Katılım Bankası A.Ş.	–	–	–	–	–	–	0.12%	**0.26%**

Source: Derived from Appendix 1 and 2

Appendix 4 Banks' credit sales to asset management companies in Turkey

Year	Seller (banks)	Bank type	Buyer (asset management companies)	Portfolio volume (TL)	Sale price (TL)	Sale price/portfolio volume
2008	Ak	Deposit	Güven	339,000,000	42,000,000	12.39%
2008	Ak	Deposit	Güven	331,000,000	86,500,000	26.13%
2008	Şeker	Deposit	Türkasset	243,700,000	61,000,000	25.03%
2008	Türk Ekonomi	Deposit	Güven	75,600,000	10,850,000	14.35%
2008	Türkiye Garanti	Deposit	Bebek (Deutsche)	98,000,000	28,900,000	29.49%
2008	Yapı ve Kredi	Deposit	Türkasset	532,351,710	60,500,000	11.36%
2009	Fortis	Deposit	Türkasset	115,800,000	6,500,000	5.61%
2009	HSBC	Deposit	Bebek (Deutsche)	161,460,000	9,300,000	5.76%
2009	Türk Ekonomi	Deposit	Türkasset	29,950,000	1,950,000	6.51%
2009	Türkiye İş	Deposit	İstanbul	186,000,000	8,500,000	4.57%
2009	Türkiye İş	Deposit	Türkasset	37,823,000	9,550,000	25.25%
2009	Yapı ve Kredi	Deposit	Güven	393,867,278	26,525,000	6.73%
2010	Ak	Deposit	Güven	326,000,000	38,500,000	11.81%
2010	Alternatif	Deposit	Güven	59,600,000	11,500,000	19.30%
2010	Citi	Deposit	Güven	89,000,000	9,376,000	10.53%
2010	Deniz	Deposit	İstanbul	50,200,000	4,900,000	9.76%
2010	Deniz	Deposit	İstanbul	32,100,000	3,200,000	9.97%
2010	Deniz	Deposit	Türkasset	47,700,000	2,900,000	6.08%
2010	Eurobank Tekfen	Deposit	Türkasset	41,441,000	1,550,000	3.74%
2010	Fortis	Deposit	Güven	30,400,000	1,700,000	5.59%
2010	Fortis	Deposit	Türkasset	54,450,000	2,100,000	3.86%
2010	HSBC	Deposit	Türkasset	158,000,000	44,000,000	27.85%
2010	Türk Ekonomi	Deposit	İstanbul	39,900,000	4,125,000	10.34%
2010	Türkiye İş	Deposit	Güven	300,400,000	50,800,000	16.91%
2010	Türkiye İş	Deposit	Türkasset	41,900,000	6,400,000	15.27%

(continued)

Year	Seller (banks)	Bank type	Buyer (asset management companies)	Portfolio volume (TL)	Sale price (TL)	Sale price/portfolio volume
2010	Yapı ve Kredi	Deposit	Güven	381,973,395	32,435,000	8.49%
2010	Yapı ve Kredi	Deposit	Güven	170,867,418	24,435,000	14.30%
2010	Yapı ve Kredi	Deposit	İstanbul	74,606,491	6,450,000	8.65%
2010	Yapı ve Kredi	Deposit	Türkasset	224,390,404	31,232,323	13.92%
2010	Yapı ve Kredi	Deposit	Türkasset	298,741,496	7,518,378	2.52%
2010	Yapı ve Kredi	Deposit	Türkasset	256,955,075	31,610,000	12.30%
2011	Deniz	Deposit	Güven	111,000,000	10,500,000	9.46%
2011	Deniz	Deposit	İstanbul Varlık / Efes	136,000,000	17,500,000	12.87%
2011	Finans	Deposit	Türkasset	288,000,000	17,500,000	6.08%
2011	Şeker	Deposit	Güven	144,000,000	12,000,000	8.33%
2011	Türk Ekonomi	Deposit	Türkasset	55,500,000	4,250,000	7.66%
2011	Türkiye Garanti	Deposit	Bebek (Deutsche)	483,800,000	53,900,000	11.14%
2011	Türkiye İş	Deposit	Efes	221,000,000	42,100,000	19.05%
2011	Türkiye İş	Deposit	İstanbul	88,400,000	13,900,000	15.72%
2011	Yapı ve Kredi	Deposit	Türkasset	290,276,671	45,801,000	15.78%
2012	Ak	Deposit	Güven	500,000,000	95,000,000	19.00%
2012	Alternatif	Deposit	Final	58,433,767	7,750,000	13.26%
2012	Alternatif	Deposit	Güven	93,082,028	18,000,000	19.34%
2012	Citi	Deposit	Türkasset	107,000,000	14,900,000	13.93%
2012	Deniz	Deposit	Güven	38,895,258	6,208,101	15.96%
2012	Deniz	Deposit	Türkasset / Final	70,256,349	7,200,000	10.25%
2012	Deniz	Deposit	Türkasset / Efes	75,089,077	7,250,000	9.66%
2012	HSBC	Deposit	Güven	146,200,000	25,100,000	17.17%
2012	ING	Deposit	İstanbul	66,141,000	12,300,000	18.60%
2012	Şeker	Deposit	Güven	23,960,698	5,050,000	21.08%

2012	Şeker	Deposit	Güven	172,642,882	16,000,000	9.27%
2012	Türk Ekonomi	Deposit	Güven	124,000,000	16,800,000	13.55%
2012	Türkiye Garanti	Deposit	Güven	200,564,023	32,600,000	16.25%
2012	Türkiye İş	Deposit	Güven	136,600,000	28,600,000	20.94%
2012	Türkiye İş	Deposit	Türkasset	285,600,000	50,100,000	17.54%
2012	Yapı ve Kredi	Deposit	Anadolu	60,022,358	11,760,000	19.59%
2012	Yapı ve Kredi	Deposit	Güven	119,729,742	24,005,000	20.05%
2012	Yapı ve Kredi	Deposit	İstanbul	73,711,193	15,058,000	20.43%
2012	Yapı ve Kredi	Deposit	Türkasset	174,839,932	1,000,001	0.57%
2012	Yapı ve Kredi	Deposit	Türkasset	197,775,543	15,000,000	7.58%
2013	Ak	Deposit	Efes	250,500,000	58,300,000	23.27%
2013	Alternatif	Deposit	Güven	91,738,986	19,200,000	20.93%
2013	Asya	Participation	Birleşim	467,872,160	18,100,000	3.87%
2013	Deniz	Deposit	Final	51,332,638	6,000,000	11.69%
2013	Deniz	Deposit	İstanbul	122,579,295	25,100,000	20.48%
2013	Finans	Deposit	Anadolu	182,888,228	32,600,000	17.83%
2013	Finans	Deposit	Final	182,918,204	35,000,000	19.13%
2013	Finans	Deposit	İstanbul	182,908,878	32,500,000	17.77%
2013	ING	Deposit	Final	41,571,000	6,471,000	15.57%
2013	Türkiye Finans	Participation	Birleşim	4,522,000	425,000	9.40%
2013	Türkiye Garanti	Deposit	Türkasset	314,157,760	58,400,000	18.59%
2013	Türkiye İş	Deposit	Güven	164,000,000	32,000,000	19.51%
2013	Türkiye İş	Deposit	Türkasset	85,000,000	10,000,000	11.76%
2013	Yapı ve Kredi	Deposit	Anadolu	53,822,013	9,810,000	18.23%
2013	Yapı ve Kredi	Deposit	Final	107,704,809	20,230,000	18.78%
2013	Yapı ve Kredi	Deposit	Türkasset	53,287,754	9,610,000	18.03%
2014	Ak	Deposit	Efes	250,500,000	41,000,000	16.37%
2014	Ak	Deposit	Güven	252,000,000	44,000,000	17.46%

(continued)

Year	Seller (banks)	Bank type	Buyer (asset management companies)	Portfolio volume (TL)	Sale price (TL)	Sale price/portfolio volume
2014	Asya	Participation	Destek	180,859,631	36,600,000	20.24%
2014	Deniz	Deposit	Güven	251,552,159	38,150,000	15.17%
2014	Deniz	Deposit	Türkasset	88,836,782	7,100,000	7.99%
2014	Fiba	Deposit	Final	13,961,182	300,000	2.15%
2014	Fiba	Deposit	Vera	4,572,909	260,000	5.69%
2014	Finans	Deposit	Anadolu	180,547,723	35,600,000	19.72%
2014	Finans	Deposit	Final	153,455,084	20,000,000	13.03%
2014	Finans	Deposit	Final	21,371,647	2,200,000	10.29%
2014	Finans	Deposit	Güven	109,393,961	20,800,000	19.01%
2014	Finans	Deposit	Türkasset	180,509,013	34,600,000	19.17%
2014	Finans	Deposit	Türkasset	180,652,909	33,000,000	18.27%
2014	Finans	Deposit	Türkasset	39,213,252	4,400,000	11.22%
2014	Finans	Deposit	Türkasset	151,379,545	1,100,000	0.73%
2014	Finans	Deposit	Türkasset	99,180,909	6,700,000	6.76%
2014	Finans	Deposit	Türkasset	37,433,375	750,000	2.00%
2014	Finans	Deposit	Türkasset	254,000,000	8,600,000	3.39%
2014	Finans	Deposit	Türkasset	109,499,905	19,200,000	17.53%
2014	Finans	Deposit	Türkasset	109,316,441	21,800,000	19.94%
2014	ING	Deposit	Destek	92,000,000	4,900,000	5.33%
2014	ING	Deposit	Türkasset	47,861,000	7,250,000	15.15%
2014	Tekstil	Deposit	Türkasset	22,623,250	1,500,000	6.63%
2014	Tekstil	Deposit	Vera	60,489,325	200,000	0.33%
2014	Türk Ekonomi	Deposit	Türkasset	174,635,000	19,800,000	11.34%
2014	Türkiye Garanti	Deposit	Birleşim	69,925,529	12,401,123	17.73%
2014	Türkiye Garanti	Deposit	Final	69,954,701	11,911,456	17.03%

2014	Türkiye Garanti	Deposit	İstanbul	106,500,000	18,700,000	17.56%
2014	Türkiye İş	Deposit	Efes	218,000,000	22,000,000	10.09%
2014	Türkiye İş	Deposit	Güven	272,517,432	44,016,816	16.15%
2014	Yapı ve Kredi	Deposit	Birleşim	61,127,536	8,300,000	13.58%
2014	Yapı ve Kredi	Deposit	Destek	54,314,875	8,230,000	15.15%
2014	Yapı ve Kredi	Deposit	Efes	116,488,999	15,600,000	13.39%
2014	Yapı ve Kredi	Deposit	Efes	53,344,179	7,800,000	14.62%
2014	Yapı ve Kredi	Deposit	Güven	49,490,282	7,310,000	14.77%
2014	Yapı ve Kredi	Deposit	Türkasset	56,393,746	2,500,000	4.43%
2014	Yapı ve Kredi	Deposit	Vera	56,128,729	2,530,000	4.51%
2015	Ak	Deposit	Güven	248,500,000	40,300,000	16.22%
2015	Alternatif	Deposit	Güven	115,834,710	4,650,000	4.01%
2015	Asya	Participation	Destek	180,859,631	36,600,000	20.24%
2015	ING	Deposit	Anadolu	22,921,360	1,130,000	4.93%
2015	ING	Deposit	Güven	39,000,000	100,000	0.26%
2015	ING	Deposit	Sümer	91,700,000	10,200,000	11.12%
2015	ING	Deposit	Vera	31,000,000	1,000,000	3.23%
2015	Odea	Deposit	Sümer	35,626,627	3,800,000	10.67%
2015	Odea	Deposit	Sümer	35,626,627	3,800,000	10.67%
2015	Odea	Deposit	Türkasset	47,786,000	6,749,000	14.12%
2015	Şeker	Deposit	Destek	29,943,774	3,600,000	12.02%
2015	Şeker	Deposit	Destek / Güven / Final	209,057,111	15,100,000	7.22%
2015	Türk Ekonomi	Deposit	Final	215,354,933	27,950,000	12.98%
2015	Türk Ekonomi	Deposit	Final	41,823,124	7,500,000	17.93%
2015	Türkiye Finans	Participation	Final	22,545,408	4,750,000	21.07%
2015	Türkiye Garanti	Deposit	Destek	79,114,484	14,500,000	18.33%
2015	Türkiye İş	Deposit	Final	189,223,526	29,000,000	15.33%
2016	Ak	Deposit	Güven	149,924,935	14,800,000	9.87%

(continued)

Year	Seller (banks)	Bank type	Buyer (asset management companies)	Portfolio volume (TL)	Sale price (TL)	Sale price/portfolio volume
2016	Ak	Deposit	Güven	150,046,132	17,100,000	11.40%
2016	Ak	Deposit	Güven	150,040,965	17,200,000	11.46%
2016	Anadolu	Deposit	Güven	92,437,992	2,850,000	3.08%
2016	Burgan	Deposit	Mega	72,579,606	1,500,000	2.07%
2016	Deniz	Deposit	Final	204,690,204	25,400,000	12.41%
2016	Deniz	Deposit	Final	79,900,000	5,600,000	7.01%
2016	Deniz	Deposit	İstanbul	107,186,585	11,700,000	10.92%
2016	Deniz	Deposit	Sümer	107,477,784	11,600,000	10.79%
2016	Fiba	Deposit	Hedef	13,956,004	1,250,000	8.96%
2016	Fiba	Deposit	Hedef	40,046,049	700,000	1.75%
2016	Fiba	Deposit	Hedef	64,736,130	400,000	0.62%
2016	Finans	Deposit	Destek	146,800,000	10,000,000	6.81%
2016	Finans	Deposit	Destek	147,000,000	10,000,000	6.80%
2016	Finans	Deposit	Final	297,020,548	41,200,000	13.87%
2016	Finans	Deposit	Güven	123,900,000	19,100,000	15.42%
2016	Finans	Deposit	Güven	124,000,000	19,200,000	15.48%
2016	Finans	Deposit	Türkasset	198,011,539	28,200,000	14.24%
2016	Finans	Deposit	Türkasset	124,100,000	19,400,000	15.63%
2016	Finans	Deposit	Türkasset	123,900,000	19,300,000	15.58%
2016	HSBC	Deposit	Final	285,000,000	31,350,000	11.00%
2016	ICBC Turkey	Deposit	Final	8,858,397	800,000	9.03%
2016	ICBC Turkey	Deposit	Mega	45,596,182	575,500	1.26%
2016	ING	Deposit	İstanbul	115,000,000	13,050,000	11.35%
2016	ING	Deposit	Mega	45,000,000	850,000	1.89%
2016	Odea	Deposit	Güven	77,730,505	12,000,000	15.44%

2016	Şeker	Deposit	Final	87,800,000	4,500,000	5.13%
2016	Şeker	Deposit	Hedef	228,880,293	8,650,000	3.78%
2016	Şeker	Deposit	Hedef / Mega / Birleşim	102,645,171	3,900,000	3.80%
2016	Şeker	Deposit	Mega	51,787,429	2,650,000	5.12%
2016	Tbank	Deposit	Sümer	32,649,863	300,000	0.92%
2016	Türk Ekonomi	Deposit	Destek	213,000,000	23,000,000	10.80%
2016	Türk Ekonomi	Deposit	Güven	201,777,021	20,000,000	9.91%
2016	Türkiye Finans	Participation	Birleşim	104,571,426	13,000,000	12.43%
2016	Türkiye Finans	Participation	Birleşim	104,117,323	13,000,000	12.49%
2016	Türkiye Finans	Participation	Birleşim	104,619,172	15,000,000	14.34%
2016	Türkiye Finans	Participation	Güven	25,203,814	3,800,000	15.08%
2016	Türkiye Finans	Participation	Güven	31,933,385	6,000,000	18.79%
2016	Türkiye Finans	Participation	Mega	178,263,311	14,000,000	7.85%
2016	Türkiye Garanti	Deposit	Güven	207,030,767	14,600,000	7.05%
2016	Türkiye Garanti	Deposit	Sümer	175,174,390	28,000,000	15.98%
2016	Türkiye Garanti	Deposit	Sümer	81,047,703	10,100,000	12.46%
2016	Türkiye Garanti	Deposit	Sümer	203,583,441	2,500,000	1.23%
2016	Türkiye Garanti	Deposit	Türkasset	158,740,834	2,250,000	1.42%
2016	Türkiye Garanti	Deposit	Türkasset	139,045,179	16,600,000	11.94%
2016	Türkiye Garanti	Deposit	Türkasset	92,600,000	1,250,000	1.35%
2016	Türkiye İş	Deposit	Final	233,800,000	29,800,000	12.75%
2016	Türkiye İş	Deposit	Sümer	171,200,000	5,500,000	3.21%
2017	Alternatif	Deposit	Mega	105,189,860	2,100,000	2.00%
2017	Deniz	Deposit	Güven	100,747,357	5,400,000	5.36%
2017	Deniz	Deposit	Sümer	150,802,527	12,900,000	8.55%
2017	Türk Ekonomi	Deposit	Hayat	102,751,844	5,900,000	5.74%
2017	Türkiye Garanti	Deposit	Sümer	109,750,396	9,010,000	8.21%
2017	Yapı ve Kredi	Deposit	Güven	531,026,113	27,500,000	5.18%

(continued)

Year	Seller (banks)	Bank type	Buyer (asset management companies)	Portfolio volume (TL)	Sale price (TL)	Sale price/portfolio volume
2017	Yapı ve Kredi	Deposit	Güven	316,030,170	17,700,000	5.60%
2017	Şeker	Deposit	Destek / Efes	109,365,393	3,100,000	2.83%
Grand Total				**25,558,523,576**	**3,106,658,698**	**12.16%**

Source: Derived from Internet

References

Acar, O. (2013). *Varlık Yönetim Şirketleri: Asya Ülkeleri Uygulaması*. 15.08.2017. http://www.okanacar.com/2013/01/varlk-yonetim-sirketleri-asya-ulkeleri.html

Ağaoğlu, A. (2011). 2001 Krizi Sonrasında Sorunlu Aktiflerin Çözümlenmesinde Kamunun ve Varlık Yönetim Şirketlerinin Önemi, İstanbul Kültür Üniversitesi, Sosyal Bilimler Enstitüsü, İktisat Anabilim Dalı, Yüksek Lisans Tezi.

Aktaş, R. (2000). Sorunlu Krediler, TBB Eğitim ve Tanıtım Grubu Seminer Notları, İstanbul, 25–26 Mayıs.

Alhassan, A. L., Brobbey, F. O., & Asamoah, M. E. (2013). Does asset quality persist on bank lending behaviour? Empirical evidence from Ghana. *Global Journal of Management and Business Research Finance, 13*(4), 1–2.

Aydoğan, K. (1990). An investigation of performance and operational efficiency in Turkish banking industry. *Türkiye Cumhuriyet Merkez Bankası, 9022*(5), 1–33.

Banking Law. (2005). 5411 sayılı, 01.11.2005 tarih ve 25983 sayılı Resmi Gazete.

Barr, R. S., Seiford, L. M., & Siems, T. F. (1994). Forecasting bank failure: A non-parametric frontier estimation approach. *Recherches Économiques de Louvain/Louvain Economic Review, 60*(04), 417–429.

BDDK. (2006). Varlık Yönetim Şirketlerinin Kuruluş ve Faaliyet Esasları Hakkında Yönetmelik, 01.11.2006 tarih ve 26333 sayılı Resmi Gazete.

BDDK. (2017a). Türk Bankacılık Sektörü Temel Göstergeleri Haziran 2017. 11.08.2017. http://www.bddk.org.tr/WebSitesi/turkce/Raporlar/TBSGG/16208tbs_temel_gostergeler_raporu_haziran_2017.pdf

BDDK. (2017b). Türkiye'deki Bankalar. 11.08.2017. http://www.bddk.org.tr/WebSitesi/turkce/Kuruluslar/Bankalar/Bankalar.aspx

BDDK. (2017c). Kamu Sermayeli Bankalar İle Bu Bankaların Bağlı Ortaklığı Niteliğini Haiz Finansal Kuruluşların Alacaklarının Varlık Yönetim Şirketlerine Satışı Hakkında Yönetmelik, 11.08.2017 tarih ve 30151 sayılı Resmi Gazete.

Berger, A. N., & DeYoung, R. (1997). Problem loans and cost efficiency in commercial banks. *Journal of Banking & Finance, 21*(6), 849–870.

Çan, E. (2014). Sorunlu Kredi Transferi ve Fiyatlaması Üzerine Bir Çalışma. *Bankacılar Dergisi, 90*, 3–18.

Castro, V. (2013). Macroeconomic determinants of the credit risk in the banking system: The case of the GIPSI. *Economic Modelling, 31*, 672–683.

Chaibi, H., & Ftiti, Z. (2015). Credit risk determinants: Evidence from a cross-country study. *Research in International Business and Finance, 33*, 1–16.

Ćurak, M., Pepur, S., & Poposki, K. (2013). Determinants of non-performing loans–evidence from Southeastern banking systems. *Banks & Bank System, 8*(1), 45–54.

Duvan, B. (2001). Türk Bankacılık Sisteminde Tahsili Gecikmiş Alacakların Tasfiyesi ve Şirket Borçlarının Yapılandırılması, TC Başbakanlık Devlet Planlama Teşkilatı Müsteşarlığı Uzmanlık Tezi.

Dziobek, C. (1998). *Market-based policy instruments for systemic bank restructuring*. IMF Working Paper.

Espinoza, R. A., & Prasad, A. (2010). *Nonperforming loans in the GCC banking system and their macroeconomic effect*. IMF Working Papers, 1–24.

Gülhan, Ü., & Uzunlar, E. (2011). Bankacılık Sektöründe Kârlılığı Etkileyen Faktörler: Türk Bankacılık Sektörüne Yönelik Bir Uygulama. *Atatürk Üniversitesi Sosyal Bilimler Enstitüsü Dergisi, 15*(1), 341–368.

Güngör, B. (2007). Türkiye'de Faaliyet Gösteren Yerel ve Yabancı Bankaların Kârlılık Seviyelerini Etkileyen Faktörler: Panel Veri Analizi. *İktisat İşletme ve Finans Dergisi, 22*(258), 40–63.

Kartal, M. T., & Demir, C. H. (2017a). Türkiye'de Katılım Bankacılığının Sektör Payı Hedefi Üzerine Bir Analiz, *Route Educational & Social Science Journal*, Sayı: 14, *4*(3), 33–58.

Kartal, M. T., & Demir, C. H. (2017b). Türkiye'de Katılım Bankacılığında Sorunlu Kredilerin Varlık Yönetim Şirketlerine Satışı Üzerine Bir İnceleme ve Yöntem Önerileri. *İslam Ekonomisi ve Finansı Dergisi, 3*(1), 89–115.

Kaya, Y. T. (2002). Türk Bankacılık Sektöründe Karlılığın Belirleyicileri, MSPD Çalışma Raporları, *BDDK Yayınları*, 1–21.

Kaya, Z., Şahin, L., Hacıevliyagil, N., & Ekşi, İ. H. (2016). Bankaların Kredi Verme Davranışlarında Varlık Kalitesinin Etkisi. *Finansal Araştırmalar ve Çalışmalar Dergisi, 8* (14), 1–10.

Koyuncu, C., & Saka, B. (2011). Takipteki Kredilerin Özel Sektöre Verilen Krediler ve Yatırımlar Üzerindeki Etkisi. *Dumlupınar Üniversitesi Sosyal Bilimler Dergisi, 31*, 113–124.

Makri, V., Tsagkanos, A., & Bellas, A. (2014). Determinants of non-performing loans: The case of Eurozone. *Panoeconomicus, 61*(2), 193–206.

Mesutoğlu, B. (2001). Sorunlu Aktiflerin Varlık Yönetimi Şirketlerince Tasfiyesi-Ülke Örnekleri, BDDK MSPD Çalışma Raporları, 1–50.

Şahbaz, N. (2010). Türk Bankacılık Sektöründe Sorunlu Krediler ve Makro Ekonomik Etkileri, Afyon Kocatepe Üniversitesi Sosyal Bilimler Enstitüsü, İktisat Anabilim Dalı, Yüksek Lisans Tezi.

Şahbaz, N., & İnkaya, A. (2014). Türk Bankacılık Sektöründe Sorunlu Krediler ve Makro Ekonomik Etkileri. *Optimum Ekonomi ve Yönetim Bilimleri Dergisi, 1*, 69–82.

Selimler, H. (2006). Türk Bankacılık Sektöründe Sorunlu Kredilerin Varlık Yönetim Şirketlerince Tasfiyesi, Seçilmiş Ülkeler ve Türkiye Uygulaması, Marmara Üniversitesi Bankacılık ve Sigortacılık Enstitüsü, Bankacılık Anabilim Dalı, Doktora Tezi.

Selimler, H. (2015). Sorunlu Kredilerin Analizi, Banka Finansal Tablo ve Oranlarına Etkisinin Değerlendirilmesi. *Finansal Araştırmalar ve Çalışmalar Dergisi, 7*(29), 131–172.

Suadiye, G. (2006). Sorunlu Kredilerin Yeniden Yapılandırılmasında İstanbul Yaklaşımı. *Mustafa Kemal Üniversitesi Sosyal Bilimler Enstitüsü Dergisi, 3*(6), 1–25.

Turkish Banking Association. (2017). Veri Sorgulama Sistemi. 10.08.2017. https://www.tbb.org.tr/ tr/bankacilik/banka-ve-sektor-bilgileri/veri-sorgulama-sistemi/mali-tablolar/71

Yuca, H. (2012). Bankacılık Sektöründe Takipteki Krediler-Teminat İlişkisi: Türk Bankacılık Sektörü Üzerine Bir Uygulama, Kadir Has Üniversitesi Sosyal Bilimler Enstitüsü, Doktora Tezi.

Yücememiş, B. T., & Sözer, İ. A. (2010). Türk Bankacılık Sektöründe Takipteki Krediler: Mukayeseli Kriz Performansı. *Avrupa Araştırmaları Dergisi, 18*(1–2), 89–119.

Yüksel, S. (2016). Bankaların Takipteki Krediler Oranını Belirleyen Faktörler: Türkiye İçin Bir Model Önerisi. *Bankacılar Dergisi, 98*, 41–56.

Yüksel, S. (2017). Determinants of the credit risk in developing countries after economic crisis: A case of Turkish banking sector. In *Global financial crisis and its ramifications on capital markets* (pp. 401–415). Springer.

Chapter 13
Economic Contributions of the Ottoman Bank in the Ottoman Empire and the Turkish Republic

Seçil Şenel

Abstract The Ottoman Bank had a special place in the Ottoman Empire during the development of monetary and credit institutions. Founded in 1863, the Ottoman Bank functioned as the central bank for many subjects in the Ottoman Empire, and the bank is an interesting example of the role of foreign capital control over finance and the economy. The Ottoman Bank handled treasury operations until the establishment of the Central Bank and continued to protect the state bank statue. In this chapter, the duties and economic effects of the Ottoman Bank, which started in the Ottoman Empire and continued in the Republic of Turkey, will be discussed in the historical process.

Introduction

In the Ottoman Empire, trade was promoted, and the credit required for trade was widely used, with the money foundations, established especially for social solidarity, considered one of the important elements providing credit supply (Tabakoğlu 2003: 277). Monetary foundations are types of foundations formed by the devotion of a certain amount of money rather than a real estate commodity. Within these foundations, money is handled by a responsible party "board of trustees," and the profits obtained are spent according to the establishment purpose of the foundation (Çizakça 1993: 67). In fact, 1161 monetary foundations were established in Istanbul between 1456 and 1551 (Döndüren 2008: 4).

In the Ottoman Empire, the majority of the banking activities began with the money changers, Galata bankers who were mostly Levantine, who carried out all the monetary and credit works for the state and gained corporate entity status (The Development of National Banking in Turkey 1938: 4–5). Bankers, in turn, had to

S. Şenel (✉)
İstanbul Medipol University, Istanbul, Turkey
e-mail: secilsenel@medipol.edu.tr

© Springer International Publishing AG, part of Springer Nature 2018   271
H. Dincer et al. (eds.), *Global Approaches in Financial Economics, Banking, and Finance*, Contributions to Economics, https://doi.org/10.1007/978-3-319-78494-6_13

resort to European capital, with the understanding that a state bank could not be established after several unsuccessful tries.

Initially, the Ottoman Bank was founded in 1863 with equal shares of British and French capital and had a special place in the Ottoman Empire during the development of monetary and credit institutions. Additionally, it functioned as a central bank in the Ottoman state in multiple matters (Pamuk 2005: 234–235). Due to these unique conditions, the Ottoman Bank together with the Ottoman Public Debt Administration constitutes an interesting example of foreign capital control over finance and economy (Toprak 1982: 136).

Among the main reasons leading to the establishment of the Ottoman Bank was the desire to create an environment of monetary stability, thus enabling European capital to develop foreign trade and find solutions to the financial difficulties of the central state. At the beginning of the nineteenth century, though, the deepening financial crisis led to the frequent debasements[1] of the central state and a fluctuation in the currency's value. Additionally, the introduction of new debasements without a withdrawal of the old currency from the market left the coin system in a stalemate. As time continued, it became clear that the process of printing money (started in 1840) would not solve the financial dilemma and was only exacerbating the situation.

By the 1850s, the central state continued to borrow short-term debts from Galata bankers, although it also began to sell bonds in European currencies as well. With the expansion of foreign trade, Galata bankers engaged in import and export financing in major port cities, opening a new field of activity. However, the growing needs of the central government exceeded the capabilities of Galata bankers and necessary short-term credit requirements, thus leading the state to enter into a search for more powerful institutions.

The Ottoman Bank, or Bank-ı Osmanî-i Şahane as it was known in those days, was established under these conditions. With the establishment of the Ottoman Bank, the state gave the bank the power to issue banknotes in the empire, thereby abandoning the right to have an independent monetary policy. Now, the limited amount of banknotes the Ottoman Bank had within the market could be turned into gold in Istanbul. Payment of principal and interest of domestic and foreign state debts and the removal of worn out money from circulation were left to the Ottoman Bank. In addition, the bank took on the role of granting short-term loans to the state.

In fact, the Ottoman Bank became a partner with foreign capital investors and an influential advocate of interests of foreign capital, especially the interests of French capital. The bank, together with the Ottoman Public Debt Administration, played an important role in supervision and direction of the Ottoman economy and its finance by European capital.

Still, despite working as a state bank, significant disagreements between the Ottoman Bank and the state would arise related to war expenditures. Shortly after the Ottoman Empire declared that it was stopping the payment of foreign debt, the

---

[1]Debasement means the depreciation of precious metal content in the coins.

1877–1878 Ottoman-Russian war broke out. The Ottoman Bank refused to lend to the central state during this war, and as a result, the central state began printing paper currency in order to meet its war expenditures, thereby pushing aside the privileges granted to the Ottoman Bank. These actions were repeated twice more; the third and the last attempt occurred during World War I.

The stability of Ottoman money, in terms of European capital, was one of the most important purposes. For this reason, the Ottoman Bank printed a very limited amount of paper money in the period until World War I. Yet, instead of carrying out foreign trade under stable conditions, it would have been possible for a central bank, which regarded the revitalization of the Ottoman economy as its main objective, to stimulate the economy by printing more money in certain periods (Pamuk 2005: 234–235).

Requirement for Banks

The Ottoman economy, in fact, was predominantly agricultural. Taxes collected from the agricultural sector represented a significant portion of the state revenues—57.9% of the collected taxes. The indirect and direct taxes paid by the farmer were 87% of all taxes. In agriculture, agricultural-based taxes constituted a large part of state revenues. And, since crops could only be cultivated at a certain time of year, as a result, taxes could also be collected during certain periods of the year (Sevimay 1995: 238–239). As a result, silver money flown from Istanbul to boroughs increased the value of this metal during the harvest time, while the shortage of money in Istanbul made it easier for the money changers to speculate. Also, the money changers were taking these to the boroughs, despite the action of taking more than one hundred copper coins to the boroughs being illegal—as was the selling of these coins at a high price, which caused coin shortages in Istanbul (Biliotti 1909: 120–123). In addition, the shortage of transportation facilities delayed the collection of budget revenues and the appropriation of what was collected into the treasure. In defiance of all this, the state continued spending.

Actually, until the midway through the nineteenth century, total revenues were sufficient for expenses. But, appropriation of the income for the treasury and treasury payments did not coincide in terms of time. Since the Ottoman treasury was emptied, it was not possible for the delays in the appropriation of the income to be eliminated with liquid assets. As a result, it was difficult to make government expenditures. In fact, the most important reason for this is the fact that the Ottoman Empire remained an unindustrialized country of agriculture.

The empire took great responsibility in 1830 by resorting to paper money to rectify the time incompatibility of their income with their expenditures, which lead to an emptying of the treasury. In addition, the copper money that had been in circulation since the time of Sultan Mahmud II had rapidly lost its value.

The government needed an organization that would, until the revenues were collected, give advances for budgetary expenditures, release paper money into circulation for this purpose, and be able to solve the problems of paper and copper money. This requirement was expressed very clearly in the Edict of Reform dated the 18th of February, 1856. In fact, Mustafa Reşid Pasha had convinced his friends that a bank had to be established to protect the value of the money during the announcement of the Edict of Gülhane (Sevimay 1995: 238–239).

The initiative to establish the first bank in the Ottoman state was voiced by the British in 1836 and later proposed to the British Bursa Consul, Mustafa Reşid Pasha, to establish a bank under the name of Reed Irving and Company. Although another proposal was brought in 1840 under the name of General Bank of Constantinople, it was inconclusive (Akgüç 1992: 98).

Development of Banking

The beginning of banking in our country is identical to the beginning of banking in the world. Banking in the world, in its closest sense to today's meaning, began with money changers and then money changers turned into bankers and then to banks as institutions. Money changing, which developed after the Middle Ages in the Ottoman Empire, allowed money changers to undertake the task of exchanging the Ottoman and foreign currencies with each other. Primarily undertaken by minorities, the money changing task eventually transitioned into banking in the fullest sense. Undoubtedly, in this transformation, new efforts of money changers, such as lending to the state and issuing credits against tax revenues, became very effective.

Toward the 1850s, the fact that the Ottoman state had to negotiate all its tax revenues with the Galata bankers led to another development—bankers started to set down the discount rates by establishing "unions" (Ulutan 1957: 137–139).

In 1985, an agreement was signed between the government and the well-known members of the Galata bankers in order to prevent the further decline in the value of paper money (first issued in 1840). With this agreement, the government agreed to give these bankers two million kuruş annually and the bankers agreed to sell policies on London and Paris—1 British sterling a year, per 110 kuruş. Upon the successful realization of the agreement with its implementation in 1847, these bankers established the first bank under the name of Istanbul Bank (Dersaadet—Banque de Constantinople). The aim of the bank was to protect the parity between the sterling and the kuruş (Kuyucak 1948: 154). It is especially understood that the British wanted to establish a bank to develop trade and the Ottoman administration wanted to meet their cash needs. It can be said that the attempt to establish a bank in the Ottoman territories began after the first quarter of the nineteenth century, at a time when the reflection and manifestations of the industrial revolution within the Ottoman economy were just beginning to arise (Clay 1993: 22–23).

Despite various internal and external difficulties, the Istanbul Bank continued until 1852 and maintained the value of kuruş for a long time. However, the inability to prevent the continuous value decline that had started in the beginning of 1852 caused the Istanbul Bank to close that year (Akyıldız 2003: 58). In the period when the bank was in operation, it withdrew paper money from the market with 3% discount and lent money to the government, while the government helped the founders in the same way when the bank had cash shortages. Despite this, some traders drew policies without actually trading, thereby shaking the reputation of the bank. In addition, this corruption increased the costs of the exchange that the state had undertaken. Secondarily, the value of the coins in circulation continued to fluctuate since the government had failed to fulfill its commitment to regulate the money market as it had agreed to (Clay 1993: 22–23).

In particular, the heavy bill that the Crimean War imposed on the Ottoman economy further aggravated the situation of the treasury (Akyıldız 2003: 58). In 1854, the Ottoman Empire had a domestic debt of 15 million sterling, inflation in the supply of money and price increases, a foreign trade balance deficit, and a large budget deficit (Kıray 1995: 27). The years following the Crimean War were years of borrowing in the Ottoman Empire, as well as the years during which foreign banks came. In 1856, the Bank-ı Osmanî (Ottoman Bank) headquarters in London was established; nevertheless, the Ottoman Bank's first attempt at success was short-lived, and it eventually failed. During this time frame, the era of foreign banking, which lasted and continued its exploitation for many years, had begun (Artun 1980: 22–23).

Indeed, the establishment of the Ottoman Bank was followed by the establishment of other foreign banks who aimed to exploit currency speculation and lend money to the Ottoman government at high interest rates. In 1860, Türkiye Bankası, founded by Union Financiere and Mires groups, tried to acquire the privilege of issuing paper money from the Ottoman government but closed in 1861 before it could obtain this exclusive right. Eventually, the privilege of issuing paper money was granted to the Ottoman Bank, to which the French also participated in its capital. In 1864, the Şirketi Umumiye-i Osmaniye Bank (the first participant in Turkish banking) was founded by a joint venture between the Ottoman Bank and some minority bankers with the primary aim of giving temporary advances to the treasury.

Şirketi Maliye-i Osmaniye Bankası, founded by the British in 1865, in contrast, had a twofold aim: (1) increase raw material for the British textile industry which was in a raw material shortage due to the American Civil War and (2) increase the cotton production in Anatolia. This bank closed after a few years, following the establishment of banks like the Şirketi Umumiye-i Osmaniye Bankası, and handed over its works to the Ottoman Bank.

İtibari Umumi Osmani Bankası (Credit General Ottoman) was founded in 1869 by a financial group—a competitor of the founders of the Ottoman Bank. In 1868, a year before the Ottoman Bank's foundation, this bank issued a significant amount of treasury bonds to the Ottoman government's account. The establishment of the bank, regarded as the concession for the mission carried out by its founders, obtained tremendous gains from financial transactions to the account of the treasury (especially with the advances it gave to the treasury). It closed in 1839 (Artun 1980: 23).

Establishment of the Ottoman Bank

M. Forster, who came to Istanbul before the borrowing of 1862, reported to the government of the United Kingdom that the financial situation of the Ottoman Empire was suitable for improvement. Indeed Sultan Abdulaziz continued to implement the healing program that Sultan Abdulmecid had begun. Therefore, the 1862 borrowing was rather easy: during the borrowing Deveaux Company in Central London and Ottoman Bank founders were promised that they would be allowed to set up a bank in the Ottoman Empire to function as a state bank.

Upon these promises, a group consisting of Emile Perrier, the head of Spain organization of Credit Mobiliere; famous people such as İsaac Perrier, duc de Galliera, F. Darke; and companies such as Fould and Partner, Hottinger and Partner, Malet Brothers and Partners, Pillet-Ville and Partner, A.J. Stern and Partners founded a union to organize the establishment of a bank. On February 4, 1863, an edict was issued regarding the establishment of a bank in the name of Bank-ı Osmanî-i Şahane as a state bank. Thus, the Ottoman Bank entered the establishment phase (Sevimay 1995: 242).

Why Ottoman Bank?

In the Ottoman Empire, the fact that imports twice surpassed exports not only brought a payment deficit but also a concern of how to close such deficits and prevent the interventions in favor of industrial countries. These countries were not content with selling goods, and the need for raw materials and goods such as tobacco and salt was increasing day by day. After the USA stopped cotton exports to Europe and steam vessels started to cruise, the cost of shipping freight paid to Mediterranean cotton was one-fifth of the shipping freight paid to the USA. Cotton led Britain to search for new cotton areas in the Mediterranean. Additionally, the fact that salt started to be used as a chemical input and tobacco smokers increased in Europe (every year by about 10%) catapulted the demand for Ottoman salt and tobacco causing the industrializing countries to rethink the Ottoman economy and foreign trade. By then, it was possible to become rich by importing agricultural materials such as salt, cotton, tobacco, figs, grapes, etc. and exporting all kinds of industrial materials.

In line with this goal, the problem of banknote issuing monopolization in the Ottoman Empire was gaining importance, especially in terms of European finance capital. Since 1845, the Ottoman government succeeded in lowering interest rates in the domestic market with its banknotes. First with interest, then without interest, then with bonds which were called "konsolid," which were gaining a reputation of being the bonds which were most susceptible to speculation. In fact, all these banknotes and bonds provided speculative profits to both Galata bankers and European finance capital but also turned out to be a great risk. For this reason, they wanted to manage the risks and revenues by letting the bank assume the liability, thereby taking this opportunity from the Ottoman Empire and making the Ottoman country a favorable area in terms of finance capital (Kazgan et al. 1999: 307).

Clearly, Western statesmen, industrialists, and finance capital expected the bank to guarantee the principal and interests of payment deficits caused by foreign debts and foreign trade deficits. For this, they wanted the government to open a current account in the bank and this account to have a nature that protected the foreign and domestic receivables of the current. Until this point, there had been problems and delays in the payment of principal and interest of the debts to the Galata bankers (since the Tanzimat and borrowings were made as a state from Europe), as well as political disagreements resulting from Ottoman authorities' failure to accept the compound interest accounts related to these debts (Kazgan 1997: 80).

Benefits Expected from the Foundation of the Bank

The most important thing for the Ottoman government, in terms of the benefits expected from the foundation of the Ottoman Bank, was the partial elimination of the damage caused by the tax farming procedure. Taxes (such as tithing and cattle collected from agriculture) constituted 80% of state income, and these were assumed by means of auction methods. Generally, the bankers of Galata closed jobs as first taxmen and gave money to the government in cash, at which point they would transfer their rights to the second taxmen, that is, to the money changers in the provinces. Furthermore, they were transferring their rights to recognized people, generally to the landowners. So, only half or in some cases one-fourth of the tax paid by the peasants reached the coffers of the government. The founders of the Ottoman Bank were interested in this key issue. With this bank, it would be possible to collect taxes from the Ottoman Empire, while European finance capital entered into the Ottoman Empire as a new kind of taxman. The Ottoman Bank would collect taxes by taking a small fee or commission, when compared to the old taxmen, but in reality the government would pay the interest to the bank continuously and the Ottomans would have to share the tax revenues with the others because the Ottoman government would continue to be indebted to the current account (Kazgan 1997: 80).

Authorities of the Ottoman Bank

The Ottoman Bank had two boards of directors: ten French members in Paris and the other ten English members in Britain. According to Article 7 of the concession charter, the board of directors were able to direct and inspect all transactions of the Ottoman Bank. But, the most effective authorities were assembled in the subcommittee, which consisted of four British and four French members. A general manager and an executive board, composed of two directors under the chairmanship of the general manager, were at the helm of the Istanbul organization of the Ottoman Bank. According to the concession charter, the Ottoman Bank would operate under the auspices of the sultan and under the supervision of the government (Sevimay 1995: 242).

The capital of the bank was 67,500,000 francs, 135,000 stock certificates, each having a value of 500 francs on condition that half of its capital was to be paid up. Of these stock certificates, 80,000 were under the control of the English capital group (the majority were former Ottoman Bank shareholders), 50,000 were under the control of the French group, and 5000 were allocated to the Ottoman subjects (Kazgan 2005: 45).

The distribution of the profits in the Ottoman Bank was regulated as follows:

- "Five percent of the capital of the issued share certificates to be distributed to the shareholders in exchange for dividends."
- "Ten percent of it to be reserved for the purpose of allocating to contingency."
- Nine-tenths of the remainder of the profit would be reserved as dividend stocks; one-tenths would be split up; one-half would be distributed among the founders; and the other half would be distributed among the members of the committee and the board of directors.

The first committee, determined in part by the statute and the rest of the members, was completed by the first electors:

- T.C. Bruce, Sir William Clay, Lord Hobart, P. du Pre Grenfell, L.M. Rate, W.R. Drake, J. Alexander, J. Anderson, G.T. Clark, J.W. Larking, J. Stewart in London;
- Emile ve Isaac Pereire, Ch. Mallet, H. Hottinguer, C. Salvador, A. Fould, Count Pillet-Will, A.J. Stern, duc de Galliera, A. Andre, J. Buffarini, F. Greininger in Paris.

Sir Wiliam Clay in London and Charles Mallet in Paris undertook the presidency, and in accordance with the agreement made with the Government, Marquis de Ploeuc became the bank's general manager. Former Ottoman Bank general manager, Ed. Gilbertson, was also assigned as his vice-president. Other members of the executive board in Istanbul were J. Stewart, an administrator authorized by the committee, and local bankers A. Alleon and CS Hanson (Autheman 2002: 42).

Concessions Granted to Ottoman Bank

- To solve the money problems of the Empire, to regulate and manage the monetary policy, to stabilize the money
- To issue banknotes to pay for the provisions of the issued banknotes
- To be the financial agent of the state in home or abroad
- To mediate the state's external borrowing and to repay the installments of the foreign debts with interest at a rate of 1%
- To keep accounts of the income in the treasury

- To discount the bonds with terms up to 6 months to be issued by the Ministry of Finance
- To carry out the tellership of the treasury and to make payments on behalf of the treasury according to the orders of the minister of finance
- To make loans to the state with interest of 6% per annum up to 500.000 TL
- To issue and market bonds on their behalf, up to three times the cash resources
- To carry out other general banking transactions
- To obtain economic concessions (Sevimay 1995: 243)

The bank and its branches would be exempted from all kinds of taxes, duties, and charges during its activities. Also, the bank would be given free land by the government to build a central building in Istanbul, and help would be provided to secure land for branches opened in other cities. According to this agreement, the concession period was 30 years (Kazgan 2005: 45).

The bank became a treasurer of the empire with the amendment of the agreement dated February 17, 1875; and, in response to its increasing financial support, the bank was also involved in the preparation and implementation of the budget and, therefore, treasury transactions (Ekinci 2008: 391).

With this agreement, the bank obtained the authorities of the Central Bank with very advantageous conditions. As a matter of fact, at the general assembly meeting of the Ottoman Bank in 1875, the administrators themselves admitted that there was no similar situation to the success of the Ottoman Bank of the existing companies and financial institutions throughout the world (Avcıoğlu 1969: 93).

First Banknote Issue of Ottoman Bank and Aftermath

The first banknote designed by the Ottoman Bank is a 200 kuruş banknote. On this banknote it said "when this banknote is presented it will be paid in gold or silver," and it was dated June 3, 1863. However, the first 6000 banknotes of 200 kuruş were only issued in Istanbul on November 16, 1863, over 3 consecutive days—November 16, 17, and 18 of 1863. A total of 14,996 banknotes representing a very modest sum of 2,999,200 kuruş or 29,992 pounds were issued. Prior to that, the government issued millions of pounds in total, and when compared, the Ottoman Bank made a cautious start as a banknote-issuing bank.

However, there were various reasons to justify this cautious behavior, primarily of which was the weight of the conditions for granting the bank the banknote issuance concession. In particular, it was ruled that the bank should have reserve funds equal to at least one-third of the value of the banknotes in circulation. There was also a feeling that a large volume would not be welcomed publicly because at this time there was a distrust of paper money.

Despite these difficulties, the Ottoman Bank made its first attempt at circulating banknotes in provinces a few months after the first issue in Istanbul. They chose İzmir for this, since İzmir was the most developed city of the empire in economic

Table 13.1 Ottoman Bank issuance and circulation, 1863–1875

	Total Istanbul issuance (lira)	Total İzmir issuance (lira)	Total issuance (lira)	Total circulation (lira)	Circulation/ issuance (%)
1863	29,992		29,992	8726	29.09
1864	29,992	10,000	39,992	7436	18.59
1865	29,992	26,000	55,992	25,230	45.06
1866	29,992	46,000	75,992	39,885	52.49
1867	29,992	51,686	81,678	42,494	52.03
1868	50,002	57,686	107,688	96,551	89.66
1869	239,985	65,686	305,671	246,440	80.62
1870	239,907	65,686	305,593	68,531	22.43
1870	239,907	65,686	305,593	68,531	22.43
1871	239,903	65,686	305,589	134,000	43.85
1872	239,896	65,686	305,582	247,600	81.03
1873	239,890	65,686	305,576	222,800	72.91
1874	339,540	65,686	405,226	324,500	80.08
1875	438,498	65,686	504,184	109,000	21.62

Source: Edhem Eldem, Osmanlı Bankası Tarihi, Istanbul: Ofset Yapımevi, 1999, p. 482

terms after Istanbul and it had a wide commercial relations network with both the inner regions of Anatolia and the Western world. Furthermore, the presence of a strong domestic and foreign trade bourgeois increased the chances of achieving results similar to those achieved in Istanbul. In İzmir, 200 kuruş banknotes were issued very slowly over a period of almost 6 years, with the total amount of this issuance reaching 33,000 banknotes or 66,000 liras (Eldem 1999: 117).

Table 13.1 shows that the Ottoman Bank issued 305,671 liras from 1863 to the end of 1869 and seized 89.66%, a substantial extent of the total money in circulation. The future of the bank seemed brilliant, and the public accepted the name and credibility of the bank. However, when Napoleon III waged a war against Prussia in June 1870, there was panic in Istanbul, and the government was forced to close the stock exchange. The Ottoman Bank also took its share of the crisis. Upon coming face to face with a crisis in a period when the banknotes in circulation were three times as many, the bank managed the conversion of 220,000 liras worth of banknotes within a period shorter than 2 weeks. Thus the nominal circulation fell to 68,500 liras. Fortunately, the Ottoman Bank survived this crisis with banknotes in the cash reserves.

The bank did not issue banknotes until 1874, but with the issuance in 1874, the bank's total issuance reached 340,000 liras. The agreement that the bank signed with the Ottoman Empire also influenced this issuance as the bank was given new duties and responsibilities. It was accepted by the government that not only would the bank be the sole financial intermediary of the Ottoman Empire but also the supervision of organization of payment installments of government debts would be given back to the bank. Additionally, the bank was encouraged to open branches in the territory of the whole Ottoman Empire with the financial support of the state and a 20-year concession extension, which was approved by the sultan's edict in 1875 (Autheman 2002: 74).

Yet, instead of focusing on the investments that could enable the resources of the country to be evaluated and developed with the money borrowed, the bank focused on closing budget deficits and the interest and principal payments of the money borrowed previously. In spite of the increase in internal and external debt, the Ottoman Empire had been unable to pay the interest and principal of its debts because of the inability to create a budget surplus and inability of the socioeconomic system to increase the investment and production (Yılmaz 2002: 195).

These developments paralyzed the Ottoman financing and lead to a steady decline in the demand for Ottoman bonds in international markets. The situation became worse with the uprising in Herzegovina in 1875, and the military measures taken by the Ottoman state to suppress this uprising made financial bankruptcy inevitable. For a period of 5 years, the payments of the Ottoman bond coupons would be made half in cash, with half being paid in 5% interest bonds. This statement meant a kind of moratorium and destroyed the reputation of the state. After this explanation, the circulation decreased to 109,000 liras, i.e., 21.62% of the circulation.

Serbia and Montenegro's intervention in the Bosnia-Herzegovina conflict further worsened the political situation of the Ottoman Empire, and the financial situation of the state reached desperate levels. The state was no longer able to pay the salaries of civil servants and armies, and in 1875, attempts to borrow from the European markets were not possible because debt payments could not be made. When an advance of 2,000,000 liras was rejected by the Ottoman Bank, the Ottoman government resorted to paper money issuance. Unfortunately, according to the 1863 concession, the Ottoman government had already given the authority to issue banknotes to the Ottoman Bank; and, according to the agreement made with the bank, the Ottoman government would give 1% of the issuance to the bank, while the Ottoman Bank would control the issuance itself (Eldem 1999: 131). The details are given on Table 13.2.

The crisis that resulted in the issuance of banknotes was partly solved by the demonetization of paper money, but the priority of monetary reform was the stabilization and standardization of coin money. With the law enacted in 1880, the monetary standard of the Ottoman Empire was accepted as 100 kuruş gold lira (Eldem 1999: 142).

Table 13.2 Ottoman Bank issuance, demonetization, and circulation, 1875–1880 (Except 200 kuruş banknotes issued in İzmir)

	Issuance (lira)	Demonetization (lira)	Cumulative total issuance (lira)	Total circulation (lira)	Circulation/ issuance (%)
1875	100,000	1042	438,498	109,000	21.62
1876		586	437,912	24,500	5.59
1877		122	437,790	18,100	4.13
1878			437,790	17,700	4.04
1879		35	437,755	70,000	15.99
1880	8000	196,475	249,280	136,000	54.56

Source: Edhem Eldem, Osmanlı Bankası Tarihi, Istanbul: Ofset Yapımevi, 1999, p.485

Table 13.3 Ottoman Bank issuance, demonetization, and circulation, 1880–1895

	Issuance (lira)	Demonetization (lira)	Cumulative total issuance (lira)	Total circulation (lira)	Circulation/ issuance (%)
1880	8000	196,475	249,280	136,000	54.56
1881	150,000	39,936	359,344	264,000	73.47
1882		183	359,161	190,000	52.90
1883	112,000	167,192	303,969	260,000	85.53
1884	95,000	82	398,887	344,000	86.24
1885	155,000	10	553,877	384,000	69.33
1886		7	553,870	387,000	69.87
1887		12	553,858	483,000	87.21
1888		785	553,073	497,000	89.86
1889		399	552,674	541,000	97.89
1890	260,000	6	812,668	732,000	90.07
1891	425,000	175,000	1,062,668	751,000	70.67
1892	15,000	5	1,077,663	957,000	88.80
1893	100,000		1,177,663	952,000	80.84
1894	375,000	125,006	1,427,657	923,000	64.65
1895	225,000	225,000	1,427,657	688,000	48.19

Kaynak: Edhem Eldem, Osmanlı Bankası Tarihi, çev: Ayşe Berktay, Istanbul: Ofset Yapımevi, 1999, s.486

The relationship of the bank with monetary policy can be followed to the purchase of gold bullion, which was to be printed as lira by the mint. The Ottoman government was receiving short-term advances from the Ottoman Bank to buy the necessary gold for gold coin, and for these advances, the government paid 7% interest on the bank, making considerable profit for the bank (Eldem 1999: 151).

Table 13.3 indicates that as a result of the financial crisis of the Ottoman Empire, the bank took an active role in the establishment of the Public Debt Administration in 1881 (Kazgan 1997: 178). The Ottoman Bank, which entered the process of restructuring with the takeover of a significant part of the state's borrowing burden by Public Debt Administration, turned to trade and investment banking. In those years, it participated in Müşterek-ül Menfa Tobacco Regie (1884), Rumelia Railways (1885), Beirut Harbour Company (1888), Salonica-Istanbul Railway Connection, Extension of İzmir-Kasaba Railway (1984), Ereğli Coal Mines (1896), Beirut-Damascus-Hawran Railway, and its extension (1892–1900) Baghdad Railway investments. In addition to its infrastructure initiatives, the bank began to assume the identity of a commercial bank, gaining access to a growing customer portfolio. Following this pathway, starting from 1890, the bank attached great importance to increasing the number of its branches and further strengthened its influence on the market thanks to its increasing number of branches after 1910 (http://www.obarsiv. com/ob-harih.html).

The Chronological List of Ottoman Branches Before the Republic

- 1856 London, Istanbul, İzmir, Galati (closed in 1866), Beirut (closed in 1921)
- 1861 Bucharest (closed in 1921)
- 1862 Thessaloniki, Aydın, Afyonkarahisar (closed in 1880), Manisa, Larnaca
- 1865 Isparta
- 1867 Alexandria
- 1868 Paris
- 1869 Antalya
- 1872 Port Said
- 1875 Rousse (closed in 1880), Edirne, Bursa, Damascus (closed in 1880)
- 1878 Plovdiv (closed in 1899)
- 1879 Nicosia, Limassol
- 1880 Varna (closed in 1882)
- 1881 Nazilli (closed in 1898)
- 1886 Istanbul—Yeni Cami
- 1889 Adana, Konya
- 1890 Sofia (closed in 1899), Denizli, Muğla
- 1891 Istanbul—Beyoğlu, Balıkesir, Uşak, Samsun, Trabzon
- 1892 Rousse (reopened, closed in 1921)
- 1898 Mytilini (closed in 1921)
- 1899 Kastamonu, Sivas
- 1903 Monastir (closed in 1914), Skopje (closed in 1914)
- 1904 Alexandroupoli (closed in 1914), Kavala, Eskişehir, Akşehir, Tripoli (Alexandroupoli 1921), Jerusalem
- 1905 Nazilli (reopened), Bandırma, Bilecik, Jaffa
- 1906 Xanthi (closed in 1914), Erzurum, Giresun, Kütahya, Antep, Silifke (closed in 1907), Famagusta, Haifa, Tripoli (closed in 1912)
- 1907 Adapazarı, Mosul, Miniyeh
- 1908 Tarsus, Homs (closed in 1921)
- 1909 Komotini (closed in 1914), Tekirdağ
- 1910 Soufli, Drama (closed in 1921), Serres (closed in 1921), Ioannina (closed in 1921), Kayseri, İnebolu, Ordu, Geyve, Bolvadin, Mansureh
- 1911 Manchester, Scutari (closed in 1914), Rhodes (closed in 19031921), Diyarbekir, Harput/Mamuret-ül-Aziz, Bitlis, Van, Ceyhan, Saida (closed in 1921), Hodeida (closed in 1921), Benghazi (closed in 1912)
- 1912 Bolu, Urfa, Sandıklı, Söke, Jeddah (closed in 1916)
- 1913 İskenderun (closed in 1921)
- 1914 Çanakkale, Zahleh (closed in 1921)
- 1915 Marseille
- 1919 Hamah (closed in 1921)
- 1920 Kirkuk, Ashar, Tunis, Kermanshah
- 1921 Paphos, Troodos

- 1922 Bethlehem, Ramallah, Nabulus, Hamadan, Tehran (http://www.obarsiv. com/ob-tarih.html).

The Ottoman Bank aspired to increase savings in the Ottoman Empire, where 80% of the population was dealing with agricultural activities. For this purpose, it was announced to the public that the poor should save as well as the rich. The bank declared that it aspired to even the smallest savings account and that it would evaluate these savings to begin with at least 3 months maturity. The interest rates to be applied to these savings varied according to the maturity and deposit amount just like today (Kazgan 2005: 51).

The bank also opened current merchant accounts by establishing a merchant fund for merchants. The fact that the Ottoman Bank offered all of these services in the standard and quality offered by Western banks to European merchants increased the attention of traders to the bank, which was trying to get these services from Galata bankers by paying higher commissions earlier. Offering these services at a lower cost than before had a positive effect on the consumers by lowering the transaction prices of the merchants and, parallel to this, the prices of the goods. The bank also played an important role in ensuring the stability of the exchange, which caused many problems in import and export transactions by predeclaring the foreign exchange rates that it had conducted (Kazgan 1997: 52–53). The rules set by the bank for commercial notes and credits helped settle modern banking procedures on the market and also opened up the use of interest rates and discount rates as an instrument in expanding and narrowing the credit volume (Bayraktar 2002: 99).

In February 1893, the "Ottoman General Insurance Company" *(Osmanlı Umum Sigorta Şirketi/La Societe Generale d'Assurances Ottomane)* was established with the participation of the Ottoman Bank, Public Debt Administration, and Regie Administration, and with the capital of 44,000, Ottoman liras divided into 40,000 shares—each having a value of 10 Ottoman lira. Thus, the first domestic insurance company established in the Ottoman state was started with foreign capital: the company's agency run by the branches of the Ottoman Bank and the Tobacco Regie. With this new company, the number of fire insurance companies increased to 38 in Istanbul. The *Ottoman General Insurance Company*, which intended to operate in the fire, life, and transport insurance branches, was considered small by the British Consul. The consul, at the time, thought "it has a capital seeming rather small for insurance in this city where the risks are great." Notwithstanding, it was soon understood that the Ottoman Company was a serious market competitor. Thanks to the fact that its name and transactions are in Turkish, the company attracted domestic customers, and it had the power to make quick payments in case of damages with the support of the Ottoman Bank and Public Debts Administration (Başkıcı 2002: 7).

Paper Money

The failing Ottoman economy was constantly in a budget deficit because of the military spending that began to rapidly increase before World War I. The budget deficit, which was 775 thousand Ottoman lira in the 1911–1912 fiscal year, reached almost three million Ottoman lira in the fiscal year 1917–1918 (Güran, 2006: 71). During World War I, the Ottoman Bank refused the government's request to issue advances and banknotes. This dispute was overcome, though, when the bank explained that it would not use the issuance privilege of banknotes during the war. Soon thereafter, the Ottoman administration began issuing banknotes (over a total of 160 million liras) in seven stages over a 4-year period starting from 1915, using gold and German treasury bills as provision. These banknotes were transferred to the Republic of Turkey under the name "evrak-ı nakdiye," and these banknotes were in circulation until the end of 1927, since money was not printed in the first years of the republic.

After the declaration of the republic, certain provisions of the concessions of 1924 and 1925 that were signed with the Ottoman Bank (and the privilege documents of 1863 and 1875) were abolished, while some obligations for the bank were also being introduced. Among the abolished provisions were important provisions such as having representatives in budget commissions, prohibiting the government to issue paper money, and recording extraordinary appropriations. The most important obligation was that the Ottoman Bank had to pay 1.5% interest to the treasury for the paper money it issued. It also made it possible for the Republic of Turkey to establish a central bank at any time. In fact, the Central Bank of the Republic of Turkey, established in 1930, was founded on the basis of this provision in the 1924 agreement (Artun 1980: 29).

The Idea of Founding a National Bank

The idea of establishing a national state bank was introduced at the Turkish Economy Congress, convened in 1923. In the congress, emphasis was on the establishment of a central bank, which would both determine the government's banking policy while also regulating the banknote issuance and state credits. In 1924, the Turkish government made some attempts to transform the Ottoman Bank into a state bank. However, the economic and fiscal conditions of that time were not appropriate. Then, in the same year, an agreement was made between the republican government and Ottoman Bank. Accordingly, the bank's privilege of issuing banknotes, which was expected to expire at the end of 1925, was extended until 1935. Clearly though, if a national central bank had been established during this period, the Ottoman Bank would have had no objection to it. According to the agreement:

- Circulation of existing banknotes was made compulsory. The amount of the advance to be issued to the government was raised from 1.5 million liras to 5 million liras. In addition, it would give Ziraat Bank a loan of two million liras.

- The bank would have the privilege of issuing banknotes but would keep a gold reserve in a ratio of 1:3.
- The appointment of the general manager to the bank would be subject to the permission of the Ministry of Finance. The number of Turkish-Muslim personnel working at the bank would be gradually increased every year.
- The bank would bring 500,000 sterling to Turkey as capital.
- The bank undertook the task of replacing the banknotes issued in the Ottoman period with the republican banknotes (TCMB History, http://www.tcmb.gov.tr/ yeni/banka/tarihce.html).

Yet, with the advent of World War I, the activities of the bank were greatly affected. As the Ottomans entered the war, the bank, which acquired the character of an "enemy organization" in the eyes of France and England, began to be seen as unreliable by the Ottoman Empire as a result of their British and French capital. Therefore, in this period, the bank was only allowed to continue its activities provided the French and British directors left their posts and gave up the privilege of printing money (http://www.obarsiv.com/ob-tarih.html).

With the establishment of the national government, two important facts emerged: first, state money could not be managed by a foreign institution; second, there was no possibility of transferring the paper money taken over from the Ottoman Empire period and making it into banknotes, especially as it had no provisions from the Ottoman Bank. In this case, they chose to solve the problem by giving this work to a national organization (Kayla 1981: 28).

Although the Ottoman Bank transferred the privilege of printing money to the Turkish republic with an agreement signed on March 10, 1924, the Ottoman Bank continued to maintain treasury transactions and its status as a state bank until the establishment of the Central Bank. In this period, it was called the "Ottoman Bank," in accordance with the new political regime. The Ottoman Bank was established as private trade bank through a contract signed in June 1933, and with the addition of another contract in 1952, they received new status, which lasted until the 1990s.

The Ottoman Bank, at this time, had over 80 branches in 1914: 37 of which were in Anatolia, 11 in Syria and Palestine, 5 in Egypt, 3 in Istanbul, 5 in Thrace, 6 in Macedonia, and others in Cyprus, Mesopotamia, Arabia, and Albania—all of which closed both during the war and immediately afterward. In the meantime, starting in the Middle East between 1920 and 1930, the bank branches quickly spread in the direction of British shareholders. But, as a result of the nationalization and seizure of the Egyptian branches in 1956, there was a significant loss of activity in the Middle East. In the same period, the bank continued to work in Kenya, Uganda, Tanzania, Rhodesia, Qatar, Abu Dhabi, Sudan, and Qatar under British investors. Meanwhile, the Ottoman Bank, which transferred its branches in Europe, Middle East, and Africa to Grindlays Bank (in line with the request of the main shareholder Group Paribas in 1969), started to serve only within the borders of Turkey and continued serving only Turkey from that time forward. In 1993, the shares of the bank which were restructured as a joint stock company status were purchased by Clover Investments which belonged to Garanti Bank, and the Garanti Bank joined Doğuş Group. As of

August 31, 2001, the Ottoman Bank merged with Körfezbank (within the Doğuş Group) and was included in the organizational structure of its main shareholder Garanti Bank on December 21, 2001.

Garanti-Ottoman Bank Merger

Before the Garanti-Ottoman Bank merger, the Ottoman Bank had increasingly been losing capital, working with operational losses, and in danger of being transferred to the Savings Deposit Insurance Fund in accordance with Article 14 of Bank Law. The transfer of the Ottoman Bank to the Savings Deposit Insurance Fund would obviously have negatively affected the prestige of the group in which the Ottoman Bank was included. So, the Ottoman Bank was transferred to the Garanti Bank within the scope of an intragroup banking association, in order to expand its market share (Şahözkan 2003: 52).

Moreover, the economic crisis Turkey faced in 2001 further exacerbated the Ottoman Bank's economic standing. After the economic crisis faced, the bank ended the working period with high interest rates and high profit margins. In this period, the best banks of Turkey started to merge one by one. In 2001, the banking sector suffered severe losses as some banks were caught unprepared for the crisis. Even still, some banks had already started preparations with the idea that the period of high inflation in Turkey would eventually end. In early 2001, the Doğuş Group, which included the Körfezbank, the Ottoman Bank, and the Garanti Bank, began taking measures in lieu of the changing economic climate. The most important measure taken was to make the merger decision, specifically to make Garanti Technology a service provider to all the banks of the group. This start provided considerable convenience in future merger transactions because during the economic crisis the three banks owned by the group were operating in different areas and working in different information substructures. As a result of this situation, the Ottoman Bank merged with the Körfezbank, and then the Garanti-Ottoman Bank merger was realized.

Finally, the merger of the Garanti-Ottoman Bank benefited economies of scale. Garanti, the most widespread brand in the Doğuş Group, allowed the name of the mentioned group to be accepted as an identity in the financial sector (Şahözkan 2003: 54).

Result

Upon entering the nineteenth century, the Ottoman Empire had suffered political and economic power losses against Europe and carried out important reforms before and after the Tanzimat. As a result of a series of changes made in social, administrative, political, and economic areas, the central administration was able to escape the classical mind and the institutional structure. On the other hand, the policy of centralization allowed the power of the state to expand, most pointedly against the local centrifugal powers, which were led by the bureaucracy in accordance with the existing model of nation state in Europe. By creating resources, the Ottoman administration was trying to increase income in order to finance the reform works that were being carried out. The central government, which had increased tax revenues—especially those collected from agriculture—managed to subsidize the reform program with income-increasing measures. Notwithstanding, two long-term external borrowings from foreign markets had upset the income-expenditure balance which was already on the knife's edge: the loans from Greek and Armenian bankers and the 1840 increase in the issuance of paper money which was distributed to finance the Crimean War with the Russians in the late 1853 and could only be won with the political and military interventions of Britain and France.

At the same time, in the Islahat Fermanı (Edict of Reformation), many promises had been made to Europe where the bank would be founded. The driving force of the banking efforts carried out, until this time, was to overcome the exchange problem stemming from the import-export imbalance caused by increased foreign trade with Europe after the British Industrial Revolution. Furthermore, the bank was working toward withdrawing worthless paper money (devalued from overprinting and causing price increases) from the market in an attempt to eliminate its negative effects on foreign trade. During the Crimean War, due to the abovementioned reasons, the wish to establish a bank to cover the war expenditures of the treasure increased.

A number of proposals were submitted by domestic and foreign investors to the government for the establishment of a national bank until the Ottoman Bank became operational, but no final result could be obtained due to an inability to remove the paper money in circulation or the indecision as to which side would be dominant in the board of directors. In the end, the final result could not be reached due to the intervention of the countries, where the bidders were nationals of the proposals and the mutual influence struggles in the Ottoman state. On the eve of the establishment of the Ottoman Bank, the treasury was now faced with a serious domestic debt problem, especially the problem of banknotes. In 1861–1862, about 20% of treasury revenues were allocated to debt payments. As the debt burden increased, it became difficult for the treasury to borrow from the outside. When applying for external borrowing, requests were made to increase the current incomes and to provide sound income as a provision for compensating the interest of debt.

Also, from the beginning of the 1860s, unrest and rebellions had begun taking place, particularly in the Balkans where the Christian population was intense. During the same interval, the shipment of troops to these locations produced an increase in the demand for cash. On the other hand, the schedule of the government's expenditure of income and expenses consistently differed. The Ottoman Bank was established in order to meet both the urgent need of money and as an intermediary for borrowing money from foreign markets on favorable terms. In fact, Fuad Pasha, one of the leading bureaucrats of the Tanzimat, conducted negotiations with the Westerners during the bank's establishment phase. Interestingly for Europe, the operationality of the Ottoman Bank allowed the owners of the Ottoman bonds to domestically collect their receivables on behalf of them and transfer them abroad, ensuring a regular flow of capital and goods through the integration of the Ottoman Empire with the international money markets.

The foundation of the Ottoman Bank, first established under the name Bank-ı Osmanî-i Şahane, was realized with an agreement signed on February 4, 1863. Bank-ı Osmanî-i Şahane, which took over Ottoman Bank's inheritance, started to serve with its new identity after June 1, 1863. And, improvement of the monetary system and the establishment of Bank-ı Osmanî-i Şahane was among the first reforms of Tanzimat's financial activities. The bank created a borrowing source for the Ottoman Empire, assumed the role of intermediary in borrowing and used the right to issue money, which is one of the most important concessions of state banks. With a new agreement signed on February 17, 1875, the bank became the treasure of the empire. Thus, for increasing financial support, it had become a monopoly in treasury transactions as a proprietor in the preparation and implementation of the budget.

Although the Bank-ı Osmanî-i Şahane transferred the privilege of printing money after World War I to the Turkish republic through an agreement signed on March 10, 1924, it continued to maintain treasury transactions and its status as a state bank until the establishment of the Central Bank. In this period, it was called the "Ottoman Bank" in accordance with the new political regime. With the agreement signed in June 1933, the official bank of the state was transferred to the Central Bank of the Republic of Turkey, and the Ottoman Bank was structured as a private trade bank.

But, as a result of the nationalization and seizure of the Egyptian branches in 1956, there was a significant loss of activity in the Middle East for the Ottoman Bank. In the same period, it continued to work in Kenya, Uganda, Tanzania, Rhodesia, Qatar, Abu Dhabi, Sudan, and Qatar under the British investors. The Ottoman Bank transferred its branches in Europe, the Middle East, and Africa to Grindlays Bank in 1969 and started to serve only within the borders of Turkey after this.

The Ottoman Bank AS, which continued to operate as one of the most important banks in Turkey until 1993, was restructured that year with the status of the joint stock company where the shares of the bank were purchased by Clover Investments belonging to Garanti Bank and the bank joined Doğuş Group. As of August 31, 2001, the Ottoman Bank merged with Körfezbank within the organizational structure of Doğuş Group. The Ottoman Bank was incorporated into Garanti Bank, which is its main shareholder on December 21.

The Ottoman Bank emblem was redesigned in 1947 by Edmund Dulac, a renowned artist and orientalism expert, within the context of the advertising approach of that day. The point of movement in the emblem has a very rich content in terms of symbols, most pointedly of which is the olive tree—widely grown in the countries where the Ottoman Bank operates and a symbol of "peace." The olive tree symbolizes multiple themes, fertility with its fruits, protection with its shadow, peace with its leaves, and resistance against time with its roots, and is also known as the symbol of "continuity." Likewise, the symbol of the diamond is an extension of the Eastern influence, and is frequently seen in Islamic art and miniatures. Pointedly, it was used in the emblem design in such a way that it frames the olive tree as an expression of "valuableness." The emblem-logo, simplified by various revisions over time, has been protected in its latest shape by the new shareholders after the transfer in June 1996 (http://www.finhat.com/finhat/menu4/osmanli.html).

Chronology

1856	The Ottoman Bank was founded in England under the name Ottoman Bank.
1863	It became a multi-partnered company with the participation of French and Ottoman Empire where its name changed to Bank-ı Osmanî-i Şahane. It received the privilege of issuing banknotes in the Ottoman territory.
1874	It took over the task of Ottoman Central Bank.
1875	Its issuance privileges were extended for 20 years; it took over the task of the empire's general treasurer.
1881	It actively played a role in the establishment of the Public Debts Administration.
1881	With the Muharrem Resolution, it undertook the first large-scale state debt restructuring in the world.
1884	It took part in the establishment of Istanbul Regie Administration.
1888	It financed the establishment of Beirut Harbor.
1896	It financed the establishment of Ereğli Coal Mines in Zonguldak.
1897	It financed the construction of the Syria-Anatolia railway.
1933	It transferred its official state bank status to the Central Bank of the Republic of Turkey and became a private commercial bank.
1952	Its charter changed and it earned its current status.
1956	Its 90-year existence in Egypt ended with nationalization.
1969	It sold its branches in Europe, Middle East, and Africa to Grindlay at the request of its main shareholder Group Paribas.
1993	It became a joint stock company.
1996	Its shares were purchased by Clover Investments, which belonged to Garanti Bank, and the bank joined the Doğuş Group.
1999	(February) Moved to the new headquarters building in Maslak from Karaköy building where it served for 107 years.
2001	(August 31) Merged with Körfezbank.
December 20, 2001	It merged with Garanti Bank and ended its banking activities.

References

Akgüç, Ö. (1992). Türkiye'de Bankacılık, Gerçek Yayınevi, 3.b. İstanbul Kasım.
Akyıldız, A. (2003). *Para Pul Oldu, Osmanlı'da Kağıt Para, Maliye ve Toplum.* İstanbul: İletişim Yayınları.
Artun, T. (1980). *İşlevi, Gelişimi, Özellikleri ve Sorunlarıyla Türkiye'de Bankacılık.* İstanbul: Tekin Yayınevi.
Autheman, A. (2002). Tanzimat'tan Cumhuriyet'e Osmanlı Bankası Bank-ı Osmani-i Şahane. çev: Ali Bertay, İstanbul: Ofset Yapımevi.
Avcıoğlu, D. (1969). *Türkiye'nin Düzeni (Dün-Bugün-Yarın).* Ankara: Bilgi Yayınevi.
Baskıcı, M. (2002). Osmanlı Anadolusunda Sigorta Piyasası: 1860-1918. Ankara Üniversitesi Siyasal Bilgiler Fakültesi Dergisi, Cilt 57, Sayı 4.
Bayraktar, K. (2002). Osmanlı Bankasının Kuruluşu, C.Ü. İktisadi ve İdari Bilimler Dergisi, Cilt 3, Sayı 2.
Biliotti, Adrien Pierre Marie. (1909). La Banque İmpériale Ottomane, Paris.
Çizakça, M. (1993). Risk Sermayesi Özel Finans Kurumları ve Para Vakıfları, İslami İlimler Araştırma Vakfı Yayını, Tartışmalı ilmi Toplantılar Dizisi, İlmi Neşriyat, İstanbul.
Clay, C. (1993). The Bank Notes of the Imperial Ottoman Bank, 1863-1876. New Perspectives on Turkey, No. 9, Fall 1993.
Döndüren, H. (2008). Osmanlı Tarihinde Bazı Faizsiz Kredi Uygulamaları ve Modern Türkiye'de Faizsiz Bankacılık Tecrübesi, Uludağ Üniversitesi, İlahiyat Fakültesi Dergisi, Cilt: 17, Sayı:1, Bursa.
Ekinci, M. F. (2008). *Türkiye'nin Mali İntiharı Kapitülasyonlar ve 1838 Balta Limanı Ticaret Sözleşmeleri'nden Sevres Andlaşması'na.* Ankara: Barış Platin Kitapları.
Eldem, E. (1999). Osmanlı Bankası Tarihi. çev: Ayşe Berktay, İstanbul: Ofset Yapımevi.
Güran, T. (2006). Osmanlı Kamu Maliyesi 1839-1918, haz. Mehmet Genç ve Erol Özvar, Osmanlı Maliyesi Kurumlar ve Bütçeler 1. İstanbul: Osmanlı Bankası Arşiv ve Araştırma Merkezi Yayınları.
http://www.obarsiv.com/ob-tarih.html
http://www.finhat.com/finhat/menu4/osmanli.html
Kayla, Z. (1981). "Merkez Bankası İşlemleri", Ankara İktisadi ve Ticari İlimler Akademisi Yayınları, No: 149.
Kazgan, H. (1997). Osmanlı'dan Cumhuriyet'e Türk Bankacılık Tarihi. İstanbul: Creative Yayıncılık.
Kazgan, H. (2005). Galata Bankerleri. 1. Cilt, Ankara: Orion Yayınevi.
Kazgan, H., Ateş, T., Koraltürk, M. (1999). "Osmanlı Devleti'nde Finansal Faaliyetler ve Kurumlar", Osmanlı'dan Günümüze Türk Finans Tarihi içinde. c.1. İstanbul: İstanbul Menkul Kıymetler Borsası.
Kıray, E. (1995). *Osmanlı'da Ekonomik Yapı ve Dış Borçlar.* İstanbul: İletişim Yayınevi.
Kuyucak, H. A. (1948). *Para ve Banka.* İstanbul: İstanbul Üniversitesi Yayınları.
Pamuk, Ş. (2005). *Osmanlı-Türkiye İktisadi Tarihi 1500-1914.* İstanbul: İletişim Yayınları.
Şahözkan, Burak Cem. (2003). Banka Birleşmeleri, Türkiye Bankalar Birliği, Yayın No: 233.
Sevimay, H. R. (1995). *Cumhuriyete Girerken Ekonomi Osmanlı Son Dönem Ekonomisi.* İstanbul: Kazancı Hukuk Yayınları.
Tabakoğlu, A. (2003). *Türk İktisat Tarihi.* İstanbul: Dergah Yayınları.
Tarihçesi. http://www.tcmb.gov.tr/yeni/banka/tarihce.html
The Development of National Banking in Turkey. (1938). Ankara: Press Department of the Ministry of Interior.
Toprak, Z. (1982). *Türkiye'de Milli İktisat (1908-1918).* İstanbul: Yurt Yayınları.
Ulutan, B. (1957). Bankacılığın Tekamülü. Ankara.
Yılmaz, B. E. (2002) Osmanlı İmparatorluğu'nu dış borçlanmaya iten nedenler ve ilk dış borç. *Akdeniz İ.İ.B.F. Dergisi* (4).

Chapter 14
Bankruptcy: An Examination of Different Approaches

Fatih Yigit

Abstract This chapter mentions etymology and history of bankruptcy and discusses serious bankruptcy-related problems such as measuring bankruptcy costs
and predicting bankruptcies. The magnitude of bankruptcy costs is a critical issue
in terms of capital structure theories. It has also crucial importance to predict
probability of bankruptcy in the assessment of companies' creditworthiness. The
enormous increase in large corporate failures in the last decades has revealed the
importance of bankruptcy prediction and enforced to improve new techniques. The
keystone studies of bankruptcy literature, different findings and views regarding
problematic issues of bankruptcy are presented in this chapter. The inconclusive
results of these studies indicate that bankruptcy will remain an attractive field for all
parties of financial world.

Introduction

Financial distress is a general financial concept that can be used to describe lack of
control and success in satisfying financial obligations for an individual or an entity.
Distress may occur in case of cash shortage or negative net firm value. While the
latter is more serious as compared to the former one, permanently experienced cash
shortages may lead to relatively critical events which may even result in the
termination of economic activities.

Whenever a company experiences financial distress, it can incur specific costs
associated with distress which limit and erode cash flows available to investors.
Moreover, firm value is also negatively affected by those costs. To avoid such an
undesirable case, an optimal capital structure should be maintained by management.
The choice on optimal structure can influence the likelihood to fall in financial
distress especially in case of market imperfections; therefore leverage may have
significant consequences as it is relatively high.

F. Yigit
Istanbul Medeniyet University, Istanbul, Turkey
e-mail: fatih.yigit@medeniyet.edu.tr

© Springer International Publishing AG, part of Springer Nature 2018   293
H. Dincer et al. (eds.), *Global Approaches in Financial Economics, Banking, and
Finance*, Contributions to Economics, https://doi.org/10.1007/978-3-319-78494-6_14

Debt financing results in some obligations that a firm must meet. Excessive risk-taking through extreme use of debt financing and ineffective and unprofitable investments carried out by managers with these debts are expected to carry the firm to financial bottlenecks by increasing financial risks to which it is exposed. Financial crises are also another factor that may deepen and strengthen unfavourable consequences of those financial problems. If the firm is unable to pay interests on debts or principal amounts, it is deemed to be in default, which eventually give debtholders some rights over the defaulting firm's assets. They may perform legal actions to take over the ownership of the assets via an extreme process called bankruptcy.

Bankruptcy is a financial and legal result of personal or organizational failure to pay up outstanding debts. It has become a very prevalent phenomenon all over the world because of the rapid economic growth and the serious problems caused by this new economic condition. In recent years, huge corporate bankruptcies have been observed such as Lehman Brothers bankruptcy with $619 billion in debt and $639 billion in assets. Policymakers have strived to find the best way to overcome serious economic problems caused by increasing bankruptcies. While the USA has adopted some reforms designed to limit access to the bankruptcy procedures, the UK and Japan have implemented distinctive reforms to encourage more filings.

Four generic terms that are used for unsuccessful business enterprise are failure, insolvency, default and bankruptcy. Though they are related with unsuccessful business enterprise, these terms have important differences. If capital costs happen to be higher than the approximate return on investment, then this would result in the failure of a company. A company may experience economic failure for a long time, but never fail to satisfy its financial obligations due to the lack of the debt that is enforceable by law.

When a company couldn't satisfy its obligations resulting from lack of liquidity, technical insolvency surfaces. Though it is usually the direct reason of official bankruptcy statement, it may be a temporary situation. A more serious situation arises when insolvency is tied to bankruptcy. This situation takes place when total liabilities of a company surpass its total assets. Deepening insolvency occurs when an otherwise bankrupt company is kept afloat unnaturally (Altman and Hotchkiss 2006).

Default involves a relationship between debtor firm and creditors and may be technical and/or legal. Technical default occurs when the debtor violates the agreement with a creditor. But it is usually solved by negotiations. These violations are rare in triggering more formal default or bankruptcy. Legal default occurs in the case whereby the debtor firm misses a scheduled payment.

Bankruptcy generally relates to the net worth position of a business. Bankruptcy is also used to describe a firm's formal declaration which involves the demand to liquidate its assets or attempt a reorganization plan. Both liquidation and reorganization are options available to exercise for unsuccessful entities. If entity's liquidation value is less than its economic value, reorganization will be the best option. Besides, if the liquidation value happens to be more than the economic value, then the firm should be permitted to liquidate. Bankruptcy is a long and challenging process with some costs to the firm in default.

The terms bankruptcy and insolvency are often mixed up and used interchangeably, but there is a subtle difference between them. While insolvency is a financial state of inability to repay the debts, bankruptcy stems from a legal adjudication that arises from this failure. Contrary to the common view, bankruptcy doesn't mean disappearance of company. It is a legal process which allows creditors to have control over the assets of debtor. The main aim of modern practices is to repay the debt from the point of creditor and to give a chance for a fresh start from the point of debtor.

In case of insolvency, creditors may file a bankruptcy petition. However bankruptcy is often initiated by debtors. Bankrupts generally have some assets to pay some of their debts. But assets of bankrupt are not enough for all debts. Bankruptcy court adjudicates bankruptcy by appointing a trustee who closes the company and sells the assets by auction. Then appointed trustee creates a list, and according to which debtors collect their money under the control of bankruptcy estate.

Etymology

The origin of word bankruptcy is the Italian *banco rotto* (broken bench) which comprises of the classical Latin terms *bancus* (bench) and *ruptus* (broken), symbolizing one whose place of business was broken or gone. In the early 1800s, people used to come together in market places. Merchants would set up their businesses either on tables or benches at these common areas. Even bankers at that time had also a bench and operated their transactions on it. When a merchant or a banker could no longer afford to stay in business, they broke their bench to declare to the public their activities were ended. Therefore the meaning of this word comes from the habit of breaking the bench of bankrupts.

Some argue that the word has been derived from French *banque* (table) and *route* (trace) by attributing the trace of a table on the ground. Advocators of this idea establish the relationship to the ancient Roman *mensarii* or *argentarii*, who had their *tabernae* or *mansae* in the marketplace. When they escape with the money that belongs to others, they left the trace of their table behind them.

History

Bankruptcy used to be considered a shameful last resort. However, later on, its important role to solve serious financial problems has been accepted. The rise of debt in recent decades has caused the development of bankruptcy systems in jurisdictions of several countries. Even the countries that have had bankruptcy systems for many years such as the UK and the USA have needed major reforms in their jurisdictions due to increasing levels of bankruptcy in recent years.

In Ancient Greece, if a man could not repay his debt, his family members and servants were compelled into a form of debt slavery until the creditor is compensated with the debt that is owed. Debt slavery was restricted to a span of around 5 years, and debt slaves were granted the rights of being protected. But servants of the debtor could be retained more than 5 years and even forced into lifelong service. Their masters couldn't kill or remove any of the debt slaves' limbs unlike other types of slaves.

Bankruptcy was considered a crime when the first bankruptcy laws were brought into effect in England during the sixteenth century. In the modern era, bankruptcy laws have been formed from the modifications in the historical process. Roots of US bankruptcy laws come from English laws in sixteenth century. England first introduced a law (Act of Henry VIII) in 1542 related with the issue of bankruptcy. A criminal statute directed against men who made very prodigal expenditures and then failed to repay. Until the eighteenth century, the punishment of debtors by imprisonment was being practised in England. In eighteenth century, development of debt discharge became the main point of interest. Thus bankruptcy law which aims to inflict punishment upon the debtor developed into a form of legislation that protected the debtor as well as encouraging the outstanding debt resolution. Modern laws focus less on the actual punishment of the debtor and more so on the rehabilitation of person or organization. So the debtors will be able to manage their financial balances, and the economy will be protected from adverse effects of bankruptcies.

Bankruptcy Act of 1800 in the USA stressed upon creditor relief and therefore would not give way for debtors to file to relief willingly. Because of the huge disagreement this caused in public, this legislation was repealed 3 years later. The first modern Bankruptcy Act in the USA was entered into force in 1898, and it developed into the foundation of present day bankruptcy laws. The Bankruptcy Act of 1898 provided only for a firm's liquidation and had no provisions allowing reorganization. But if an entity's economic value is greater than its liquidation value, the firm should be allowed to reorganize and remain in existence. In 1934, the US Supreme Court put forward the motion that bankruptcy laws were designed to give the debtor a fresh start by removing previous financial burdens. The aim was to provide a new opportunity that was no longer related to former errors. The "Chandler Act" of 1938 replaced the inadequate earlier statute and gave unique authority to the Securities and Exchange Commission for the administration of bankruptcy processes. Bankruptcy Act of 1941 offered debtors more protections and allowed them to file for bankruptcy relief voluntarily. The Bankruptcy Reform Act of 1978, which entered in force in 1979, substituted old bankruptcy laws and is still in effect today. This law made it too easy for consumers and companies to file bankruptcy and recover their debts. The Bankruptcy Abuse Prevention and Consumer Protection Act of 2005 constructed a number of significant changes to the US Bankruptcy Code. The US government designed the act to limit consumers' access to and increase the cost of liquidation-type bankruptcy procedures. Chapter 7 of the US Bankruptcy Act usually leads to liquidation. Chapter 11 helps to aid a business to stay alive by encouraging negotiation. Chapters 12 and 13 are reorganization programmes designed for individuals. Chapter 12 is intended for owners of family farms, while Chap. 13 aims at everyone else. As of March 2015, total filings in US bankruptcy courts have reached to 911,086. If we look at the density of implementing different procedures, 596,867 filings are in the scope of the Chap. 7 while 306,729 filings are in the Chap. 13 (Yigit 2015).

Martin (2005) examines social attitudes toward debt and financial failure and concludes that culture leads the way in terms of the efficacy of bankruptcy systems. Even countries which share a common legal tradition, for example, the USA, England, Australia as well as Canada, adopt diverse approaches in personal and corporate bankruptcies. Although most of them are moving to US model, Continental Europe and Japan have divergent systems. Different states will modify their own legal systems according to different levels of intensity. Davydenko and Franks (2008) rely upon a sample of small businesses that defaulted on their bank debt and review the bankruptcy regimes in the UK, Germany and France. They assert that banks change their lending and reorganization methods in order to mitigate costly areas of creditor-unfriendly bankruptcy legislation.

Personal Bankruptcy

Bankruptcy filings are separated into two categories: consumer (personal) and business (corporate) filings. As of June 2017, there are 23,433 business and 772,594 consumer bankruptcy filings; 489,011 filings for Chap. 7, 6999 for Chap. 11 and 299,398 for Chap. 13.

Personal bankruptcy is a legal procedure for people who don't have any chance to pay off their debts. Modern legal systems allow an individual to declare bankruptcy and include a debt relief. Debt is a result of spending more than one's income in a certain period. If anybody continues to spend more than affordable limit, bankruptcy will be inevitable. Some groups of society are more prone to debt problems than others. For example, young people have been pointed as the most vulnerable group. There is no doubt that excessive amounts of consumer credit have played a significant role on bankruptcies. The increasing debt problems of households have led governments all over the world to create efficient personal bankruptcy procedures. Personal bankruptcy procedures which are leading to partial or total relief of outstanding debt have been the solution to depressing debt problems in Anglo-Saxon jurisdictions. This solution process also has been increasingly common in European countries as well as in the industrialized Asian countries (Mann 2009).

In all modern legal systems, a key question is why debtors file to bankruptcy. Unemployment, family breakdown and losing one's own financial overview are to be considered the primary reasons that cause personal bankruptcy. As national income and consumer spending rise, the personal debt level increases. When personal debt becomes common, household financial distress rises. This situation is the important antecedent of high bankruptcy rates.

In countries with bankruptcy systems that offer less generous relief, fewer debtors file for bankruptcy. When legal system offers more generous relief, more debtors file for bankruptcy. Mann (2009), who has conducted an extensive study of variation in levels of consumer credit in several countries, compares the filing rates in several jurisdictions with a view to explaining what factors impact the different bankruptcy per capita rates. As of 2004, there were 930 filings per million residents in the UK, 1300 filings per million residents in Australia, 3100 filings per million residents in Canada and 5500 filings per million residents in the USA. Personal debtors in the USA file consumer bankruptcy more often than other countries. This difference is not because they have a lax attitude to repayment of debts but because they have more debt. However, legal and cultural factors have influenced filing behaviour. For example, when Canadians are overindebted, they seem to have a lower threshold of filing for bankruptcy than debtors in comparable countries. The easy access to bankruptcy in Canada with low upfront payments and fewer requirements for a judicial determination may be the reasons for this situation.

In the USA, people can use two different ways for personal bankruptcy. It is possible to meet all or part of debt with the direct liquidation under Chap. 7. This way is suitable for people who have large amounts of debt and insufficient income. The second way is suitable for people who have enough income to repay their debt in reasonable time. In this situation debtors repay all or part of their debt within a payment plan under Chap. 13. In spite of the advantages of personal bankruptcy, it has negative consequences as remaining on personal credit report for 7–10 years. People with low credit scores usually face problems obtaining loan, or higher interest rates are applied to them due to their financial risk.

Bankruptcy laws allow the personal debtors to keep certain assets such as common domestic items kept in the household. Therefore, one is provided with their basic living necessities, while creditors are repaid. For this reason if a debtor has no wages and no property, they are called judgement proof, meaning a judgement would have no impact on their financial situation.

Corporate Bankruptcy

The primary reason behind the distress of a firm and its potential downfall is inadequacy in management. The apparent reason is usually payment inability, but there are some other reasons which contribute to high number of bankruptcies and other distressed conditions Altman and Hotchkiss (2006).

Corporate bankruptcies take place when shareholders exercise their right to default. Because of the limited liability of shareholders, they can avoid to meet all debt obligations. Limited liability structure allows assets of a company to be considered separate from owner. Thus, personal assets of an owner are prevented from bankruptcy process which has some direct and indirect costs for companies. The bankruptcy costs which are to be classed as direct are fees that are paid to lawyers, accountants, consultants as well as other professionals involved in the process. Other expenses which are directly related to bankruptcy process and administration of this process are accepted as costs of bankruptcy that are direct. Weiss (1990) has found the average cost of bankruptcy to be around 3% of total book assets and 20% of the market value of equity in the year prior to bankruptcy. Bankruptcy is more costly for small firms and firms which have more growth opportunities.

Indirect bankruptcy costs are economic losses incurred during bankruptcy process. These losses may be caused by inefficiency at decision-making in company due to the required approval of bankruptcy court on business decisions. Additionally focusing on bankruptcy process instead of the main activities of company by managers gives birth to inefficiency. Indirect bankruptcy costs are also inclusive of losing key employees, losing important suppliers, losing customers or consumers as well as the potential for investment that have been missed. It is nearly impossible to measure the costs of bankruptcy that are indirect.

As a result of the threat that bankruptcy presents, this led to minimizing the debt financing. Bankruptcy is more likely to arise for leveraged firms that should make more interest and principal payments. Therefore, cost of bankruptcy is an important factor of capital structure. More debt creates a larger tax shield but leads to higher bankruptcy costs. According to the trade-off theory of capital structure, optimal capital structure is determined through the balance between benefit of tax shield and cost of bankruptcy. Tangibility is an important factor to determine how the bankruptcy is serious. A company with more tangible assets is exposed to less bankruptcy costs in contrast to the company with more intangible asset. It is easy to convert tangible assets to cash, but the conversion is difficult for intangible assets. According to Miller (1977), the apparent trade-off between tax shields and bankruptcy costs looks like a recipe for the fabled horse and rabbit stew. In other words, bankruptcy costs are unimportant compared to the tax shields. But some other scholars reject this idea and emphasize the importance of bankruptcy costs.

The bankruptcy process within the USA could be introduced through the creditor. However, for public corporations, it is the business that will usually decide to file or not. Two procedures which are commonly used are Chaps. 7 and 11 of the Bankruptcy Act. The objective of Chap. 7 is to supervise the firm's collapse, while Chap. 11 sets out the aim to rehabilitate companies. Chapter 7 is used for small firms and frequently are initiated not by the company but instead it is done by the creditor. Large companies which cannot meet their debt obligations try to rehabilitate the business with the procedures described in Chap. 11. A total of 34 corporations in the 1989–1991 period and nearly 100 corporations in the 2001–2003 period, with liabilities greater than $ 1 billion, filed for Chap. 11. Conseco, WorldCom and Enron are the major samples of US corporate bankruptcy history (Brealey et al. 2011). Altman and Hotchkiss (2006) argue that it is more relevant to analyse bankruptcies in terms of liabilities rather than assets due to fraud-related bankruptcies.

Bankruptcy Costs

According to the model which is developed by Kraus and Litzenberger (1973), trade-off between tax savings and bankruptcy costs will determine the optimal capital structure. Myers (1984) refers to the hypothesis whereby firms balance their tax savings against bankruptcy costs, the trade-off theory. A tax shield will increase the optimal leverage, and bankruptcy costs will decrease the optimal leverage. So magnitude of expected bankruptcy costs is crucial to decide how much debt is optimal for the firm. Miller (1977) argues that bankruptcy costs are not important relative to the tax savings. He describes the analysis of tax savings and bankruptcy costs as the recipe of horse and rabbit stew. The bankruptcy costs (the rabbit) appear disproportionately small to offset the large tax savings (the horse). Haugen and Senbet (1978) have shown that the costs related with liquidating the assets of unprofitable firm are not related to capital structure of the state of the firm (bankrupt or not). They suggest that bankruptcy costs are not so important because creditors negotiate outside of court without affecting the actual value of the debtor firm.

When bankruptcy transpires, there occurs a formal reorganization and a transmission of ownership. The particular costs that one associates with this type of transmission can be categorized as either being direct or indirect (Haugen and Senbet 1978). The costs which are direct are inclusive of accountants' and lawyers' fees, the value of the time in the bankruptcy process as well as other professional fees. However, indirect costs relate to a wide range of unobservable opportunity costs and include the loss of profits, loss of sales and inability of companies to issue securities or get credit. It is the case that several businesses suffer from the loss in terms of their profits and sales as a result of customer behaviours such as not to deal with bankrupt firms. These firms also suffer from a result of increased costs, for example, weaker positions with suppliers or higher debt costs.

It is easier to identify the direct costs than indirect costs which are mainly lost opportunities. It is generally accepted that the direct costs may be less than the indirect costs. Therefore, it is really difficult to determine total bankruptcy costs due to the difficulties in quantifying indirect costs. So most studies focus on direct costs only and undervalue indirect bankruptcy costs. There have been several estimation techniques which are constructed to identify unobservable indirect costs.

While direct costs identification is easier, it may be difficult from the perspective of a researcher to gather all of the necessary data required to examine these particular costs. The main problem related to costs which are direct is due to there being no centralized source that lists all of the companies that went bankrupt and their costs. The only way to collect this information is to investigate each individual case (Altman and Hotchkiss 2006).

The literature about the costs of bankruptcy when a reorganization plan is applied is mixed because of the variation of sample size and time span. Some studies consider the costs to be high, whereas others consider to be low. Warner (1977) uses direct cost, for example, professional services, trustees' fees, legal fees as well as filing fees for 11 bankrupt railroads between 1933 and 1955. He concludes that the direct costs of reorganization process for 11 railroads are nearly 4% of the market value 1 year prior to default. Altman (1984) finds these costs to be approximately 7.5% using 19 bankrupt companies between 1974 and 1978. Weiss (1990) examines 37 bankruptcy cases for the period between 1980 and 1986. He approximates that the direct costs of bankruptcy are 3.1% of the book value of debt plus the market value of equity at the end of fiscal year prior to bankruptcy filing. LoPucki and Doherty (2004) find out that professional fees are 1.4% of the total assets at the beginning of the bankruptcy process. Bris et al. (2006) examine small and large bankruptcies between 1995 and 2001 in Arizona and New York. Their study distinguishes from prior research with two features. First, it covers both reorganization and liquidation cases. Second, it considers smaller non-public firms in contrast to previous studies which examine large public companies. They observe that the direct bankruptcy costs have a mean of 9.5% of pre-bankruptcy assets at reorganization cases and 8.1% of pre-bankruptcy assets at liquidation cases. According to the results, bankruptcy costs are very heterogeneous and sensitive to the measurement method.

The literature about the costs of bankruptcy when a liquidation plan is applied is scarce. Pulvino (1999) investigates commercial aircraft sales and concludes that asset fire sales decrease asset values. Also Strömberg (2000) finds that asset fire sales cause to important inefficiencies in the liquidation process. Bris et al. (2006) conclude that liquidations are not faster or cheaper than reorganizations.

All of these studies provide some important facts. First and foremost, it is probably going to be a significant scale effect. Most studies have focused upon the public companies which one would consider to be large. The companies which are smaller perhaps are not able to apply plan for reorganization due to the large amount of fees relative to their assets. Moreover, while the quantity of fees for large businesses could be relatively large, the percentage of these fees to total assets is low. But the costs which are indirect as a result of financial stress could still be substantial for large companies. Furthermore, when the data is made available, the ability to measure these costs improves (Altman and Hotchkiss 2006).

Indirect costs are not observable such as direct costs. However, researchers have estimated the probable size that such costs would generate using several approaches. Primarily the issue comes down to the fact that it is difficult to differentiate whether the substandard performance of the business be related to financial distress or if it be related to the economic factors that cause the financial distress. Therefore, researchers attempt to determine whether poor performance is related to economic distress, financial distress or perhaps a connection of both (Altman and Hotchkiss 2006). Altman (1984) presents a proxy methodology for the first time to measure the costs of bankruptcy that are indirect and compares the present value of expected bankruptcy cost with the present value of expected tax benefits generated from interest payments. If bankruptcy costs are significant, it should be seen to determine the optimal capital structure. But if these costs are trivial, it may be argued that capital structure decisions couldn't explain with bankruptcy cost. He uses two ways to estimate financial distress costs for each individual firm: decline in sales relative to others in the same industry and deviation between actual earnings and estimates of earnings over the 3 years prior to bankruptcy. He concludes that indirect costs are 10.5% and combined direct and indirect costs are 16.7% of firm value prior to bankruptcy. These findings indicate that bankruptcy costs are not trivial.

After Altman's (1984) pioneer study, several researchers have focused on this issue using several different methodologies and data sets. While Altman (1984) does observe large costs which are indirect, he does not separate them from negative operating shocks. Using firms which are not only financially distressed but also economically distressed makes it difficult to measure the magnitude of financial stress (Andrade and Kaplan 1998). Andrade and Kaplan (1998) study 31 highly leveraged transactions between 1980 and 1989 to identify the cost of financial distress. They examine only financially distressed, not economically distressed, firms selecting the sample from the firms that have positive operating margins at the distress time. Thus, their methodology provides an opportunity to distinguish costs of financial distress. They present the direct and indirect costs of financial distress and their determinants. They also estimate the cost financial distress to be between 10% and 23% of firm value.

Opler and Titman (1994) address a problem referred to as the reverse causality problem which is between the financial distress and assumed results. If the financial distress is costly, the firms which are highly leveraged would experience the highest of operating difficulties during distressed periods. Otherwise, if financial distress enforces companies to efficient operating changes, then this will result in the firms which are highly leveraged to increase their performance considerably. They have found the firms which are highly leveraged to lose a significant portion from their market share they possess and experience lower operating profits than conservatively financed competitors in distressed periods. Their findings are consistent with other studies that argue for the significance of the costs from financial distress which are indirect.

Almeida and Philippon (2007) propose a new method in order to estimate the net present value of financial distress costs. Their method is easy to implement and takes into consideration the systematic component. They argue that the existing literature ignores capitalization and underestimates the magnitude of ex ante distress costs. Elkamhi et al. (2012) use around 500,000 firm-quarter observations and find that the present value of ex ante distress costs occurred after bankruptcy are less than 1% of current firm value. Their findings differ from results gathered by Almeida and Philippon (2007) that estimate the ex ante distress cost in the range of 4–6%.

Hortaçsu et al. (2013) investigated the costs of financial distress that are indirect for auto manufacturers. They approximate that an increase in the levels of financial distress of a manufacturer results in a decrease in the prices of its secondhand cars. This effect is determined stronger for those cars which expect a longer life in use. They conclude that the costs of financial distress which are indirect are substantial and surpass the tax savings for General Motors and Ford.

Bankruptcy Prediction

Corporate failure leads to undesirable effects on the parties with any stakes in a firm. Therefore, assessing corporate failure risk prior to existence of failure event can enable those parties to take remedial measures against probable unfavourable consequences of such a risky situation. Most of the previous studies carried out on financial distress and bankruptcy-related issues merely aim to derive functional prediction models in order to forecast failure within a corporate perspective.

The development of bankruptcy prediction models has been a significant and extensively studied topic in both academic and business environments. The right prediction makes lending decisions easier and increases the profitability of financial institutions. Because of its economic effect, academics, practitioners and regulators are interested in bankruptcy prediction for decades. Regulators aim to monitor the financial health of financial sector. Practitioners focus on pricing the corporate debt.

Prevalent and trendy interest in developing properly working prediction models for corporate financial distress and bankruptcy has paved the way to derivation of numerous linear and non-linear models. The fundamental assumption which these prediction models rely on is the belief that firm's current and financial accounts can be utilized to foresee the manifests of any impending business failure event. This belief has motivated many academicians and practitioners to use related financial data and ratios as model predictors with some econometric techniques while it is possible to mention some distinct studies that can be considered exceptional in that firm-related non-financial data were employed as independent variables through more complicated techniques apart from the econometric models.

The failure prediction models derived using financial statement data can be discussed under four main titles: (a) the models based on industry averages, (b) the models based on stock returns and return variation, (c) the models based on cash flows and (d) the models based on financial ratios (Mossman et al. 1998). Among the researchers backing the paradigm to use of financial statements data in failure prediction are Beaver (1966), Altman (1968) and Deakin (1972) as well as many others. In addition to financial statement data, some non-financial statement data such as macroeconomic indicators, commodity price changes, nature of management structure, accounting information system quality and alike have been included in those models.

Beaver (1966) investigates the predictability of 14 financial ratios using 158 failed and non-failed firms. After the pioneering research of Beaver (1966), many studies investigate whether the financial ratios provide information about bankruptcy. But most of this research adopts a discriminant analysis approach instead of the univariate approach which is used by Beaver (1966). Altman (1968) uses multivariate discriminant analysis to predict the bankruptcies and concludes that bankruptcy could be explained by a means of using five financial ratios (sales/total assets, market capitalization/total debt, earnings before interest and taxes/total assets, retained earnings/total assets, working capital/total assets). These financial ratios are extensively used in the following studies. Multivariate discriminant analysis is a technique designed to classify an observation into one of the established groups according to the characteristics of the observation. The importance of this technique is its ability to distinguish the groups through multiple means of measurement. Altman's (1968) results are 95% effective 1 year before the bankruptcy. But predictive power of the model declines through the fifth year prior to failure. Beaver's (1966) model using only a cash flow/total debt ratio performs better in the fifth year prior to failure. Although Beaver's (1966) results show more predictive ability, Altman's (1968) model has more intuitive appeal (Deakin 1972). Deakin (1972) replicates the Beaver study and searches for the linear combination of the 14 ratios to determine the best predictor. He concludes that discriminant analysis can be used for bankruptcy prediction as far as 3 years in advance with high accuracy.

Ohlson (1980) contributes to the literature by using logistic regression approach in bankruptcy prediction problem. This approach provides specific contribution of each individual variable and gives a direct measure of probability. The study relies on sample of 105 bankrupt firms and 2058 non-bankrupt firms for the period between 1970 and 1976. The advantages of using conditional logit analysis are not to make assumptions regarding prior probabilities of bankruptcy and/or distribution of predictors. Zmijewski (1984) points out two potential biases of financial distress studies. These are called choice-based sample bias and sample selection bias. The probit models are used to compare the performance of estimations. However, all these conventional methods have assumptions such as the linearity, normality and independence among predictor or input variables. Considering the violations of these assumptions, the conventional methods can have limitations to obtain the effectiveness and validity (Shin et al. 2005).

Some studies have been argued that artificial intelligence such as neural networks may be an alternative to the conventional methods. Neural networks have been widely studied in financial problems including bankruptcy prediction, because of their capabilities of identifying and representing non-linear relationships. Odom and Sharda (1990) develop a neural network model to predict the bankruptcies and compare the predictive abilities of neural network and discriminant analysis. They conclude that neural networks predict the likelihood of a firm getting into bankruptcy better and provide an applicable solution to the bankruptcy risk prediction by using Altman's (1968) financial ratios as indicators. The prediction capability of neural networks is 81.81% while it is 74.28% for multivariate discriminant analysis.

Tam and Kiang (1992) compare a neural network model with multivariate discriminant analysis and logit model using bank default data for the period between 1985 and 1987. They have concluded that the neural network is a promising method in terms of its adaptability accuracy as well as its robustness while noting that the method does have several limitations.

Atiya (2001) argues that non-linear approach is superior to a linear approach due to several reasons. One of these reasons is saturation effects in the connection between the probability of bankruptcy and financial ratios. But it is necessary to improve neural networks through better training methods, better architecture selection or better inputs. Atiya (2001) concludes that the new indicators improve the prediction power of the method.

Although much research did report an effectiveness of the back-propagation neural network (BPN) in classification problems, a number of issues must still be taken into consideration. Shin et al. (2005) point out these limitations and examine the efficacy of using support vector machines (SVM) to corporate bankruptcy prediction. They conclude that SVM approach outperforms BPN to the bankruptcy prediction problem. According to the results, SVM has been noted as having the greatest level of accuracy and a greater generalization performance as the sample size is getting smaller.

Jones et al. (2017) conducted an examination of the predictive performance of 16 classifiers that ranges from traditional ones (multivariate discriminant analysis, logit and probit) to more advanced ones (neural networks, support vector machines) and "new age" statistical learning models (generalized boosting, AdaBoost and random forests). They conclude that traditional classifiers such as multivariate discriminant analysis and logit perform well in bankruptcy prediction. But they recommend "new age" classifiers due to several reasons. Firstly, they have been seen to predict better than the other classifiers on both cross-sectional and longitudinal samples. Secondly, they are relatively easy to estimate and implement. Finally, these classifiers also have a level of interpretability that ought to be considered good.

Some researchers have estimated single-period classification (static) models with multiple-period bankruptcy data. These models produce biased and inconsistent estimates because of the nature of bankruptcy data. Since bankruptcy occurs fairly infrequently, researchers estimate their models with the samples that span over several years. These models consider only a set of explanatory data, but they don't consider that companies evolve over time (Shumway 2001).

Queen and Roll (1987) and Theodossiou (1993) propose dynamic models of forecasting. Shumway (2001) who follows them develops a simple hazard model which uses all available information to determine the bankruptcy risk of each firm at each point of time. The traditional models use accounting data from publicly available financial statements. But accounting data has historical nature and is subject to reporting standards that might not reveal the true economic value of assets. The problems in accounting-based bankruptcy prediction models enforce an approach that argues to combine both accounting and market information sources. The most of the hazard models combine accounting and market information in simple discrete time logit models (Bauer and Agarwal 2014). According to Shumway (2001), there are three basic superiorities of hazard models compared to static models. Firstly, while static models do not adjust period at risk, hazard models adjust it automatically. Secondly, unlike static models, hazard models incorporate explanatory variables that change over time. Finally, hazard models produce more efficient forecasts because they use much more data.

Chava and Jarrow (2004) investigate the forecasting accuracy of hazard models for US firms between 1962 and 1999 using both yearly and monthly observations. They validate the forecasting performance of the hazard model and conclude that industry effect is significant in model estimation. They demonstrate that the predictive power of accounting variables reduces when the variables of the market are also included to the model.

Bauer and Agarwal (2014) examine a comprehensive test comparing the performance of accounting and contingent claim-based approaches against hazard models which are using both market and accounting information. They assess the predictive power of models with three dimensions: the ability of discrimination between non-bankrupt and bankrupt companies, the marginal information gathered via different models and the misclassification costs. Bankruptcy prediction approaches are compared in terms of all these dimensions using the UK data for the period between 1979 and 2009. According to the findings, hazard models outperform the other models.

Conclusion

In this chapter, it is aimed to provide a comprehensive and comparative picture of financial distress and bankruptcy concepts within a global perspective, especially concentrating on bankruptcy costs and prediction issues. The discussion points out the truth that while this field has been on the focus of scholars for decades and has a wide literature, there still exist some gaps that future studies should address. For instance, most of the existing findings on bankruptcy costs have been produced using the data of developed countries, particularly the USA. Therefore, the magnitude of bankruptcy costs should be measured in various cultural and institutional environments. It is also important for literature development to derive more sophisticated prediction models that could yield robust and more accurate results.

Keyword Definitions

Failure: The situation where the average return on investment is lower than firm's cost of capital.

Insolvency: The situation where total liabilities of a firm or person exceed the value of total assets.

Default: The situation where the debtor firm or person misses a scheduled payment.

Bankruptcy: Financial and legal result of failure to pay off outstanding debts by a person or an organization.

Direct bankruptcy costs: Fees paid to lawyers, accountants, consultants and other professionals involved in the bankruptcy process.

Indirect bankruptcy costs: Economic losses incurred during bankruptcy process.

References

Almeida, H., & Philippon, T. (2007). The risk-adjusted cost of financial distress. *The Journal of Finance, 62*(6), 2557–2586.

Altman, E. I. (1968). Financial ratios, discriminant analysis and the prediction of corporate bankruptcy. *The Journal of Finance, 23*(4), 589–609.

Altman, E. I. (1984). A further empirical investigation of the bankruptcy cost question. *The Journal of Finance, 39*(4), 1067–1089.

Altman, E. I., & Hotchkiss, E. (2006). *Corporate financial distress and bankruptcy: Predict and avoid bankruptcy, analyze and invest in distressed debt* (3rd ed.). Hoboken, NJ: Wiley.

Andrade, G., & Kaplan, S. N. (1998). How costly is financial (not economic) distress? Evidence from highly leveraged transactions that became distressed. *The Journal of Finance, 53*(5), 1443–1493.

Atiya, A. F. (2001). Bankruptcy prediction for credit risk using neural networks: A survey and new results. *IEEE Transactions on Neural Networks, 12*(4), 929–935.

Bauer, J., & Agarwal, V. (2014). Are hazard models superior to traditional bankruptcy prediction approaches? A comprehensive test. *Journal of Banking & Finance, 40*, 432–442.

Beaver, W. H. (1966). Financial ratios as predictors of failure. *Journal of Accounting Research*, 71–111.

Brealey, R. A., Myers, S. C., & Allen, F. (2011). *Principles of corporate finance* (10th ed.). Singapore: McGraw-Hill Irwin.

Bris, A., Welch, I., & Zhu, N. (2006). The costs of bankruptcy: Chapter 7 liquidation versus Chapter 11 reorganization. *The Journal of Finance, 61*(3), 1253–1303.

Chava, S., & Jarrow, R. A. (2004). Bankruptcy prediction with industry effects. *Review of Finance, 8*(4), 537–569.

Davydenko, S. A., & Franks, J. R. (2008). Do bankruptcy codes matter? A study of defaults in France, Germany, and the UK. *The Journal of Finance, 63*(2), 565–608.

Deakin, E. B. (1972). A discriminant analysis of predictors of business failure. *Journal of Accounting Research, 10*(1), 167–179.

Elkamhi, R., Ericsson, J., & Parsons, C. A. (2012). The cost and timing of financial distress. *Journal of Financial Economics, 105*(1), 62–81.

Haugen, R. A., & Senbet, L. W. (1978). The insignificance of bankruptcy costs to the theory of optimal capital structure. *The Journal of Finance, 33*(2), 383–393.

Hortaçsu, A., Matvos, G., Syverson, C., & Venkataraman, S. (2013). Indirect costs of financial distress in durable goods industries: The case of auto manufacturers. *The Review of Financial Studies, 26*(5), 1248–1290.

Jones, S., Johnstone, D., & Wilson, R. (2017). Predicting corporate bankruptcy: An evaluation of alternative statistical frameworks. *Journal of Business Finance & Accounting, 44*(1-2), 3–34.

Kraus, A., & Litzenberger, R. H. (1973). A state-preference model of optimal financial leverage. *The Journal of Finance, 28*(4), 911–922.

LoPucki, L. M., & Doherty, J. W. (2004). The determinants of professional fees in large bankruptcy reorganization cases. *Journal of Empirical Legal Studies, 1*(1), 111–141.

Mann, F. C. (2009). Making sense of nation-level bankruptcy filing rates. In J. Niemi, I. Ramsay, & W. C. Whitford (Eds.), *Consumer credit, debt and bankruptcy: Comparative and international perspectives* (pp. 225–247). North America: Hart Publishing.

Martin, N. (2005). The role of history and culture in developing bankruptcy and insolvency systems: The perils of legal transplantation.

Miller, M. H. (1977). Debt and taxes. *The Journal of Finance, 32*(2), 261–275.

Mossman, C. E., Bell, G. G., Swartz, L. M., & Turtle, H. (1998). An empirical comparison of bankruptcy models. *Financial Review, 33*(2), 35–54.

Myers, S. C. (1984). The capital structure puzzle. *The Journal of Finance, 39*(3), 574–592.

Odom, M. D., & Sharda, R. (1990). *A neural network model for bankruptcy prediction.* Paper presented at the International Joint Conference on Neural Networks.

Ohlson, J. A. (1980). Financial ratios and the probabilistic prediction of bankruptcy. *Journal of Accounting Research, 18*, 109–131.

Opler, T. C., & Titman, S. (1994). Financial distress and corporate performance. *The Journal of Finance, 49*(3), 1015–1040.

Pulvino, T. C. (1999). Effects of bankruptcy court protection on asset sales. *Journal of Financial Economics, 52*(2), 151–186.

Queen, M., & Roll, R. (1987). Firm mortality: Using market indicators to predict survival. *Financial Analysts Journal, 43*(3), 9–26.

Shin, K.-S., Lee, T. S., & Kim, H.-j. (2005). An application of support vector machines in bankruptcy prediction model. *Expert Systems with Applications, 28*(1), 127–135.

Shumway, T. (2001). Forecasting bankruptcy more accurately: A simple hazard model. *The Journal of Business, 74*(1), 101–124.

Strömberg, P. (2000). Conflicts of interest and market illiquidity in bankruptcy auctions: Theory and tests. *The Journal of Finance, 55*(6), 2641–2692.

Tam, K. Y., & Kiang, M. Y. (1992). Managerial applications of neural networks: The case of bank failure predictions. *Management Science, 38*(7), 926–947.

Theodossiou, P. T. (1993). Predicting shifts in the mean of a multivariate time series process: An application in predicting business failures. *Journal of the American Statistical Association, 88* (422), 441–449.

Warner, J. B. (1977). Bankruptcy costs: Some evidence. *The Journal of Finance, 32*(2), 337–347.

Weiss, L. A. (1990). Bankruptcy resolution: Direct costs and violation of priority of claims. *Journal of Financial Economics, 27*(2), 285–314.

Yigit, F. (2015). Bankruptcy. In F. F. Wherry & J. B. Schor (Eds.), *The SAGE encyclopedia of economics and society* (pp. 176–179). SAGE.

Zmijewski, M. E. (1984). Methodological issues related to the estimation of financial distress prediction models. *Journal of Accounting Research*, 59–82.

Chapter 15
Behavioral Finance Models, Anomalies, and Factors Affecting Investor Psychology

İstemi Çömlekçi and Ali Özer

Abstract In traditional finance theories and in the efficient market hypothesis, human beings are regarded as rational entities. It has been accepted that people exhibit rational behavior in investment decisions. However, various anomalies have been observed as a result of the inability of these theories to explain the change in the markets. These anomalies have led to criticism of traditional finance theories and have been regarded as the beginning of behavioral finance.

Behavioral finance theories and models argue that the definition of stock prices is influenced by psychological, cognitive and emotional factors of investors. The presence of investors, who do not act rationally on the stock market, and the fact that psychological and emotional factors are effective in the decision-making process distract the stock market from being effective.

Determining the investor behaviors that cause the anomalies detected in the stock market and putting out the possible reasons is important in terms of estimating the share price. In this study, information was given on traditional finance theories that accept individuals as rational. Behavioral finance models and theories were examined to investigate irrational behavior. In addition, anomalies resulting from irrational behavior of investors and investor behavior were examined, and also the relationship between investor behaviors and anomalies was examined.

Introduction

In Effective Market Hypothesis and other traditional finance theories, individuals are considered as rational assets. In many studies, the theoretical and empirical validity of these theories has been tested and supported. However, later studies have shown that they deviate from rationality, and individuals cannot always make rational

İ. Çömlekçi (✉)
Düzce University, Düzce, Turkey
e-mail: istemicomlekci@duzce.edu.tr

A. Özer
Erzincan University, Erzincan, Turkey

© Springer International Publishing AG, part of Springer Nature 2018
H. Dincer et al. (eds.), *Global Approaches in Financial Economics, Banking, and Finance*, Contributions to Economics, https://doi.org/10.1007/978-3-319-78494-6_15

decisions. These results have led researchers to examine the effects of individual behavior on investment decisions and have led to the emergence of a new field of behavioral finance. The abnormal price and return movements caused by these irrational movements are also called anomalies.

In the decision process of investment, individuals first reach to information and analyze and later decide between alternatives according to results of analyzing. However, as soon as the process of analyzing of information gets more complicated and uncertainty in the market increases, rational evaluations leave their places to emotional thinking. In the emotional thinking mechanism, former events, mental shorts, and psychological and sociological factors are influential. As the number of factors engaged in the process increases, the decision-making process becomes more complicated. In the field of finance, it is seen that behavioral factors are effective; the identification of behavioral factors, the mechanism of functioning and the evaluation of the results of the factors have been compulsory.

In this study, the information that are about conventional finance theories based on rationality which is effective on investment decisions, assumptions of behavioral finance and anomalies emerging from irrational movements are given. It is thought that these information support theoretical and empirical studies that will be done.

Finance Theories

Finance theories characterize individuals as rational, irrational, and restricted rational. While conventional finance theories describe individuals as rational, behavioral finance theories use the concepts of irrational and restricted rational when characterizing. Being rational is a type of mechanic movement for maximum benefit by evaluating information effectively. Nevertheless, with the effects of beliefs, values, traditions, psychology, and society, types of behaviors may advance from rationality to irrationality. It is even easy to be detected types of irrational behaviors that are far away from rationality. So, while tackling with financial theories, by the framing of rationality, it is studied under two headings as conventional finance theories and behavioral finance theories.

Conventional Finance Theories

Before explaining behavioral finance models, which are based on investors' irrational behaviors and movements, traditional finance theories that try to explain the risk-return relationship by describing investors as rational assets have been explained.

Capital Asset Pricing Model

Capital Asset Pricing Model (CAPM) is one of the models which tries to explain the risk and return relationship in the investment alternatives that investors face with and in which the risk is expressed with a variable. It was developed for the first time by Sharpe (1964) on the basis of Markowitz's portfolio theory, and the theory has become feasible in financial assets by providing the necessary contributions by Lintner (1965) and Mossin (1966). Since this model can be implemented separately for each financial asset, it also gives an idea of the risk and the return of the portfolio.

In CAPM, in addition to the risk and return concepts developed in the light of the assumptions of the efficient market hypothesis (EMH), many investors during an investment period, in their investment or use, are based on the assumptions of EPH on many issues such as having investors have the same risk-free interest rate and free and instant access to knowledge (Merton 1973:867).

In this model, which examines the relationship between market return and expected return on an asset or portfolio, there is a linear relationship between the return of any financial asset and the systematic risk. Systematic risk is measured by the beta coefficient indicating the sensitivity of the financial asset to the market index return.

CAPM:

$$R_i = R_f + \beta_i(R_m - R_f) \tag{15.1}$$

It is described as R_i, expected return of financial assets; R_f, the risk-free interest rate; R_m, the expected return on the market; and β_i, the sensitivity of the financial asset to the movement of the whole market. The CAPM, which accepts the market portfolio as the only variable, tries to explain the market portfolio and the returns of all risky financial assets with the returns of the market portfolio. The model, which indicates that the only factor affecting the systematic risk of return expressed as the beta coefficient, is considered to be the province of the asset pricing models (Brealey et al. 2007:272).

Certain assumptions that are valid in the financial asset pricing model were applied.

These are (Fabozzi et al. 2006:208–209):

- Since the security market is big, investors do not affect the price alone.
- There is a systematic relationship between risk and expected return.
- Investors who agree with issues related to expected returns, standard deviations, and covariance of financial assets have homogeneous expectations.
- Investors using Markowitz's efficient portfolio model are the majority. The utility function determines how the investor will be positioned on the market.
- For investors who are trying to maintain effective diversification developed by Markowitz, they are able to find their positions in their investments without the cost of cash. Every financial asset has infinite divisibility. There is full liquidity in the market.

- Apart from market interest rate, investors do not face with any interest and borrow the required amount of cash on the market with the risk-free interest rate.
- There are no tax-related financial asset returns, commissions on transfer, and transfer costs, or they are zero.
- The investors have the same risk-free interest rate in the same investment period.
- All investors can access the information easily.

Arbitrage Pricing Model

Arbitrage is the sale of financial assets purchased today from different prices temporally or spatially. It is a model developed as an alternative of CAPM and less hypothetical model. Developed on the basis of law of one price, this model focuses on systematic risk factors by asserting that prices will be on balance as spatial arbitrage is not possible. There is also no assumption about investor behavior (Amenc and Sourd 2003:101).

Arbitrage Pricing Model (APM), with its many factors, affects all financial assets in the market with the factors it has in its possession. It is argued that a number of factors can affect the expected return of the financial asset. The result is that the expected return of a security is a function of the sensitivity of the factors affecting the return. APM has a beta set in it that takes into account every factor (Francis 1993:638–642). Arbitrage pricing model can be shown as follows (Elton and Gruber 1991:369):

$$E(R_i) = R_f + \beta_{i1}(F_1 - R_f) + \beta_{i2}(F_2 - R_f) + \ldots + \beta_{im}(F_m - R_f) \qquad (15.2)$$

$E(R_i)$: the required return rate of financial asset "i"
R_f: risk-free interest rate (return rate of portfolio with "0" beta)
β_{ij}: the sensitivity of financial asset "i" to the factor of "j"
F_j: return rate of factor number "j" (periodic rate of change)
$(F_j - R_f)$: risk premium of factor number "j"
m: number of factors

The APM has three basic assumptions. These are (Ross 1976):

1. Full competition conditions apply in the markets.
2. Investors prefer more returns, rather than less returns.
3. The stochastic process (k) shows how the expected return of financial assets is realized with the factor model.

Efficient Market Hypothesis and Random Walk

Random walk theory is based on the assumption that current prices of financial assets have no relation with previous prices and that it is not possible to put forward an idea about future or current prices; in short, there is no memory of prices, and they occur in a random fashion (Dimson and Mussavian 1998:92). Random walk theory was developed with the work of Fama (1970), becoming the efficient market hypothesis (EMH). In Fama (1970), EMH claimed that information on various forms in the market is reflected in prices, that it is not possible to obtain abnormal returns by using this information, that buyers and sellers can easily access information, and that information can be accessed simultaneously and at low cost.

The assumptions of EPH are as follows (Kiyılar 1997:9):

1. All investors can access all information about the financial asset without a cost.
2. There is no charge for the transactions carried out, and there is an objective tax system for the market.
3. There are enough buyers and sellers in the markets to not have a share that will affect prices.
4. Investors are likely to make rational decisions on risk-return.
5. All financial assets are divisible.

Portfolio Approach

Portfolio is called as basket which is composed of various financial assets. There are two approaches developed according to investors' risk and return expectations. The first one is conventional portfolio approach based more upon assumption purposing to make benefit maximum by diversification between risk and return but ignoring the relationship of financial assets one another that composing portfolio. The second is a modern portfolio theory based on mathematical models derived from the criticisms of the traditional portfolio theory. The traditional portfolio theory is still used because of its practical application in spite of criticism. As in the first approach, the modern portfolio theory aims at maximizing the utility of the risk-return relation, but choosing the appropriate number of mathematical models and qualitative financial products instead of increasing the number of financial assets in order to reduce the risk of portfolio. In addition, it is generally aimed at choosing the most appropriate one among portfolios by creating different portfolios instead of a single portfolio (Ceylan and Korkmaz 2006:116).

Basic Analysis

Basic analysis is a method based on analysis of publicly disclosed economic, sectoral and company information. This method analyzes the past and current information and makes estimates about the future of the company and the stock. In addition, mathematical models for the analysis of this information can be used to analyze the price of the financial product, and buying and selling decisions regarding the financial product can be made (Thomsett 1998:2). The basic analysis is a three-step analysis of economy, industry, and firm analysis. In the economic analysis, the general situation of the country and the relationship between macroeconomic indicators and financial markets are tried to be revealed. In the sector analysis, the general situation of the sector and its future are evaluated. Finally, with company analysis, information about the company to which the financial product belongs is evaluated, and ultimately last decision is made.

Technical Analysis

Technical analysis, also referred to as market analysis, visual analysis, or graphical analysis, focuses on how the future fluctuations in prices will move by its past movements rather than reasons of fluctuations in prices. Technical analysts concentrate on forecasting current and future trends, rather than factors that are influential by macro, micro, and psychological factors affecting prices and trends affecting past prices. It is possible to distinguish technical analysts to two groups as subjective analysts who interpret their own results and objective analysts who make use of a certain model-program (Aronsan 2007:14). Technical analysis analyzes the trends and trends expressed by current price graphs, using graphical models of statistical methods used in price movements of past periods. It evaluates past market data such as price, transaction volume, and open positions. Price movements in the past periods tend to be observable and recurrent. The investor will sell the financial asset at the high points where the prices are going up and going to decline and buy the financial asset at lowest points where the prices fall and are going to rise (Edwards et al. 2013:4–10).

Behavioral Finance Theories

Together with EMH, Fama (1970), the rationality of investors is generally accepted. When bubbles and collapses in the markets are not unclosed with rationality, it is commenced to be discussed that investors always cannot be rational and that situation may change in terms of time and places. This debate has led to the emergence of behavioral financing that studies investor behavior and psychology.

The Expected Utility Theory

The expected utility theory (EUT) focuses on the behavior and reactions of individuals when uncertainty prevails. EUT describes human behavior with a measurable utility function. In the uncertain future, when investors decide, they do not fully know the end result of this decision. For this reason, it is argued that risk avoidance increases by the EUT. EUT tries to explain investors' subjective behavior as a consequence why they avoid investment in large-scale investments. The EUT examines how investors make rational choices in unconditional terms when their economic outcomes are realized (Luce and Raiffa 1989:14). The EUT suggests for individuals to take into consideration when making subjective assessments among different alternatives that the likelihoods and probabilities of the case involving risky alternatives can be measured simultaneously and independently of each other. According to this theory, one should be formulated to measure the gains of events, provided that it remains indifferent among alternatives that are risky.

Kahneman and Tversky's Expectation Theory

The expected utility theory has been accepted for decades under uncertainty, but Kahneman and Tversky (1979) proposed new approaches to the emergence of behaviors that rejected their basic assumptions, supplemented by the lack of expected utility theory and formulated and supported by the empirical results (Shiller 2001:1309). The most important criticism of the expected utility theory was in the field of individuals, and in this theory, individuals were not always able to make rational decisions, and it shows psychological factors as a matter of reason. In this theory, individuals will calculate the benefits they will have when deciding between alternatives and will prefer the alternative that provides the most benefit. There are, however, similarities between the two theories: in both theories, it is assumed that the individual tries to maximize the benefits and accepted that benefit must be measured not as monetary but as satisfactory level and individuals avoid risk for their earnings. Besides the similarities, theories have different aspects. These differences constitute the basis of Kahneman and Tversky's Expectation Theory (KTET) (Ding et al. 1993:2–3):

1. The expected utility theory deals with the final state of the earnings of the persons. When earnings are generated, not only previous acquisitions will be efficient, but also sum of earnings of last alternative in return will be efficient. KTET is interested in how the last alternative will affect the total wealth.
2. The EUT uses predetermined probabilities in the calculation of the expected utility and places emphasis on alternatives according to these possibilities. On the other hand, KTET uses decision weights when calculating utility and evaluates alternatives accordingly. The decision weights used in the weight function developed by Kahneman and Tversky (1979) are lower than the determined probabilities of the EUT.
3. EUT allocates three groups according to their attitudes toward risk. These are investors: risk-averse, indifferent toward risk, and willing to take risks. In addition, the investor will be included in one of these three groups and will not have the same feature of more than one group. On the other hand, the KTBT has divided the investors into two groups, one that avoids the risks of profit and the one who does not avoid the risk of loss.

Behavioral Finance Models and Market Anomalies

Anomalies are price and return movements that emerge as a result of irrational movements and are compatible with theory. Therefore, anomalies in which conventional finance theories are also hard to explain are tried to be explained by behavioral finance theories and models. In this part, the information which is about anomalies and models trying to explain anomalies will be given.

Behavioral Finance Models

According to behavioral finance models, markets are not active and the most important proof of this is market anomalies. Behavioral finance tries to explain these anomalies theoretically and empirically. This study will focus on three widely accepted models in the literature.

Barberis, Shleifer, and Vishny's Representative Investor Model

The representative investor model explains irrational behaviors in two approaches: conservatism and representation. Conservatism is that information that is new to the market does not change the patterns of behavior and mental shortcuts of individuals in the past. Representative effect refers to emphasizing situations where individuals are most affected when making decisions, not considering the analysis of other situations and making decisions under this effect. In this model, the incomplete response is explained by conservativeness, and the extreme reaction is explained by representation.

Studies of the incomplete reaction have claimed that individuals responded to the news reflected in the marketplace for 1–12 months. Thus, there is a slow interaction between prices and market news, leading to positive autocorrelation. In addition, good news now has the power to predict future positive returns. Findings related to overreaction show that securities prices are overreacting in the same direction as related news in the longer periods of 3–5 years. It also causes overvaluation and drop in average returns because securities hold good news-related effects for a long time in memory. In other words, securities with high-performance trends and overvalued securities will eventually return to their average values. These findings contradict the efficient market hypothesis, which argues that investors can make high profits using the advantages of extreme and incomplete reaction without taking any risk (Barberis et al. 1998:307–308).

Barberis et al. (1998) stated that the firm profits in fact have a random structure but that they are distorted by the effect of conservatism and representation. Investors have the belief that firms that have picked up the uptrend will gradually return to average and enter a certain trend. With the belief that the securities that catch the uptrend of incomplete reaction will return to the average, the overreaction occurs with the belief that certain trend will occur after the increase. In their studies, they also described the positive correlations of the security incomes that arise in the studies that prove the momentum strategy with the past periods as the incomplete reaction, and they have shown that the information coming to the market is reflected in the prices over time.

Daniel, Hirshleifer, and Subrahmanyam's Excessive Confidence and Self-Attribution Bias Model

This model is based on investors' self-overconfidence and self-affecting types of trust. Theories of investor overconfidence are based on cognitive psychology (Daniel et al. 1998:1841), which provides evidence for individuals who exaggerate their abilities in many manners. Excess confidence is the overwhelming confidence that individuals have in their personal knowledge. Attribution to oneself is based on the confidence that they have and the relationship between investment decisions and the investment decisions taken with this confidence. Individuals are biased by claiming that the decisions that result from the gain come from themselves and that the decisions that are the result of the damage are from external factors (Lawrance 2001:18). Studies by Daniel et al. (1998) are based on the fact that securities prices are overreacting to private information and that the public is incapable of responding to disclosed information. They also argue that overreaction models are related to the negative correlation of long-term stock returns, unconditional excess volatility, and more inferences for the state of volatility. In this model, the investor stated that the confirmed public increased their confidence with the disclosed information, but the unconfirmed information caused only the loss of confidence. If individual investors act on the market in a way that is far from prejudices about their capabilities, the new information disclosed to the public will, on average, confirm their proprietary information. This, in turn, will cause more and more excessive reaction to previous private information. Thus, the ongoing overreaction will cause momentum in securities prices, but the public will gradually return to the main point with the announced information falling. Thus, self-attribution bias will cause momentum in the short term but will reverse in the long term (Daniel et al. 1998:1842).

Hong and Stein's Interactive Relationship Model Among Heterogeneous Investors

Hong and Stein (1999) mentioned two types of investors, their momentum investors and news hunters, in their work on the interactive relationship model. Momentum investors are investors who do not take into account publicly disclosed information or their proprietary information and accept past price movements as basic information and invest accordingly. News hunters are investors who are not interested in current or past price movements, publicly disclosed or disclosed information, and estimates of the future with their own private information (Hong and Stein 1999:2144–2145). Both investors are not completely rational in style and are considered to be rationally limited.

In both investors, the public may act on certain parts of the disclosed information. Private information is spread slowly among news hunters. So the information on the market, where only the news hunters are, will slowly reflect on the prices and cause the missing reaction. In this case, there will certainly be no overreaction. With momentum investors entering the market, the incomplete reaction caused by news hunters will be forced away from the market due to arbitrage with adequate risk tolerance and will be forced to be activated by market momentum investors. But this change will cause excessive reaction after a point. Because those investors who are not interested in basic information and only take into account price movements do not know the price that should be, they will not even notice it. Investors who arrive at early awareness will make profits from the late ones (Hong and Stein 1999:2145).

Investor Biases

Behavioral finance models have shown that the rationality of individuals from the basic assumptions of traditional finance models is deteriorated by various psychological and sociological factors, while the other side has tried to explain the reasons of irrationality. Here, concepts of "investor sensitivity" arise because of the concept of "noise" based on rumors based on real information and because individuals can be overly optimistic or pessimistic about the information and the reaction to the rumors. These investors are also called noise transactions. The noise transactions of noise traders from time to time contain extreme reactions and may cause significant fluctuations in the market (Binswanger 1999:146–148).

The concept of investor sensitivity is the excessive optimism and pessimism of investors' reaction to expectations about the return of financial assets or against good or bad news received. In the emergence of investor sensitivity, it is possible to talk about two basic rationales as the beliefs about the price trends and the expectations. These two must be together; if the belief is not strong despite the expectation, the decisions of the individuals can change quickly (Plummer 2003:1).

Those who will make financial decisions are faced with many factors that will influence these decisions. Economists argued that mistakes made by individuals in decision-making were independent of each other. However, studies in the field of experimental psychology show that individuals have similar prejudices and that similar mistakes fall when they decide. The mistakes made in the decision-making process are based on four basic reasons. These reasons are self-deception, cognitive bias, emotion, and social interaction (Hirshleifer 2001).

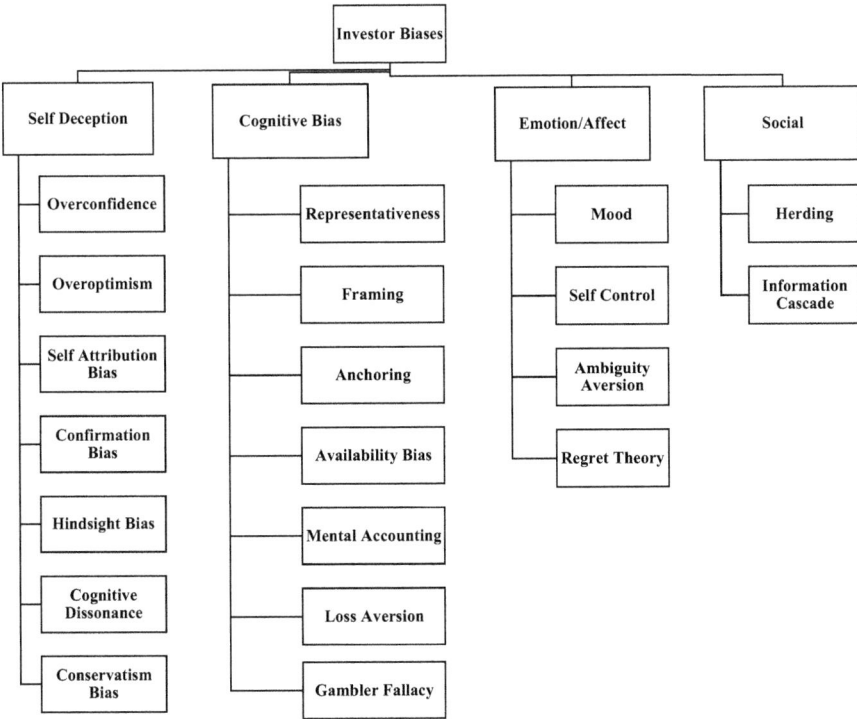

Fig. 15.1 The categorization of the problems caused by prejudices and bias

The prejudices and bias that cause this error are categorized and shown in Fig. 15.1 (Pompian 2006; Özan 2010; Jaya et al. 2010).

Self-Deception

Economists assume that people take lessons from mistakes they have made in the past and shape their future behavior according to these conclusions. However, psychologists have shown that learning from past mistakes and learning are a process involving fraudulent situations. It hinders the ability of self-deceiving people to take lessons from past mistakes. Because these trends cause people not to fully understand their situation. They think themselves in a better situation than they are. Self-deception causes various tendencies to emerge in people (Hirshleifer 2001). These can be ranged as overconfidence bias, optimism bias, self-attribution bias, confirmation bias, hindsight bias, cognitive dissonance, and conservative bias.

Overconfidence Bias

The tendency to believe that people know more than they actually know, and to see their own abilities superior to what they actually are, is called "overconfidence bias" (Pompian 2006:51). People who are over-reliant blames others for their mistakes but they see the achievement as their own successes (Peterson 2007). Rational investors are seeking to obtain the highest return with the least risk. An investor who is overly confident puts an emphasis on the information they have and thinks that the investment instruments he/she selects will perform well. Overconfidence may lead to incorrect estimation of the level of risk of investments (Pompian 2006).

Optimism Bias

The best possible outcome expectation from individual investment decisions is expressed as optimism (Iqbal 2015). This tendency is a prejudice that causes people to over-reliance on information and overestimate their knowledge, exaggerate their ability to control events, and underestimate risks (Barak 2008).

Self-Attribution Bias

The tendency to misinterpret the mistakes is expressed as the fact that the success of the investment decisions depends on their own skills and their failures depend on external factors. The tendency to misjudge mistakes causes people not to see mistakes, and mistakes cause them to fail to notice the resulting adversities. This situation is likely to fall back to the same fault again because it prevents them from seeing their mistakes (Özan 2010).

Confirmation Bias

Confirmation bias is the result of people searching for information that overlaps with their existing beliefs and neglecting conflicting information about their beliefs. Although the tendency to confirm and the tendency to conservatism are similar, the tendency of conservatism leads people to react less to all the new information they learn. On the other hand, the tendency of confirmation is low reaction to people's beliefs in parallel with their beliefs and conflicting beliefs with their beliefs (Dave and Wolfe 2003).

Hindsight Bias

Hindsight bias is expressed that people believe that this event can be predicted when the results of an event happened in the past. This behavior arises as a result of easier comprehension of the actual outcomes of the infinite outcomes that have not been realized by people's minds. This leads investors to believe in the correctness of their prediction (Pompian 2006).

Cognitive Dissonance

If people are contradictory to one of the two concepts in their minds, "cognitive dissonance" comes into play. Investors experience internal discomfort and anxiety as a result of this dissonance. Investors with cognitive dissonance are trying to change past values, feelings, or thoughts or justify their own decisions. Against this backdrop, investors may choose to invest in wrong and faulty investments and may be able to make a loss (Ricciardi and Simon 2000).

Conservatism Bias

Conservatism bias can be defined overlooking information when new information is in conflict with previously given decisions, taking into account information that is in harmony with the decisions they have made, when evaluating information that will help people to make their decisions. Conservatism tends to cause people to react poorly to new knowledge (Dave and Wolfe 2003).

Cognitive Bias

Human brain analyzes the signals it receives via information using some shortcuts (hedonic) and shortens the analysis process. Although the shortcuts provide advantages in terms of saving time, they increase the possibility of making mistakes as all information cannot be passed through the evaluation filter (Böyükaslan 2012). The most frequent occurrences of cognitive bias can be listed as bias to represent, bias to frame, bias to anchor, bias to loss aversion, cognitive dissonance, bias to confirm, and bias to conserve.

Representativeness Heuristic

The tendency to represent emerges as a result of investors placing more emphasis on the most recent or most multiplier factors in the decision-making process and neglecting the characteristics of population distribution (Ülkü 2001). In terms of investors, the representation shortage also includes good stocks and good companies. It also implies that large companies prefer stocks without regarding to aggregate returns (Nofsinger 2001).

Framing Effect

Framing misconceptions or bias is the way in which individuals react differently to perceiving and responding differently to the different interpretation of the same problem in the decision-making phase (Pompian 2006). The two options with the same probability of occurrence and the same can be evaluated differently due to differences in expression.

Anchoring Heuristics

When the human brain solves complex problems, the bias to designate an initial reference point and then to arrange this reference point in the direction of additional information received is called the "anchoring heuristics" (Kahneman and Tversky 1974). This bias to anchor may lead to incorrect pricing of financial assets. For example, investors anchoring past stock prices can view buying opportunities without much consideration for the price of the stock.

Availability Heuristic

Availability heuristic is defined as "the first reason for the sample concerned with the event in order to determine the probability or frequency of any event" (Pachur et al. 2012).

Loss Aversion

Loss aversion is a trend that determines the attitudes of individual investors toward risk. One of the main assumptions of behavioral finance is that investors are reluctant to lose, not to risk. Investors have shown that they are willing to take more risk to get rid of the possibility of losing. In other words, the negative effect of loss on the individual is more important than the effect of the gain, and it is called loss aversion (Benartzi and Thaler 1993).

Mental Accounting

Individuals like businesses record monetary transactions and decisions they make in separate accounts and independently evaluate each other. This is called mental accounting (Thaler 1985). Mental accounting also influences investors' risk perception. Mental accounting leads to misunderstanding of risk and consequently low diversification of portfolio investments (Nofsinger 2002:85).

Gambler Fallacy

The gambler fallacy is a false belief that an event occurring independently and randomly is less likely to happen again if it has recently come true. Those people who play for hours at the beginning of gambling machines that are programmed to perceive all the games in a way that is independent of each other think that they are getting a little closer to jackpot in every lost game. This fallacy applies to investors (Suetens and Tryan 2012).

Emotional Bias

Emotion is the perception of physical stimuli or mental processes. Emotional tendencies are the comprehension and decision-making disorders caused by emotional factors. An event that is actually a negative effect due to emotional tendencies can be perceived as having a positive effect. Cognitive tendencies are more effective when short-term decisions are made, whereas emotional tendencies are more effective when long-term decisions are made (Özan 2010). These emotional biases cause individuals to interpret the error and therefore make erroneous decisions. The main biases are mood, ambiguity aversion, regret aversion, and self-control.

Mood

Anticipations for the future of people under uncertainty are affected by the mood. People become optimistic in a good (happy) spirit and become pessimistic if you are in a bad (sad) mood (Wright and Bower 1992). This mood is also reflected in the expectations and interpretations of the market. Investors believe that if they are in a good mood they will provide high returns, and in a bad mood their asset prices will decrease.

Self-Control

Difficulties in mastering movements, behaviors, and thoughts of individuals, in other words, the events that occur in the way of leaving themselves to developing events, mean that people have difficulties not to control themselves. Failure to control oneself shows that you are deprived of an inner self-discipline and feelings are heavy in your attitudes. Individuals who have difficulties in keeping themselves under control can eventually make mistakes and mistakes that can be disadvantageous to them in the future, such as giving more importance to short-term goals and making too many transactions without considering the timing (Böyükaslan 2012).

Ambiguity Aversion

Ambiguity aversion is that people prefer to take risks rather than unknown odds, according to the known probabilities. In other words, investors avoid uncertainties or situations where they cannot predict the outcome (Ahn et al. 2014). Investors may buy financial assets for which they can estimate the probability distribution and prefer the lowest risk at the same level of return as an example of ambiguity aversion behavior.

Regret Aversion

Regarding investments, regret is defined as the pain that people feel when they know that they have a better result of the choice of alternatives to their preference in the past and they are late to change it. Regret is a strong negative emotion. It is called "regret aversion," in which people move by adding a remorse that they can live in the future. This feeling is seen as investors hold stocks in their portfolio while selling stocks that earn in order not to regret their decisions about their investments (Özan 2010).

Social Bias

Social biases are behavioral tendencies shared by a majority of members of a society or group. These biases influence, direct, or even restrict people's thoughts, decisions, and activities. Instead of acting as a separate individual, people tend to act as a majority with the group that they are a member of, because of the fear of exclusion from the group or thinking that majority decision is healthier. Investors are constantly curious about what most people are doing and tend to make their investments parallel to this case. Even if he/she invests in opposition in a matter of opinion, most of them will question themselves psychologically. If he/she thinks like a majority and has invested or will make investments in this direction, then he will be sure about his/her decision (Özan 2010).

Herding Behavior

Herding behavior is that investors act on behalf of other investor's movement, not on their own knowledge and evaluations. Because of herding behavior, investors are leaving their knowledge and beliefs to imitate other investor behaviors (Chang et al. 2000). Reasons, such as the belief that other investors have different knowledge that is not same with himself/herself, imitate people who are more professional than himself/herself and the desire to follow that comprises in the subconscious of people whom the person appreciates inherently (Rizzi 2008).

Common act emerging as a result of analyzed knowledge and news by persons is considered as falsified herding behavior. It is difficult to differentiate between real herding behavior without rational reasons and analysis because there are many variables that influence the herding behavior, the market, and the individual. Actual herding behavior can always arise not only through the rational analysis of information and data but also by the imitation of the professionals. Falsified herding behavior is always influenced by psychological factors (Chang et al. 2000).

Information Cascade

It is said that investors tend to ignore their own information when they make a decision and tend to follow those investors while thinking that investors who have already made investment decisions use more useful information (Bikhchandani et al. 1992). Information cascading effect occurs in several stages. For example, if the price of a share rises (or falls) in a way that cannot be explained by any economic event, some investors think that other investors have a different knowledge and that these increases (or decreases) are caused by the purchases (or sales) of other investors. Investors' buying (or selling) based on these considerations leads to the continuation of the increase (or decrease) in the stock price. This new movement ensures that other investors who have not been influenced by the cascade up until now will be able to see that the increase (or decrease) trend will be continuous; this should be a good cause and take action. Thus, prices increase (or decrease) again. The increase (or decrease) of prices continues for a while with the participation of new investors in the process of cascade effect (Özan 2010).

Anomalies in Stock Market

The efficient market hypothesis argues that stock prices reflect all kinds of information on the market and that it is not possible for investors to earn extra income.

Deviations in market efficiency are expressed as anomalies (Pompian 2006:8–9). It is possible to investigate the anomalies seen in the markets as periodical anomalies, firm anomalies, and price anomalies. Periodic anomalies occur in the form of hourly, daily, weekly, monthly, yearly, or pre- or post-specific periods. Price anomalies appear as excessive and low reactions. Firm anomalies can be diversified as firm size anomalies and neglected firm anomalies (Barak and Demirelli 2006).

Periodic (Seasonal) Anomalies

The situation in which the securities perform differently according to normal times at any period is generally expressed as a periodical anomaly. Periodic anomalies can be classified as day anomaly, moon anomaly, and holiday anomaly (Barak 2008). Day anomalies: anomalies are the result of securities getting different returns according to other days and hours during certain days or in a day.

Day anomalies, weekly anomalies, weekend anomalies, and intra-day anomalies are examined in three different ways.

The month anomalies are the difference of the stock returns according to the other month in any month of the year. Month anomalies are covered under the title of January, the end of month, and the end of year.

Holiday anomalies are anomalies in that stock returns are different before, during, and after holiday in official, religious, and weekend holidays.

Firm Anomalies

Firm anomalies are formed by the size of the firms and by the transaction numbers on the market where the stock returns differ. Firm size can be diversified as anomaly and neglected firm anomaly (Ergün 2009:30).

Firm size anomaly means that stocks with small market value have a higher return than stocks with high market value.

Neglected firm anomaly is the state that stocks that is less advised by investors and specialists earn more than stocks that have high transaction volumes and trading less.

Price Anomalies

Price anomalies of stocks can be classified under two headings: incomplete reaction and extreme reaction anomalies (Barak 2008).

Incomplete reaction As a result of investors reaching to news late, it is the anomaly that emerges from the result of stocks that earns (losses) in the past continue to earn (loss) in the future.

Overreaction The average return after positive news may be lower than the average return after bad news. The anomaly which occurs in this case is called the over-reaction.

Conclusion

In Fama (1970) in the assumptions of effective market hypotheses and classical finance theories, individuals are considered as rational entities. Many studies in the 1970s have produced results that support the assumptions of classical financial theory, but later on crises, bubbles and other reactions that have taken place in the markets have begun to be unexplained by these theories, which in turn have raised objections. These objections led to the emergence of new approaches and theories called behavioral finance. Although many studies in the field of psychology have discussed the impact of psychology on the decisions of individuals, psychological influences on financial decisions have come to the fore with the work of Kahneman and Tversky (1979). In Kahneman and Tversky's (1979) expectation theory, taking into account the criticized sides of the expected utility theory, it has shown that individuals cannot always make rational decisions, and reasons of this situation are psychological factors. With this in mind, many models and theories have been developed in the field of behavioral finance.

In behavioral finance models, Barberis, Shleifer, and Vishny explain the irrational behavior of the model of the investor in terms of conservatism and representation. Conservatism is that information which is new to the market does not change individuals' past behavior patterns and mental shortcuts. Representation effect refers to emphasizing situations where individuals are most affected when making decisions, not considering the analysis of other situations and making decisions under this effect. In this model, the incomplete reaction is expressed by conservatism, and the extreme reaction is expressed by representation.

Daniel, Hirshleifer, and Subrahmanyam's excessive confidence and self-attribution models are based on the kind of confidence that affected self-attribution and self-excessive confidence of investors. According to model, individuals attribute partial by asserting that decisions resulted by earnings emerged by themselves; however, decisions resulted losses emerged by external factors.

According to Hong and Stein's interactive relationship model between investors, there are two investor types: momentum investors and news hunters. Momentum investors are investors who accept previous price movements as a fundamental knowledge. News hunters are investors who act by knowledge that is explained to the public or will be explained. Both types of investors which are not rational totally are accepted limited rational.

Behavioral finance models reveal that individuals' rationality which is basic assumption of conventional finance models are destroyed because of the kind of sociological and psychological factors. Individuals fall into the same mistakes since they have similar prejudices. Mistakes in decision-making process are based on four main reasons. These can be ranged as self-deception, cognitive bias, emotion, and social interactions.

Self-deception brings about emerging of bias such as overconfidence bias, optimism bias, self-attribution bias, confirmation bias, hindsight bias, cognitive bias, and conservatism bias. The most prevailed bias among cognitive bias causing that individual's fall into mistake while deciding can be ranged as representativeness heuristic, framing effect, anchoring heuristics, loss aversion, cognitive conflict, confirmation bias, conservative dissonance, and conservatism bias. Emotional bias ranges as mood, ambiguity aversion, regret aversion, and self-control. Influencing of individuals' decisions as a result of behavioral bias which society shares is clarified by herding behavior and information cascade.

Anomalies which point out as deviations in efficient market hypothesis are scrutinized as periodical anomalies, firm anomalies, and price anomalies. Periodical anomalies comprise of hourly, daily, weekly, monthly, and yearly or before or later of a periodic term. It is possible to diversify the price anomalies as firm size anomalies and neglected firm anomalies.

Anomalies emerge as a result of divergence of rationality and investor bias. For example, it can be asserted that, as a result of overoptimism bias, excessive reaction anomaly is seen in the stock price. When thinking that the shortcut of representation is the matching of good stocks and good companies, it could be fenced that it could be the manner of firm size anomaly. The view of supportive side of the day of a week anomy could be seen as spirit mood of emotional bias. Generally speaking, investors' bias cause their wrong decisions. In this situation, it is resulted as departing of markets from effectiveness and emerging of kind of anomalies. From this point of view, investors' bias could be said the import reason of anomalies seen in markets. The relationship between anomalies and investor must be revealed by empirical studies.

References

Ahn, D., Choi, S., Gale, D., & Kariv, S. (2014). Estimating ambiguity aversion in a portfolio choice experiment. *Quantitative Economics, 5*, 195–223.

Amenc, N., & Sourd, V. L. (2003). *Portfolio theory and performance analysis*. West Sussex: Wiley.

Aronson, D. (2007). *Evidence based technical analysis*. Hoboken, NJ: Wiley.

Barak, O. (2008). *Davranışsal Finans Teori ve Uygulama*. Ankara: Gazi Kitabevi.

Barak, O., & Demirelli, E. (2006). İMKB'de Gözlemlenen Fiyat Anomalilerinin Davranışsal Finans Modelleri Kapsamında Değerlendirilmesi, 10.Ulusal Finans Sempozyumu: Küreselleşme Sürecinde İşletmelerin Finans Yönetimi, 1–4 Kasım 2006, İzmir.

Barberis, N., Shleifer, A., & Vishny, R. (1998). A model of investor sentiment. *Journal of Financial Economics, 49*(3), 307–343.

Benartzi, S., & Thaler, R. H. (1993). *Myopic loss aversion and the equity premium puzzle* (pp. 1–27). NBER Working Paper, No: 4369.

Bikhchandani, S., Hirshleifer, D., & Welch, I. (1992). A theory of fads, fashion, custom and cultural change as information cascade. *Journal of Political Economy, 100*(5), 992–1026.

Binswanger, M. (1999). *Stock markets, speculative bubbles and economic growth: New dimensions in the co-evolution of real and financial markets.* Northampton: Edward Elgar.

Böyükaslan, A. (2012). Bireysel Yatırımcıları Finansal Yatırım Kararına Yönlendiren Faktörlerin Davranışsal Finans Açısından İncelenmesi: Afyonkarahisar Örneği, Afyon Kocatepe Üniversitesi Sosyal Bilimler Enstitüsü, Afyon.

Brealey, R. A., Myers, S. C., & Marcus, A. J. (2007). *İşletme Finansının Temelleri.* (Beşinci Basım), (Çevirenler:Ünal Bozkurt, Türkan Arıkan, Hatice Doğukanlı), Literatür Yayıncılık.

Ceylan, A., & Korkmaz T. (2006). *İşletmelerde Finansal Yönetim.* Ekin Kitapevi, Güncelleştirilmiş 9. Baskı, Bursa.

Chang, E., Cheng, J., & Khorana, A. (2000). An examination of herd behavior in equity markets: An international perspective. *Journal of Banking and Finance, 24*(10), 1651–1679.

Daniel, K., Hirshleifer, D., & Subrahmanyam, A. (1998). Investor psychology and security market under- and overreactions. *Journal of Finance, 53*(6), 1839–1885.

Dave, C., & Wolfe, W. K. (2003, March 21). On confirmation bias and deviations from Bayesian updating. Retrieved from www.peel.pit.edu/esa2003/papers/wolfe_confirmationbias.pdf.

Dimson, E., & Mussavian, M. (1998). A brief history of market efficiency. *European Financial Management, 4*(1), 91–103.

Ding, Z., Granger, C. W. J., & Engle, R. F. A. (1993). Long memory property of stock market and a new model. *Journal of Empirical Finance, 1,* 83–106.

Edwards, D. R., Magee, J., & Bassetti, W. H. C. (2013). *Technical analysis of stock trends* (10th ed.). Boca Raton, FL: CRC Press.

Elton, E. J., & Gruber, M. J. (1991). *Modern portfolio theory and investment analysis* (4th ed.). New York: Wiley.

Ergün, B. (2009). *Piyasa Anomalileri ve Aşırı Tepki Hipotezinin İMKB'de Araştırılması.* Adana: Çukurova Üniversitesi Sosyal Bilimler Enstitüsü.

Fabozzi, F. J., Sergio, M. F., & Peter, N. K. (2006). *Financial modeling of the equity market: From CAPM to cointegration.* New York: Wiley.

Fama, E. F. (1970). Efficient capital markets: A review of theory and empirical work. *Journal of Finance, 25,* 338–417.

Francis, J. C. (1993). *Management of investments* (3rd ed.). New York: McGrawHill.

Hirshleifer, D. (2001). Investor psychology and asset pricing. *Journal of Finance, 56*(4), 1533–1597.

Hong, H., & Stein, J. C. (1999). A unified theory of underreaction, momentum trading and over-reaction in asset markets. *Journal of Finance, 54*(6), 2143–2184.

Iqbal, N. (2015). Impact of optimism bias on investment decision: Evidence from Islamabad Stock Exchange – Pakistan. *Research Journal of Finance and Accounting, 6*(19), 74–79.

Jaya, M. P., Kapoor, S., & Sengupta, J. (2010). Theory of behavioral finance. In Z. Çopur (Ed.), *Handbook of research on behavioral finance and investment strategies: Decision making in the financial industry.* Hershey: IGI Global.

Kahneman, D., & Tversky, A. (1974). Judgements under uncertainty: Heuristics and biases. *Science, 185*(4157), 1124–1131.

Kahneman, D., & Tversky, A. (1979). Prospect theory: An analysis of decision under risk. *Econometrica, 47*(2), 263–292.

Kıyılar, M. (1997). Etkin Pazar Kuramı ve Etkin Pazar Kuramının İMKB'de İrdelenmesi, SPK Yayınları No:86, Ankara.

Lawrance, A. (2001). *Behavioral finance and investor governance.* CardPublic Law and Legal Theory Research Paper Series, Working Paper, 18.

Lintner, J. (1965). Security prices, risk and maximal gains from diversification. *Journal of Finance, 20*(4), 587–615.

Luce, R. D., & Howard, R. (1989). *Games and decisions: Introduction and critical survey.* New York: Dover Publications.

Merton, R. C. (1973). An intertemporal capital asset pricing model. *Econometrica, 41*(5), 867.

Mossin, J. (1966). Equilibrium in a capital asset market. *Econometrica, 34*(4), 768–783.

Nofsinger, J. R. (2001). *Investment madness: How psychology affects your investing and what to do about it.* Hoboken, NJ: Pearson Education.

Nofsinger, J. R. (2002). *The psychology of investing.* Hoboken, NJ: Pearson Education.

Özan, M. H. (2010). İşletmelerde Alınan Finansal Kararların Yatırımcı Davranışları Üzerindeki Etkilerinin İncelenmesi, Dokuz Eylül Üniversitesi Sosyal Bilimler Enstitüsü, Yayımlanmamış Yüksek Lisans Tezi, İzmir.

Pachur, T., Hertwig, R., & Steinmann, F. (2012). How do people judge risks: Availability heuristic, affect heuristic, or both? *Journal of Experimental Psychology: Applied, 18*(3), 314–330.

Peterson, R. L. (2007). *Inside the investor's brain: The power of mind over money.* Hoboken, NJ: Wiley.

Plummer, T. (2003). *Forecasting financial markets: The psychology of successful investing.* London: Koran Page Ltd.

Pompian, M. M. (2006). *Behavioral finance and wealth management: How to build optimal portfolios that account for investor biases.* Hoboken, NJ: Wiley.

Ricciardi, V., & Simon, H. K. (2000). What is behavioral finance? *Business, Education & Technology Journal, 2*(2), 1–9.

Rizzi, J. V. (2008). Behavioral basis of the financial crisis. *Journal of Applied Finance, XVIII*(2), 84–96.

Sharpe, W. F. (1964). Capital asset prices: A theory of market equilibrium under conditions of risk. *Journal of Finance, 19*(3), 425–442.

Shiller, R. J. (2001). *Human behaviour and the efficiency of the financial system* (pp. 1305–1340). Cowles Foundation Paper No.1025.

Suetens, S., & Tyran, J. R. (2012). The gambler's fallacy and gender. *Journal of Economic Behavior and Organization, 83*(1), 118–124.

Thaler, R. (1985). Mental accounting and consumer choice. *Marketing Science, 4*(3), 199–214.

Thomsett, M. C. (1998). *Mastering fundamental analysis.* Chicago: Dearborn Financial Publishing.

Ülkü, N. (2001, Ocak/Şubat/Mart). Finansta Davranış Teorileri ve İMKB'nin Dezenflasyon Programının Başlangıcında Fiyat Davranışı. İMKB Dergisi, c.5, sy.17, pp. 101–132.

Wright, W., & Bower, G. (1992). Mood effects on subjective probability assessment. *Organizational Behavior and Human Decision Process, 52*(2), 276–291.

Chapter 16
Global Macroeconomic Determinants of the Domestic Commodity Derivatives

Cagatay Basarir and Mehmet Fatih Bayramoglu

Abstract Countries compete with products which have an absolute advantage in foreign trade operations. Also, there are derivative financial instruments derived from these products in many developing financial markets. Thus, these products provide opportunities for investors such as speculation, arbitrage, and particularly hedging with the help of trading in derivative markets. The trading of these products on derivative markets also brings about the impact of global parameters on spot markets, as well as on futures markets. Hence, it is important for both real investors and financial investors to determine and observe the major macroeconomic variables that affect these products.

This chapter aims to determine macroeconomic variables which affect domestic (local) commodity derivatives such as banana (Central America and Ecuador), palm oil (Malaysia), rice (Thailand), and tea (Kenya). Thereby when the market efficiency is weak or almost absent, the ability to lower the fragility against risks faced by the investors and the other related parties by maintaining advance information is analyzed. For this purpose, K* (K Star) algorithm as a data mining method which is one of the knowledge-based analysis techniques is used in the analysis. In this chapter, four derivative products were estimated by the K* algorithm, which predicts whether their direction will decrease or increase during the next 18 months. The results show that the K* algorithm predicts an accuracy of 66.7–72.2% for three of the four domestic commodity derivatives so that this algorithm is successful in identifying similar properties between global macroeconomic variables and domestic commodity derivatives.

C. Basarir
Bandirma Onyedi Eylul University, Bandirma, Turkey
e-mail: cbasarir@bandirma.edu.tr

M. F. Bayramoglu (✉)
Bulent Ecevit University, Zonguldak, Turkey
e-mail: fatih.bayramoglu@beun.edu.tr

© Springer International Publishing AG, part of Springer Nature 2018   331
H. Dincer et al. (eds.), *Global Approaches in Financial Economics, Banking, and Finance*, Contributions to Economics, https://doi.org/10.1007/978-3-319-78494-6_16

Introduction

Broadly defined, derivative contracts are financial agreements made between two or more parties based upon the predetermined asset or assets to purchase or sell some other type of financial instrument or nonfinancial asset on today depending on the future value of this asset or assets. Derivative markets are the markets in which those contracts are traded. In other words, these markets can be defined as the markets in which commerce of some goods or financial instruments on today due to a future delivery or cash settlement is merchandised (Aydın et al. 2007: 520, 531). An options contract is an agreement between a buyer and seller that gives the buyer side of the option or the right to buy or sell a particular asset at a later date at an agreed-upon price in a return of a price called option premium (Akgüç 1998: 732).

Investors make their decisions under a permanent environment of the uncertainty of the prices of commodity, interest rates, and exchange rates to get a stable level in the future. Derivative products have emerged from the efforts of decision-making investors trying to hedge the risks arising from the uncertainty of the financial environments. Derivative products can be held both to hedge derived from the uncertainty and price movements and to aim arbitrage and speculation operations.

Parties of the financial system that are under the influence of globalization aim to keep their activities in a safe place where it is most suitable for them. Therefore, financial risks occur as a result of taking place in global product trade and financial or direct investments. As known by everyone interested in finance, all businesses aim to protect their capital and maximize profits. But there are obstacles in front of these goals such as exchange rate risk, market risk, credit risk, interest rate risk, and liquidity risk (Coşkun 2007: 60). Hence, taking a position in different financial markets is seen as a way to hedge faced risks and preserve profit maximization (Kurar and Çetin 2016: 404).

Past financial crises have led investors to use differentiated financial ways to eliminate risks. The economic downturn has contributed investors who want to hedge their profits and investments against all financial risks to search for new profitable ways such as arbitrage, speculation, and derivatives like forwards, futures, swaps, and options. Aside from the advantages of arbitrage and speculation by gaining benefits from price movements, derivatives are seen as game-changing financial instruments to assist investors to spread and prevent the risk. In this context, derivatives are used to reduce borrowing costs and borrowing capacity and to increase firm's net flows. Especially in developed countries, the prevalence of derivative instruments in the use of risk protection is mostly related to exchange rate, interest rate, and price risk (Akgiray 1998: 10).

When hedging methods shine out and the use of derivatives becomes a question, it is crucial to have enough knowledge about the market. According to the efficient market hypothesis, prices of all securities on the market include whole information, news, and related anticipations (Bayraktar 2012: 38). In other words, the concept of market efficiency is defined as complete procurable information that refer to and influence prices of the securities (assets) (Karan 2001: 268). This definition means that every investor in the market would have almost the same data which means gaining extraordinary profits with the same knowledge could not be possible. In brief, it is right that forecasting prices of the derivatives and maintaining advance information have a vital role in getting the edge on markets.

After the emergence and the use of derivatives in financial markets, usage of derivatives in commodity markets did not take ages to become available (Ghosh 2011: 287). Commodity derivatives are known as innovative financial instruments for commodity market participants (Masood and Chary 2016: 131). Including futures and options as well as forwards, commodity derivatives promise a fairly wide range of financial investment choices (Basu and Gavin 2011: 37).

It is known that many financial managers added commodity derivatives to their portfolios as an asset because of their potential benefits. Lately, financial agenda is respective about commodity derivatives, and that brings substantial growth to the commodity derivative markets. Since every commodity is a part of exemplary international spot trade system, derivatives are seen as a profitable replacement for international spot commodity trade (Geman 2005: 6). As almost all well-known characteristics of financial derivatives are valid in the commodity derivative markets, the influence of maintaining information on reducing risks and fragility of investors is a subject which is worthy to investigate.

For this reason, in this chapter, the authors seek to analyze the relationship between the international macroeconomics indicators and domestic commodity derivatives using K* algorithm which is considered as a lazy learning-based data mining method and machine learning technique. Thus, it has been tested whether the derivatives with a comparative advantage in certain regions can be modeled with international macroeconomic variables with a glocal approach.

The organization of the rest of the chapter is as follows. Second section provides a quick glance on derivatives and commodity derivatives. Third section provides a general, albeit a brief, theoretical framework and literature review. Fourth section provides definition and description of the concept of the $K*$ (K Star) algorithm which is one of the data mining methods and machine learning techniques. Fifth section consists of the aim of the application, the data, modeling, and application of the model. Sixth section presents the findings and evaluations. Last section provides conclusions.

The Derivatives and the Commodity Derivatives

The derivatives are financial instruments defined in the context of commodity prices, foreign exchange rates, interest rates, and stock indices. Those instruments can be traded in organized stock markets or even in over-the-counter markets restricted between bank and investors. Many products take place in derivative markets depending on interest rates, exchange rates, stock markets, equity shares, and commodity prices.

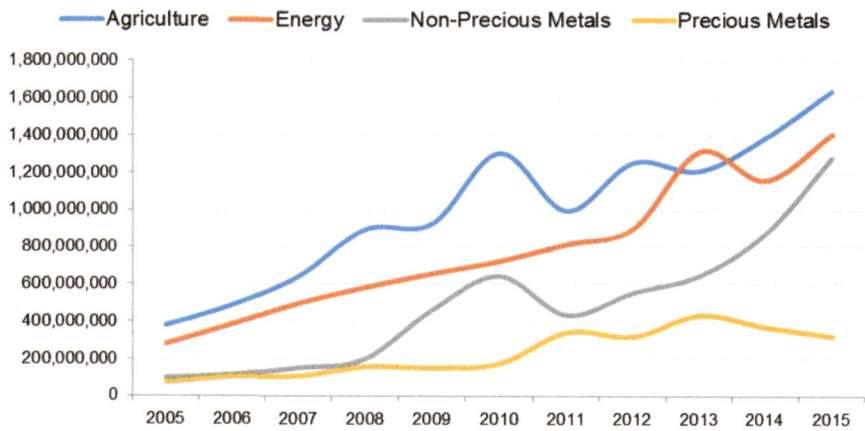

Fig. 16.1 Contracts traded (US dollars). *Source*: W. Acworth (2016). *Asia Takes the Lead*. FIA 2015 Annual Survey: Global Derivatives Volume

Initial examples of futures contracts are the agreements depending on goods or commodities. First examples are observed in Osaka stock market in the 1600s and become a regular operation after the introduction of Chicago stock exchange in the 1880s. After the 1980s, derivative markets have reached high transaction volumes by financial managers, have become increasingly popular, and have widely used hedging and investment method (Ersan 2003: 7).

Global derivative instruments are seen to reach record levels in 2016 (Acworth 2017). Recognizing that most of the money flows in the world is based on capital and financial flows, hence trade-based money flow has a petty share in money flow of the global economy. In this sense, it seems fairly normal for the hedge fund structure of financial derivatives to reach a record level in 2016; for this reason, there is no natural condition than the wealthy investors wanting to protect themselves from the risk in this money stream surrounding the world (Commodity Fact 2017). At the point where derivative products reached, investments on futures are seen remarkable since it is regularly increasing every year for the last 5 years (Acworth 2017).

Contracts traded in world markets between 2005 and 2015 are given in Fig. 16.1. When looking at Fig. 16.1, commodity contracts of futures and options of energy, agriculture, precious metals, and non-precious metals increased by 22.6% from $0.9 billion to $4.6 billion. These four categories made a peak point for the four sorts of them. At present, commodity futures and options are 19% of total global trading volume. Agricultural category increased from 18.1% which makes $1.6 billion contracts, energy category increased to 21.2% which makes $1.4 billion, and non-precious metals category increased to 46.8% which makes $1.3 billion. After this peak points of these three sectors, trading of derivative operations has proceeded much more. After this increasing trend, more futures and options traded worldwide based on commodities than interest rates and almost as many as individual equities in our day (Acworth 2016).

Today, developed international commodity markets have been leading the growth of derivative products with their growth trends (Khosla 2012: 7). As a result, the growth of derivative products has become one of the determinants of exchange rates in the world with the anticipation of future investments through occurring expectations about prices. This has become a paradox and has led to hedge the foreign currencies obtained or expected from sold goods and services with derivative products. In this context, it is considered impossible to distinguish between capital markets and trade.

Derivatives offer financial managers great advantages in risk management by hedging against price differences. Determining futures prices in derivative markets regarding market efficiency makes it easier for investors to make safer investments. Also, as derivative products have an insurance function regarding returns, hedging transaction made at low cost causes transaction fees to decrease (Francis 2012).

With all these features, derivative products grew by 1.7% in 2016 (Acworth 2017) compared to the previous year, and transaction volume increased to $25.22 billion (BIS 2016). Looking at the world trade, it is seen that the total trade volume of the world is $16.055 trillion (World Bank 2017). The volume of the commodity derivative market is about $1.35 billion (BIS 2016) which shows that it is prone to protect the returns from risks or for profit-making investments of the commodities that are related to world trade.

Futures, options, or swap contracts may be the subject of commodity derivatives. Traders who invest in this market are different from traders who trade in spot markets. The main reason for this difference is that large companies that make international spot trading are acting as intermediaries between consumer and producer. In commodity derivative markets, traders are composed of hedgers, speculators, and arbitrageurs (Kowalski 2017; Khosla 2012: 8). The role of these participants is already known in the financial system.

Therefore, financial and commodity derivative products, which are clearly aimed at using in the financial system, are also important in the commodity trading system. The analysis of the opportunities and threats to be presented to investors regarding size and content of these markets stands as a matter to be studied in the field of the academy or the business world in economics and finance. In this context, the analysis of the factors affecting the prices of some commodities on which this study is based will shed light on future researchers who will study commodity derivatives.

Table 16.1 shows the most traded futures and options contracts in agricultural products. We can conclude from the table that the most widely traded agricultural product is soybean meal futures having a volume of US$290 million, and the tenth traded agricultural product is sugar futures having a volume of US$34 million in 2015. When we analyze the year of 2014, we see that the most widely traded agricultural product is rapeseed meal futures contracts having a volume of US$304 million, and the tenth traded agricultural product is corn futures. When we compare the rate of changes from 2014 to 2015, we see that all the futures contracts except rubber and rapeseed meal futures increased, and the biggest share of this increase results from corn futures with a 351% increase. While these futures contracts had the least volume in 2014, they had the biggest rise in 2015. It can be emphasized that

Table 16.1 Top ten agricultural futures and options contracts (million USD)

Rank	Contracts	Jan–Dec 2015	Jan–Dec 2014	Change
1	Soybean meal futures	289,496,780	204,988,746	41.20%
2	Rapeseed meal (RM) futures	261,487,209	303,515,966	−13.80%
3	White sugar (SR) futures	187,323,456	97,726,662	91.70%
4	RBD palm olein futures	111,515,010	79,996,388	39.40%
5	Soybean oil futures	92,504,264	64,082,631	44.40%
6	Corn futures	83,094,271	69,437,304	19.70%
7	Rubber futures	83,067,547	88,631,586	−6.30%
8	Soybean futures	54,095,051	49,169,361	10.00%
9	Corn futures	42,090,235	9,329,939	351.10%
10	Sugar futures	34,394,482	29,396,597	17.00%

Source: Acworth, W. (2017). Global Futures and Options Volume Reaches Record Level. FIA 2016 Annual Volume Survey: Global Futures and Options Volume Reaches Record Level

commodity contracts have drawn a rising interest increasingly. Investors now pay attention to not only financial derivative products but also commodity products such as energy agriculture and metals.

Theoretical Framework and Literature Review

After the 1990s, many investors empowered their portfolios with domestic (local) commodity derivatives (Valle et al. 2017: 1). Especially in last decade, commodity derivative markets multiplied its importance (Cheng et al. 2017: 2). With this interest in domestic commodity derivatives, trade volume of related products and financial instruments showed enormous growth (Lai and Mellios 2016: 402). Why did international trade and finance system need a commodity derivative choice? This question must be on the front burner of people who are concerned about finance after the realization of great importance originated by commodity derivatives. Dummu (2009: 335) explained the cause of the existence of domestic commodity derivatives in an easy way with remarking agricultural production capacity. This issue can be addressed with production intensity of domestic goods in gross domestic product (GDP). According to past studies, production of the domestic agricultural goods led to a search for new financial hedging methods in an attempt to maximize profits in commodity industry (Dummu 2009; Karamala 2013; Ghosh 2009). Observed increases in financial investments in agricultural commodity derivatives showed financial sphere a new approach to the assessment of intense agricultural production (Clapp and Helleiner 2012: 183). With this approach, agricultural products regarded as ordinary food are now seen as commodities.

Well-developed commodity spot markets are seen as authentic places to find out decent prices for related commodities. When price inspections began, information about markets becomes a big deal. However, gaining information is quite important for investors. Almost all parties in the market get the same amount of information, except some advanced receivers. While a spot commodity market could be seen as a market which effectiveness is related to its structure, commodity derivative markets considered as effectiveness is about possessed information contained and distributed in the market (Nath and Lingareddy 2008: 2).

Previous studies in the literature indicate that most domestic spot commodity markets have existed in the past with their alternative derivative markets (Masood and Chary 2016; Geman 2005; Goodwin and Schnepf 2000). Domestic commodity derivative markets include mostly futures contracts (Karamala 2013; Nair 2004; Goodwin and Schnepf 2000; Dummu 2009). For example, Masood and Chary (2016: 137) investigated 21 commodity futures exchanges in India including such as almond, barley, bajra, castor seed, coconut oil, palm oil, and wheat. Natanelov et al. (2011: 4980) analyzed some domestic derivatives consisting of cocoa, rice, soybeans, corn, coffee, and sugar. Arismendi et al. (2016: 58) took a light on the relationship between corn derivative prices and gasoline prices. As can be seen in the literature, the domestic derivatives highly diversified concerning agricultural production. Therefore, it is of crucial importance to know what influences prices in local and global commodity derivative markets. Consequently, in the next part of this section, authors handled related empirical studies that have been done in the past.

The effect of seasons on the production of agricultural products is the fact that everyone knows. Domestic commodity derivative prices and markets are influenced by geographical location conditions as well as each domestic good. Valle et al. (2017) brought a light on this issue and investigated the effects of the seasonal components on commodity option and futures prices in New York Mercantile Exchange (NYMEX). Also, they found that there are considerable key differences in the prices related to seasonality. On the other hand, the need to earn money and gain profit is not a seasonal target. Obtaining yields is one of the primary objectives of all financial transactions. Lai and Mellios (2016) wanted to reach the little-known and tried to forecast commodity futures prices by using unobservable yields.

What about speculators? Any professional could say that buying commodities or using derivatives in a risky trend might bring some benefits such as high return opportunity if forestalling is possible. Accordingly, taking risks and aiming profits by price and condition differences can be highly profitable. Hence, Haase et al. (2016) observed 100 empirical studies to reveal the impact of speculation on commodity futures markets including wheat, soybeans, corn, coffee, rice, feeder cattle, cocoa, orange, and sugar. Results show that speculation does not affect domestic agricultural commodity futures. Miffre and Brooks (2013) supported this study with finding out that speculators could not alter prices and risks by their trades. Speculation is also about spot prices of commodities. Causality between futures and spot prices of domestic commodity markets and its strength, extent, and direction is examined by Joseph and his work group in 2014. The study uses data of selected commodity futures prices such as soybean and reveals that there is a strong relationship between futures and spot prices which is directed from futures to spot. The study suggests that futures have a function of forecasting in commodity derivative markets by meaning indication of the efficiency of domestic commodity derivative markets.

In a study investigating the effect of different variables on prices in domestic commodity derivative markets, forecasting power, market structure, and seasonality variables are used to understand agricultural derivative prices just as cocoa, coffee, corn, cotton, orange juice, soybean, and wheat. Brooks et al. (2013) found that while forecasting power has a reinforcing effect on price changes and market structure is related to prices, there is no evidence to infer that seasonal changes ease forecasting process. The study also conveys that commodity derivative prices might differ according to geopolitical and economic conditions of countries.

Lazy Learning and K Star Algorithm

Lazy learning is a machine learning method in which generalization beyond the training data is deferred until a request is sent to the system, in contrast to in eager learning, where the system tries to generalize the training data before receiving requests (Hormozi et al. 2012: 562). In other words, lazy learning is a local learning method that stores the training instances and does no real work till classification time (Vijayarani and Muthulakshmi 2013: 3121).

As a local learning approach, lazy learning has a useful approach to a wide variety of tasks, particularly those characterized by an evolving training distribution where frequent retraining is inapplicable and those tasks where the training set is too large to train global learners (Garcia et al. 2010: 1283).

Lazy learning algorithms have three behaviors that distinguish them from other learning algorithms: (1) they store all instances as a training data and defer processing of the instances until they receive requests for information, (2) they respond to information requests by combining their recorded data, and (3) after responding a question, the answer and interim results are discarded (Wettschereck et al. 1997: 274–275).

Instance-based learners, like lazy learning, classify an instance by comparing it to a database of pre-classified examples. "The basic assumption is that similar instances will have similar classifications. The questions are asked lies in how to define similar instance and similar classification?" (Cleary and Trigg 1995: 110–113). As an instance-based algorithm, the K* (K Star) seeks to answer this question.

The K* algorithm can be defined as an instance-based learning algorithm of classification analysis which mainly aims at the partition of "n" instances into "k" classes in which each instance belongs to the class with the nearest mean (Vijayarani and Muthulakshmi 2013: 3121).

The K* algorithm uses entropy-based distance function which calculates the mean of the complexity of transforming an instance into another, which makes itself different from other classifiers. The K* algorithm make classification using sums of the probabilities from the instance to all of the members of a category. Finally, the K* algorithm selects the highest probability (Hernandez 2015: 14). So, the K* algorithm has two advantages for users. First, the K* algorithm operates rapidly which only needs to find out the stored vertices by searching in the memory. Second, the K* algorithm uses a heuristic evaluation function for a target-guided search (Haufe 2017: 3).

N is a set of instances, and M is a finite set of transformations of N. Each $m \in M$ maps instances to instances: $m : N \rightarrow N$. M has a distinguished number σ which for completeness maps instances to themselves ($\sigma(x) = x$). P is the set of all prefix codes from M^* which are terminated by σ. Members of M^* uniquely define a transformation on N (Cleary and Trigg 1995: 110–113):

$$\bar{m}(a) = m_n(m_{n-1}(\ldots m_1(a)\ldots)), \bar{m} = m_1, \ldots, m_n \qquad (16.1)$$

p is a probability function which is defined on M^* and fulfills the following properties:

$$0 \leq \frac{p(\bar{m}u)}{p(\bar{m})} \leq 1 \qquad (16.2)$$

$$\sum_u p(\bar{m}u) = p(\bar{m}) \qquad (16.3)$$

$$p(\Lambda) = 1 \qquad (16.4)$$

As a result, it meets in below:

$$\sum_{\bar{m} \in P} p(\bar{m}) = 1 \qquad (16.5)$$

P^* is defined as the probability of all paths from instance x to instance y

$$P^*(y|x) = \sum_{\bar{m} \in P : \bar{m}(x)=y} p(\bar{m}) \qquad (16.6)$$

So, P^* performs the following properties:

$$\sum_y P^*(y|x) = 1 \qquad (16.7)$$

$$0 \leq P^*(y|x) \leq 1 \qquad (16.8)$$

Then, the K^* function can be defined as

$$K^*(y|x) = -\log_2 P^*(y|x) \qquad (16.9)$$

Then, we can specify the effective number of instances with the function given below:

$$s_0 \leq \frac{\left(\sum\limits_{y} P^*(y|x) \right)^2}{\sum\limits_{y} P^*(y|z)^2} \leq S \tag{16.10}$$

where s_0 is the number of training instances at the smallest distance from a and S is the total number of training instances. Formerly, we can make category prediction with the following equation:

$$P^*(H|x) = \sum_{y \in H} P^*(y|x) \tag{16.11}$$

We calculate the probability of an instance x being in category H by summing the probabilities from x to each instance that is a member of H (Cleary and Trigg 1995: 110–113).

Application

The Aim of the Chapter

The financial assets traded in the market are influenced by many economic and financial factors according to both theoretical and empirical literature. Therefore, determining the economic and financial factors that are affecting on a financial product, especially in the markets that are in inefficiency or weak-form efficiency, can positively affect the ability of investors to be protected from risks through a proactive approach and to have abnormal returns.

In this chapter, the authors focused on the determination of international macro-economic variables affecting domestic (local) commodity derivatives by using K* algorithm which is a data mining method and machine learning technique. Thus, it has been tested whether the derivatives with a comparative advantage in certain regions can be modeled with international macroeconomic variables with a glocal approach. By this purpose; the global macroeconomic input variables shown in Table 16.1 were used to estimate the direction of the price movements for the next 18 months for domestic commodity derivatives which are banana (Central America and Ecuador), palm oil (Malaysia), rice (Thailand), and tea (Kenya). Also, it has been investigated that domestic derivatives could be foreseen using the input variables employed in this chapter.

Table 16.2 Input and output variables

Input (independent) variables	
Macroeconomic variables	Data source
Brent Europe crude oil spot price (per barrel)	US Energy Information Administration (EIA)
DAX 100 stock market index	Yahoo Finance
FED monthly interest rate	Federal Reserve Economic Data (FRED)
Gold price (USD per ounce)	CBRT EDDS
Index of industrial production of the USA	Federal Reserve Economic Data (FRED)
CNY/USD exchange rate	Reuters
Nikkei 225 stock market index	Yahoo Finance
S&P 500 stock market index	Yahoo Finance
EUR/USD exchange rate	Reuters
JPY/USD exchange rate	Reuters
Output (dependent) variables	
Domestic commodity derivatives	Data source
Banana futures prices	Index Mundi Country Facts
Palm oil futures prices	Index Mundi Country Facts
Rice futures prices	Index Mundi Country Facts
Tea futures prices	Index Mundi Country Facts

The Data

The data set covers from January 1999 to June 2017 to classify the price movements of the input (independent) and output (dependent) variables. Input and output variables and the data sources for these variables are shown in Table 16.2.

As can be seen Table 16.2, all input variables are international macroeconomic variables including oil price, interest rate, gold price, industrial production index, exchange rates, and stock market indices. Output variables are four domestic (local) commodity derivatives from the food industry group: banana is in the fruits group, palm oil is in the vegetable oils group, rice is in the cereals group, and tea is in the beverages group.

The input variables which are international macroeconomic indicators used in this study are selected based on macro-finance literature and geographically approach. For all variables, the frequency period is monthly price averages and used in analysis without any statistical transformations. Another characteristic of the input variables is that they contain numerical data. Output variables contain verbal (string) data as "decrease" and "increase," and their nominal transformations were made.

The values of the input variable are obtained for the period between January 1999 and May 2017, and the values of the output variable are obtained for the period between February 1999 and June 2017. Period of output variables start and end 1 month later because the output variable depends on the previous month values of the input variables. The length of the data set is determined as 221 months, and data in the 1–203 interval (92% of the database) are used as the test data set for model development. 204–221 interval is used for prediction (classifying the price directions of the domestic commodity derivatives).

Table 16.3 shows that the correlation between the ten international macroeconomic variables (input variables) and the four domestic commodity derivatives (output variables). The variables that are seen in the positive correlations except for FED monthly interest rates and Nikkei 225 stock market index. While there is a negative correlation between FED monthly interest rates and all domestic commodity derivatives, the Nikkei 225 index is negatively correlated with palm oil and rice futures. Correlations among the international macroeconomic variables are negative or positive, while correlations between the domestic commodity derivatives are positive.

Modeling

In this section, an application has been made to classify the price movements of the next 18 months of derivatives with the K* (K Star) algorithm. As explained in the fourth part, the K* algorithm has a sample-based classification technique and works on a simple method based on the principle of categorizing samples with similar properties to the same classes. For this purpose, the K* algorithm identifies the features in the test data set; then it classifies the instances in the class accordingly.

In this study, a matrix of "11 × 221" length consisting of ten input and one output variables shown in Table 16.1 is prepared as a database. Since there are four output variables in the study, this matrix is prepared separately for each output variable. This database is intended for determining the features of the input variables by K* algorithm and classifying the price movements of output variables as "decrease" or "increase" according to the determined features of the input variables.

Therefore, this process is repeated for each output variable with four different databases being prepared.

Thus, these properties obtained by the K* algorithm as a result of the test process are also used when estimating that the price movements of the local derivatives over the next 18 months by the K* algorithm. The application was made with Weka 3.8 which is the world's most widely used open source data mining and machine learning software.

Empirical Findings and Evaluation

Since the analysis by K* algorithm is performed for four domestic (local) commodity derivatives, the research findings in Tables 16.4, 16.5, 16.6 and 16.7 should be evaluated separately for each domestic derivative.

When looking at the prediction results of the banana futures from Table 16.4, the K* algorithm has classified the price movements over the next 18 months with an

Table 16.3 Correlation coefficients between input and output variables

ρ	Brent oil	DAX 100	FED I. R.	Gold	IIP of the USA	CNY/ USD	JPY/ USD	EUR/ USD	Nikkei 225	S&P 500	Banana	Palm oil	Rice	Tea
Brent oil	1.00													
DAX 100	0.33	1.00												
FED I. R.	−0.44	−0.23	1.00											
Gold	0.80	0.59	−0.70	1.00										
IIP of the USA	0.47	0.71	−0.08	0.45	1.00									
CNY/USD	0.75	0.67	−0.72	0.94	0.47	1.00								
JPY/USD	0.67	0.02	−0.48	0.71	−0.09	0.56	1.00							
EUR/USD	0.78	0.05	−0.36	0.55	0.31	0.50	0.54	1.00						
Nikkei 225	−0.17	0.69	0.38	−0.06	0.56	0.05	−0.50	−0.23	1.00					
S&P 500	0.20	0.95	−0.17	0.46	0.75	0.54	−0.13	−0.05	0.75	1.00				
Banana	0.68	0.64	−0.65	0.88	0.49	0.88	0.50	0.47	0.04	0.52	1.00			
Palm oil	0.85	0.35	−0.55	0.83	0.35	0.75	0.70	0.74	−0.19	0.22	0.72	1.00		
Rice	0.79	0.26	−0.54	0.76	0.22	0.75	0.67	0.74	−0.23	0.10	0.72	0.80	1.00	
Tea	0.52	0.50	−0.46	0.76	0.19	0.69	0.62	0.33	0.03	0.37	0.69	0.59	0.65	1.00

Table 16.4 Prediction results for banana futures

Confusion matrix			Class-based results (decrease and increase)		Overall results		
	Decrease	Increase	Correctly classified	True number of instances	Correctly classified (MAPE)	Correctly classified	Kappa statistic[a]
Decrease	3	4	0.4286%	3/7	0.3889%	7/18	−0.1928
Increase	7	4	0.3636%	4/11			

Source: A. J. Viera & J. M. Garrett (2005). Understanding Interobserver Agreement: The Kappa Statistic. *Fam Med*, *37*(5), 360–363
MAPE mean absolute percentage error
[a]$\kappa < 0$ "poor agreement"; $0.01 < \kappa < 0.20$ "slight agreement"; $0.21 < \kappa < 0.40$ "fair agreement"; $0.41 < \kappa < 0.60$ "moderate agreement"; $0.61 < \kappa < 0.80$ "substantial agreement"; $0.81 < \kappa < 1.00$ "almost perfect agreement"

Table 16.5 Prediction results for palm oil futures

Confusion matrix			Class-based results (decrease and increase)		Overall results		
	Decrease	Increase	Correctly classified	True number of instances	Correctly classified (MAPE)	Correctly classified	Kappa statistic[a]
Decrease	6	3	0.6667%	6/9	0.7222%	13/18	0.4444
Increase	2	7	0.7778%	7/9			

MAPE mean absolute percentage error
[a]$\kappa < 0$ "poor agreement"; $0.01 < \kappa < 0.20$ "slight agreement"; $0.21 < \kappa < 0.40$ "fair agreement"; $0.41 < \kappa < 0.60$ "moderate agreement"; $0.61 < \kappa < 0.80$ "substantial agreement"; $0.81 < \kappa < 1.00$ "almost perfect agreement"

Table 16.6 Prediction results for rice futures

Confusion matrix			Class-based results (decrease and increase)		Overall results		
	Decrease	Increase	Correctly classified	True number of instances	Correctly classified (MAPE)	Correctly classified	Kappa statistic[a]
Decrease	9	1	0.9000%	9/10	0.6667%	12/18	0.2895
Increase	5	3	0.3750%	3/8			

MAPE mean absolute percentage error
[a]$\kappa < 0$ "poor agreement"; $0.01 < \kappa < 0.20$ "slight agreement"; $0.21 < \kappa < 0.40$ "fair agreement"; $0.41 < \kappa < 0.60$ "moderate agreement"; $0.61 < \kappa < 0.80$ "substantial agreement"; $0.81 < \kappa < 1.00$ "almost perfect agreement"

accuracy of 38.9%. Table 16.4 also demonstrates the results for the change in the direction of banana futures; in other words, results show whether the price of the banana futures will decrease or increase in comparison with rates in the previous month. If the model shows that the real value and predicted value change (increase or decrease) in the same direction for the related month, the classification is successful. However, if the model shows that the real value and predicted value change in

Table 16.7 Prediction results for tea futures

Confusion matrix			Class-based results (decrease and increase)		Overall results		
	Decrease	Increase	Correctly classified	True number of instances	Correctly classified (MAPE)	Correctly classified	Kappa statistic[a]
Decrease	8	1	0.8889%	8/9	0.7222%	13/18	0.4444
Increase	4	5	0.5556%	5/9			

MAPE mean absolute percentage error

[a]$\kappa < 0$ "poor agreement"; $0.01 < \kappa < 0.20$ "slight agreement"; $0.21 < \kappa < 0.40$ "fair agreement"; $0.41 < \kappa < 0.60$ "moderate agreement"; $0.61 < \kappa < 0.80$ "substantial agreement"; $0.81 < \kappa < 1.00$ "almost perfect agreement"

different directions, the classification is wrong. According to Table 16.4, K* algorithm was performed with 39.9% precision (7 months accuracy out of 18 months) the classification of directions.

This accuracy below the 50% level is important to show investors that international macroeconomic variables in this application are not descriptive in modeling banana futures prices. Because of this poor forecasting success, the Kappa statistic (κ) is -0.19 for 18 months, so it was found that there was a "poor agreement" between real classes and forecasted classes. Also, as can be seen from Table 16.4, the K* algorithm estimated the price decreases with 42.9% precision (3 months accuracy of 7 months), while the price increases with 36.4% precision (4 months accuracy of 11 months). Therefore, K* algorithm can be considered unsuccessful on forecasting of banana futures prices.

Regarding palm oil futures prices, as can be seen from Table 16.5, the K* algorithm was able to classify (estimate) the price movements of the next 18 months with an accuracy of 72.2%. Thus, the K* algorithm was performed with 72.2% precision (13 months accuracy out of 18 months) the classification of directions. The Kappa statistic (κ) was 0.44 for 18 months, indicating a "moderate agreement" between real classes and forecasted classes. Also, the K* algorithm estimated the price decreases with 66.7% precision (6 months accuracy of 9 months), while the price increases with 77.8% precision (7 months accuracy of 9 months). Therefore, K* algorithm can be considered successful on forecasting of palm oil futures prices. This accuracy level shows that the international macroeconomic variables in this application are descriptive in the modeling of the palm oil futures prices.

Table 16.6 shows that the K* algorithm has classified the price movements of rice futures over the next 18 months with 66.7% precision. Thus, the K* algorithm was performed with 67.7% precision (12 months accuracy out of 18 months) the classification of directions. The Kappa statistic (κ) was 0.29 for 18 months, indicating a "fair agreement" between real classes and forecasted classes. Also, the K* algorithm estimated the price decreases with 90.0% precision (9 months accuracy of 10 months), while the price increases with 37.5% precision (3 months accuracy of 8 months). Therefore, K* algorithm can be considered quite successful on forecasting of the decrease in rice futures prices, but the increase in prices is forecasted with a high deviation.

Lastly, according to Table 16.7, the K* algorithm has classified the price movements of tea futures over the next 18 months with an accuracy of 72.2%. Thus, the K* algorithm was performed with 72.2% precision (13 months accuracy out of 18 months) the classification of directions. The Kappa statistic (κ) was 0.44 for 18 months, indicating a "moderate agreement" between real classes and forecasted classes. Also, the K* algorithm estimated the price decreases with 88.9% precision (8 months accuracy of 9 months), while the price increases with 55.6% precision (5 months accuracy of 9 months). Therefore, K* algorithm can be considered quite successful on forecasting of the decrease in tea futures prices, but the increase in prices are forecasted with a high deviation. Therefore, K* algorithm was found to be quite successful in predicting the decline in tea futures prices, while it was successful in predicting the increases, but this was not as good as the downward forecast.

Conclusion

The financial assets traded in the market are influenced by many economic and financial factors according to both theoretical and empirical literature. Therefore, identifying the economic and financial indicators that are affecting on a financial product, particularly in the markets that are in inefficiency or weak-form efficiency, can positively affect the ability of investors to be protected from risks through a proactive approach and to have abnormal returns. In this chapter, the relationship between domestic commodity derivatives and international macroeconomic variables was analyzed for the investor's side on this topic with K Star (K*) algorithm which is accepted both in data mining method and machine learning techniques.

In accordance with this purpose, ten international macroeconomic variables including oil price, interest rate, gold price, industrial production index, exchange rates, and stock market indices; and domestic commodity derivatives; banana (Central America and Ecuador), palm oil (Malaysia), rice (Thailand) and tea (Kenya) futures prices are analyzed comparatively. Thus, it has been tested whether the commodity derivatives with a comparative advantage in certain regions can be modeled with international macroeconomic variables using a glocal approach.

In this application, each domestic derivative was analyzed separately by K* algorithm, which was run with databases prepared separately for each domestic derivative. The results for the change in the direction of derivatives over the next 18 months can be summarized as follows:

1. Three of the four domestic commodity derivatives (palm oil, rice, tea) were successfully classified by international macroeconomic variables used as input variables with an accuracy of 66.7–72.2%, while the other derivative (banana) is classified with 38.9% low precision.

2. It is seen that the prediction of the decrease in the price of domestic derivatives is more successful than the increase in prices. Predictions of the decrease in domestic commodity derivatives (banana, palm oil, rice, tea) were, respectively, made with 42.9%, 66.7%, 90%, and 88.9% precision, while the increase estimates were, respectively, done 36.4%, 77.8%, 37.5%, and 55.6% precision. These results show that the prediction of the decrease in domestic commodity derivatives except banana is more successful than the prediction of the increases. Therefore, domestic commodity derivatives have been found to be more successful in declining forecasts.
3. The K* algorithm, which is evaluated by both the data mining methods and the machine learning techniques, has led successfully this study to reveal the relationship between international macroeconomic variables and domestic commodity derivatives, by the achieving forecast success three out of four domestic commodity derivatives. Thus, it has been shown that the K* algorithm can identify similar characteristics between global macroeconomic variables and domestic commodity derivatives, and this can be done more accurately, especially in the case of the decrease in the prices.

As a conclusion, the success of the K* algorithm in identifying similar characteristics between global macroeconomic variables and domestic commodity derivatives is important because it demonstrates the usefulness of data mining methods and machine learning techniques in solving glocal problems related to economics and finance. From this point of view, it is seen that the results of this chapter can be a guide for both individual and institutional investors by increasing the studies related to data mining and machine learning in the field of the academy or the business world in economics and finance.

Keyword Definitions

Derivatives markets The *derivatives market* is the financial market for derivatives, financial instruments like futures contracts or options, which are derived from other forms of assets.

Macro-finance Macro-finance is a new area of open economy macroeconomics that brings portfolio choice and asset pricing considerations into models of international macroeconomics.

K* (K Star) algorithm The K* algorithm can be defined as an instance-based learning algorithm of classification analysis which mainly aims at the partition of "n" instances into "k" classes in which each instance belongs to the class with the nearest mean.

Lazy learning Lazy learning is a machine learning method in which generalization beyond the training data is deferred until a request is sent to the system, in contrast to in eager learning, where the system tries to generalize the training data before receiving requests.

Data mining Data mining is the process of discovering actionable information from large sets of data.

References

Acworth, W. (2016). *Asia takes the lead*. FIA 2015 Annual Survey: Global Derivatives Volume.
Acworth, W. (2017). *Global futures and options volume reaches record level*. FIA 2016 Annual Volume Survey.
Akgiray, V. (1998). Finansal Yeniliklerin ve Risk Yönetiminin Ekonomik Kalkınmaya Katkıları. *İMKB Dergisi, 2*(5), 1–14.
Akgüç, Ö. (1998). *Finansal Yönetim, 9*. Istanbul: Baskı, Avcıol Basım Yayın.
Arismendi, J. C., Back, J., Prokopczuk, M., Paschke, R., & Rudolf, M. (2016). Seasonal stochastic volatility: Implications for the pricing of commodity options. *Journal of Banking and Finance, 66*, 53–65.
Aydın, N., Başar, M., & ve Coşkun, M. (2007). *Finansal Yönetim* (İkinci Baskı). Eskişehir: Genç Copy Center.
Bank for International Settlements. (2016). *Global OTC derivatives market statistics*. Accessed January 9, 2017, from http://www.bis.org/publ/rpfx16.htm.
Basu, P., & Gavin, W. T. (2011). What explains the growth in commodity derivatives? *Federal Bank of St. Louis Review, 93*(1), 37–48.
Bayraktar, A. (2012). Etkin piyasalar hipotezi. *Aksaray Üniversitesi İktisadi ve İdari Bilimler Fakültesi Dergisi, 4*(1), 37–47.
Brooks, C., Prokopczuk, M., & Wu, Y. (2013). Commodity futures prices: More evidence on forecast power, risk premia and the theory of storage. *The Quarterly Review of Economics and Finance, 53*(1), 73–85.
Cheng, B., Nikitopoulos, C. S., & Schlögl, E. (2017). Pricing of long-dated commodity derivatives: Do stochastic interest rates matter? *Journal of Banking and Finance*, 1–19 (in press).
Clapp, J., & Helleiner, E. (2012). Troubled futures? The global food crisis and the politics of agricultural derivatives regulation. *Review of International Political Economy, 19*(2), 181–207.
Cleary, J. G., & Trigg, L. E. (1995). *K*: An instance-based learner using an entropic distance measure* (pp. 108–114). Proceedings of the 12th International Conference on Machine Learning.
Commodity Facts. (2017). Accessed March 9, 2017, from http://www.commodityfact.org/about-commodity-derivatives/.
Coşkun, Y. (2007). *Bankalarda Öz Disiplin Süreçlerinin Etkinliğinin Değerlendirilmesi*. Master Thesis, Gazi Üniversitesi, Eğitim Bilimleri Enstitüsü, Ankara.
Dummu, T. R. (2009). Commodity futures markets in India: Its impact on production and prices. *Indian Journal of Agricultural Economics, 64*(3), 333–356.
Ersan, İ. (2003). *Finansal Türevler*. İstanbul: Literatür Yayınları.
Francis, A. (2012). *What are the reasons for the use of derivatives?* Accessed May 9, 2017, from https://www.quora.com/What-are-the-reasons-for-the-use-of-derivatives.
Garcia, E. K., Feldman, S., Gupta, M. R., & Srivastava, S. (2010). Completely lazy learning. *IEEE Transactions on Knowledge and Data Engineering, 22*(9), 1274–1285.
Geman, H. (2005). *Commodities and commodity derivatives: Modeling and pricing for agriculturals, metals and energy*. Chichester: Wiley.
Ghosh, N. (2009). Issues and concerns of commodity derivative markets in India: An agenda for research. *Commodity Vision, 3*(4), 8–19.

Ghosh, J. (2011). Implications of regulating commodity derivatives markets in the USA and EU. *PSL Quarterly Review, 64*(258), 287–304.

Gómez-Valle, L., Habibilashkary, Z., & Martínez-Rodríguez, J. (2017). A multiplicative seasonal component in commodity derivative pricing. *Journal of Computational and Applied Mathematics*, 1–13 (in press).

Goodwin, B. K., & Schnepf, R. (2000). Determinants of endogenous price risk in corn and wheat futures markets. *Journal of Futures Markets, 20*(8), 753–774.

Haase, M., Zimmermann, Y. S., & Zimmermann, H. (2016). The impact of speculation on commodity futures markets–A review of the findings of 100 empirical studies. *Journal of Commodity Markets, 3*(1), 1–15.

Haufe, S. (2017). *A Workbench for the K* algorithm*. Konstanz: Bachelor Thesis in Information Engineering. University of Konstanz Department of Computer and Information Science.

Hernandez, D. C. T. (2015). An experimental study of K* algorithm. *International Journal of Information Engineering & Electronic Business, 7*(2), 14–19.

Hormozi, H., Hormozi, E., & Nohooji, H. R. (2012). The classification of the applicable machine learning methods in robot manipulators. *International Journal of Machine Learning and Computing, 2*(5), 560–563.

Joseph, A., Sisodia, G., & Tiwari, A. K. (2014). A frequency domain causality investigation between futures and spot prices of Indian commodity markets. *Economic Modelling, 40*, 250–258.

Karamala, P. (2013). Growth and challenges of commodity derivative market in India. *International Journal of Management, Information Technology and Engineering, 1*(3), 205–218.

Karan, B. (2001). *Yatırım Analizi ve Portföy Yönetimi*. Ankara: Gazi Kitabevi.

Khosla, S. (2012). *Commodity futures trading in Kenya-Are we ready for the future?* Master Thesis, Faculty of Actuarial Science and Insurance Cass Business School City University, London.

Kowalski, C. (2017). *The importance of the commodities market*. Accessed May 9, 2017, from https://www.thebalance.com/commodity-exchanges-are-still-a-necessity-to-the-economy-809378.

Kurar, İ., & Çetin, A. C. (2016). Türev Araçlarının Risk Yönetim Fonksiyonu: Vadeli İşlem Piyasası Risk Yönetimi Üzerine Bir Araştırma. *Süleyman Demirel Üniversitesi İktisadi ve İdari Bilimler Fakültesi Dergisi, 21*(2), 403–425.

Lai, A. N., & Mellios, C. (2016). Valuation of commodity derivatives with an unobservable convenience yield. *Computers and Operations Research, 66*, 402–414.

Masood, S., & Chary, T. S. (2016). Performance of commodity derivatives market in India. *Amity Journal of Finance, 1*(1), 131–148.

Miffre, J., & Brooks, C. (2013). Do long-short speculators destabilize commodity futures markets? *International Review of Financial Analysis, 30*, 230–240.

Nair, C. K. G. (2004). *Commodity futures markets in India: Ready for "Take off?* (pp. 1–9). National Stock Exchange of India Limited, Mumbai, India.

Natanelov, V., Alam, M. J., McKenzie, A. M., & Van Huylenbroeck, G. (2011). Is there co-movement of agricultural commodities futures prices and crude oil? *Energy Policy, 39*(9), 4971–4984.

Nath, G. C., & Lingareddy, T. (2008). *Commodity derivative market and its impact on spot market*. Accessed May 8, 2015, from https://doi.org/10.2139/ssrn.1087904.

Viera, A. J., & Garrett, J. M. (2005). Understanding interobserver agreement: The kappa statistic. *Family Medicine, 37*(5), 360–363.

Vijayarani, S., & Muthulakshmi, M. (2013). Comparative analysis of bayes and lazy classification algorithms. *International Journal of Advanced Research in Computer and Communication Engineering, 2*(8), 3118–3124.

Wettschereck, D., Aha, D. W., & Mohri, T. (1997). A review and empirical evaluation of feature weighting methods for a class of lazy learning algorithms. In *Lazy learning* (pp. 273–314). Netherlands: Springer.

World Bank. (2017). Accessed February 9, 2017, from https://data.worldbank.org/topic/trade.

Chapter 17
Evaluation of Elderly Financial Stability: Evidence from European Countries

Marta Borda and Patrycja Kowalczyk-Rólczyńska

Abstract The financial situation of elderly people in Europe has been strongly influenced by demographic trends, changes in macroeconomic situation and reforms of existing pension systems. Increasing lifetime, relatively low replacement rate from the public pension systems and little pension savings or even a lack of them can cause an increasing number of elderly people to be exposed to financial instability or even poverty risk. The present chapter tries to analyse whether the financial situation of elderly people in countries located in two different parts of Europe—Western Europe and Central and Eastern Europe—is similar or not. In this chapter, the authors applied Ward's method and the *k*-means method in order to classify the examined countries according to the financial standing of senior citizens. The obtained results allow to indicate countries with similar financial situation of elderly people in 2007, 2010 and 2014 as well as changes in clusters over the analyzed period. Moreover, the variance analysis was applied to indicate the influence of particular variables on the clustering results. The main findings show that the financial situation of the senior citizens in particular European states is very differentiated and changeable; however, over the analyzed period, the financial standing of the senior citizens seems to be the most similar in Italy, Portugal and France, Poland and Hungary, the Czech Republic and Slovakia, Latvia and Lithuania as well as Finland and Sweden.

Introduction

Recently, European countries have been facing significant demographic changes directly influencing the structure of the population according to age and determining the directions of further socio-economic development. As the European Commission (2015) notes, the demographic trends projected over the long term reveal that Europe

M. Borda (✉) · P. Kowalczyk-Rólczyńska
Wroclaw University of Economics, Wroclaw, Poland
e-mail: marta.borda@ue.wroc.pl; patrycja.kowalczyk@ue.wroc.pl

© Springer International Publishing AG, part of Springer Nature 2018   351
H. Dincer et al. (eds.), *Global Approaches in Financial Economics, Banking, and Finance*, Contributions to Economics, https://doi.org/10.1007/978-3-319-78494-6_17

is 'turning increasingly grey' in the coming decades. Due to the dynamics in fertility, life expectancy and migration, the age structure of the European Union population will change strongly in the coming decades including an increasing share of elderly people. It is also worth mentioning that in the case of countries located in Central and Eastern Europe, progressive demographic trends have run parallel to systemic and structural changes that began in the 1990s; however, the dynamics of those changes are often higher than in Western European countries. For example, until 2060 the largest growths in life expectancy at birth, for both males and females, are expected to be observed in Bulgaria, Estonia, Latvia, Lithuania, Hungary and Romania (European Commission 2015). These trends have resulted in long-term effects on the nationwide situation and the economic growth, what predominantly constitutes the area of scientific research. In the narrow context, demographic processes have a significant impact on the financial situation of particular households and individuals. As Antczak and Zaidi (2016) noted, in 2014 over 16 million citizens aged 65 or over were at risk of poverty in 28 European Union member states. The observed demographic changes cause increasing interest in developing products addressed to the senior consumer segment. Consequently, the financial standing of elderly people in Europe requires comprehensive examination from both scientific and practical perspectives.

The main contribution of the present chapter is that the authors made an attempt to conduct a comprehensive analysis of the financial situation of elderly people in different European countries with the application of the selected classification methods. The authors decided to analyse and evaluate the financial situation of senior citizens in both Western European and Central and Eastern European countries. It should be emphasized that countries located in Central and Eastern Europe have gone through similar transformation path to market economy in their socio-economic development, and currently they are faced with similar demographic and economic problems. The financial situation of the elderly in this region has been strongly influenced by demographic trends, changes in macroeconomic situation and reforms of existing pension systems. Increasing lifetime, low replacement rate from the public pension systems and little pension savings or even a lack of them lead to the growing exposure of pensioners to poverty risk. The research question arises if the financial situation, including probability of poverty risk, of senior citizens living in Central and Eastern Europe is similar to those observed in Western Europe or not. In the study the authors applied research hypothesis that the countries belonging to Western Europe and Central and Eastern Europe are differentiated according to the financial stability of elderly people. The results of the research presented in this chapter can be useful for both scientists and practitioners interested in the implementation of social policy solutions as well as financial services addressed to the elderly.

The structure of the chapter consists of six main parts. After this introduction, a review of scientific literature is presented, and the objective of the study is identified. Then, a description of the applied research methods and data is presented. Next, the main results of the analysis of the elderly financial standing in European countries using Ward's method and the k-means method are considered. Moreover, the obtained clustering results are examined with the use of variance analysis. Finally, the main conclusions are presented and discussed.

Review of Related Literature

The financial situation of an individual is affected by a number of factors, including among others disposable income, consumption expenditure, savings as well as the number of persons in a family (household). First of all, income is considered to be an important factor determining the financial decisions of each individual, both in terms of consumption and savings. The level, structure and dynamics of income influence the capabilities and consumption profiles of people, including the amount of financial resources intended to cover various types of consumer spending.

An important criterion for differentiating the level and structure of income, expenditure and savings is the age of an individual. With respect to elderly people, specific changes in consumption and savings profile can be observed, typical for this stage of an individual/household financial life cycle. In European countries, the amount of pension benefits received from the public system usually constitutes the main component of an individual's income, possibly supplemented by an additional private income available at retirement period. With respect to the senior citizens, a characteristic change in the consumption structure can be noted. Elderly people usually spend relatively more money on health care, long-term care services and rehabilitation services. Moreover, they are relatively less likely to accumulate new savings for future. All the above-mentioned aspects contributing to the level of financial stability require continuous examination from both the social policy and market perspective.

In the international scientific literature, the issues related to financial standing of elderly people are considered from various approaches. The attention of researchers is mainly focused on the specific changes in consumption and savings profile, which are typical for the considered group of population. Problems related to sources of income in households of pensioners, health-care expenses of elderly people as well as possibilities of accumulation of savings during retirement period have been examined, among others, by Palumbo (1999), Alemayehu and Warner (2004) and De Nardi et al. (2010). In Poland, so far relatively few authors have been dealing with the issues concerning the financial situation of the elderly; however, this topic gained more and more interest during last years. Ćwiek and Wałęga (2014) carried out the analysis of financial standing of households of elderly people in Poland (in 2000–2012) with the use of regressive modelling. Piekut (2016) analysed the level of expenditure on restaurants and hotels incurred in the Polish households of the elderly, with the application of variance analysis and regression analysis. The results of her study showed that the level of examined expenditures is mainly influenced by income *per capita* and the education level of a family head. Incomes and savings of the elderly in Poland were also examined by Zalega (2016).

Review of the scientific literature indicates that much more attention is put on various aspects related to the household financial standing (including, among others, elderly households). For example, saving and investment decisions of households in Poland have been examined recently by Fatuła (2010), Anioła and Gołaś (2013), Kolasa and Liberda (2014) and Kowalczyk-Rólczyńska (2017). Moreover, Kośny

(2013) analysed the determinants of economic security and its impact on decisions made by the Polish households. Świecka (2009) conducted a comprehensive research on indebtedness and insolvency of households in Poland. Borda (2015) examined the financial situation of households in Poland in 2000–2013 in the context of development of private voluntary methods of health-care financing. Moreover, Anioła-Mikołajczak (2017) conducted a study concerning the influence of age on the financial standing, especially indebtedness and over-indebtedness of the Polish households. In the above-mentioned studies, the authors focused on the financial standing of households in Poland, however, without broader international comparison.

The problems related to the financial situation of individuals or households in Central and Eastern Europe are getting more and more attention. For example, Perek-Białas (2012) in her research found significant differences in the financial situation of elderly households in Central and Eastern Europe based on data from the EU-SILC (European Union—Survey of Income and Living Conditions). Next, Piekut (2014) examined the consumption of households in Poland in comparison to other European states. An analysis of the connection between the household saving rate and consumer confidence in the selected Eastern European countries has been recently conducted by Klapkiv (2016). There are also comprehensive studies in the area of household financial situation comprising states from different European regions. Tai and Treas (2009) conducted cross-national research comprising 22 countries (Southern European, post-communist European and East Asian states) in order to examine the exposure to the risk of poverty from both macro-level state approach and micro-level composition of households. The risk of poverty among elderly people in European Union countries was also investigated by Zaidi (2010), who distinguished the profiles of poverty among senior citizens in European countries and analysed the trends in elderly people poverty risk in 2004–2008. In the next study, Antczak and Zaidi (2016) examined the stability of elderly pension benefits taking into account the negative impact of the financial crisis.

Summarizing, the provided literature review indicates that although many researchers deal with problems related to financial standing of elderly people (households) in Europe, there is a need to conduct studies on the comparison and assessment of the financial situation of elderly people living in different European regions—especially to compare Central and Eastern European countries with Western European states.

Objective of the Chapter

The objective of the present chapter is to analyse and compare the financial situation of elderly people in the selected European countries. The authors decided to compare the financial standing of pensioners from the Central and Eastern European states to the senior citizens living in Western Europe in years 2007, 2010 and 2014, with the application of the selected classification methods. The authors also applied the variance analysis to indicate the influence of particular variables on the clustering results.

Methodology and Data

In order to examine the financial situation of the senior citizens, two methods of classification were applied: the first method was Ward's method, whereas the second method was the k-means method. The main advantage of the use of these two methods is that they allow to compare the examined objects according to given criteria and to create groups of objects which are characterized with similar values of analyzed variables. In this study these methods allow to compare the financial situation of elderly in European countries. The authors believe that the results of research will permit to identify similarities in the level of financial standing of elderly in these European countries which will be in the same class as well as the differences between the level of financial standing of elderly in these European countries which will be in separate clusters.

Ward's method belongs to the agglomerative hierarchical methods, which are discussed in details in the scientific literature (Ward 1963; Johnson 1967; Lance and Williams 1967a, b; Punj and Steward 1983; Milligan and Cooper 1987; Rencher 2002; Zivadinovic et al. 2009; Everitt et al. 2011). This method can be used for clustering the objects according to their similarities as well as separation of them according to the differences. It should be noted that hierarchical methods assume that a distance matrix of a set of objects is given. The grouping scheme of objects is as follows: it is initially assumed that every object creates a class (cluster) on its own. Afterwards, a pair of classes with the smallest distance is found at each grouping stage. Both classes are combined, as a result of which the number of classes is reduced by one. Then, the distance between the newly created class and other classes is determined. The procedure is repeated $n-1$ times until all classes are combined in one (Mooi and Sarstedt 2011). In Ward's method, the variance analysis approach is used for estimating the distance between classes. The method aims at minimizing the within-cluster sum of squared variance (Ward 1963).

The k-means method belongs to nonhierarchical methods. It is a type of iterative optimization method used to "improve" the initial division of a set of objects into k classes from the point of view of a certain defined function of the classification quality criterion. This criterion can be defined, e.g. as the sum of the Euclidean distance of objects from the centres of their respective class gravity. Depending on the initial division of the objects into classes, defining the function of the quality classification criterion and the rules of determining the number of resultant groups, there are different versions of the k-means method, with the most commonly used variant having been developed by Hartigan (1975). It should be mentioned that in the k-means method, the researcher assumes what should be the number of classes, while in the case of Ward's method, the number of classes is established using the dendrogram results.

The procedure of the k-means method used in the study is as follows:

1. The maximum number of iterations is set as well as the number of k clusters into which the set of objects is to be divided.

2. The initial k clusters are defined; in the applied variant of the method, they consist of objects selected in such a way as to maximize the distances between clusters.
3. The measure of the correctness of division is calculated, which is the sum of the squares of the Euclidean distance between the centres of gravity of the distinguished classes.
4. For the first unallocated object, the distance from each class' gravity centre is calculated and then classified as the nearest grade.
5. The classes' gravity centres are calculated, and the correctness of the division is measured; if the value of the division measure has improved, the object remains in the group, otherwise the change is not made, and the next object is considered.
6. The first iteration of the procedure is closed with the decision on the last unassigned object.
7. Consecutive iterations are carried out until all objects are qualified for a class or until the set number of iterations is carried out.

In the research the variance analysis was used to verify the classification results obtained with the use of the k-means method. A comparison of the variation within clusters to the variation in the clusters was performed. It is desirable that the variation within the clusters is smaller than the variation between clusters.

In the study the authors selected six diagnostic variables which allow to describe the financial situation of elderly. The stress is put on measures indicating the adequacy of income and expenditure incurred by the elderly, their exposure to poverty risk as well as gender differences in disposable income. The set of diagnostic variables is formed by the following ratios:

- **Expenditure on pensions** (X_1)—defined as the sum of social benefits such as disability pension, early retirement benefits due to reduced capacity to work, old-age pension, partial pension, survivor's pension and early retirement benefits for labour market reasons, expressed as a percentage of GDP.
- **Severe material deprivation rate 65 years or over** (X_2)—this indicator expresses the enforced inability to afford some items considered by most people to be desirable or even necessary to lead an adequate life (e.g. to pay their mortgage bills, to face unexpected expenses, to go on holiday, to have a car), measured as a percentage of total population.
- **At-risk-of-poverty rate for pensioners** (X_3)—defined as the share of retired persons with an equivalised disposable income (after social transfer) below the at-risk-of-poverty threshold, which is set at 60% of the national median equivalised disposable income after social transfers, in the total population.
- **Relative median income ratio (65+)** (X_4)—ratio of the median equivalised disposable income of people aged above 65 to the median equivalised disposable income of persons aged below 65.
- **Gender differences in the relative median income ratio (65+)** (X_5)—expressed as relative median income ratio (65+) broken down by group of sex.
- **Housing cost overburden rate (65+)** (X_6)—defined as percentage of persons aged 65 or over (in the total population) living in households where the total housing costs represent more than 40% of disposable income.

Variable X_1 is a macroeconomic characteristic referring to the adequacy of pensions by comparing the amount of pension benefits to the level of GDP, whereas variables X_2–X_6 represent indicators used in the EU-SILC survey. All variables have been applied for this research. Their values as well as their statistical characteristics are shown in Appendix. It should be added that the criterion for selecting the variables for the study was the variation coefficient. The authors assumed the critical value of the coefficient at a level $|CV^*| = 0.1$, which lead to all variables being included in the study.

Moreover, the correlation analysis of diagnostic variables was conducted for each year separately. The values of correlation coefficient between six variables for each of analyzed years were calculated. The critical value of correlation coefficient was assumed at the level $|r| = 0.8$. Because the values of correlation coefficient between variables for each of analyzed years did not exceed 0.8, all these variables were used in the next step of the research. The next step in the analysis was an application of Ward's method and the k-means method in order to classify European countries based on the financial situation of senior citizens. The data for the following years 2007, 2010 and 2014 was included into the analysis.

In the conducted research, data from the Eurostat database for 2007, 2010 and 2014 was used. The analysis covered the following countries: Belgium, Bulgaria, the Czech Republic (in 2016 the Czech Republic changed into Czechia), Denmark, Germany (with the exception of 2007), Estonia, Ireland, Greece, Spain, France, Croatia (with the exception of 2007), Italy, Cyprus, Latvia, Lithuania, Luxembourg, Hungary, Malta, the Netherlands, Austria, Poland, Portugal, Romania, Slovenia, Slovakia, Finland, Sweden, the United Kingdom, Iceland, Norway and Switzerland (with the exception of 2007).

Results and Discussion

Ward's method was used as a first method in the study. The results of grouping with the use of this method allow to discern six classes of countries in 2007 and 2010, as well as eight classes in 2014 (Figs. 17.1, 17.2 and 17.3 and Table 17.1, respectively).

Classification results obtained by application of Ward's method indicate that in each of the examined years, the financial situation of elderly people in Belgium, Finland, Slovenia and Sweden, Estonia and Latvia, Hungary and Luxemburg was very similar. As presented in Table 17.1, the first four countries as well as two next pairs of countries are always in the same group. It is worth to highlight that Belgium, Finland, Slovenia and Sweden are characterized by almost the same values of expenditure on pensions, relative median income ratio (especially in 2010) and gender differences in the relative median income ratio (which are similar to the average values of this indicator presented in Appendix). Estonia and Latvia recorded almost the same values of gender differences in the relative median income ratio and

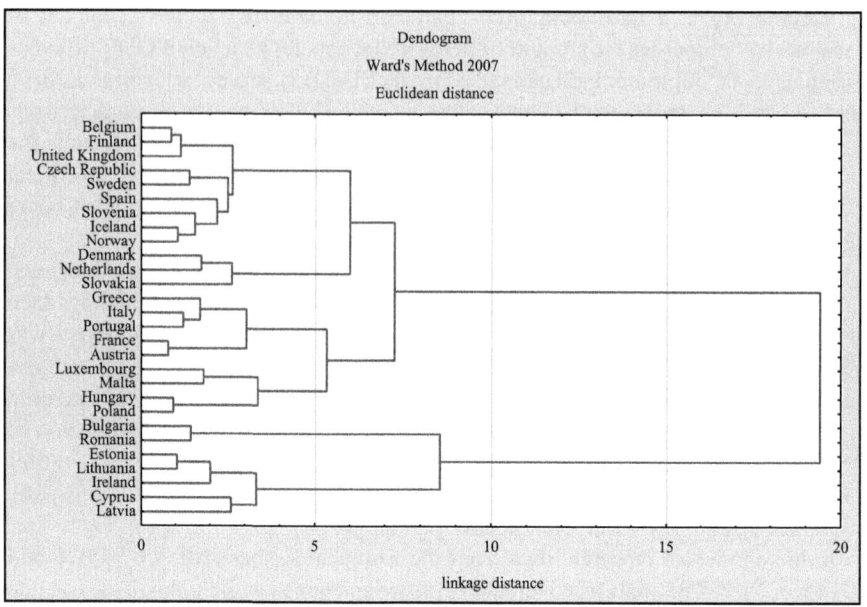

Fig. 17.1 Classification of European countries according to the financial standing of the elderly in 2007 (Ward's method). Source: Authors' work with the use of Statistica software

the at-risk-of-poverty rate for pensioners. Moreover, in these two countries, a difference in the value of severe material deprivation rate for people aged 65 or over can be observed.

It should be noted that the highest value of percentage of elderly people who was exposed to poverty risk was recorded in Estonia and Latvia in 2007 and 2014. Moreover, approximately 30% of pensioners who live in Switzerland were exposed to poverty risk in each of analyzed years. The second pair, Hungary and Luxembourg, is characterized by very similar values of expenditure on pensions as well as relative median income ratio and gender differences in the relative median income ratio; however, these two countries are differed widely when comparing the values of severe material depravation rates 65 years or over and housing cost overburden rates. It should be noted that the above two countries are characterized by the smallest value of the at-risk-of-poverty rate for pensioners in 2014. It was the reason that Hungary and Luxembourg belonged to separate class in 2014.

When analysing the grouping results of application of Ward's method, it should be mentioned that the financial situation of elderly people who live in Italy, Portugal and France was very similar in 2007 and 2014. In these three countries, the values of expenditure on pensions were almost the highest. At the same time, the values of expenditure on pensions in Greece were also very high, but in 2014 Greece created a separate cluster. The reason for that situation was the highest value of housing cost overburden rate, which increased two times in comparison with corresponding value noted in 2010.

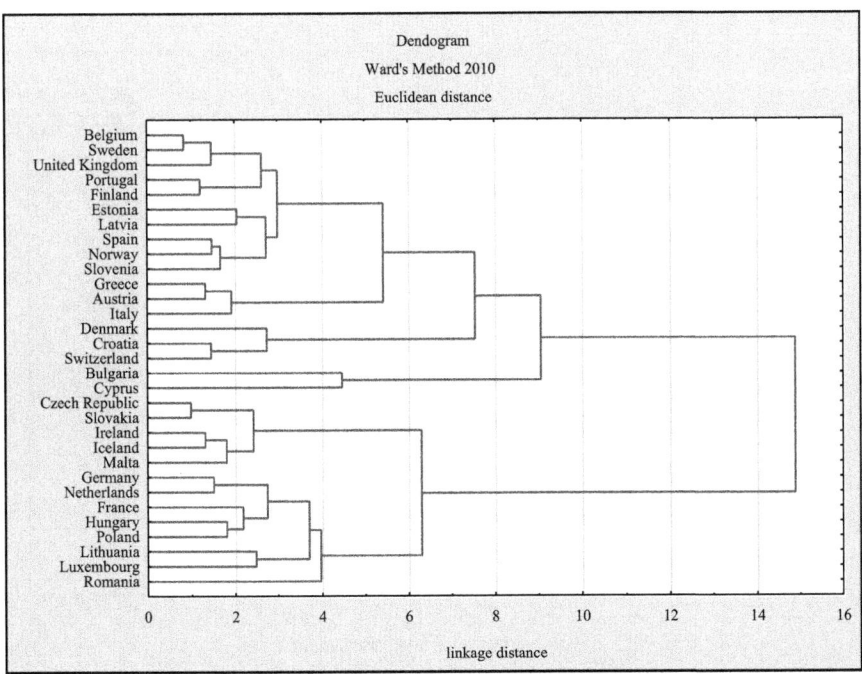

Fig. 17.2 Classification of European countries according to the financial standing of the elderly in 2010 (Ward's method). Source: Authors' work with the use of Statistica software

It should also be stressed that in 2010 and 2014, the financial situation of elderly people who live in the Czech Republic and Slovakia was very similar. These two countries are characterized by similar values of the at-risk-of-poverty rate for pensioners as well as expenditure on pensions, which were not high in comparison with others European countries. The values of the at-risk-of-poverty rate for pensioners in the Czech Republic and Slovakia were almost two times lower than average values of this indicators for all European countries. This could suggest that the financial situation of the elderly in these two countries was quite good.

In 2007 and 2014, Denmark and the Netherlands belonged to the same class. These two countries are characterized by very similar values of expenditure on pensions in 2007 as well as almost the same values of severe material deprivation rate for people aged 65 years or over in 2007 and 2014. It should be noted that these two countries as well as Sweden, Iceland and Norway are characterized by the smallest values of severe material deprivation rate for people aged 65 years or over in all analyzed years.

The *k*-means method was the second method which was used in the study. The result of classification with the application of this method is presented in Table 17.2. This result corresponds to those obtained using Ward's method, but in some case, other similarities can be noticed.

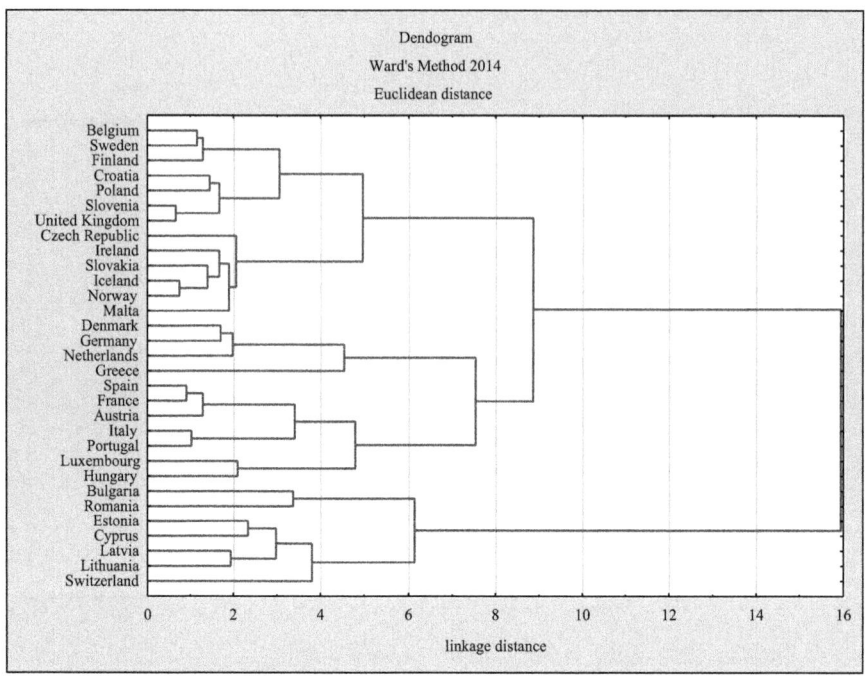

Fig. 17.3 Classification of European countries according to the financial standing of the elderly in 2014 (Ward's method). Source: Authors' work with the use of Statistica software

Based on the presented above classification results, one can observe that the financial situation of senior citizens living in the UK, Belgium and Finland was very similar in 2007 and 2014. In 2007 the values of the relative median income ratio were exactly the same for these three countries. In 2014 the values of the at-risk-of-poverty rate for pensioners were almost the same for the UK and Finland, while in 2007 the values of this ratio were very similar for Belgium and Finland. It should be also stressed that in these states, values of the at-risk-of-poverty rate for pensioners decreased from 2007 to 2014.

By analysing of classification results, it should be mentioned that financial situation of elderly people in Poland and Hungary was very similar in 2007 and 2010. In 2007 in these two countries, the values of gender differences in the relative median income ratio, housing cost overburden rate as well as the at-risk-of-poverty rate for pensioners were similar, and in this case, the values of the at-risk-of-poverty rate for pensioners were almost three times smaller than average for all analyzed countries. In 2010 the values of severe material deprivation rate for people at age 65+ as well as the values of expenditure on pensions were close to each other's.

The next pairs of countries in which the financial situation of elderly people were similar were the following: Latvia and Lithuania in 2007 and 2014 as well as Sweden and Spain in 2007 and 2010. Latvia and Lithuania belonged to the same class in 2007 because of the similar values of the relative median income ratio and the gender

Table 17.1 Results of grouping with the application of Ward's method

	2007	2010	2014
Class 1	Belgium Finland United Kingdom Czech Republic Sweden Spain Slovenia Iceland Norway	Belgium Sweden United Kingdom Portugal Finland Estonia Latvia Spain Norway Slovenia	Belgium Sweden Finland Croatia Poland United Kingdom Slovenia
Class 2	Denmark Netherlands Slovakia	Greece Italy Austria	Czech Republic Slovakia Iceland Ireland Malta Norway
Class 3	Greece Italy Portugal France Austria	Denmark Croatia Switzerland	Denmark Netherlands Germany
Class 4	Luxemburg Malta Hungary Poland	Bulgaria Cyprus	France Austria Spain Italy Portugal
Class 5	Bulgaria Romania	Czech Republic Slovakia Iceland Malta Ireland	Bulgaria Romania
Class 6	Estonia Lithuania Ireland Cyprus Latvia	Germany Netherlands France Hungary Poland Lithuania Luxemburg Romania	Estonia Cyprus Latvia Lithuania Switzerland
Class 7	—	—	Greece
Class 8	—	—	Luxemburg Hungary

Source: Authors' work with the use of Statistica software

differences in the relative median income ratio as well as very similar and the high values of the at-risk-of-poverty rate for pensioners. In 2014 the values of expenditure on pensions in Latvia and Lithuania were almost the same. In 2007 Sweden and Spain belonged to the same class because of the very similar values of relative

Table 17.2 Results of grouping with the application of the *k*-means method

	2007	2010	2014
Class 1	Belgium Finland United Kingdom Sweden Spain Greece Italy Portugal	Belgium Czech Republic Estonia Spain Latvia Portugal Slovenia Finland Sweden Norway	Spain France Luxemburg Italy Austria Poland Portugal
Class 2	Denmark Netherlands Slovakia	Greece Germany France Italy Austria Netherlands	Czech Republic Slovakia Iceland Ireland Malta Norway
Class 3	France Luxemburg Austria Hungary Poland	Denmark Croatia Switzerland United Kingdom	Denmark Germany Netherlands
Class 4	Czech Republic Malta Norway Slovenia Iceland	Slovakia Luxemburg Iceland Malta Ireland	Belgium Croatia Slovenia Finland Sweden United Kingdom
Class 5	Bulgaria Romania	Bulgaria Cyprus	Cyprus Switzerland Estonia
Class 6	Estonia Lithuania Ireland Cyprus Latvia	Hungary Poland Lithuania Romania	Bulgaria Lithuania Latvia
Class 7	—	—	Greece
Class 8	—	—	Hungary Romania

Source: Authors' work with the use of Statistica software

median income ratio which were almost the same as average value for all European countries. In 2010 the values of gender differences in the relative median income ratio were nearly the same for Sweden and Spain.

In 2010 and 2014, the elderly living in Iceland, Ireland and Malta had the similar financial situation. In these countries in two analyzed years, the values of expenditure on pensions were not only similar but also relatively low in comparison with other examined countries.

It should also be stressed that the conducted variance analysis indicates the correctness of the classification performed with the application of the k-means method. The variances within the classes were usually smaller than the variances between classes. At the same time, it points out which variables constituted the main criteria determining the obtained clustering results. These were, respectively, in 2007 relative median income ratio (65+), in 2010 expenditure on pensions and at-risk-of-poverty rate for pensioners and in 2014 at-risk-of-poverty rate for pensioners and relative median income ratio (65+).

Summarizing the discussion on the classification results as well as analysis of values of applied variables (ratios), the following finding can be noticed: Italy, Portugal, Austria, Greece and France are characterized by the highest values of expenditure on pensions; the highest values of the at-risk-of-poverty rate for pensioners were recorded for Estonia, Latvia and Switzerland; the highest values of rates of severe material deprivation in people aged 65 or over and housing cost overburden rate were noticed for Bulgaria and Romania in 2007 and 2010; the lowest value of housing cost overburden rate was recorded for Cyprus, the highest—for Switzerland.

Conclusion

Taking into account the demographic trends (ageing societies) observed practically in all European countries, one can expect that further changes in population age structure will lead to an increasing number of senior citizens. Undoubtedly, ageing societies and related problems, such as financial standing of elderly people, require continuous examination from both the social policy and market perspective. The examination of financial standing of this special type of consumers seems to be crucial for both scientists and practitioners interested in developing products and services addressed to this age group. In the authors' opinion, this study contributes to the development of the silver economy and constitutes a part of a greater research on the financial standing of elderly people in Europe.

The conducted analysis shows that the comparison and evaluation of the financial standing of elderly people living in different European regions is not an easy task, especially in midterm- and long-term horizon. One of the biggest problems the authors had to face was a lack of complete and detailed data, mainly due to the different moments of accession to the European Union and the need to provide relevant data. However, based on the classification results obtained with the use of Ward's method and the k-means, some important conclusions can be formulated. The results seem to reflect regional similarities and differences in the level of socio-economic developments of the examined states. The countries located in the same geographic area such as Italy, Portugal and France are characterized by very similar financial situation of elderly citizens, and as a result, they usually belong to the same cluster. The same is true for Poland and Hungary, the Czech Republic and Slovakia, Latvia and Lithuania as well as Finland and Sweden. It should be added that among

Central and Eastern European states, the financial situation of elderly people seems to be the most difficult in Romania and Bulgaria.

In general, the obtained results confirm the research hypothesis that the countries belonging to Western Europe and Central and Eastern Europe are differentiated according to the financial stability of elderly citizens. What seems to be worrying is that according to Eurostat forecasts (until 2060), life expectancy will be the greatest in developing countries, especially in Latvia, Lithuania, Romania and Bulgaria (European Commission 2015). Taking this into account, the research findings indicate a very serious challenge for the above-mentioned states.

The variables which mostly determined the obtained classification results were as follows: relative median income ratio, expenditure on pensions and at-risk-of-poverty rate. These ratios measure a relative level and/or adequacy of income (especially pension benefits) received by the senior citizens as well as their exposure to poverty risk. At the next stage of the research, the authors intend to conduct a further analysis of socio-economic factors (such as the rules of existing pension systems and macroeconomic indicators) that can affect the main reasons for the observed similarities and differences between countries belonging to the same cluster.

Keywords Definitions

Elderly people For the purpose of this study, it means a population group of people at age 65 or over.

Financial stability It means that an individual's or family's financial situation is sustainable and resilient to temporary shocks and setbacks. There is no precise measure of financial stability, but it is likely to be positively related to a family's net worth, its stock of liquid assets and its anticipation of cash flows paid from employment, trust funds, pensions or other sources.

Poverty risk This is the situation in which individuals live in households where equivalised disposable income is below the threshold of 60% of the national equivalised median income. This measurement approach is adopted in all European Commission's recent reports, which also uses the same data source, EU-SILC, as used in this chapter.

Europe It is a continent located entirely in the Northern Hemisphere and mostly in the Eastern Hemisphere; it is bordered by the Arctic Ocean to the north, the Atlantic Ocean to the west and the Mediterranean Sea to the south.

Cluster analysis It is one of the methods of multivariate analysis in which the examined objects are divided into groups (clusters) according to their similarities; the method of grouping a set of objects in such a way that objects in the same group are more similar (in some sense or another) to each other than to those in other groups.

Appendix

Table 17.3 Values and statistical characteristic of applied variables in years 2007, 2010 and 2014

Country	Expenditure on pensions as percentage of GDP			Severe material deprivation rate 65 years or over			At-risk-of-poverty rate for pensioners		
	2007	2010	2014	2007	2010	2014	2007	2010	2014
Belgium	10.5	11.8	12.5	3.6	2.8	2.4	22.8	17.4	13.8
Bulgaria	6.5	8.7	8.8	67.2	58.1	40.3	30.2	37.8	26.2
Czech Republic	7.6	8.8	9	6.5	4.3	5.1	7.9	10.6	9.1
Denmark	11.7	12.7	14.2	0.8	0.9	0.9	19.2	18.8	10.8
Germany	12	12.4	11.8	2.2	2.1	3.2	19.1	14.1	18.1
Estonia	5.7	8.7	7.6	7.9	6.6	6.4	42.9	20.1	42.2
Ireland	5	6.9	6.4	1.2	1.5	2.9	25.9	7.8	12.2
Greece	12.3	14.8	17.1	17.4	12.4	15.5	29.3	24.5	14.6
Spain	9	10.5	12.8	3.6	2.2	2.4	17	15.2	8.4
France	13.1	14.3	15.2	3.4	3.4	2.4	12.1	9	9
Croatia	n.a.	10.6	11	n.a.	15.7	14.7	n.a.	30.7	21.6
Italy	14	15.5	16.5	6.5	6.3	9	18.6	14.5	11.1
Cyprus	6	7.5	10.5	19.4	7.3	7.4	57	43.2	26.9
Latvia	4.9	10.1	7.9	35.8	27.5	22	43.7	21.5	35.5
Lithuania	6.5	8.4	7	20.8	24	17.8	38.8	11	25.1
Luxembourg	8.4	9.2	9.4	0.6	0.1	0.1	10.8	5.6	3.1
Hungary	10.3	10.8	9	17.2	14.1	16.5	7.5	4.3	4.7
Malta	8.6	9.4	8.6	3.1	5	8.1	13.6	11.1	8.9
Netherlands	11.5	12.4	11.5	0.7	0.3	1	10.3	6	7
Austria	13.4	14.6	14.9	2.1	1.9	2	15.5	19.2	15.9
Poland	11.5	11.8	11.8	24	16.5	9.7	8.9	17.7	14
Portugal	12.2	13.7	15.6	10.7	9.6	9.8	25.3	22.8	14.1
Romania	6.4	9.3	8.2	50	32	26.5	31.2	20.6	18.5
Slovenia	9.6	11	11.2	6.6	6.3	6.7	24.8	27.2	21.4
Slovakia	7.1	8.2	8.7	17.7	11.1	9.2	11.4	10	7.6
Finland	10.4	12.2	13.4	2.6	1.7	1.7	24.6	22.9	20
Sweden	10.9	11.3	11.5	0.6	0.7	0.2	12.9	22.2	22.3
United Kingdom	9.8	11.4	11.3	1.9	1.3	1.9	30.7	25.6	21
Iceland	6.7	7.5	9	0.7	0.4	0.5	23.3	10.1	10.2
Norway	7.5	8.3	9.3	0.5	0.5	0.2	22.8	20.6	16.4
Switzerland	11.1	11.4	11.8	1	0.6	0.2	30.3	30.8	30.4
Average	9.34	10.78	11.08	11.20	8.95	7.95	22.95	18.48	16.78
Standard deviation	2.63	2.29	2.81	15.49	12.21	9.03	11.67	9.18	8.94
Variation coefficient	0.28	0.21	0.25	1.38	1.36	1.14	0.51	0.50	0.53

Source: Authors' work based on data from Eurostat, http://ec.europa.eu/eurostat/web/income-and-living-conditions/data/database

Table 17.4 Values and statistical characteristic of applied variables in years 2007, 2010 and 2014

Country	Relative median income ratio (65+)			Gender differences in the relative median income ratio (65+)			Housing cost overburden rate (65+)		
	2007	2010	2014	2007	2010	2014	2007	2010	2014
Belgium	0.74	0.75	0.77	0.76	0.75	0.82	11.4	11.9	11.9
Bulgaria	0.78	0.74	0.82	0.65	0.58	0.65	22.6	10.2	16.4
Czech Republic	0.81	0.82	0.84	0.79	0.77	0.77	14.8	13.1	13.9
Denmark	0.7	0.71	0.78	0.86	0.87	0.95	18.9	27.6	18.1
Germany	0.87	0.89	0.9	0.9	1.02	0.97	n.a.	19.3	22
Estonia	0.65	0.73	0.63	0.62	0.72	0.61	6.5	4.1	5.6
Ireland	0.69	0.85	0.89	0.64	0.87	0.78	1.5	2.9	4.6
Greece	0.83	0.84	1	0.76	0.8	0.88	15	14.3	33.2
Spain	0.79	0.88	1.03	0.57	0.7	0.96	4	3.8	3.5
France	0.91	0.98	1.02	0.91	0.97	1	6.2	4	3.7
Croatia	n.a.	0.78	0.88	n.a.	0.72	0.85	n.a.	23.5	9
Italy	0.86	0.92	0.99	0.7	0.74	0.84	8.1	5.8	5.3
Cyprus	0.57	0.65	0.75	0.44	0.5	0.67	3.1	2	2.8
Latvia	0.64	0.78	0.71	0.6	0.76	0.67	14.9	9.7	11.8
Lithuania	0.69	0.93	0.77	0.65	1.1	0.82	5.8	5.4	9.2
Luxembourg	0.96	1.05	1.11	0.91	1.05	1.01	2.3	2.4	3.1
Hungary	0.97	1.01	1.05	0.95	0.94	0.97	9.5	9.1	9.2
Malta	0.78	0.81	0.78	0.96	0.97	0.89	3.4	4.1	1.5
Netherlands	0.83	0.87	0.89	0.95	1	1.07	24	10.8	13.6
Austria	0.93	0.9	0.95	0.82	0.87	0.97	5.2	13	5.4
Poland	1.04	0.93	0.99	0.97	0.89	0.88	10.5	11.2	9.4
Portugal	0.8	0.82	0.94	0.74	0.67	0.75	4.4	1.8	4.4
Romania	0.76	0.97	1.04	0.71	0.84	0.89	28.9	18	16.7
Slovenia	0.87	0.87	0.91	0.83	0.85	0.9	7.4	5.8	6.4
Slovakia	0.81	0.83	0.91	0.86	0.83	0.88	28.2	8.6	8
Finland	0.74	0.78	0.79	0.72	0.76	0.83	5.2	3.1	5
Sweden	0.81	0.79	0.83	0.78	0.73	0.82	12	9	11.7
United Kingdom	0.74	0.81	0.87	0.7	0.82	0.91	13.8	16.1	7.5
Iceland	0.79	0.96	0.9	0.68	0.91	0.89	7.9	5	6.5
Norway	0.81	0.85	0.92	0.81	0.81	0.88	6.8	6.8	5.1
Switzerland	0.84	0.8	0.82	0.67	0.64	0.68	n.a.	26.1	21.4
Average	0.80	0.85	0.89	0.76	0.82	0.85	10.80	9.95	9.87
Standard deviation	0.10	0.09	0.11	0.13	0.13	0.11	7.57	6.98	6.87
Variation coefficient	0.13	0.11	0.12	0.17	0.16	0.13	0.70	0.70	0.70

Source: Authors' work based on data from Eurostat, http://ec.europa.eu/eurostat/web/income-and-living-conditions/data/database

References

Alemayehu, B., & Warner, K. E. (2004). The life distribution of health care costs. *Health Services Research, 39*(3), 627–642.

Anioła, P., & Gołaś, Z. (2013). *Zachowania oszczędnościowe gospodarstw domowych w Polsce* [Savings behaviour of households in Poland]. Poznań: Poznań University of Life Sciences Publishing House.

Anioła-Mikołajczak, P. (2017). The impact of age on Polish households financial behavior – indebtedness and over- indebtedness. *Optimum Studia Ekonomiczne, 1*(85), 106–116.

Antczak, R., & Zaidi, A. (2016). Risk of poverty among older people in EU countries. *CESifo DICE Report, 14*(1), 37–46.

Borda, M. (2015). *Medyczne konta oszczędnościowe w finansowaniu opieki zdrowotnej. Koncepcja, modele, uwarunkowania* [Medical savings accounts in health care financing. Concept, models and determinants]. Warsaw: Poltext.

Ćwiek, M., & Wałęga, A. (2014). *Financial situation of households of elderly people in Poland.* Proceedings of IAC-EMM 2014: International Academic Conference on Economics, Management and Marketing in Prague

De Nardi, M., French, E., & Jones, J. B. (2010). Why do the elderly save? The role of medical expenses. *Journal of Political Economy, 118*, 39–75.

European Commission. (2015). The 2015 ageing report. *European Economy, 3*, 1–424.

Everitt, B. S., Landau, S., Leese, M., & Stahl, D. (2011). *Cluster analysis.* Chichester: Wiley.

Fatuła, D. (2010). *Zachowania polskich gospodarstw domowych na rynku finansowym* [Behaviour of the Polish households in the financial market]. Cracow: Cracow University of Economics Publishing House.

Hartigan, J. A. (1975). *Clustering algorithms.* New York: Wiley.

Johnson, S. C. (1967). Hierarchical clustering schemes. *Psychometrika, 32*(3), 241–254.

Klapkiv, L. (2016). Household saving rate including life insurance premiums and consumer confidence index in selected Eastern European countries. *Journal of Insurance, Financial Markets and Consumer Protection, 22*(3), 16–33.

Kolasa, A., & Liberda, B. (2014). *Determinants of saving in Poland: Are they different than in other OECD countries.* University of Warsaw Working Papers, No. 13/2014 (130).

Kośny, M. (2013). *Determinanty bezpieczeństwa ekonomicznego rodzin* [Determinants of economic security of families]. Wroclaw: Wroclaw University of Economics Publishing House.

Kowalczyk-Rólczyńska, P. (2017). Czynniki warunkujące posiadanie dobrowolnych oszczędności emerytalnych przez gospodarstwa domowe w Polsce [Factors determining the possession of voluntary retirement savings by households in Poland]. *Wiadomości Ubezpieczeniowe, 2*, 41–57.

Lance, G. N., & Williams, W. T. (1967a). A general theory of classificatory sorting strategies I. Hierarchical system. *The Computer Journal, 9*, 373–380.

Lance, G. N., & Williams, W. T. (1967b). A general theory of classificatory sorting strategies II. Hierarchical system. *The Computer Journal, 10*, 271–277.

Milligan, G. W., & Cooper, M. C. (1987). Methodology review: Clustering methods. *Applied Psychological Measurement, 11*(4), 329–354.

Mooi, E., & Sarstedt, M. (2011). *A concise guide to market research.* Berlin: Springer.

Palumbo, M. G. (1999). Uncertain medical expenses and precautionary saving near the end of the life cycle. *Review of Economic Studies, 66*(2), 395–421.

Perek-Białas, J. (2012). The possibilities analysis of the financial situation of the elderly households in Central and Eastern Europe. *Wiadomości Statystyczne, 12*, 53–60.

Piekut, M. (2014). Konsumpcja w polskich gospodarstwach domowych na tle krajów europejskich. *Problemy Zarządzania, 11*(1), 23–39.

Piekut, M. (2016). Restaurants and hotels expenditure in Polish households of the elderly. *Economics and Management, 8*(1), 80–90.

Punj, G., & Steward, D. W. (1983). Cluster analysis in marketing research: Review and suggestions for application. *Journal of Marketing Research, XX*, 134–148.

Rencher, A. C. (2002). *Methods of multivariate analysis*. Chichester: Wiley.

Świecka, B. (2009). *Niewypłacalność gospodarstw domowych. Przyczyny – skutki – przeciwdziałanie* [Insolvency of households. Causes – effects – prevention]. Warsaw: Difin.

Tai, T.-o., & Treas, J. (2009). Does household composition explain welfare regime poverty risk for older adults and other household members? *Journal of Gerontology: Social Sciences, 64B*(6), 777–787.

Ward, J. H. (1963). Hierarchical grouping to optimize an objective function. *Journal of the American Statistical Association, 58*, 236–244.

Zaidi, A. (2010, January). *Poverty risk for older people in EU countries – an update*. European Centre Vienna Policy Brief (11).

Zalega, T. (2016). Incomes and savings of Polish seniors in view of research outcomes. *Problemy Zarządzania, 14*(2), 135–155.

Zivadinovic, N. K., Dumicic, K., & Casni, A. C. (2009). Cluster and factor analysis of structural economic indicators for selected European countries. *WSEAS Transactions on Business and Economics, 6*(7), 331–341.

Chapter 18
An Overview of Measuring and Reporting Intellectual Capital

Buket Atalay, Soner Gokten, and Medine Turkcan

Abstract Value creation process is based on intellectual capital or intangibles rather than tangible assets in today's business environment. Therefore, measuring and reporting of intellectual capital for different issues has become a hotly debated issue in the literature. Currently, it is fair to say that existing financial reporting framework has an inadequacy in disclosuring intellectual capital and there is no consensus on a method to measure intellectual capital correctly as well as a generally accepted model has not been emerged in the literature yet. This chapter aims to cover main methods employed in measuring and evaluating the value of intellectual capital by considering its effect on company value and to assert the inadequacy of traditional accounting to report intellectual capital on financial statements. Moreover, applicability of methods is also discussed in terms of their ability to benefit from accounting numbers. The study is concluded by showing the need on developing new and innovative methods to overcome the challenge of measuring and reporting intellectual capital.

Introduction

Measuring intangible assets currently create a challenge in terms of accounting and finance phenomenon, namely, that there are various valuation approaches based on different cases. Thus, several innovations have occurred in financial markets since the last two decades, but methods of corporate valuation have not undergone a change substantially (Berzkalne and Zelgalve 2014). Methods generally used in practice only represent historical performance. In other words, traditional methods of corporate valuation mostly depend on accounting numbers. On the other hand, off-balance sheet value should be also considered.

B. Atalay · S. Gokten (✉) · M. Turkcan
Management Department, Baskent University, Ankara, Turkey
e-mail: buketatalay@baskent.edu.tr; sgokten@baskent.edu.tr

© Springer International Publishing AG, part of Springer Nature 2018   369
H. Dincer et al. (eds.), *Global Approaches in Financial Economics, Banking, and Finance*, Contributions to Economics, https://doi.org/10.1007/978-3-319-78494-6_18

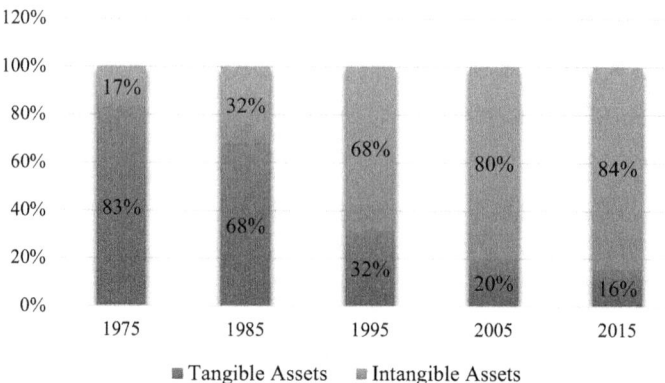

Fig. 18.1 Components of S&P 500 market value (Source: Ocean Tomo—January 1, 2015)

Intellectual capital (IC) is one of the most important basic sources for signals concerning the future potential of a company in today's business environment, while there is no worldwide definition (Berzkalne and Zelgalve 2014). In this sense, IC needs to be taken into account in order to reach an inclusive value.

The adequacy of current financial reporting framework to full disclosure of IC is a hotly debated issue as well. In the related literature, there are several studies which conclude that IC accounting does not accomplishedly comply with the traditional financial reporting framework and accounting needs to be amended in order to provide a standardized approach on IC (Gowthorpe 2009; Cronje and Moolman 2013). In short, the value generated by IC cannot be entirely presented in traditional financial statements, and so, this inability creates a significant gap between market and book values.

Confronting with the restrictions of financial statements in accounting for corporate value emphasizes that sources of economic value depend on generating intellectual capital instead of producing tangible goods (Chen et al. 2005). Most researches have indicated that due to its importance in sustaining a competitive advantage, the value of a company relies on its intellectual capital rather than its tangible assets (Okan Gökten and Marşap 2017). Figure 18.1 shows the components of S&P 500 market value where intangibles have significantly increased from 1975 to 2015. In that period, intangible assets have become the main component of market value for companies.

In addition, recent views especially emerged in comparative economic development literature have supplied theoretical and empirical evidences which support the importance of intellectual capital. Glaeser et al. (2004), Hanushek and Woessmann (2008, 2012a, b) and Gennaioli et al. (2013) supply empirical evidences suggesting that human capital which represents one of the basic sources for IC has a significant effect on economic development. Therefore, it is clear that the importance of IC has increased especially in recent years and should be considered in corporate valuation.

Wide range of methods has been used in IC valuation. However, all of them have some limitations, and since IC contains intangible components, it is not easy to measure it accurately. So, there is no consensus on one of the methods as a best one, while a generally accepted model has not been emerged in the literature yet.

This chapter covers and discusses the methods employed to measure IC from past to future and is organized as follows: First section defines the IC components by providing related literature review. Second section asserts and discusses the inadequacy of current accounting framework to report IC in terms of full disclosure. Third section overviews existing methods applied for measuring IC and provides comparisons among them by giving details on most widely used ones. Moreover, this section discusses applicability of IC measurement methods from the accounting perspective, considering the significance of intellectual capital on company value. Fourth section concludes.

IC Components and Related Literature

Intellectual capital defines the knowledge-based sources of an entity, or IC refers to the intangibles which provide competitive advantages. Dumay (2016) identifies IC as intellectual material, intellectual property, knowledge and experience which can be used to generate value in an entity. In this sense, IC can be defined as the value created by the intellectual assets that include all intangibles of an entity. Similarly, Brooking (1996) has regarded IC as a company's unobservable assets, that is, intangibles, which allows the company to carry on its activities. He indicated that the intangible assets classified into four groups as human-based assets, intellectual property assets, information infrastructure assets and market-based assets. On the other hand, Edvinsson (1997) describes IC as the knowledge which can be converted into value. Alike Brooking (1996), he emphasizes the assets which cannot be observed on the balance sheets.

Stewart (1991) defines IC as the knowledge of employees within a company, which provides the company with competitive advantage. He enlarged the scope of IC in 1997 and identifies IC as the knowledge on which each entity relies heavily such as patents, technologies, managerial adepts, past experiences, procedures concerning suppliers and customers (Stewart 1997b). Therefore, IC refers to organizational and knowledge-based intangible assets that include intellectual property and organizational capital. Software rights, copyrights, licences and patents are cited as examples of intellectual property, while protocols, implicit information, systems and processes are some of the components of organizational capital (IIRC 2013: 12).

In the financial perspective, IC is identified as the gap which occurs between the company's market value and its book value (Ordóñez de Pablos 2004). From the accounting perspective, IC shows the value of intangibles such as patents, trademarks, copyrights, goodwills, etc. However, financial statements are unable to report all components of IC. Therefore, intangibles represent only some part of IC. That is, IC includes the assets which generate value for the company (Petty and Guthrie 2000).

Structural capital, human capital and relational capital are the main components of IC that have been dealt with in the literature (Bontis 1998; Roos and Roos 1997; Sánchez et al. 2001; Stewart 1997a). Structural capital is related with an organization's structures that favour its employees with searching for the optimal intellectual performance (Bontis 1998; Mouritsen and Roslender 2009). Structural capital relies on the productivity and capacity to develop new things of a company. Human capital includes competencies, information, attitudes of a company's employees and their capacities to make decisions and cope with problems quickly (Gogan and Draghici 2013). Social and relationship capital refers to the institutions and the relationships within and between societies, groups of related parties and other networks and the talent of sharing knowledge in order to improve individual and common welfare (IIRC 2013: 12).

Although identifying IC components have been researched by many authors, IC has become crucial following the studies of Sveiby (1997) in Sweden. The author brought a different perspective to IC, regarding the intangibles as the principal strategic subject which needs to be included in the entities. Since then, most of the authors have assumed that measuring IC is an important issue for a company (Matos 2013: 340).

It is fair to say that traditional corporate valuation methods cannot meet the needs of today's business environment. Most of these methods pay attention to tangible assets of a company. However, it is essential to recognize intellectual capital on balance sheet as well (Berzkalne and Zelgalve 2014: 888). In this sense, it is required to put more emphasis on IC in the frame of the modern value creation process.

Inadequacy of Accounting

IAS 1, presentation of financial statements, states that the aim of the financial statements is to enable its users to obtain useful information concerning the financial position and performance of entities. Thus, required information concerning an entity is provided to its investors and stakeholders by full IC disclosure on financial statements.

In IAS 38, an asset is defined as a resource controlled by a corporation in consequence of past events and expected to provide economic benefits to the corporation in the future. The notion of intangible asset is described as a nonmonetary asset with identifiable, separable and nonphysical characteristics in IAS 38. Intangibles can be recognized only when three conditions are fulfilled at the same time according to IAS 38. Then, appropriate valuation model can be chosen by an entity. Recognition of intangibles is shown in Table 18.1.

IAS 38 indicates that computer software, patents, copyrights, licence, market rights, customer and supplier relationships are among the potential examples of assets. These items generally regarded as intellectual assets cannot meet the so-called conditions. In that, most of the intangibles are impossible to be controlled.

Table 18.1 Recognition of intangibles

Condition	Answer	Result
Is asset separable and controlled?	No	Not recognized
	Yes	First condition is fulfilled
Will it generate future economic benefits?	No	No valuation
	Yes	Second condition is fulfilled
Can value be reliably determined?	No	Component of goodwill
	Yes	Third condition is fulfilled
Selection of suitable valuation method	Yes	All the conditions are fulfilled

Therefore, the concept of asset needs to be redefined to report the real value of a company on balance sheets.

Human capital is the most challenged component of IC to be identified and recognized. Although this component includes intangible assets, human potential cannot be expressed in monetary units. Therefore, current financial statements do not reflect the human capital. Thus, traditional financial reporting cannot definitely disclose value of IC created by organizations. Moreover, traditional financial statements are prepared on the grounds of historical costs. In this sense, traditional accounting approaches give importance to controlling costs (Svanadze and Kowalewska 2015). Therefore, they cannot reflect the future cash flows of companies. Also, according to the traditional accounting principles, most intangibles, especially internally developed ones, cannot be displayed in the balance sheets. Only if the specific conditions are fulfilled, expenditures on development shall be recognized.

Capitalizing development expenditures lead to increase the tax base, so the financial result appears low in income statement. Smaller companies have a tendency to capitalize development expenses in order to increase their net profit, while larger ones are likely to recognize these expenditures as period expenses with the aim of reducing their taxable income and providing a tax advantage. Thus, this causes investors to make irrational decisions.

Determination, measurement and reporting of internally generated intangibles such as goodwills are difficult issues for the accounting that is based on historical costs and the traditional accounting principles. When patents and copyrights are purchased, they are recorded on balance sheets of companies. Apart from intellectual property such as patents and trademarks, acquired assets such as goodwills can be traditionally recognized in financial statements, while information cannot be correctly reported on the balance sheet or cannot completely reflect the reality of the economic and financial positions of firms. On the other hand, the value of internally generated intangible assets still has not been determined in monetary units. Thus, internally generated goodwill shall not be recognized as an intangible asset since the aforementioned recognition criteria cannot be fulfilled. When incurred, internally generated goodwill, start-up, advertising and training costs are considered as period expenses.

It is obvious that only a part of intangible assets has been represented in traditional financial statements. This induces external and internal parties of a company not to obtain useful information about the financial and economic performance of the company. Thus, traditional accounting has limitations on IC reporting, though there are no widely accepted standards for IC reporting (Karimi and Gholami 2014).

Guthrie (2001) realized that there exists a continuous search for creating a better system in order to spread knowledge within organizations since the value of IC still cannot be accurately recorded and reported through traditional accounting systems. Managing IC and overcoming the insufficiency of reporting intangible assets properly, a number of models for evaluating the IC of corporations have been developed by several authors. Once IC is measured by using one of the IC measurement methods, IC can be reported in financial statements.

What We Have in Hand: Methods Overview

A wide-range of models used for IC measurement has been developed over the last decades with the keen on running the intellectual capital. Generally, methods were developed for the internal use of specific companies, and so, we cannot find a standardized approach on IC measurement which can be widely used. Thus, choosing an appropriate method among developed ones play an important role on determining the financial situation or performance of the firm.

Luthy (1998) and Williams (2000) offer a classification which categorizes the IC measurement methods: (1) market capitalization methods (MCM), (2) return on assets methods (ROAM), (3) direct intellectual capital methods (DICM) and (4) scorecard methods (SCM). MCM and ROAM, known as market models, measure IC at the aggregate organizational level. In these models, market and annual reports of companies are the sources for obtaining the data used to calculate the value of IC. The other ones, DICM and SCM, identify IC measurement methods at the component level. Therefore, they are regarded as management methods in which the data for measuring IC value acquired from within companies (Nazari 2014). In order to find out attempts to measure IC, current models which are chronologically categorized depending on the Williams' (2000) classification are shown in Tables 18.2, 18.3, 18.4 and 18.5 (adapted from Sveiby 2010). This part of the chapter reviews the most widely used methods for measuring IC based on the Williams four-method categorization.

Table 18.2 Market capitalization methods

Year	Method
1990	The invisible balance sheet
1997	Tobin's Q
1997	Calculated intangible value
1998	Investor-assigned market value (IAMV)
2002	FiMIAM

Table 18.3   Return on assets methods

Year	Method
1997	Economic value added (EVA)
1997	Value added intellectual coefficient (VAIC)
1998	Calculated intangible value
1999	Knowledge capital earnings

Table 18.4   Direct intellectual capital methods

Year	Method
1996	Citation-weighted patents
1996	Technology broker
1996	Human resource costing and accounting
1998	Accounting for the future (AFTF)
1998	HR statement
2000	Intellectual asset valuation
2000	The value explorer
2000	Total value creation (TVC)
2001	Inclusive valuation methodology (IVM)
2002	FiMIAM
2007	Dynamic monetary model
2008	EVVICAE

Market Capitalization Methods

Market capitalization methods estimate the value of IC by computing the difference between market capitalization of a firm and its shareholders' equity (Sveiby 2010). Capital market values are employed in order to predict the IC value of companies (Nazari 2014). These methods presume that forecasting the value of IC based on capital market is beneficial for organizations.

Calculated intangible value (CIV) method, which is illustrated by Stewart (1995), is categorized under both ROA and MC methods. Calculated intangible value indicates the difference between the sustainable profit and the expected return on the tangibles of the company (CIMA 2005). This method is designed to cope with the companies' problems in providing financial resources. Credit organizations provide companies with credits by considering the tangible assets which they own regardless of their intangible assets (Stewart 1997a). This poses a challenge especially for the knowledge-based companies that own few tangible assets. It is obvious that a company's market value is affected not only by the tangibles but also by the intangibles of the company.

Tobin's Q ratio is regarded as one of the MC methods developed by James Tobin (1969). This ratio equals the market value divided by the value of assets replacement (Gogan and Draghici 2013: 870–871). Many researchers have used this ratio so as to measure the performance of companies. Stewart (1997a) discussed that this ratio was not introduced to measure the value of IC, though it has become a useful indicator of IC (Nazari 2014).

Table 18.5 Scorecard methods

Year	Method
1992	Balanced scorecard
1997	IC Index™
1997	Skandia Navigator™
1997	Intangible assets monitor
1998	Intellect model
1999	Holistic accounts
1999	Modelo Nova
2000	Value creation index (VCI)
2000	IC rating
2000	Intangible value framework
2000	Intellectual capital rating
2001	Value chain scoreboard
2001	Based on EFQM model
2001	Heng model
2001	Meritum guidelines
2001	Intangible assets statement
2001	Knowledge audit cycle
2003	Dynamic valuation of intellectual capital (IC-dVAL)
2003	Danish guidelines
2003	Public sector IC
2004	Chen, Zhu e Xie model
2004	Intellectual asset-based management (IABM)
2004	Topplinjen/business IQ
2004	National intellectual capital
2004	Index SICAP-EU project
2004	Intellectus
2005	Intellectual Capital Value Creation
2007	Intellectus model
2008	Regional intellectual capital index (RICI)
2009	ICU report

Source: Adapted from Sveiby (2010)

Although market-to-book ratio does not exist under the Williams classification (2000), it is one of the methods mostly used for measuring IC. According to this model, IC refers to the difference between the market and the book values of a company (Stewart 1997a; Luthy 1998). As the ratio increases, the value of IC of a company is getting higher. This ratio has become a reasonable method in order to evaluate IC (Nazari 2014) because in the framework of the traditional accounting, the value of intangibles, particularly internally generated ones, cannot be reported on the balance sheets of companies.

Return on Assets Methods

Return on assets equals a firm's average earnings before taxes divided by the firm's average tangibles according to ROA methods. Namely, product of the average tangibles and the difference between ROA and industrial average of a company gives the average annual earning from the intangible assets; then the above-average earnings are divided by the average cost of capital of the company. As a consequence, the expected value of its intangibles or intellectual capital is derived (Sveiby 2010: 3).

Economic value added (EVA), value added intellectual coefficient (VAIC) and the intellectual capital model (ICM) are the most widely used ROA methods.

Economic value added (EVA), proposed by Stern and Stewart Co, does not only consider as one of the methods designed for measuring intangibles; it is also used as an indicator in the accounting literature (Nazari 2014). EVA, developed in 1997, equals the difference between return on investment (ROI) and the value calculated as a result of multiplying weighted average cost of capital (WACC) with the invested capital.

The other method used for measuring IC of a company is value added intellectual coefficient (VAIC) proposed by Pulic (2000). This method depending on accounting figures is appropriate for measuring the efficiency of value generation in the organizations. A company has a chance to measure the added value based on IC formation by applying this model (Stahle et al. 2011). In other words, this is an analytical method which enables the interest groups of a company such as its managers, employees, shareholders and investors to measure the efficiency of value added created by all components of the company. This method measures IC by using the accounting numbers of companies (Pulic 2004b).

VAIC is defined as one of the IC valuation methods that measures the efficiency of the main resources, which generate value added in entities (Andriessen 2004). Figure 18.2 shows that physical and financial capital constitutes capital employed (CE), while IC includes human and structural capital. It is obvious that this model takes into consideration two important components, human and structural capital, of intellectual capital from the accounting perspective. This model aims to measure the effectiveness of these resources. In order to determine value added intellectual coefficient, it is necessary to calculate three kinds of efficiency: capital employed

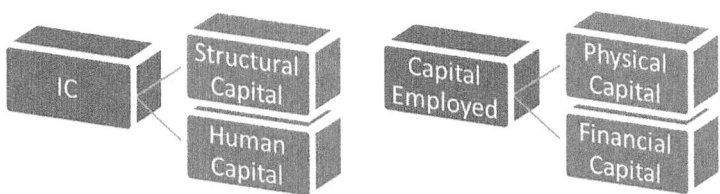

Fig. 18.2   Contents of IC and capital employed. Source: Andriessen (2004)

efficiency (CEE), structural capital efficiency (SCE) and human capital efficiency (HCE) (Pulic 2004b).

In the framework of this model, human capital (HC) is regarded as the expenses of employee (Pulic 2004a). In this sense, labour expenses are considered as an asset on the balance sheet of a company. Human capital efficiency equals added value (VA) divided by HC (Pulic 2004b). The difference between VA and HC equals structural capital (SC). Structural capital efficiency is derived as a result of dividing SC by VA. Capital employed efficiency is calculated by dividing VA with capital employed (Berzkalne and Zelgalve 2014: 889).

Pulic (2004b) explains that value added intellectual coefficient (VAIC) is the sum of three kinds of efficiency aforementioned. This coefficient indicates the amount of value created per invested resources in terms of monetary units. If a company increases the value generated by employing its resources, the coefficient becomes higher (Berzkalne and Zelgalve 2014). VAIC provides a standardized and consistent measure (Firer and Williams 2003), which enables companies to compare their performances with other companies' efficiency in intellectual capital. On the other hand, the study by Stahle et al. (2011) indicates that VAIC parameters are not related with IC. These parameters only show that the extent to which a company is efficient in its labour and capital investments.

Direct Intellectual Capital Methods

Direct intellectual capital methods predict the value of intangibles or intellectual capital by determining its elements. Technology broker, developed by Brooking (1996), classifies IC into four groups as intellectual property assets, human-centred assets, infrastructure assets and market assets and calculates IC by taking the sum of them. Dynamic valuation of intellectual capital, developed by Bounfour (2003), brings a dynamic perspective to intellectual capital by its indicators which are derived from four dimensions of competitiveness: resources, processes, intangible assets and outputs (Aitouche et al. 2015). Pursuant to this model, providing a competitive advantage for a company and a nation via four dimensions of competitiveness is probable (Nazari 2014).

The value explorer is offered by KPMG in 1998 as a new accounting methodology for measuring IC (Andriessen and Tissen 2000; Andriessen 2005). In this model, a set of core competencies is identified in order to indicate the significance of IC for an entity. Andriessen (2005) implies that to apply this model, a company should pursue five steps: (a) create a categorization of core competencies to determine IC; (b) evaluate these competencies by using a checklist; (c) allocate a part of expected normalized earnings to these competencies in order to identify the value of IC; (d) provide advice to management so as to enhance the value of IC; and (e) prepare a report by using a value dashboard (Nazari 2014). It aims to determine and assign value to five kinds of intangible assets: assets and grants, competencies and implicit information, common values and norms, technology and explicit knowledge and primary and management procedures (Andriessen and Tissen 2000). There exist some successful applications of the Value Explorer in practice; however, determining the aforementioned core competencies and allocating the value of IC to these competencies pose a challenge (Nazari 2014).

The model, FiMIAM, proposed by Rodov and Leliaert (2002) associates the IC value to the gap between the market and book value of a company. In this model, measurement of tangible and intangibles have been incorporated (Sveiby 2010). FiMIAM evaluates IC value measured in monetary values. The model takes into consideration three main IC components: human, customer and structural capital (Nazari 2014). In this model, the strategic significance of IC in value generation has been emphasized. However, certainty in identifying the value of IC components has not been provided yet (Nazari 2014).

Scorecard Methods

Scorecard methods measure IC by using nonfinancial indicators and determine the IC indicators reported in scorecards. In this sense, a dollar value for the elements of IC cannot be estimated in these methods (Nazari 2014).

Balanced scorecard is the first model to measure IC classified under SCM (Kaplan and Norton 1992, 1996a, b) where IC equals the sum of client, internal, employee and financial perspectives (Gogan and Draghici 2013: 870–871). In this model, it is tried to determine what companies should really measure by balancing the internal and external criteria for evaluating IC performance. Corporate performance is appraised in terms of four perspectives: learning and development, client, financial and internal business processes (Kaplan and Norton 1996b). While determining these criteria, strategic objectives of a company are taken into consideration. After measurement, the targets of the company are identified. In accordance with these targets, necessary actions are taken by the company (Kaplan and Norton 1996b). In this sense, this method redresses a strategic balance between the tangibles and intangibles in the framework of causation.

Skandia Navigator was developed by Edvinson and Malone (1997). It is one of the pioneer models to evaluate IC by using nonfinancial indicators (Edvinsson and Sullivan 1996). In this model, IC includes human capital and structural capital (Gogan and Draghici 2013: 870–871). This model employs five basic indicators for measuring and reporting IC and focuses on financial, replacement and development, client, process and human-based dimensions (Edvinsson 1997; Mouritsen et al. 2001: 405).

Developed by Sveiby (1997), intangible assets monitor is one of the methods categorized under the scorecard methods. In this model, the intangible assets were separated into three categories: individual competency, external structure and internal structure. This model depends on quantitative and qualitative indicators in order to evaluate IC and has been employed by several corporations all over the world that propose a conspectus of intellectual capital (Sveiby 1997).

National intellectual capital index, developed by Bontis (2004), aims to evaluate IC of a nation (Bontis 2002) which includes human capital, market capital, process capital and renewal capital. In this sense, it is modified from Skandia Navigator in terms of nations. National wealth constitutes financial wealth and IC (Aitouche et al. 2015). Bontis (2004) made an analysis of IC in terms of five core scopes: human, process, renewal, financial and market capital (Nazari 2014). Bontis (2004) identified various indices for each component.

Comparison of Methods

IC measuring methods can be divided into two groups: those which measure intellectual capital using with financial indicators and those which use nonfinancial indicators like scorecard methods. It is significant that companies need to be consistent in applying the method which they choose for measuring IC. This allows dynamic IC analysis and comparisons of the yearly results (Gogan and Draghici 2013: 869).

It is given in the Table 18.6, a comparison of four categories of methods used for IC measurement in terms of their pros and cons (Marr and Roos 2005). And Table 18.7 represents comparison of existing models mostly used for IC assessment in terms of their strengths and weaknesses (Gogan and Draghici 2013: 870–871).

Applicability of Methods by Accounting Numbers

SCM and DICM which are also known as the management methods measure IC by using the data acquired from within companies. In addition, SCM use nonfinancial indicators to measure and evaluate IC of a company[1]. Therefore, methods in these categories could not be applied by accounting numbers and cannot be considered as useful tool from the accounting perspective.

On the other hand, MCM and ROAM are nearly fully applicable to accounting because the necessary data is obtained by the market, annual reports and financial statements of the company in order to calculate the IC value of a company. Classified as one of the MCM methods, the market-to-book ratio and Tobin's Q ratio were offered to be regarded as more trustworthy measures from the perspectives of

---

[1]Due to the fact that SCM measure IC by using nonfinancial indicators, they are insufficient in making financial analysis in terms of accounting approach. From the perspectives of investors, there are some drawbacks related with the SCM such as the balanced scorecard, Skandia Navigator and national intellectual capital index. The most important disadvantage of these methods is the lack of comparability among firms and industries, which causes the usefulness of the information to diminish. Similarly, direct intellectual capital methods are not suitable for benchmarking or comparison with the other companies.

Table 18.6 A comparison of methods depending on Williams categorization

Category	Pros	Cons
MCM	• Suitable for comparison of companies in a given scope • Measures IC in monetary values • Suitable for benchmarking • Beneficial in the situations of merger and acquisitions and stock valuation	• Not due to provide a conspectus of IC progress in companies • Limited to focus on economic perspective
ROAM	• Suitable for benchmarking • Makes companies operated within the same sector comparable • Depends on the traditional accounting principles • Beneficial in the situations such as merger and acquisitions and stock valuation	• Limited knowledge in constituting intellectual capital • Limited to focus on economic perspective • Easily affected by interest rate and the assumptions of discounting rate
DICM	• Provides a separately measurement of the components of IC • Enables a far-reaching portrait of an entity's IC • Measures IC depending on events. Thus, this model enables companies to quickly prepare IC reports and is more reliable than the other pure financial measures • Can be better identified with organizational strategy when compared with the other methods • Can be easily applied to all units of a company	• Peculiar to certain companies • Not suitable for benchmarking or comparison with the other companies • Not include all the components of IC
SCM	• Allows an extensive analysis of intellectual capital compared with the other methods depending on measuring monetary values • Easy to apply to all units of a company • Suitable for non-profit and public sector organizations	• Affected by the changes occurred in the content of IC • Hard to get a quantitative result by applying this method • Indicators are based on context and have to be adapted to meet the needs of every organization. This makes comparisons difficult

investors (Stewart 1997a). Although these methods were not essentially developed on the purpose of measuring IC, they have been used as measures of IC.

The Tobin's Q method relies on traditional accounting principles but can measure IC more accurately when compared with other methods. Replacement costs instead of historical ones are used to measure the value of IC in this method, eliminating the negativities emerged from the application of amortization. By contrary, there are some disadvantages of this method. First of all, the necessary information for measuring IC cannot be easily accessible. Secondly, Tobin's Q is difficult to calculate the replacement costs. Finally, it only allows for comparisons among companies within the same sector.

Table 18.7 Comparison of existing models mostly used for IC evaluation

Method	Strengths	Weaknesses
Calculated intangible value	• Suitable for benchmarking and comparisons among industries on the grounds of audited financial outcomes • Can be easily computed	• Takes into consideration the industry ROA as a main indicator • Cannot assess the components of IC • Depends on cost of capital in calculating the net present value of intangible assets. This causes financial statements not to reflect the real potential of companies • Not putting forward an opinion concerning the management of intellectual capital • Not providing information about the future performance of companies
Value added intellectual coefficient	• Can be easily computed • Allows for a confirmable, easily accessible and objective data • Provides a standardized and consistent measure • Suitable for making comparisons among companies	• Its parameters are not related with IC • Argued in virtue of its method to separate expenses from assets
Dynamic valuation of intellectual capital	• Can be employed at the macroeconomic and country level • Suitable for benchmarking and comparison of business performance • Can improve the overestimates of market's possible value • Can develop performance indicators directly adherent to operational responsibilities	• Subjective in identifying certain indexes • The certain problem which the model deals and copes with is not obvious • Not clear what the indicators represent and the way they are joined • The way the overall index needs to be interpreted and the reason why it is multiplied by the market value is not examined in this model • Not obvious how the calculations of human, structural and market capital are made and the reason why the sum of them equals to the firm's market value
Tobin's Q ratio	• Proposes a worldwide view • Appropriate for benchmarking • Depends on the traditional accounting principles • Measures IC more accurately, because it employs replacement costs instead of historical ones • Eliminates the negativities which arise from the application of amortization because this ratio takes into consideration replacement costs	• Not easy to get the required information • Relies on the market • Difficult to calculate the replacement costs • Only allows for comparisons among companies within the same sector
Market-to-book value	• Easy to get the necessary information • Can be easily computed	• Only applied by the companies whose shares are publicly traded

(continued)

Table 18.7 (continued)

Method	Strengths	Weaknesses
Economic value added	• Gives an opportunity for making an analysis of individual business units such as departments and products • Easily applied by companies • Is due to benchmarking	• Not take into consideration the future performance of entities • The profitability of companies needs to be above the financing costs of them
Balanced scorecard	• Gives importance to the meets of the stakeholders • Applicable for the companies	• Insufficient in making financial analysis • Inflexible model. In this sense, the categorizations that are rigid and peculiar to companies need to be created. This causes companies not to be externally compared • Restricted model in terms of the classification of the factors which affect the performance of companies • Employees of a company have an indirect effect on its incomes rather than fundamental one
Skandia Navigator	• Not constitute financial components • Allows for a comprehensive standpoint about companies	• Applied only by the experienced staff • Cannot make an analysis of synergies between regions
National intellectual capital index	• The most well-known regional IC measurement method • A method generally accepted in macroeconomic literature on IC	• Merely financial and industrial indicators are proposed in this model. Nevertheless, due to the originality of qualitative indicators, companies can face with some methodological problems when applying this method • Human capital can directly affect the economic performance of a nation. On the other hand, market capital has an impact on it via other elements of IC

Overall, both the market-to-book ratio (equals the ratio the market value to the book value of a company) and the Tobin's Q ratio (equals the market value divided by the value of assets' replacement) depend on the market value of a company. This situation poses a challenge in terms of calculating IC properly because in emerging countries where the capital markets can be subject to the economic fluctuations.

Value added intellectual coefficient, categorized under the ROAM, is the mostly used methods in practice by the reasons of its simplicity in terms of computability, accessibility, objectiveness and confirmability. The calculation of the coefficient depends on the audited information, which provides a standardized and consistent measure and gives a chance to compare several companies easily in terms of their IC value.

Apart from the advantages of value added intellectual coefficient, some authors argue that determining the efficiency of IC by using ratios causes the effect of IC elements on value generation not to be observed, and value added is not only the outcome of the components used in this model (Svanadze and Kowalewska 2015). A questionable conclusion can be drawn when this method is applied for measuring IC. Because, in order to find the value of coefficient, one of the components needed to be calculated is capital employed efficiency which equals the ratio of the total added value created by the company to the book value of the company's assets (Pulic 2004b). Thus, high value added intellectual coefficient scores are calculated for the firms with a high debt to asset ratio, which indicates an insignificant result.

Moreover, labour expenses are regarded as an asset in this model. Pursuant to the definition of asset in IAS 38, an asset would provide economic benefits to the company in the future. Some of the labour expenses such as research and development expenses can provide benefits to the entity in the following accounting period; however, this kind of expenses are mostly not expected to bring benefit to the company (Svanadze and Kowalewska 2015). Capitalizing all labour expenses within an accounting period as an asset leads to an increase in the depreciation expenses within that period, which affects the income statement by decreasing the profit.

In spite of the so-called limitations of VAIC, this method has been applied in practice in order to attempt to report IC in financial statements. Furthermore, it has been a research subject of several studies in the literature concerning the measurement of intangibles and the effect of IC on the performance of corporations.

Conclusion

Traditional corporate valuation methods depend on the balance sheet and statement of income, that is, accounting figures of company. Historical costs are taking into account in traditional accounting reporting. Thus, it focuses on controlling costs. Furthermore, it relies on estimated value such as forecasting free cash flows and weighted average cost of capital for following periods. From the accounting perspective, intellectual capital is defined as the value of intangibles such as patents, trademarks, copyrights, goodwills, etc. However, intangible assets constitute only a part of intellectual capital. Thus, all components of intellectual capital cannot be reported in financial statements.

IAS 38 indicates that computer software, patents, copyrights, licence, market rights, customer and supplier relationships are among the potential examples of assets. These items generally considered as intangible assets cannot fulfill the aforementioned recognition conditions. Therefore, the concept of asset needs to be redefined in order to report the real value of intellectual capital which companies generates on balance sheets.

The value created by intellectual capital is too crucial for an indicator of companies' performance. Users of financial statements have a chance to evaluate how effectively a company operates in its sector and whether or not it realizes its objectives, only if intellectual capital is accurately reported in the financial statements.

Intellectual capital is regarded as the key indicator of a successful company, with the arrival of knowledge-based economy. Recently, there has been a growing unanimity on the significance of intangibles with a view to competitive edge of enterprises. Therefore, managing, reporting and evaluating intellectual capital have become crucial for companies in terms of their future potential.

Companies' increasing interest on managing intellectual capital and reflecting the real value of intangible assets on the balance sheets and income statements has provided the development of several methods used for measuring and evaluating intellectual capital in recent years. Although there have been a number of methods essentially developed for complementing accounting standards, it is not easy to arrive at a consensus which model is better to be used for measuring and reporting intellectual capital from the accounting perspective. In addition, a generally accepted model has not been emerged in the literature yet. Also, the existing methods have various pros and cons when compared with each other. It can be possible to consider value added intellectual coefficient, one of the return on assets methods, as the most applicable method used for measuring intellectual capital to accounting.

The required data to measure intellectual capital by using this method can be easily accessible and confirmable and objective as it is obtained from the company's audited financial statements and annual reports. On the other hand, the model is criticized by some authors in terms of its' using parameters not related with intellectual capital and the method which it uses to separate expenses from assets. In this sense, this model takes into consideration only two components of intellectual capital, structural and human capital. The number of studies applying this method is increasing in spite of the limitations of the value added intellectual coefficient model. However, it is better to improve this method by eliminating its limitations or develop new methods in order to measure and, thereby, to report the value of intellectual capital properly.

The comprehensive theoretical analysis of existing measurement intellectual capital methods indicates that there still has been a need to develop innovative models for intellectual capital evaluation with the aim of overcoming the inadequacy in the financial reporting relying on traditional approaches.

References

Aitouche, S., Mouss, N. K., Mouss, M. D., Kaanit, A., & Marref, T. (2015). Comparison and prioritisation of measurement methods of intellectual capital; IC-dVal, VAIC and NICI. *International Journal of Learning and Intellectual Capital, 12*(2), 122–145.

Andriessen, D. (2004). *Making sense of intellectual capital: Designing a method for the valuation of intangibles*. Abingdon: Routledge.

Andriessen, D., & Tiessen, R. (2000). *Weightless Weight–Find your real value in a future of intangible assets*. London: Financial Times Prentice Hall.

Andriesson, D. (2005). Implementing the KPMG value explorer: Critical success factors for applying IC measurement tools. *Journal of Intellectual Capital, 6*(4), 474–488.

Berzkalne, I., & Zelgalve, E. (2014). Intellectual capital and company value. *Procedia-Social and Behavioral Sciences, 110*, 887–896.

Bontis, N. (1998). Intellectual capital: An exploratory study that develops measures and models. *Management Decision, 36*(2), 63–76.

Bontis, N. (2002). *National intellectual capital index: Intellectual capital development in the Arab Region.* Ontario: Institute for Intellectual Capital Research.

Bontis, N. (2004). National intellectual capital index: A United Nations initiative for the Arab region. *Journal of Intellectual Capital, 5*(1), 13–39.

Bounfour, A. (2003). *The management of intangibles: The organisation's most valuable assets* (Vol. 16). Hove: Psychology Press.

Brooking, A. (1996). *Intellectual capital: Core asset for the third millennium enterprise.* London: International Thomson Business Press.

Chen, M. C., Cheng, S. J., & Hwang, Y. (2005). An empirical investigation of the relationship between intellectual capital and firms' market value and financial performance. *Journal of Intellectual Capital, 6*(2), 159–176.

CIMA. (2005, March 24). *Understanding corporate value: Managing and reporting intellectual capital.* Retrieved from http://www.cimaglobal.com/Documents/ImportedDocuments/intellectualcapital.pdf

Cronje, C. J., & Moolman, S. (2013). Intellectual capital: Measurement, recognition and reporting. *South African Journal of Economic and Management Sciences, 16*(1), 1–12.

Dumay, J. (2016). A critical reflection on the future of intellectual capital: From reporting to disclosure. *Journal of Intellectual Capital, 17*(1), 168–184.

Edvinsson, L. (1997). Developing intellectual capital at Skandia. *Long Range Planning, 30*(3), 320–373.

Edvinsson, L., & Malone, M. S. (1997). *Intellectual capital: Realizing your company's true value by finding its hidden brainpower.* New York: Harper Business.

Edvinsson, L., & Sullivan, P. (1996). Developing a model for managing intellectual capital. *European Management Journal, 14*(4), 356–364.

Firer, S., & Mitchell Williams, S. (2003). Intellectual capital and traditional measures of corporate performance. *Journal of Intellectual Capital, 4*(3), 348–360.

Gennaioli, N., La Porta, R., Lopez-de-Silanes, F., & Shleifer, A. (2013). Human capital and regional development. *Quarterly Journal of Economics, 128*, 105–164.

Glaeser, E., LaPorta, R., López-de-Silanes, F., & Shleifer, A. (2004). Do institutions cause growth? *Journal of Economic Growth, 9*, 271–303.

Gogan, L. M., & Draghici, A. (2013). A model to evaluate the intellectual capital. *Procedia Technology, 9*, 867–875.

Gowthorpe, C. (2009). Wider still and wider? A critical discussion of intellectual capital recognition, measurement and control in a boundary theoretical context. *Critical Perspectives on Accounting, 20*(7), 823–834.

Guthrie, J. (2001). The management, measurement and the reporting of intellectual capital. *Journal of Intellectual Capital, 2*(1), 27–41.

Hanushek, E., & Woessmann, L. (2008). The role of cognitive skills in economic development. *Journal of Economic Literature, 46*, 607–668.

Hanushek, E., & Woessmann, L. (2012a). Schooling, educational achievement, and the Latin American growth puzzle. *Journal of Development Economics, 99*, 497–512.

Hanushek, E., & Woessmann, L. (2012b). Do better schools lead to more growth? Cognitive skills, economic outcomes, and causation. *Journal of Economic Growth, 17*, 267–321.

International Integrated Reporting Council (IIRC). (2013). *The international framework.* London: IIRC.

Kaplan, R. S., & Norton, D. P. (1992). The balanced scorecard: Translating strategy into action. *Harvard Business Review, Jan–Feb*, 71–79.

Kaplan, R. S., & Norton, D. P. (1996a). Using the balanced scorecard as a strategic management system. *Harvard Business Review, Jan–Feb*, 75–85.

Kaplan, R. S., & Norton, D. P. (1996b). *The balanced scorecard: Translating strategy into action.* Boston: Harvard Business Press.

Karimi, A., & Gholami, K. (2014). How to measure the intellectual capital (IC) of an organization or financial institutions? *Bulletin of Environment, Pharmacology and Life Sciences, 3*(2), 291–295.

Luthy, D. H. (1998, August). *Intellectual capital and its measurement* (pp. 16–17). Proceedings of the Asian Pacific Interdisciplinary Research in Accounting Conference (APIRA), Osaka, Japan.

Marr, B., & Roos, G. (2005). A strategy perspective on intellectual capital. In *Perspectives on intellectual capital* (pp. 28–41). Amsterdam: Elsevier.

Matos, F. (2013). A theoretical model for the report of intellectual capital. *The Electronic Journal of Knowledge Management, 11*(4), 339–360.

Mouritsen, J., Larsen, H. T., & Bukh, P. N. (2001). Valuing the future: Intellectual capital supplements at Skandia. *Accounting, Auditing & Accountability Journal, 14*(4), 399–422.

Mouritsen, J., & Roslender, R. (2009). Critical intellectual capital. *Critical Perspectives on Accounting, 20*, 801–803.

Nazari, J. A. (2014). Intellectual capital measurement and reporting models. In *Knowledge management for competitive advantage during economic crisis* (pp. 117–139). Hershey, PA: IGI Global.

Ocean Tomo. (2015). *Annual study of intangible asset market value.* Retrieved from http://www.oceantomo.com/blog/2015/03-05-ocean-tomo-2015-intangible-asset-market-value/

Okan Gökten, P., & Marşap, B. (2017). Paradigm shift in corporate reporting. In S. Gokten (Ed.), *Accounting and corporate reporting-today and tomorrow* (pp. 3–14). London: InTech.

Ordóñez de Pablos, P. (2004). Measuring and reporting structural capital: Lessons from European learning firms. *Journal of Intellectual Capital, 5*(4), 629–647.

Petty, R., & Guthrie, J. (2000). Intellectual capital literature review: Measurement, reporting and management. *Journal of Intellectual Capital, 1*(2), 155–176.

Pulic, A. (2000). VAIC™–an accounting tool for IC management. *International Journal of Technology Management, 20*(5–8), 702–714.

Pulic, A. (2004a). Do we know if we create or destroy value? *International Journal of Entrepreneurship and Innovation Management, 4*(4), 349–359.

Pulic, A. (2004b). Intellectual capital–does it create or destroy value? *Measuring Business Excellence, 8*(1), 62–68.

Rodov, I., & Leliaert, P. (2002). FiMIAM: Financial method of intangible assets measurement. *Journal of Intellectual Capital, 3*(3), 323–336.

Roos, G., & Roos, J. (1997). Measuring your company's intellectual performance. *Long Range Planning, 30*(3), 413–426.

Sánchez, P., Asplund, R., Stolowy, H., Roberts, H., Johanson, U., & Mouritsen, J. (2001). *Measuring intangibles to understand and improve innovation management* (MERITUM Final Report). European Commission, Brussels. Retrieved from http://www.pnbukh.com/files/pdf_filer/FINAL_REPORT_MERITUM.pdf

Ståhle, P., Ståhle, S., & Aho, S. (2011). Value added intellectual coefficient (VAIC): A critical analysis. *Journal of Intellectual Capital, 12*(4), 531–551.

Stewart, T. A. (1995). Trying to grasp the intangible. *Fortune Magazine, 26*, 157–161.

Stewart, T. A. (1997a). *Intellectual capital: The new wealth of organisations.* New York: Doubleday/Currency.

Stewart, T. A. (1997b, July 3). Brain power. How intellectual capital is becoming America's most valuable asset. *Fortune*.

Stewart, T. A. (1991). Brainpower. *Fortune, 123*(11), 44–50.

Svanadze, S., & Kowalewska, M. (2015). The measurement of intellectual capital by VAIC method–example of WIG20. *Online Journal of Applied Knowledge Management, 3*(2), 36–44.

Sveiby, K. E. (1997). *The new organizational wealth: Managing & measuring knowledge-based assets*. San Francisco: Berrett-Koehler Publishers.

Sveiby, K. (2010, April 27). *Methods for measuring intangible assets*. Retrieved from http://www.sveiby.com/files/pdf/intangiblemethods.pdf

Tobin, J. (1969). A general equilibrium approach to monetary theory. *Journal of Money, Credit and Banking, 1*(1), 15–29.

Williams, M. (2000). *Is a company's intellectual capital performance and intellectual capital disclosure practices related? Evidence from publicly listed companies from the FTSE 100*. Paper Presented at Mcmasters Intellectual Capital Conference, Toronto, January 2001.

Chapter 19
The Financial Analysis of the Ottoman Cash Waqfs

Çiğdem Gürsoy

Abstract From the sixteenth century onwards and along with the increase in the velocity of money, every state diversified its own financial sources. During the related centuries, the Ottoman state created the "cash waqfs", an outcome of local settlement, out of its trust institution as an alternative financial source. Cash waqf is the sort of foundation in which the money devoted by persons is managed through the profit/usury rates determined by the state so that the necessary charities are performed. The process can be summarized as the transfer of the total remaining amount into charity services (the primary objective) after the removal of foundation expenses from the incomes of the funds that were made use of as credit.

In endowments, treated as the deeds of foundations, the information regarding how the foundation will be operated and where its revenues will be used is recorded with all its details. Endowments are organized by foundations that are administered by trustees. The arranged section is intended for explaining the functioning of cash waqfs through the financial terms of our present day based on the details involved in endowments. Within this framework, the decisions made by foundations in preparing their endowments with close attention to the economic situations of the related period are associated with such concepts like financial management strategy, trustees' use of instruments like bonds and bills in evaluating the funds and cash management. Besides, the cash waqfs gathered in funds are addressed in relation to fund management, while the sureties and the pledged assets received during the credit phase are discussed within risk management.

Ç. Gürsoy (✉)
Department of Economics, İstinye University, Istanbul, Turkey
e-mail: cgursoy@istinye.edu.tr

© Springer International Publishing AG, part of Springer Nature 2018   389
H. Dincer et al. (eds.), *Global Approaches in Financial Economics, Banking, and Finance*, Contributions to Economics, https://doi.org/10.1007/978-3-319-78494-6_19

Introduction

From the years when financial relations started to replace exchange until today, financial sources have been required in every period. The process that advanced slowly in the earlier stages gained speed with the geographical discoveries and the capture of precious metals. Easy transportation, population growth and the prevalence of production directed at new markets accelerated the need for financial sources by expanding the trade volume. Bruno Hilbebrand classified the economic stages under three titles (Güçer 1983, p. 29).

Natural economy (the first stage)
Financial economy (the second stage)
Credit economy (the third stage)

In natural economy, production is managed on the basis of needs and possibilities, and trading is achieved on the principal of exchange. In the stage of financial economy, money started to be used in trading. As for credit economy, the need for money gradually increased and necessitated the use of alternative financial instruments. In this third stage which corresponded to the early sixteenth century, it is observed that money abounded in people's pockets and commercial partnerships were formed rapidly. The mercantile activity continuing from the sixteenth to the eighteenth century during which the trade maintained its dynamism and the first signs of globalization became apparent is also known as the Commercial Revolution (Güran 2014, p. 115).

During their first experiences of getting into the global market within these years, the states demonstrated various economic attitudes stemming from the differences related to geography, population, political regime, institutions, customs and traditions, value judgements and sense of religion (Güçer 1983, p. 12–13). The reflection of the experienced economic developments on the Ottoman state led to the emergence of "cash waqfs" which were the outcome of local settlements. This alternative financial source newly formed on the basis of foundations that sustained their services as of the early years of Islam played a major role in the assessment of the savings gained through commercial activity. Later on, the cash waqfs set up with all kinds of fund in little or large amounts showed a rapid expansion as no restriction was imposed.

Foundations are divided into two classes as movable and immovable in relation to the type of the endowed property. Within the scope of this division which is based on property portability, cash waqfs are included in the category of movable foundations, or portable foundations in other words. The foundations established in special cases in which the money and property were endowed together were also treated in the status of cash waqfs. Regardless of gender discrimination, persons who belonged to the Ottoman citizenship, reached puberty and held criminal responsibility could found cash waqfs at their own will. All establishers of movable or immovable foundations were named as "founders".

Cash waqfs established by more than one person are also available along with those founded by a single person. In this respect, whether the amounts endowed by the founders were less or more than the others did not constitute a problem. The endowed sum, growth rate, operating procedure, trustee election and other task descriptions as well as the details of the charity services to be held were recorded in the endowments upon the request of founders. In other words, founders designed their financial management strategies based on endowments. Endowments are the deeds of foundations. It is possible to state that the financial management strategy will remain unchanged once its outline is determined considering the principle that endowments cannot be changed as stated by the foundation law.

In addition to the founders who operated their foundations themselves, there also existed founders who directly handed the management over the trustees they had elected. The elected trustees worked as fund managers in line with the strategies determined by the founders. In some foundations, the founders gave initiative to trustees regarding the use of the amount they endowed. In this case, the trustees had the right to evaluate the endowed sum in accordance with their own decisions considering the economic conditions of the related period of time. The foundations that started to function right after the official approval of the endowments following the determination of trustee authorities operated in all service areas of the states, municipalities as well as private, public and non-governmental organizations of our present time including education, public works, economy, culture, social services and transportation. Within the Ottoman state known as "foundation civilization", cash waqfs occupied approximately 40% of the system in question.

The working principle of cash waqfs can be summarized as the operating of the money endowed by persons upon the usury/profit rates as defined by the state and the transfer of its revenues to the services determined in endowments. The cash waqfs were given as a credit to people asking for a loan at the fixed rates specified beforehand. The credits were used in the financing of commercial activities as well as in meeting personal needs. Within this framework, the cash waqfs identified to have been functioning in parallel with the financial need of markets from the sixteenth century onwards gradually increased both in number and in terms of the endowed amount as of the date they were first established. The cash waqfs for which new application fields were discovered in accordance with emerging needs were joined under the titles of "neighbourhood avariz funds", "artisan funds" and "janissary funds". The wealth of the cash waqfs collected under the same category were brought together in a fund pool.

It is possible to trace the alteration and transformation of cash waqfs over the years from the details of endowments and accountings. Accordingly, the cash waqfs and the basic common fields related to the companies today have primarily been identified out of the collected data. Secondly, the functionality of such financial practices like financial management strategy, cash management, fund management and risk management within cash waqfs has been questioned. Also, the common points between the procedure called "sell and leaseback" and "Bey'lil-istiglal", one of the financial methods of cash waqfs, have been touched upon under the title of risk management. The archive documents used in the making of this study have been provided from T.R. Ottoman Archives of the Prime Ministry, Court Records Archive of the Provincial Office of Mufti in Istanbul and Istanbul Kadi Records.

The Basic Common Fields of Foundations and Companies

Companies operating in financial markets are classified in various ways with regard to their field of activity, size, ownership of production means, production structures, legal structures and national origins as well as the technology they use (Sayın 2016, p. 50–71). When companies are categorized as industrial, commercial and service business according to their areas of activity, it is possible to evaluate cash waqfs under the category of service business. Social work, transportation, communication, education and financial activities listed under the title of service business are only some of the areas of interest related to cash waqfs. When businesses are categorized according to their size, cash waqfs can be analyzed under two titles. Micro-scale businesses that involve less than 10 employees and small-scale businesses with 10–50 employees can be used in defining the sizes of cash waqfs. Cash waqfs operate within a simple organization structure such as micro- and small-scale businesses and under the responsibility of a single administrator. In another business classification in accordance with the ownership of production means, cash waqfs can be qualified under the category of private businesses (Sayın 2016, p. 54). Just as all or some of the capital belonged to the company founder in private businesses, a single person endows all the money in most cash waqfs.

Businesses are divided into three as private, public and foreign-capital businesses according to their legal structure. Those in the form of partnership that exist as the subclass of private businesses are founded by either one or more than one real or artificial person within the scope of the contract and for the same purpose. In the light of this information, it is possible to regard the foundations established with the inclusion of one (or more) person as companies. Businesses in the form of companies are classified into two groups as unincorporated companies and trading companies. Trading companies are assessed as legal entities within the context of their capital structures, polities, rights and responsibilities related to the partners and divided into two as private companies and equity companies (Sayın 2016, p. 60–61). In accordance with the endowments and accounting samples, the funds into which cash waqfs were endowed were operated in conformity with the structure of the equity companies in question. All foundations gathered together in the same category after being endowed to the funds possessed legal entity and were administered by a single elected trustee. Within this framework, just as the withdrawal or death of the company partners did not affect the sustainability of the company, the death of one of the fund founders or the nonfunctionality of a foundation within the category did not influence the fund operations.

The Financial Analysis of Cash Waqfs

The proliferation of money and the increase in its velocity of circulation diversify the financial notions with each passing day. Considering the idea that all conditions are interrelated, more than one concept has been analyzed in the following chapter. Just as the fund management designed upon the proper financial management strategy cannot be dissociated from cash management, it is quite difficult to get optimum efficiency from cash and fund management performed without risk management. Within this perspective, the evaluation of cash waqfs by means of the modern financial concepts features financial management strategy as its starting point. The pursuing chapter that involves cash and fund management ends with risk management which is a required element in all three stages.

Financial Management Strategy

The financial management strategies of companies centre upon three major titles which include the supply, financing and management of the assets in the business. In order to maintain their sustainability following the establishment phase, companies embarked on a quest of new finance while, on the other hand, expanding their investment portfolio. As for the process management, it is assumed that the decision makers must have adopted rational behaviour and taken into account the possible risks and expected gainings (Karan et al. 2013, p. 3–4).

Cash waqfs were managed in a similar way to modern businesses in financial terms. The movables and immovables endowed by the founders for the purpose of bringing in money, namely, the foundation assets, were recorded in the endowments as "the essential money/capital". Most cash waqfs were established merely upon cash capital. Likewise, the banks, intermediary institutions as well as insurance and financial leasing companies and the like were founded on cash assets. In some cash waqfs, immovables were endowed along with cash. This situation, which is not a frequent case in cash waqfs, took place reversely during the establishment phase of companies. The assets of most companies comprised of movables and immovables.

The issue regarding the ownership of assets is one of the major points distinguishing foundations from companies. The whole assets in foundations are the personal property of the founder, and from the moment of their endowment on, the founder eternally renounces his or her ownership of the related property which is then offered to the public interest (Pakalın 1983, p. 577). The property in question is irrevocable, unsaleable, uninheritable, untransferable and banned from misuse. In companies, however, it is possible to bequeath, transfer and sell the property which is used as capital in the establishment phase.

The financing need of the company that continued with its activities was met with the equities and/or foreign assets within the business. The finance of the cash waqf was most often supplied with the revenues received from its equities. These included accretion revenues received from such endowed movables like money and bond as well as rental income acquired from immovables in case of endowment. In some foundations, it has been detected that the small amounts remaining after the expenses were added to the capital of the foundation in order to provide extra source of finance for the following year. In cases of the failure of revenues in making up for the charges, the founders had the opportunity to mark up movables and/or immovables on behalf of the foundation if they were still alive. In this respect, the new property was not treated within the status of foreign source since it had been added by the founders themselves. When examined in terms of the similarity in functioning, the capital increases in companies, and the mark-ups in foundations are not that much different from each other. Besides, the addition of the sum remaining after the annual expenditures to the capital in foundations can be related to the capital increase as performed by companies without distributing the net profits to their partners. Apart from these, it is possible to view the establishment of foundations upon joined cash by multiple persons and the foundation of associated companies from the same perspective.

The fact that mark-ups could be performed more than once has been identified from the endowments of Alyanakzade who marked up his foundation six times between the years 1838 and 1860. The assets of the foundation which was established with 1000 kurush in 1838 reached 11500 kurush following the mark-ups applied until 1860. Each implemented mark-up emerged out of necessity on behalf of the foundation and was recorded in the endowment in detail. The repairment of the waterways of Alyanakzade's mosque and monastery as well as the food expenses of those who accommodated in the monastery and of the needy ones among the neighbourhood residents was all reserved a share from the revenues. The mark-ups performed over the initially endowed 1000 kurush, respectively, involved 500 kurush for the staff wages, 2000 kurush for food purchase, 1000 kurush for the increase in food expense, 1500 kurush for supporting the same expenditure again, 2500 kurush for water-carrier wages and helping the monastery residents and 3000 kurush for the required mendings and the addition to food fees (Gürsoy Ç. 2015, p. 130–132). As most of the mark-ups were allocated to food expenses, it is clearly understood that the monastery offered service to even more people throughout the years.

As it became impossible to mark up the foundation upon the death of founders, different persons established new cash waqfs in order to meet the required expenses of the same foundation. These usually involved those who benefited from the opportunities of the foundation or the close relatives of the founder. In 1740, Atif Efendi established a foundation for the required expenses of the library he was about to build. Later on, his relatives set up foundations many times until the year 1865 so as to secure the sustainability of the services offered by Atif Efendi Library. In 1744, Haci Omer Efendi (Atif Efendi's son-in-law) endowed his books to the library. In 1751, Omer Vahit Efendi (Atif Efendi's son) endowed the property and revenues of his two houses in Edirne. In 1751–1752, Abdulkadir Efendi reserved the gainings of the foundation he established as the library janitor's payment. Likewise, Ahmet Bey, Mehmet Vahit Efendi and Husamettin Efendi established different foundations so as to meet the other expenses of the library in the years 1786, 1864 and 1868 (Gürsoy Ç. 2015, p. 139–140).

One of the principal points to be emphasized while determining the financial management strategy in foundations is the issue of which management procedure to be used in the evaluation of funds. The cash waqf management procedures are the true copy of borrowing procedures used in the Ottoman commercial transaction (Bilmen). Among these, "Muamele-i Ser'iyye" and "Bey" are the most frequently used lending procedures in cash waqfs. Moreover, from the second half of the nineteenth century onwards, the purchase of bonds comes into play as the operating procedure (Gürsoy Ç. 2015, p. 186).

Muamele-i ser'iyye, which means legal treatment, is the procedure in which money is lent in return for a particular period of time and amount of profit. A transaction of purchase and sale was included within the process of lending, and in this way, it was secured that the extra sum during the repayment of money resulted from this procedure. In this buying and selling process, interest and usury were carefully avoided while an item like a watch, fur or dress changed hands. Meanwhile, the necessary precaution to solve possible conflicts in the future through official means was taken beforehand by gaining the approval of the kadi (Gürsoy Ç. 2015, p. 68). The item sold by the trustee to the borrower on credit returns to the trustee again by changing hands several times with the inclusion of a third person intervening the process after the procedure (Özcan 2003, p. 54–55). Here, the item is sold not at its real value but at a price equal to the accretion of the borrowed money that needs to be repaid. A person who borrows from the trustee 1000 kurush at the rate of 15% for 1 year needs to repay 1150 kurush at the end of the year. The 150 kurush in between is the accretion revenue of the foundation and, at the same time, the value of the item sold during the borrowing.

Bey', which is another frequently used operating procedure, means exchange and signifies dealings in trade and sale in Islamic law (Özcan 2003, p. 69–70). This procedure involves two fields of practice as "bey'bi'l-vefa" and "bey'bi'l-istiglal". Bey'bi'l-vefa, a type of sales agreement, is the act of selling in which the need for a pledge overweighs and the item is given back only on the condition that its charge is returned. The development of economic life and the rise in commercial relationships brought forward even more debt-credit relationships. The implementation of pledge-inclusive debt transactions became difficult over time, and thus, sales in exchange for the borrowed money were deemed suitable instead. In other words, persons pledged their goods as security in order to find loans from the market. This act of selling was also evaluated as a sort of mortgage throughout the duration of the debt. When the loan is paid back, the sale transaction is removed, and the item is returned to its former owner. During this period of time, the money lender only holds the right of use regarding the pledged asset. The borrowed money is most often less than the real price of the good (Özcan 2003, p. 70–71). Likewise, the immovables pledged as security in return for a loan today are assessed under the status of pledge.

Bey'bi'l-istiglal "Istiglal" which means receiving the profit and revenue of a property is the type of sale in which an item is rented to the debtor for the purpose of benefiting from its income (Bayındır A. 1992, p. 22). The rent received during the sale transaction equals not to the real rental value of the property but to the accretion of the money lent. Thanks to this procedure, the debtors not only met their cash need but also continued to make use of their property. In this way, usury was avoided in loan procedures just as in the case of muamele-i ser'iyye. The related process has been analyzed in detail under the title of "sell and leaseback".

Another major point related to the operating procedure in determining financial management strategy is the issue of which accretion rate is to be taken into consideration while providing credit for the funds. It is known that the state defined the rates in question by means of usury laws and monitored the whole process to secure obedience to the rules. Thanks to the rates identified between 10% and 20%, the state was also able to struggle against the high rates of usury that reached 60% (Gürsoy Ç. 2015, p. 72). While small fluctuations of about 1–2 points were visible in the usury rates during the sixteenth, seventeenth and eighteenth centuries, from the second half of the nineteenth century onwards, these changes went up to 4–5 points. The frequency of the fluctuations in the nineteenth century increased the tendency towards not stating accretion rates in endowments.

One of the fundamental differences between foundations and companies is the issue of social responsibility. It is observed that the businesses of our present day underestimate social responsibility projects although they perform dense and effective financial operations in order to maintain their existence. The disadvantageous situation resulting from the calculation of the extra burdens that are likely to be bred by the projects in question has estranged businesses from the related issue for many years. The socially and environmentally harmful effects of these ignored projects rise to the surface afterwards and increase incrementally with each passing day. Contrary to companies, the most significant element underlying the establishment of all foundations, movable or immovable, is the idea of social responsibility. By virtue of the endowments, the supports offered to the poor, orphans, the disabled, those who are about to start a business or get married and other needy people were followed closely. The foundations served just like the social security institutions or pension funds in our day also provided for the repair and maintenance of architectural works of art and infrastructural investments. As a notable indicator of the care for environment, the underground and overland natural sources in the Ottoman state functioned as foundation enterprises.

In the light of all the above-mentioned information, the secret of success concerning the financial management strategies of businesses owes much to well-directed prediction and planning, ensuring the coordination and control among all sections of the business, and collaboration with money and capital markets. On the other hand, the triumph of the financial management strategies of foundations depends a great deal upon long-term planning by the founders so as to maintain the sustainability of their foundations, the activation of control mechanism by means of coordinating the incomes and expenses of foundations and the diversification of economic instruments in accordance with the market conditions.

Cash Management

An effective cash management aims at balancing between the payments and collections of businesses as well as taking the optimum advantage of cash (Çankaya 2012). Businesses need to keep cash for three main reasons: transaction, caution and speculation. The first two of these seek achieving the routine operations and avoiding the unexpected economic and/or extraordinary natural developments. As for the investments made in risky areas so as not to miss the advantageous investment opportunities, they constantly involve speculative risk (Çankaya 2012).

On the other hand, cash waqfs' need of holding cash stems from the causes related to transaction and caution. Based on the principle of maintaining the amount of funds, speculation-oriented money use is unfavourable according to the foundation law. For those foundation managers who violate the law, punishments like discharge from the managing position and recovery of the losses were imposed. Apart from the speculative activities, other issues that dominated the cash management of foundations involved the effort to prevent the funds from remaining inactive and reducing in amount, the mark-ups applied when necessary and the regulation of expenses in the case of diminished accretion rates. How the cash flow of the foundation should proceed was recorded in detail in the endowments. The trustee could gain the optimum benefit based on his or her ability in handling the management and control in accordance with the circumstances in the endowment. Trustees who could not maximize cash flows had difficulty in meeting the expenses of the foundation.

The endowed movables and/or immovables were apparently defined in all of the cash waqfs. Similarly, the operating procedures and accretion rates are recorded in most endowments until the mid-nineteenth century apart from the exceptions. In this way, it became possible to calculate the annual maximum income of the foundation (Gürsoy 2017, p. 178). The operating of all the endowed money at the defined rate in the way to reach the targeted revenue was the prior condition so as to maintain the sustainability of the foundation services. It is a significant detail that transactions could be performed below the determined rates if required, and yet, exceeding the rates was allowed in no way. The income losses were targeted to be minimalized by lending money at rates that are lower than the defined ones in order to prevent the inactivity of the money.

In the aftermath of the mid-nineteenth century when the state started to change the accretion rates more frequently in compliance with the increase in economic fluctuations, tendency towards defining accretion rates reduced in foundations. Following the second half of the nineteenth century, it is understood that the founders who established foundations did not determine accretion rates in the making of their financial management strategies considering the market conditions. Some founders preferred not to state rates within the framework of effective cash management as the defined rate could not be exceeded according to the foundation law. A foundation that determined a rate of 10% in its endowment was sure to lose by about 2% with an increase in the usury rate up to 12% as imposed by the state. Also, the act of not stating specified rates in endowments brought along rapid conformity to market conditions and made the cash management of the trustee more efficient (Gürsoy 2017, p. 179).

The expenses of foundations, as well as the revenues, were recorded in endowments in detail apart from some exceptions. The total charges match up with the expected gainings of the endowed money. In this way, the accretion rate could be approximately calculated by means of expense totals in foundations that did not state a particular accretion rate. In a foundation established in 1825, 1000 kurush were endowed without an accretion rate, and the foundation was requested to be run through the operating procedures called "istirbah" and "istiglal". The total expenditures of the foundation were 94 kurush (Endowment 1882). When the endowed 1000 piastres were operated by at least 10% annually, an accretion of 100 kurush was to be gained, and the expenses were to be met accordingly. As is clear from the example, in such foundations where the revenues were more than the charges, the request concerning the addition of the remaining extra money to the capital was absolutely recorded at the end of the endowments.

In another endowment, the 80,000 asper endowed in 1640 was requested to be operated by the accretion rate of 15% based on the procedure of muamele-i ser'iyye. The annual income of the foundation was 12,000 asper. The annual expense has been calculated to be 11,160 asper on the basis of the total recorded expenditures. The remaining 840 asper was preserved for the unexpected and sudden charges or, in other words, as a precautionary measure. If the share allocated for potential expenses was not spent within the year, it would be added to the capital of the foundation (Endowment 1640). When the extra accumulated money reached a particular amount, it was directed into the purchase of revenue-generating assets. Such sort of additions made into the equity of the foundation led to changes in the ongoing cash management. The rents received from the newly bought property were used in the salary rise of foundation employees, construction and repair of architectural works as well as other charity works. In addition to these properties that was bought with the money saved after the establishment of the foundation, a second or third property was similarly purchased over time as well.

As can be seen clearly, the founders developed long-term strategies. In this stage, the question of how well the rules in the endowments were obeyed as years went by comes into prominence. The answer to the question resides in the foundation accountings. The endowments display what ought to be, or the theory in other words, whereas the periodically checked accountings reveal what actually is, or the practice. The efficiency of cash management can be measured by a comparison between the endowment and foundation accounting. Based on the accounting and endowment of the foundation established by Nefise Hatun in 1771, the efficacy of cash management was questioned (Endowment 1771). An accretion rate was not defined in the endowment, and istirbah and istiglal were requested to be used as the operating procedures. This situation indicates that Nefise Hatun was conscious of the economic fluctuations in the second half of the seventeenth century and took precautions against possible rises and falls in accretion rates. It is possible to state that the decision was well directed based on the accounts pursued for 17 years.

Nefise Hatun endowed 500 kurush and demanded that the extra money remaining after the foundation expenses be saved in the course of time and a new income-generating property be bought. The rental income received from this property would be used in the salary rise of the employees available in the foundation. Attendants that were likely to be employed in the foundation over time together with their wages were also recorded. Provided that the necessary amounts were saved, it is understood that the cycle of new property purchase would be repeated several times and the same procedures would be performed. It is possible to point out that Nefise Hatun made forward-looking decisions and designed a long-term financial management strategy for the perpetuity of foundation.

When the accounting is examined in relation to cash management, it was foreseen that 500 kurush endowed money would breed a revenue of 518.30 kurush by being operated at an accretion rate of 15% during the first accounting period of 7 years between 1771 and 1778. Later on, the foundation charges were listed, and 358.30 kurush expenditure in total was detailed. Within this outlay, the expense of 111.5 kurush under the title of export is noteworthy. In the explanation provided upon this issue, it was stated that the accretion loss that emerged as a result of the inability in getting all of the endowed money of 500 kurush to be operated was shown to be among other expenses as export cost. When the expenses are subtracted from the foundation's expected profits of 7 years (518.30–358.30), an extra amount of 160 kurush comes in view. If all of the fund could have been operated (160 + 111.5), the remaining extra sum would have been 271.5 kurush. At the end of the accounting, the extra money of 160 kurush was added to the 500 kurush capital, and the fund was transferred to the next accounting period as 660 kurush.

During the second accounting period of the foundation between the years 1778 and 1787, the 660 kurush transferred from the first period was operated over 10% accretion rate, and a revenue of 660 kurush was envisioned by the end of 10 years. As the accounting did not refer to export expenditures, it is understood that the foundation directed all its money at transaction. The accretion discount that falls from 15% to 10% between the two accounting periods is a dramatic decrease that corresponds to one third of the first rate. It is clearly seen that the trustee made a well-directed decision by defining a lower rate in the second accounting period.

When the 411.5 kurush cost is subtracted from the total income of 660 kurush at the end of 10 years, an amount of 248.5 kurush turned out to be an excess. This extra sum was added to the capital in accordance with the requirements of the endowment, and (660 + 248.5) 908.5 kurush was transferred to the following period. The fund starting with 500 kurush in 1771 reached 908.5 kurush by undergoing an increase of 82% in 1787. Table 19.1 shows the incomes and expenses as well as the transferred amounts in both accounting period (İMŞSA. DM. Register nr: 95., p. 16).

Table 19.1 The incomes and expenses of Hodja Nefise Hatun foundation (1771–1787)

Accounting period	Capital	Rate %	Income	Expenses	Spread	Transferred amounts
1771–1778	500	15	518.30	358.30	160	660
1778–1787	660	10	660	411.20	248.5	908.5
Total			1178.30	770.10	408.5	

The declaration in the endowment stating that an appropriate property ought to be bought and rented when conditions were available was not identified in the 17-year accounting records. Considering the fact that the fund was increasingly transferred every year, the fulfilment of the condition regarding property purchase in the forthcoming years seems possible.

One of the considerations concerning cash waqfs within the context of cash management is the knowledge that the amounts given as credit could not be reclaimed until they fell due. Within this framework, the trustee managed the debt terms so as to meet the foundation expenditures. When unexpected delays took place during the return of the due money, different alternatives stepped in. It has been detected that the money saved for precautionary reasons was either used, or its accretion shares were taken so that the term of the capital was extended. As the annual expenses of the foundation were met by use of the accretion shares, the capital was not returned, and it did not constitute a problem in terms of cash management when the same person was relent money within the determined term. However, whether the delays stemmed from the debtors' payment difficulty or the credit need for another period still remains inexplainable. The cases in which the loans could be repaid under no circumstances, on the other hand, have been discussed under the title of risk managements.

In the Ottoman economic system, the circulation of multiple currencies at the same time posed a problem in terms of effective cash management. In order to maximize cash management, the requirement that the lent money be repaid in kind as a solution was definitely recorded in the endowments. In some endowments, the fund was also redefined in relation to another currency, and its value regarding that period of time was precisely specified. As of the second half of the nineteenth century in particular, the fund was recorded in detail as gold and kurush. Serife Ummugulsum Hanim and her husband Mustafa Efendi determined the kurush-denominated value of the money they endowed as *mecidiye* gold in the foundation they established in 1875 and recorded 1 mecidiye gold as equal to 100 kurush. The founders affected by the uncertainty in the market not only redefined the money they endowed in different currency but also applied alternative economic means.

The five foundations established by Ummugulsum Hanim and the one foundation set up by her husband Mustafa Efendi were approved on the same day as dated 29 May 1875 (Endowment 1875). The sort of fund, the operating procedures and the condition which allows demand for new stock shares from the State Treasury when necessary are common in all the six foundations. The founders administrated their foundations themselves while alive and handed over the management of all their foundations to a single trustee after death. It was identified that the revenues of each foundation were made use of in taking services to various places. Ummugulsum Hanim established her foundations in order to afford the charges of the staff in Cerrahpasa Mosque and meet the needs of the water reservoir she built in The Sultan's School near the mosque. The foundation set-up by Mustafa Bey, on the other hand, was meant for contributing to the wages of the employees working in his wife's foundation.

Table 19.2 The obtained stock profit shares (16 March 1877/22 November 1881)

Installment	Profit share (kurush)	Installment	Profit share (kurush)
March 1877	903	September 1879	812.5
June 1877	903	December 1879	812.5
September 1877	903		**1625**
December 1877	903	March 1880	812.5
	3612	June 1880	812.5
March 1878	903	September 1880	812.5
June 1878	903	December 1880	812.5
September 1878	903		**4875**
December 1878	903	March 1881	812.5
	7224	June 1881	812.5
March 1879	903	September 1881	812.5
June 1879	903	December 1881	812.5
	9030		**8125**
Total income		**17,155**	

Table 19.3 The annual expenses of foundations (16 March, 1877/ 22 November, 1881)

March 1877–June 1879 Before the reduction		September 1879–December 1881 After the reduction	
Expenditure	Kurush	Expenditure	Kurush
The staff wage	8947.5	The staff wage	8042.5
Fund cost	82.5	Fund cost	82.5
Total expense	9030	Total expense	8125

Eight shares of Anadolu Railway Company equal to 52,550 kurush in total were purchased with all the money of the six foundations. It is recorded in the accounting that profit share would be gained from all of the bills in brackets of 903 kurush four times a year in March, June, September and December for the next 5 years. However, it was understood that the profit shares were not distributed over the same rates during these 5 years and they continued to be given as 812.5 kurush with a deficiency by 10% after 2.5 years. The reason for the decrease was explained to be the 10% discount applied by the State Treasury to all stock profit shares. The foundation received a profit share of 17,155 kurush at the end of 5 years. Table 19.2 displays the payment dates of the profit shares in question together with the paid amounts (BOA.EV. MH. 2148. 336. 1881).

The trustee purchased bonds with all the endowed money by taking security price risk. The year-end accounting records indicate that no precautions were taken for potential risks. In this case, the revenue losses were compensated for by juggling with the staff wages. Despite the fact that the personnel were paid 8947.5 kurush in the first period, they received 8042.5 kurush in the second period with regard to the wage reduction based on the decreasing profit shares. Table 19.3 reveals the adjustments in the foundation expenses before and after the reducement of profit shares.

Total expense before and after the reduction = *17,155 kurush*

It is possible to regard the expense item defined to be "fund cost" in Table 19.3 as safe deposit box rent of our present time. From the mid-seventeenth century onwards, the valuable documents, money and all other papers that required safety concerning the large- and medium-sized foundations were preserved inside the chests available in Bezistan within the covered bazaars. The chests found in the Bezistan which existed in the covered bazaar of each city were under the state guarantee and available for public use (İnalcık 1997, p. 121).

Considering all the executed cash transactions, it is clearly viewed that the planning of the foundations was done based on the idea of their perpetuity. Thanks to an active cash management strategy, any potential decrease in the fund was prevented. In this stage, there was no room for speculation-oriented activities in these planning. Also, no records have been identified about any foundation that allowed borrowing from the markets at low rates and performing credit transactions at higher rates for the purpose of deriving profit from any money which was not its own. In other words, no foundations which benefited from financial leverage have been detected.

Fund Management

When the globalization tendencies in financial markets that started in 1970s gained acceleration after 1990s, the use of alternative financial instruments besides cash has become widespread. Fund managements are concerned with managing cash and cash equivalents, or in other words, the alternative financial means. The use of the instruments in question provided different opportunities for the investors who sought protection from market fluctuations. The investors who desired to take optimum advantage of the funds expanding through the gradual diversification of financial means needed professional fund managers in time. In this stage, the fund managements which performed transactions by gathering the cash belonging to multiple investors within the same fund pool and the radius of action regarding the fund managers expanded a great deal (Büyükağaoğlu 2011, p. 8).

When examined within the frame of fund managements, the funds in which cash waqfs were accumulated are the pools that brought the cash of more than one foundation together. The Ottoman foundation system involved three different waqf funds under the titles of artisan funds, *avariz* funds and Janissary squad funds. These funds whose common purpose was to sustain the socio-economic and sociocultural needs of their members functioned as today's retirement systems, unemployment insurances and other relief funds. Considering the existence of at least one waqf fund in every neighbourhood, guild, bazaar and Janissary squad (yeniçeri ortası) available in all rural and urban areas, it becomes possible to hold an idea on the prevalence of the related system. It should be kept in mind that each fund operated as a separate legal entity and was managed in this way. The fund managers who also functioned as fund trustees were elected from among the notables of fund members, and the decision concerning who would replace them once they resigned from their position was made beforehand. The trustee appointments regarding the waqfs endowed to the funds were recorded in endowment deeds with such declarative expressions like "Ali Efendi, the second-hand bookseller artisan fund trustee".

The fund trustees of the related period served as the fund managers of our present day and managed all the waqfs collected in the fund pool from as the single authority. The amount endowed by each founder, the accretion rates he or she finds appropriate, the rents received from the properties and the demanded services differed from one another. Within this view, the accounting of each waqf endowed to the funds was recorded in the same book but on separate pages. Until the nineteenth century when the alternative financial instruments were not yet sufficiently diversified, the fund trustees managing property rents and cash revenues conducted different funds in the following years.

It is possible to keep track of the executed transactions from the periodically kept accounts. In the 9-year accounting of the second-hand bookseller artisans, a fund was created through the joining of the assets transferred from the earlier period and the new period incomes (Evkaf Register 1881). The fund revenue is the sum total of the accretions of the endowed money, property rents, fees received from the artisans who were members of the fund and bond incomes. It is understood that the bond returns corresponded to rates enough to meet the foundation expenses and were used as a long-term investment means. Apart from this, it is detected that securities convertible to cash if needed were utilized as an alternative financing instrument in the evaluation of inoperative money.

The fund accounting also involves 14 bonds that belonged to the former period and whose par value equaled to 700 liras. Furthermore, new bonds were bought with the money transferred from the earlier period and all the revenues within the period. In addition to the 14 bonds on hand, another bond purchase of 79,834 kurush in total took place during the accounting period between the years 1873 and 1875. The maturity par value of the bonds that were usually bought in 50-lira coupons was clearly stated in the accounting. Within this perspective, the number of the 50-lira bonds which were purchased with 79,834 kurush and whose par value was 1300 liras is 26. With the inclusion of the earlier purchases, 40 bonds equal to 2000 liras were present in the whole fund in 1875.

In Table 19.4, the dates and purchase prices of the bonds bought within the accounting period can be viewed. Two activities performed 8 days apart during the

Table 19.4 Second-hand bookseller artisan fund bonds (1873–1875)

Date	Par value (lira)	Purchase prices (kurush)
10 August 1873	350	24,106
16 October 1873	400	25,912
20 February 1874	200	11,011
4 November 1875	50	2965
12 November 1875	300	15,840
10 August 1873	350	24,106
Accounting period: total	1300	79,834

last bond purchase are quite attention-grabbing. The 50-lira bonds cost 2965 kurush on 4 November 1875, whereas 2640 kurush was paid for them on 12 November 1875. Huseyin Al stated in his study that bond prices bottomed out after the Ottoman state declared on October 1875 (Hijri Ramadhan) that it stopped payments related to credits (Al 2005, p. 41). The dates concerning the last two bond purchases made by the fund are shortly after the Ramadhan Decree on October 1875. It is understood from the account activities that the trustee followed the market closely and made a purchase again right after the decline in bond prices for the purpose of increasing the profit maximization.

The fund expenses were spared for the nutritional and residential requirements of the poor, dervishes and passengers, the necessary aids for maintaining the occupations of poor artisans, those who are about to set up a shop or get married, those who have retired, the orphans, the disabled, the elderly, the burial procedures, the wages of water bearers and carriers, the readings of the Koran and the performance of memorial services as well as the salaries of the trustees, ministers, chamberlains, foremen, clerks and well-wishers. The expenditures also involved the expenses made during the traditional ceremonies known as "waistband wear" and performed in particular periods every year, the building rentals and equipment of the guilds and the staff wages. In addition to all these outgoings, accounting fees paid to the state, provincial treasurer wages and taxes demanded in the event of war and went by the name of "subsidy" were in question as well. In this sense, it is recorded in the accounting of second-hand bookseller artisans that the amounts falling to the tax share of the bazaar that provided workplaces for these artisans included 4500 kurush for the ground forces and 224 kurush for the fleet. Considering the specific date, the related payments were collected and the 4724 kurush in total was the tax the state received from the second-hand bookseller artisans in Istanbul for the Ottoman-Russian War, or in other words, the 1993 War that started in 1877.

Despite the uncertainty regarding the dates the aforementioned funds first appeared, it is known that they served in the late sixteenth century. The funds owe their 300 years of sustainability to the ultralow levels of asper depreciation as well as a well-conducted fund management. According to the researches carried out in the related area, the average annual loss in value concerning asper between the years 1326 and 1740 was around 0.2% (Tabakoğlu 2008, p. 328). The fluctuations observed in monetary value after the eighteenth century directed the fund trustees to alternative financial instruments, particularly the state guaranteed bonds. Moreover, the systematic operation of the funds and the minimalization of management weaknesses were targeted by means of keeping the civilian and official supervision mechanism channels incessantly open.

As can be seen clearly, the fund trustees focused on deriving the maximum benefit from the funds collected in the pools within the frame of the rate and time determined by the founders. The different positions adopted by trustees when necessary provide insight into the assumption that the trustees followed the market closely. Their difference from modern fund managers not only involves their management of funds in the way to get the optimum profit possible but also their use of the received revenues in line with the needs of fund members. In this context, the fund trustees can be claimed to have contributed to the shaping of the socio-economic life during their operating cycle on the basis of the attitude they adopted in management.

Risk Management

The aim of risk management is to protect the movables and immovables within the organization and help minimize the potential losses at minimum cost. A well-conducted risk management is expected to diminish the risk by effective use of sources and provide an environment of dignity and trust by through the operation of supervision mechanism as well. In this way, the services offered were intended to enhance in quality and secure sustainability (Emhan 2009).

The purpose of risk management in foundations is the sustainability of the endowed assets without decreasing and the maintenance of foundation permanency. Within this view, the first risk the founder would take into consideration was the risk that featured the question whether the trustee he or she would appoint was able to manage the foundation properly, or in other words, the administrative risk. The responsibility given to the trustee, the limits of his or her mobility and the flexibility of the supervision mechanism constitute the coverage zone of the administrative risk in foundations. In order to define the limits of the area in question, the powers of the trustee were recorded down to the last detail. Even though the trustee's authorities were restricted in many ways, free spaces were provided at times in the way to make cash management run smoothly. In this respect, a private foundation trustee could let the liquid fund of the foundation be used by a single person (or more than one person for the sake of reducing the return risk. The division of the fund into parts brings along the possibility of some of the money to be left over. When the fund was left to the use of a single person, on the other hand, the risk of disorder with regard to the balance of income and expenses prevailed in such cases of failed returns. Based on the related data, the trustees of large foundations and the fund trustees that incorporated multiple foundations undertook more risks compared to the trustees of small foundations.

The administrative risk also contained the possibility of malpractice and corruption. The trustee who skipped performing risk management in the implementation of the decisions made by the founder in accordance with the financial management strategy was accepted to have misconducted (Bilmen, p. 49). The trustees were made to withdraw from their posts either temporarily or permanently from the moment they abused their duties on. The data concerning the persons to replace the positions of trustees who had to resign due to such obligations or natural causes like disease or death were recorded in endowment deeds. The trustees were responsible for the accountings of their own period. When needed, they could be held accountable in the aftermath of their resignation for the retrospective deeds which encompassed their own phases. With regard to past time disagreements, either the trustee of the related period, if alive, or the heirs were to assume the responsibility.

Another risk faced by foundations is the problems created in the markets by the foreign-sourced or domestic-based political and diplomatic events. All kinds of fluctuations named as market risk and likely to emerge out of the normal course lead to negative non-linearities in financial markets. As the revenues and expenses of foundations match up with one another, possible deviations in the incomes directly affect the expenditures. Such results extend to the following periods and cause decreases in the assets endowed and delays in the services provided. The gradual reduction in the profit shares of the bonds bought by Ummugulsum Hanim as discussed under the previous title can be evaluated within the context of market risk encountered by foundations. The trustee resorted to reducing the staff wages instead of using the net assets of the foundation for the required expenses in the case of a decline in profit shares. Thanks to risk management, the perpetuity of the foundation was taken into account, and impairment of the capital was prevented. Such and similar problems were tried to be overcome with minimum damage imposed by being solved within the phase they came about and without being forwarded to the next periods as far as possible. Similarly, the possibility that the risk characterized by a situation in which money might not be given as credit could become real was observed in the foundation of Nefise Hatun. Accordingly, the trustee strived to compensate for the process with minimum loss by reducing the accretion rates so as to prevent the money from remaining totally inoperative in the second accounting period. Specific to foundations, the problem was solved in the related period itself without being prolonged to the following phases as the revenues were more than the expenses. It could not be made certain whether the nonpermissibility that denied the whole money from being used as credit in the first accounting period stemmed from the management of the trustee or the market circumstances.

It is a known fact that fluctuations became frequent and the fluctuation length increased in the Ottoman economy at times. Such market risks reflected on the accretions rates in the market and, thus, on the bond prices prompted the founders to take different precautions. The founder named Karabet Matavyan adopted a quite different financial management strategy and arranged the expenses of the foundation in direct proportion to its revenues (Endowment 1895). He demanded that the foundation income be spent on the expenditures of the school built by his father Serkis in Kayseri, the poor in the church vicinity and hospital charges. Matavyan, who endowed 1,000,000 kurush, did not specify an accretion rate and distributed the foundation expenses in percentage terms and in parallel with the profit gained without expecting fixed income. The percentage of the revenues to be spared for meeting different needs involved 5% for the requirements of the Armenian Hospital, 40% for the nutritional needs of the school in Kayseri, 10% for the food allowance on behalf of the poor of the three churches in the province of Berivan, 10% for other needs of the same poor, 15% for the officers of foundation supervision and the remaining 20% for the mark-up to the capital. The potential financial risks in the years to come were taken precaution against by means of the 20% amount saved for precautionary means and added to the foundation capital. It is understood that the founder kept track of the economic conditions of the period and formed a flexible financial management strategy. This flexibility manifested itself in cash and risk managements as well. The situation which might be considered disadvantageous here is the fact that the foundation services could not be maintained in the same level every year due to the lack of fixed income.

The survival of the endowed money without being reduced is the necessary condition for both the sustainability of the foundation and the operability of the system. In this stage, the risk management encloses the probability, uncertainty and decision-making processes and expands its sphere of influence. The possibility that the results might be different from what is expected, or the uncertainty in other words, forces persons to take precautions. Although the maintenance of the optimum balance through a well-conducted analysis of the possible risks concerning the monetary foundations and funds was the task of the trustees, the necessary warnings were included in the endowment deeds against uncertainties. Among all, the characteristics of those asking for a loan were the leading warning. Ghazi Husrev Bey warned the trustees in his endowment deed by stating that the endowed money meant to be lent should be given to the well-off merchants, artisans and farmer as well as those who were well-known and well-loved by their fellows. While it was specifically suggested in the following statements that those in debt, the ill-natured people, the greedy, the extravagant, the arrogant and the imposters should not be lent money, such people like soldiers, kadis, ameers and governors were also included among those to be avoided in terms of lending (Şuceska 1990, p. 273).

Through the second warning within the context of risk management, it was requested that no money should be lent without the presence of a strong guarantor and/or a valuable good against the uncertainties. Despite possible opportunity costs, the necessity that loans should not be offered in the absence of a warranter and a pledged asset is a significant point which requires close attention by the trustee. Special attention was paid in picking the guarantors from among the close acquaintances of the borrower such as relatives, spouse or colleagues. One of the two names written under the phrase "debtor" in the accounting books was most often the name of the warranter. The goods taken as the pledged assets usually involved such storable items like silver combs, belts, gold watches and jewellery. When it came to the nineteenth century, notes payables and bonds stood out among the pledged assets as well. Following the second half of the century, the immovables taken during the procedure of Bey' in the status of pledged assets were insured against potential natural risks. The insurance expenses initially met by the foundation were made to be covered by the debtors themselves later on. Apart from the immovables held in pledge, the possible wear and tear of other immovables owned by the foundation were evaluated within the context of insurance risk, and the required amount was spared among the foundation outgoings. Another practice within the frame of insurance was the endowment of immovables along with movables. The founders divided between the risk related to the loss and depreciation of money in time and the risk regarding the wear, burning and collapse of the endowed immovable in this way.

By means of the third warning, precautions were taken against the risks likely to result from potential disvaluation of the endowed money in the course of time.

Through this warning which can also be associated with cash management, the loans lent in the markets in which multiple currencies were transacted were asked to be returned in the same kind of currency. The foundation expenses were also defined by the endowed currency type. As the income and expense balance in foundations were almost well-suited, even the slightest fluctuation could lead to problems. Considering the transaction of 36 different currencies in the Ottoman economy in the early nineteenth century, the importance of the desire to transact upon the same sort of currency becomes apparent.

The last warning, on the other hand, involves the section which is available at the end of the endowment deeds and which requests the voluntary supervision of the functioning of the foundation by reliable people. The controlling was not usually limited to a single person, and it was voluntarily conducted by such people like well-known people in the neighbourhood, artisan masters and Janissary headmen. The double checks performed played an important role in preventing the deficiencies and corruptions escaping the attention. Also, the trustees had to show all foundation accountings to any requestor. The checking of the accountings at intervals by official supervisors was another risk-reducing precaution. Provided that no complaints were available against foundation accountings, they did not require to be checked by official authorities every year. In line with the conditions of endowments, the control of the accountings was demanded at such different intervals like 2, 4, 5, 9 and 11 years. As can be seen clearly, even though the concept of risk management was not directly used in foundations, precautions were taken in several transactions considering the potential risks. In this way, the optimum output gained out of the risk management processes manifested itself in all areas of the trust institution. Obedience to the foundation conditions, source management, accountability when necessary, right decision-making and preservation of the foundation image might be counted among the yields in question.

Sell and Leaseback

Within the context of risk management, the similarities between "sell and lease-back", the lower version of the procedure called "leasing" today and the procedure of "Bey' bi'l-istiglal", which is frequently used in operating monetary foundations, have been emphasized. Leasing is an agreement signed between the leasor of an item and the leasee for a particular period of time during the stage in which the related item is purchased. Here, the property chosen by the leasee is purchased by the leasor. The ownership of the property is held by the leasor, whereas the right of use belongs to the leasee in exchange for a specific amount of rent (Şenyurt 2015). Companies that perform leasing acquire the goods, the utilization of which will be offered to the leasee by means of two different methods. The first method is single stage, and it involves the purchase of the rented item by the leasing company from a third person. The other method known as "sell and leaseback", on the other hand, takes place in two stages within itself. In the first stage, the business which is short of cash sells an immovable item within its property to a leasing company in order to get rid of its cash problem. Later, a rental agreement is signed between the two parties for the usage of the related item, and the business in difficulty becomes the leasee of the item it has sold. In the aftermath of the contract expiry, the immovable is returned to the leasee, or the original owner of the item, by the leasing company. In this respect, the money oriented on the item is released for a while, and needs are met with the income received during this period. The procedure of "sell and leaseback", which began to be used in Europe in 1970s, has been legalized in Turkey as of the year 2012 (Şenyurt 2015).

This transaction is held exempted from corporation tax, stamp tax, value-added tax and title deed fees on the condition that the property is returned to its former owner at the end of the rental agreement. In this way, the procedure has achieved extensive use. Otherwise, in the case of a failure in paying the debts, all the above-mentioned taxes are collected with interest (Ilgar 2017).

The procedure of "Bey' bi'l-istiglal", on the other hand, was used as the Ottoman cash waqf operating procedure as of the early sixteenth century. The use of this procedure as one of the credit methods of the Islamic economy dates back to older times than cash waqfs. Bey' represents the reception of pledges assets in return for a given debt, which is a frequent practice in the use of credits. As for the term "istiglal", which means the collection of the profit and revenue of a property, it refers to the sale in which a property is rented to a debtor so as to benefit from its incomes. The rent received at the end of the transaction does not equal to the value of the property but to the accretion of the loan made. Thanks to this procedure, the debtors not only met their cash needs but also continued to make use of their property. Even though the procedure of bey' is a sale transaction, based on the principle that the properties bought by the foundation could not be sold back as clearly stated by the foundation law, sales performed through bey' bi'l-istiglal did not go beyond the status of pledged assets (Bayındır S. 2015).

The Kadi Records contain various documents regarding the procedure of bey' bi'l-istiglal frequently used in the Ottoman credit market and cash waqfs. Ayse Hatun sold her house for 1 year through bey' bi'l-istiglal in exchange for the 6550 kurush debt she took on from the Janissary fund in 1686. Later on, she continued to inhabit the house she had sold in return for a rent of 975 kurush in total. The received debt and the repayment of the rent at the end of 1 year are recorded as 7525 kurush. At the end of the transaction, the 975 kurush rent paid by Ayse Hatun who held the right of use regarding the house approximately corresponded to 1-year accretion of the debt she was given at 15%. Ayse Hatun could only offer 2525 kurush when the dueness of the debt took place and became indebted again for the remaining 5000 kurush. In order to get the loan in question, she sold her garden to the foundation by means of bey' bi'l-istiglal this time. It is recorded in the accounting that the house and the garden were rented to Ayse Hatun again in exchange for 750 kurush rent for 1 year after the last sale. Similar to the former indebtedness, the rent here was defined in accordance with 15% accretion rate again, and the total debt reached 5750 kurush. It is understood that reborrowing was possible provided that some of the debts were already paid and the pledged assets to be offered were valuable (Atay et al. 2011).

Table 19.5 Total debt and collection (1902–1936)

Accounting for Omer Husamettin Efendi foundation (kurush)	
The given debt	237,550
Insurance, execution, brokerage	24,230
Total debt	261,780
The collected	
Debts	181,670
Insurance, execution, brokerage	7000
Total	188,670
Overplus	73,110

The debts were collected by the guarantors when unpaid by the debtors, the bills taken were put into operation, the assets pledged through public sale were sold at its true value and the foundation money was received back. During the sale transaction, all kinds of expenses related to the property like repair, upkeep, tax, insurance and execution were paid by the foundation and written on the debtor's tab (Gürsoy Ç. 2015, p. 155).

Table 19.5 is composed of the accounting records between the years 1902 and 1936 concerning the foundation established by Omer Husamettin Efendi (Evkaf Muhasebesi 1902–1936). It can be inferred from the table that the pledged assets in return for the money lent from the riches of execution and brokerage expenses and the credits given through bey'bi'l-istiglal were not returned. The insurance expense, on the other hand, is the indicator of the expenditures made for the purpose of preserving the pledged immovables, discussed under the title of risk management, against potential natural risks. All three expenses and the debts given are written separately. The foundation met the expenses of cost items itself first, and then it collected the related expenses from the debtor. The 73,110 kurush owed debt in Table 19.5 involves execution, insurance and brokerage expenses equal to 17,230 kurush in total.

Conclusion and Assessment

Within the frame of time, setting and value judgements that have undergone changes throughout the history from the use of money onwards, savers and entrepreneurs have met by means of financial systems. The financial systems have made the economic sources accessible, distributed them to the required places and contributed to their incremental and extensive usage. The financial activities which started with local movements, continued at urban scale and finally reached the national degree have mounted the international level over time and recently begun to operate within global dimension.

The cash waqfs that started to be involved in the Ottoman financial system by the end of the fifteenth century continued their existence for about 450 years. The cash waqfs which increased in number in time and underwent changes in accordance with the emerging needs turned out to be indispensable elements in the Ottoman economic life. They particularly occupied, as their field of application, the broad spectrum extending from the rural to urban areas within the Anatolian and Balkan territories of the Empire. While the cash waqfs offered financial service with easily accessed and cheap credit opportunities thanks to their prevalence on the one hand, they contributed to the sociocultural domains on the other. Besides all these, they showed ultimate attention so as not to neglect the social responsibilities towards society and environment.

The economic instruments used by the cash waqfs, one of the agents meeting the financing needs of the capital and service markets, share similarities with today's financial practices. Although the financial concepts have undergone changes and transformations throughout years, no big differences dwell on the basis. In this regard, such details like pledge and guarantor requests, the preservation of the valuable pledged assets and the insurance of the immovables, bond issues and the control of the operation and accounting can be emphasized as the featured elements during crediting.

Apart from private foundations, the roles played by the financial pools created within the context of charity funds in collective credit activities can be regarded as the pioneers of the fund managements today. Besides, these funds assumed various services offered by today's private organizations and public institutions as well as non-governmental organizations. In this way, the problems were solved on a local scale before the situation became graver, and the maintenance of the incessant operating of the system was secured.

All of the above-mentioned activities were arranged under the legal rules of trust institution. The foundations functioned in accordance with the requests of founders and within the frame of judicial laws. The trustees, on the other hand, managed foundations within the limits defined by founders, or in other words, in parallel with the financial management strategy determined by founders. In the financial management strategies planned for long-term use, activities similar to the cash, fund and risk management practices of our present day have been identified.

Throughout the chapter, the similarities between the cash waqfs, discussed under four main titles in financial terms, and the businesses today have been ascertained. Accordingly, it has been detected that the financial notions in question are not separated from one another by rigid limits, fund management designed upon direct financial management strategy is inseparable from cash management and risk management also shows parallelism with cash and fund managements. It is possible to diversify financial titles by means of different examples of foundation accountings. Furthermore, the common points between companies and foundations in terms of other service areas like social work, education and transportation are also worth analyzing aside from financial activities.

Bibliography

Al, H. (2005). *Ondokuzuncu Yüzyılda Ülke Riski, Finans Politik, İngiliz Tahvil Sahipleri ve Babıâli*. Unpublished PhD Thesis, Department of Economic History, Istanbul University Institute of Social Sciences, İstanbul.

Atay, S., Kılıç, H., & Karaca, Y. (2011). *İstanbul Kadı Sicilleri Bab Mahkemesi C. 19*. İstanbul: İSAM.

Bardakoğlu, A. (1992). *Bey'*. İstanbul: TDVİA.

Bayındır, A. (1992). *Bey'bi'l-istiğlâl*. İstanbul: TDVİA.

Bayındır, S. (2015). *Fıkhî ve İktisadî Açıdan İslamî Finans (Para ve Sermaye Piyasaları)*. İstanbul: Süleymaniye Vakfı Yayınları.

Bilmen, Ö. *Hukuki İslâmiyye ve Islahatı Fıkhiyye Kamusu, C.5*. Bilmen Yayınevi.

Büyükağaoğlu, Ş. (2011). *Ticari Bankalarda Fon Yönetimi ve Fon Yönetiminde Karşılaşılan Finansal Riskler*. PhD Thesis, Dokuz Eylül University Institute of Social Sciences, İzmir.

Çankaya, S. (2012, Nisan 5). *Finansal Yönetim*. Beykent University. Retrieved from http://kampus. beykent.edu.tr/Paylasim/Dosyalar/8.hafta_129806173005830000.pdf

Emhan, A. (2009). Risk Yönetim Süreci ve Risk Yönetmekte Kullanılan Teknikler. *Atatürk University Journal of Economıcs And Admınıstratıve Scıences, 23*, 209–220.

Güçer, L. (1983). *İktisat Tarihi Ders Notları*. İstanbul: Filiz Kitabevi.

Güran, T. (2014). *İktisat Tarihi*. İstanbul: Der Yayınları.

Gürsoy, Ç. (2015, Haziran). *Osmanlı'da Para Vakıflarının İşleyişi ve Muhasebe Uygulamaları: Davudpaşa Mahkemesi Para Vakıfları*. Unpublished PhD Thesis, Istanbul University Institute of Social Sciences, İstanbul.

Gürsoy, Ç. (2017, Nisan). Para Vakıfları Kapsamında Sosyo-Ekonomik Bir Analiz: Davutpaşa Mahkemesi Kayıtları (1634–1911). *Belleten*, 159–190.

Ilgar, E. (2017, Temmuz 18). Retrieved from http://www.roedl.com/tr/tr/yayinlar/yazilar/sat_ve_ geri_kirala_sale_leaseback_leasing_islemi_ve_vergisel_avantajlari.html. roedl.com

İnalcık, H. (1997). *İstanbul'un İncisi Bedesten. İktisat Ve Din*. İstanbul: İz Yayıncılık.

Karan, M., Doğukanlı, H., Güler, A., & Korkmaz, T. (2013). *Finansal Yönetim*. Eskişehir: Anadolu University.

Korkmaz, T., Aydın, N., & Sayılgan, G. (2013). *Portföy Yönetimi*. Eskişehir: Anadolu University.

Özcan, T. (2003). *Osmanlı Para Vakıfları Kanûnî Dönemi Üsküdar Örneği*. Ankara: TTK.

Pakalın, M. (1983). *Tarih Deyimleri ve Terimleri Sözlüğü C.3*. İstanbul: Milli Eğitim Basımevi.

Sayın, C. (2016). *İşletme İlkeleri*. Eskişehir: Anadolu University.

Şenyurt, A. (2015). Osmanlı Para Vakıflarında Kullanılan Bir Finasman Yönteminin Batılı Anlamda Karşılığı: Sell and Lease Back (Sat ve Geri Kirala). *Sosyologca*, 83–97.

Şuceska, A. (1990). Sarayova'da XVI. Asırda Vakıf Kredileri. *V. Milletlerarası Türkiye Sosyal ve İktisat Tarihi Kongresi Tebliğler (21–25 Ağustos 1989)*, 721–726.

Tabakoğlu, A. (2008). *Türkiye İktisat Tarihi*. İstanbul: Dergah.

Archive Sources

BOA. EV.MH. 2148. 336. (1881).

Evkaf Muhasebesi, Register no. 1698. (1902–1936). Court Records Archive of the Provincial Office of Mufti in Istanbul.

Evkaf Register. (1881). *Evkaf Register nr. 22632*. T.R. Ottoman Archives of the Prime Ministry.

İMŞSA. DM. Register nr: 95.

Endowment, 3/52 (Evkaf Muhasebeciliği Court 1640).

Endowment, 95/15 (Davut Paşa Court 1771).
Endowment, 145/23b. (Davut Paşa Court May 29, 1875).
Endowment, 145/21-21b-23-23b-25-26. (Davut Paşa Court May 29, 1875).
Endowment, 107/71 (Evkaf Muhasebeciliği Court 1882).
Endowment, 166/76 (Mahmut Paşa Court 1895).

Chapter 20
Performances of Emerging Stock Exchanges During the Fed's Tapering Announcements

Onur Enginar, Mehmet Baha Karan, and Göknur Büyükkara

Abstract This paper investigates abnormal returns of 19 emerging market equity portfolios during the Fed's tapering period. Event study methodology is used during the early Fed's announcements at 2013. The aim of the study is to evaluate both the event study methodology and abnormal return performance of the emerging market stock exchanges during tapering period. The authors also check for abnormal volatility during tapering announcements, specifying it with GARCH (1,1) model. The results indicate that, together with China and Greece, the fragile five economies are differentiated from the rest of the emerging markets during tapering announcements. Moreover, the striking result that the authors see is Turkey is affected more negatively than any other fragile five members in this period. Yet, the authors did not find any significant abnormal volatility effect brought by tapering announces. In addition, the authors find emerging markets are not semi-strong form efficient during tapering period.

Introduction

After the 2008 financial crisis, US Federal Reserve (Fed) employed the quantitative easing (QE) policy to rehabilitate and rebound the US economy. As the Fed was increasing the amount of dollar-denominated currency in the market, the value of common stocks in the world exchanges including emerging economies moved to upper levels. Meanwhile, most of the portfolio managers in developing countries were exploiting the favorable conditions of QE program. The first signal about the end of purchases under the Fed's QE program which is called tapering was given in May 22, 2013. Following the first announcement of Fed, foreign investors in the emerging countries started to withdraw their holdings in stock exchanges leading to capital outflows, a drop in stock markets, and a rise in bond yields (Rai and Suchanek 2014). The reactions of all emerging stock exchanges to the tapering program of Fed

O. Enginar (✉) · M. B. Karan · G. Büyükkara
Hacettepe University, Ankara, Turkey
e-mail: onuren08@hacettepe.edu.tr; mbkaran@hacettepe.edu.tr; goknur@hacettepe.edu.tr

© Springer International Publishing AG, part of Springer Nature 2018   415
H. Dincer et al. (eds.), *Global Approaches in Financial Economics, Banking, and Finance*, Contributions to Economics, https://doi.org/10.1007/978-3-319-78494-6_20

were not the same. As the stock prices of some countries dramatically dropped, stock indices of (Kuepper 2016, thebalance.com) some other countries were not affected significantly. Some of them gave a profound reaction to every Fed's announcements; a few countries were only influenced by one or two of the Fed's decisions. The different economic conditions and structure of the economies might be the reason behind this issue. Thus, the reports of international institutions have discussed this point (Bank of England 2013).[1]

It is apparent that Fed's tapering announcement had a set of impact on emerging markets, yet the impact was not the same for all markets. A class of countries called "fragile five" more explicitly felt the impact of the announcement. During the period of 2013–2014, these reports were underlying the financial fragilities in the economies of five countries: Brazil, India, Indonesia, Turkey, and South Africa. Additional to BRICS, fancy abbreviation, the term "fragile five" is coined by a Morgan Stanley analyst in his research note.[2] These particular five countries have the following economic conditions: high inflation rates, weakening growth, large external deficits, and high dependence to foreign inflows. In 2013 and 2014, after tapering decision, fragile five relied on foreign investments to cover their current account deficits and finance their growth began to see capital outflows. Specifically, Turkey experienced sharp outflows and has been primary on target.[3] These countries have larger foreign financing needs and macroeconomic imbalances. Particularly the market reactions of those countries for Fed's announcements during 2013 were striking. Not only these countries but also some other emerging economies have shown significant decreases in stock prices. It can be questioned that these reactions were normal according to the past volatilities of market or more than expected. In other words, how big were the abnormal returns of the stock exchanges? Therefore, the authors conduct an event study to assess the effects of Fed's tapering decision on stock exchanges of emerging markets. Moreover, it is natural to extend analysis to investigate the effects of tapering decision on the variance, by which volatility is measured, of the emerging equity markets. Therefore, the authors seek for a structural change (jump) on variance of stock exchanges of emerging markets defined as a process by GARCH (1,1) model.

Additional to assessing abnormal returns in tapering period by performing an abnormal return analysis, implicitly, provides us to test the semi-strong form efficiency (Fama 1969) in emerging markets by employing event study since it is the general method to assess abnormal return. Even though it is accepted as a common methodology to assess the impacts of exogenous happenings on asset returns, event study has received significant amount of critics and thus its ability to capture abnormal returns extensively challenged. In literature, it is well explained by Brown (1980, 1985) and several others (Karafiath and Spencer 1991; Boehmer et al. 1991;

---

[1]Bank of England (27 May 2013). "Quantitative easing – injecting money into the economy" (PDF). bankofengland.co.uk

[2]http://www.morganstanley.com/institutional/research/pdf/FXPulse_20130829.pdf

[3]https://www.thebalance.com/what-are-the-fragile-five-1978880

Savickas 2003; Schipper and Thompson 1983; Binder 1998) in which hypothesis testing with simple OLS model results in misspecification and therefore has a low statistical power, when heteroscedasticity and autocorrelation problem occur. In order to assess abnormal returns, the authors believe that not only employing event study but also deeper analysis of the event study methodology is required. Following the eye-opener know-how in literature and according to preliminary analysis of data, the authors employ event study methodology with a GARCH (1,1) specification (Savickas 2003) to set the parameter estimation correctly, i.e., estimating parameters unbiased and efficiently, since it's the determinant of statistical inference by which the authors conclude the market efficiency results. The authors also give a thorough analysis on statistical theory of the methodology the authors employed (see Appendix). And also, simply adding a dummy variable to GARCH (1,1) model provides to investigate possible effects of tapering decision on volatility of emerging stock exchanges which is also taken into consideration by authors.

In literature, event study is used in order to gage the effects of tapering announcements (Aizenman et al. 2014; Rai&Suchanek 2014; Mishra et al. 2014; Sahay et al. 2014; Chen 2016; Bouraoui 2015). As event study is a parametric method, the authors need this parameter estimation to be correctly set. As mentioned above, there are several papers in literature on assessing the power of event study to set the correct specification of hypothesis tests employed. Thus, in order to assess properly the tapering effect on emerging markets, the authors put special attention on parameter estimation since it's the determinant for the abnormal and thus efficiency results. Therefore, authors' effort is to specify event study model thoroughly, i.e., the authors check for serial correlation and heteroscedasticity in error terms and make model specifications accordingly. To do so, with a step-by-step approach, the authors employ a model, analogous to Savickas (2003), by which the authors consider error analysis and thus efficiently estimate the parameters of model and doing as such provide results of the emerging equity market reactions to Fed's announcements by which the authors inspect the behavior of emerging markets, i.e., the authors check market efficiency.

Addition to the above, the authors examine how fragile five differentiated from rest of the emerging markets. This basically gives a short summary of authors' contribution to existing literature. Therefore, the main research question of this study is that to test the abnormal return performance of the main emerging market stock exchanges and how fragile five differentiated than the rest of the emerging markets via using event study methodology with employing a general model of Savickas (2003) who employs GARCH (1,1) specification for prediction model for return process. The reasoning for this approach stems from relative weakness of market model (simple one-factor model) compared to ARIMA and GARCH models, since latter ones relax the restrictions/assumptions on error terms, and therefore provide robust results in hypothesis testing (for details, see Appendix). Moreover, the authors also check for abnormal volatility affect due to Fed's announcements during tapering, and the authors employ GARCH (1,1) for parameter estimation. Reasoning for employing GARCH model to assess abnormal volatility is that it is known that

GARCH models do provide good forecasts (Andersen 1998; Bollerslev 1986). This, actually, means that GARCH models fit financial data well. Hansen (2005) find out that GARCH (1,1) specification outperforms several other GARCH model specifications.

In general, authors' contribution can be summarized as follows: using event study methodology, authors assess the reactions of emerging markets to tapering announcements and also by employing Garch (1,1) specification, reactions in market volatility are considered as well; and in addition to this, the authors implicitly check whether emerging markets react efficiently to those Fed's tapering announcement. The authors use the term reacting efficiently rather than efficient market since markets can move away from efficiency time to time. As Ito (2014) use the term time-varying efficiency and conclude market efficiency changes over time. Yet in this study, the authors don't directly examine market efficiency since employing such small sample could not provide efficiency results. However, the authors can check market reaction to Fed's announcements and see market reaction efficiently or not to those announcements.

The rest of the paper is organized as follows. Second section explains the impact of Fed's tapering announcements on EMEs, third section summarizes previous studies, and fourth section describes methodology. Data and empirical results are given in fifth section. The paper concludes in sixth section.

Fed's Tapering Announcements and Performance of Emerging Market Exchanges

Fed implemented the quantitative easing (QE) program to stimulate the US economy by buying debt instruments from financial institutions after the 2008 global financial crisis. While simultaneously increasing the money supply, prices of financial assets including common stocks are raised, and interest rates of borrowing instruments decreased (Bank of England 2016). The positive market conditions for not only developed economies but also emerging ones pushed the indices of stock exchanges to higher bands, so investors took out significant returns as much as the market let. The policy of Fed employed in different phases from 2008 to 2013, and particularly emerging countries claimed the advantages of the quantitative easing because of the profitable trade and confidence stemming from stronger economic activity (Lavigne 2014). On the other hand, some researchers argue that QE could create financial instability in some emerging economies. The study of Bowman (2015) reveals that the Federal Reserve's quantitative easing (QE) program may deteriorate EME's financial or macroeconomic conditions and cause unexpected, and sometimes unwelcome, effects on domestic asset prices. It can be particularly true for some emerging countries which are called fragile five which have been addicted to the excess liquidity of QE policy by greedily exploiting the positive market conditions. These countries, namely, Brazil, India, Indonesia, Turkey, and South Africa, are seen as more hooked on foreign capital flows and as displaying higher risk of currency depreciation against the dollar (Morgan Stanley 2016).[4] Bhattarai (2015) investigate that QE program of Fed drives to an exchange rate appreciation, a decline in bond interest rates, and an increase in stock market indices for these emerging market economies. Although the fragile five countries are influenced more, other emerging market economies are also affected.

Fed has given the first signal for the end of QE program in late 2012, and the international institutions like IMF and World Bank began to advise about the change of Fed politics after the beginning of 2013 (IMF 2014) by warning the risk of capital flow reversal and higher borrowing costs for EMEs.

The first important declaration is given by the governor of Fed on May 22, 2013, during the speech at US Congress, about the likely change in QE program. The impact of this testimony was very destructive for emerging markets; many economies in Asia and Latin America lived dramatic capital flow returns and falls in stock exchanges. Particularly the countries that have significant financial or macroeconomic weaknesses have felt more market strain (Rai and Suchanek 2014). Fed continues similar announcements since then; however, the 2013 declarations had more impact on EMEs, and reaction of the market decreased over time. Notably, some of the emerging countries have improved some macroeconomic indicators during the time. As of the year 2015, India and Indonesia rehabilitate their economies by implementing reforms in last years, and international financial analysts are noticing investors for only the three fragile emerging economies; these are Turkey, Brazil, and South Africa.

The significant Fed's announcements in 2013 are given below (Rai and Suchanek 2014):

1. Federal Reserve Chairman Ben Bernanke declared that the likelihood of the Fed reducing its security purchases had a sharp negative impact on emerging markets on **May 22, 2013**. MSCI Emerging Markets Index decreased 0.5%, much of it recovered over the past 3 months, while the S&P 500 rose 13.57%.
2. Bernanke noticed that reducing the bond purchases is contingent upon run-on positive economic data on **June 19, 2013**, and the Fed could scale back its monthly bond purchases from $85 billion to $65 billion during the next September 2013 meeting. The minutes of the meeting created a volatility in emerging markets, and returns of stock markets decreased by nearly 4.3% over the three trading days following Bernanke's declaration.
3. Fed's monetary policymaking body baffled markets with the decision to avoid from reducing the amount of monthly bond purchases it makes under its quantitative easing (QE) program on **September 19, 2013**. The general response of the markets was positive. European markets rise more than 1% after the US Federal Reserve surprised markets and chose not to start tapering its $85bn asset

---

[4]http://www.morganstanley.com/institutional/research/pdf/FXPulse_20130829.pdf

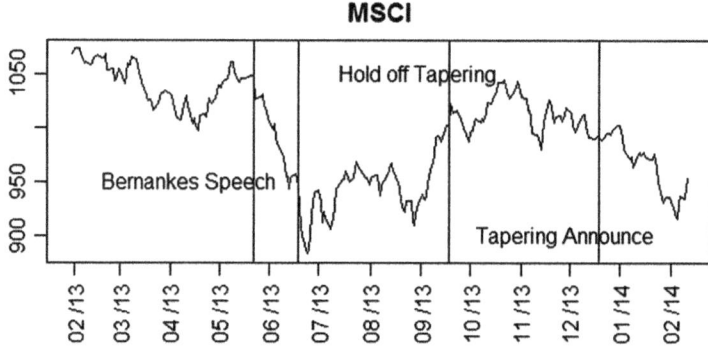

Fig. 20.1 Reaction of emerging equity markets during tapering period is given in this figure. Source: Rai, V., & Suchanek, L. (2014). *The Effect of the Federal Reserve's Tapering Announcements on Emerging Markets*. Bank of Canada WP

purchases. Japan's Nikkei closed 1.8% higher, and the Australia ASX All Ordinaries Index increased 1.1%. Hong Kong's Hang Seng rise 1.7%.
4. Bernanke announced plans to cut its monthly bond purchases to $75 billion from $85 billion on **December 18, 2013**. The emerging markets in Asia were the most sensitive to the Fed's tapering program; however the reaction among investors was very mild. The Hang Seng Index dropped 1.1%, and South Korea's benchmark indicator, the KOSPI, and the Straits Times Index in Singapore have little changed (Fig. 20.1).

Literature

As mentioned in the previous section, after dramatic global crisis in 2008, Fed employed the unconventional monetary policy called "quantitative easing" that came to an end in May 2013 with a "tapering" speech of Fed chair Bernanke. Starting with this tapering speech, emerging markets found themselves in a more volatile financial environment leading to severe losses in emerging asset markets. This sudden happening drew a good deal of scholars' attention.

The existing literature on effects of tapering announcements on emerging markets is focused on macroeconomic fundamentals of emerging markets. However, the authors think that to be stuck in those fundamentals will result in a miss on market efficiency. In a world of high-tech and fast-traveling information, it is anticipated that those information contents are to be priced in markets in context of event study and market efficiency (Fama 1969). Therefore, some attention should be put on event study, by which the authors assess the expected returns and hence abnormal returns and market efficiency as well as on macroeconomic fundamentals.

Eichengreen and Gupta (2014) find out that the suffering of stock exchange, currency, and bond markets in emerging markets doesn't depend on fundamental macroeconomic foundations which are consisting of several variables such as current account balance, GDP growth, reserves account in central bank, interest rate, FDI, portfolio inflows, public debt and fiscal balance, financial depth, and openness of markets.[5] Apart from that, in their study, they implicitly assume that there is a significant effect of tapering announcement on prices, and then in order to capture this relation, they regress these effects in markets to macroeconomic fundamentals.

Aizenman et al. (2014) have an interesting conclusion as emerging countries with strong fundamentals experienced severe losses than those with weaker fundamentals, and therefore there is no profound differentiation between emerging markets with strong and with weak fundamentals. They conduct an event study with mean model to capture the effects of tapering announcement on emerging markets. And based on characteristics of country, they divide emerging markets into robust and fragile group, and thus their conclusion follows from this separation.

However, Rai and Suchanek (2014) state that strong fundamental macroeconomic conditions do provide an insulation for emerging countries having those strong fundamentals. Additionally, what made their research notable, on authors' point of view, is they first conduct an event study to estimate the effect of tapering announcement and report that there is no serial correlation or GARCH effect in error terms.

Mishra et al. (2014) find contrary to Eichengreen and Gupta (2014), strong macroeconomic fundamentals and financial depth provide a buffer for emerging countries with strong fundamentals during tapering session of emerging markets.

Sahay et al. (2014) conclude that, initially, all emerging markets reacted poorly to tapering; yet countries with strong fundamentals get over the shock more rapidly.

According to working paper of FRBSF (2016),[6] it is stated that reactions to tapering announcement of emerging countries are related to economic conditions and that sudden stop or capital reversals are depending not only on external conditions but also internal prospects. In other words, their findings, consistent with Mishra et al. and Rai and Suchanek (2014), suggest that with weak fundamentals, especially "fragile five" suffered most.

Ahmed (2017) also go after whether strong fundamentals provide a safety against tapering announcement and found out that it does. And also, countries that inflowed larger capital during QE also experienced more deterioration in their economic conditions leading to sharp drops in asset markets during tapering. It is called "more in more out."[7]

Chen (2016) conclude that emerging countries with stronger fundamentals and having more liquid markets reacted fairly relative to those with weak fundamental

---

[5]Definition and variables of macroeconomic fundamentals may vary through out literature yet having a lot in common.

[6]http://www.frbsf.org/economic-research/publications/economic-letter/2014/march/federal-reserve-tapering-emerging-markets/

[7]https://papers.ssrn.com/sol3/papers.cfm?abstract_id=2671043

countries and that differentiation among countries was salient when shock is powerful.[8]

Díez (2014) finds out increasing current account and real exchange rate appreciation are key factors in explaining observed adjustments in emerging country markets.

Bouraoui (2015) employs event study to estimate the effect of tapering announcement on currencies of fragile five countries. He points out that, especially at the day after tapering announcement, currencies reacted negatively. He also states, FDI outward played significant role in currency depreciation.

What seems problematic with existing literature from the point of view of event study approach is the following: existing literature only focuses on macroeconomic fundamentals which are assumed to be determinants of effect of tapering announce, yet the authors think event study should also be conducted. In other words, naively speaking, existing literature has a myopia on fundamentals.

To see further the authors' reasoning for this approach is the following. By definition, scholars assess abnormal returns as the difference between actual and predicted returns. At this point, there needs to be a model for prediction of return process, and this model, ideally, should represent the return process to have a precise prediction. And it might be the case that the prediction model may foresee the expected drop in market index as it's expected since in a world of technology where information travels faster than most of any other objects. Thus, prediction model might forecast possible drops in asset classes, and therefore the authors might not have significant abnormal return due to efficiency of markets. Thus, authors believe, conducting event study is crucial. To put it in different words, instead directly regressing returns on macroeconomic variables, i.e., employing multifactor models, might not be sufficient on explaining the determinants of abnormal returns. And as a result of this, before considering the effects of macroeconomic variables on returns, conducting event study is pivotal. Then, at this point, parametrization and estimation of the abnormal returns should be performed thoroughly, since the statistical power of these models is proved to be weaker. The authors will explain the employed model in methodology section more comprehensively.

Data and Methodology

In this study, authors aim is to investigate the effect of Fed's tapering decision on emerging market stock returns by event study methodology. The event study methodology is selected since it is an appropriate model to detect outside effects on price movements (MacKinley 1997). The authors use daily data of 19 countries for 252 days forecasting window and 7 days event window (3 days before the event day, event day, and the 3 days after the event). Countries subject to this study is

---

[8]https://www.imf.org/external/pubs/ft/wp/2014/wp14240.pdf

Table 20.1 Summary
statistics

Country	Mean	Std. dev.	Skew.	Kurt.
Turkey	0.0005	0.0153	−1.2706	11.7145
Brazil	−0.0002	0.0129	0.1143	3.5009
Chile	−0.0004	0.0078	0.0477	4.4389
Mexico	0.0003	0.0087	−0.134	4.2066
Colombia	−0.0003	0.0083	−0.2773	5.2089
Czech	0.0003	0.0089	−0.2844	3.3833
Egypt	0.0009	0.0148	−0.5992	10.9949
Greece	0.0019	0.0207	−0.2353	4.7628
Hungary	0.0003	0.01	0.0418	4.1141
Poland	0.0008	0.009	−0.3826	5.8975
Russia	0.0003	0.0101	0.2561	4.2179
South Africa	0.0007	0.0072	−0.1073	4.9477
China	−0.0003	0.0107	0.0118	5.9464
India	0.0006	0.0099	0.0105	4.3852
Indonesia	0.0003	0.0142	−0.0526	5.7663
South Korea	0.0001	0.01	−0.9465	6.7087
Malaysia	0.0004	0.0049	0.0702	10.0431
Philippines	0.0004	0.0117	−0.3246	5.7902
Thailand	0.0003	0.011	−0.2837	5.7415

chosen from the list that forms MSCI Emerging Market Index excluding Qatar, Taiwan, United Arab Emirates, Peru, and Pakistan. Specific events the authors selected are as in section "Fed's Tapering Announcements and Performance of Emerging Market Exchanges": May 22, 2013–June 19, 2013–September 19, 2013, and December 18, 2013.

Due to these selected four events, dataset covers the period between May 20, 2012, and December 23, 2013, by considering the 252 days forecasting window are taken from "Datastream" of Reuters. Stock market returns are calculated as follows:

$$R_t = \ln\left(\frac{t_i}{t_{i-1}}\right), i = 2, 3, 4, \ldots, 259.$$

t_i is the price in day i. In Table 20.1, summary statistics of 19 countries are presented.

According to Table 20.1, the data is not normally distributed as expected from the financial data usually set since skewness value is not closer to value of 0 and kurtosis value is not closer to value of 3 in all countries. Particularly, the authors observe excess kurtosis in Turkey, Egypt, and Malaysia.

Parameter Estimation

As parallel notation with MacKinley (1997), the expected returns of prices of "*i*th" county in the event window are calculated:

$E[R_{i\tau}|R_{m\tau}] = \widehat{\alpha}_i + \widehat{\beta}_i R_{i\tau}$, $\tau = -3, -2, -1, 0, 1, 2, 3$ and where "0" shows the event day.

Then abnormal return is the difference between the expected return of "*i*th" country and realized return on the event date:

$$\widehat{AR}_{i\tau} = R_{i\tau} - E[R_{i\tau}|X]$$

By adding the abnormal returns in the event window, the total effect of the event for the firm is calculated as cumulative abnormal return (CAR):

$$\widehat{CAR}_i = \sum_{\tau=-3}^{3} \widehat{AR}_{i\tau}.$$

The authors parameterize abnormal returns as γ_{is} by simply adding dummy for every event "*s*" D_{st} same as Binder (1998), and step-by-step modification of one-factor market model for event study is as follows:

$$R_{it} = \alpha_i + \beta_i R_{mt} + \sum_{s=1}^{S} \gamma_{is} D_{st} + u_{it} \tag{20.1}$$

$$E[u_{it}] = 0$$

$$Var(u_{it}) = \sigma_{ui}^2$$

From the above equation, R_{it} is the day t returns of firm i; R_{mt} is the return of the market portfolio. The authors use MSCI Emerging Markets Index for the market portfolio as an independent variable. MSCI Emerging Markets Index which is constructed as a weighted average of the returns of emerging markets is a good candidate for the market portfolio. D_{st} is the dummy variable that takes the value of 1 for the event day and 0 otherwise, u_{it} is the error term, and σ_{ui}^2 is the variance of the error term. The linear regression assumptions are also relevant for the model. So the authors analyze error terms and make adjustments in the model accordingly.

In the second step, the authors search whether there is an autocorrelation between error terms to authenticate that error terms are IID (Godfrey 1978). If the authors find autocorrelation, the authors add the lag variable of the dependent variable, and the model becomes as follows (for details check Appendix):

$$R_{it} = \alpha_i + a_i R_{it-1} + \sum_{s=1}^{S} \gamma_{is} D_{st} + \sum_{i=0}^{q} \beta_i R_{mt} + u_t \tag{20.2}$$

In the third step, the authors analyze the variance for the problem of heteroskedasticity by Breusch and Pagan (1980). Since the authors come across to heteroskedasticity problem in dataset, in order to estimate the parameters in an unbiased and efficient way, the authors use the GARCH (1,1) modeling process, since it allows variance to be nonconstant over a period, as in the Eqs. (20.3) and (20.4) below (for details check Appendix):

$$R_{it} = \alpha_i + a_i R_{t-1} + \sum_{s=1}^{S} \gamma_{is} D_{st} + \sum_{i=0}^{q} \beta_i R_{mt} + u_t \tag{20.3}$$

$$E\left[\left(u_{it}^2 | \Omega\right)\right] = h_{it} = \alpha'_{i0} + \sum_{i=1}^{q} a'_i u_{t-i} + \sum_{i=1}^{p} \beta'_i h_{t-i} \tag{20.4}$$

Additionally, the authors investigate reflections of tapering decision on unconditional variance (long-term variance) of emerging markets. The authors seek for possible jump/jumps on long-term variance by simply adding dummy variable to GARCH (1,1) model on event days or a structural change after May 22, 2013. This specification is set in two ways: adding dummy equal to "1" on pre-specified event days and "0" otherwise and equal to "1" after May 22, 2013, and "0" otherwise.

To do so, the authors specify dummy variable in variance process modeling accordingly. Then, variance model GARCH (1,1) model becomes:

$$E\left[\left(u_{it}^2 | \Omega\right)\right] = h_{it} = \alpha'_{i0} + \sum_{s=1}^{S} \gamma'_{is} D'_{st} + \sum_{i=1}^{q} a'_i u_{t-i} + \sum_{i=1}^{p} \beta'_i h_{t-i} \tag{20.5}$$

where D_{st} measures the shift in the unconditional variance of the market within same manner in mean model and Ω is condition information up to time t.

The authors specify dummy variable in two ways which can be considered as robustness check: (a) same as the authors employ to measure the abnormal return in event window and (b) its equal to zero until May 22 and equal to 1 thereafter. With this specification the authors check for abnormal variance within event window and for a permanent shift in long-term variance of emerging markets.

As a summary of this section, it is essential to conduct error term analysis since the authors employ linear models. All effort is to make a straight modeling for expected returns which is the determinant of abnormal returns. Under desired conditions, i.e., white noise error terms, linear models are convenient to conduct event study. Authors' model approach follows from this effort.

Findings

The authors represent the preliminary results and model specification results in this section. First, the authors check autocorrelation and then heteroscedasticity. After that, the authors report the results both for abnormal return and for abnormal variance model.

Godfrey (1978) test results for autocorrelation are presented in Table 20.2. According to Table 20.2, autocorrelation problem occurred in Turkey, Brazil, Chile, Egypt, Russia, South Africa, Indonesia, South Korea, Malaysia, and the Philippines. The null hypothesis as "no autocorrelation" is rejected for above countries meaning that p values are smaller than 0.1 for these countries.

As seen in Table 20.2, more than half of the dataset, autocorrelation problem appeared. Then the authors add the lag variable of the dependent variable to solve this problem. On the other hand, heteroskedasticity test of Breusch and Pagan (1980) is presented in Table 20.3.

Table 20.3 indicates that great majority of the dataset suffers from heteroskedasticity problem except for Brazil, Mexico, Czech Republic, Russia, China, and Malaysia. In same manner, the null hypothesis homoscedasticity is rejected for these countries having p value smaller than 0.1. As a result of Table 20.3, GARCH (1,1) model is determined to use.

Event Study Results

In this study, the authors examine four events specified in section "Data and Methodology" separately, since Fed's tapering decisions could not be considered as regular events as earning announcements, inflation announcements, and stock splits. Instead, these four events can be treated as separately in itself.

Respectively, Tables 20.4, 20.5, 20.6, and 20.7 exhibits the event study analysis result for May, June, September, and December announcement. And the average of these four announcements is shown in Table 20.8.

May Announcement

For the May announcement, the authors see that more than half of the emerging markets reacted negatively in pre-event window in which the authors expect those markets to react. Yet in event day, the authors only see some positive responses, which are statistically significant, to losses in pre-event window or weak/random reactions to event. Yet the authors don't conclude markets are efficient in this period since signs of the returns in pre-event and post-event window are different. For the fragile five, South Africa, India, and Indonesia affected negatively in the pre-event period and in the event day. Also, the authors see that markets with negative reactions covered up for their losses in pre-event period.

June Announcement

In June, the authors observe again more than half of the markets reacted negatively to the June announcement but in greater magnitude relative to May. And the authors

Table 20.2 Godfrey test results

Turkey	Brazil	Chile	Mexico	Colombia	Czech Rep.	Egypt	Greece	Hungary	Poland
0.0004***	0.0007***	0.0041***	0.375	0.9998	0.829	0.0002***	0.5348	0.3418	0.6163
Russia	South Africa	China	India	Indonesia	South Korea	Malaysia	Philippines	Thailand	
0.0277**	0.0143**	0.635	0.4232	0.0002***	0.0216**	0.0670*	0.0572*	0.4384	

Significance level: (***) %1, (**) %5, and (*) %10

Table 20.3 Breusch test results

Turkey	Brazil	Chile	Mexico	Colombia	Czech Rep.	Egypt	Greece	Hungary	Poland
0.0078***	0.4966	0.0009***	0.5795	0.0043***	0.5159	0.0197**	0.0002***	0.0001***	0.0572*
Russia	South Africa	China	India	Indonesia	South Korea	Malaysia	Philippines	Thailand	
0.4267	0.0023***	0.2526	0.0016***	0.0000***	0.0859*	0.3459	0.0000***	0.0000***	

Significance level: (***) %1, (**) %5, and (*) %10

Table 20.4 Event study analysis result for May announcement

	−3	−2	−1	0	1	2	3	Sum(−3,0)	Sum(−3,+3)	Sum(0,+3)
Turkey	−0.0015**	−0.0236	0.0195	0.0033	0.0194	0.0435	−0.0934	−0.0056	−0.0328	−0.0305
Brazil	0.0078***	0.0083***	0.0107***	0.0036***	0.0184***	0.0012**	−0.0025**	0.0268***	0.0473***	0.01702**
Chile	0.0006	−0.006***	0.0046***	0.0046***	0.0004	−0.009***	−0.0044	0.0014**	−0.0101**	−0.0133*
Mexico	0.0011***	−0.018***	−0.013***	−0.011***	0.0173***	−0.0003	−0.011***	−0.0311***	−0.0362***	0.0058**
Colombia	0.0018***	−0.005***	0.0018***	0.0023***	0.0152***	0.0043***	0.0004	−0.0021***	0.0201***	0.0120**
Czech Rep.	−0.002***	−0.002***	0.0028***	0.0036***	0.0023**	−0.008***	0.008***	−0.0018***	0.0035***	0.0016***
Egypt	−0.008***	0.002	−0.005***	−0.006***	0.0009	−0.015***	−0.009***	−0.0121**	−0.0422**	−0.0239*
Greece	0.013***	−0.019***	−0.043***	−0.012***	−0.026***	−0.006***	0	−0.0484***	−0.0932***	−0.0329*
Hungary	0.0006	−0.002***	−0.0006	0.0166***	0.0062***	0.0095***	0.0037***	−0.0026*	0.0334*	0.0194*
Poland	0.0015***	−0.003***	−0.005***	0.001**	0.0063***	0.0087***	0.0222***	−0.0064***	0.0317***	0.0371***
Russia	0.0197***	0.0021***	0.0115***	0.0178***	−0.020***	−0.012***	−0.002***	0.0333***	0.0167***	−0.0343***
South Africa	−0.005***	0.0004	0.002***	−0.0005	−0.003***	0.0005	−0.005***	−0.0027**	−0.012*	−0.0087
China	0.0138***	0.0064***	0.0024***	−0.001**	0.0004	0.0054***	0.0008	−0.0226***	0.0282*	0.0066
India	0.003***	−0.006***	−0.007***	−0.003***	−0.008***	0.0021***	0.0152***	−0.0108***	−0.0051**	0.0091**
Indonesia	0.0176***	0.0125***	−0.005***	−0.0005	0.0048***	−0.0006	−0.011***	0.0243***	0.0162*	−0.0076
South Korea	0.0005	0.0007	0.0092***	0.0025***	−0.0013	0.0077***	0.0008	0.0104***	0.0200	0.0070
Malaysia	0.0019**	0.0034***	0.0051***	−0.002***	−0.002***	−0.001***	−0.004***	0.0104***	0.0000**	−0.0077**
Philippines	−0.004***	−0.002***	0.0067***	0.0073***	0.0063	−0.0178	−0.0108	0.0001***	−0.0150*	−0.0222
Thailand	0.0057***	0.0076***	−0.0006*	−0.008***	−0.004***	−0.0066	−0.014***	−0.0127*	−0.0207*	−0.0253

Significance level: (***) %1, (**) %5, and (*) %10

Table 20.5 Event study analysis result for June announcement

	−3	−2	−1	0	1	2	3	Sum(−3,0)	Sum(−3,+3)	Sum(0,+3)
Turkey	0.0369***	−0.017***	−0.014***	0.0167***	−0.047***	−0.0012	−0.0151**	0.0049***	−0.0419**	−0.0635*
Brazil	−0.024***	−0.008***	0.0118***	−0.025***	0.0446***	−0.016***	−0.0012	−0.0211***	−0.0194**	0.0269*
Chile	−0.003***	−0.005***	0.002***	−0.004***	−0.015***	0.0023***	0.0027	−0.0072***	−0.0218**	−0.0106*
Mexico	−0.01***	0.0054***	−0.0012**	−0.008***	−0.024***	0.0167***	−0.007***	−0.0058**	−0.0291***	−0.0150***
Colombia	0.001	0.0007*	0.0172***	−0.003***	−0.006***	−0.010***	−0.013***	0.0188	−0.0143***	−0.0298***
Czech Rep.	−0.007***	−0.005***	0.0024***	0.0047***	−0.0045**	−0.018***	−0.014***	−0.0109***	−0.0432***	−0.0370***
Egypt	0.0243**	−0.0081	0.0115***	0.0098***	−0.0053	−0.013***	−0.022***	0.0277*	−0.0042*	−0.0418*
Greece	0.0131***	−0.018***	0.0118***	0.0023	−0.0094	−0.059***	0.0214***	0.007***	−0.0378*	−0.0471*
Hungary	0.0002	−0.015***	−0.003***	−0.005***	0.0061*	−0.017***	0.0079***	−0.0182**	−0.0268*	−0.0034*
Poland	−0.004***	−0.006***	0.0011**	−0.004***	−0.016***	−0.020***	0.0125***	−0.0093***	−0.0389***	−0.0251***
Russia	0.0059***	0.0169***	0.0103***	−0.003***	0.0107***	0.0081***	0.0082***	0.0331***	0.0567***	0.0269***
South Africa	−0.010***	0.0061***	0.002***	0.01***	−0.0049**	−0.0049	−0.0084*	−0.0023***	−0.0105	−0.0181
China	0.0005	−0.004***	0.0037***	−0.003***	−0.0049	−0.0002	−0.043***	−0.0003*	−0.0519*	−0.0484
India	0.012***	0.0047***	−0.004***	0.0057***	−0.0037*	0.0073***	−0.002**	0.0125***	0.0196*	0.0015
Indonesia	0.0312***	−0.005***	0.0193***	−0.0015*	−0.015***	−0.0215**	0.0159	0.0448***	0.0225**	−0.0207*
South Korea	−0.012***	−0.023***	0.0196***	−0.003***	−0.0028	0.0076	0.012	−0.0156***	−0.0019	0.0167
Malaysia	0.0097***	0.0043***	0.0012***	0.0003	0.0027**	−0.002***	−0.003***	0.0153***	0.0121*	−0.0034*
Philippines	0.0154***	0.0134***	0.029***	0.0017***	−0.011***	−0.019***	−0.027***	0.0578***	0.0005**	−0.059**
Thailand	0.0366***	0.0014***	−0.028***	0.0103***	−0.0039	0.0028***	−0.016***	0.0092***	0.0019*	−0.0175*

Significance level: (***) %1, (**) %5, and (*) %10

Table 20.6 Event study analysis result for September announcement

	−3	−2	−1	0	1	2	3	Sum(−3,0)	Sum(−3,+3)	Sum(0,+3)
Turkey	−0.014***	0.025***	0.005***	−0.002***	0.0478***	−0.0165***	−0.0171***	0.0153***	0.0271***	0.0142***
Brazil	0.0125***	−0.012***	0.0083***	0.0279***	−0.025***	−0.009***	0.0074***	0.0084***	0.0049***	−0.0314***
Chile	−0.006***	0.0063***	−0.003***	0.0064***	−0.002*	0.0093***	0.0164***	−0.0041***	0.0260*	0.0237*
Mexico	0.01***	−0.006***	−0.0006	0.0186***	−0.012***	−0.009***	0.0006*	0.0036*	0.0012*	−0.0210*
Colombia	0.0007*	−0.008***	0.0049***	0.0026***	−0.007***	0.0052***	0.002***	−0.0029	−0.001***	−0.0005***
Czech Rep.	−0.007***	0.0038***	−0.004***	−0.002***	−0.013***	−0.017***	0.0034***	−0.008***	−0.0392***	−0.0293***
Egypt	0.0045***	0.002	0.0036***	−0.0004	−0.008***	0.0006	0.0056***	0.0100**	0.0074**	−0.0022*
Greece	−0.005***	−0.011***	0.0037***	−0.0005	0.0035	−0.034***	0.0005	−0.0137***	−0.0445**	−0.0302*
Hungary	0.0086***	0.0028**	−0.0006	−0.009***	−0.010***	−0.007***	−0.004***	0.0107	−0.0207**	−0.0224
Poland	−0.007***	−0.018***	0.0093***	−0.0004	0.0046***	0.0047***	−0.009***	−0.0166***	−0.0175**	−0.0004***
Russia	−0.003***	0.0093***	0.0013***	−0.0008	−0.0008	−0.0001	−0.008***	0.0067***	−0.0067**	−0.0091
South Africa	0.0058***	−0.0005	−0.004***	−0.004***	0.0106***	0.0081***	0.0016***	0.0006**	0.0165***	0.0202***
China	−0.006***	−0.010***	−0.021***	0.0039***	−0.009***	0.008***	0.0064***	−0.0381***	−0.0289***	0.0053***
India	0.0016***	−0.011***	0.001***	0.009***	0.0225***	−0.011***	−0.022***	−0.0087***	−0.0114***	−0.0117***
Indonesia	0.003***	0.0279***	−0.004***	−0.016***	0.0369***	−0.009	0.0041	0.0265***	0.0418*	0.0320
South Korea	0.0034***	−0.014***	0.0013**	0.0003	−0.007***	0.003**	−0.001***	−0.0095**	−0.0154**	−0.0061*
Malaysia	−0.001***	−0.002***	−0.0003	−0.002***	0.0066***	0.0064***	−0.004***	−0.0036*	0.0026***	0.0085***
Philippines	−0.009***	0.0202***	0.0057***	−0.001***	0.0179***	−0.01***	0.0065***	0.0168***	0.0297***	0.0143***
Thailand	0.0033***	0.0224***	−0.002***	−0.003***	0.0223***	0.0027***	−0.037***	0.0238***	0.0086***	−0.0120***

Significance level: (***) %1, (**) %5, and (*) %10

Table 20.7 Event study analysis result for December announcement

	−3	−2	−1	0	1	2	3	Sum(−3,0)	Sum(−3,+3)	Sum(0,+3)
Turkey	0.0127***	0.0089***	−0.055***	0.0036***	−0.033***	0.0066***	−0.026***	−0.0336***	−0.0827***	−0.0527***
Brazil	0.0023***	0.0048***	−0.003***	0.008***	0.0234***	−0.006***	−0.0001	0.0039***	0.02930**	0.01737***
Chile	−0.003***	0.0087***	−0.004***	−0.002***	0.0051***	0.0082***	−0.008***	0.0007***	0.0033***	0.0047***
Mexico	−0.005***	0.0037***	−0.007***	0.0064***	0.0032***	0.0002	0.0056***	−0.0087***	0.0066**	0.0089**
Colombia	−0.003***	−0.015***	0.0023***	−0.007***	0.0043***	0.014***	−0.013***	−0.0160***	−0.0187***	0.0051***
Czech Rep.	−0.010***	0.0106***	−0.004***	0.0106***	0.0022***	0.0036***	0.0022***	−0.0046***	0.0140***	0.0080***
Egypt	0.0154***	0.0094***	−0.006***	0.0098***	−0.001	0.0022**	−0.003***	0.0180***	0.0255***	−0.0022**
Greece	−0.027***	−0.011***	−0.002***	−0.004***	0.0071***	−0.028***	−0.016***	−0.0411***	−0.0833***	−0.0377***
Hungary	0.0079***	0.0188***	−0.009***	−0.001***	0.0018***	−0.008***	−0.009***	0.0175***	−0.0003***	−0.0160***
Poland	−0.003***	−0.001***	−0.019***	0.0017***	−0.006***	0.0097***	0.0017***	−0.0244***	−0.0176***	0.0051***
Russia	0.0028***	0.0121***	0.0062***	0.0035***	0.0091***	0.0014***	0.0036***	0.0211***	0.0386***	0.0140***
South Africa	−0.002***	−0.001***	−0.0011**	0.0038***	0.012***	−0.012***	0.0033***	−0.0048	0.0020***	0.0031***
China	−0.002***	−0.016***	−0.004***	−0.002***	−0.008***	−0.019***	0	−0.0228***	−0.0524***	−0.0271**
India	−0.010***	−0.002***	−0.003***	0.011***	−0.007***	0.0185***	−0.001***	−0.0160***	0.0049***	0.0099***
Indonesia	−0.011***	−0.014***	0.0154***	0.0013***	0.0168***	−0.011***	−0.004***	−0.0106***	−0.0078***	0.0013***
South Korea	−0.003***	−0.012***	−0.004***	−0.002***	−0.002***	0.0094***	0.0007	−0.0202***	−0.0146**	0.0075**
Malaysia	0.0034***	−0.002***	0.0064***	−0.003***	−0.001***	−0.002***	−0.006***	0.0077***	−0.0052***	−0.0100***
Philippines	0.0006	0.0074***	0.0193***	0.004***	−0.006***	−0.014***	0.0009**	0.0273**	0.0117***	−0.0195***
Thailand	−0.011***	−0.010***	0.0059***	0.0076***	−0.002***	−0.002***	−0.015***	−0.0155***	−0.0275***	−0.0196***

Significance level: (***) %1, (**) %5, and (*) %10

Table 20.8 The average of event results

	−3	−2	−1	0	1	2	3	Sum(−3,0)	Sum(−3,+3)	Sum(0,+3)
Turkey	0.0083	−0.0017	−0.0114	0.0053	−0.0034	0.0081	−0.0379	−0.0047	−0.0326	−0.0332
Brazil	−0.0004	−0.0020	0.0069	0.0035	0.0142	−0.0076	0.0009	0.0045	0.0155	0.0075
Chile	−0.0033	0.0007	−0.0004	0.0012	−0.0030	0.0026	0.0015	−0.0030	−0.0007	0.0011
Mexico	−0.0010	−0.0039	−0.0057	0.0014	−0.0040	0.0018	−0.0030	−0.0105	−0.0144	−0.0053
Colombia	0.0000	−0.0072	0.0066	−0.0015	0.0012	0.0033	−0.0059	−0.0006	−0.0035	−0.0013
Czech Rep.	−0.0071	0.0017	−0.0008	0.0042	−0.0038	−0.0101	−0.0002	−0.0063	−0.0162	−0.0142
Egypt	0.0088	0.0013	0.0008	0.0033	−0.0035	−0.0065	−0.0076	0.0109	−0.0034	−0.0176
Greece	−0.0016	−0.0149	−0.0075	−0.0037	−0.0064	−0.0320	0.0014	−0.0241	−0.0648	−0.0370
Hungary	0.0043	0.0009	−0.0033	0.0002	0.0008	−0.0060	−0.0005	0.0019	−0.0036	−0.0056
Poland	−0.0035	−0.0071	−0.0035	−0.0006	−0.0031	0.0006	0.0067	−0.0142	−0.0106	0.0042
Russia	−0.0008	0.0053	−0.0006	−0.0021	0.0011	−0.0032	−0.0028	0.0040	−0.0031	−0.0049
South Africa	0.0061	0.0101	0.0073	0.0034	−0.0003	−0.0007	0.0003	0.0236	0.0263	−0.0006
China	−0.0030	0.0011	−0.0004	0.0022	0.0035	−0.0021	−0.0023	−0.0023	−0.0010	−0.0009
India	0.0003	0.0070	−0.0038	0.0014	−0.0029	−0.0012	−0.0083	0.0035	−0.0075	−0.0124
Indonesia	0.0013	−0.0062	−0.0048	−0.0007	−0.0054	−0.0014	−0.0090	−0.0097	−0.0263	−0.0159
South Korea	0.0015	−0.0039	−0.0033	0.0056	0.0009	0.0041	−0.0027	−0.0058	0.0020	0.0022
Malaysia	0.0100	0.0051	0.0062	−0.0044	0.0109	−0.0106	0.0010	0.0213	0.0182	0.0013
Philippines	−0.0028	−0.0124	0.0064	−0.0006	−0.0036	0.0069	0.0030	−0.0088	−0.0030	0.0063
Thailand	0.0035	0.0009	0.0031	−0.0019	0.0016	−0.0001	−0.0046	0.0075	0.0024	−0.0031

This table only has an exhibition purpose, it's not statistically evaluated don't observe the cover-up pattern in June and loss proceeds in post-event window, and even countries not having negative reactions in pre-event window also turns negative. Therefore the authors say that the announcement made in June is tough for emerging markets. Moreover, emerging markets didn't efficiently react to the announcement in June, since market reactions can be followed by pattern the authors recognize, i.e., the authors don't see cumulative reactions in post-event window, which should be zero in case of market efficiency and is equal to zero. Also, the authors see that, particularly in fragile five, Brazil, Turkey, and South Africa affected negatively from the announcement made in June by Fed in pre-event period yet India and Indonesia remain quiet in this period. Together with May event, authors observe emerging markets in Europe are negatively affected from Fed than those in Asia.

September Announcement

The authors observe negative reactions with bigger magnitude are rare in pre-event period as it is expected. Since, Fed announces to delay tapering actions in September. Mostly, the authors see mixed reactions in emerging markets in post-event window; one might relate it with market efficiency. Also the fragile five was positive for this announcement except for India. The authors conclude the September announcement is a relief for emerging markets.

December Announcement

The authors find as in the previous announcements more than half of the emerging markets reacted negatively in pre-event period to the announcement made in December, with greater magnitude than afore announcements. Particularly, fragile five expect Brazil to give negative reactions to this announcement. Interestingly, the authors see Turkey had a severe lost in its equity market. What is more interesting for Turkey is Greece has a huge lost in its markets. The authors interpret this as, Turkey perceived risky as Greece who was having default issues and troublesome times in its economy at that time. Moreover, the authors don't see cover-up pattern for this announcement in fragile five. At a glance, June and December announcements have similar effects on fragile five, both are negative and permanent. Also, as in May and June, emerging markets in Asia are negatively affected in September and December.

The Average Effects of Tapering

The average of the four tapering announcements is reported in the table below. However, the authors don't evaluate this table statistically since positive and negative responses might balance out and the authors might not have any reasonable results, yet the authors demonstrate the result below. Yet it can be seen that Turkey and Greece are negatively differentiated among other markets in magnitude of the market loss. Meaning that the magnitude of the negative returns sweeps any positive reactions. This basically describes the investors' attitudes toward to these countries.

Variance Model Results

The variance model results are shown in Table 20.9 and in Table 20.10.

For the model that authors specified to measure the variance shift during tapering announcements (event days), there are no robust results. In other words, there are no jumps in long-term variance of emerging market returns due to tapering decision in event days. Therefore, it can be concluded that Fed's tapering decisions have impacts only on emerging market returns but not on variance of those markets.

For robustness, authors also check whether the long-term variance of emerging markets has been effected after the May 22, 2013, not only on event days. This specification measures the regime shift in variance of emerging markets due to the tapering signal in May 22, 2013. Findings indicate that there is also not a systematical shift in long-term variance of emerging markets returns.

Conclusion

Emerging markets are expected to get through a stressful period after the revocation sign of the QE program that makes currency more abundant. This policy change was expected to reverse the capital flows directed to the EME. In accordance with the estimations, market indices dramatically declined during the taper-talk period. Particularly the economically fragile EMEs are affected the most.

The authors test the abnormal return performance of the main emerging market stock exchanges using event study methodology. In brief, this study has three important findings; first all of the emerging markets are affected from the decision of Fed during the early announcements in 2013. Secondly, the influence of the Fed's decision has decreased in time except for June. The last but not least, fragile five, specifically Turkey, economies plus China and Greece are influenced the most.

At first sight, the authors find that there is a differentiation in the reactions of emerging markets between four events. Events happened in June and December affect most of the emerging markets, especially "fragile five," severely and negatively. On the other hand, May reactions are ambiguous, and September event is a relief for all. Actually, this result is expected since the September announcement is a hold-off for tapering action. Thus markets react positively to this announcement.

Secondly, the authors observe a distinction in reactions of emerging markets based on locations. In the June and May announcements, emerging market situated in Europe negatively reacts, and Asian countries are not; but for December announcement, the situation is vice versa. That is, Asian emerging markets respond negatively, and European emerging markets are not affected in this way.

Table 20.9 Average volatility shift separately measured for each event

	Estimate	Std. dev.	t value	Prob.
Turkey				
May	0.000000	0.000003	0.011285	0.990996
June	0.000000	0.000003	0.000748	0.999403
September	0.000000	0.000015	0.000000	1
December	0.000000	0.000010	0.000030	0.999976
Brazil				
May	0.000000	0.000002	0.004956	0.996046
June	0.000000	0.000000	21.647.250	0.000000
September	0.000000	0.000000	0.014692	0.988278
December	0.000000	0.000009	0.000004	0.999996
Chile				
May	0.000000	0.000000	68.792.800	0.000000
June	0.000000	0.000000	0.232485	0.816161
September	0.000000	0.000001	0.008443	0.993263
December	0.000000	0.000039	0.000000	1
Mexico				
May	0.000000	0.000000	9.569.328	0.000000
June	0.000000	0.000000	0.080664	0.935709
September	0.000000	0.000001	0.061427	0.951019
December	0.000000	0.000012	0.000000	1
Colombia				
May	0.000000	0.000004	0.012180	0.990282
June	0.000000	0.000000	0.230400	0.817781
September	0.000000	0.000000	0.073908	0.941084
December	0.000000	0.000010	0.000000	1
Czech				
May	0.000000	0.000000	0.021573	0.982789
June	0.000000	0.000000	0.016939	0.986485
September	0.000000	0.000001	0.035010	0.972072
December	0.000000	0.000020	0.000882	0.999297
Egypt				
May	0.000000	0.000039	0.000381	0.999696
June	0.000000	0.000157	0.000265	0.999789
September	0.000000	0.000035	0.000507	0.999596
December	0.000000	0.000031	0.000000	1
Greece				
May	0.000000	0.000004	0.014818	0.988177
June	0.000000	0.000003	0.001017	0.999188
September	0.000000	0.000006	0.003201	0.997446
December	0.000000	0.000068	0.000096	0.999924

(continued)

Table 20.9 (continued)

	Estimate	Std. dev.	t value	Prob.
Hungary				
May	0.000000	0.000011	0.000000	1
June	0.000000	0.000009	0.000979	0.999219
September	0.000000	0.000027	0.000054	0.999957
December	0.000000	0.000007	0.001890	0.998492
Poland				
May	0.000000	0.000010	0.000564	0.999550
June	0.000000	0.000011	0.001526	0.998782
September	0.000000	0.000012	0.000803	0.999360
December	0.000000	0.000012	0.000000	1
Russia				
May	0.000000	0.000007	0.000691	0.999449
June	0.000000	0.000008	0.004161	0.996680
September	0.000000	0.000015	0.000692	0.999448
December	0.000000	0.000015	0.001432	0.998857
South Africa				
May	0.000000	0.000000	0.054572	0.956479
June	0.000000	0.000000	0.921911	0.356575
September	0.000000	0.000046	0.000000	1
December	0.000000	0.000280	0.000002	0.999999
China				
May	0.000000	0.000000	0.000903	0.999279
June	0.000000	0.000002	0.024139	0.980742
September	0.000000	0.000000	0.031147	0.975152
December	0.000000	0.000006	0.006798	0.994576
India				
May	0.000000	0.000006	0.002173	0.998266
June	0.000000	0.000008	0.002951	0.997645
September	0.000000	0.000007	0.000686	0.999453
December	0.000000	0.000004	0.000000	1
Indonesia				
May	0.000000	0.000002	0.002559	0.997958
June	0.000000	0.000000	0.491499	0.623073
September	0.000000	0.000000	0.163027	0.870497
December	0.000000	0.000007	0.000000	1
South Korea				
May	0.000000	0.000325	0.000017	0.999987
June	0.000000	0.002210	0.000008	0.999994
September	0.000000	0.000165	0.000000	1
December	0.000000	0.000138	0.000001	0.999999

(continued)

Table 20.9 (continued)

	Estimate	Std. dev.	t value	Prob.
Malaysia				
May	0.000000	0.000004	0.004200	0.996649
June	0.000000	0.000029	0.000647	0.999484
September	0.000000	0.000015	0.000000	1
December	0.000000	0.000021	0.000519	0.999586
Philippines				
May	0.000022	0.000020	1.076.545	0.281684
June	0.000000	0.000012	0.003748	0.997010
September	0.000000	0.000012	0.000595	0.999525
December	0.000000	0.000002	0.000000	1
Thailand				
May	0.000000	0.000003	0.073172	0.941669
June	0.000000	0.000012	0.003085	0.997539
September	0.000000	0.000002	0.010230	0.991838
December	0.000000	0.000086	0.000000	1

Significance level: (***) %1, (**) %5, and (*) %10

Table 20.10 Average volatility shift results

	Estimate	Std. dev.	t value	Prob.
Turkey	0.000000	0.000003	0.000000	1
Brazil	0.000000	0.000000	0.000000	1
Chile	0.000000	0.000000	0.000000	1
Mexico	0.000005	0.000002	2.023850	0.042986**
Colombia	0.000000	0.000000	0.000000	1
Czech Rep.	0.000000	0.000006	0.003304	0.997364
Egypt	0.000000	0.000016	0.000000	1
Greece	0.000000	0.000015	0.000000	1
Hungary	0.000000	0.000002	0.000000	1
Poland	0.000000	0.000003	0.000000	1
Russia	0.000000	0.000000	0.971056	1
South Africa	0.000000	0.000000	0.000000	0.331520
China	0.000000	0.000006	0.000995	1
India	0.000000	0.000001	0.000000	1
Indonesia	0.000000	0.000000	0.001498	0.999206
South Korea	0.000000	0.000022	0.000000	1
Malaysia	0.000000	0.000000	0.004252	0.998805
Philippines	0.000012	0.000015	0.824732	1
Thailand	0.000002	0.000009	0.189572	0.996607

Significance level: (***) %1, (**) %5, and (*) %10

Thirdly, narrowing the focus on fragile five, the May announcement influences them negatively except for Brazil. Additionally, the authors recognize a pattern as follows: at first they are negatively affected, and then they cover up for their losses. And also, with fragile five, Greece, Egypt, and Mexico hit badly in May. In June the authors find Turkey—not in the sum of the pre-event window but in last 2 days—Brazil, and South Africa have negative reactions to the Fed's declaration. What is striking with those countries is they compensate up for their losses except for Turkey which continues suffering in post-event period. For the September announcement, as for most of the countries, fragile five remain positive or with trivial negative reaction. For December, Turkey is negative in both pre- and post-event window. Brazil is positive, and South Africa, India, and Indonesia are negative in pre-event period and turn positive in post-event window. The authors conclude that Turkey is perceived the most risky among fragile five and that fragile five countries first negatively affected and then cover up for their losses due to announcements except for Turkey which continue suffering from this losses after announcements and same observation holds for Greece, China and Egypt.

For the variance model, the authors ask whether Fed's tapering decision brings additional volatility on emerging equity markets. Since, rising uncertainty among emerging markets might increase the volatility. Results indicate that there are no shift in unconditional variance of emerging equity markets. For both of the dummy variable specification, the authors could not find significant shift in long-term variance. Therefore, the authors cannot conclude any significant variance shift pattern due to Fed announcements between emerging markets. That might be related to robustness of GARCH $(1,1)$ model (Andersen 1998; Bollerslev 1986) which can cover the movements in variance and even possible jumps. Also, estimated values are so close to zero indicating no variance shifts in emerging markets.

To sum up, Turkey is the most negatively affected emerging market in fragile five, on average. Particularly for June and December announcements, Turkey takes a hit which is a hard one. Also, with Turkey, South Africa, India, and Indonesia are also negatively affected from these two events, but then they cover up their losses. However Turkey couldn't compensate the damage. There is also Greece that is having troubles to cover its losses in post-event period. The authors can see that Turkey is perceived risky as Greece. The developments indicate that Turkey is the most breakable among the fragile five countries. Lastly, efficiency results indicate that emerging markets do not behave efficiently during tapering announcement period and Fed's tapering decision has no effects on volatility of emerging equity markets.

For a further study, with high-frequency data, non-synchronous trading might be considered for event study methodology, and for the macroeconomic variables that might be related with the reactions of tapering announcement, a twofold study might be considered: at first, with an event study metric, markets could be group into 1–0 category according to negative reactions. And for second stage, given this negative 1–0 reaction data, logistic regression might be performed in order to classify the macroeconomic variables.

Appendix

Basically, the authors add lagged variable in linear regression to overcome autocorrelation between error terms which leads to statistical inference conducted fallaciously in least squares.

Now let us clarify the technicality of the autocorrelation problem with some matrix notation. As it's well known, abnormal returns are by definition prediction errors:

$$AR = y - y^*$$

where AR is the vector of abnormal return, $y = X\beta + u$ is the vector of actual return, $y^* = Xb$ is the normal return vector, and X is the market returns on event window.

Rearranging terms the authors have

$$AR = X(\beta - b) + u$$

where u is the vector of residuals with variance $\sigma_u^2 \Omega$.

The authors are now interested in variance, and since the authors are dealing with statistical inference, the authors need variance terms to be well specified.

Variance of abnormal returns is

$$var(AR) = Xvar(b)X' + \sigma_u^2 \Omega$$

First part of the rhs of above equation is additional variance due to prediction error. Asymptotically, that first part goes zero, and the authors are left with $\sigma_u^2 \Omega$ term, if the authors have uncorrelated error terms in event period. Yet it may not be the case or the authors may not have variance of error terms equal to a constant, the authors will come to latter one soon.

For the case:

$$\sigma_u^2 \Omega = \sigma_u^2 I$$

where I is identity matrix, i.e., uncorrelated error terms, then statistical inference based on $\sigma_u^2 I$ will be correctly specified. But for the case below:

$$\sigma_u^2 \Omega \neq \sigma_u^2 I$$

i.e., correlated error terms, statistical inference that the authors made will be misleading since cross correlations in between error terms are underestimated with least squares, since least squares assumes $\Omega = I$ above equation.

Additionally, variance of the estimated parameters of OLS:

$$var(b) = \sigma_u^2 (X'X)^{-1}$$

Actually it's simplified to above equation when

$$E(e'e) = \sigma_u^2 I$$

But in case of autocorrelation, this assumption leads to problematic conclusion in hypothesis testing due to biased estimation of last equation above. That is, this conclusion is well specified when errors are white noise.

When

$$E(e'e) = \sigma_u^2 \Omega$$

the authors have

$$\text{var}(b) = (X'X)^{-1} X' \sigma_u^2 \Omega X (X'X)^{-1}$$

Then the hypothesis testing based on $\sigma_u^2 \Omega$ will fail obviously. If correlation between error terms is persistent, then bias will be severe. The authors know that $\sigma_u^2 (X'X)^{-1}$ is biased estimation for $(X'X)^{-1} X' \sigma_u^2 \Omega X (X'X)^{-1}$. T or F distributions that are calculated by this $\sigma_u^2 (X'X)^{-1}$ will be misleading.

Other than that, there are no problem with unbiasedness; consistency, i.e., plimb=beta; or asymptotically normality of least square estimation. However, the authors cannot conclude it's an efficient estimation, since heteroscedasticity leads us some fallacious conclusion in hypothesis testing due to biased estimation of variance of error terms.

Again, if the authors assume error terms as above,

$$E(e'e) = \sigma_u^2 \Omega$$

Again least square estimate will be misleading. Since variance is not equal to some constant σ_u^2, least squares estimation will fail, therefore MLE should be employed for parameter estimation. The authors replace the variance of error terms in the conditional density with conditional variance; it's a generic way.

The statistical reasoning behind this specification above is the following:

The authors now, in addition to autocorrelation problem, constant variance assumption may lead some misleading inference.

Having nonconstant variance requires modeling the variance as a process:

$$u_t = v_t h_t$$

where

$$h_t^2 = \alpha_0 + \alpha'_1 u_{t-1}^2 + \beta' h_{t-1}^2$$
$$E[v_t] = 0 \text{ and } E[v_t^2] = 1$$

$$f(u_t|\Omega) = \frac{1}{\sqrt{2\pi h_t^2}} \exp\left[-\frac{u_t^2}{2h_t^2}\right]$$

The log likelihood becomes

$$L(\alpha_0, \alpha_1, \beta, \gamma) = -\frac{n}{2}\log(2\pi) - \frac{1}{2}\sum_{t=1}^{n}\left\{\log\left(h_t^2\right) + u_t^2/h_t^2\right\}$$

And the authors know MLE is unbiased, consistent, asymptotically normal, and efficient in this specification. Therefore hypothesis testing will be correctly specified in this way.

References

Ahmed, S. C. (2017). International financial spillovers to emerging market economies: How important are economic fundamentals? *Journal of International Money and Finance, 76,* 133–152.

Aizenman, J., Binici, M., & Hutchison, M. M. (2014). *The transmission of Federal Reserve tapering news to emerging financial markets* (No. w19980). National Bureau of Economic Research.

Andersen, T. G. (1998). Answering the skeptics: Yes, standard volatility models do provide accurate forecasts. *International Economic Review, 39,* 885–905.

Bank of England. (2016, June 1). *Quantitative easing – injecting money into the economy.* Retrieved from bankofengland.co.uk.

Bhattarai, S. C. (2015). *Effects of US quantitative easing on emerging market economies.* Retrieved from www.dallasfed.org/assets/documents/institute/wpapers/2015/0255.pdf.

Binder, J. (1998). The event study methodology since 1969. *Review of Quantitative Finance and Accounting, 11*(2), 111–137.

Boehmer, E., Masumeci, J., & Poulsen, A. B. (1991). Event-study methodology under conditions of event-induced variance. *Journal of Financial Economics, 30*(2), 253–272.

Bollerslev, T. (1986). Generalized autoregressive conditional heteroskedasticity. *Journal of Econometrics, 31*(3), 307–327.

Bouraoui, T. (2015). The effect of reducing quantitative easing on emerging markets. *Applied Economics, 47*(15), 1562–1573.

Bowman, D. L. (2015). US unconventional monetary policy and transmission to emerging market economies. *Journal of International Money and Finance, 55,* 27–59.

Breusch, T. S., & Pagan, A. R. (1980). The Lagrange multiplier test and its applications to model specification in econometrics. *The Review of Economic Studies, 47*(1), 239.

Brown, S. J. (1980). Measuring security price performance. *Journal of Financial Economics, 8*(3), 205–258.

Brown, S. J. (1985). Using daily stock returns: The case of event studies. *Journal of Financial Economics, 14*(1), 3–31.

Chen, J. M. (2016, June 1). *Spillovers from United States monetary policy on emerging markets: Different this time?* Retrieved from https://papers.ssrn.com/sol3/papers.cfm?abstract_id=2561285.

Díez, F. J. (2014). *The emerging market economies in times of taper-talk and actual tapering.* Current Policy Perspectives No. 14-6.

Eichengreen, B., & Gupta, P. (2014). Tapering talk: The impact of expectations of reduced Federal Reserve security purchases on emerging markets. *Emerging Markets Review, 25,* 1–15.

Fama, E. F. (1969). The adjustment of stock prices to new information. *International Economic Review, 10*(1), 1–21.

Federal Reserve Bank of San Francisco. (2016, March 15). *FRBSF Economic Letter.* Retrieved from http://www.frbsf.org/economic-research/publications/economic-letter/2014/march/federal-reserve-tapering-emerging-markets/.

Godfrey, L. G. (1978). Testing against general autoregressive and moving average error models when the regressors include lagged dependent variables. *Econometrica: Journal of the Econometric Society, 40,* 1293–1301.

Hansen, P. R. (2005). A forecast comparison of volatility models: does anything beat a GARCH (1, 1)? *Journal of Applied Econometrics, 20*(7), 873–889.

IMF. (2014). IMF Working Paper No:240.

Ito, M. N. (2014). International stock market efficiency: A non-bayesian time-varying model approach. *Applied Economics, 46*(23), 2744–2754.

Karafiath, I., & Spencer, D. E. (1991). Statistical inference in multiperiod event studies. *Review of Quantitative Finance and Accounting, 1*(4), 353–371.

Kuepper, J. (2016, March 20). *What are the fragile five?* Retrieved from https://www.thebalance.com/what-are-the-fragile-five-1978880.

Lavigne, R. S. (2014). Spillover effects of quantitative easing on emerging-market economies. *Bank of Canada Review, 2014,* 23–33.

MacKinlay, A. C. (1997). Event studies in economics and finance. *Journal of Economic Literature, 35*(1), 13–39.

Mishra, P., Moriyama, K., & N'Diaye, P. (2014). *Impact of Fed tapering announcements on emerging markets.* IMF Working Paper No. 14/109.

Morgan Stanley. (2016, May 20). *Fx pulse.* Retrieved from http://www.morganstanley.com/institutional/research/pdf/FXPulse_20130829.pdf.

Rai, V., & Suchanek, L. (2014). *The effect of the Federal Reserve's tapering announcements on emerging markets.* Bank of Canada WP.

Sahay, R., Arora, V., Arvanitis, T., Faruqee, H., N'Diaye, P., & Griffoli, T. M. (2014). *Emerging market volatility: Lessons from the taper tantrum.* IMF Staff Discussion Notes.

Savickas, R. (2003). Event-induced volatility and tests for abnormal performance. *Journal of Financial Research, 26*(2), 165–178.

Schipper, K., & Thompson, R. (1983). The impact of merger-related regulations on the shareholders of acquiring firms. *Journal of Accounting Research, 21,* 184–221.

Chapter 21
Determining the Priorities of CAMELS Dimensions Based on Bank Performance

Mehmet Pekkaya and Figen Erol Demir

Abstract Banks' performances are important not only for the stability/growth of the firms and economic situation of a country; it is also important for the stability/growth of the world economy. The aim of this study is to determine the priorities of CAMELS dimensions with respect to bank performance via AHP method and to present the results as an information to researchers, investors and decision-makers. Furthermore, this study shows the feasibility of many statistical hypothesis tests by separately generated priority series from expert's views based on performance and bankruptcy risk of banks.

CAMELS, used for bank performance appraisal, is a financial ratio analysis comparing the ratios of banks with the industries. Along with evaluating the determined priorities of CAMELS dimensions based on performance of banks, the differences of the views between the priorities based on risk of bankruptcy and performance of banks, the view differences according to the demographic characteristics of the experts, etc., are also examined. According to analysis, "Asset" (24.75%) is the most important dimension of CAMELS, and then "Earnings" (19.16%), "Liquidity" (18.54%) and "Management" (17.68%) are thought as following important dimensions with respect to bank performance. Dimensions of "Sensitivity to market risk" (11.11%) and "Capital" (10.03%) are observed as weak dimensions.

Introduction

The banking industry is acting almost in all industries, ranging from construction, textile, agriculture, manufacturing, etc., to finance industry. The banking industry plays an important role on the economic resource allocation and the financial stability of countries, namely, promoting economic growth of the countries. The

M. Pekkaya (✉)
Business Administration, Bülent Ecevit University, Zonguldak, Turkey

F. E. Demir
Bülent Ecevit University, Zonguldak, Turkey

© Springer International Publishing AG, part of Springer Nature 2018   445
H. Dincer et al. (eds.), *Global Approaches in Financial Economics, Banking, and Finance*, Contributions to Economics, https://doi.org/10.1007/978-3-319-78494-6_21

banks accept deposits and funding, in order to fund business and individuals who need capital. Within the framework of (re)structuring the economic systems of the countries, evaluating the activity of banks as capital actors of economic growth has a vital pathfinder for the future-proper decisions of decision-makers. Moreover, for the sake of sustainability of ordinary function of banks, banks admire to be in a profitable region, and their financial performance need to be good in order to offer the shareholders a profit or a value increase in their investments. So, poor banking performance may lead to banking failure which is bad news for investors and negatively affects the country's economy. Then, measuring and controlling bank performances are very important for the investors and the stable growth of the country. The financial performance researches, which focus on commercial banks, attract attention of academics, researchers, managers and decision-makers. Since there is more than one factor/variable/criteria in evaluating process of the financial performance of banks, multi-criteria decision-making (MCDM) techniques can be appropriate in such researches.

In related literacy about bank performance, so many recent research papers are conducted in measuring the financial performances of banks and also determining the factor priorities or factors which are important for this measuring. Some of these studies use selected financial ratios and some variables selected from financial statements, and/or most of them use financial ratios of CAMELS dimensions as factors for their research objectives. As few of them use descriptive statistics, namely, mean, some of them use (panel) regression analysis, and some of them use MCDM methods. In application part of these researches, regression analysis is generally used for determining the factors which are important for performance evaluation; on the other hand, MCDM methods can be used for determining the priorities of the factors (AHP (analytical hierarchy process), entropy, etc.) and selecting/ordering/grouping the banks according to their performances (AHP, WASPAS, TOPSIS, GRA, Promethee, etc.) with respect to determined priorities.

The purpose of this study is to determine the priorities of CAMELS dimensions based on the bank performance via AHP method and to present the results as an information to researchers, investors and decision-makers. Furthermore, this study shows the feasibility of many statistical hypothesis tests by separately generated priority series from expert's views based on performance and bankruptcy risk of banks.

According to the literacy of AHP, AHP is used for determining the priorities and/or selecting/ordering the alternatives. The reasons of preferring AHP technique for determining the priorities of CAMELS dimensions are common usage of AHP in priority calculations and its opportunity of consistency calculation with respect to other MCDM techniques. And also, AHP technique has the potential to be more popular than the Likert scale by style of approaching to AHP in this study. This study also shows that generating the priority series from each expert's views with checking whether they are making consistent pairwise comparisons and then statistical tests can be carried out on generated priority series via AHP. In this study, the expert sample volume is quite big according to related literacy of AHP, and this relatively big sample and generated priority series let us use parametric statistical tests for different purposes. These features of the study can take this study as original.

In order to determine the priorities of CAMELS dimensions, a survey is conducted to 108 experts who study finance and especially on banks in Turkey. Obtained scores from pairwise comparisons of experts, based on bank performance and bankruptcy risk of banks, are used for separately generating priority series via AHP. Calculated priorities based on bank performance are interpreted according to literacy and compared with the priorities based on bankruptcy risk of banks. Moreover, some statistical hypothesis tests in terms of characteristic groups of experts are conducted on generated priority series of expert's views based on performance banks.

The rest of the paper is organized as follows: second part of the study overviews CAMELS approach and literacy summary of CAMELS approach, and the third part presents the MCDM and AHP method briefly. In the fourth part, application, analysis procedure and results are reported for determining the priorities of CAMELS dimensions based on bank performance via AHP method. Finally, conclusion is presented.

CAMELS Approach and Literacy Summary

The profitability of the assets (return on assets and return on equities) and the net margin interest can be accepted as the two key indicators in order to measure the banking performance. Banking performance is related to internal factors (specific to banks such as risk, market share, the interest rates and the financial ratios) and external factors (macroeconomic and macrofinancial) which reflect the economic environment in which the bank operates (Nouaili et al. 2015; Atyeh et al. 2015).

The CAMEL model, in order to assess the financial position of the banks, was formed in the end of the 1970s. The CAMEL model emphasizes on the five parameters of the banking system by looking at its profit and loss statement for assessing financial performance and balance sheet. Nowadays, CAMELS approach with S dimension for evaluating banks' performances is commonly preferred by academicians and banking supervisors. This model is recommended for assessing bank performance by the US Federal Reserve and the Uniform Financial Institutions Rating System (Ishaq et al. 2016). CAMELS' dimensions are capital adequacy (CAP), asset quality (ASS), management quality (MAN), earnings quality (EAR), liquidity performance (LIQ) and sensitivity to market risk (SMR) explained at Table 21.1. These dimensions generally consist of financial ratios acquired from balance sheet and financial statements.

In related literacy about bank performance, so many recent research papers are conducted for measuring the financial performances of banks and also determining the factors which are important for the financial performances of banks. Some of these studies use selected financial ratios, and some variables selected from financial statements (Atyeh et al. 2015; Nouaili et al. 2015; some other studies reported at Table 21.2), and/or most of them use financial ratios of CAMEL(S) dimensions (Aspal and Dhawan 2014; Chatzi et al. 2015; Mohiuddin 2014; Rostami 2015;

Table 21.1 CAMELS dimensions

Dimension	Explanation
Capital adequacy (CAP)	The ratio of capital shows the strength of a bank by the adequacy of its capital in relation to their risk-weighted exposures. The CAP is an important dimension to help the bank in understanding the shock attractive capability during risk. CAP enables a bank to meet any financial unexpected condition due to FX risk, credit risk, market risk and interest rate risk
Asset quality (ASS)	The ASS is an important dimension to help the bank in understanding the risk on the exposure of the debtors. We accept the loans have the highest default risk; an increasing number of non-performing loans may produce a deterioration of asset quality. By monitoring this parameter, we may see the amount of funds that have been reserved in the bad investments
Management quality (MAN)	Since management is a qualitative issue, measuring the MAN is usually difficult to conduct. The management acts as a safeguard to operate the bank in a stable manner. The MAN is the ability of the management to restrict each form of risk inherent in any activity of the bank, whenever it controls its cost and increases productivity, ultimately achieving higher profits
Earnings quality (EAR)	Earning is the most crucial (financial) performance measurement of banks. EAR mainly takes into account the profitability and productivity of the bank and explains the growth and sustainability of future earnings capacity. The earnings ratio is usually represented by two individual financial ratios, ROA (return on asset) and ROE (return on equity)
Liquidity performance (LIQ)	Liquidity ratio in a bank measures and shows the bank's ability to pay its current obligations. When any bank faces liquidity crisis, which can be accepted as the image of banks, bank may not supply its short-term obligations. An adequate LIQ of bank means a situation where institution can obtain sufficient funds, either by raising liabilities or by converting its assets quickly at a reasonable cost. Liquidity ratio may represent at least two individual ratios, namely, "total loans total customer deposits" and "current assets average total assets." Liquidity ratios may be positively or negatively related to the likelihood of failure in those that are set in model
Sensitivity to market risk (SMR)	Sensitivity ratios can be accepted as prominent for CAMEL model. SMR is related to risk and covering power of organization that are assessed to finalize bank's performance model because of risk indicators. SMR shows the performance obtained by the portfolio of securities of the bank

Source: Rostami (2015); Chatzi et al. (2015); Ahsan (2016)

Ahsan 2016; Ishaq et al. 2016) for their research objectives. As few of them use descriptive statistics, namely, mean (Mohiuddin 2014; some other studies reported at Table 21.2), some of them use (panel) regression analysis (Socol and Dănulețiu 2013; Rostami 2015; Atyeh et al. 2015; Nouaili et al. 2015; Ishaq et al. 2016; some other studies reported at Table 21.2), some of them use data envelopment analysis (Barr et al. 2002; Jha et al. 2013; Bhatia and Mahendru 2015; Tata and Nimmagadda 2016), some of them use performance evaluation models (Table 21.2), and some of

Table 21.2 Some researches about bank performance

Researchers	Approach	Method
Kılıç and Fettahoğlu (2005); Tunay and Silpar (2006); Azizi and Serkani (2014); Ongore and Kusa (2013)	CAMELS	Regression analysis
Adeusi et al. (2014); Nuriyeva (2014); Reddy (2012)	CAMELS	Panel regression analysis
Ayadi and Elloze (2015); Helhel (2014)	Selected ratios	Panel regression analysis
Bandaranayeke and Jayasinghe (2013)	Efficiency and profitability models	Panel regression analysis
Sakarya (2010); Kandemir and Arıcı (2013); Ifeacho and Ngalawa (2014); Mukhtarov and Çağıl (2014); Thirunavukkarasu and Parthiban (2015)	CAMELS	Performance evaluation models
Çinko and Avcı (2008)	CAMELS	Logistic regression and ANN
Çağıl (2011)	CAMELS	MCDM (ELECTRE)
Uçkun and Girginer (2011); Ecer (2013)	CAMELS	MCDM (gray relational analysis)
Dinçer (2011); Altan et al. (2014); Aftab et al. (2015); Ferrouhi (2014); Misra and Aspal (2013)	CAMELS	Descriptive statistics or simple mean
Gupta (2014)	CAMELS	ANOVA
Abdullayev (2013)	CAMELS	Scaling and index conversion
Tükenmez et al. (2009)	CAMELS	Reference and index value
Karapınar and Doğan (2015); Kabir and Dey (2012)	CAMELS	Comparative (performance) analysis

Source: Adapted from Toplu's (2017) report

them use MCDM methods (Ecer 2013; Akkoç and Vatansever 2013; Gökalp 2015; Rezaei and Ketabi 2016; Ghasempour and Salami 2016; Akçakanat et al. 2017; Panja 2017; Wanke et al. 2017; Dash 2017). Data envelopment analysis is sometimes used for banks' performance evaluation and generally used for banks' efficiency calculations taking into account especially input and output variables instead of only financial ratios. Regression analysis is generally used for determining the factors which are important for performance evaluation of the banks and determining the effect direction of the factors on the performances. On the other hand, MCDM methods can be used for determining the priorities of the factors (AHP, entropy, etc.) and selecting, ordering and grouping the decision unit, such as banks based on their performances (AHP, WASPAS, TOPSIS, GRA, Promethee, etc.) with respect to determined priorities and their financial ratios. In determining the prominence of a factor, AHP produces priorities based on banks' performance by using expert's views, but regression analyses detect factors which have effects on banks' performance in a statistically significant manner using variables which usually consist of financial ratios obtained from financial statements or market values of banks. However, regression analyses have some delicate assumptions which must be satisfied, for example, multicollinearity may generally be observed among CAMELS dimensions, and this multicollinearity problem may prevent to detect factors' effects separately. According to these results, for the sake of determining the priorities of CAMELS main dimensions separately or especially sub-dimensions which may have high correlations, MCDM methods can be accepted as a more useful method than regression analysis.

Ishaq et al. (2016) declared that, "the literature review on the determinants of the CAMEL model to assess the performance of banks has shown mixed results with respect to the significance and direction of their association. Some of the studies have shown significant and positive results of these variables with the firm's performance, whereas significant and negative results have also been found. The studies in the literature review showed that all components of CAMEL model have a significant effect on the bank's performance. In case of capital adequacy, asset quality and earnings & profitability, most of the studies showed these variables were positive and negative, but significantly related to the bank's performance, whereas studies on management efficiency and liquidity showed a positive and significant relationship with the bank's performance." These results are derived from some studies which use regression analysis. The purpose of this study is determining the priorities of CAMELS dimensions instead of determining the dimensions' direction or existence which can be accepted as similar with these regression studies that have the purpose of investigating the significant effect on the bank performance but not determining the direction of effect by using the experts' views. As the studies which use regression let to investigate variables/ factors which have significant effects, effect direction and magnitude on the bank performance, AHP method used in this study let to investigate priorities of the variables/factors on the bank performance.

MCDM and AHP

When people encounter complex or even ordinary problems, they usually take into account more than one criterion/variable/goal simultaneously instead of only one criterion/variable/goal. MCDM techniques are improved for solving these kinds of problems via concrete, analytical (mathematical) and systematical path. There are so many MCDM techniques that each of them may have various advantages developed for solving the MCDM problems. Some of these techniques can be listed, namely, AHP, analytic network process (ANP), Elimination et Choix Traduisant la Realite (ELECTRE), preference ranking organization method for enrichment evaluation (PROMETHEE), Technique for Order Preference by Similarity to Ideal Solution (TOPSIS), gray relational analysis (GRA), etc. The researches which use MCDM technique may have an application on product design, product selection, facility location and facility layout planning, achievement order, financial applications, etc.,

(Hamzacebi and Pekkaya 2011) and also bank performance evaluation (Ecer 2013; Mohiuddin 2014; Ghasempour and Salami 2016; Akçakanat et al. 2017; Panja 2017; Wanke et al. 2017; Dash 2017).

Accordingly, almost all citizens/decision-makers may inevitably (consciously or unconsciously) take into account simple or modern MCDM techniques, when the problems that have more than one dimension/criteria/factor/variable in decision/solution process are encountered. For example, weighted mean calculation can be accepted as the simplest MCDM technique that is commonly used in daily life in selecting/ordering alternatives or units. Modern MCDM techniques at least take into account the distances between the score of one alternative and other alternatives and/or both minimum-maximum scores of the alternatives for each criteria in selecting/ordering alternatives or units.

MCDM techniques can be used for determining priorities of the criteria, exploring the interrelations between the criteria and/or selecting, ordering and grouping the alternatives/units which exist in the decision-making process. In this study, AHP, one of the MCDM techniques, is used for determining the priorities of CAMELS dimensions.

AHP was improved by Satty (1980) and can be defined simply as an eigenvalue approach to the pairwise comparisons. By making pairwise comparisons, each criteria/alternative is compared to one another, and the pairwise compared judgments' scores which indicate how many times more important or dominant one criteria/alternative is over another criteria/alternative are attributed by interviewee. AHP produces ratio scaled values by using generally qualitative double-directed 9-point scaled (1, equal importance; 3, moderate importance; 5, strong importance; 7, very strong importance; 9, extreme importance; 2-4-6-8, intra-values) views of people. The comparison matrix can be created from the scores of the pairwise comparisons, and the priorities can be obtained from the comparison matrix. After obtaining the priorities, the consistency of the comparison matrix can be calculated. The consistency calculation is one of the prominent advantages of the AHP method. According to the consistency of the comparison matrix, researcher can decide to declare the acceptability of obtained priorities, since consistency score [consistency ratio (CR)] represents the consistency of all the pairwise comparisons as an index.

AHP method calculation can be summarized as in the following steps (Saaty 2008; Hamzaçebi and Pekkaya 2011):

1. Define the problem.
2. Determine the frame of the decision hierarchy.
3. Construct the pairwise comparison matrix (A) for n criteria.
4. Obtain the priorities/weights (W) from the comparison matrix (AW=λmaxW, where λmax is the largest eigenvector of A matrix).
5. Calculate the consistency index [CI $= (\lambda max - n)/(n-1)$] and CR (=CI/RI). RI is random index values which change according to the matrix dimension or n (RI values: 0.00 for $n = 2$; 0.58 for $n = 3$; 0.90 for $n = 4$; 1.12 for $n = 5$; 1.24 for $n = 6$; 1.32 for $n = 7$; 1.41 for $n = 8$; etc.).

Moreover, AHP technique can be more popular than the Likert scale, since (1) AHP has a 17-point scale which has much more sensitive measurement of views, (2) AHP contains easy calculation process of consistency from all the pairwise comparisons which produce more reliable measurement in consistency than Likert scale, and the consistency of all pairwise comparisons can be monitored/controlled by a generated index, and (3) AHP calculation converts interval scale measured data to ratio scaled priorities (Pekkaya and Başaran 2011; Pekkaya and Çolak 2013; Pekkaya and Aktogan 2014). AHP technique is preferred according to other MCDM techniques, since (1) AHP is more common and accepted technique among other MCDM techniques and (2) AHP calculation procedure contains consistency calculation from all the pairwise comparisons which produce more reliable measurement in consistency than other MCDM techniques.

AHP techniques have various applications on determining the priorities. Some of them are determining the priorities of service quality of SERVQUAL dimensions (Pekkaya and Başaran 2011), factors of stock selection (Hamzaçebi and Pekkaya 2011), factors that affect in choosing professions (Pekkaya and Çolak 2013), factors of laptop selection (Pekkaya and Aktogan 2014), factors in the assessment process of commercial credit (Pekkaya and Zilifli 2016), factors in the production functions (Ogunyemi et al. 2011), and factors of decision-support system in the housing sector (Chauhan et al. 2008).

Determining the Priorities of CAMELS' Dimensions for Bank Performance

CAMELS, used for bank performance appraisal, is a financial ratio analysis of comparing ratios of banks/industries. In this study, the analysis is based on a survey conducted to 108 experts on bank/finance and working at institutions such as "Banking Regulation and Supervision Agency", "Central Bank of Turkey", and top managers of some banks and academicians who study finance and especially on banks in Turkey. The survey consists of some demographic questions and pairwise comparison questions of CAMELS dimensions used for determining priorities of CAMELS dimensions based on bank performances. In addition to these, the survey contains pairwise questions of CAMELS dimensions used for determining priorities based on bank's bankruptcy risk, in order to compare the priorities obtained based on bank performances.

Since there are six dimensions/criteria in CAMELS, then MCDM methods are applicable for bank performance measurement processes. AHP method, which is one of the MCDM methods, can be used for determining priorities of criteria and selecting and ordering the alternatives/units. In this study, the priorities of CAMELS' dimensions based on the bank performances and bankruptcy prediction are determined via AHP method.

In related literature about AHP, little volume sample of experts are commonly used for the calculations. Inconsistent pairwise comparisons can be accepted as they are unconsciously fulfilled, unwillingly fulfilled or fulfilled with restricted specific information of interviewee. In this study, since some inconsistent pairwise comparisons may deviate the whole views which contain respectable information, these inconsistent pairwise comparisons fulfilled by such people are not taken into account for the common views.

Saaty's consistency boundary can be thought as too strict (Pekkaya and Başaran 2011; Pekkaya and Çolak 2013; Pekkaya and Aktogan 2014; Pekkaya and Zilifli 2016). According to Saaty (1980), CR score of pairwise comparisons must be below 0.10. Numerically for criteria pairwise comparisons, comparisons of 21 experts among 108 can be accepted as consistent. However, according to Dodd et al. (1993), 95 pairwise comparisons are not randomly scored pairwise comparisons which consistency boundary is 0.4113 for six criteria (Pekkaya and Demir 2016). The critic value of 0.4113 for six criteria is calculated by dividing 0.50996 (critic table value generated by Dodd et al. from simulation at the 95% confidence level for six criteria) to 1.24 (RI value for six criteria). Thus, the view of Dodd et al. is accepted for taking into account much more opinions from experts in priority calculations as in the studies of Pekkaya and Başaran (2011), Pekkaya and Çolak (2013), etc. Accordingly, consistency-tolerated pairwise comparisons are used in the priority calculations and analyses of this study.

AHP, one of the MCDM methods, is commonly used for determining the priorities via pairwise comparisons. With regard to incorporating more experts' views in the analysis and reducing the loss of information obtained, rather than strict limit of Saaty's (1980) consistency boundary, the approach of Dodd et al. (1993) has been taken into account. Along with evaluating the determined priorities of CAMELS dimensions based on performance of banks, the differences of the views between the priorities based on risk of bankruptcy and performance of banks, the view differences in terms of the demographic characteristics of the experts, etc., are also examined.

Priorities of CAMELS dimensions based on the performance of banks is presented at Table 21.3. These descriptive statistics are produced by generating priority series from consistent tolerated pairwise comparisons according to Dodd et al. approach via AHP method. When each dimension mean is compared with other dimensions, ASS dimension of CAMELS is accepted as the most important dimension with 23.10% priority based on the performance of banks according to 95 experts.

Table 21.3 Priorities of CAMELS dimensions based on the performance of banks

	Minimum	Maximum	Mean	StdDev	CoV	Skewness	Kurtosis
CAP	0.0226	0.4524	0.1215	0.1066	87.74	1.133	0.341
ASS	0.0280	0.4963	0.2310	0.1235	53.46	0.464	−0.975
MAN	0.0216	0.5771	0.1768	0.1303	73.70	0.975	0.199
EAR	0.0190	0.4805	0.1898	0.1159	61.06	0.559	−0.458
LIQ	0.0279	0.5032	0.1743	0.0974	55.88	0.944	1.059
SMR	0.0232	0.4022	0.1065	0.0656	61.60	1.722	4.125

StdDev standard deviation, *CoV* coefficient of variation

For investigating whether the difference of these priority series exists in means of six dimensions, one of the parametric tests called one-way repeated measures ANOVA test for such situations can be conducted. When each priority series have bigger sample than 30 units, these series can be accepted as normally distributed according to central limit theorem. Then, parametric tests which have usual assumptions of ratio scaled and normal distributed data set can be conducted on these series.

One-way repeated measures ANOVA test F statistics (Wilks' Lambda) for the priority series is 22,488, and p value is 0.000. Since Mauchly's test of sphericity p value is 0.000 and Huynh-Feldt's test p value is 0.818, within-subjects effects are taken into consideration which has p value of 0.000. Then, it is decided that at least two dimensions' priorities among six dimensions of CAMELS cannot be accepted as equal.

However, none of the priority series can be accepted as normally distributed at 0.05 significance level according to Lilliefors corrected Kolmogorov-Smirnov test and Shapiro-Wilk test of normality. Then, Friedman test, non-parametric alternative of repeated measures ANOVA test, is also conducted, and its chi-square statistic (76,588; p value, 0.000) gives the same conclusion with repeated measures ANOVA test. In this study, the results of parametric tests in case of bigger sample than 30 in volume are taken into account; even conclusion usually does not change.

Next to ASS dimension in priority, EAR (18.98%), MAN (17.68%) and LIQ (17.43%) dimensions can be accepted as quite important in banks' performance evaluations. However, CAP (12.15%) and SMR (10.65%) dimensions can be accepted as the least important ones among CAMELS dimensions.

Coefficient of variation (CoV) values is calculated by dividing the standard deviation value to its mean. CoV represents the homogeneity of views on the priorities like standard deviation especially in case of existence of different means and/or scale units among series whose homogeneities are comparing. According to CoV series at Table 21.3, most homogenous or the highest common mindedness can be observed on priority series of ASS with respect to the smallest CoV value, but most heterogeneous or the lowest common mindedness can be observed on priority series of CAP with respect to the highest CoV value.

Priorities of CAMELS dimensions are calculated according to various scenarios; some of them are reported at Table 21.4 for conducting evaluations among each other and results of similar researches in literacy. The generated priority series based on bank performance (at Table 21.3) is called Perf-95a at Table 21.4. The name Perf-95a scenario originates from the following properties: (obj; objective) the priority determining is based on bank performance; (approach) arithmetic mean of generated priority series according to Dodd et al. approach and (n) sample volume or number of experts as interviewee. In the scenario of Perf-21a, the arithmetic mean calculation is conducted by using the generated priority series for each dimension, from the views of 21 experts whose pairwise comparisons are consistent according to Satty. Scenarios named such as Perf-76a, Risk-76g, etc., contain views of 76 experts sample, and the sample volume of 76 is consisted of views of experts whose pairwise comparisons have common consistency depending on both bank performance and bankruptcy risk of banks according to Dodd et al. approach.

Table 21.4 Priorities based on bank performance and bankruptcy risk of banks

Scenarios	Obj.	Approach		n	CAP	ASS	MAN	EAR	LIQ	SMR	Const.
Perf-21a	Perf.	M	Saaty	21	.1250	.2113	.1994	.1883	.1559	.1201	.0584
Perf-95a	Perf.	M	Dodd	95	.1215	.2310	.1768	.1898	.1743	.1065	.1940
Perf-95g	Perf.	GM	Dodd	95	.1003	.2475	.1642	.1916	.1854	.1111	.0133
Risk-76a	Risk	M	Dodd	76	.2017	.2067	.1579	.0818	.2295	.1225	.1832
Perf-76a	Perf.	M	Dodd	76	.1232	.2321	.1742	.1920	.1705	.1079	.1690
Risk-76g	Risk	GM	Dodd	76	.1940	.2244	.1334	.0832	.2447	.1204	.0098
Perf-76g	Perf.	GM	Dodd	76	.1018	.2506	.1657	.1900	.1791	.1128	.0152
Researcher					**CAP**	**ASS**	**MAN**	**EAR**	**LIQ**	**SMR**	**Others**
Doumpos and Zopounidis (2010)					.30	.20	.15	.15	.10	.10	
Ginevičius and Podviezko (2013)					.223	.208	.166	.225	.178		
Gökalp (2015)					.300	.200	.150	.150	.200	–	
Güneysu et al. (2015)					.20	.20	.21	.24			.15
Chatzi et al. (2015)					.2000	.2000	.2000	.1000	.2000	.1000	
Ghasempour and Salami (2016)					.192	.205	.158	.221	.122	.102	
Wanke et al. (2017)					.1648	.0934	.1471	.1628	.1524	.2795	

Obj: objective; Perf.: bank performance; Risk: bankruptcy risk of banks; M: arithmetic mean of generated priority series via AHP; GM: geometric mean of pairwise comparisons is used for calculating priorities via AHP; Const.: consistency

According to academic literacy of AHP calculations, determining the priorities by getting geometric means (GM) of pairwise comparisons' grades has a general usage. However, different from the common usage of AHP method, we used much bigger sample in volume, in order to decrease the losing information by using Dodd et al. approach, and we can generate some priority series (Perf-95a, Risk-76a and Perf-76a) of each CAMELS dimensions for paving the way for conducting statistical tests on these priority series. Thus, priority results of GM approaches can be reported as ultimate results for priority series; in accordance with literacy of AHP, priority results of arithmetic mean (M) approaches can be used for conducting statistical test applications on priority series.

For example, the priorities of Perf-95g (GM) scenario and Perf-95a (M) scenario can be compared whether their dimensions' priority values are equal or not by using one sample t tests. These t tests are conducted by taking priorities calculated via scenario of Perf-95g as reference values, since as the priorities Perf-95g are fixed values but priorities Perf-95a are generated priority series according to views of the same sample (95 experts) and objective of the priority calculations of these scenarios are the same which are based on the bank performance of CAMELS dimension. According to one sample t tests' results, CAP (p value, 0.055), ASS (p value, 0.195), MAN (p value, 0.347), EAR (p value, 0.881), LIQ (p value, 0.272) and SMR (p value, 0.496) priority values cannot be accepted as different at 0.05 significance level for the results of scenarios of Perf-95g and Perf-95a.

The determined priorities of CAMELS dimension according to different scenarios based on the bank performance are not changing significantly. Then, the priorities of Perf-95g and/or Perf-95a scenarios can be accepted as representing general structure of priorities, because these scenarios take into account much more views of experts than other scenarios.

Accordingly, in reporting the priorities of CAMELS dimensions based on the performance of banks, Perf-95g scenario results are preferred instead of Perf-95a scenario results as in the academic literacy of AHP. Then, ASS dimension with 24.75% has the highest priority based on the banks' performance, followed by EAR (19.16%), LIQ (18.54%) and MAN (17.68%) dimensions which can be accepted as quite important in banks' performance evaluations. SMR (11.11%) and CAP (10.03%) dimensions can be accepted as the least important ones among CAMELS dimensions.

When these priorities are compared with related literacy, it can be declared that there are no consensus on the priorities of CAMELS dimensions and also our results. The determined CAMELS priorities of this study can be accepted as similar (some of them in priority orders) with the CAMELS priorities of Ghasempour and Salami's (2016) study but inversely associated with the CAMELS priorities of Wanke et al.'s (2017) study. However, there is a very important point that must be considered. Such kinds of studies do not project to determine the priorities of CAMELS dimensions; they usually need the priorities of CAMELS for evaluating the banks performances which is the objective of these studies. For this reason, in evaluations of banks, they sometimes take priorities almost equal or equal. According to the survey and its results, since most of the experts declare and/or note that the priorities of CAMELS

Table 21.5 Views in term of gender

	Means ($n = 63, 27$)		S-W		Independent sample	Mann-Whitney
	Male	Female	Male	Female	t test (p value)	U test (p value)
CAP	0.1119	0.1395	0.000	0.001	0.267	**0.506**
ASS	0.2374	0.2171	0.002	0.012	0.482	**0.512**
MAN	0.1850	0.1763	0.000	0.015	0.774	**0.761**
EAR	0.2015	0.1572	0.066	0.283	**0.086**	0.099
LIQ	0.1683	0.1831	0.000	0.171	**0.512**	0.231
SMR	0.0958	0.1268	0.000	0.157	**0.061**	0.064

S-W: p value of Shapiro-Wilk test which has null hypothesis of "Series is normally distributed"
When the sub sample volume is less than 30, S-W test is conducted for which test is the decider of statistical test for difference in means of sub group views. The tests that taking account, are bold in the Table 21.5 to 21.10

Table 21.6 Views in term of education degree

	Means ($n = 42, 43$)		Independent sample
	Bachelor	Graduate	t test (p value)
CAP	0.1130	0.1312	**0.445**
ASS	0.2512	0.2002	**0.054**
MAN	0.1898	0.1767	**0.645**
EAR	0.1848	0.1931	**0.738**
LIQ	0.1608	0.1868	**0.225**
SMR	0.1003	0.1120	**0.430**

Table 21.7 Views in term of experts' job

	Means ($n = 47, 44$)		Independent sample
	Experts	Other	t test (p value)
CAP	0.1309	0.1114	**0.392**
ASS	0.1958	0.2719	**0.003**
MAN	0.1818	0.1807	**0.968**
EAR	0.1839	0.1900	**0.799**
LIQ	0.1848	0.1600	**0.219**
SMR	0.1227	0.0860	**0.007**

dimensions depend on banks performances and should be different from each other, then this study can be thought as conducting an important mission in terms of its position.

The generated priority series for the scenario of Perf-95a are investigated whether there is a difference of views in terms of the subgroups of experts (Table 21.5, 21.6, 21.7, 21.8 and 21.9). If the subgroup consists of less than 30 experts in volume and normal distribution is not satisfied for that subgroup, then non-parametric tests are conducted (Mann-Whitney U test for two subgroups); otherwise parametric tests are conducted (independent sample t test for two subgroups).

Table 21.8 Views in term of age groups

	Means ($n = 25, 41$)		S-W		Independent sample	Mann-Whitney
	26–34	35–61	26–34	35–61	t test (p value)	U Test (p value)
CAP	0.1202	0.1314	0.001	0.000	0.684	**0.890**
ASS	0.2266	0.2007	0.033	0.015	0.389	**0.496**
MAN	0.1764	0.1917	0.007	0.001	0.649	**0.592**
EAR	0.1977	0.1797	0.139	0.127	**0.567**	0.797
LIQ	0.1572	0.1882	0.021	0.002	0.252	**0.188**
SMR	0.1219	0.1083	0.002	0.000	0.479	**0.838**

The views of experts are not statistically differentiated between subgroups of gender (Table 21.5), education status (Table 21.6), age groups (Table 21.8) and experience (Table 21.9) of experts at 0.05 significance level. Then, the priorities determined from the scenario of Perf-95a (Tables 21.3 and 21.4) cannot be changed in case of subgroups of gender, education status, age and experience of experts. However, as the male experts can attach 28.2% more importance to EAR dimension than female counterparts, the female experts can attach 32.4% more importance to SMR dimension than male counterparts statistically at 0.10 significance level (weak level). And the bachelor degree experts can attach 25.5% more importance to ASS dimension than graduate counterparts statistically at 0.10 significance level.

The views of experts are statistically differentiated for the dimension of ASS and SMR between subgroups of experts' jobs which they defined at 0.05 significance level. As the experts can attach 42.7% more importance to SMR dimension than other counterparts, the others can attach 38.9% more importance to ASS dimension than expert counterparts at 0.05 significance level.

At Table 21.10, whether there is a difference between determined priorities of CAMELS dimensions based on bank performance and bankruptcy risk of banks is investigated for each dimension. When the sample volume is 76, the distribution can be accepted as normal which let us to conduct parametric tests, named repeated sample t test for such situations. The normality of series is also investigated, and none of them is accepted as statistically normally distributed at 0.05 significant level according to Shapiro-Wilk test. So, non-parametric equivalent of Wilcoxon test is also conducted, but non-parametric test results should be well advisedly considered because of their tendency to wrong decision or error (Pekkaya and Akıllı 2013). For this reason, parametric tests should be taken into account when their assumptions are satisfied.

According to the results of Table 21.10, the experts attach 63.7% more importance to CAP dimension and 34.6% more importance to LIQ dimension in case of bankruptcy risk evaluations of banks than bank performance evaluations which are statistically significant at 0.05 level with respect to both repeated sample t test and its equivalent Wilcoxon test. On the other hand, the experts attach 134.7% more (about one and half times more) importance to EAR dimension in case of bank performance evaluations than bankruptcy risk evaluations of banks. These results show

Table 21.9 Views in terms of experience

	Means ($n = 18,23,29,16$)				Lev	F	Wel	Br-F	S-W				K-W
	1–5	6–10	11–15	16–30					1–5	6–10	11–15	16–30	
CAP	0.1261	0.1243	0.1273	0.1053	0.834	0.924	0.921	0.923	0.003	0.000	0.000	0.000	**0.752**
ASS	0.2933	0.2138	0.2189	0.2353	0.062	0.169	0.215	0.195	0.075	0.746	0.083	0.032	**0.206**
MAN	0.1480	0.1717	0.1847	0.2107	0.625	0.542	0.574	0.540	0.001	0.083	0.004	0.087	**0.346**
EAR	0.1827	0.1812	0.1964	0.1820	0.430	**0.954**	0.950	0.955	0.160	0.118	0.074	0.455	0.895
LIQ	0.1391	0.1836	0.1865	0.1556	0.426	0.278	0.283	0.265	0.001	0.364	0.266	0.183	**0.116**
SMR	0.1108	0.1255	0.0861	0.1111	0.003	0.208	0.134	0.237	0.109	0.003	0.238	0.001	**0.645**

Lev.: p value of Levene test for testing homogeneity (variances of subgroups). F: p value of independent samples of one-way ANOVA F statistics. Wel. and Br-F: p value of Welch test and Brown-Forsythe test which is alternative of F Test when the homogeneity is not satisfied. K-W: p value of Kruskal-Wallis test which is an alternative of F Test when the normality is not satisfied

Table 21.10 Views based on bank performance and bankruptcy risk of banks

	Means		Repeated sample	Wilcoxon test
	Risk-76a	Perf-76a	t test (p value)	(p value)
CAP	0.2017	0.1232	**0.000**	0.000
ASS	0.2067	0.2321	**0.040**	0.179
MAN	0.1579	0.1742	**0.198**	0.020
EAR	0.0818	0.1920	**0.000**	0.000
LIQ	0.2295	0.1705	**0.001**	0.008
SMR	0.1225	0.1079	**0.157**	0.508

significant evidence about evaluation differences in case of bank performance evaluations and bankruptcy risk evaluations of banks. It can be also conferred but well advisedly needed that the experts attach 12.3% more importance to ASS dimension and 10.3% more importance to MAN dimension in case of bank performance evaluations than bankruptcy risk evaluations of banks at statistically 0.05 significance level with respect to orderly repeated sample t test and equivalent Wilcoxon test.

Conclusion

Some important results are acquired from this study about priorities of CAMELS based on bank performance evaluations. According to the analysis, "Asset (ASS)" (24.75%) is the most important dimension of CAMELS, then "Earnings (EAR)" (19.16%), "Liquidity (LIQ)" (18.54%) and "Management (MAN)" (17.68%) can be thought as following important dimensions based on the bank performance. These four dimensions have the total priority of 78.86% among CAMELS dimensions. Dimensions of "Sensitivity to market risk (SMR)" (11.11%) and "Capital (CAP)" (10.03%) are observed as weak dimensions. According to gender, education status, experience level and age groups of experts and view differences are not significant. However, those who are employed as experts accept SMR as 42.7% more important than other counterparts, while others accept that ASS has 38.9% more importance.

The experts attach 63.7% more importance to CAP dimension and 34.6% more importance to LIQ dimension in case of bankruptcy risk evaluations of banks than bank performance evaluations. On the other hand, the experts attach 134.7% more importance to EAR dimension in case of bank performance evaluations than bankruptcy risk evaluations of banks. These results show significant evidence about evaluation differences in case of bank performance evaluations and bankruptcy risk evaluations of banks. Thus, managers, researchers and decision-makers should be aware of these obtained priorities, since these priority statistics can be accepted as representing the views of 95 selected experts who are top managers, researchers and decision-makers about finance and especially banks in Turkey.

This study also guides in paving the way of AHP, in popularity of the Likert scale, because AHP has a more sensitive scale than Likert and its joint consistency calculation property. Moreover, this study also has a different style of approaching to AHP by generating the priority series from each expert's views and conducting lots of statistical tests on these separately generated priority series.

Appendix: Characteristics of Experts

	Count	%		Count	%
Gender			*Experience*		
Male	63	66.3	1–5 years	18	18.9
Female	27	28.4	6–10 year	23	24.2
Total	90	94.7	11–15 year	29	30.5
Education			16–30 year	16	16.8
Bachelor	42	44.2	Total	86	90.5
Master	39	41.1	*Experts' job*		
PhD	4	4.2	Academician	2	2.1
Total	85	89.5	(Assistant) Expert	47	49.5
Age (year)			(Assistant) Manager/inspector	3	3.2
26–34	25	26.3	(Assistant) Consultant	1	1.1
35–61	41	43.2	Special auditor	1	1.1
Total	66	69.5	Other	37	38.9
			Total	91	95.8

References

Ahsan, M. K. (2016). Measuring financial performance based on CAMEL: A study on selected Islamic Banks in Bangladesh. *Asian Business Review, 6*(13), 47–56.

Akçakanat, Ö., Eren, H., Aksoy, E., & Ömürbek, V. (2017). Performance evaluation by entropy and WASPAS methods at banking sector. *SDU the Journal of Faculty of Economics and Administrative Sciences, 22*(2), 285–300.

Akkoç, S., & Vatansever, K. (2013). Fuzzy performance evaluation with AHP and TOPSIS methods: Evidence from Turkish banking sector after the global financial crisis. *Eurasian Journal of Business and Economics, 6*(11), 53–74.

Aspal, P. K., & Dhawan, S. (2014). Financial performance assessment of banking sector in India: A case study of old private sector banks. *The Business & Management Review, 5*(3), 196–211.

Atyeh, M. H., Yasin, J., & Khatib, A. M. (2015). Measuring the performance of the Kuwaiti banking sector before and after the recent financial crisis. *Business & Financial Affairs, 4*(3), 1–3.

Barr, R. S., Killgo, K. A., Siems, T. F., & Zimmel, S. (2002). Evaluating the productive efficiency and performance of US commercial banks. *Managerial Finance, 28*(8), 3–25.

Bhatia, A., & Mahendru, M. (2015). Assessment of technical efficiency of public sector banks in India using data envelopment analysis. *Eurasian Journal of Business and Economics, 8*(15), 115–140.

Chatzi, I. G., Diakomihalis, M. N., & Chytis, E. T. (2015). Performance of the Greek banking sector pre and throughout the financial crisis. *Journal of Risk and Control, 2*(1), 45–69.

Chauhan, K. A., Shah, N. C., & Rao, R. V. (2008). The analytic hierarchy process as a decision-support system in the housing sector: A case study. *World Applied Sciences Journal, 3*(4), 609–613.

Dash, M. (2017). A model for bank performance measurement integrating multivariate factor structure with multi-criteria PROMETHEE methodology. *Asian Journal of Finance & Accounting, 9*(1), 310–332.

Dodd, F. J., Donegan, H. A., & McMaster, T. B. M. (1993). A statistical approach to consistency in AHP. *Mathematical and Computer Modelling, 18*(6), 19–22.

Doumpos, M., & Zopounidis, C. (2010). A multicriteria decision support system for bank rating. *Decision Support Systems, 50,* 55–63.

Ecer, F. (2013). Türkiye'deki Özel Bankaların Finansal Performanslarının Karşılaştırılması: 2008–2011 Dönemi. *AIBU Sosyal Bilimler Enstitüsü Dergisi, 13*(2), 171–189.

Ghasempour, S., & Salami, M. (2016). Ranking Iranian private banks based on the CAMELS model using the AHP hybrid approach and TOPSIS. *International Journal of Academic Research in Accounting, Finance and Management Sciences, 6*(4), 52–62.

Ginevičius, R., & Podviezko, A. (2013). The evaluation of financial stability and soundness of Lithuanian banks. *Ekonomska Istraživanja-Economic Research, 26*(2), 191–208.

Gökalp, F. (2015). Comparing the financial performance of banks in Turkey by using Promethee method. *Ege Strategic Research Journal, 6*(1), 63–82.

Güneysu, Y., Er, B., & Ar, İ. M. (2015). Türkiye'deki Ticari Bankaların Performanslarinin AHS ve GIA Yöntemleri ile Incelenmesi. *KTU SBE Sosyal Bilimler Dergisi, 9,* 71–93.

Hamzaçebi, C., & Pekkaya, M. (2011). Determining of stock investments with grey relational analysis. *Expert Systems with Applications, 38*(8), 9186–9195.

Ishaq, A. B., Karim, A., Ahmed, S., & Zaheer, A. (2016). Evaluating performance of commercial banks in Pakistan: "An application of Camel model". *Journal of Business & Financial Affairs, 5* (1), 1–30.

Jha, S., Hui, X., & Sun, B. (2013). Commercial banking efficiency in Nepal: Application of DEA and Tobit model. *Information Technology Journal, 12*(2), 306–314.

Mohiuddin, G. (2014). Use of CAMEL model: A study on financial performance of selected commercial banks in Bangladesh. *Universal Journal of Accounting and Finance, 2*(5), 151–160.

Nouaili, M., Abaoub, E., & Ochi, A. (2015). The determinants of banking performance in front of financial changes: Case of trade banks in Tunisia. *International Journal of Economics and Financial Issues, 5*(2), 410–417.

Ogunyemi, O., Ibiwoye, A., & Oyatoye, E. O. (2011). Analytic hierarchy process for prioritizing production functions: Illustration with pharmaceutical data. *Journal of Economics and International Finance, 3*(14), 749–760.

Panja, S. (2017). Multivariate bank performance analysis using standardized CAMEL methodology and fuzzy analytical hierarchical process. *Indian Journal of Science and Technology, 10*(23), 1–17.

Pekkaya, M., & Akıllı, F. (2013). Statistical analysis and evaluation of airline service quality by SERVPERF-SERVQUAL scale. *The International Journal of Economic and Social Research, 9* (1), 75–96.

Pekkaya, M., & Aktogan, M. (2014). Dizüstü bilgisayar seçimi: DEA, VIKOR ve TOPSIS ile Karşılaştırmalı bir Analiz. *Ekonomik ve Sosyal Araştırmalar Dergisi, 10*(1), 107–125.

Pekkaya, M., & Başaran, S. (2011). Konaklama İşletmeleri Hizmet Kalitesi Boyutları Önem Derecelerinin AHP ile Belirlenmesi ve İşletmelerin Hizmet Kalitesine göre TOPSIS ile Sıralanması. *Mali Ufuklar Dergisi, 5,* 111–136.

Pekkaya, M., & Çolak, N. (2013). Determining the priorities of ratings via AHP for the factors that effects in choosing professions for the University students. *The Journal of Academic Social Science Studies, 6*(2), 797–818.

Pekkaya, M., & Demir, F. E. (2016). Determining the priorities of criteria in assessing the bankruptcy risk of the banks via AHP. *International Journal of Management Economics and Business*, ICAFR 16 Special Issue, 40–45.

Pekkaya, M., & Zilifli, V. (2016). Determining the priorities of the criteria which the banks take in consideration in the assessment process of commercial credit. *International Journal of Management Economics and Business*, ICAFR 16 Special Issue, 201–210.

Rezaei, M., & Ketabi, S. (2016). Ranking the banks through performance evaluation by integrating fuzzy AHP and TOPSIS methods: A study of Iranian private banks. *International Journal of Academic Research in Accounting, Finance and Management Sciences, 6*(3), 19–30.

Rostami, M. (2015). Determination of Camels model on bank's performance. *International Journal of Multidisciplinary Research and Development, 2*(10), 652–664.

Saaty, T. L. (1980). *The analytic hierarchy process*. New York: McGraw-Hill.

Saaty, T. L. (2008). Decision making with the analytic hierarchy process. *International Journal of Services Sciences, 1*(1), 83–98.

Socol, A., & Dănuleţiu, A. E. (2013). Analysis of the Romanian banks' performance through ROA, ROE and non-performing loans models. *Annales Universitatis Apulensis Series Oeconomica, 15*(2), 594–604.

Tata, H. K., & Nimmagadda, V. S. (2016). Performance evaluation of banks through four phased DEA – A case study. *International Journal of Industrial Engineering Research and Development, 7*(1), 24–34.

Toplu, H. Y. (2017). *Effective ratios on financial performance with CAMELS approach: An application of panel regression on commercial banks in Turkey*. Unpublished PhD Thesis, BEU Institute of Social Sciences, Zonguldak.

Wanke, P., Kabir Hassan, M., & Gavião, L. O. (2017). Islamic banking and performance in the Asean banking industry: A TOPSIS approach with probabilistic weights. *International Journal of Business and Society, 18*(S1), 129–150.

Chapter 22
What Are Relations Between the Domestic Macroeconomic Variables and the Convertible Exchange Rates?

Cem Kartal and Mehmet Fatih Bayramoglu

Abstract Worldwide foreign trade operations and financial investment activities are realized as convertible currencies. The level of exchange rate volatility may be higher in developing countries than in developed countries. This situation can be seen both in the real sector and in the financial sector. In the real sector, especially companies that meet their raw material and intermediary needs through import are affected by the exchange rate volatility, while the financial sector is more affected by exchange rate volatility in the markets with weak-efficiency levels. These determinant attributes reflect the characteristics of developing countries. Therefore, the identification of parameters that can provide knowledge about changes in exchange rates is important for both the real sector and the financial sector. Also, this knowledge is also important regarding increasing the effectiveness of exchange rate interventions, one of the instruments of monetary policy in modern central banking practices. This chapter aims to attain explanation capacity of domestic macroeconomic factors of convertible exchange rates and rules for the application made by OneR algorithm which is one of the data mining methods and the machine learning techniques. The reason for using only domestic macroeconomic variables and the exclusion of international macroeconomic variables in the study is that it is more frequent to attain knowledge about domestic macroeconomic variables which are estimated within the countries. Thus, it is aimed to increase the frequency of observing convertible exchange rates with the rules acquired by the OneR algorithm. It is also aimed to investigate whether the exchange rate movements included in this study can be modeled by using only domestic macroeconomic variables as a glocal approach. EUR/USD, GBP/USD, JPY/USD, and TRY/USD exchange rates are analyzed within the scope of the chapter. The findings of the chapter show that (1) the problem of estimation of the exchange rate movements is insufficient to solve by OneR algorithm; (2) it is seen that the success rate of the models with a relatively small number of input variables is higher in this application; therefore, the importance of the use of lean models is supported by the results of the chapter; and (3) in

C. Kartal · M. F. Bayramoglu (✉)
Bulent Ecevit University, Zonguldak, Turkey
e-mail: cem.kartal@beun.edu.tr; fatih.bayramoglu@beun.edu.tr

© Springer International Publishing AG, part of Springer Nature 2018
H. Dincer et al. (eds.), *Global Approaches in Financial Economics, Banking, and Finance*, Contributions to Economics, https://doi.org/10.1007/978-3-319-78494-6_22

terms of the primary aim of the survey, Turkey's domestic macroeconomic variables are not sufficient to explain convertible exchange rates. As the reasons for these findings, it can say that the Turkish economy is a developing economy and that the economy is small compared to developed country economies.

Introduction

A large volume of transactions takes place in currency markets every day. Exchange rates can be defined as the price of one currency with regard to another currency. Exchange rates which are an important component of these transactions are highly affected by many economic, political, and psychological factors. Therefore, exchange rate prediction is a crucial but tough issue. The principal motivation of financial analysts for exchange rate prediction is earning maximization and avoidance (minimization) of exchange rate risk. In this regard, the primary problem that needs to be addressed is predictability of the exchange rates.

Investors focus on predicting foreign exchange prices, but volatility is high in currency markets. Also, global financial crises have increased the volatility in these markets. The increase in the volatility may lead to possible sharp increases in both gains and losses of the investors who do business in the currency markets. However, the prediction is more difficult when volatility is high. Therefore, the prediction models become more important.

Studies in the literature use the following five exchange rate prediction methods: (1) fundamental analysis, (2) technical analysis, (3) classical time series analysis, (4) machine learning techniques, and (5) data mining (Zhang and Xuhui 2007: 1149). These methods have been developed by using statistical and data mining technologies. These methods are also utilized for the prediction of exchange rates as a money market instrument.

Foreign exchange rate transactions in the world are creating a large trading volume. Foreign exchange, which as it can be seen in Table 22.1, reaches a transaction volume of $5.1 trillion every day across the world, being the subject of many financial transactions, and the rise in the velocity of circulation between financial markets causes it to enter reciprocal interaction between the markets where transactions are made. Therefore, foreign exchange rate transactions have the ability to both influence the markets in which they are transacted and to be influenced by the developments in these markets. In markets in countries that have a flexible exchange rate regime that degrades only the market interventions to the limit of the reduction of volatility, in particular, exchange rate and macroeconomic parameters such as money supply, inflation rate, interest rate, share certificates, etc. affect each other more and more.

The primary function of currency markets is the execution of international trade and capital flows. Today, the biggest financial markets in the world are currency markets. Among the currency markets in the world, the largest transaction volumes are generally in developed financial markets such as London, New York, Singapore, Hong Kong, and Tokyo. It is known that the foreign exchange rate has a wide

Table 22.1 OTC foreign exchange turnover by currency (million $, April 2016, daily averages)

	Total	Foreign exchange swaps	Spot transactions	Outright forward	FX options	Currency swaps
Total, "net-net" basis[a]	5,066,955	2,378,304	1,652,349	699,676	254,414	82,151
By currency						
USD	4,437,554	2,160,211	1,385,410	599,764	218,350	73,820
EUR	1,590,573	807,131	519,363	177,530	64,259	22,290
JPY	1,095,562	457,929	394,931	151,068	73,516	18,119
GBP	648,576	305,393	211,054	92,005	29,765	10,360
AUD	348,312	137,877	142,932	40,877	19,574	7052
CAD	260,408	103,060	104,551	34,482	14,060	4256
CHF	243,419	149,727	57,286	29,833	4870	1702
CNY	202,055	86,030	67,555	27,984	17,868	2618
SEK	112,321	59,081	33,710	13,386	5272	872
Other currencies	1,195,130	490,168	387,906	232,425	61,293	23,213

Source: http://www.bis.org/publ/rpfx16.htm
[a]Adjusted for local and cross-border interdealer double-counting

range of usage in the financial markets and is subject to spot trading, futures transactions, option contracts, forward transactions, swap transactions, and forex (FX) transactions, in which investors today have an increasing interest; in particular, foreign exchange swaps and spot transactions constitute and make up a large part of the foreign exchange transactions.

Table 22.2 indicates that the appreciation of the US dollar from 2013 to 2016 decreased the US dollar value of turnover in other currencies than the US dollar. As the turnover was valued at stable exchange rates (April 2016), it increased only around 4% from April 2013 through April 2016. The euro's role in FX markets has kept diminishing since 2010, which shows the beginning of the euro area sovereign debt crisis. It has altered trading activity unevenly across the main FX instrument categories. Trading volumes of the two largest instrument categories, such as spot trades and FX swaps particularly, have grown into opposite directions. In April 2016, spot market trading activity fell by 19% and became $1.7 trillion per day.

The quick giving of reactions of the exchange rate, which has such importance regarding financial markets, to national and international developments as it exists in many risky financial assets is discussed. The volatility in exchange rates, which are subject to spot and derivative transactions in addition to exports and imports, in particular, presents an additional risk factor for the holders of foreign currency. In other words, the appearance of reactions given by foreign exchange rates quickly affected from many global or local political, economic, and financial developments to these developments and the determination of which parameters, in particular, are

Table 22.2 OTC foreign exchange turnover by instrument (Net-net basis[a], daily averages in April 2016, billion $)

Instrument	2001	2013	2016
Foreign exchange instruments	1239	5357	5067
Spot transactions	386	2047	1652
Outright forward	130	679	700
Foreign exchange swaps	656	2240	2378
Currency swaps	7	54	82
Options and other products[b]	60	337	254
Memo			
Turnover at April 2016 exchange rates[c]	1381	4917	5067
Exchange-traded derivatives	12	145	115

Source: http://www.bis.org/publ/rpfx16.htm
[a]Regulated for local and cross-border interdealer double-counting (i.e., "net-net" basis)
[b]"Other FX products" category contains considerably leveraged transactions and/or trading which have the variational notional amount. For this reason, a decomposition into individual plain vanilla components was unworkable or impossible
[c]Average exchange rates for April of every survey year were used for non-US dollar parts of foreign exchange transactions which were turned into original currency amounts. Then, these amounts were again turned into US dollar amounts at average exchange rates for April 2016

influential in defining the behavior of foreign exchange rates creates important information in terms of those carrying out the foreign exchange rate transactions.

The foreign exchange rate is a domestic and international economic indicator. In developed countries, it is possible to reach a broad range of literature related to it rapidly responding to events such as war, terrorism, and political changes and general economic indicators such as unemployment, interest rate, and inflation (Anlas 2012: 34–35). In this context, the systems used to determine the exchange rates are also called exchange rate regimes.

The exchange rate regimes are basically examined in two groups as flexible and fixed exchange rate regimes. In practice, however, there are different systems between the flexible exchange rate system, which currencies exchange freely depending on market forces, and the fixed exchange rate systems, which exchange rates are determined by official institutions (Melvin and Norrbin 2013: 40–41).

There is a close relationship between the instabilities that may arise in exchange rates and crises. The fixing of the exchange rate by tying it to a certain diameter or keeping it below the real value makes the financial sector more vulnerable to crises (Corbett and Vines 1999: 156–158). Therefore, countries prefer mostly flexible exchange rate regimes.

Exchange rate volatility is often considered as a risk. A higher risk creates a higher cost for investors who avoid risk. As a result, volatility causes more uncertainty and cost of the transaction (Chang 2011: 66).

The organization of the rest of the chapter is as follows. Second section provides a general, albeit, a brief, theoretical review of the relationship between exchange rate and macroeconomic factors and also provides a brief literature review. Third section provides definition and description of the concept of the OneR algorithm which is one of the data mining methods. Fourth section consists of the aim of the application, the data, modeling, and application of the model. Fifth section presents the results and discussion. Lastly, Sixth section provides conclusions.

Theoretical Background and Literature Review

Nowadays, the foreign exchange market is the market with the highest volatility and liquidity among all financial markets (Kotai 2013: 897). Hence, exchange rates are highly influenced by various economic and political conditions such as interest rates, international trade, inflation, and political stability. The exchange rate is one of the most important macroeconomic variables, especially in developing countries.

Like every other product sold in the market, the price of the currency is determined by the demand for that currency. The rate of exchange between two currencies in a given time period varies according to supply and demand conditions. Changes in demand or supply to a currency affect price level of the currency directly. Foreign exchange supply and demand is influenced by many economic variables such as export and import demand, interest rates, income levels, and inflation rate of countries. At the point where the foreign exchange supply and demand intersects, the exchange rate price is determined. In a country's economy where demand is sought, exchange rates move downward. In contrast with this, in a country where the demand is high, exchange rates move upward. Moreover, changes in the relative inflation rate will affect the international trade operations that affect supply and demand for money and therefore the exchange rate. Relative interest rates also affect securities investments affecting foreign exchange rates due to money supply and demand (Madura 2014: 108–127).

There are some who claim in the literature that the relationship between the interest rate and the exchange rate is strong, as well as those who argue that it is weak and ineffective. For this reason, studies that investigated the interrelationship between interest rate and exchange rate revealed contradictory results. Furman and Stiglitz (1998) reviewed the effect of interest rates and inflation on exchange rates for nine developing countries between 1992 and 1998 and indicated that consequently high interest rates were associated with a fall in the nominal exchange rate. Thomas (2012) examined the relation between the exchange rate and the local interest rates in sub-Saharan countries with a flexible exchange rate regime, and no result that supported the relationship between them came out. Mouna and Anis (2016) investigated the relationship between interest rate and exchange rate volatility using the MGARCH model in eight countries where the US, Europe, and Chinese economies were involved in the 2006–2009 financial crisis period and found that there was a significant relationship between these two variables in financial markets. Dekle et al. (2002) examined whether or not the high interest rates affected nominal exchange rates in three Asian countries and found that the increase in interest rates during the crisis had a low impact on the nominal exchange rates.

Karaca (2005) could not find any statistically significant relationship between exchange rate and short-term interest rates in analysis encompassing the 1990–2005 period in Turkey. In analyses made for the 2001–2005 period, where only the flexible exchange rate period was considered, a statistically significant positive but weak relationship was found between the interest rate and the exchange rate.

The relationship between inflation and the exchange rate is important owing to their impact and volatility on the economic stability. Although the relationship between inflation and exchange rate cannot be determined regarding developed countries, it is revealed that the relationship between inflation and exchange rate is more meaningful regarding developing countries.

Kurihara and Fukushima (2014) examined the relation between stock prices and the exchange rate for Japan and the euro area. In the study they carried out using unit root tests and augmented Dickey-Fuller tests, the result for both regions is that the relation between exchange rates and stock prices is meaningless.

The exchange rate is one of the most important factors of the economic growth of a country, and the fluctuations in the currencies are an important influence in international trade. Ali et al. (2015) examined the effect of inflation and, as a result, interest rate and money supply on the volatility of the exchange rate in Pakistan and revealed that inflation has a positive relationship with the exchange rate and there is a negative relationship between interest rate and money supply.

Abbas et al. (2012) investigated in ten African countries the relationship between inflation, GDP, and real exchange rate; it was determined that the only GDP has a significant linkage with the exchange rate and that the relationship between real interest rate and inflation and exchange rate is not significant. However, it turns out that interest rates in Comoros and inflation in Gambia have had a significant impact on the exchange rate. Also, Albulescu (2010) found that the influence of the exchange rate and inflation did not have an immediate effect in the case of Romania but a delayed effect after testing the mathematical model.

With the influence of globalization since the 1980s, there is an interrelationship between capital markets and currency markets as a result of the interlinking of capital markets, the gradual abolition of capital entry barriers, and the application of the developed and flexible exchange rate mechanism in transition economies (Aydemir and Demirhan 2009: 207–215).

These developments have led to the carrying out of some studies investigating the relationship between stock markets and exchange rates. There are also studies in the literature that show exchange rates affect stock prices and there is a long-term relationship between the two variables, and studies show that there is no relationship between them. Therefore, it is not possible to mention a consensus among the studies carried out in this respect. Some studies have found two-way causality between stock returns and exchange rates, but some have concluded that there is no significant relationship between these two variables (Stefanescu and Dumitriu 2011: 61–65).

Mgammal (2012) examined the relationship between stock returns and exchange rates in Saudi Arabia and the United Arab Emirates and found short- and long-term relationships. According to the results of the study, in the short term, there was no correlation between the two variables in Saudi Arabia, while there was a positive effect of the exchange rate on the stock market index in the United Arab Emirates. When assessed for the long term, the results show that the exchange rate negatively influenced the stock market index in the United Arab Emirates, even though there was no significant correlation with the stock market index in Saudi Arabia.

Ayvaz (2006) examined the relationship between stock prices and the exchange rate in the Turkish financial markets. In the study, the relationship between the BIST100, BIST Financial, BIST Industrial, BIST Services Index, and the US exchange rate was analyzed. The existence of a long-term relationship between the exchange rate and stock indices was revealed.

Pekkaya and Bayramoglu (2008) analyzed the causality test between stock indices and the exchange rate. The results of the study where the causality between TRY/USD, BIST100 Index, and S&P 500 index was analyzed concluded that, except for the crisis periods, there was Granger causality between stock indices and exchange rates.

Although there are exchange rates floating among industrialized countries during the last three decades, there is still no agreement related to the effect of exchange rate volatility on macroeconomic variables. The empirical literature to study entire data has usually found small or minor impacts of exchange rate fluctuations on the export quantity. Since there are lacking parts regarding the interrelationship between exchange rates and export volumes, researchers are supported to develop models that generally depend on local currency pricing assumption which limits the response of export prices to exchange rate volatility (Dekle et al. 2016: 435–436).

The relationship between foreign exchange and foreign trade is an essential element in defining the exchange rates. Theoretically, export is a function of local prices, exchange rates, and production levels. Changes in exchange rates may cause changes in export and import quantities. As a result of the change in the production quantity, the amount of import will decrease because the price of imported products will increase due to the increase of exchange rate (like devaluation). As a result of this, domestic products will replace imported products, thus increasing employment (Gharavi 2002: 170–171).

In literature, empirical studies to determine the relationship between foreign trade and exchange rate appear to focus more on the exchange rate and foreign trade balance and exchange rate volatility on foreign trade. Arize (1995) found that the uncertainty in the exchange rate had a negative effect on the US real exports. Kroner and Lastrapes (1993) showed that fluctuations in local currency had a negative effect on exports on the USA and the UK and a positive effect on the exports of Germany, France, and Japan.

The findings found by Thorbecke and Kato (2012) indicate that there is a long-term equilibrium relationship between Germany's entire export, its real exchange rate, and its income in importing countries. In each indication, the evidence shows that an appreciation of the German REER would decrease exports. Findings gained by using a panel data set point out that consumption exports are much more sensitive to exchange rate changes than capital goods exports are. German capital goods exports are in the tendency to high-quality goods that compete more on quality than price.

Another parameter related to the exchange rate is the level of unemployment. The existence of a centrical relationship between exchange rates and unemployment has been discussed in the literature for many years. It is widely accepted in the literature that flexible exchange rate in particular influences the labor market through the money market (Gordon 1981: 40–45).

De Grauwe (1988) examined the relation between exchange rate volatility and the unemployment rate. The results of his research show that fluctuations in exchange rates have led to the appearance of investors investing less and avoiding risk, and as a result of this, there is a decrease in the employment rate. For this reason, it can be said that the increase or decrease in exchange rate has some effects on unemployment.

In recent years, it has been witnessed that foreign exchange crises in many countries have had serious effects on unemployment. The unemployment rate in countries exposed to the crisis has increased significantly in a short period of time. For example, due to the crisis it experienced in 1994, there has been a huge increase in real exchange rates and the unemployment rate in Mexico (Bratsiotis and Robinson 2002: 1–2).

The OneR Algorithm

OneR algorithm stands for "One Rule Algorithm," is a machine learning classifier in data mining problems, and is one of the simple and most effective classifier algorithms (Alam and Pachauri 2017: 1738) that generates a one-level decision tree (Kavitha et al. 2012: 1105). In this method, a set of classification rules on certain tested attributes will be generated by OneR algorithm depending on the value of a single attribute. OneR algorithm selects attribute with a minimum error rate as its "One Rule" (Muda et al. 2011: 193). So, OneR algorithm can derive simple but correct classification rules from a set of instances creating one rule for each attribute in the training data and then chooses the One Rule with the lowest error rate. Creating a rule for an attribute, the most frequently class for each attribute value must be identified. A rule is a set of attribute values that depend on the majority class; the attribute that the rule is based on establishes such a link for each attribute value (Kavitha et al. 2012: 1105).

The steps of the OneR algorithm, using the Weka 3.8 data mining software, can be described as follows (Alam and Pachauri 2017: 1738–1739):

Input

- Set of tuples $= Dn$.
- Each tuple is an "n"-dimensional vector.
- Set of attribute values $= Aj$.
- Attribute value is a "j"-dimensional attribute vector.

OneR BUILD (*D, *A)

For each attribute.
For each value of the attribute:

- Decide rule: count how often each class appears.
- Find the most frequent class.
- Assign that class to this attribute value.

Calculate the error rate of the rules.

Select the rules with the minimum error rate.

Application

Objective of the Chapter

This chapter seeks to analyze the relationship between the domestic macroeconomic parameters of Turkey and convertible exchange rates. For this purpose, the OneR algorithm, which is considered as a data mining method and machine learning technique, is employed to determine the effect of domestic macroeconomic indicators on convertible exchange rates. The reason for the use of only domestic macroeconomic variables in the study, in other words, the exclusion of international macroeconomic variables from the application, is that the frequency to be able to be informed about the domestic macroeconomic variables that are calculated within the country is greater. Thus, the aim is to increase the frequency of observing convertible exchange rates with the rules obtained by the applied OneR data mining method. Investigating whether or not the exchange rate movements included in the study can be modeled with only domestic macroeconomic variables as a glocal approach is also aimed. For this purpose, the exchange rates which have the highest transaction volume in the currency markets are included in the scope of the study. These exchange rates are EUR/USD, GBP/USD, and JPY/USD. Also, since Turkey's domestic macroeconomic variables were used in the study, TRY/USD exchange rate was included in the study. Therefore four convertible exchange rates were analyzed by the related method within the scope of the study.

Data Set

The application covers a period of approximately 10.5 years from January 2006 to May 2017 to classify the directions of EUR/USD, GBP/USD, JPY/USD, and TRY/USD exchange rates. Input (independent) and output (dependent) variables and the data sources for these variables are shown in Table 22.3.

Table 22.3 Input and output variables

Input (independent) variables	Acronym	Data source
BIST100 return index	BIST100	CBRT EDDS
Consumer price index of Turkey	INFRATE	CBRT EDDS
Export to import rate of Turkey	EXtoIMP	TSI
Index of industrial production of Turkey	IIP	CBRT EDDS
M2 money supply of Turkey	M2	CBRT EDDS
Unemployment rate in Turkey	UNEMPRATE	TSI
Weighted average interest rates for USD deposits of Turkish banks	INTRATE	CBRT EDDS

Output (dependent) variables	Acronym	Data source
EUR/USD exchange rate	EUR/USD	REUTERS
GBP/USD exchange rate	GBP/USD	REUTERS
JPY/USD exchange rate	JPY/USD	REUTERS
TRY/USD exchange rate	TRY/USD	REUTERS

The input variables which are domestic macroeconomic indicators of Turkey used in this study are selected based on literature review. When identifying these variables, the authors of the chapter followed the fundamental analysis approach. Another characteristic of the input variables is that they contain numeric data. Output variables include verbal (string) data as "rise" and "fall" and their nominal transformations were made.

Table 22.4 shows the correlations between the input variables and the output variables. It can be seen that there is a negative correlation in different levels between IIP, UNEMPRATE, EXtoIMP, and the output variables, while no correlation between BIST100, INFRATE, M2, and the output variables. Also, there is a negative correlation between the interest rate and GBP/USD and a positive correlation with other exchange rates.

For all variables, the frequency period is monthly averages and used in analysis without any statistical transformations. The values of the input variables are obtained for the period between January 2006 and April 2017, and the values of the output variable are obtained for the period between February 2006 and May 2017. Period of output variables start and end 1 month later because the output variable depends on the previous month values of the input variables. The length of the data set is determined as 136 months, and data in the 1–124 intervals which can be called as test data are used for model development. 125–136 intervals (12 months) are used for prediction (classifying the directions of the exchange rates).

Table 22.4 Correlations between input and output variables

ρ	BIST 100	INFRATE	INTRATE	M2	IIP	UNEMPRATE	EXtoIMP	EUR/USD	GBP/USD	JPY/USD	TRY/USD
BIST 100	1.00										
INFRATE	-0.07	1.00									
INTRATE	-0.11	0.02	1.00								
M2	-0.39	-0.07	0.08	1.00							
IIP	-0.10	0.03	-0.53	0.04	1.00						
UNEMPRATE	0.19	-0.03	-0.34	-0.02	-0.18	1.00					
EXtoIMP	0.02	0.15	-0.17	-0.09	0.04	0.52	1.00				
EUR/USD	0.01	0.01	0.38	0.00	-0.51	-0.13	-0.36	1.00			
GBP/USD	0.02	-0.06	-0.20	-0.07	-0.13	-0.08	-0.31	0.37	1.00		
JPY/USD	0.04	-0.04	0.70	0.02	-0.75	-0.16	-0.35	0.80	0.16	1.00	
TRY/USD	0.01	0.00	0.76	0.02	-0.46	-0.45	-0.36	0.66	-0.21	0.80	1.00

Methodology of the Application

In this part of the chapter, an application has been made to classify the price movements of the next 12 months of exchange rates with the OneR algorithm. As described in the third part of the chapter, the OneR algorithm aims to determine the input variable that best estimates the target class and by taking into account the frequencies in the database. For this reason, it evaluates each input variable individually, and as a result of this evaluation, a simple model that classifies according to a single variable comes out.

There are two target classes in this analysis: (1) fall and (2) rise of the convertible exchange rates in the next 12 months. In this chapter, it is focused on determining which one of the input variables, which will accept as the best predictor by OneR algorithm, can classify more accurately according to the target classes. In other words, which one of the selected input variables predicts the exchange rate movements more accurately in the next 12 months was analyzed with OneR algorithm.

The flowchart of the OneR algorithm for this study is shown in Fig. 22.1. As can be seen, OneR algorithm generates simple rules based on a single attribute (Singh 2009: 482). Firstly, the algorithm starts by selecting a single predictor attribute. Then, it calculates the frequency of appearance of each target class value for each predictor value. After that, it makes a rule that associates each predictor value with the maximum target class value. Then, it calculates the total error of the rules of each predictor. The rule with the minimum rate is selected as the One Rule for classification by OneR algorithm. If there is more than one rule with the same minimum

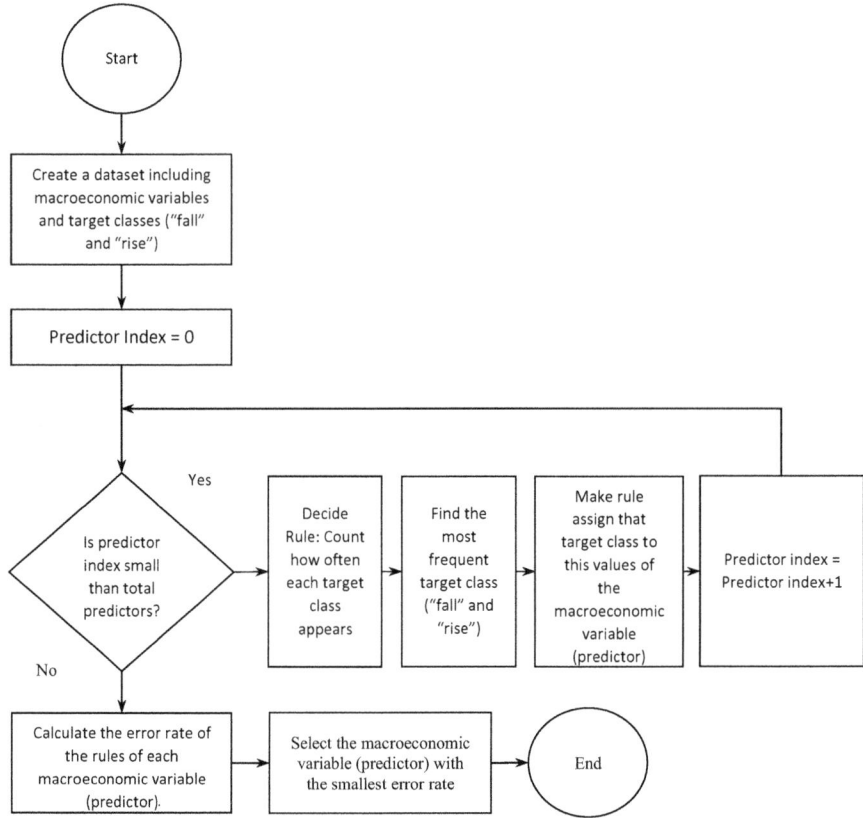

Fig. 22.1 Flowchart of the OneR algorithm. *Source*: Rajendiran, S., (2015). *Learning classification algorithms in data mining*. Project Report in Master of Science, California State University, Sacramento, p. 9

error rate, one of them is selected randomly by the algorithm (Rajendiran 2015: 18–19).

In this application, seven domestic macroeconomic variables were used as input variables while running the OneR algorithm, and the best estimator (classifier) was determined according to their frequencies. The application was made with Weka 3.8 which is one of the world's most widely used open-source data mining software. The application has been repeated separately for four exchange rates.

In the application, a database consisting of seven input variables and one output variable was presented to the OneR model, and 91.5% (124 intervals) of the data set was divided into the test database. The OneR algorithm determines the best estimator from the seven input variables based on the test data and then uses this best estimator to determine the target classes (fall or rise) for the next 12 months of the exchange rates. This process is repeated for each exchange rate.

At this point, the writers ask themselves: "Which is the second, third, or last best predictor that classifies best?" Therefore, writers repeated the application described in steps above by omitting the variable that the OneR model determined as the best predictor (variable) in the previous application out of the database and try to answer the questions by these means. In other words, while there are seven input variables in the first run of the OneR algorithm for any exchange rate, there are only six in the second run, five in the third run, and only one input variable in the seventh (last) run. This process was repeated for each exchange rate separately, so the OneR algorithm for each exchange rate was run seven times. Therefore, the OneR algorithm was run 28 times totally. The results obtained for each exchange rate by this method are given in the section titled as "Findings and Evaluations."

Results and Discussion

For EUR/USD exchange rate, the input variable (class) determined by the OneR model as the (first) best classifier (predictor) was the BIST100 Index, and the classification success of this input variable was 58.33% (Table 22.5). The second

Table 22.5 Results for EUR/USD exchange rate

x^{th} best predictor (x^{th} best class)	EUR/USD exchange rate	Correctly classified instances (CCI)	Instances correct (frequency)
1	BIST100	58.33%	99/136
2	M2	33.33%	97/136
3	INFRATE	33.33%	95/136
4	IIP	66.67%	95/136
5	UNEMPRATE	66.67%	91/136
6	INTRATE	66.67%	90/136
7	EXtoIMP	25.00%	87/136
Confusion matrix (the best results according to OneR's best predictor)			
BIST100	Fall	Rise	Total (7/12)
	3	2	Fall (**3/5**)
	3	**4**	Rise (**4** /7)
	Kappa statistic $(\kappa)^a$	0.1667	
Confusion matrix (the best results according to CCI)			
IIP	Fall	Rise	Total (8/12)
	4	1	Fall (**4/5**)
	3	**4**	Rise (**4/7**)
	Kappa statistic $(\kappa)^a$	0.3514	

[a]Kappa statistic (κ): $\kappa < 0$ "poor (less than chance) agreement"; $0.01 < \kappa < 0.20$ "slight agreement"; $0.21 < \kappa < 0.40$ "fair agreement"; $0.41 < \kappa < 0.60$ "moderate agreement"; $0.61 < \kappa < 0.80$ "substantial agreement"; $0.81 < \kappa < 1.00$ "almost perfect agreement" (Viera and Garrett 2005: 362)

Table 22.6 Results for GBP/USD exchange rate

x^{th} best predictor (x^{th} best class)	GBP/USD exchange rate	Correctly classified instances (CCI)	Instances correct (frequency)
1	EXtoIMP	58.33%	101/136
2	INFRATE	58.33%	99/136
3	INTRATE	58.33%	99/136
4	IIP	41.67%	96/136
5	BIST100	66.67%	95/136
6	M2	83.33%	93/136
7	UNEMPRATE	83.33%	92/136
Confusion matrix (the best results according to OneR's best predictor)			
EXtoIMP	Fall	Rise	Total (7/12)
	7	1	Fall (**7**/8)
	4	**0**	Rise (**0**/4)
	Kappa statistic (κ)[a]	-0.1538	
Confusion matrix (the best results according to CCI)			
M2	Fall	Rise	Total (10/12)
	8	0	Fall (**8**/8)
	2	**2**	Rise (**2**/4)
	Kappa statistic (κ)[a]	0.5714	

[a]For an explanation of Kappa statistic, please see the footnotes of Table 22.5

best estimator for EUR/USD was determined as the M2 money supply, and the classification done with this input variable was seen at a 33.33% success rate. The most successful classifications for EUR/USD were seen at a rate of 66.67% with the fourth (index of industrial production), fifth (unemployment rate), and sixth (interest rate) best estimators. The Kappa statistic is 0.17 for the 12-month forecasting period, based on the BIST100 Index, which was designated as the (first) best classifier by the OneR algorithm. Therefore, Kappa statistic shows that there is a "slight agreement" between the real classes and the forecasted classes. Table 22.5 indicates that the forecasting results with the fourth-best classifier (IIP) have 0.35 Kappa statistic, which means there is a "fair agreement" between the real classes and the forecasted classes.

For GDP/USD exchange rate, the input variable identified by the OneR model as the (first) best classifier is the export to import rate (EXtoIMP), and the classification success of this input variable is 58.33% (Table 22.6). The second best estimator for GDP/USD was identified as inflation rate (INFRATE), and the classification done with this input variable was seen at a 58.33% success rate. The most successful classifications for GDP/USD were found to be 83.33% with the sixth (M2 money supply) and seventh (unemployment rate) best predictors. The Kappa statistic is -0.15 for the 12-month forecasting period, based on the export to import rate (EXtoIMP), which was designated as the (first) best classifier by the OneR

Table 22.7 Results for JPY/USD exchange rate

x^{th} best predictor (x^{th} best class)	JPY/USD exchange rate	Correctly classified instances (CCI)	Instances correct (frequency)
1	EXtoIMP	66.67%	99/136
2	INFRATE	66.67%	95/136
3	IIP	66.67%	94/136
4	INTRATE	66.67%	91/136
5	M2	66.67%	89/136
6	BIST100	41.67%	87/136
7	UNEMPRATE	41.67%	84/136
Confusion matrix (the best results according to OneR's best predictor and CCI)			
EXtoIMP	Fall	Rise	Total (8/12)
	3	3	Fall (**3**/6)
	1	**5**	Rise (**5**/6)
	Kappa statistic (κ)[a]	0.3333	

[a]For an explanation of Kappa statistic, please see the footnotes of Table 22.5

algorithm. Therefore, Kappa statistic shows that there is a "poor (less than chance) agreement" between the real classes and the forecasted classes. Table 22.6 shows that the forecasting results with the sixth-best classifier (M2) have 0.57 Kappa statistic, which means there is a "fair agreement" between the real classes and the forecasted classes.

For JPY/USD exchange rate, the input variable identified by the OneR model as the (first) best classifier is the export to import rate (EXtoIMP), and the classification success of this input variable is 66.67% (Table 22.7). The second best estimator for JPY/USD was identified as inflation rate (INFRATE), and the classification done with this input variable was seen at a 66.67% success rate. It is considered that the same classification performance (66.67% classification success) is also exhibited by the following four best guessers (inflation rate, index of industrial production, interest rate, and M2 money supply). The Kappa statistic is 0.33 for the 12-month forecasting period, based on the export to import rate (EXtoIMP), which was designated as the (first) best classifier by the OneR algorithm. Therefore, Kappa statistic shows that there is a "fair agreement" between the real classes and the forecasted classes.

For TRY/USD exchange rate, the input variable identified by the OneR model as the (first) best classifier is M2, and the classification success of this input variable is 33.33% (Table 22.8). The second best estimator for TRY/USD was identified as the export to import rate (EXtoIMP), and the classification is done with this input variable was seen at a 33.33% success rate. The most successful classification for TRY/USD was seen by interest rate (INTRATE) which is the third-best estimator with a success rate of 58.33%. The Kappa statistic is −0.50 for the 12-month forecasting period, based on the M2 money supply, which was designated as the

Table 22.8 Results for TRY/USD exchange rate

x^{th} best predictor (x^{th} best class)	TRY/USD exchange rate	Correctly classified instances (CCI)	Instances correct (frequency)
1	M2	33.33%	99/136
2	EXtoIMP	33.33%	97/136
3	INTRATE	58.33%	96/136
4	IIP	50.00%	94/136
5	BIST100	50.00%	93/136
6	INFRATE	50.00%	92/136
7	UNEMPRATE	50.00%	88/136
Confusion matrix (the best results according to OneR's best predictor)			
M2	Fall	Rise	Total (4/12)
	0	4	Fall (**0**/4)
	4	**4**	Rise (**4**/8)
	Kappa statistic $(\kappa)^a$	−0.5000	
Confusion matrix (the best results according to CCI)			
INTRATE	Fall	Rise	Total (6/12)
	3	1	Fall (**3**/4)
	5	**3**	Rise (**3**/8)
	Kappa statistic $(\kappa)^a$	0.1000	

[a]For an explanation of Kappa statistic, please see the footnotes of Table 22.5

(first) best classifier by the OneR algorithm. Therefore, Kappa statistic shows that there is a "poor (less than chance) agreement" between the real classes and the forecasted classes. As can be seen in Table 22.8, forecasting results with the third-best classifier (INTRATE) have 0.10 Kappa statistic, which means there is a "slight agreement" between the real classes and the forecasted classes.

Conclusion

When the results obtained within the scope of the application are evaluated in general, it is possible to make many deductions from the findings. Some of these deductions are as follows:

Regarding OneR algorithm, the algorithm finds the best classifier (best predictor) considering frequency interval. However, this method is supported by the findings of the study that the problem of classification of the exchange rate movements for the next 12 months is insufficient to solve. For example, although it was determined as the export to import rate (EXtoIMP) with 101/136 instances according to the best estimating frequency for the GBP/USD exchange rate, the success of this classifier was 58.33%. Moreover, the success rate of the unemployment rate, whose instances correct rate was 92/136 and which was determined as the seventh best predictor by OneR algorithm, was 83.33%. From this, it can be deduced that the classification should not be decided by looking only at the frequency interval.

In terms of data mining methods and machine learning techniques, it is seen that the success rate of the models with a relatively small number of input variables is higher in this application. When the application results are examined, even the third, fourth, and seventh best input variables can produce higher results than the first best input variable (best predictor). Therefore, the importance of the use of lean models is supported by the findings of the study.

Regarding the primary aim of the survey, this chapter aimed to reveal the explanation capacity of Turkey's domestic macroeconomic variables on the convertible exchange rates. When the results are evaluated for this purpose, although satisfactory classification success was achieved between 58.33% and 83.33%, these percentages have been achieved with a lower percentage between 33.33% and 66.67% when evaluated from the first best predictor standpoint.

Therefore, it has been concluded that Turkey's domestic macroeconomic variables are not sufficient to explain convertible exchange rates. As the reasons for these findings, it can be shown that the Turkish economy is a developing economy and that the economy is small compared to developed country economies. Therefore, it can be said that the Turkey's domestic macroeconomic variables do not have a capacity to explain the international foreign exchange markets.

Keywords Definitions

Currency markets Currency market is a market in which banks and traders purchase and sell foreign currencies.

Exchange rate Exchange rates can be defined as the price of one currency with regard to another currency.

Macro-finance Macro-finance is a new area of open economy macroeconomics that brings portfolio choice and asset pricing considerations into models of international macroeconomics.

Glocal approaches in finance Glocal approaches in finance are the adaptation of international financial instruments around the particularities of a local culture.

Classification Classification is an ordered set of related categories used to group data according to its similarities.

Data mining Data mining is the process of discovering actionable information from large sets of data.

Machine learning Machine learning is the field of study that gives computers the ability to learn without being explicitly programmed.

OneR algorithm OneR algorithm is one of the simple and most effective classifier algorithms that generate a one-level decision tree.

References

Abbas, Q., Javid, I., & Ayaz, L. (2012). Relationship between GDP, inflation and real interest rate with exchange rate fluctuation of African countries. *International Journal of Academic Research in Accounting, Finance and Management Sciences, 2*(3), 132–139.

Alam, F., & Pachauri, S. (2017). Comparative study of J48, Naive Bayes and One-R classification technique for credit card fraud detection using WEKA. *Advances in Computational Sciences and Technology, 10*(6), 1731–1743.

Albulescu, C. T. (2010). Forecasting the Romanian financial system stability using a stochastic simulation model. *Romanian Journal of Economic Forecasting, 13*(1), 81–98.

Ali, T. M., Mahmood, M. T., & Bashir, T. (2015). Impact of interest rate, inflation and money supply on exchange rate volatility in Pakistan. *World Applied Sciences Journal, 33*(4), 620–630.

Anlas, T. (2012). The effects of changes in foreign exchange rates on ISE-100 index. *Journal of Applied Economics & Business Research, 2*(1), 34–45.

Arize, A. C. (1995). The effects of exchange-rate volatility on US exports: An empirical investigation. *Southern Economic Journal, 62*(1), 34–43.

Aydemir, O., & Demirhan, E. (2009). The relationship between stock prices and exchange rates: Evidence from Turkey. *International Research Journal of Finance and Economics, 23*(2), 207–215.

Ayvaz, Ö. (2006). Döviz kuru ve hisse senetleri fiyatları arasındaki nedensellik ilişkisi. *İktisadi ve İdari Bilimler Fakültesi Dergisi, 8*(2), 1–14.

Bank for International Settlements. *Triennial Central Bank Survey of foreign exchange and OTC derivatives markets in 2016*. Retrieved from http://www.bis.org/publ/rpfx16.htm.

Bratsiotis, G. J., & Robinson, W. (2002). *Economic fundamentals and self-fulfilling crises: Some evidence from Mexico* (pp. 1–30). Discussion Paper Series, Centre for Growth and Business Cycle Research, University of Manchester.

Chang, S. C. (2011). The interrelationship between exchange-rate uncertainty and unemployment for South Korea and Taiwan: Evidence from a vector autoregressive approach. *International Economics, 125*, 65–82.

Corbett, J., & Vines, D. (1999). Asian currency and financial crises: Lessons from vulnerability, crisis and collapse. *The World Economy, 22*(2), 156–158.

De Grauwe, P. (1988). Exchange rate variability and the slowdown in growth of international trade. *Staff Papers, 35*(1), 63–84.

Dekle, R., Hsiao, C., & Wang, S. (2002). High interest rates and exchange rate stabilization in Korea, Malaysia, and Thailand: An empirical investigation of the traditional and revisionist views. *Review of International Economics, 10*(1), 64–78.

Dekle, R., Jeong, H., & Ryoo, H. H. (2016). Firm-level heterogeneity and the aggregate exchange rate effect on exports. *Economic Record, 92*(298), 435–447.

Furman, J., & Stiglitz, J. E. (1998). Economic consequences of income inequality. In *Income inequality: Issues and policy options* (pp. 221–263). Proceedings of a Symposium Sponsored by the Federal Reserve Bank of Kansas City.

Gharavi, N. S. (2002). Unemployment crisis in Iran. *Economic Research Review Summer, 2*(5), 171–184.

Gordon, R. J. (1981). *Inflation, flexible exchange rates, and the natural rate of unemployment* (pp. 1–96). NBER Working Paper No. 708.

Karaca, O. (2005). *Türkiye'de faiz oranı ile döviz kuru arasındaki ilişki: faizlerin düşürülmesi kurları yükseltir mi?* (pp. 1–18). Discussion Paper, Turkish Economic Association, No. 14.

Kavitha, A. S., Kavitha, R., & Viji, G. J. (2012). Empirical evaluation of feature selection technique in educational data mining. *ARPN Journal of Science and Technology, 2*(11), 1103–1112.

Kotai, V. (2013). An empirical study on currency volatility in foreign exchange market. *Global Journal of Management and Business Studies, 3*(8), 897–904.

Kroner, K. F., & Lastrapes, W. D. (1993). The impact of exchange rate volatility on international trade: Reduced form estimates using the GARCH-in-mean model. *Journal of International Money and Finance, 12*(3), 298–318.

Kurihara, Y., & Fukushima, A. (2014). Exchange rates, stock prices, and commodity prices: Are there any relationships? *Advances in Social Sciences Research Journal, 1*(5), 107–115.

Madura, J. (2014). *International financial management* (12th ed.). Boston: Cengage Learning.

Melvin, M., & Norrbin, S. C. (2013). *International money and finance* (8th ed.). London: Academic Press.

Mgammal, M. H. H. (2012). The effect of inflation, interest rates and exchange rates on stock prices comparative study among two GCC countries. *International Journal of Finance and Accounting, 1*(6), 179–189.

Mouna, A., & Anis, J. (2016). Market, interest rate, and exchange rate risk effects on financial stock returns during the financial crisis: AGARCH-M approach. *Cogent Economics & Finance, 4*(1), 1–16.

Muda, Z., Yassin, W., Sulaiman, M. N., & Udzir, N. I. (2011). *Intrusion detection based on K-means clustering and OneR classification* (pp. 192–197). IEEE 7th International Conference on Information Assurance and Security (IAS), Malaysia, 5–8 December.

Pekkaya, M., & Bayramoglu, M. F. (2008). Hisse senedi fiyatları ve döviz kuru arasındaki nedensellik ilişkisi: YTL/USD, İMKB 100 ve S&P 500 Üzerine Bir Uygulama. *Muhasebe ve Finansman Dergisi, 38*, 163–176.

Rajendiran, S. (2015). *Learning classification algorithms in data mining.* Project Report in Master of Science, California State University, Sacramento, CA.

Singh, P. (2009). Comparing the effectiveness of machine learning algorithms for defect prediction. *International Journal of Information Technology and Knowledge Management, 2*(2), 481–483.

Stefanescu, R., & Dumitru, R. (2011). Interactions between the exchange rates and the differential of the stock returns between Romania and US during the global crisis. *Economics and Applied Informatics, XVII*(2), 61–66.

Thomas, A. H. (2012). *Exchange rate and foreign interest rate linkages for Sub-Saharan Africa floaters* (pp. 1–21). IMF Working Paper No. 12/208.

Thorbecke, W., & Kato, A. (2012). *The effect of exchange rate changes on Germany's exports* (pp. 1–29). RIETI Discussion Paper Series 12-E-081.

Viera, A. J., & Garrett, J. M. (2005). Understanding interobserver agreement: The kappa statistic. *Family Medicine, 37*(5), 360–363.

Zhang, Y.-Q., & Xuhui, W. (2007). Statistical fuzzy interval neural networks for currency exchange rate time series prediction. *Applied Soft Computing, 7*(4), 1149–1156.

Printed by Printforce, the Netherlands